USING COMPUTERS: MANAGING CHANGE

USING COMPUTERS:
MANAGING CHANGE

Levi Reiss
ALGONQUIN COLLEGE

Edwin G. Dolan
GEORGE MASON UNIVERSITY

J76
PUBLISHED BY
SOUTH-WESTERN PUBLISHING CO.
CINCINNATI   WEST CHICAGO, IL   CARROLLTON, TX   LIVERMORE, CA

Cover and Chapter-Opening Illustrations: Mitchell Confer
Title Page and Part-Opening Photographs: Reginald Wickham

Copyright © 1989 by South-Western Publishing Co., Cincinnati, Ohio

All Rights Reserved

The text of this publication, or any part thereof, may not be reproduced or transmitted in any form or by any means, electronic or mechanical, including photocopying, recording, storage in an information retrieval system, or otherwise, without the prior written permission of the publisher.

ISBN: 0-538-10760-X
Library of Congress Catalog Card Number: 87-82210

1 2 3 4 5 6 7 8 9 RM 5 4 3 2 1 0 9 8 7

Printed in the United States of America

BRIEF CONTENTS

Preface xiii

PART 1 OVERVIEW 1
1. Computers and Their Impact 3
2. Some Basic Concepts 31

PART 2 HARDWARE 67
3. Computers Large and Small 69
4. Input and Output 99
5. The Central Processing Unit and Storage 131
6. Data Communication 171

PART 3 SOFTWARE 209
7. Programming: Process, Tools, Techniques 211
8. Programming Languages and Operating Systems 249
9. Personal-Productivity Software 291
10. File-Processing and Data-Base Systems 345

COMPUTERS: THE IMPACT 384

PART 4 PEOPLE AND SYSTEMS 407
11. Introduction to Business Systems 409
12. Management and Systems Analysis 439
13. Management Support and Expert Systems 481
14. The Automated Office 523
15. Automating Production 559

PART 5 OUR AUTOMATED LIVES 591
16. Uses of Computers: Some Applications 593
17. Privacy, Computer Crime, and Security 623
18. The Future of Computing: Trends and Prospects 653

Appendix: Programming in BASIC 678
Glossary 720
Index 728

DETAILED CONTENTS

Preface	xiii
PART 1 OVERVIEW	1
1 Computers and Their Impact	3
The Computer Revolution	5
A Brief History of Computing	6
Early Calculating Devices	7
The First Computing Devices	8
The First Three Generations	11
Personal Computers	13
Advantages and Limitations of Computers	14
Advantages	15
Limitations	16
Data Processing	19
Data Processing Functions	21
Computer Users and Specialists	22
Computer Users	22
Computer Specialists	23
Organization of the Book	24
2 Some Basic Concepts	31
Hardware	33
Input	34
Output	38
The Central Processing Unit	39
Auxiliary Storage Devices	42
Data Communication	45
Software	46
Applications Software	46
Systems Software	49
The Data Hierarchy	51
Bit	51
Byte and Character	51
Field	52
Record	52
File	53
Data Base	53
File Processing	53
Batch Processing	53
Interactive Processing	55
People as an Element of Computer Systems	55
Ergonomics and Hardware Design	55
User-Friendly Software	58
PART 2 HARDWARE	67
3 Computers Large and Small	69
Microprocessors and Microcomputers	71
The IBM PC	72
Other IBM Personal Computers	76
Compatibles	77
Portable Computers	78
Minicomputers	82
Micros vs. Minis	82
Mainframe Computers	84
Supercomputers	88
Appendix: Buying a Personal Computer	90
4 Input and Output	99
Input	101
Data Entry	101
Input Devices	103
Keyboards	104
Terminals	107
Other Data Entry Devices	108
Scanners	111
Other Input Devices and Techniques	114
Output	117
Output Devices	118
Video Display Terminals	118
Printers	120
Plotters	123
Computer Output Microfilm Systems	124
Audio Response Units	124

5 The Central Processing Unit and Storage — 131
The Central Processing Unit — 133
The Control Unit — *133*
The Arithmetic-Logic Unit — *134*
Primary Storage — *134*
Codes — *137*
Storage — 139
Storage Devices for Microcomputers — *139*
Special Storage Techniques — *145*
Auxiliary Storage for Larger Computers — *146*
File Organization — 153
Sequential Files — *155*
Random-Access Files — *156*
Indexed-Sequential Files — *158*
Appendix: Inside the Computer — 160

6 Data Communication — 171
Data Communication Systems — 173
Data Communication Applications — 175
Information Utilities — *175*
Internal Uses — *176*
Basic Data Communication Concepts — 178
Communication Channels — *178*
Communication Terminology — *182*
Communication Equipment and Software — *185*
Networks — 189
Network Configurations — *189*
Network Suppliers — *194*
Teleprocessing — *195*
Distributed Data Processing — *198*
Local Area Networks — *200*
Multiuser Systems — *202*

PART 3 SOFTWARE — 209

7 Programming: Process, Tools, Techniques — 211
The Program Development Process — 213
Programmers and Systems Analysts — *214*
Steps in the Programming Process — *215*
Programming Tools and Techniques — 224
Structured Programming — *225*
Defining the Problem — *227*
Designing the Solution — *231*
Coding the Program — *233*
Testing and Debugging the Program — *241*
Implementing and Maintaining the Program — *243*

8 Programming Languages and Operating Systems — 249
Programming Languages — 251
Low-Level Programming Languages — *252*
High-Level Programming Languages — *254*
Very-High-Level Programming Languages — *268*
Selecting a Programming Language — *274*
Operating Systems — 277
Types of Operating Systems — *277*
Functions of Operating Systems — *278*
Operating System Commands — *279*
Special Features of Operating Systems — *283*
Standardization — *285*

9 Personal-Productivity Software — 291
Data-Base Management Programs — 293
File Management versus Data-Base Management — *293*

Mechanics of Data-Base Management Programs	297
Word Processing	**307**
Using Word-Processing Programs	309
Mechanics of Word Processing	309
Additional Features	318
Electronic Spreadsheets	**320**
Using Electronic Spreadsheets	322
Mechanics of Electronic Spreadsheets	322

10 File-Processing and Data-Base Systems 345

File-Processing Systems	**347**
Types of File Organization	347
Drawbacks of Traditional File Processing	351
Data-Base Management Systems	**352**
DBMS Personnel	354
The Data Dictionary	356
Data Models	358
Structured Query Language	363
Advantages of Data-Base Management Systems	372
Disadvantages of Data-Base Management Systems	373
Technical Challenges	374
Selecting a DBMS	374
Installing a Data-Base Management System	377
COMPUTERS: THE IMPACT	384

PART 4 PEOPLE AND SYSTEMS 407

11 Introduction to Business Systems 409

Personal versus Organizational Applications	411
Personal Applications	411
Organizational Applications	412
Systems	**414**
Businesses as Systems	416
Computer Information Systems	416
Business Subsystems	**419**
Typical Business Subsystems	423
Computer Information Systems in Business	424
Commonly Used Computer Information Systems	**427**
Accounting Systems	428
Inventory Control and Management Systems	432
Sales Analysis Systems	433

12 Management and Systems Analysis 439

Systems and Change	**441**
A Brief Review	441
System Personnel	442
The System Development Life Cycle	**444**
System Investigation	445
Systems Analysis	452
System Design	459
System Acquisition	465
System Implementation	469
System Maintenance	471
Prototyping	473

13 Management Support and Expert Systems 481

Operations Information Systems	**483**
On-Line Transaction-Processing Systems	483
Uses of Operations Information Systems	487
Operational Control	489
Management Information Systems	**491**

Uses of Management Information Systems	494	**Appendix: Computer Graphics**	550
External Data and the MIS	495		
The MIS Department	497	**15 Automating Production**	**559**
Decision Support Systems	**500**	**Computer-Aided Design**	561
Types of Decisions	501	*Elements of a CAD System*	562
Characteristics of Decision Support Systems	502	*Features of CAD Systems*	562
		Advantages and Disadvantages of CAD	564
Uses of Decision Support Systems	504	*An Application*	564
Executive Information Systems	506	**Computer-Aided Manufacturing**	565
Expert Systems	**508**	*Advantages and Disadvantages of CAM*	566
Benefits of Expert Systems	511	*An Application*	566
Drawbacks of Expert Systems	511	**Materials Requirements and Manufacturing Resource Planning**	567
Information Centers	**513**	*Elements of an MRP System*	567
Guidelines for Information Centers	515	*Manufacturing Resource Planning*	568
		An Application	568
14 The Automated Office	**523**	**Robots**	569
Benefits of Office Automation	**526**	*Programming Robots*	570
Tools of Office Automation	**528**	*Robot Vision Systems*	570
Word Processing	529	*Touch-Sensitive Robots*	572
Electronic Mail	529	*An Application*	573
Electronic Filing	531	**Flexible Manufacturing Systems**	574
Image Processing	532	*Implementing FMS*	574
Teleconferencing	536	*Advantages and Disadvantages of FMS*	575
Telecommuting	538	*An Application*	575
Integrated Workstations	**539**	**Just-In-Time**	577
Characteristics of Integrated Workstations	540	*Advantages and Disadvantages of JIT*	578
Office Automation Systems	**541**	*An Application*	579
The Impact of Office Automation	**542**	**Computer-Integrated Manufacturing**	579
Changes in Secretarial and Clerical Work	543	*Advantages and Disadvantages of CIM*	581
Effects on Managers, Professionals, and Technical Personnel	544	*An Application*	582
New Support Functions	546	**Manufacturing Automation Protocol**	582
Desktop Publishing	**547**	*An Application*	584
Limitations	548		
Types of Systems	549		

PART 5 OUR AUTOMATED LIVES — 591

16 Uses of Computers: Some Applications — 593
Computers and Health Care — 595
Home Health Care — 595
Decision Support Systems for Hospitals — 596
Data Bases for Health-Care Professionals — 597
The Centers for Disease Control — 598
Computers and Sports — 599
Computers and Football — 600
Computers and Boating — 602
Computers and Skiing — 605
Computers and Education — 606
Computer-Assisted Instruction — 606
Computer-Managed Instruction — 609
Challenges to the Use of Computers in Education — 609
Computers and Music — 610
Computers and Finances — 612
Personal Finances — 613
Investment Software — 614
Electronic Funds Transfer — 617

17 Privacy, Computer Crime, and Security — 623
Privacy — 625
The Meaning of Privacy — 626
Privacy in Business Situations — 627
Standard Universal Identifiers — 628
Electronic Funds Transfer Systems — 630
Privacy Legislation — 630
Computer Crime — 632
Types of Computer Crime — 633
Legislation to Reduce Computer Crime — 639
Security — 640
Administrative Measures — 641
Physical Measures — 641
Technological Measures — 642
Individual Awareness — 645
Data Security for Microcomputer Users — 645
Data Integrity — 646

18 The Future of Computing: Trends and Prospects — 653
Trends in Hardware — 655
The IBM PS/2 — 658
Gallium Arsenide — 660
Superconducting Computers — 660
Optical Computing — 661
The Future of Desktop Computing — 662
Trends in Software — 663
Personal-Productivity Software — 663
Artificial Intelligence — 665
But Can Computers Think? — 669
Risks in the Computerized Future — 671
Computers Are Only as Good as Their Programmers — 671
Threats to Privacy and Freedom — 672
Is Anything Safe from Computers? — 672

Appendix: Programming in BASIC — 678
Rudimentary BASIC — 678
First Program — 678
Second Program — 679
Third Program — 683
Programs to Modify — 685
Programs to Write — 685
Branching to Another Instruction — 685
Intermediate BASIC — 687
First Program — 687
Second Program — 691

Third Program	*693*	Additional Topics	709
Programs to Modify	*700*	*Nested FOR . . . NEXT Loops*	*709*
Programs to Write	*700*	*Two-Dimensional Arrays*	*710*
Arrays	**701**	*Subroutines*	*713*
Second Program	*702*	*Other Features*	*713*
Third Program	*706*		
Programs to Modify	*707*	**Glossary**	**720**
Programs to Write	*707*	**Index**	**728**

CHAPTER BOXES

BOX 1–1 MANAGING CHANGE
Computer Errors Are People Errors 18
BOX 1–2 USING COMPUTERS
Matching Products with Customer Needs 20
BOX 2–1 USING COMPUTERS
Legibility of Computer Output 40–41
BOX 2–2 MANAGING CHANGE
Mary Parker Follett on Getting Things Done Through People 57
BOX 3–1 FRONTIERS IN TECHNOLOGY
Growing Up With the Personal Computer 74–75
BOX 3–2 MANAGING CHANGE
PCs Aren't Always the Answer 83
BOX 4–1 FRONTIERS IN TECHNOLOGY
Teaching Computers to Read 113
BOX 4–2 MANAGING CHANGE
Direct Product Profitability 115
BOX 5–1 USING COMPUTERS
Be Nice to Your Storage Media 144
BOX 5–2 FRONTIERS IN TECHNOLOGY
Optical Storage Media for PCs 154

BOX 6–1 USING COMPUTERS
Dow Jones News/Retrieval 177
BOX 6–2 FRONTIERS IN TECHNOLOGY
Fiber Optics for Local Area Networks 201
BOX 7–1 USING COMPUTERS
A Programming Superstar Talks About Balance and Elegance 226
BOX 7–2 FRONTIERS IN TECHNOLOGY
Programs that Help Programmers Program 236
BOX 8–1 MANAGING CHANGE
Cost-Justifying a Very-High-Level Language 270–271
BOX 8–2 USING COMPUTERS
Choosing a Language for *Econograph* 276
BOX 9–1 MANAGING CHANGE
When to Computerize a Data Base 294
BOX 9–2 FRONTIERS IN TECHNOLOGY
Integrating Personal-Productivity Software 336–337
BOX 10–1 MANAGING CHANGE
Overcoming the Conversion Barrier 364

BOX 10–2 FRONTIERS IN TECHNOLOGY
Special Hardware Helps Meet the Relational-DBMS Challenge 375
BOX 11–1 MANAGING CHANGE
The Middle Manager in the Factory of the Future 420–421
BOX 11–2 MANAGING CHANGE
What's in a Name? 425
BOX 12–1 MANAGING CHANGE
Help! Our Network Is Out of Control 446–447
BOX 12–2 MANAGING CHANGE
When to Throw Your System Away 474–475
BOX 13–1 MANAGING CHANGE
Uses and Misuses of Information Systems 505
BOX 13–2 FRONTIERS IN TECHNOLOGY
Personal Workstations 512
BOX 14–1 FRONTIERS IN TECHNOLOGY
Hardware for Image Processing 534–535
BOX 14–2 USING COMPUTERS
Corporate Electronic Publishing Saves the Ace Catalog 551
BOX 15–1 FRONTIERS IN TECHNOLOGY
Why Do Robots Need to See? 571
BOX 15–2 MANAGING CHANGE
Flexible Manufacturing, a Step at a Time 576
BOX 16–1 FRONTIERS IN TECHNOLOGY
Computers Help Teach the Deaf to Speak 607
BOX 16–2 USING COMPUTERS
Artificial Intelligence Aids Financial Planners 616
BOX 17–1 USING COMPUTERS FOR CRIME
Who Does It? Who Gets Hurt? 634–635
BOX 17–2 MANAGING CHANGE
Programs in Escrow 638
BOX 18–1 FRONTIERS IN TECHNOLOGY
Downward Migration of Computer Technology 656–657
BOX 18–2 USING COMPUTERS
AI Integration 666–667

Preface

The computer revolution continues unabated. Every year it affects larger numbers of people more profoundly both in their careers and in their everyday lives. Whereas in the past it was sufficient for nontechnical students to take a vaguely defined "computer appreciation" course, today both employers and students expect graduates to be "computer competent"—to be able to use computers to help solve problems in any field of endeavor. Computer competence is not limited to using a computer program to ask "what if?" questions. It also involves making choices, such as when to access the computer oneself and when to seek the aid of an expert, or whether to use a microcomputer or a larger computer for a particular application. This book focuses on helping students learn how to make such choices in a rapidly changing world.

The rate of change in computer technology is astronomical; certainly the design and manufacturing cycle for many computer products is shorter than the cycle for writing and publishing a textbook! It clearly is not enough for an introductory textbook to describe the present reality of computers; students must be given the tools to acquire such knowledge themselves. The isolated facts that students learn today will be hopelessly out of date within a few years. But students who have mastered the principles of computers and their application will continue to profit from advances in computer technology. The goal of this book, therefore, is to present computer technology and its impact on people in a balanced manner.

If students are to be fully prepared for their computerized future, however, they must also be made aware of the drawbacks and shortcomings of computers. The computer revolution has not been an unmitigated success, and it would be a disservice to students to pretend that it has. This book discusses the disadvantages as well as the advantages of computerized solutions. Moreover, while the text devotes considerable space to the ubiquitous and popular personal computer, it also recognizes the increasing importance of larger computers and the need to link personal computers with other computers of all sizes.

The text is designed to be useful to a wide variety of students. Many of the examples and applications have been chosen from the business world in the belief that a large proportion of readers are interested in careers in business. The nonthreatening writing style, the numerous examples from everyday life, and the lively pedagogical features will attract students who are not "turned on" by traditional computer textbooks. At the same time, technical issues such as structured programming and data-base management systems are discussed in sufficient depth for students planning to major in computer science. Yet even these subjects are discussed from a "people" perspective—their impact on both technical and nontechnical personnel is explained.

Textbooks, particularly introductory textbooks, should inspire students. We hope that this book, with its balanced presentation of the world of computers, will inspire students to profit from and help shape the ongoing computer revolution.

Special Features

The text is enhanced by numerous pedagogical features, some of which are unique to this book. Among them are the following:

Opening Vignettes. Each chapter opens with a short vignette that sparks the reader's interest. The vignettes raise points that will be discussed in the chapter and often provide raw material for review and discussion questions.

Cases. A case at the end of each chapter can be used to review key points made within the chapter. Both the vignettes and the cases generally focus on the impact of technology on people. They often illustrate potential pitfalls of computerization.

Boxes. The boxed features are organized into three groups. One group, entitled "Using Computers," presents real-world examples of ways in which people use computers in their daily life and work. A second group, titled "Managing Change," focuses on how computers affect business managers in their functions of planning, organizing, leading, and controlling. A third group, "Frontiers in Technology," shows how new technologies will help people solve problems in the future.

Focus on People. The text discusses technology not for its own sake but as a tool to help people solve information problems. The discussion of people and their relationship to technology is not left to a concluding chapter but integrated into the entire text.

Vocabulary. Terminology plays a major role in the mastery of many disciplines, and this is particularly true in the case of computer competence. This text uses a four-level system of vocabulary reinforcement. Each key term is printed in boldface type the first time it appears in the text, with its definition in the margin next to it. A list of key terms appears at the end of each chapter, and the marginal definitions are included in a glossary at the end of the book.

State-of-the-Art Coverage. We have included extensive discussions of such subjects as local area networks, expert systems, and the automated office, including the pros and cons of each and their implications for both specialists and nonspecialists. In fact, an entire chapter is devoted to automating production, presenting real-world applications that students will understand and appreciate.

BASIC Appendix. The appendix on BASIC programming is unique in that it presents a series of programs for calculating the true rate of interest on a loan. Students can actually run these programs to analyze the cost of obtaining a loan. Within each application, several graduated examples are considered, showing the relationship between a computational need and the syntax that helps meet that need.

Supplementary Materials

This book is accompanied by a complete set of instructional materials, including the following items:
- An instructor's manual
- A student study guide
- A lab manual of applications tutorials
- Educational software
- A test bank
- Computerized test banks (Apple and IBM)
- A resource guide
- Acetate transparencies

The *Instructor's Manual* was developed by the authors and represents a distillation of two decades of experience in teaching various computer- and business-related subjects. It contains a detailed lecture outline, instructional goals, teaching suggestions and possible problem areas, answers to review questions, additional questions, an annotated list of additional sources of information, and short items of interest to add to your lectures.

The student *Study Guide,* authored by Edward G. Martin of Kingsborough Community College, provides students with a carefully thought out system for reviewing each chapter of the text. The guide includes chapter outlines, key concepts, fill-in-the-blank chapter reviews, matching exercises, and self-tests.

The *Lab Manual,* also developed by Edward Martin, enables students to learn how to use some frequently encountered personal-productivity software packages, including DOS, spreadsheets, word processing, and data-base management programs. The manual is accompanied by its own instructor's manual that provides mastery lists, screen dumps and files, and solutions to the practice sets. Adopters of the *Lab Manual* may receive free copies of the educational versions of V-P Planner, WordPerfect, and dBASE III+.

The *Test Bank,* prepared by Karen A. Forcht of James Madison University, contains over 100 multiple-choice, true/false, short-answer, and essay questions for each chapter of the text. Apple and IBM versions of the test bank are provided free to adopters of the text.

Acknowledgments

Only with the help of a panel of thoughtful, experienced reviewers is it possible to offer a balanced text that truly reflects the complicated and exciting reality of computers today. The following reviewers outdid themselves in offering constructive criticism of almost every page of the manuscript.

Alan Chmura
Portland State University

Dennis Clarke
Hillsborough Community College

Ed Cross
Old Dominion University

John Dwyer
University of Detroit

Karen A. Forcht
James Madison University

George Fowler
Texas A&M University

George McMeen
University of Nevada

George Miller
Seattle Community College

Robert Norton
San Diego Mesa College

Marilyn Repsher
Jacksonville University

Peter Simis
California State University

Surya B. Yadav
Texas Technology University

In addition, we received many excellent suggestions from the participants who attended two informative focus group sessions.

Finally, special thanks are due to three people whose understanding and cooperation were absolutely necessary to the success of this project. This book is dedicated to Noga Reiss in gratitude for her unflagging support and thoughtful criticism, and to Sami and Maya Reiss.

To the Student

You belong to a generation for whom computer competence is not a luxury but a necessity. The goal of this book is to enable you to understand computers and their impact on people well enough to participate in the ongoing computer revolution. To reach this level of competence, it is important to go beyond mere facts and assimilate the basic principles of computers and computer applications.

With this goal in mind, we have attempted to convey the excitement of the computer revolution. At the same time, we do not hesitate to point out the shortcomings of computers and instances in which they have been applied inappropriately. Whatever your chosen field, a concrete understanding of the benefits and drawbacks of computers and the ability to harness their power will be a significant advantage.

To derive the greatest possible benefit from this text, we recommend that you read each chapter twice: the first time to get a general idea of the subject matter and the second time to retain specific details. Many successful students have adopted the following approach:

1. Read the learning objectives at the beginning of the chapter.
2. Read the chapter through, paying particular attention to the terms in boldface type.
3. Look carefully at each chart and photograph, and read the captions.
4. Read the chapter summary.
5. Skim through the review questions. This step will help you determine which parts of the chapter to focus on in your second reading.
6. Repeat steps 1 – 4, noting any areas of difficulty.
7. Answer the review questions.
8. Review any material that you do not understand fully.

We also recommend that you purchase the *Study Guide,* which has been specially developed to help you maximize your performance.

P

PART 1

Overview

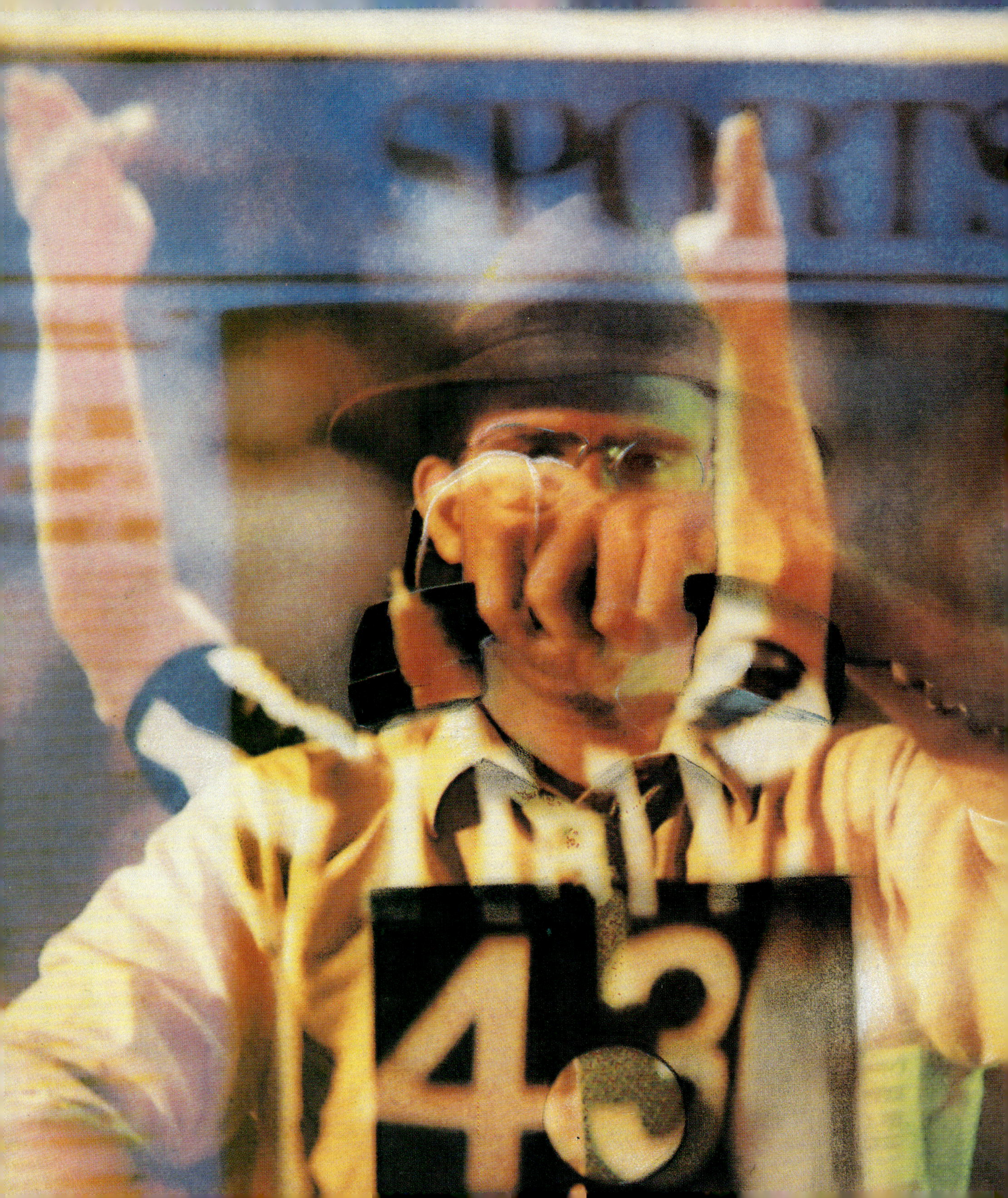
43

Computers and Their Impact

CHAPTER

1

It is late afternoon in Los Angeles. The Washington Redskins are battling the Los Angeles Rams. From high in the press box, *Washington Post* sports reporter Gary Pommerantz follows the play. Perched on the table in front of him is his trusty Tandy model 200 computer—a portable unit the size of a large book.

Back in Washington, D.C., it is evening already. The press deadline for the early-morning edition of the *Post* is fast approaching. Pommerantz has already written much of his story, but the game is not yet over. As the final seconds tick away with the Rams leading by one point, the Redskins fight their way into position for a field goal attempt. Up goes the kick—and it's good!

As the disgruntled Los Angeles fans head for the exits, Pommerantz adds a final paragraph to his story and heads for the nearest phone. He dials a special number in Washington. The computer in the basement of the *Post*'s home office, 3000 miles away, answers with a steady tone. Pommerantz hooks his Tandy 200 to the handset, and moments later the story has crossed the continent.

Pommerantz next dials the number of assistant sports editor Sandra Bailey. He lets her know that the story has been sent. In seconds, Bailey has called the Redskins story up on the screen of the desktop computer in her office on the fifth floor of the *Post*'s Fifteenth Street headquarters. While she checks the story for style and grammar and edits it if need be to fit the available space, another editor adds a headline on his terminal.

At the speed of light, the story, headline and all, heads back downstairs, where the *Post*'s computer instantly sets it in type. The story is then printed onto a clean sheet of paper and pasted into a position held for it on page 1 of the sports section. Fifteen minutes after the final kick, before the fans in Los Angeles have even reached the parking lot, the *Post*'s early edition is ready to roll off the presses, complete with Pommerantz's account of the game.

Sportswriting is just one among thousands of occupations on which computers have had an impact. Chapter 1 introduces the computer and discusses its impact on people and society. After reviewing the history of computers and data processing, it presents some of the advantages and limitations of computers. The chapter goes on to describe the nine functions of data processing, comparing their use in a computer application and a manual one. In addition, several categories of computer users and specialists are discussed. The chapter ends with a brief preview of the rest of the book.

When you have read this chapter, you should be able to:
1. Describe the impact of computers on individuals and society.
2. Outline the key advances in the history of computers and data processing.
3. Discuss the advantages and limitations of computerized data processing.
4. Describe the nine data processing functions.
5. Characterize the important categories of computer users and specialists.
6. Understand and use the key terms listed at the end of the chapter.

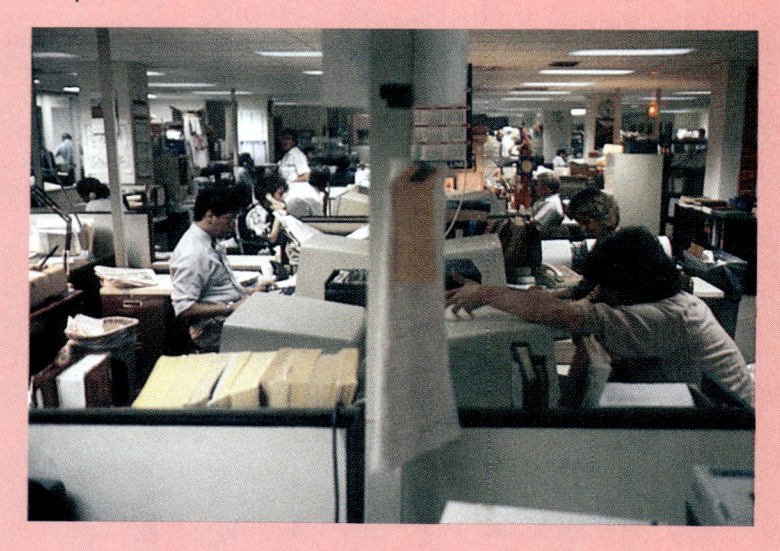

Armed with portable computers, sportswriters can transmit their stories to newspaper offices located across the continent. In the editorial office, computer screens display reporters' stories ready for editing. (© Robert McElroy, Woodfin Camp.)

The Computer Revolution

Computer
An electronic machine that processes raw data to produce information for people or for other machines.

The computer revolution is upon us. Its impact on the way we work, the way we learn, the way we play—in short, the way we live—is tremendous. The **computer**, an electronic machine that processes raw data to produce information for people or for other machines, affects our lives hundreds of times a day. To see how it does this, let's start with your clothes.

Take a close look at yourself. Computers played a role in producing, marketing, and selling virtually everything you are wearing. A *minicomputer* (medium-sized computer) designed the running shoes you are so proud of. Computer-controlled machinery cut the reddish-brown windbreaker you bought on sale last week. The manufacturer's marketing department determined the colors for the windbreaker after reviewing a survey of customer preferences, which was analyzed by its *mainframe (full-sized) computer*. The clothing store where you bought your jacket on sale calculated the value of its inventory with a *microcomputer (a small computer)*. The same computer was used to evaluate the cost of maintaining that inventory before the decision was made to reduce the price on several items.

You read about the sale in the local newspaper, whose ads

Computer reports allow busy executives to have data at their fingertips when they make decisions. (© Lawrence Migdale, Photo Researchers.)

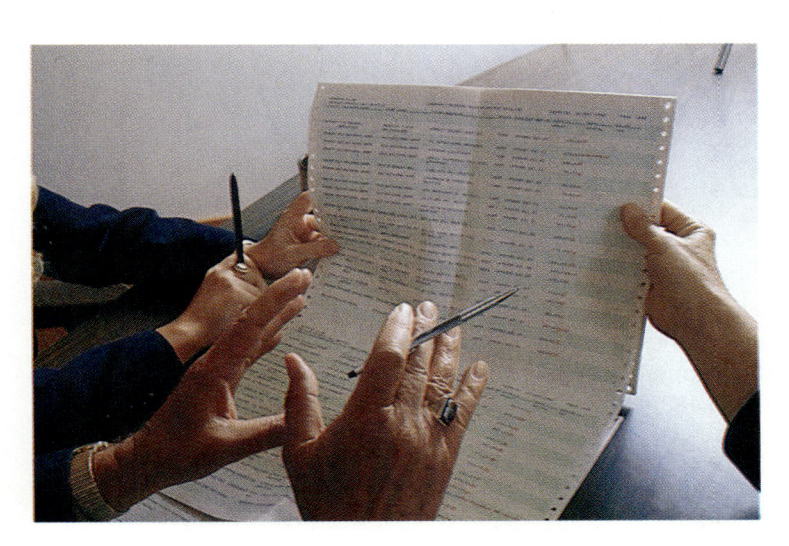

CHAPTER 1   5   COMPUTERS AND THEIR IMPACT

were typeset by computer, and paid for the windbreaker from your automatic teller account (also handled by computer). When the jacket was sold, the store's computerized cash register automatically modified its inventory information. You decided to wear the windbreaker this morning after hearing the weather forecast, which had been prepared by the weather bureau using a *supercomputer* (an extra-large computer) and transmitted electronically to the local radio station.

For the past several years, we have all been living in the age of computers: The clothes we wear, the food we eat, the magazines and books we read, and the television shows and movies we see are all prepared, produced, and distributed by computer. Even the garbage we generate is likely to be managed by computer. From the maternity ward to the cemetery, computers record and influence our lives.

Anyone who was born in a hospital, went to kindergarten or elementary school, or received a government benefit during the past twenty or thirty years is on at least one computer *file* (collection of data). **Data** such as your name, Social Security number, address, and facts related to your education is stored on dozens, if not hundreds, of computer files. Computers can process this data to provide **information** such as your college transcript or your credit rating. (See Figure 1-1.)

It is possible to escape from the computer, but only at the price of withdrawing from society. Even if you chose to retreat to the mountains and breed goats, you might find yourself using a computer to keep records on the herd, improve its diet, and communicate with other goat breeders.

Data
The facts and figures that make up the raw material supplied to a computer for processing.

Information
Processed data that is available for use by an individual.

A Brief History of Computing

Computers have not always played such an important role in our lives. In fact, until quite recently most people's only interaction with computers was via science fiction and movies. To fully appreciate the significance of computers both today and in the future, let's take a brief look at the evolution of computing devices from prehistoric times to the present. It will quickly become clear that in spite of their great variety, all computing devices have something in common: They were invented to meet record keeping and data processing needs.

FIGURE 1-1

Processing of Files

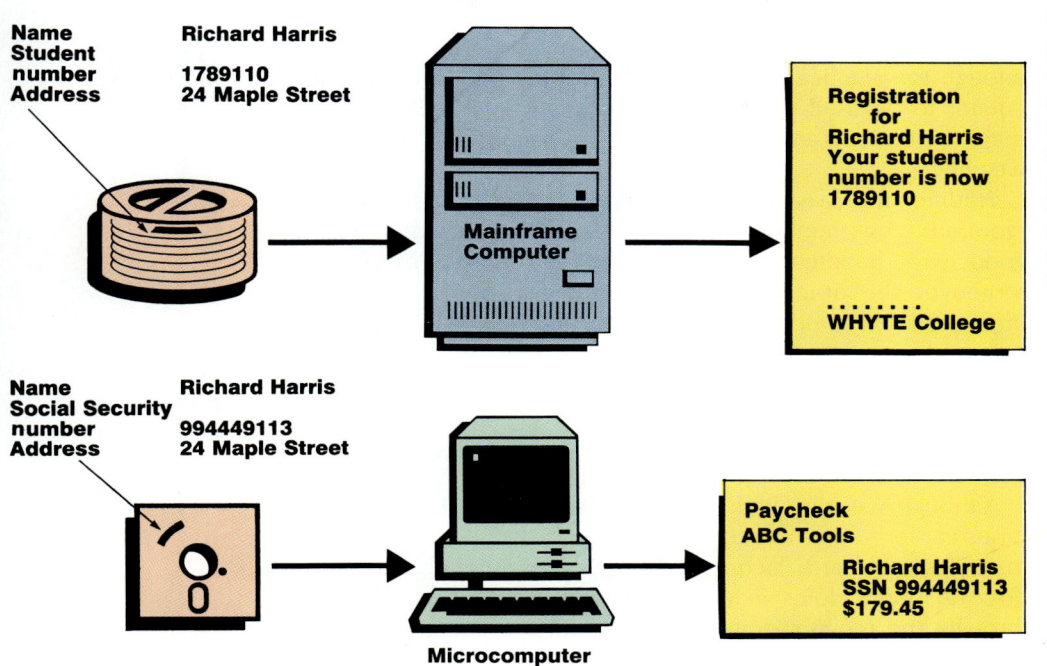

Name Richard Harris
Student number 1789110
Address 24 Maple Street

Mainframe Computer

Registration for Richard Harris Your student number is now 1789110

....
WHYTE College

Richard Harris is described in different files, two of which are shown in part here. Many files include several pages of data for each individual described and may describe thousands of individuals.

Name Richard Harris
Social Security number 994449113
Address 24 Maple Street

Microcomputer

Paycheck
ABC Tools

Richard Harris
SSN 994449113
$179.45

Early Calculating Devices

The abacus, the oldest known calculating device, is still in use in parts of Asia. (© Erin Calmes.)

The origins of computing predate the dawn of civilization. Even prehistoric people had basic data processing needs. They had to keep track of the seasons and the locations of herds of game animals. Undoubtedly they began by counting on their fingers. The first tools for data processing and record keeping were rudimentary—sticks to draw lines on the ground, pebbles for counting, and carved stone for record keeping.

In the Orient the *abacus* has been used for calculating for several thousand years. It is still used extensively in some parts of Asia. Skilled operators can calculate rapidly on an abacus. In fact, in the hands of an expert this device can process data faster than anything invented in the West prior to the 1940s.

The first calculating machine used in the Western world was an adding machine invented in 1642 by a Frenchman, Blaise Pascal. Pascal, who was 18 at the time, wanted to simplify the tedious work performed by his father, the Superintendent of

Taxes. This machine, sometimes called the *Pascaline,* consisted of a series of interconnected wheels. By means of a lever the Pascaline was able to "carry" a digit to the next-higher wheel.

About fifty years after the invention of the adding machine, a German, Gottfried von Leibnitz, invented a machine that could perform the four basic arithmetic operations: addition, subtraction, multiplication, and division. This device was not reliable enough for practical use, however. The first four-function calculator to be used commercially appeared in the 1820s. This major invention came from the seemingly unrelated domain of weaving.

Traditionally, weaving had been performed by artisans who required long training to master the trade. Because woven goods were handmade, they tended to be relatively expensive. Moreover, the intricacy of their design meant that it was almost impossible to reproduce items exactly. Mechanization of weaving would increase the speed of production, reduce the number of employees required, enable relatively unskilled workers to replace skilled artisans, and provide for a uniform product. It is interesting to note that these are the goals of many automation projects today.

Although weaving had been automated in the Far East centuries earlier, it was not commercially successful until a Frenchman, Joseph Marie Jacquard, began using punched cards to drive a loom. Holes in each card allowed a needle to pass through and move specific threads to form a pattern. We can get an idea of the complexity of this loom when we realize that it used about 24,000 cards, each of which contained over 1000 holes. By the 1830s there were tens of thousands of Jacquard looms and the weaving industry had been transformed. Before long, punched cards would be used in the earliest machines that could be called computers.

The Jacquard loom was the first application of punched cards to industrial automation. (Culver Pictures.)

The First Computing Devices

The Analytical Engine. During the 1800s sailors relied on navigational tables to steer ships. Calculating these tables by hand was time-consuming, and the chance of errors was high. In 1822 Charles Babbage, a professor of mathematics at Cambridge University, started working on the *difference engine,* a machine that would calculate navigational tables mechanically. During the next ten years he continued to work on this machine, which was far ahead of the technology of its day, but without success.

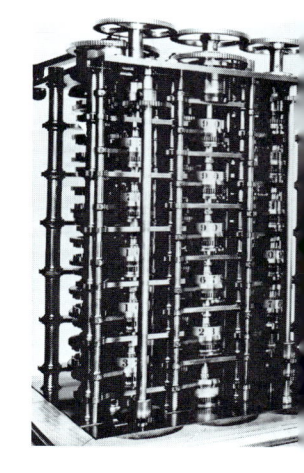

In 1834 Babbage became aware of the Jacquard loom. He reasoned that if punched cards could produce an intricate pat-

This photograph shows part of Charles Babbage's difference engine. (Bettmann Archive.)

tern, they could also be used to drive a calculating machine. When the cards were changed, the machine could perform a different calculation. He called this new machine the *analytical engine*.

In many ways the analytical engine was the first computer. It received data and generated output on punched cards. It was designed to perform the four arithmetic operations, and it had a memory unit in which numbers could be stored. Although Babbage spent the rest of his life developing the analytical engine, he was unable to produce a functioning model. He died in 1871, and the idea of a computer died with him, to be revived more than half a century later.

The analytical engine owes many of its aspects to Babbage's collaborator, Lady Ada Lovelace. Lovelace popularized Babbage's work, corrected several technical errors, convinced him to use binary rather than decimal storage (see Chapter 5), and provided financial assistance. In addition, she was the first programmer. Foreseeing the flexibility of Babbage's invention, she predicted that it would one day play music.

The Hollerith Tabulator. Every ten years the U.S. Bureau of the Census conducts a study of the population, determining the total number of people in the nation and various other useful information, such as the age, sex, and family income of each citizen. The data gathered in the 1880 census was processed manually over a period of seven years. Because of the increase in population and the larger number of questions asked, officials estimated that it would take at least ten years to process the data from the 1890 census, by which time a new census would be under way.

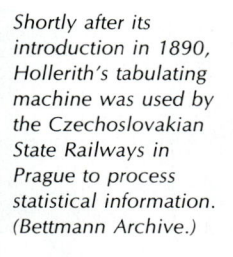

Shortly after its introduction in 1890, Hollerith's tabulating machine was used by the Czechoslovakian State Railways in Prague to process statistical information. (Bettmann Archive.)

Under contract to the Census Bureau, Herman Hollerith developed a machine that compiled and tabulated census data recorded on punched cards. This machine was able to process data from the 1890 census in 2½ years. Hollerith later founded a company to manufacture tabulating machines. Eventually, after a few mergers and a change of name, Hollerith's company became International Business Machines.

Mark I and ENIAC. As is the case with many major inventions, there is considerable debate over who actually invented the first computer. Many people consider the *Mark I* to be the first functioning computer. It dates back to the late 1930s, when Howard Aiken of Harvard University started work on a mechanical calculator. In 1939 his project received financial backing from IBM, and in 1944 it was delivered to Harvard University, where it remains on permanent display. The Mark I was over 50 feet long and 8 feet high. Unlike later computers, it was electromechanical and relied on relays and switches. It was painfully slow by today's standards, requiring about three seconds per multiplication. But it was a giant step forward.

Between 1943 and 1946 John Mauchly and J. Presper Eckert developed the *Electronic Numerical Integrator and Computer (ENIAC)* at the University of Pennsylvania. ENIAC was designed to meet a very specific need: calculating tables of numbers for firing weapons, taking into account such factors as wind speed, temperature, and elevation. Before the development of ENIAC, the Army's Ballistics Research Lab employed more than 200 people working full time with desktop calculators to prepare these tables.

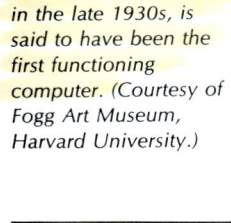

The Mark 1, developed in the late 1930s, is said to have been the first functioning computer. (Courtesy of Fogg Art Museum, Harvard University.)

ENIAC was one of the first computers. In spite of its tremendous size, its processing power was far less than that of a modern home computer.

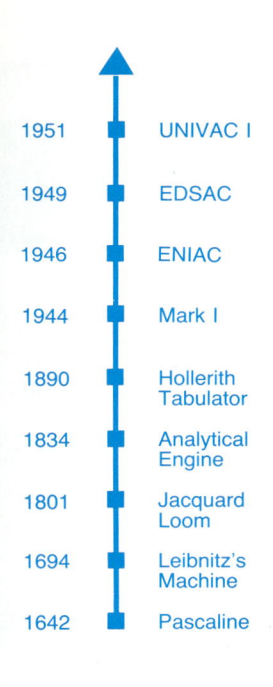

1951	UNIVAC I
1949	EDSAC
1946	ENIAC
1944	Mark I
1890	Hollerith Tabulator
1834	Analytical Engine
1801	Jacquard Loom
1694	Leibnitz's Machine
1642	Pascaline

From Calculating Machine to Computer

ENIAC was a vast improvement over the Mark I because it was fully electronic. It had no moving parts but was composed of about 17,000 vacuum tubes. This more advanced technology made it approximately 1000 times faster than the Mark I. For example, ENIAC could carry out 5,000 additions of 10-digit numbers in a second. However, ENIAC operated quite differently than modern computers. Each step in a calculation had to be prepared manually by attaching wires between the various units. Thus, it could easily take one or two days to prepare a calculation. Once the computer was wired, it received its orders from punched cards at the rate of about two per second. Hence, there was a tremendous difference between the time taken to determine what to do next (about half a second) and the time required to carry out the operation (a few thousandths of a second).

The next step in computer development was to find a way of storing the instructions within the computer itself. This would enable the computer to determine what to do next at "computer" speed rather than at "punched-card unit" speed. Equally important, a group of instructions could be prepared in advance, thereby practically eliminating the long delay for "wiring" the computer.

The Hungarian-born mathematician John von Neumann first recognized the need for a *stored-program computer*. If the computer contains both the data to be processed, such as a set of customer bills, and the instructions for processing this data, the entire operation can be carried out rapidly without human intervention. The first electronic stored-program computer was developed by Maurice Wilkes at Cambridge University in 1949. It was called the *Electronic Delay Storage Automatic Computer (EDSAC)*. All computers developed since EDSAC have been stored-program computers.

The First Three Generations

In the 1960s and 1970s it was common to refer to *computer generations*. A generation of computers was defined by the type of circuitry used at the time. Today, while there is general agreement on what is meant by the first, second, and third generations of computers, the notion of computer generations is no longer clearly defined.

The First Generation. The first generation of computers was based on vacuum-tube technology similar to that used in old radios. Vacuum-tube computers were bulky and gave off a

UNIVAC, now called UNIVAC I, brought computers to public prominence in 1952, when it correctly predicted the election of Dwight Eisenhower to the presidency. (Courtesy of Unisys.)

The vacuum tube, which replaced electronic relays, was used in computers until the late 1950's. It could multiply five 10-digit numbers forty times per second. (Courtesy of IBM Archives.)

great deal of heat. A typical first-generation computer filled an entire city block. Perhaps the best-known model was the UNIVAC I, which introduced the general public to computers when it predicted Dwight D. Eisenhower's victory in the 1952 presidential election. All first-generation computers were mainframe computers. Few, if any, remain in use today.

The Second Generation. The second generation of computers used the transistor and the magnetic core memory as its basic building blocks. Although the transistor had been invented in 1948, second-generation computers did not come into being until 1959. About a year later, minicomputers came onto the scene. Typical second-generation computers include the mainframe IBM 1401 and the minicomputer PDP-1, manufactured by Digital Equipment Corporation. Most second-generation computers were designed to perform either scientific or commercial data processing. Although they were smaller, more powerful, and easier to use than first-generation computers, their use was still restricted largely to specialists.

The Third Generation. The basic building block of third-generation computers was the integrated circuit. The most important third-generation computers were introduced by IBM in 1964 and were known as the System/360. Purchasers of a small model in this series were assured of a path for future growth— their programs could run on larger models with few or no changes.

The third generation extended until about 1970, when more sophisticated technologies came into widespread use. The terms *fourth-* and *fifth-generation computer* are sometimes used in referring to modern computers. In fact, a major Japanese project that is currently under way is known as the Fifth-Generation Computing Project.

FIGURE 1-2

Applications of Home Computers

Entertainment. Home computers can run video games and play old favorites like chess, checkers, poker, and blackjack. In addition, many hobbyists use computers to catalog their collections of stamps, coins, or stereo albums. Artists enjoy the outstanding graphics capabilities of some home computers, and musicians appreciate the computer's sound reproduction capabilities.

Home Management. Home computers can help manage many tasks involved in running a home. They can wake you up to computer-generated music, accompanied by the day's list of things to do displayed on the screen. Computers can also be used for record-keeping activities such as maintaining an inventory for insurance purposes and managing home finances, and for maintaining telephone lists such as a list of baby-sitters.

Personal Finance. Many programs are available to help in managing budgets, preparing income tax returns, and keeping financial records. Many personal-finance programs are powerful enough to help manage the financial operations of a small business.

Education. Owners of popular computers such as the Apple II can buy educational programs on many subjects. There are also computerized courses that teach users how to program the computer in languages such as Pascal and BASIC.

Information Services. Specially equipped computers can access a variety of information services such as CompuServe and TheSource. For a fairly small charge, subscribers can use their computers to shop for bargains, study the stock market and invest extra money, exchange ideas with people who share their interests, reserve a table at a restaurant, or make a flight reservation, all without leaving home.

Personal Computers

Since the mid-1950s computers have steadily become smaller and easier to use, as well as vastly more powerful. The mid-1970s saw the birth of the *microcomputer*, a computer that was inexpensive enough for use by individuals or small businesses. Within a few years hundreds of thousands and then millions of microcomputers were sold for use in homes, businesses, and schools. (The term **personal computer** expresses how people feel about these computers.) Smaller models used in the home are often called *home computers*. Figure 1-2 describes some applications of home computers, while Figure 1-3 describes applications of personal computers in businesses.

Personal computer
A microcomputer that can be used by individuals in homes, schools, and offices.

FIGURE 1-3

Applications of Personal Computers in Offices

Word Processing. Word-processing programs allow users to enter text via the computer, store it, process it, and produce desired output. The more sophisticated programs have the capacity to check spelling and grammar, produce footnotes, and generate indexes.

Electronic Spreadsheets. Electronic spreadsheets are programs that display and manipulate rows and columns of numbers and text. A department manager can set up a spreadsheet for the department's budget and try different ways of allocating funds. The same program can be used to consolidate all of the firm's departmental budgets and make changes in them.

Data Management. Easy-to-use data management programs make it possible for inexperienced users to manipulate files in order to obtain information rapidly. For example, it is quite simple to sort data in any order desired, such as by customer name, by customer number, by city, by ZIP code, by vendor, or by amount owed. It is also easy to obtain customized reports, such as a list of all clients who haven't paid for more than sixty days or who haven't paid for more than thirty days and owe more than $10,000.

Graphics. Graphics programs enable managers and others to view data in the form of bar charts, pie charts, and other diagrams. The better programs allow the user to play with the data, changing headings, labels, and even the type of graph, until it looks right. Then the user presses one or two keys to obtain a printed copy that is good enough for a sales presentation.

Graphics extend the applications of personal computers both at work and at home. While this engineer is testing a newly designed circuit, her children can play computer games. [(top) © Hank Morgan, Rainbow; (bottom) Courtesy of Tandy Corp.]

Advantages and Limitations of Computers

The history of computers is one of extremely rapid change. Except for the electronics industry, few areas of human endeavor have seen such rapid, almost uninterrupted progress. However, it is essential not to overestimate the power of the computer. It is a tool, and like any other tool it has both advantages and disadvantages.

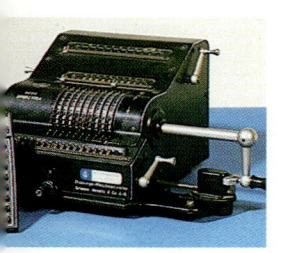

The mechanical calculator has been replaced by the modern electronic calculator on its left. Many programs convert the computer into an electronic calculator with a one-line screen. (© Sheila Terry, Photo Researchers.)

Advantages

There are five major advantages of computerized data processing compared with the use of electronic calculators or manual processing. They are speed, reliability, precision, flexibility, and economy.

Speed. How long does it take you to calculate 2 × 2? How long does it take you to calculate 7354.1 × 7865.34? An electronic calculator speeds up the process considerably, but for complex problems it would still take a very long time. The computer works so fast that its basic time unit is measured in **milliseconds** (thousandths of a second), **microseconds** (millionths of a second), and even **nanoseconds** (billionths of a second). One of the first computers, which could perform 300 multiplications per second, was retired to a museum in the mid-1950s because it was "too slow." Any computer purchased today will be many times faster. A properly programmed computer can calculate in a few seconds a problem that would take weeks to do by electronic calculator and years to do with only pencil and paper.

All this speed has some very practical applications. For example, an engineer designing a new interstate highway can carry out extensive calculations in a few seconds. Businesspeople can obtain up-to-date stock market quotes or inventory reports almost instantaneously.

The computer's lightning-fast calculation speed is accompanied by rapid data retrieval and transmission capabilities. For example, a customer can make over-the-phone airline ticket reservations instead of having to call back the next morning to confirm seat availability. The high speed of computer calculations, data retrieval, and transmission is essential for many applications in which a late answer is useless.

Reliability. Did you try to multiply 7354.1 × 7865.34? Did you get the answer 57,842,496.894? (We used the computer as a calculator to generate the result.) Try doing similar calculations hour after hour, and before long you'll be making mistakes. People are not suited to such tedious arithmetic. Computers do not get tired; many are designed for around-the-clock operations without ever taking a coffee break or making a mistake. As our society becomes more and more complex, the need for error-free processing increases. Computers can greatly reduce the number of errors and may even pinpoint the cause of an error. If a single computer is not reliable enough, as is true for many military and industrial users, two or more computers can be used.

Millisecond
One one-thousandth of a second.

Microsecond
One one-millionth of a second.

Nanosecond
One one-billionth of a second.

CHAPTER 1　15　COMPUTERS AND THEIR IMPACT

Precision. Check your answer to the arithmetic problem again. Did you get exactly 57,842,496.894? Or did your calculator round it off to 57,842,496.89? Or even 57,842,496? Is 0.004 or 0.894 in over 50 million important? It depends on the specific application. Sometimes a seemingly tiny difference in arithmetic can have grave implications. Recall that one of the first computers was invented to perform ballistics calculations during World War II. A small arithmetic error would cause the shells to fall on the wrong target. In other instances, a slight inaccuracy would render an aircraft engine useless and perhaps bankrupt the manufacturer. Special techniques enable modern computers to carry out calculations to almost any degree of precision desired.

Flexibility. A computer is more flexible than an electronic calculator. Besides processing numbers, it can process words and images. This makes it useful in the typing pool and the executive suite as well as in the payroll department and the engineering lab. As we will see later, the same basic data can be processed to provide information to a variety of users. For example, in a major department store computers might be used to generate the following types of information:
- For the accounting department, the sales and payment information needed to do billings.
- For the credit department, a report listing all accounts due for more than sixty days in order to reduce credit losses.
- For the marketing department, information concerning all accounts for customers buying more than $100,000 worth of merchandise a year; it will send them a questionnaire.
- For the sales department, a list of customers who did not buy anything during the last three months; it will send them advertising fliers.

Economy. You might expect that because the computer is fast, reliable, precise, and flexible, it must be expensive. But this is not true. Even the smallest personal computers will score high in each of these qualities when compared to processing by hand or by electronic calculator. People in the computer industry are fond of saying that if the automobile industry had progressed to the same extent that the computer industry has in the past thirty years, a Rolls Royce would cost $20 and get 2 million miles to the gallon.

Limitations

Although computers have many advantages, they have some limitations as well. Basically, a computer can only do what people tell it to do, and there are some things for which it is not suitable. Let's take a brief look a few of the limitations of computers.

Needs to Be Programmed. A computer must be programmed; that is, it has to be told precisely what to do. If a computer runs into an unforeseen situation, it cannot figure out what to do by itself. In other words, there is no such thing as computer common sense. The inability of computers to do things other than those they are told to do is the source of virtually all of the annoying and sometimes dangerous "computer errors" that are an unwelcome feature of life in the late twentieth century. (See Box 1-1.)

It is hoped that computers of the fifth generation and beyond will be less susceptible to programming errors than computers in use today. Such computers often will be able to understand instructions in plain English, eliminating the errors that arise when a specialist translates a user's requests into a code that can be understood by the computer. Also, fifth-generation computers will sometimes be able to learn from their own mistakes. Already some chess-playing computers can do this. They get better the more they play, and can sometimes even beat the people who programmed them.

Performs Limited Tasks. Computers may get better at doing the things for which they have been programmed, but they cannot apply what they have learned to a quite different task. For example, chess programs usually cannot play checkers or backgammon. And don't try to use a chess program to solve an inventory problem or prepare a home budget; the program would not know where to begin. Some popular business programs will carry out several tasks, such as accounting, letter writing, and graphics, but only if they have the specific instructions to do so.

Cannot Evaluate Intangibles. Although a computer can make decisions such as when to send a dunning letter, it does so by applying unambiguous rules. But many human activities cannot be represented in terms of rules. For example, few companies would let a computer make final decisions in selecting personnel. Given the present level of technology, computers cannot evaluate the intangibles involved in hiring. A clever interviewer can detect when an applicant is trying to exaggerate his or her job experience or is covering up several years of unemployment and aimless wandering. A computer cannot.

Not Always the Best Solution. Even though computers can be fast, reliable, precise, flexible, and economical, they do not

BOX 1-1

MANAGING CHANGE

Computer Errors Are People Errors

Vernon Kidd, an East Texas bus driver, was making progress against his skin cancer last spring when his computerized radiation-therapy machine went haywire and killed him. Federal and state regulators say a defect in the machine's programmed instructions—its "software," in computer jargon—caused the machine to burn Kidd with radiation 80 times more potent than the prescribed dose. Atomic Energy of Canada, Ltd., the manufacturer, acknowledges that its equipment may have been partly to blame but says that it can't possibly catch every "bug" or programming error.

The tiniest software bug can fell the mightiest machine—often with disastrous consequences. During the past five years, software defects have killed sailors, maimed patients, wounded corporations, and threatened to cause the government securities market to collapse. Such problems are likely to grow as industry and the military increasingly rely on software to run systems of phenomenal complexity, including President Reagan's proposed "Star Wars" anti-missile defense system.

Software bugs breed as quickly as cockroaches and are as difficult to stamp out. A computerized banking system, for instance, may consist of millions of lines of computer code written by hundreds of people who each work on small segments of the program. Software experts say that they can't ever know with certainty whether all the segments will work in harmony; an error as tiny as a misplaced semicolon can cause a system to malfunction. In 1985 an error in such a system blocked a government securities transaction by the Bank of New York. The bank had to borrow $23.6 billion from the Federal Reserve, and pay $5 million in interest on the loan, before the trouble was straightened out two days later.

"Imagine writing a large book, but instead of three authors, you have 300 and they're all writing a few paragraphs—try putting that together and getting it to make sense," says John Musa, a software expert at Bell Laboratories.

Some software bugs can be traced to mistakes by individual programmers, who may omit part of an instruction or make a mistake in logic. However, when big systems are involved, software flaws go beyond the mistakes of individuals or the shortcomings of technology. "Most software problems are management problems," says Will Smith, formerly the chief technical officer at ITT Corporation. "When you run into technical problems, that's when you expose weaknesses in management."

Meanwhile a computer carries out whatever instructions are given it, without any awareness of whether it is producing the desired results or not. Thus, one frustrated programmer scrawled on a computer center wall: "I hate this @#**! computer/I wish that they would sell it/It won't do what I want it to/It just does what I tell it!"

Source: Based in part on Bob Davis, "As Complexity Rises, Tiny Flaws in Software Pose a Growing Threat," *Wall Street Journal*, January 28, 1987, p. 1. Reprinted by permission of *The Wall Street Journal*, © Dow Jones & Company, Inc. 1987. All Rights Reserved.

always represent the best solution to a particular problem. Moreover, for many applications a computer is not financially feasible.

Data Processing

No matter what the application, a computer follows a set of precise steps or instructions in order to transform raw data into useful information. The transformation of data into information is known as **data processing**. Its exact nature depends on the specific information required, the data available, and both the computer and the people involved. The person requesting the information is called a **user** or *end-user*. The user is not necessarily a computer specialist.

The data that is put into the computer is called **input**; it is entered by means of a specialized device, such as a keyboard. The information that comes out of the computer is called **output**; it appears on a specialized device such as a screen, which is like a television screen, or on paper from a printer. A computer's input and output devices are often contained in a single unit known as a *workstation*. The workstation may be a microcomputer that processes the input to generate the output, or it may be a computer *terminal* that transmits the input to a computer in another location, which then processes it and generates output.

As a concrete example of data processing, consider the case reported in Box 1-2. In this case, both the salesperson and the young couple are users of a program written for an automobile dealership. The salesperson enters input (data). The computer processes the input and responds with output (information). The users examine the output together, and if necessary more input is entered. This procedure continues until the users receive enough information to make a decision.

As any computer user will testify, computers do not always provide valuable information. For example, in Box 1-2, instead of providing the Lloyds with an indication of which truck to buy, the computer might convince them that no available truck meets their needs. Another possible negative outcome occurs when the computer program is unable to provide the requested information. In this case the salesperson will try to process the data manually.

Every day millions of dialogs like the one in Box 1-2 take

Data processing
The manipulation of data to produce information.

User
A person who requests information from a computer.

Input
The data that is entered into a computer.

Output
The information that is generated by a computer.

BOX 1-2

USING COMPUTERS

Matching Products with Customer Needs

On a warm spring afternoon, John and Ada Lloyd walk into the showroom of JKJ Chevrolet. They are greeted by salesperson Hal Miller.

MILLER: What can I do for you?
ADA: We're looking for a pickup to pull our boat trailer.
MILLER: Well, we've got about 200 trucks in stock, so we ought to have one that will do your job. Let's see what the computer shows.
(Together, they step to the front of the store, where the computer sits on a convenient table. Miller turns on the machine. The screen displays a series of blanks to be filled in.)
MILLER: How much does your trailer weigh with the boat on it?
JOHN: About 3500 pounds, I think.
MILLER: A half-ton truck will do the job if it has the right equipment. We'll put CCC10—that's a half-ton—in this blank that says "model." For "required options" we'll put the LE9 engine—that's a V-8—and the heavy-duty J55 brakes. Now, tell me, are you looking for just a basic truck or something fancy?
ADA: We'd like an automatic transmission, but other than that, we'd like the most basic thing that will do the job.
MILLER: OK, then, we'll fill in MM1—that's the manual transmission—in the blank for "excluded options." We'll put in air conditioning as an excluded option, too. That will make sure we get a basic truck, because everything that isn't just a work truck will have AC. Now we'll just punch the enter key and see what we come up with.
(A list of four trucks with brief descriptions appears on the screen.)
MILLER: Ah, there's a blue one, a beige one, and two white ones. Which one would you like to see the details on?
JOHN: Let's look at the cheapest one first.
(At the push of another key, a detailed description of one of the white trucks flashes onto the screen. Miller pushes the print key, and a few seconds later he hands the Lloyds a printed copy of the description.)
MILLER: OK, this one has the V-8, the automatic transmission, heavy-duty brakes, springs, shocks, tinted glass, blue seats—and it lists for $10,435.
ADA: I don't see why that wouldn't do the job. Now tell us, the machine says it lists for $10,435, but what will you really sell it for?
MILLER: How about going out and taking it for a drive? Then I'll see what I can do for you on the price.

The computer has done its work and it's time for some hard bargaining—a job that is still left to humans at JKJ Chevrolet.

place. We'll see many examples of dialogs between users and computers in the following chapters. In each case, the computer is able to process the users' requests correctly because it has been programmed to do so.

Data Processing Functions

A computer program is a set of precise steps, or instructions, that tell the computer what to do. The computer performs the instructions contained in a program to process data and produce information. To do this, it uses different *data processing functions*.

There are nine functions that the computer uses to process data and produce information. These functions are similar whether data is processed by hand, by calculator, or by computer. They are often divided into three categories: data input, processing, and information output. The functions and their definitions are as follows:

Inputting: Entering data into the computer.
Retrieving: Recalling stored data at a later time.
Classifying: Placing similar items in categories.
Sorting: Arranging data in a specified order.
Calculating: Carrying out the standard arithmetic operations—addition, subtraction, multiplication, and division.
Summarizing: Providing an abstract of the data.
Storing: Keeping data for future use.
Communicating: Transferring information from one place or person to another.
Reproducing: Making a copy of the information.

The first two functions in this list constitute data input. The next four are processing functions, and the last three are in the information output category.

The case of the Lloyds' visit to JKJ Chevrolet (Box 1-2) illustrates how the nine data processing functions are performed by computers. Hal Miller initiates these functions when he *inputs* data pertaining to the model and options that the Lloyds want. The computer has already *classified* JKJ's inventory of vehicles into pickups, sedans, and so on.

The computer *calculates* the list price of each truck on the basis of the factory price, options, shipping charges, and dealer markup. Upon request it *sorts* the pickups by price. It then displays a *summary* of trucks that meet the Lloyds' needs.

Detailed descriptions of all the vehicles in stock at JKJ have already been *stored* in the computer's memory. When the Lloyds ask for details on the white truck, the computer *retrieves*

Inputting
Retrieving

Data Input

Classifying
Sorting
Calculating
Summarizing

Processing

Storing
Communicating
Reproducing

Information Output

The Data Processing Functions

CHAPTER 1   21   COMPUTERS AND THEIR IMPACT

the appropriate information. It *communicates* the information to the users by displaying it on the screen. In response to another command, it *reproduces* the information in printed form so that the Lloyds can carry it with them while they take a test drive.

As noted earlier, these nine functions are not unique to data processing by computer. To illustrate this point further, let's compare these functions to the data processing functions that Miller performs in his head at the same time that he is using the computer to find a truck for his customers. Miller *inputs* the sales activity by asking, "What can I do for you?" After a short conversation with the Lloyds, he quickly *classifies* them as serious customers who know what they are looking for. He then *sorts* his current prospects in order of probability of buying. He might place this couple second, ahead of the older man looking for a pickup truck but behind the middle-aged couple who said they'd be back later in the day for a station wagon. Even before the Lloyds ask about price, he *calculates* the lowest offer he can accept. As he talks with his customers, he mentally *summarizes* his impressions. After they leave the showroom, he will *store* this information in his file of active customers. He can quickly *retrieve* it from this file to make a follow-up *communication* by telephone. In the course of that follow-up call, he will verbally *reproduce* the offer to sell the white pickup at a price substantially below list, hoping to close the sale.

Computer Users and Specialists

We mentioned earlier that computers cannot do anything without being programmed, that is, told in great detail what to do and how to do it. But once programs have been written, many users can apply them, often without having to rely on the services of a specialist. In this section we will consider several categories of computer users and specialists.

Computer Users

Users are the people for whom computers supply information. They vary greatly in terms of frequency of computer use, technical skills, and interest. A major element of the computer revolution is a dramatic increase in users' computer skills. An interested user may rival a specialist in applying some kinds of programs.

John and Ada Lloyd are indirect users of JKJ Chevrolet's computer; they communicate with it via the salesperson, Hal Miller. Miller is an unsophisticated user of JKJ's computer. He is not familiar with the internal functioning of the computer or any of the programs that run on it. The only program he knows how to run is the one that displays information about available trucks.

Several employees in the accounts receivable department at JKJ Chevrolet are also unsophisticated computer users. They access computer-generated reports to determine which clients are behind in their payments. When these users want to generate new reports or change existing ones, they must contact a computer specialist. Eva Rogers, a sales manager who is using a popular program, Lotus 1-2-3, to develop a new commission plan for her sales force, is a more sophisticated user. As Rogers gains experience with Lotus 1-2-3 and uses its advanced features to meet new challenges, she may become a *power user*, a specialist in the use of one or more computer programs.

Computer Specialists

Computer specialists are people who earn a living by working with computers (as opposed to people who use the computer as a tool). The people who designed and wrote the programs that run on JKJ Chevrolet's computer are computer specialists.

Although growing numbers of people are able to use computers without requiring the services of specialists, computer specialists remain in demand. This is true for the following reasons, among others: (1) some applications are extremely technical and require the skills of a specialist; (2) some applications are simply too big for even sophisticated users and powerful personal computers to handle alone; (3) millions of people are not yet ready to apply the computer directly to meet their needs; and (4) some applications require the entry of vast amounts of data. It is often inefficient to have nonspecialists enter this data.

There are several kinds of computer specialists. Some work directly with users, while others spend more of their time communicating with the computer. *Computer programmers* communicate with the computer by means of special languages such as COBOL and BASIC. Programmers are paid for programming and spend most of their time working with the computer. JKJ Chevrolet does not employ any programmers. It purchases specialized programs from Automotive Computer Services, Inc., a company that develops computer programs for automobile dealerships. Automotive Computer Services employs several programmers to write programs and modify them to meet its clients' needs.

Since programmers are not always business specialists, another type of computer specialist, the systems analyst, is necessary. *Systems analysts* are people who know not only computer languages but also specific business functions such as accounting or marketing. They act as a bridge between computer users and programmers, translating users' needs into terms that programmers can understand. Systems analysts, aided by users, develop or modify *computer information systems*, systems that coordinate computers with users in order to meet users' information needs. Systems analysts must be able to explain technical aspects of computerization in terms that users can appreciate.

Ideally, a systems analyst has extensive experience in a particular field, such as the automotive industry. For example, all the systems analysts at Automotive Computer Services have experience in developing computer applications for automobile dealers. Two are former owners of automobile dealerships. Because of their background, they are familiar with the needs of a wide variety of automobile dealership personnel.

Once a business begins using a program, other computer specialists may be needed. *Computer operators* run the computer programs and notify the programmers or analysts if there are any problems that they cannot solve themselves. *Data entry operators* enter data that the programs process. *Field engineers* are responsible for keeping the various types of computer equipment in working order. In later chapters we will introduce additional categories of computer personnel, both technical and administrative.

Organization of the Book

This chapter and the following one make up Part 1 of this book. The next chapter presents some basic concepts, including an introduction to computer equipment (hardware) and programs (software) and the main ways in which data is organized and processed. Part 2 is devoted to computer hardware and consists of four chapters. Chapter 3 examines the main categories of computers, ranging from personal computers to supercomputers. Chapter 4 discusses input and output devices in greater depth. Chapter 5 discusses the central processing unit and devices used to store data. Chapter 6 presents the methods and devices used to communicate data and programs.

The four chapters in Part 3 describe computer software in detail. Chapter 7 presents the process and techniques used in computer programming. Chapter 8 examines a variety of programming languages and introduces the operating system, the master program through which users communicate with personal computers. Chapter 9 presents useful examples of programs that run on personal computers. Chapter 10 examines in greater detail the various ways in which data may be organized to meet business needs.

Part 4 looks at the relationships among people and information systems. Chapter 11 introduces the subject of information systems, and Chapter 12 examines the process through which systems are designed and put into use. Chapter 13 describes computer information systems designed to serve various levels of management. Chapter 14 is concerned with information systems in offices, while Chapter 15 explores the use of information systems in the production process.

Part 5 goes beyond commercial applications of computers to examine the impact of computers on everyday life, both now and in the future. Chapter 16 applies principles learned in previous chapters to computer applications in such fields as medicine and sports. Chapter 17 describes two negative applications of computers and discusses ways of reducing their impact. Finally, Chapter 18 considers trends and future developments in computer technologies and applications.

SUMMARY

1. A **computer** is an electronic machine that processes raw data to produce information for people or for other machines. **Data** of many kinds is stored on computer files. The computer can be used to process this data to provide **information**.

2. The oldest calculating device, the abacus, has been used in the Orient for several thousand years. The first calculating machine used in the Western world was an adding machine invented in 1642 by Blaise Pascal. About fifty years later Gottfried von Leibnitz invented a calculating machine that could handle basic arithmetic operations. In the early 1800s Joseph Marie Jacquard used punched cards to drive a loom.

3. The analytical engine designed by Charles Babbage received data and generated output on punched cards, could perform the four arithmetic operations, and had a memory unit. Babbage was unable to produce a functioning model, however. In the 1880s Herman Hollerith developed a punched-card machine that was able to process data from the 1890 census in 2½ years.

4. Many people consider the Mark I, developed by Howard Aiken in the early 1940s, to be the first computer. In the mid-1940s John Mauchly and J. Presper Eckert developed the Electronic Numerical Integrator and Computer (ENIAC). The first electronic stored-program computer, EDSAC, was developed by Maurice Wilkes in 1949.

5. The first generation of computers was based on vacuum-tube technology. The second generation used the transistor as its basic building block. The basic building block of third-generation computers was the integrated circuit. The mid-1970s saw the birth of the relatively inexpensive microcomputer, or **personal computer**.

6. Computerized data processing has five advantages compared with electronic calculators or manual processing. They are speed, reliability, precision, flexibility, and economy. However, computers also have important limitations: they need to be programmed, perform limited tasks, cannot evaluate intangibles, and are not always the best solution to a particular problem.

7. The transformation of data into information is known as **data processing**. The person who requests the information is the **user** or end-user. The data that is put into the computer is called **input**, while the information generated by the computer is called **output**. The data input functions are input and retrieval; processing consists of classifying, sorting, calculating, and summarizing; and information output involves the functions of storing, communicating, and reproducing.

8. Computer specialists earn a living by working with the computer. Computer programmers communicate with the computer by means of special computer languages. Systems analysts deal with both computers and specific business functions. They translate users' needs into terms that programmers understand. Computer operators run programs and notify programmers or analysts if there are any problems that they cannot solve themselves. Data entry operators enter data, and field engineers are responsible for keeping computer equipment in working order.

KEY TERMS

computer
data
information
personal computer
millisecond
microsecond
nanosecond
data processing
user
input
output

REVIEW QUESTIONS

1. Define *computer*, *data*, and *information*, and give an example of each.

2. Describe the abacus, the Pascaline, the Jacquard loom, the analytical engine, and the Hollerith tabulator. Are any of these devices still in use today?

3. Describe the Mark I, ENIAC, and EDSAC. Distinguish among first-, second-, and third-generation computers.

4. Identify four advantages of computerized data processing. Which do you feel is most important? Why?

5. What are the limitations of computerized data processing?

6. Describe the nine data processing functions and give an example of each.

7. Describe three categories of computer specialists.

APPLICATIONS

1. Make a list of all the ways in which you interact with computers during a typical day.

2. If you own a microcomputer, describe what you do with it. If not, talk to a friend or classmate who owns one and describe what he or she does with it.

3. Find out how a local small business uses computers. What does the owner say about the advantages and limitations of using a computer?

4. Discuss the following statement: The world as we know it could not exist without computers.

CASE FOR DISCUSSION

You are applying for a job as a marketing research analyst with the Acme Computer Company, your first job after finishing college. You are eager for the job because Acme is a fast-growing company that offers many opportunities for advancement. However, Acme receives so many job applications that it cannot process them all by hand. It uses a computer to make a preliminary screening in order to provide department heads with a short list of promising candidates to be interviewed.

When your application arrives at Acme, a data entry operator creates an electronic record into which data regarding your age, your college education and major, your previous work experience, and so on, is entered. Depending on the data entered, the computer groups your application with others for similar jobs. Your application is automatically grouped with applications for positions in the marketing department. Within this group, the computer identifies your application and eleven others for the position of marketing research analyst.

This is only the beginning of the process. After data is entered from all of the applications, the computer executes a program that assigns a certain number of points to each one according to such factors as college courses taken in subjects related to the job, grades received, years of work experience, and so on. Fortunately, your qualifications fit Acme's requirements reasonably closely. Your application and six of the eleven others for the position are found to meet an established minimum of points.

On the basis of the point-rating procedure, a report is sent to the marketing department to let them know that twelve applications have been received and that seven candidates should be interviewed. The details of your application remain, for the time being, in the computer's memory.

Your interview has been scheduled for 10:00 A.M. Tuesday. That morning, a computer operator locates your application in the machine's memory bank. The data is recalled and sent to a terminal in the marketing department, which is on another floor of Acme's headquarters building. When the information arrives in the marketing department, the information is printed on paper and placed on the desk of the marketing manager, Rosemary Pfeiffer.

You arrive early for the interview. You wait, nervously thumbing through old copies of *Datamation* and *Advertising Age*. At 10 o'clock, Pfeiffer comes to the door of her office and calls you in. As you talk, she quickly sees that you are a serious candidate. She compares you with the others she has already interviewed for the same job, weighing your strong and weak points. Some of the other candidates have more semester hours of study in marketing courses. However, you have a better background in quantitative analytical techniques and three years of experience as a salesperson in a computer store. Pfeiffer jots some notes on a yellow pad for future reference.

It is late in the day before Pfeiffer has finished interviewing all seven of the candidates. While other Acme employees are leaving for home, she stays at her desk. She wants to go over her notes while her impressions of the candidates are fresh in her mind. Several of the candidates she has interviewed meet the minimum qualifications for the job, but you made by far the strongest impression. She scribbles a note to her secretary, who uses her word processor to write a standard letter to you formally offering the job.

Naturally, you accept. Your visit to Acme left you with a good impression as well. The following Monday you report to a training program that is the first step in your new career as an employee of Acme Computer.

CASE QUESTIONS

1. Each of the nine data processing functions is represented in the preliminary computer evaluation of your application. Highlight and number each of these steps in the case, or make a list on a separate piece of paper.

2. The same nine functions also represented in the noncomputerized interviewing procedure. Number and highlight them as well.

3. What are the advantages and disadvantages of the computerized and noncomputerized phases of the application procedure? Why is it advantageous to use a combination of the two approaches?

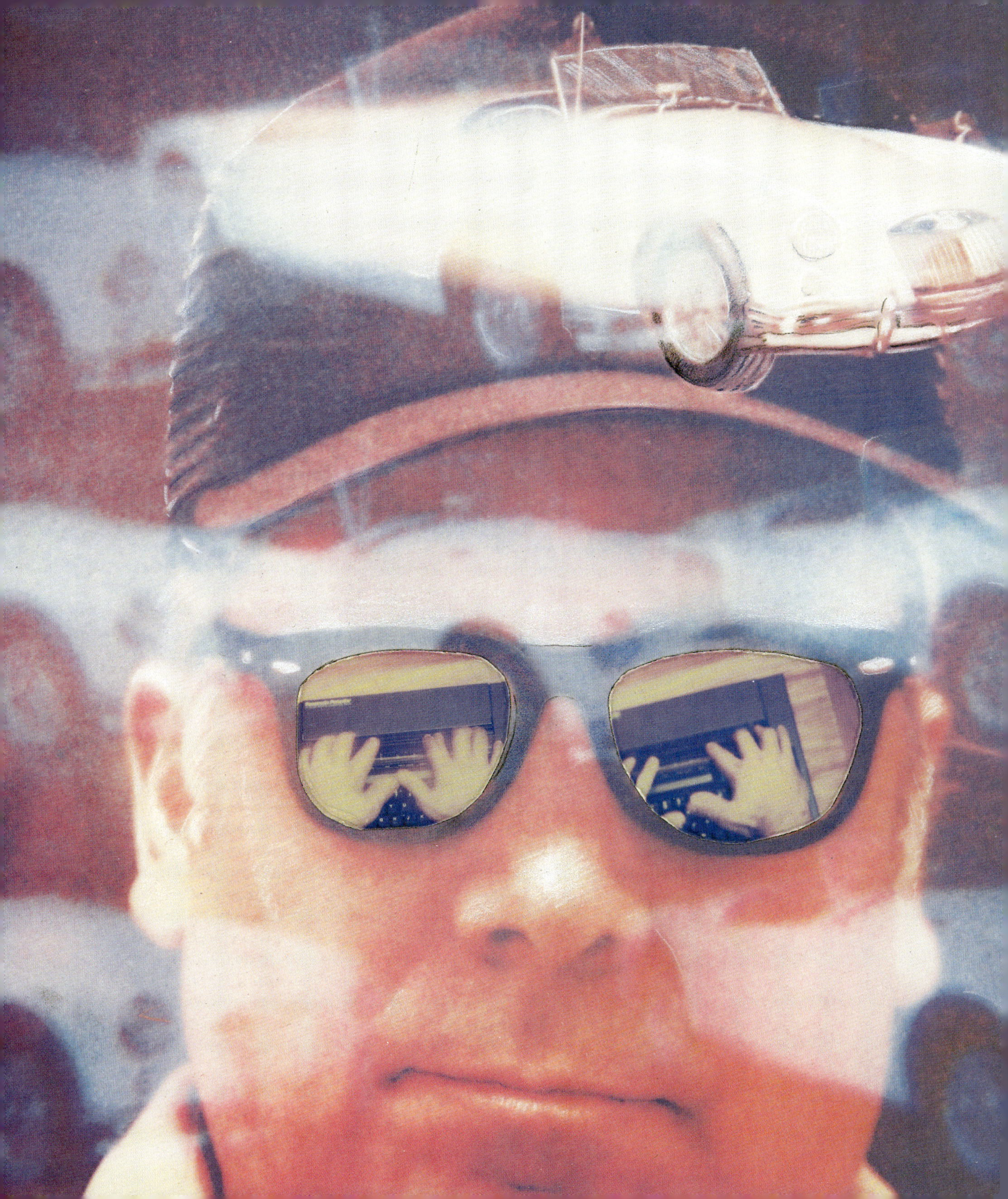

Some Basic Concepts

CHAPTER

2

At first the shop seems cluttered. A closer look shows that it is merely full and busy and that it is quite orderly in its own way. A long tube removes exhaust gases from a bright red MGB. A battered TR3 roadster sits in a corner, waiting for a part to arrive. Through the door you can see a vintage Jaguar waiting to donate its last remaining parts. On a lift is a gleaming new XJ6.

The shop is R&R Motors, which specializes in the repair and restoration of classic British cars. A customer steps through a door from the shop into an inner office. Co-owner David Carter is behind a counter. Carter pulls a repair order from a pigeonhole and hands it to the customer. "Your little MG is doing just fine," he says. "We put a grose jet in the front carburetor, replaced a bad radiator hose, and put in a new fuel pump. The whole job, with a tune-up, comes to $369.85."

At this point Carter is interrupted by a phone call. "Hello, R&R. . . . Yes, we do that kind of work. . . . When? Monday? Let me check. . . . I'll put you down for Monday." As he talks, Carter calls up data about scheduling on his computer terminal and enters the new appointment into the computer's memory.

What Carter did was a routine example of the application of computers to small-business record keeping, except for one detail: The Brailink terminal that he used has no screen. Carter is blind. Instead of a screen, this terminal has a flexible plastic bar on which raised dots representing Braille characters appear and disappear. The operator reads the bar with a fingertip. Input is made through a typewriter keyboard, and special software allows the operator to move quickly through large files even though the plastic bar can display only forty characters at a time.

"The computer age is the golden age for the visually handicapped," says Carter. The Brailink terminal puts information literally at his fingertips that previously had to be filed on hand-punched Braille note sheets. Those sheets could not be written or retrieved by employees who were not skilled in Braille. However, the notes that Carter now makes on his terminal can be displayed on a computer screen or printed on paper as well as displayed in Braille on the plastic strip.

The job of managing a small business like R&R Motors is not an easy one, even in the best of circumstances. But in Carter's case, as in many others, a computer can help keep a hard job from becoming an impossible one.

This chapter presents some basic concepts related to computers and data processing. We begin with the notion of a system—machines, programs, and people working together to meet specific goals. We then proceed to an overview of the five main components of computer hardware as implemented in microcomputers and larger computers. We next examine two types of computer programs and describe the data hierarchy, that is, the organization of data within the computer. Two methods of processing files, batch processing and interactive processing, are discussed, and the chapter concludes with an examination of ergonomics, or ways of adapting computer hardware and software to the user.

When you have read this chapter you should be able to:
1. Describe the components of a computer system.
2. Identify the major input and output devices and the types of people who use them.
3. List the three components of the central processing unit and their functions.
4. Distinguish among the major auxiliary storage devices for microcomputers and larger computers.
5. Distinguish between applications software and systems software.
6. Illustrate the data hierarchy.
7. Define ergonomics and indicate its importance.
8. Compare and contrast batch and interactive processing.
9. Understand and use the key terms listed at the end of the chapter.

Without software packages like those illustrated here, a computer would be a useless piece of furniture. Notice the printed manual, which helps the user run the software efficiently and effectively. (Courtesy of Apple Computer Inc.)

System
An organized set of machines, people, and procedures designed to meet one or more specific objectives.

We saw in Chapter 1 that in the past thirty years computers have steadily become more powerful, more reliable, and smaller. These benefits have resulted from improvements in computer hardware, particularly advances in electronics technology. However, other advances have also had a major impact on the way computers are used. Although they are not as spectacular as the advances in hardware just noted, improvements in the programs that drive computers, known as *software*, are of great importance. As a result of these improvements, computers have become much easier to use. They have also become more flexible, able to handle more types of data and solve a wider range of problems.

A combination of computer hardware, software, people, data, and operating procedures is a computer **system**. Like the components of other systems (e.g., stereo systems), the various components of a computer system must work together to meet predefined goals. In the case of R&R Motors, several pieces of computer hardware, including a Brailink terminal, and related software work together to help Carter, the user, manage his business. This is an example of a small computer system with rather limited goals. Other computer systems, such as financial systems, may include more powerful hardware, more sophisticated software, and a multitude of users. They are designed to meet larger goals such as producing and analyzing the budget of a multinational corporation. Regardless of their size and purpose, however, all are composed of hardware, software, and people working together to process data and generate information.

Hardware

Hardware is the physical equipment associated with a computer system. The hardware required for a particular system may range in cost from less than $100 to more than $10 million, depending on the desired performance capabilities. But as we will see, the hardware for all computer systems shares many characteristics.

In general, computer hardware can be divided into five basic categories: input devices, output devices, the central processing unit, auxiliary storage devices, and data communication equipment and facilities. (See Figure 2-1.) In this section we will describe each category and give examples of typical equipment for microcomputer and mainframe computer systems. Part 2 (Chapters 3–6) discusses hardware in greater detail.

FIGURE 2-1

Hardware Components of a Computer System

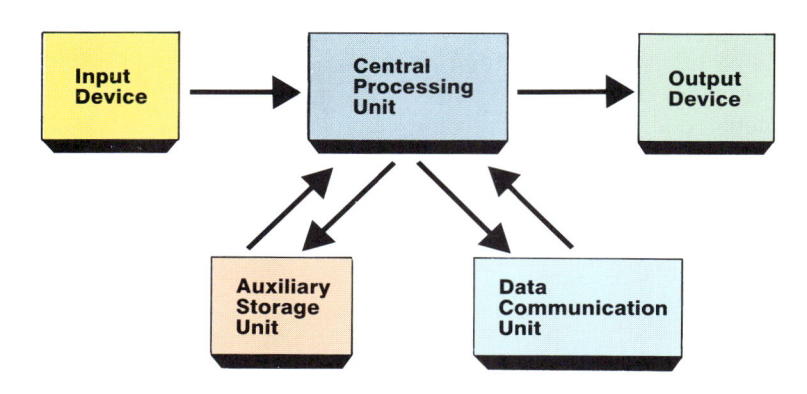

```
Input Device → Central Processing Unit → Output Device
                    ↕         ↕
            Auxiliary    Data Communication
            Storage Unit      Unit
```

Input

In any computer system, the quality of the information produced depends on the quality of the input supplied. Input has no intrinsic value; its only value lies in its potential use in generating output. The importance of good input is underscored by the popular phrase "garbage in, garbage out."

Data entry, the process of inputting data, can be a very labor-intensive activity and is a bottleneck in many computer centers.

This data entry professional earns a living by entering data into a computer. Note the wide screen that helps her check her work. (© T. Bieber, The Image Bank.)

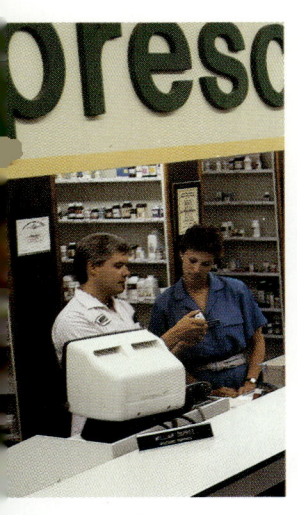

Pharmacists and checkout personnel enter data from each sale at the keyboard. They are not data entry professionals, but they use the computer as a tool in performing their jobs. [(left) © Will/Deni McIntyre, Photo Researchers; (right) © Tim Davis, Photo Researchers.]

The appropriate input devices can speed up and simplify the data entry process. The choice of an input device depends to a large extent on who is entering the data. There are three main categories of people who input data: users who work with output, data entry professionals, and people who are trained in data entry techniques for a particular application.

Examples of the first category, users who work with output, include the neighborhood pharmacist or the manager in the local bottling plant. These people enter data into computers in order to produce various kinds of reports. They don't have the time or the interest to learn many rules about data entry. For them, data entry is not an end in itself; it's a means to an end. They are more concerned with what they enter than with how efficiently they enter it. The input device should take them slowly through the steps of data entry.

Another category of users consists of data entry professionals—people who earn a living entering data into computers. They are expected to enter large volumes of data rapidly and with very few errors, and may use computers for several applications, using billing, payroll, and marketing programs with equal ease. They receive training in data entry techniques, learning specific rules and procedures to increase their efficiency and accuracy.

In between these is a third category—people like travel agents and supermarket checkout personnel who are not, strictly speaking, data entry professionals but are trained in data entry techniques for their own particular applications. They spend a lot of time entering data into the computer, work at high levels of accuracy, and expect an instantaneous response from the computer.

CHAPTER 2 35 SOME BASIC CONCEPTS

Keyboard
The most commonly used input device, similar to a typewriter keyboard.

In determining which input device to use, it is important to keep in mind who is going to enter data into the computer. Each category of users requires different methods for optimum performance. Some input devices can be programmed for different data entry methods, depending on who is using them.

In the rest of this section we will examine various input devices, starting with those that are generally used with microcomputers. Input devices can be divided into two main categories: those that rely on a keyboard and those that do not.

Keyboard. Microcomputer **keyboards** are similar to typewriter keyboards, except that they include special keys that make it easier for users to run programs or enter data. For example, many personal-computer keyboards include ten or more *function keys* that perform particular functions depending on the program used. A user running BASIC on an IBM PC need not type LIST but can press the function key F1 to generate the same lines. Many programs make extensive use of function keys to reduce the amount of typing required.

Keyboards associated with microcomputers and with terminals have a feature that increases their efficiency as input devices. As a key is depressed, the output screen displays the character that has just been entered. This allows the user to see data on the screen as it is entered, and typing mistakes can be corrected on the spot. Keyboards have a distinct limitation, however: Not everybody likes to type. Accordingly, a number of input techniques have been developed with the goal of reducing typing. They include the mouse and pointing.

Mouse. A *mouse* is a box about the size of a tape cassette that is rolled on a desk top or in the palm of the hand. As the user rolls it, different areas of the computer screen are highlighted. When the desired location is highlighted, the user pushes a button. The mouse on the Apple Macintosh has one button; other mice have two or three. For most applications, using a mouse reduces the need to use a keyboard, although it does not eliminate it entirely. The use of a mouse is generally restricted to microcomputer systems.

Pointing. The Hewlett-Packard Touch Screen computer enables users to point to what they want on the screen. Pointing can be effective for programs that involve a lot of selection, such as educational applications. Some mainframe computer systems also use terminals with touch-sensitive screens.

Keyboard Devices. Medium-sized and large computer systems may contain several keyboard devices in addition to ter-

The ten function keys at the left of the keyboard reduce the typing required when running programs. (© Erin Calmes.)

The use of a mouse reduces the amount of typing required to enter data. It is particularly well adapted to drawing pictures on the screen. (© Tom McHugh, Photo Researchers.)

The Universal Product Code is a machine-readable code designed specifically for use with point-of-sale terminals. (© Erin Calmes.)

When the old-fashioned cash register is replaced by a POS terminal, checkout personnel work faster and will make fewer errors. An added benefit to the store is improved inventory control. (© Melchior Digiacomo, The Image Bank.)

minal keyboards like those discussed earlier. One of the oldest keyboard data entry devices still in use is the *keypunch*, which is used to prepare punched cards similar to those used by the Hollerith tabulator a century ago. Unlike workstation keyboards, a keypunch is not attached to a screen, so users do not see the results of their typing. Chapter 4 describes other kinds of keyboard data entry equipment used with mainframe computer systems.

Nonkeyboard Devices. Like microcomputer systems, larger systems are increasingly providing for nonkeyboard data input. Several methods are in use, all designed to reduce typing. *Point-of-sale (POS) terminals* are cash registers equipped with scanners that read special codes such as the *universal product code (UPC)*. When the POS terminal registers a medium-sized blue cashmere sweater (item code #178-614B), it automatically prints out the price on the cash register slip and instructs the computer to reduce the appropriate inventory by one. When a predetermined number of medium-sized blue cashmere sweaters have been sold, the computer system will order more. We'll discuss the details of these operations in later chapters. The key point here is that the POS terminal picks up data such as the item code automatically, eliminating the need for a person to key in the data and perhaps make an error in doing so.

Optical character recognition (OCR) devices recognize typed or handwritten characters and convert them into electronic signals that a computer can process. The more expensive the OCR device, the more characters it can decipher and the fewer errors it makes trying to distinguish between similar characters such as 0 and O or l and 1. When consumers purchase gas at a

CHAPTER 2   37   SOME BASIC CONCEPTS

service station with a credit card, the small sliding-scale device generates a slip containing data that will be read by an OCR device at the credit card company. Inexpensive OCR devices for use with microcomputers have become available in recent years.

The unusual characters that appear on a cashed check are read by a *magnetic ink character recognition (MICR) device*. Unlike OCR equipment, an MICR device can read only numbers and a few special symbols; its application, therefore, is basically restricted to banking. This equipment has been used by the banking industry since the mid-1950s.

Output

Most computer users evaluate a system on the basis of the output it produces. If a system's output is easy to read, rapidly available, accurate, complete, concise, and relevant, they will probably approve of the system. If not, they will request improvements or ignore the output.

Output devices fall into two major categories: those that provide a temporary image of the output and those that provide a permanent printed copy. The first category consists of monitors, also known as display screens. The second consists of printers and a variety of specialized devices.

Monitors. The most widely used output device for computers of all sizes is the **video display terminal (VDT)**, also known as a *cathode-ray tube (CRT)*. VDTs display output on a screen similar to a television screen. They usually are equipped with a keyboard. There are two basic types of CRTs, one for people who work with words and numbers and the other for people who work with pictures and drawings. An increasing number of users require both kinds of VDTs. Their needs may be met by sophisticated models. The biggest drawback of VDTs is that the screen image is not portable and is not easily photographed.

Video display terminal (VDT)
A device in which output is displayed on a screen. Also known as a cathode-ray tube (CRT).

Printers. **Printers** are output devices that create permanent copy (known as *hard copy*). Printers for microcomputers run at a variety of speeds, producing anywhere from a few lines to ten or more pages per minute. They usually print a character at a time and therefore are called *character printers*. It is possible to hook up a typewriter to a computer to get printed reports. In this case legibility is no problem, but speed may be. For example, a typewriter isn't fast enough to print grade reports for 1000 students but may do an excellent job of producing accounting reports for a pizzeria. With certain types of printers,

Printer
A computer output device that produces permanent or hard copy.

on the other hand, legibility can be a problem. Box 2-1 compares the legibility of hard-copy output from four kinds of printers used with microcomputers.

In general, the larger the computer, the more powerful the printer required. Printers for mainframe computers are considerably more powerful than those for microcomputers. Mainframe printers usually print a line at a time (*line printers*) or an entire page at a time (*page printers*). Instead of producing an attractive business letter, mainframe computers may generate hundreds of bills per minute on special forms. The most sophisticated models can even generate the forms.

The Central Processing Unit

Central processing unit (CPU)
The core of the computer, composed of the arithmetic-logic unit, the control unit, and primary storage.

Chip
A single electronic circuit that serves as the building block of modern computers.

The **central processing unit (CPU)** is the "brain" or core of the computer. It is actually composed of three units: (1) the arithmetic-logic unit, (2) the control unit, and (3) primary storage. CPUs for microcomputer systems are quite small: The arithmetic-logic unit and the control unit can fit on a fingertip-sized electronic unit called a **chip**. Chips are now used in the central processing units of computers of all sizes, as well as in various types of computer hardware and computerized items such as appliances, digital watches, and toys.

Arithmetic-Logic Unit. The *arithmetic-logic unit* handles *arithmetic operations* (addition, subtraction, multiplication, and division) and *logic operations* (such as comparing two numbers to see whether they are greater than, less than, or equal to each other). Typical business applications such as producing a payroll involve countless arithmetic and logic operations. For example, an arithmetic-logic unit can determine the answer to a question such as "Did Suzanne Wolfe work more than forty hours last week?" The answer may be used in deciding whether or not Wolfe qualifies for overtime pay. In Chapter 5 we will learn more about how the computer handles arithmetic and logic operations.

Control Unit. The control unit controls the entire computer system, not just the CPU. It determines which activity to carry out next and is responsible for coordinating input devices, output devices, the central processing unit, and auxiliary storage devices.

Primary Storage. *Primary storage* contains data and programs that are currently being processed by the CPU. In most cases users need not know where an item is stored; they just ask for it by name and the computer delivers it to the CPU.

BOX 2-1

USING COMPUTERS

Legibility of Computer Output

A great many printers have been made for use with today's popular personal computers. They meet the criterion of *legibility* to varying degrees, as can be seen in the samples shown here.

Sample 1 is typical of a first-generation dot-matrix printer of the late 1970s. A dot-matrix printer uses tiny pins to strike an inked ribbon, with a pattern of dots making up a character. The legibility of this sample is poor. The characters are crudely formed, with the individual dots visible in many cases. Letters like "p" and "g" have no descenders reaching below the line. And the characters are not evenly dark. Nevertheless, many printers that produce output of comparable quality are still in use in situations in which superior legibility is not very important.

Sample 2 shows a dot-matrix printer made in the mid-1980s. Many more dots are used, descenders have been added, and the characters are darker and more uniform. This model can even mix roman, italic, and boldface type within a line. Printers that produce this type of output are fast, inexpensive, and popular.

Sample 3 shows the output of a typical daisy-wheel printer. Instead of dots, this printer uses plastic characters arranged on the spokes of a daisy-like printwheel to strike a ribbon. The characters are much crisper and clearer than those in samples 1 and 2. However, this kind of printer is slower than a dot-matrix printer and does not mix type styles easily.

Sample 4 shows what can be done with a state-of-the-art laser printer. This machine uses a laser beam to form characters directly on the drum of a device resembling a photocopier. It is very fast, printing eight or more pages a minute. The characters are clear and crisp, and an almost unlimited range of styles and sizes of type can be used.

Sample 1

```
WINNERS * WINNERS * WINNERS * WINNERS * WINNERS * WINNERS

The  weather was the pits for the Great Falls Riding Center event
on  November 3rd, but that didn't stop our gang. Ingrid deWit won
```

Sample 2

It was an old white farmhouse that stood well back from the road. On one side a modern garage had been attached. Today, though, the garage doors were tightly shut.

Sample 3

Lecture Notes and Suggestions

A minimum of one lecture session should be spent on this chapter. If necessary, much of the material on sources and uses of government funds can be left to independent reading by your students. Most of your lecture time will probably be spent on the theory of tax incidence. Depending on your preferences, you may want to spend a second session on public choice theory, but this section can be skipped without loss of continuity if you wish.

Sample 4

TABLE 1. Percentage of Positive and Negative Thoughts for University Students with Low or High Test Anxiety

Thought	Low Test Anxiety Percent	High Test Anxiety Percent
Positive Thoughts		
Will do all right on test.	71	43
Mind is clear, can concentrate.	49	26
Feel in control of my reactions.	46	23

The two most common categories of primary storage are *random-access memory (RAM)* and *read-only memory (ROM)*. Users can modify the contents of RAM, but the data and programs in RAM are erased when the computer is turned off. Users cannot change the contents of ROM—but ROM is not erased when the computer is turned off. Most personal-computer systems contain both RAM and ROM, as well as a third type of storage—auxiliary storage—which we will discuss shortly.

In the past few years the size of primary storage for all computers, and especially for personal computers, has increased at a spectacular rate. More primary storage means faster-running and easier-to-use programs.

Mainframe CPUs. The central processing units of mainframe systems are made up of the same elements as those of microcomputers, namely, arithmetic-logic unit, control unit, and primary storage. The difference is that these units are much more powerful for mainframe systems than for microcomputers. Whereas the CPU of a microcomputer can meet the needs of one or a few users at once, the CPU of a mainframe computer may serve hundreds of users at once. In many cases mainframe computer systems consist of several CPUs working together.

Auxiliary Storage Devices

We noted earlier that data and programs can be stored in primary storage within the CPU. They can also be stored in *auxiliary storage* media. A variety of auxiliary storage media and processing devices are available for computers of all sizes. They include floppy disks, hard disks, cassette tapes, magnetic tape, and magnetic disks.

Floppy Disks. The most common storage medium for personal computers used in the home is *floppy disks* (also called *diskettes* or *floppies*). These are thin pieces of magnetized plastic sealed in a protective envelope. They are read and written using specialized equipment known as *disk drives*. Floppies come in several standard sizes, one of the most popular being 5¼ inches in diameter, often storing 360K (about 360,000) characters of information. A double-spaced typed page contains 2K (2048) characters; thus, a typical floppy disk may contain about 180 typed pages of information. Diskettes are so inexpensive that they usually are sold in units of ten. Many personal-computer users have libraries consisting of hundreds of diskettes.

This Apple II Plus microcomputer includes the two floppy disk drives shown at the right. Most microcomputers in homes and offices include at least one floppy disk drive. (Courtesy of Apple Computer Inc.)

This Winchester disk, a type of hard disk, has a storage capacity equivalent to that of about fifty floppy disks. (Courtesy of International Business Machines.)

Hard Disks. *Hard disks* (also called *fixed disks* or *rigid disks*) are medium- or high-capacity metal storage media that are permanently installed in microcomputer systems. A typical hard disk contains 20M (over 20 million) characters, or the equivalent of about fifty typical floppy disks. In addition to offering much greater storage capacity, hard disks are much faster than diskettes. Today most personal computers that are sold for business use contain at least a 20M hard disk.

Cassette Tapes. Originally many home computers used *cassette tapes* to store data. Cassette tapes are slow and can be hard to work with, since it is difficult to position the tape at a precise location. Few cassette systems are sold today, but a modified form of cassette is used for making copies of data on hard disks.

Magnetic Tape. *Magnetic tape* is a widely used storage medium for large and medium-sized computers. It resembles the recording tape used for music. A typical tape is ½ inch wide and 2400 feet long. It contains magnetized spots that represent characters according to a code. These characters are *read* (input) or *written* (output) using a device known as a *magnetic-tape drive*. Magnetic tapes contain hundreds or thousands of characters per inch and therefore can hold huge amounts of information in a relatively small space.

Tapes are limited to *sequential processing,* which means that the information on them can be read only in the order in which it was written. A common example of the use of magnetic tapes is to store payroll data; typically this data is stored by employee number.

CHAPTER 2   43   SOME BASIC CONCEPTS

These magnetic tapes are identified by colored labels to permit easy access. They are mounted on magnetic-tape drives prior to processing. [(left) Courtesy of Hewlett-Packard; (right) Courtesy of International Business Machines.]

Magnetic tapes have a fundamental limitation: With standard equipment it is impossible to write on a magnetic tape as it is being read. This means that it takes at least two magnetic tapes to handle applications involving changes in recorded information. But this limitation also has a positive aspect: When processing is complete, both the previous version and the new version of the tape are available. Then if something goes wrong, there is no need to start from scratch.

Magnetic tapes have several advantages as well as disadvantages. They are inexpensive, durable, and portable. But the fact that they are sequential makes them too slow for many applications. Suppose, for example, that you have the tape containing payroll data sorted by employee number, but this time you want only employee number 423. You would have to read the data for *all* previously occurring employees to *access* (get) number 423. Because of this drawback, many organizations restrict their use of magnetic tape to making copies of essential files and storing inactive files.

Magnetic Disk. The most widely used storage medium for large and medium-sized computers is the *magnetic disk*, which is used in conjuction with a *magnetic-disk drive*. Like tapes, magnetic disks have both advantages and disadvantages.

Magnetic disks allow *random processing*, which means that the system can access data from anywhere on the disk without reading what comes before it. In the case of the employee file mentioned earlier, the computer can read or write the data for employee number 423 directly. Magnetic disks also provide for sequential processing, which is useful for some applications.

Random processing using disks makes it possible to computerize applications, such as over-the-phone airline reservations that are impractical or impossible using tapes. In the time it takes to access data for a single flight on a tape, data concerning hundreds of flights can be found and processed on a magnetic disk. Another advantage of magnetic disks is that they can be rewritten during processing. But the corresponding disadvantage is that no duplicate copy is automatically produced. As we will see in Chapter 5, systems that employ magnetic disks often rely on magnetic tapes to store copies of important files.

Data Communication

Data communication involves the transmission of data, information, and programs from one location to another. Data communication systems may include computers of all sizes, equipment such as computer terminals, and specialized transmission facilities and communication equipment. Data communication systems allow companies to transmit information between branches at different locations almost instantaneously. For example, a data communication system makes it possible for a request generated in a Chicago branch office to be transmitted in a few seconds to a warehouse in Richmond, Virginia. An employee in the warehouse can send back a reply equally fast. Data communication also allows both the branch office and the warehouse to send summary information to the head office in New York at the end of the day.

Data communication systems make use of several kinds of hardware and transmission facilities that are not found in conventional computer systems. Chief among these are telephone systems and modems.

Telephone Systems. Many data communication systems rely on the telephone network to transfer data, programs, and information from one location to another. The telephone system is useful for data communication because it is familiar to most users, is relatively inexpensive, and covers practically the entire world. However, since telephone systems were designed to carry voices, not data, they are not ideal for data communication. (Other data communication channels are described in Chapter 6.)

Modems. A *modem* is a specialized communication device that converts the type of signal that is found in computers and workstations to the type of signal that is transmitted over most telephone lines. Modems are included in most data communi-

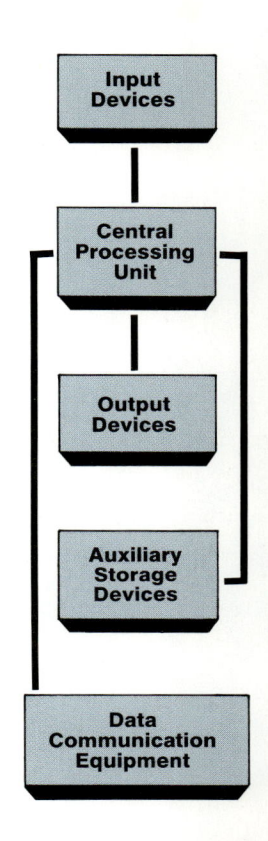

Computer Hardware

cation systems. A modem can be used to send or receive programs or data to or from a similarly equipped workstation located across the city or across the continent. Users of home computers often use modems to contact others with similar interests or to access commercial information services, for example, to do their banking or reserve hotel rooms. Modems are also used to enable employees working at home to communicate with a computer in the central office.

Software

Software refers to the programs, procedures, and documentation used to run the hardware of a computer system. Without proper software, hardware is useless. For example, David Carter's Brailink terminal displays only forty characters at a time rather than the full screen of characters that can usually be seen on a VDT. To overcome this limitation, the Brailink terminal comes with special software that makes it easy for users to scan quickly through many lines above and below those that are being worked on at any given moment. In this section we will classify software and present some examples of each type, once again distinguishing between microcomputers and other computers. In Part 3 (Chapters 7–10) we will discuss software in greater depth.

Software
The programs, procedures, and documentation used to run the hardware of a computer system.

Applications Software

Applications software is software whose function is to provide users with information or help them get a job done. It is written by applications programmers. Examples include the program that generates the list of available trucks for JKJ Chevrolet described in Chapter 1, the program that keeps records for R&R Motors described at the beginning of this chapter, and the programs used by oil companies to determine where to drill for oil. Commercially available applications programs are often called *packages*.

Applications Software for Microcomputers. The enormous popularity of microcomputers has lead to the development of a wide variety of applications software. Home computer users can purchase inexpensive programs that help them

Field computers help technicians decide whether or not to continue drilling for oil at a given location. Data from the field computers may be sent to the head office for further processing. (© John Blaustein, Woodfin Camp.)

keep track of their finances or carry out a fitness program. Other packages enable people to study almost any subject at home. Business microcomputer users can find software designed to meet all kinds of information needs. Scientists and engineers also can choose among a wide variety of packages.

A major aspect of the personal-computer revolution is the emergence of software that users can apply themselves without having to rely on the services of computer specialists. Such software is often called *personal-productivity software* because it enables users to increase their productivity in such areas as writing letters, calculating budgets, and keeping records. Chapter 9 is devoted to personal-productivity software; here we present a brief introduction to some of the most popular types of software for personal-computer users.

Word-processing programs enable users such as secretaries, typists, and managers to create, modify, and save written material ranging from simple memos to technical manuscripts several hundred pages long. Popular microcomputer word-processing programs include Word, WordStar, and MultiMate. In a typical application, co-owner Alice Nolan of R&R Motors used a word-processing program to compose a letter to each of several dozen active clients announcing a change in the company's credit policies.

Electronic spreadsheets enable users to handle rows and columns of numbers easily. The world's best-selling business program, Lotus 1-2-3, is usually purchased for use as an electronic spreadsheet, although it has other applications as well. With the aid of an electronic spreadsheet, Nolan can develop

CHAPTER 2   47   SOME BASIC CONCEPTS

a budget for R&R Motors and ask "What if?" questions such as "What is our projected profit if we increase our hourly labor charges by 5 percent?" or "What is the impact on our cash flow if we buy our building instead of continuing to lease it?"

File-management programs allow users to develop and modify files of data and extract information in several ways. Two popular file-management programs are PFS:File and PC-File III. With the aid of such a program, Nolan could list R&R's clients in alphabetical order or determine which clients have not used R&R's services in the last three months.

Data-base management programs are more sophisticated than file-management programs. For example, they can process several files at once. Popular data-base management programs include dBASE III and R:base 5000. With the aid of such a program, Nolan could combine data from a customer file, an inventory file, and a supplier file to obtain information for special orders.

Integrated software enables users to perform several types of personal-productivity functions using the same program. Examples of integrated software are Symphony, manufactured by the makers of Lotus 1-2-3, and Framework, manufactured by the makers of dBASE III. In the next section we will examine another type of software, systems software, which can help users manage several programs at once.

Applications Software for Mainframe Computers. Applications software for mainframe computers tends to be much more powerful than comparable software for microcomputers. For example, whereas a microcomputer accounts receivable program might be suitable for processing accounts for 100 clients, companies with thousands of clients are likely to use a mainframe accounts receivable program. In this case they may apply a dozen or more programs to manage and analyze their accounts receivable. Similarly, the processing capabilities of dBASE III might be more than enough for the record-keeping needs of R&R Motors, but the head office of an insurance company would probably require a mainframe data-base management system like those described in Chapter 10. Because the insurance company must process a much greater volume of data and has far more sophisticated information requirements, the cost of such a system will be much higher than that of related microcomputer software. In many cases the company itself will develop or contract for the required programs and systems. Even if an appropriate mainframe computer package is commercially available, it is usually necessary to modify the product to meet the company's specific processing and information needs.

In general, the types of personal-productivity software described earlier do not exist for mainframe computers. For example, most mainframe computers do not have easy-to-use word-processing packages. However, several electronic spreadsheets are available on popular mainframe computers. They could be used to develop a division or corporate budget by consolidating departmental budgets that have been developed on microcomputers.

There is a trend toward division of labor in the the world of computing. For example, in many businesses individual managers and technical personnel work on microcomputers. Their work is consolidated and processed further on a departmental minicomputer. The work of all of the corporation's departments, in turn, is consolidated and processed on a mainframe computer. Such a situation requires a combination of applications software and systems software.

Systems Software

Systems software is software that performs support operations for users and computer specialists. It enables users and specialists to use hardware effectively and efficiently without having to concern themselves with technical details. For example, systems software makes it possible for microcomputer users and applications programmers to save files on a diskette or a hard disk without having to know exactly how the equipment works.

Systems Software for Microcomputers. The most widely used systems software for microcomputers is the Personal Computer Disk Operating System (PC-DOS). A similar system, MS-DOS, is also in widespread use. To use either of these systems it is necessary to learn a set of basic commands. For example, a user working with a PC-DOS–based or MS-DOS–based microcomputer who wants to erase a file must enter a command such as ERA MYFILE.BAS. Most microcomputer users in businesses have learned these commands. However, the need to learn such commands has discouraged many people from making full use of personal computers.

Computers like the Apple Macintosh include an operating system that enables untrained users to perform basic operations easily. For example, to delete a file the user employs a mouse to choose the file from a list or menu of files on the screen. The user then selects the desired operation from a series of symbols or *icons* that appear on the screen. The icon for erasing a file is a picture of a garbage can. Many users find the *user interface* of the Macintosh less intimidating than that of PC-DOS–based or MS-DOS–based computers.

The difficulty of operating a microcomputer may be increased when users need to run several programs simultaneously, for example, an electronic spreadsheet and a word processor. The purpose of computerization is largely defeated if the user must copy down figures from an electronic spreadsheet and then enter them in a letter using a word processor. Integrated software may be used in such situations, but there are other solutions as well. For example, software is available that divides the monitor screen into several segments or "windows," each displaying relevant details of a particular program. With a few commands the user can transfer data from one window to another.

A major reason for the popularity of microcomputers is the relative standardization of their operating systems. With a few exceptions, a program that runs on one computer with a PC-DOS operating system will run on another with the same operating system. This factor is particularly important for organizations that have many different types of microcomputers.

Systems Software for Mainframe Computers. Systems software for mainframe computers is considerably more complicated than comparable software for microcomputers. Microcomputers typically serve only one or a few users. In contrast, mainframe systems software must coordinate computer operations for dozens or even hundreds of users working on many different applications at the same time. Mainframe systems software must optimize the use of resources such as computer hardware as well as ensure that no user is kept waiting an inordinate amount of time.

Several kinds of systems software are used to control each of the major components of a mainframe computer system. For example, magnetic disk drive operations are controlled by systems software located in the drive unit. Data communication units also may be programmable.

As one might expect, systems software for minicomputers is somewhere between microcomputer and mainframe systems software in power and complexity. Systems software for minicomputers must be able to handle several users at once, and this is increasingly true of systems software for powerful microcomputers as well. On the other hand, systems software for minicomputers is more standardized than mainframe systems software. Many minicomputers run an operating system known as UNIX that has recently become available on large microcomputers.

FIGURE 2-2

The Data Hierarchy

Data Base:	Billing File + Inventory File + +
File:	Billing File for March
Record:	14 March 19xx MG $369.85 + +
Field:	MG
Byte (character):	M
Bit:	0

The Data Hierarchy

We noted earlier that information is processed data; data consists of raw facts; and primary and auxiliary storage areas are the locations where the computer keeps data and information. If it is to be processed efficiently, data must be organized. Both primary and auxiliary storage contain data that is organized according to the *data hierarchy*, beginning with the binary digit, or *bit*, and extending through large collections of data known as *data bases*. (See Figure 2-2.)

Bit

Bit
A binary digit that can take on either of two values, arbitrarily called 0 and 1.

The smallest element in the data hierarchy is the **bit**, short for binary digit. A bit is represented by a tiny electronic circuit or piece of magnetized material that can take on one of two values such as high or low voltage. These values are arbitrarily called 0 and 1. Computer specialists may need to know the value of bits in storage, but most users never get involved at the bit level. Their data hierarchy begins with the next item, the byte.

Byte and Character

Byte
A group of bits in storage that represents a number, a character, or a program instruction.

A **byte** is a group of bits, with the exact number depending on the computer used. On most computers a byte is made up

CHAPTER 2   51   SOME BASIC CONCEPTS

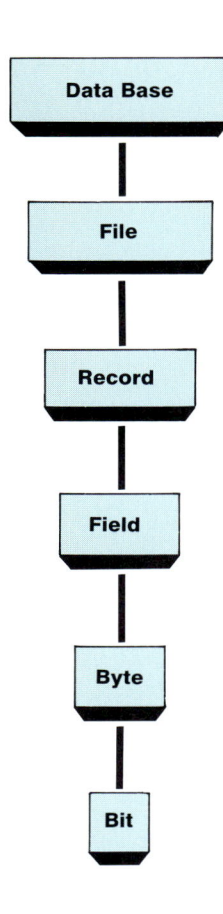

The Data Hierarchy

Data Base → File → Record → Field → Byte → Bit

of 8 bits. A byte in storage can represent a number, a character, or a program instruction. It is up to the user or programmer to define the contents of a byte; the computer only "sees" a series of bits.

In word processing and many other applications, a byte represents a character. There are three types of characters: alphabetic, numeric, and special. *A* and *a* are examples of *alphabetic characters*. *Numeric characters* are the digits 1, 2, 3, and so on, and *special characters* are symbols such as /, ?, ", %, and $.

Characters are composed of bits that are arranged according to one of several codes. The most popular code for microcomputers is *ASCII*, which stands for American Standard Code for Information Interchange. In ASCII a byte is composed of 8 bits (remember, a bit can be a 0 or a 1). For example, in ASCII the letter A is represented as 0100 0001.

Another important code is *EBCDIC*, which stands for Extended Binary-Coded Decimal Interchange Code. EBCDIC is used on large and medium-sized IBM computers. In EBCDIC, 8 bits form one character. Thus, the letter A is represented as 1100 0001. Because ASCII, EBCDIC, and other codes do not represent characters in the same way, there are programs to help users convert material from one code to another.

Field

Characters are grouped into fields in much the same way that letters are grouped into words. A **field** is a contiguous group of characters that has a meaning. The automobile name MG is an example of a field. The billed amount 369.85 is another example. Just as words contain different numbers of letters, fields contain different numbers of characters. In fact, fields can be of any length and can consist of one or more alphabetic characters, numbers, and special characters.

Field
A contiguous group of characters that has a meaning.

Record

A **record** is a collection of related fields. The bill for a client of R&R Motors is an example of a record. It consists of fields for the work order number, the client's name, the type of automobile, the parts required, the labor time incurred, the total charge, and so on. Records are often identified by a special field known as the *key field*. The key field on this record is the work order number.

Record
A collection of related fields.

OVERVIEW 52 PART 1

File

File
A collection of related records.

A **file** is a collection of related records. R&R's client bills for the month of March form a file. The inventory file at R&R Motors is composed of part records that contain background information such as cost, supplier or suppliers, and expected time to order. The number of records in a file varies according to need. Typical business files contain thousands of records.

Data Base

Data base
A collection of data that has been organized to permit ready access by both technical personnel and end-users.

Finally, several files can be combined into a **data base**. R&R's data base might contain billing files, the client file, the inventory file, and the supplier file. The ability to access a data base at the stroke of a computer key has revolutionized the way many businesses operate.

File Processing

Now that we are familiar with the data hierarchy, let's take a brief look at two ways in which the computer processes files: batch processing and interactive processing.

Batch Processing

Batch processing
A technique by which data and programs are collected in groups, known as batches, and processed periodically.

Batch processing is a technique by which data and programs are collected in groups, known as *batches*, and processed periodically. Batch processing systems are sometimes called *off-line systems*; the user has no direct line to the computer that is processing the data or the programs. Batch processing is usually done on computer systems that use magnetic tapes, but it can also be done on systems that use magnetic disks or a combination of disks and tapes.

Recall that magnetic tape is a sequential medium; therefore, rather than read half the tape or more to process a single change, known as a *transaction*, the user can collect a batch of transactions and sort them into an appropriate order. The sorted transactions are processed against a file containing semipermanent data for the application in question, or *master file*. This

CHAPTER 2   SOME BASIC CONCEPTS

FIGURE 2-3

File Update Using Batch Processing

This figure illustrates a monthly file update performed at the end of February. The old master file contains client data current to the end of January. The transaction file contains data concerning purchases, returns, and payments for the month of February. Both files are in order by client number, as is the new master file, which contains client data current to the end of February.

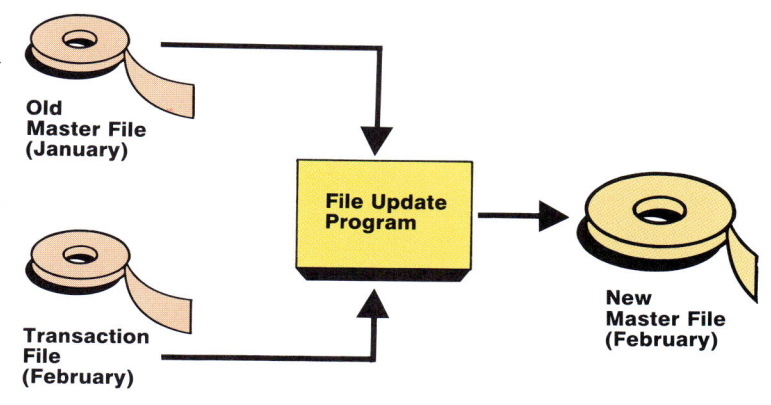

processing is known as *file updating*. In a file update, the input is called the *old master file* and the output is called the *new master file*.

As an example, suppose that we want to do a billing as shown in Figure 2-3. The old master file contains customer account information that is current to the end of January. The records on this file are in order by account number. The transactions are purchases, returns, and payments for February; they are also in order by account number. The file update produces a new master file containing customer account information that is current to the end of February, once again in order by account number. When we want to do the billing for March, we take the old master file for February and process it against the March transactions to produce the new master file for March. In this way we always have a backup file. The set of files is known as a *generation*, or grandfather (January master file), father (February master file), and son (March master file).

Batch processing inevitably causes a delay in receiving information because it takes time to collect batches of transactions and, when necessary, to sort the files. However, the cost per transaction may be fairly low because batch processing involves relatively low-cost equipment, such as magnetic tape, and handles large volumes of transactions at a time. Batch processing is used when the delay in producing information is not critical; it typically is used for applications such as biweekly payrolls.

Interactive Processing

Interactive processing
A technique by which data and programs are processed on demand.

Interactive processing eliminates the need to collect batches of transactions. It requires media that permit random processing, such as magnetic disks and floppy disks. Many systems that provide interactive processing are called *on-line systems*, reflecting the fact that the user has a line, often a telephone line, to the computer.

Although interactive systems eliminate the delays inherent in batch processing, they require expensive hardware and software and thus incur a higher cost per transaction than batch processing does.

An airline reservation system is an example of interactive processing. It enables travel agents to inform their customers of seat availability and to reserve seats while they are on the phone. Many travel agencies use the SABRE (Semi-Automatic Business Research Environment) airline reservation system supplied by American Airlines.

People as an Element of Computer Systems

Hardware and software alone cannot meet individual and organizational information needs. The third element of any computer solution is people. As computers increasingly change the way we live and work, the greatest challenge in managing those changes is shaping system hardware and software to the needs, abilities, and motivations of people. (See Figure 2-4 and Box 2-2.)

Ergonomics and Hardware Design

A key aspect of managing the changes that computer systems bring to the workplace is that of designing hardware that is healthful and comfortable to use. The increasing interest in

Ergonomically designed computer hardware and office furniture increase employee comfort and productivity. Employees can adjust the furniture, the keyboard, and the screen. (© Hank Morgan, Rainbow.)

CHAPTER 2   55   SOME BASIC CONCEPTS

FIGURE 2-4

Hardware, Software, and People

This figure shows the relationships among people, systems and applications software, and hardware.

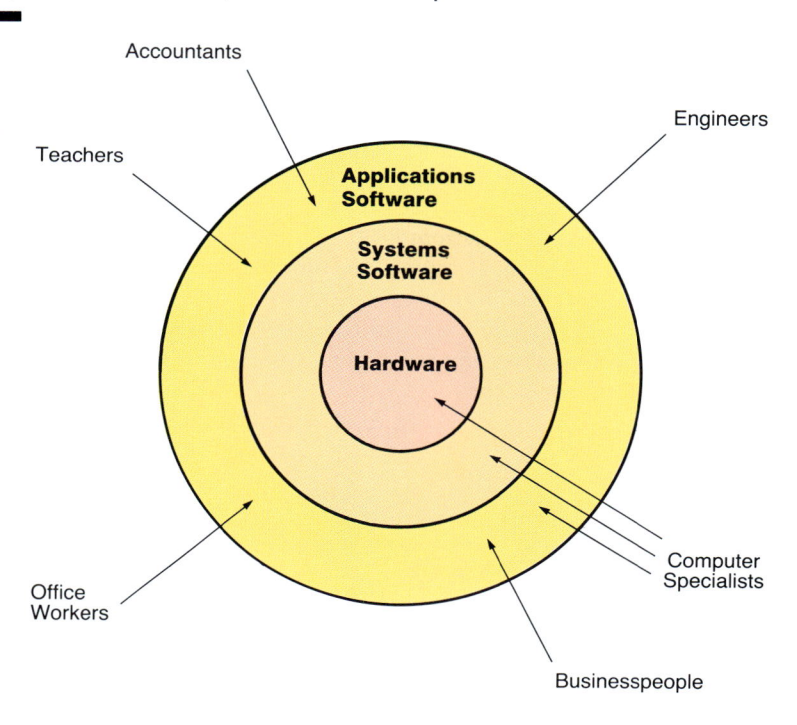

Accountants · Engineers · Teachers · Applications Software · Systems Software · Hardware · Office Workers · Computer Specialists · Businesspeople

health and fitness, together with the expanded use of computers in the workplace, has led to a new concern called ergonomics. **Ergonomics** is the study of the relationship of people to the work environment. It involves several interrelated factors, including psychology, physiology, and equipment design. Specifically, ergonomics takes into consideration people's physiological and psychological well-being in designing office furnishings and layout, lighting, air quality, color, sound, and other features of the work environment. Examples of ergonomically designed hardware include green or amber monitors and keyboards with a solid touch. Pleasant lighting and chairs that can be adjusted for maximum comfort are also important in creating a good working environment. (Symptoms often reported by data entry operators working in non-ergonomically designed environments are presented in graphic form in Figure 2-5.)

Ergonomics
The study of the relationship of people to their work environment, particularly to computing.

BOX 2-2

MANAGING CHANGE

Mary Parker Follett on Getting Things Done Through People

Mary Parker Follett is one of the leading figures in American management science. Born in 1868, in the railroad age, she lived until 1963, when the computer age was well under way. The management principles for which she is remembered, however, are in no way tied to a specific technology. They are as relevant to managers using computers as they were to managers using steam engines.

According to Follet, "management is the art of getting things done through people." She understood that people at work are motivated by the same factors that shape their lives in their leisure hours. Managers must understand this fact if they are to get things done. They must create a harmony between the people element of a business system and its physical elements. Forcing people to fit machines or driving them to work like machines will mean that the job does not get done.

Throughout this book, a series of boxes titled "Managing Change" will focus on the impact of computers on the task of getting things done through people. Computer hardware that people cannot work with will at best make a good doorstop. Software that users cannot understand and feel comfortable with is nothing but a source of problems. When efforts to computerize some aspect of business life or personal life fail, the problem most often lies in a failure to recognize the needs of the people who will be using the new computer system.

FIGURE 2-5

Data Entry Disorders

Symptoms reported by data entry operators vs. those of clerical workers in the same departments. Source: Copyright 1987 by CW Communications/Inc., Framingham, MA 01701 – Reprinted from Computerworld, May 18, 1987, p. 89.

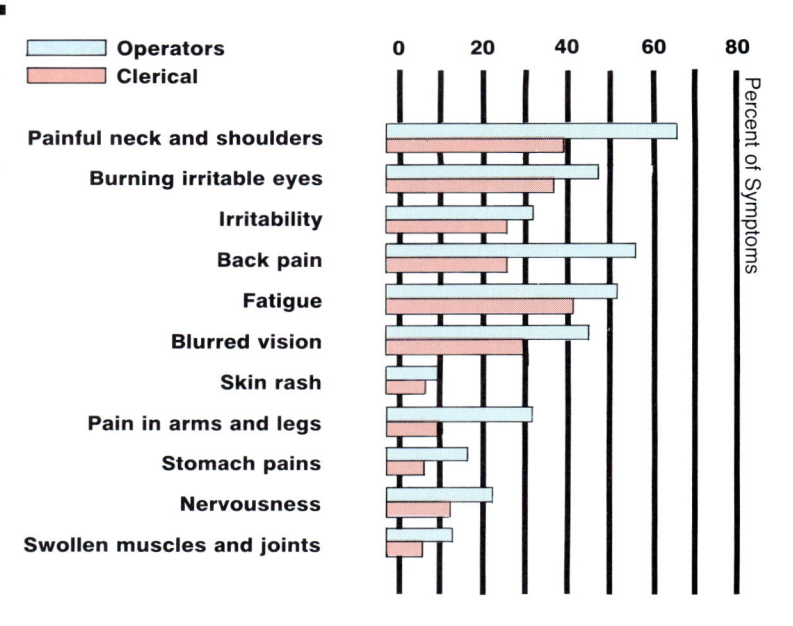

- Operators
- Clerical

0   20   40   60   80

Painful neck and shoulders
Burning irritable eyes
Irritability
Back pain
Fatigue
Blurred vision
Skin rash
Pain in arms and legs
Stomach pains
Nervousness
Swollen muscles and joints

Percent of Symptoms

User-Friendly Software

Just as hardware must be ergonomically designed so that it is easy for people to use, software must be designed to be *user-friendly*. Key features of user-friendly software are anticipation of user errors, painless correction of such errors, helpful screen messages, clear on-screen instructions for all features, and good written documentation. As an example, consider an inexperienced user who wants to print from an electronic spreadsheet for the first time. If he is using VisiCalc, the first electronic spreadsheet, he enters a "/" and the screen displays the possible choices (see Figure 2-6):

```
BCDEFGIMPRSTVW-
```

If he is not sure which one to choose, he must look in the manual or ask a coworker. If he is using a more modern program, Lotus

FIGURE 2-6

A VisiCalc Screen

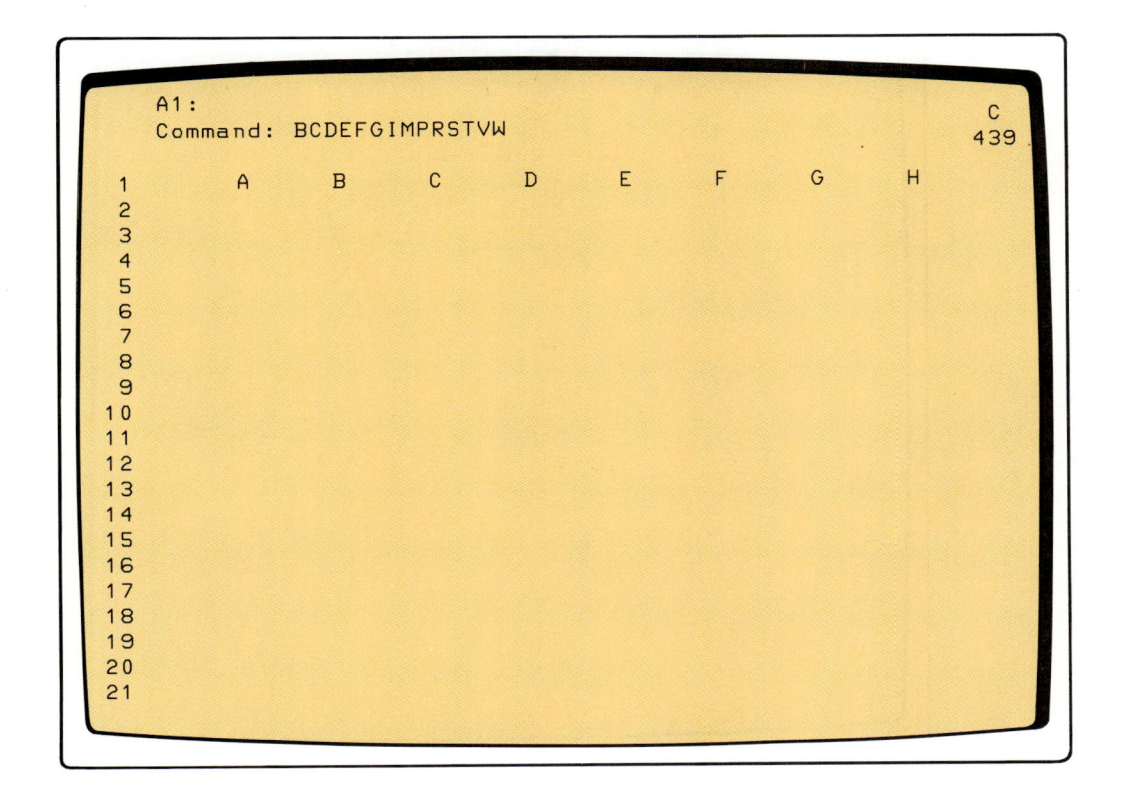

```
A1:                                                    C
Command: BCDEFGIMPRSTVW                              439
     A      B      C      D      E      F      G      H
1
2
3
4
5
6
7
8
9
10
11
12
13
14
15
16
17
18
19
20
21
```

1-2-3, the situation is much clearer. He enters a "/" and the screen displays the possible choices (see Figure 2-7):

```
Worksheet Range Copy Move File Print Graph Data Quit
```

He then either enters a "P" for "Print" or presses the right arrow key until "Print" lights up; then he presses the carriage return. Increased user-friendliness is one reason that Lotus 1-2-3 has supplanted VisiCalc as the most popular business program.

Almost all manufacturers claim that their software is user-friendly, but in reality some software packages are more user-friendly than others. Moreover, people differ in experience, expectations, and work habits. A product that one user finds

FIGURE 2-7

A Lotus 1-2-3 Screen

```
A1:                                                              MENU
Worksheet  Range  Copy  Move  File  Print  Graph  Data  Quit
Global, Insert, Delete, Column-Width, Erase, Titles, Window, Status
           A        B       C       D       E       F       G       H
    1
    2
    3
    4
    5
    6
    7
    8
    9
   10
   11
   12
   13
   14
   15
   16
   17
   18
   19
   20
```

extremely complicated, another will enjoy using. The only way to find out whether a given piece of software is user-friendly is to work with it.

Together, ergonomically designed hardware and user-friendly software can reduce eyestrain, headaches, and backaches, raise employee productivity, and decrease turnover. In short, they make business sense.

SUMMARY

1. A combination of computer hardware, software, people, data, and operating procedures is a computer **system**. The various components of the system must work together to meet predefined goals. Hardware is the physical equipment associated with a computer system and can be divided into five categories: (a) input devices, (b) output devices, (c) the central processing unit, (d) auxiliary storage devices, and (e) data communication equipment.

2. There are three basic categories of people who input data into a computer system: (a) users who work with output, for whom data entry is not an end in itself but a means to an end; (b) data entry professionals, who enter large volumes of data rapidly and with very few errors; and (c) people who are trained in data entry techniques for particular applications.

3. Microcomputer **keyboards** are similar to typewriter keyboards. Other input techniques for microcomputers include the mouse and pointing. Common input devices for larger computers are terminal keyboards, point-of-sale terminals, optical character recognition devices, and magnetic ink character recognition devices.

4. The information produced by a computer system should be easy to read, rapidly available, accurate, complete, concise, and relevant. The most widely used output device is the **video display terminal (VDT)**. **Printers** create permanent copy, or hard copy.

5. The **central processing unit (CPU)** is the core of the computer. It is composed of three units: the arithmetic-logic unit, the control unit, and primary storage. A CPU for a microcomputer system can fit on a few electronic units called **chips**. Whereas a microcomputer CPU serves one or a few users, the CPU of a mainframe computer must be able to serve hundreds of users. In many cases, mainframe computer systems consist of several CPUs.

6. Data and programs can be stored outside of the CPU in auxiliary storage. The most common storage medium for home computers is floppy disks. Hard disks are metal storage media that are permanently installed in microcomputer systems. Magnetic tape is a widely used storage device for large and medium-sized computers. However, tapes are limited to sequential processing; in contrast, magnetic disks allow random processing and hence are increasingly being used in preference to tapes.

7. Data communication is the transmission of data, information, and programs from one location to another. Data communication systems may include computers, terminals, and specialized equipment. Most data communication systems rely on the telephone network. Modems convert the signals found in computers and workstations to signals that can be transmitted over most telephone lines.

8. Software refers to the programs, procedures, and documentation used to run the hardware of a computer system. Applications software is software whose function is to provide users with information or help them get a job done. The enormous popularity of microcomputers in homes and businesses has led to the development of many kinds of personal-productivity software.

SUMMARY CONTINUED

These include word processing, electronic spreadsheets, file and data-base management programs, and integrated software.

9. Systems software is software that enables users and computer specialists to use hardware effectively and efficiently without having to concern themselves with technical details. The Personal Computer Disk Operating System (PC-DOS) and MS-DOS are the most widely used systems software for microcomputers. Some computers include an operating system that enables untrained users to perform basic operations easily. Systems software for mainframe computers is considerably more complicated than systems software for microcomputers.

10. The data hierarchy is composed of the **bit**, which can take on either of two values, 0 or 1; the **byte**, a group of bits that is often equivalent to a character; the **field**, a contiguous group of characters; the **record**, a collection of related fields; the **file**, a collection of related records; and the **data base**, which combines several files.

11. Batch processing is a technique by which data and programs are collected in groups, known as batches, and processed periodically. The sorted changes or transactions are processed against a file, known as a master file, containing semipermanent data for the application in question. **Interactive processing** eliminates the need to collect batches of transactions. It requires media that permit random processing and therefore incurs a higher cost per transaction than batch processing does.

12. Ergonomics is the study of the relationship of people to their work environment, particularly to computing. It involves several interrelated factors, including psychology, physiology, and equipment design. Ergonomically designed software is often described as user-friendly. It anticipates and corrects user errors, provides helpful screen messages and clear on-screen instructions, and is accompanied by good written documentation.

KEY TERMS

system

keyboard

video display terminal (VDT)

printer

central processing unit (CPU)

chip

software

bit

byte

field

record

file

data base

batch processing

interactive processing

ergonomics

REVIEW QUESTIONS

1. What are the components of a computer system?

2. Compare and contrast the three main categories of people who input data.

3. Identify some typical input devices for microcomputers and for larger computers. How do they differ?

4. Identify some typical output devices for microcomputers and for larger computers. How do they differ?

5. List the three components of the central processing unit and their functions.

6. Compare and contrast magnetic tapes and disks.

7. What is data communication? Identify the role of the telephone system and the modem in data communication.

8. Distinguish between applications software and systems software.

9. Distinguish among the four most popular types of personal-productivity software. Give an example of an application for each type.

10. Name and illustrate the elements of the data hierarchy.

11. Compare and contrast batch processing and interactive processing. What are the advantages and disadvantages of each?

12. Define ergonomics and give examples of ergonomic features for both hardware and software.

APPLICATIONS

1. Describe some newly developed input, output, or auxiliary storage devices for microcomputers. How do they compare to those described in the text?

2. Describe some newly developed input, output, or auxiliary storage devices for mainframe computers. How do they compare to those described in the text?

3. Describe how a user may apply a personal-productivity program to solve a problem such as drawing up a budget or composing a resume. Was the program well suited to the application?

4. Discuss the following statement: Ergonomics is a luxury that the average business cannot afford.

CASE FOR DISCUSSION

Harry Badian is the owner and manager of Shop-Er supermarkets, a local chain of seven stores in a large city in the Midwest. Over the past several years his competitors, the national chains, have put point-of-sale terminals in all of their stores. Using these machines, the checkout clerks scan each item for the pattern of black and white bars containing the universal product code. Customers like the system because it reduces checkout time and cuts down on errors by the checkout clerk. Managers like the system because it gives them data for inventory control, marketing studies, and so on.

Seeing these advantages, Badian decides to install computer systems in his stores. He buys the equipment, as well as a comprehensive training program for his clerks, from a well-known supplier. The customers are happy. The checkout process is faster and free of errors, and receipts are now printed with a list of all the items bought, instead of just the prices of the items. Also, the new machines use wider tape and blacker ink than the old ones. Several elderly customers with poor eyesight comment favorably on the change.

Badian is happy too. He spends many hours with his new "toy." He asks the seller of the computer system to write a program to supply him with a list of the quantities and prices of every item sold in the store each day, including the time of day the item was sold, whether it was sold in the ten-items-or-less express lane or a regular lane, whether it was paid for by cash or by check, and how long it was in stock before it was sold. Badian comes in early to find huge stacks of data, printed in crisp, clean characters on easy-to-read lined paper, on his desk each morning. All through the day and far into the night he pages through the stacks, making notes and tabulations on a yellow pad. He finds that many steaks are sold in the express lane in the late afternoon. He moves the display of barbeque charcoal to that corner of the store, and presto, sales of charcoal go up. He finds that not much is sold between 8:30 and 8:45 in the morning, so he decides to open later.

Fascinated by these findings, he asks for more data. He finds that people who pay by check buy more fresh produce than people who pay cash. He spends a long time wondering how to make use of this finding.

After a time, however, things start going wrong in the store. The store becomes dirty because Badian has not taken the time to make sure it is clean. Customers are rarely greeted by the owner as they shop. Without this personal touch, Shop-Er seems just like the large chains to them. Wholesalers' representatives are left to make deals with a young assistant rather than with the boss. In subtle ways, business begins to suffer despite the higher sales of charcoal.

Badian, being an observant manager, notices these things. To his credit, he once more takes the time to attend to all of his original duties. Now and then, though, he sighs when he sees those big, beautiful stacks of computer reports being thrown out, unread, along with the wilted lettuce and spoiled fish. His toy was so much fun! But how can he find the time to play with it?

CASE QUESTIONS

1. Taking the point of view of the customer, rate the output of Shop-Er's computerized checkout system. Discuss the output in terms of legibility, timeliness, accuracy, completeness, conciseness, and relevance.

2. Taking the point of view of the manager, rate and discuss the system's output according to the criteria listed in question 1.

3. In what ways did Badian use his new computer system correctly? What improvements could he have made in his use of the system?

P

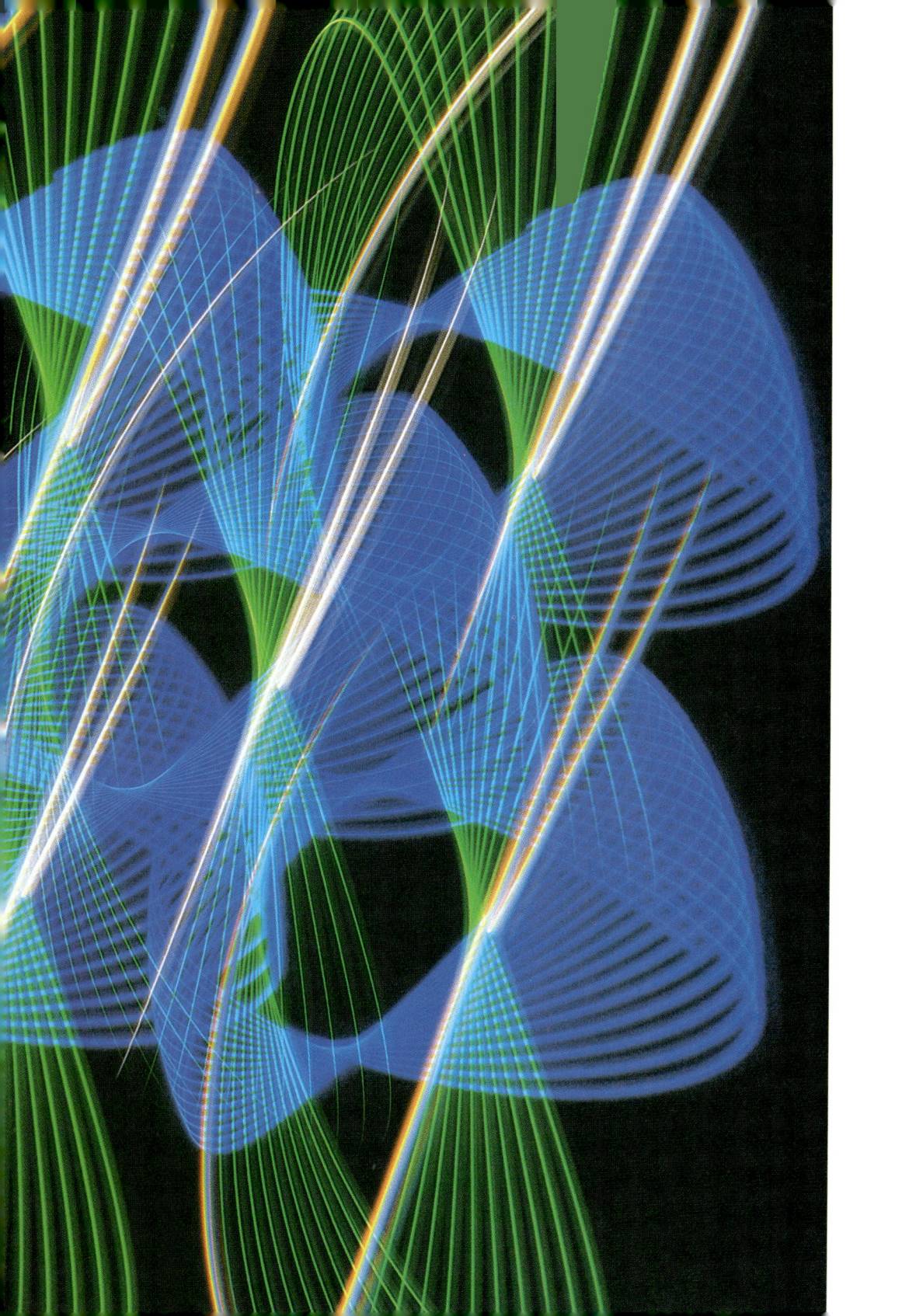

ART 2

Hardware

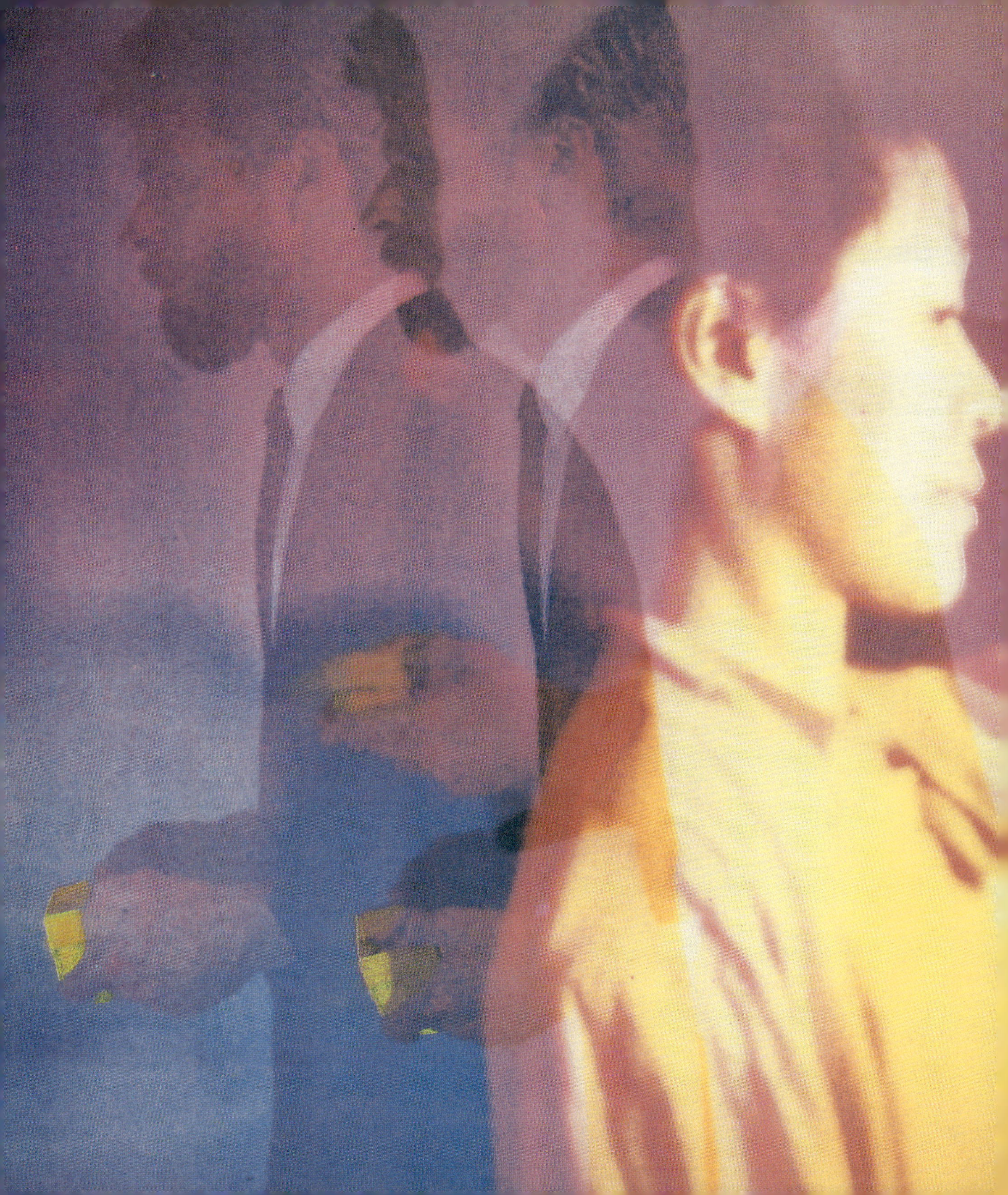

Computers Large and Small

CHAPTER 3

Up five flights of stairs, in an old building on the outskirts of Taipei, a young woman sits eating chicken and rice with chopsticks. Scattered around her are boxes of printed circuit boards and, stacked precariously in piles, plastic computer cases. The woman is taking a break from her $1.30-an-hour job testing components for the 100 IBM-compatible personal computers that her company, Aquarius Systems Inc., will turn out today.[1]

On the other side of the ocean, in Santa Clara, California, a midnight gathering of engineers awaits the first samples of a new computer chip—the Intel 80386. The new chip has cost the company $100 million and four years of prodigious effort. Computer designer Chip Krauscopf finally strides into the room with a plastic recipe box filled, he says, with these corporate crown jewels. As he enters the room he stumbles; the chips scatter, and he tramples them as he tries to regain his balance. As the crowd gasps, another designer, Pat Gelsinger, walks in with another box containing the real chips. Just a $100 million practical joke, he explains.[2]

What do these two scenes—the woman with chopsticks and the joking engineers—have in common? They are both caught up in the "clone wars"—the competitive struggle among firms that make replicas and near replicas of the ubiquitous IBM PC. Aquarius Systems is making machines that duplicate the PC's performance but cost up to four times less. Intel's chip will become the heart of a new generation of desktop computers that cost more than the old PC but are several times faster. Much hinges on the outcome. Will IBM, the world's biggest computer company, maintain its place as the leader in the market for personal-computer systems? Will Intel succeed in its fight to save the U.S. chip industry? Watch your favorite computer magazine for the latest battlefield report!

---

[1] Geoff Lewis, "The PC Wars: IBM vs. the Clones," *Business Week*, July 28, 1986, p. 62.

[2] Based on Brenton R. Schlender, "Intel's Development of 386 Computer Chip Took $100 Million and Four Years of Difficult Work," *Wall Street Journal*, August 29, 1986, p. 10.

In this chapter we will see that the clone wars are just a part of the revolution that has affected all computers, large and small. The chapter takes a detailed look at computer hardware. It begins by discussing the two types of computers—analog and digital. It discusses microprocessors—a key part of today's computers—and then classifies and describes computers according to size. Throughout the chapter the similarities as well as the differences among computers of all sizes are noted.

When you have read this chapter, you should be able to:

1. State the difference between an analog computer and a digital computer.
2. Explain what a microprocessor is and how it differs from a computer.
3. Indicate the essential features and uses of a microcomputer.
4. Describe the IBM Personal Computer, including the features that have enabled it to remain useful in the changing environment of personal computing.
5. Discuss portable computers and their roles in personal computing.
6. State what a minicomputer is and list the factors that distinguish it from a microcomputer.
7. Indicate the essential features of mainframe computers.
8. Describe supercomputers and their applications.
9. Understand and use the key terms listed at the end of the chapter.

There are two basic types of computers—analog and digital. They differ in the kinds of data they process and how they process it. **Analog computers** process data by measuring it. They are particularly useful for scientific and industrial applications, which use data that varies in continuous fashion (e.g., pressure, speed, or temperature). A thermostat is an example of an analog computer.

Digital computers process discrete items of data using a counting procedure. When you count on your fingers you can be said to be using a digital computer. The majority of computers used in business and administration are digital computers; hence, we commonly use the term *computer* when we mean digital computer.

Analog computer
A computer that processes continuous data, such as pressure or temperature, by measuring it.

Digital computer
A computer that processes discrete items of data via a counting procedure. The majority of computers used in business are digital computers.

Microprocessor
A computer on a chip; it can serve as the heart of a microcomputer or be used to computerize equipment such as microwave ovens.

Microprocessors and Microcomputers

Microprocessors are CPUs that are contained on chips smaller than a dime. In fact, they have been called computers on a chip. There are two kinds of microprocessors: those that drive computerized devices such as microwave ovens and those that drive computers. Microprocessors that control computerized devices are known as *embedded computers* since they are actually small computers that are embedded in other machines.

Unlike other computers, embedded computers can do only one thing. For example, the embedded computer that provides the action for a video game cannot drive an electronic calculator, nor will it help you do your accounting homework. On the other hand, embedded computers are an integral part of numerous familiar items. Microwave ovens, for instance, are controlled by one or more microprocessors. The fancier the oven, the more powerful and flexible its microprocessors. The computerized activities of microwave ovens include defrosting food and determining how long to cook it. Microprocessors make microwave ovens easier to use, more efficient, and safer.

Another machine that makes extensive use of embedded computers is the automobile. Each year new automotive functions are placed under the control of microprocessors. Those functions include monitoring engines for speed and fuel con-

The WE 32100 chip is a microprocessor that outperforms most advanced desktop computers. It is used in computers of all sizes. (Courtesy of AT&T Bell Laboratories.)

CHAPTER 3   COMPUTERS LARGE AND SMALL

sumption, reducing exhaust emissions, and providing vocal reminders such as "fuel supply is dangerously low" and "fasten your seatbelt."

From the day microprocessors were invented, there has been an almost continuous improvement in their speed and data-handling capabilities. A microprocessor fitted with an input device such as a keyboard, an output device such as a video monitor, and primary storage is a full-fledged computer, known as a **microcomputer**. Microcomputers are small and inexpensive enough to be used by individuals at home, in school, and in business.

As soon as microcomputers became popular, people started calling them personal computers, and they have indeed become a familiar part of the personal life of today's generation of college students. (See Box 3-1.) Such computers can perform a variety of useful everyday functions. For example, as a student, you can use a microcomputer to withdraw funds from your bank account, write your term paper, and maintain a list of addresses and phone numbers. At home, your family might use a microcomputer for entertainment, keeping track of finances, or subscribing to news information services. In business, microcomputers are used with personal-productivity software, including electronic spreadsheets; word-processing, data-management, and graphics programs; and integrated software. Personal-productivity software and other types of software are discussed in Part 3.

Microcomputer

A microprocessor that is fitted with an input device, an output device, and primary storage.

The IBM PC

The first microcomputer to be widely accepted in the business world was the IBM PC. The *8088* (pronounced "eighty eighty-eight") microprocessor, manufactured by Intel, is the computer's main chip. In August 1981, when the IBM PC was introduced, this chip was inexpensive and was available in industrial quantities, making possible rapid production of the PCs. PC users who do extensive mathematical calculations can add a related microprocessor, the *8087* ("eighty eighty-seven").

The IBM PC contains 40K (kilobytes), or about 40,000 characters, of ROM (read-only memory). (Note that for simplicity many people use K instead of KB to refer to kilobytes.) The IBM PC was originally introduced with a standard RAM (random-access memory) of 64K. This was subsequently increased to 128K and then to 256K. By 1986, the maximum primary storage directly accessible to the CPU was 640K. Because many users felt that this amount was insufficient, computer manufac-

GB = gigabyte
= 1,073,741,824MB

MB = megabyte
= 1,048,576KB

KB = kilobyte
= 1024 bytes

B = byte

The IBM PC was the first microcomputer to be widely accepted in the business world. Today millions of PCs are in use in businesses and homes. (Courtesy of International Business Machines.)

HARDWARE 72 PART 2

FIGURE 3-1

Inside the IBM PC XT

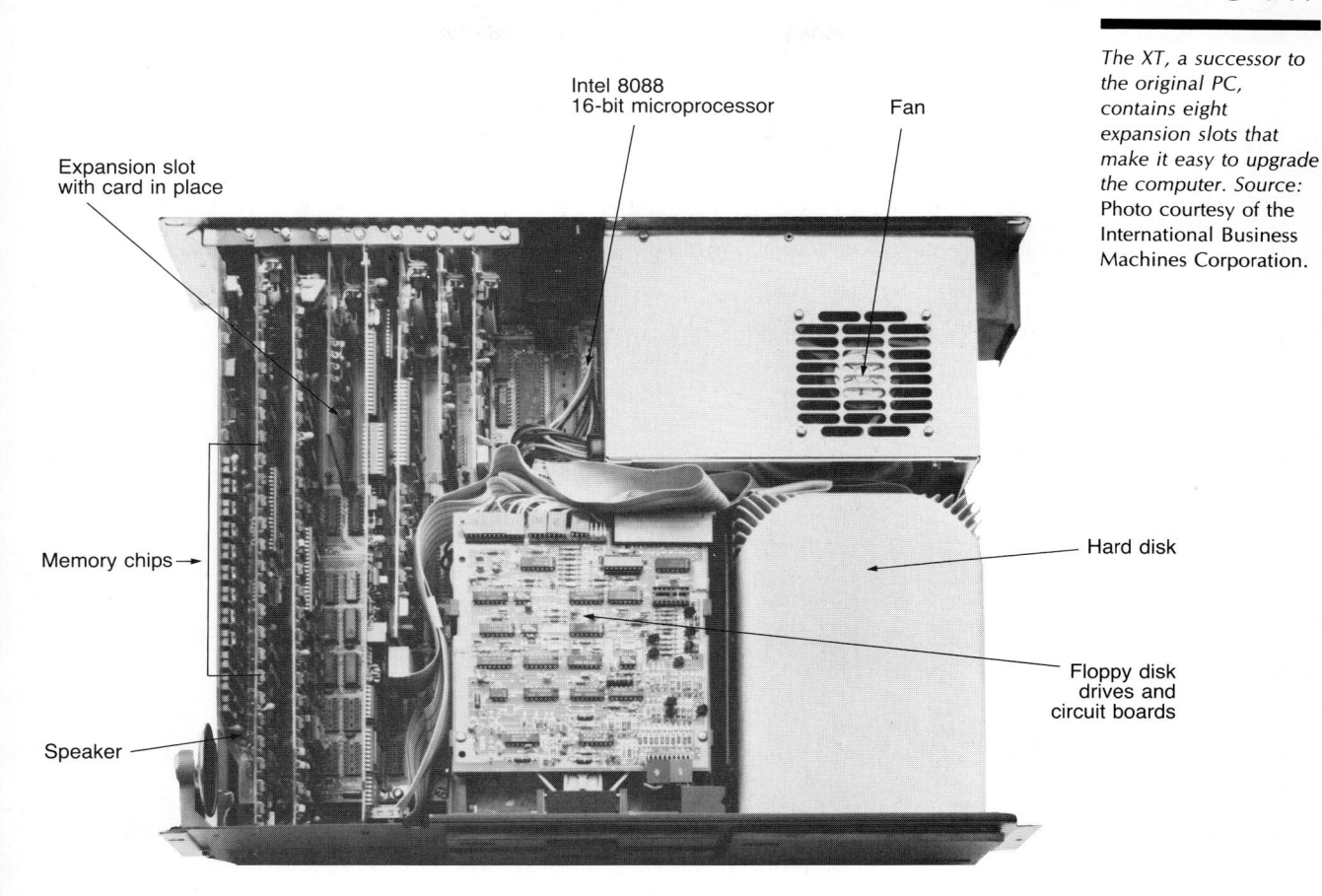

The XT, a successor to the original PC, contains eight expansion slots that make it easy to upgrade the computer. Source: Photo courtesy of the International Business Machines Corporation.

Intel 8088 16-bit microprocessor
Fan
Expansion slot with card in place
Memory chips
Speaker
Hard disk
Floppy disk drives and circuit boards

turers developed special techniques for handling considerably more memory. Today a storage capacity of 8 megabytes (equivalent to 8196 kilobytes), or 8 MB, of RAM is no longer uncommon. This is enough storage for about 4000 pages of text.

Upgrading. Many users find that they quickly outgrow their microcomputer as they apply it to solve increasingly complex problems. There are basically two choices for users who find that their personal computer no longer meets their needs. They may upgrade their present computer or buy a more powerful

BOX 3-1

FRONTIERS IN TECHNOLOGY

Growing Up with the Personal Computer

Today's frontier is tomorrow's history, and in the world of personal computing, the pace at which new frontiers flash by is astonishing. To give an idea of the pace of technological advance in this field, we set the life of the personal computer and its predecessors side by side with that of Rachel Dowling, a business major at Euphoric State University, class of '92.

1948: John Bardeen, Walter Brattain, and William Shockley of Bell Laboratories invent the transistor.

Rachel's parents are born during this year.

1964: John Kemeny and Thomas Kurtz of Dartmouth College develop the BASIC programming language.

Rachel's parents go to the Junior Prom, their first date.

1970: Intel Corp. engineers are hard at work on the 4-bit 4004 microprocessor, a breakthrough that puts the whole device on a single chip.

Rachel is born during this year.

1972: Nolan Bushnell founds Atari and develops Pong, the first video game.

Rachel is just old enough to say "Pong."

1975: *Popular Electronics* runs a cover story on the Altair 8800, the first microcomputer. The Altair has 256 bytes of memory. That's right—256 bytes, not 256 kilobytes!

Rachel has not yet learned to count to 256.

1976: Apple Computer is founded. Keuffel and Esser ends production of its slide rule and donates its last one to the Smithsonian.

Rachel enters the first grade.

1977: The introduction of Radio Shack's TRS-80 makes microcomputers (and service) much more widely available. The first of many models of this machine has 4 KB of RAM, 4 KB of ROM, keyboard, display, cassette interface, and recorder.

Rachel's father buys a TRS-80, but Rachel loses interest when she finds that it can't receive "Sesame Street."

1978: Epson America stuns the market with the high performance and low price of its MX-80 dot-matrix printer.

During this year Rachel gives up printing and learns to write cursive.

1979: Dan Bricklin and Bob Frankston of Software Arts Inc. demonstrate their VisiCalc spreadsheet program. This program persuades many people to take the microcomputer seriously as a personal-productivity tool.

1981: IBM introduces the IBM PC, with 64 KB of RAM, 40 KB of ROM, one 5¼-inch floppy disk drive, and a version of the Microsoft MS-DOS operating system. This machine legitimizes the microcomputer as a business tool and sets an industry standard for the decade.

1982: Columbia Data Products and Compaq Computer Corp. introduce the first PC clones. Compatibility becomes a way of life for the industry.

1984: Apple Computer, holding out against compatibility, introduces the Macintosh, "The computer for the rest of us." About the same time, Seiko introduces a wristwatch computer with 2 KB of RAM and 6 KB of ROM.

1986: IBM introduces its laptop PC Convertible, with 256 KB of RAM, a full 80 column by 25 line screen, and a ten-hour battery life.

1988: Optical disk storage devices for the PC start to displace magnetic storage media in many applications.

Rachel makes great strides in her ability to calculate, too—she learns long division.

Rachel's father buys one of the new PCs and donates his aging TRS-80 to Rachel's grade school.

Rachel joins the Computer Club at her junior high school.

Rachel enters high school. By this time the PC is such a common item that her teachers see nothing unusual when she turns in assignments in word-processed form.

Rachel's campaign for junior class president features flashy computer-generated posters that she and her friends have prepared in the school's computer lab.

Rachel is off to college with a laptop computer under her arm.

Source for the microcomputing timeline: Excerpted with permission from Gregg Williams and Mark Welch, "A Microcomputing Timeline," *BYTE*, September 1985, pp. 198–207. McGraw-Hill, Inc. New York. All rights reserved.

one. The IBM PC was designed for easy upgrading. However, the company that introduced the concept of upgrading was not IBM but Apple Computer, Inc. In 1977 Apple instituted a policy of **open architecture**. Unlike its competitors, it published the specifications of its computer with the express intent of enabling other companies to manufacture both hardware and software to upgrade it. This somewhat unorthodox marketing strategy proved extremely successful, and as a result IBM adopted the open architecture policy for its personal computers. However, open architecture made it easy for competitors to copy the basic computer design, and to produce the "clones" mentioned in the example that introduces this chapter. As a result, both IBM and Apple have backed away from open architecture in some of their recent models.

A feature that makes it easy to upgrade the IBM PC is the availability of *expansion boards*. An expansion board is a circuit board that can be inserted into one of a computer's *expansion slots*. A popular expansion board, the AST 6 Pack Plus, offers extra RAM (up to a total of 640K); a clock calendar that records the date and time the computer is turned on; three *ports*, or connections into which other hardware can be plugged; and software to help manage the extra memory. By 1987 over 2 million personal-computer users had purchased this expansion board, or more powerful versions of it, to upgrade their equipment.

There are several other kinds of expansion boards. These include modems (for communicating with other computers); graphics cards (which make it possible to create pictures on a VDT); and hard disks (which greatly increase a computer's storage capacity). Although different kinds of expansion boards may interfere with each other and substantial upgrading may require the installation of a larger power supply, the right expansion board can extend the useful life of a personal computer for years.

Open architecture
An approach in which a computer's specifications are made public in order to encourage independent hardware and software developers to create material that can be used on that computer, thereby increasing its market.

Other IBM Personal Computers

The IBM PC is only one member of the family of IBM personal computers. It is often possible for users to move their work from one member of this family to a larger member without any complications. A good example is the movement of work from the PC to the XT (for "extended technology"). This more powerful computer, which was introduced in 1983, is similar to the IBM PC but includes a built-in hard disk, a total of eight expansion slots, and a larger power supply. In the business world the XT has largely replaced the PC. However, users frequently carry diskettes back and forth between an XT at work and a PC at home. This is an example of a phenomenon known as compatibility, which will be discussed shortly.

Another member of the IBM computer family, the AT (for "advanced technology") was introduced in 1984. It uses an 80286 Intel processor, which does everything the 8088 chip does and more. It not only processes 16 bits at a time but also inputs and outputs 16 bits at a time. In practice, the AT is several times faster than the PC for many applications. It uses a hard disk and a 1.2-MB floppy diskette (compared to the 360-KB floppy used by the PC and the XT). However, the AT is not completely compatible with the PC or the XT. Programmers who want their programs to work on all members of the IBM PC family must apply special techniques in writing them.

In the fall of 1986 several manufacturers introduced a personal computer based on the 80386 chip. The 80386 (or 386 as it is often called) has some clear advantages over the 80286 (often abbreviated 286). Its much faster processing speed greatly increases its efficiency compared to earlier models of personal computers. Certain applications, such as processing large data bases, which were impractical on the PC and slow on the AT, are easily handled on a 386.

In April of 1987 IBM introduced the Personal System/2, or PS/2, series of microcomputers. These computers, some of which are based on the 80386 chip, promise to have a major impact on both home and business users. They are discussed further in Chapter 18.

Compatibles

Of course, not every individual or business that has a computer has a member of the IBM PC family. In fact, many businesses have more than one type of personal computer. Because the members of the IBM PC family are the industry standard and have the most widely available software, both individual and business users want to know whether different computers are **compatible** with the IBM computers and with each other. Computers are said to be compatible if they can run the same software and process data on the same diskettes. Compatibles are often called *clones*.

Many computers are compatible but not 100 percent compatible. In other words, they can run many but not all of the same programs. For example, members of the team working on this textbook exchanged diskettes for use on IBM PC, Compaq, IBM PC XT, and Leading Edge computers. They reported no compatibility problems from the standpoint of word processing.

The Leading Edge computer is a popular compatible. It may offer superior performance to that of the IBM PC for the same price. (© Erin Calmes.)

Compatible
A term used to describe a group of computers that can run all or most of the same software and process data on the same storage media.

FIGURE 3-2

Personal Computers in Use in the United States, 1987

Source: Copyright 1987 by CW Communications/Inc., Framingham, MA 01701—Reprinted from *Computerworld,* April 6, 1987, p. 107.

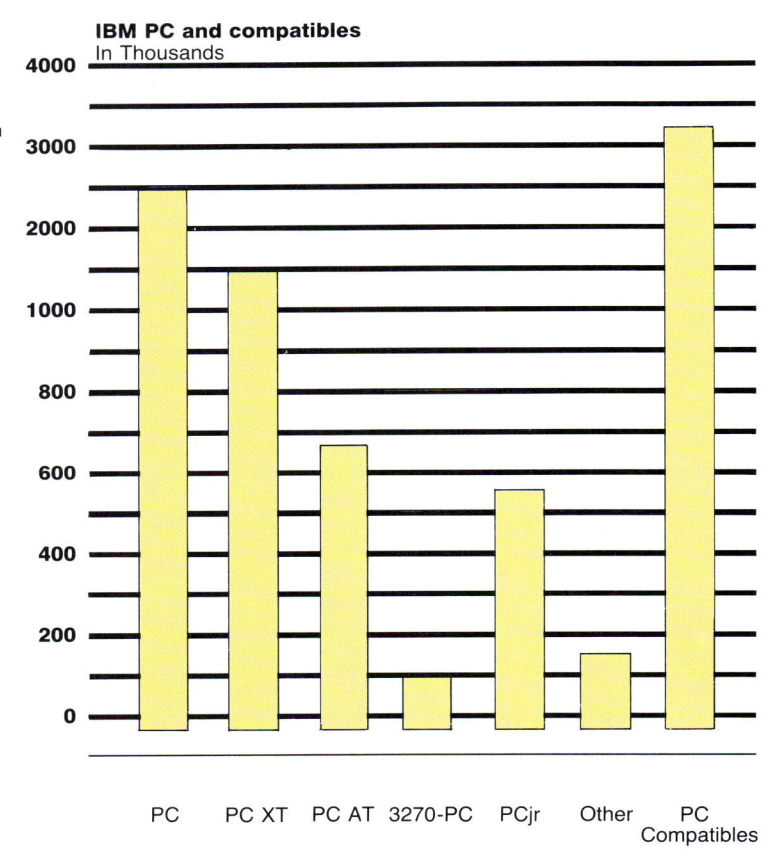

IBM PC and compatibles
In Thousands

Category	Thousands
PC	2500
PC XT	1500
PC AT	675
3270-PC	100
PCjr	550
Other	150
PC Compatibles	3250

However, this does not necessarily mean that they could exchange data from other types of programs.

Figure 3-2 shows the numbers of IBM PCs and compatible computers in use in the United States as of 1987. A typical microcomputer system is shown in Figure 3-3.

Portable Computers

Computers were first applied to solving business problems in the mid-1950s. Until the late 1960s, they were large, expensive machines that had to be programmed and operated by a profes-

FIGURE 3-3

A Typical Microcomputer System

STORAGE

Hard Disk   Floppy Disk

INPUT

Keyboard → Microcomputer → OUTPUT

Video Monitor

Printer

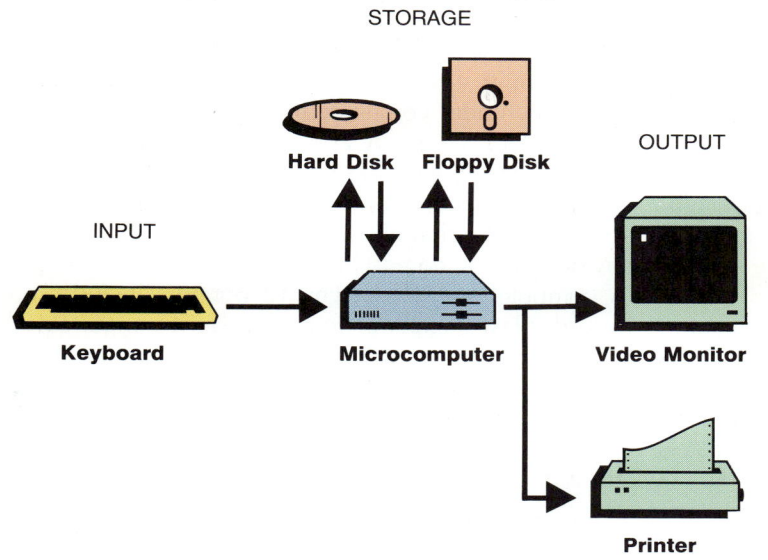

This figure depicts a typical microcomputer system. While many home systems use floppy disks for storage, most microcomputer systems used in business contain a hard disk.

sional staff. The average business user never saw a computer, much less touched one. The 1970s saw the advent of more accessible minicomputers and, eventually, the personal computer. Business users started to use computers themselves without having to rely on professionals. But they were still dependent on electrical outlets. Early in 1981 Adam Osborne introduced the first widely sold **portable computer**, the Osborne I. Since then the portable-computer market has grown substantially; it now offers models for almost every type of user. Today there are three categories of portable computers: pocket computers, laptop computers, and transportable computers.

Pocket Computers. The smallest portable computer is the *pocket computer*, also known as a *hand-held computer*. A typical model, manufactured by Tandy Radio Shack, measures about 6½ inches by 2¾ inches and is only ⅜ inch thick. It prints on a small self-contained roll of paper and is often used to replace electronic calculators. Another important use of pocket computers is *remote data collection*, for example, reading meters and recording inventory in warehouses.

Portable computer
A microcomputer that a user can transport to various locations, usually without requiring access to an electrical outlet.

CHAPTER 3   79   COMPUTERS LARGE AND SMALL

Laptop Computers. The next-larger category of portable computers, the laptops, are about the size of a large book. The opening example in Chapter 1 describes how *Washington Post* sportswriter Gary Pommerantz uses a laptop computer to write his stories. The case for discussion at the end of this chapter also describes situations in which a laptop machine can be useful.

The computer that Pommerantz uses is a Tandy model 200. This popular machine measures 12 inches by 8.5 inches by 2.2 inches. It weighs only 4.5 pounds and requires no external power supply. This model comes equipped with a disk drive and a 16-line monitor. The Tandy 200 monitor is much smaller than those found on nonportable workstations but is large enough to meet many needs. This laptop computer has proven to be quite popular with journalists.

A more powerful laptop computer is Grid Systems' GRiDCase 3 Plus. This computer, which weighs 12 pounds, includes a monitor whose display is superior to that of most nonportable workstations. Among the available options are floppy disk drives, a 10-MB hard disk, and a rechargeable battery. With all of its options, this model is comparable to the IBM XT or compatibles.

Somewhere in the middle is IBM's own PC Convertible. It is less innovative than the GRiDCase 3 Plus, but it uses 3½-inch disks and has a full-size 80 × 25 screen. Like the screens found on all but the most expensive portables, the IBM machine uses reflected light and is hard to read in some conditions. To overcome this problem, IBM makes available an optional plug-in VDT monitor that makes it easier to read the display in situations in which the user does not have to rely on battery power.

A number of accessories are available for laptop computers. For example, Hewlett-Packard makes a popular printer called the ThinkJet that is about the size of a large book and produces

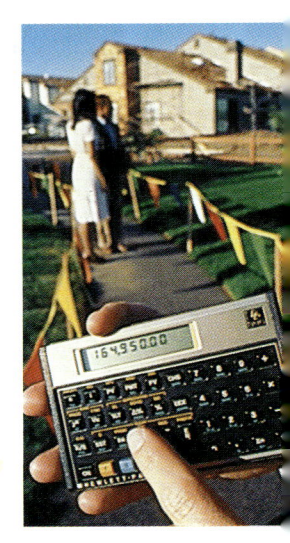

This sales agent is using a hand-held computer to calculate monthly payments for a couple's first house. (Courtesy of Hewlett-Packard.)

This executive is using a laptop computer to make last-minute calculations on the way from the airport to a business meeting. Laptop computers help make every minute count. (Courtesy of Hewlett-Packard.)

draft-quality documents. Another solution is to adapt a battery-operated electric typewriter for use as a portable printer.

Transportable Computers. Transportable computers are considerably larger and heavier than laptop computers. They weigh 20 to 25 pounds or more. Because of their relatively heavy weight, they are often called "luggables." Transportable computers can be attached to a wide variety of *peripherals*, that is, input, output, and storage devices. However, as the technology associated with laptop computers improves, laptops are replacing transportable computers in an increasing number of applications.

Compaq Computer Corporation manufactures a series of transportable computers that have become the industry standard. One Compaq portable, the 286, is compatible with the IBM PC AT. The Portable 286 is considerably larger than the laptop computers; it measures 20 inches by 8½ inches, is 16 inches thick, and weighs a hefty 33 pounds when equipped with a hard disk. The more powerful Portable III weighs only 18 pounds, not much more than a laptop computer.

Users of transportable computers include small-business owners, consultants, and professionals who want to be able to transport the computer from their home to the office to the client's place of business. For example, when Ted Jacobs, an accountant, visits Bill and Kathy Maloney to help them prepare their tax returns, he brings his transportable computer with him. Compatibility means two things to Jacobs: (1) Because his computer is IBM compatible, he can use tax return preparation software that was originally developed for the IBM PC. (2) Because his computer is compatible with Kathy Maloney's laptop computer, he can share files with her and Bill. Since all the data is ready, Jacobs can spend time analyzing investments with the Maloneys—time that he would otherwise have to spend preparing the data.

Problems with Portable Computers. In spite of the positive aspects of portable computers, sales of these machines have been somewhat disappointing. There are two main reasons for this:

1. The quality of the display on moderately priced units may be unsatisfactory, especially for people who use these computers for hours at a time.

2. Only a few portable computers have built-in printers, and the quality of their printed output is often unsatisfactory.

We can expect that as technology improves and prices drop, portable computers will occupy a larger part of the personal-computer market.

Minicomputers

The next category of computers to be discussed in this chapter consists of minicomputers. **Minicomputers** (also called minis) are usually too big to fit on a desktop. Unlike all but the most powerful micros, minicomputers can serve a dozen or more users at once. Their size, memory capacity, and processing power place them between microcomputers and mainframe computers (discussed in the next section). Typical peripherals for minicomputers include magnetic disks, magnetic tapes, terminals (which may be microcomputers), and fairly powerful printers. In general, minicomputers support faster, larger peripherals than personal computers do.

Minicomputers were introduced in the late 1960s by Digital Equipment Corporation for special-purpose applications, including science and engineering. The 1970s witnessed explosive growth in the minicomputer market, but by the end of the 1970s microcomputers were beginning to provide stiff competition for minis. Some industry observers believe that minicomputers will eventually disappear from the market, to be replaced by ever more powerful micros. However, the sheer computing power of minis is not their only advantage. At present, many organizations find that minis offer the managerial advantages of a mainframe system at a lower cost than either a true mainframe or a PC-based system. (See Box 3-2.)

The most common applications of minicomputers are in small businesses and departments of large corporations, in scientific laboratories, in engineering firms, and in educational institutions. Often end-users have direct access to these computers and do not have to rely on specialists to operate or program them. Many minicomputers offer partial compatibility with microcomputers and mainframes.

Micros vs. Minis

There are no hard-and-fast rules for distinguishing microcomputers from minicomputers, but there are some general characteristics that make it possible to classify small computers as micros or minis. Keep in mind, however, that in a changing, dynamic marketplace these distinctions are not likely to stay the same for very long.

Minicomputer
A computer whose processing power and storage capacity is between that of microcomputers and mainframe computers.

Minicomputers can drive dozens of workstations at once. This model, manufactured by WANG Laboratories, is used by an engineering firm to produce all of its technical and administrative reports. (Courtesy of Wang, Inc.)

BOX 3-2

MANAGING CHANGE

PCs Aren't Always the Answer

The Brookings Institution in Washington, D.C., is one of the most prestigious social science research centers in the country. Its economists, political scientists, and research fellows study everything from poverty trends to military strategy. They use computers for statistical analysis, for word processing, and for administrative work.

What kind of computer is best for the job? The Brookings computer center currently uses a DEC 10 and a VAX 785. The DEC 10 is a mainframe and the VAX 785 is a supermini. However, the growth in power of microcomputers has led some users at Brookings to question the wisdom of linking everyone to a single computer center. Instead, they say, why not equip each researcher with his or her own PC?

Christine deFontenay, manager of research programming at Brookings, has looked carefully at the PC alternative. Her conclusion: PCs aren't always the answer.

Technology is part of the problem. Many of the computing tasks at Brookings are just too big for even the most powerful micros. But technology isn't the whole problem. Instead, deFontenay sees the issue primarily as one of management.

"To begin with, just think about the service problem," she says. "With PCs, you have machines all over the building—printers, disk drives, things that break down. With the system we have now, most users have nothing but a terminal in their offices. The terminals have no moving parts, and almost nothing ever goes wrong with them.

"Then there's the cost. The PC enthusiasts give me a figure of about $2000 per machine, but that's unrealistic. To take full advantage of PCs, each installation has to be custom tailored to the user's needs. If you include software, you're talking about $5000 per installation. A terminal costs only $800.

"And then, how are you going to get everyone to agree on the same hardware and software? Even the people who are pushing the PCs come in every week with a different proposal for the 'ideal system.' But if everybody doesn't have the same hardware and software, compatibility problems and service problems get totally out of control.

"But from a management point of view, the biggest problem may be user service. Where do the best programmers and user service people want to go? They want to work in a mainframe type of setting. A lot of our big research jobs require extensive custom programming. Who is going to do that with a PC system? Most of the people who want a PC-based system are 'power users' who know a lot about computers, but that isn't true of all of our research fellows, by any means. We can give those other people much better service in a centralized system. And it isn't any solution to say that the power users would be able to help the guy in the next office. We don't hire those people to help their colleagues with their computer problems—we hire them to get their own research done."

Listening to deFontenay talk about managing a computer system reminds us of a basic truth: Management means getting things done through people—not just through hardware and software.

1. Minicomputers cost more than microcomputers. Most minicomputer systems—that is, the minicomputer and associated input and output devices—cost between $25,000 and $350,000, and most *superminicomputer* systems (the most powerful type of minicomputers) cost from $350,000 to $700,000. Few microcomputer systems cost more than $15,000, and most cost less than $10,000.

2. Minicomputers, which can be connected to many terminals or PCs, can be used by dozens of users at the same time, whereas most microcomputers can serve only one user at a time. Some of the larger microcomputers are powerful enough to serve additional terminals connected to the central unit.

3. In general, minicomputers can handle more data at once than microcomputers can. For example, many minicomputers can handle 32 bits or 4 characters at any one time. In contrast, the IBM PC processes 16 bits at once but can transfer only 8 bits at one time. The more data the computer can handle, the faster it can get a job done.

4. Minicomputers can work with more powerful peripherals than microcomputers can. Unlike microcomputers, minicomputers are often connected to full-size magnetic-tape drives and magnetic-disk drives. Minicomputers can also drive much faster printers than microcomputers can.

Despite the differences between them, the continued coexistence of minis and microcomputers on the market is proof that both are meeting the specific needs of the companies and individuals that use them. Chapter 6 will present some of the points to consider in determining whether one's needs can best be met by a mini- or a microcomputer–based system.

Mainframe Computers

In some settings, particularly large organizations, the appropriate computer to use is a powerful mainframe. **Mainframe computers were the original computers.** In fact, until the late 1960s they had no competitors and the word *mainframe* was synonymous with the word *computer*. Mainframe computer systems have the same components as minis and micros, but everything associated with mainframes is larger: their processing speed, their primary and secondary storage, the number

Mainframe computer
A large computer with immense primary storage capacity that can serve hundreds of users at once.

HARDWARE 84 PART 2

This mainframe computer, manufactured by Unisys, is used by a multinational corporation. It is connected to hundreds of workstations located throughout the United States and in Europe and Latin America. (Courtesy of Unisys.)

and variety of workstations they can serve, and their cost. Their processing speed, for example, is measured in *MIPS* (millions of instructions per second). This tremendous speed enables mainframe computers to serve hundreds of users at once and perform processing tasks that are far beyond the capabilities of micros and minis. Computers that process millions of instructions per second can prepare thousands of paychecks, bills, class schedules, or airline reservations each minute.

Bally's Grand Hotel in Las Vegas, Nevada, uses a relatively small mainframe, the IBM 4341, in its back office twenty-four hours a day. The applications of this equipment include the following:

1. A specialized accounting system for the casino.
2. Other accounting systems that provide information to all levels of hotel and corporate management.
3. About two dozen mailing lists that are used by the sales staff to search for new business, such as conventions.
4. A payroll system.
5. A purchasing and inventory control system.

In addition, this mainframe computer exchanges data with other computer systems in the hotel, including the hotel's reservation system, a personnel system that tracks employee attendance, a telephone system, and a fire control system. Given such large and constantly increasing workloads, it is not surprising that many companies trade in their mainframe computers for larger models on a regular basis.

Mainframe computers usually cost $1 million or more. They are very complex machines that can perform a multitude of activities at the same time. Both their cost and their complexity affect how they are used. For example, because mainframes are

CHAPTER 3   85   COMPUTERS LARGE AND SMALL

so expensive, many corporations lease them rather than purchase them outright.

Companies cannot afford to have their mainframe computers sitting idle. In fact, many companies run their mainframes around the clock. A common way of organizing the computer's workload is to provide *interactive access*. This means that during business hours hundreds of users, such as reservation agents, located at different workstations can interact with the computer. Then the computer is used to process batch jobs, such as payroll and billing, overnight. Of course, it is necessary for management to make a detailed study of the company's specific processing needs before deciding how to organize the use of the mainframe.

Mainframe computers require sophisticated input, output, and storage devices to handle the data that they process so rapidly. Input to mainframe computer systems may be supplied by heavy-duty OCR devices and a large number of data entry personnel using keyboard devices. For storage purposes, a typical mainframe computer system contains dozens of disk drives. The system's disk storage capacity is measured in *gigabytes* (billions of bytes). Twenty gigabytes of storage, which is not unusual for a mainframe computer system, is the equivalent of 1000 hard disks of storage for a personal computer; it's enough to store an 80-character record for every person living in the United States. In most cases, the mainframe's disk storage is supplemented by magnetic-tape storage.

For output, heavy-duty line printers capable of printing 2000 or more lines per minute may be supplemented by page printers, perhaps driven by lasers, which can run ten times as fast (in fact, their output can be measured in miles of paper produced per hour). But even these printers may not be able to keep up with the mainframe's workload, and they may be supplemented by computer output microfilm units.

Another important peripheral unit is the **console**, or workstation, which enables operators to communicate with the mainframe. In older systems the console was a computer terminal; in modern systems it may be a microcomputer or even a minicomputer.

In view of the tremendous amount of work produced by mainframe computers, it should not be too surprising that they generate a lot of heat. Therefore, unlike minicomputers and microcomputers, mainframe computers must be installed in specially prepared, air-conditioned rooms. The rooms usually have false floors with cables beneath them that connect the various units to each other and to their power supplies.

Manufacturers of mainframe computers present their products in families so that customers can easily upgrade their systems

Console
A workstation for an operator of a mainframe or supercomputer.

FIGURE 3-4

A Typical Mainframe Computer System

STORAGE

Disk Pack   Magnetic Tape

INPUT

Keyboard

OCR

MICR

Mainframe Computer

OUTPUT

Video Monitor

Printer

Computer Output Microfilm

Operator's Console

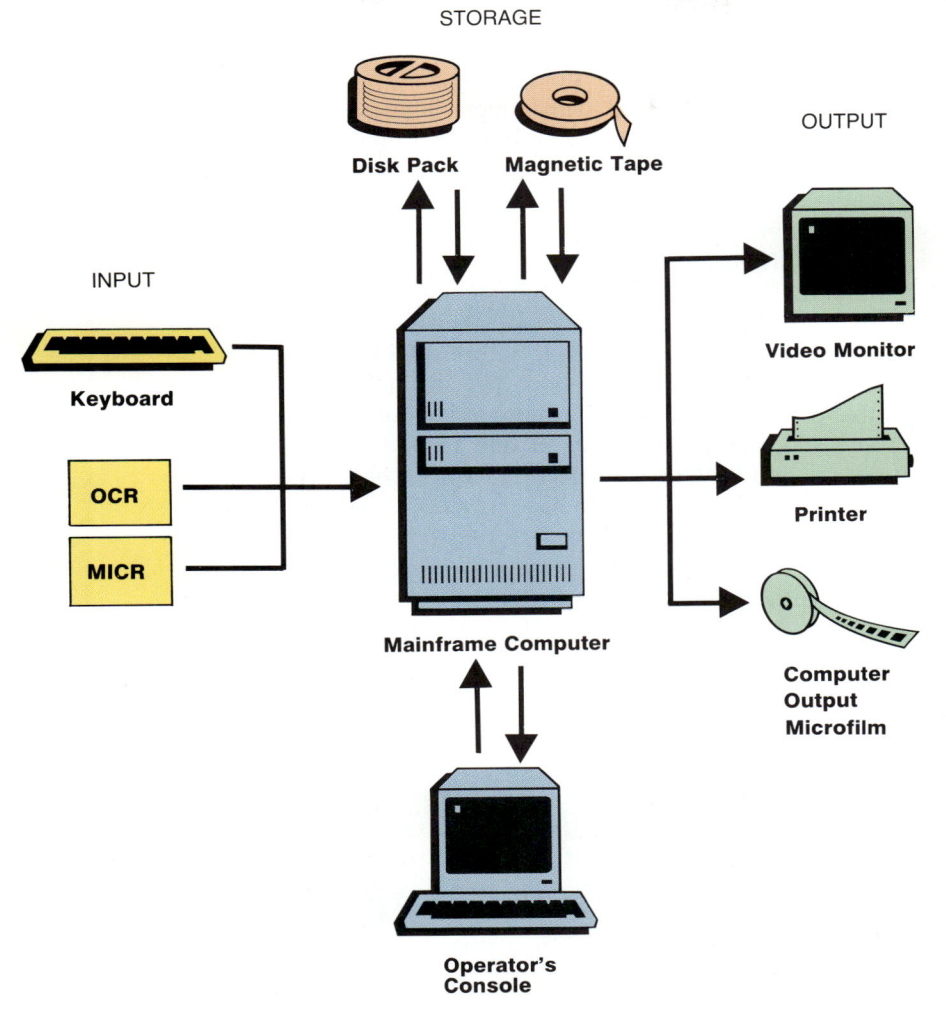

This figure depicts a typical mainframe computer system. Note that this system may use the keyboard as an input device. Printers for mainframe computer systems print a line or a page at a time compared to microcomputer printers that print a character at a time.

when their needs change. The classic example of a mainframe family of computers is the IBM Series/360, introduced in 1964; it developed into the Series/370, which was introduced in 1970 and is still in operation in many organizations. Whatever mainframe "family" they choose, companies can usually be assured of the ability to obtain more powerful computing resources as their needs expand.

A typical mainframe computer system is shown in Figure 3-4.

Microcomputers

Minicomputers

Mainframe Computers

Supercomputers

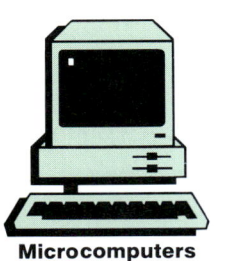

Categories of Computers

Supercomputers

Because of their immense storage capacity and processing power, their ability to deal with almost limitless amounts of data, and the fact that they can be upgraded, mainframe computers are a dynamic part of the computer industry. However, they are not the most powerful computers that exist today. **Supercomputers** are more expensive and more powerful than mainframes. Their cost ranges from about $5 million to about $20 million. The primary storage capacity of the largest models is 1 gigabyte, which is equivalent to the capacity of about 1500 IBM PCs. Their speed is measured not in MIPS but in *GFLOPS* (billions of floating-point operations per second). Calculations that take a personal computer twenty-four hours can be done by some supercomputers in about one second. On the other hand, it may cost the user $2000 or $3000 to share access to a supercomputer for just one hour. For the same amount of money, the user can purchase a personal computer.

Although there are only a few hundred supercomputers in existence, they are extremely important for defense systems and certain technological applications. Typical supercomputer users include the armed forces, scientific research institutions like the Los Alamos Scientific Laboratory in New Mexico, and the National Weather Service. Examples of commercial users are data

Supercomputer
The fastest type of computer, often used for scientific and engineering applications.

The Cray-2 supercomputer is used for extensive science and engineering calculations and can be found in a growing number of businesses. Many supercomputers are used in high-security applications. (Courtesy of Cray Research, Inc.)

HARDWARE 88 PART 2

TABLE 3-1

Categories of Computers

Computer	Memory	Size	Cost	Major Uses
Microprocessor	Small	Fingertip	A few dollars	Computerized toys and appliances
Microcomputer	4 KB – 8 MB	Pocket or desktop	Up to $10,000	Office, home, and school
Minicomputer	1 – 128 MB	Larger than desktop	$25,000 – $350,000	Multiuser and scientific
Mainframe	2 – 512 MB	Room corner or room	$1 – 10 million	Large-scale processing
Supercomputer	16 MB – 2 GB	Like mainframes	$5 – 20 million	Scientific and national security

processing services for the petroleum industry and a Hollywood filmmaker, Digital Productions, Inc.

As fast and powerful as supercomputers are, research efforts are under way to make them even faster and more powerful. In 1982 the Japanese embarked on an eight-year $100 million plan, called the National Superspeed Computer Project, whose goal is to increase the speed of supercomputers by a factor of 1000. Meanwhile, in the mid-1980s a U.S. manufacturer, Convex Computer Corporation, designed a superminicomputer, the Convex C-1. The Convex C-1's raw processing power is about half that of an early supercomputer, the Cray-1, but its price tag is a relatively modest $500,000.

Table 3-1 compares the five main categories of computers.

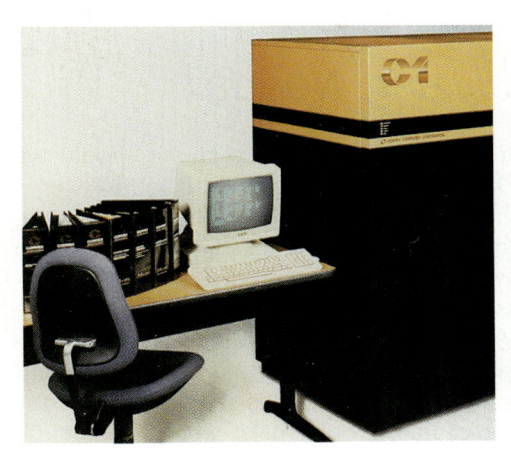

The Convex C1 is an example of a new category of computers called superminicomputers. It offers processing power approaching that of supercomputers for the cost of a large minicomputer.

CHAPTER 3   89   COMPUTERS LARGE AND SMALL

In conclusion, two things should be clear from our discussion of computer categories. First, whatever computing needs individuals and companies have, they can find an appropriate computer system to meet those needs. Second, although there are factors that distinguish each category of computer from the others, there is a great deal of overlap among the categories. Classifying a particular computer is of limited value. What is really important is knowing what a computer can do and how it can help solve specific problems. As we will see in Chapters 4 and 5, all computers, no matter what their size, share certain basic features and depend on peripherals that perform standard functions. The appendix to this chapter presents some guidelines for buying a personal computer.

Appendix: Buying a Personal Computer

This appendix sets forth some guidelines for buying a personal computer for business use. Some of the same principles can also be applied to the purchase of a computer for home use. In presenting the steps to follow in buying a personal computer, we will use what is called the *systems approach*. This approach does not necessarily proceed from one step to the next. For example, the buyer may find in step 2 that he or she lacks information that should have been obtained in step 1. In that case it is necessary to go back to step 1 before completing step 2.

Step 1: Analyzing Needs

The first question to ask is not "Which computer should we buy?" but rather, "Do we need a computer?" If the answer is "yes," the next question is, "What will we do with a computer?" This question isn't always easy to answer. Coming up with a satisfactory answer requires several procedures: reviewing business priorities; collecting data on the company and the marketplace; identifying potential applications such as accounting and word processing; and estimating potential benefits and costs. This all-important first step is often plagued by errors. Perhaps the biggest error that people make when considering the purchase of a computer is attempting to "keep up with the Joneses" by choosing the same equipment as a competitor or another department within the company. Other possible errors include unrealistic expectations regarding the benefits offered by computers, incorrect estimates of the total cost, and failure to anticipate employee resistance.

Step 2: Determining Requirements

The outcome of this step is a checklist that indicates the buyer's needs in enough detail to make it possible to approach vendors. This entails asking questions such as, "What kinds of business records must the system process?" "How many records will it process per day?" and "What type of person will use the system?" Prospective home computer purchasers might ask questions such as, "Do I want to use the system for the kids' education?" and "What are my children's aptitudes and interests?" Asking the wrong questions or giving the wrong answers at this stage reduces the likelihood that the user will benefit fully from the equipment purchased. Another common error is buying unnecessary frills for the computer system, such as a hard disk for a system that does not require extensive auxiliary storage.

Step 3: Evaluating Software

It is essential to determine the software necessary to meet the requirements listed in step 2 before choosing the hardware that will be used to run that software. Prospective buyers of software such as word processors, accounting packages, and electronic spreadsheets can choose among hundreds of programs. Determining which ones are best for a particular individual or company is not a simple matter. One solution, adopted by many neophytes and by experienced users as well, is to choose the best-selling product in each category desired. This solution has some advantages: It is easy to find people who know the product, and add-on software is readily available. But each user's needs are unique; what works for someone else may not work for you.

In this connection it is worth noting that although many people think it is easy to modify packaged software, in most cases buyers do not even have access to the program in human-readable form. Most commercial programs are written in such a way that users cannot modify them easily. Many software manufacturers consider such modification illegal and will void the warranty if they believe a program has been tampered with.

Step 4: Evaluating Hardware

Before purchasing any hardware, the buyer must make sure that it can run the software chosen in step 3. A spreadsheet or a word-processing program that runs too slowly will cause at least as many problems as it solves. At this stage it is essential to take the computer for a "test drive" in conditions similar to those in which it will be used. It is also important to talk with people who have used the same system. Users are often willing to talk about their experiences and counsel others regarding both hardware and software.

Step 5: Installing the System

Installing the system means much more than just attaching the different units with the right cables (which can be a major operation in itself). The computer system was bought to meet certain needs as defined in step 1. Now it must be installed in such a way that it will meet those needs. At this stage it is necessary for users to learn how to operate both the hardware and the software. It is also necessary to design operating procedures. In the case of word processing, for example, this involves deciding how to name documents or files, when to use hard copy (i.e., printouts), how often to make backup copies, and so forth. In a situation in which there are many users, these decisions must be put in writing. Also, it is necessary to come up with a schedule if more than one person will be using the new system.

A common error at this stage is not allowing enough time for training. Learning new ways of working always takes time; this is particularly true in the case of computer systems. Another common error is lack of management participation. The arrival of a computer often causes jurisdictional disputes that only management can resolve. When management remains aloof from the computer, it is easy for lower-level employees to stand aside also.

Step 6: Maintaining the System

In the final step, the system is evaluated in relation to the requirements determined in step 1. If those requirements have not

TABLE 3A-1

Factors in the Selection of a Computer System

Hardware costs
  Personal computers
  Expansion boards
  Input devices
  Modems and other communications equipment
  Printers
  Cables
  Graphics monitors
Software costs
  Applications software
  Systems software
  Software upgrades
  Documentation and textbooks
Furniture and site preparation
  Tables and chairs
  Bookcases
  Filing cabinets
	Wiring and lighting
	Security devices
	Water, fire, and power-supply protection
	Supplies
	  Paper
	  Ribbons
	  Diskettes
	  Diskette holders
	  Tape cartridges
	Training and miscellaneous
	  Training
	  Hiring new employees
	  Consultants
	  Parallel operations
	  Maintenance costs
	  Legal fees
	  Magazine subscriptions

been met, corrective action must be taken. But even if they have been met, it is impossible to sit back and let the system run by itself. Almost from the day the computer is installed, it will begin to be out of date. And if users like the system they will want to do more and more things with it. Under such conditions it's a good idea to consider upgrading the system. On the other hand, if the computer turns out to be inadequate to meet the user's needs, it may be necessary to start the selection process over again at step 1.

It is a mistake to rely on a single trained employee to operate the new computer. In such a case the company runs into problems whenever the employee is sick or on vacation. Also, the employee may gain excessive power and could violate rules regarding confidentiality of information. Another common error at this stage is to neglect documentation, that is, the paperwork that makes it possible for all users to understand how the system is to be operated and the procedures for doing so.

In sum, these six steps constitute a systems approach to the purchase of a microcomputer. The same approach can be applied to the creation of a computerized business information system, as discussed in Chapter 12. It can also be adapted to the purchase or lease of computers of any size, particularly minicomputers. Table 3A-1 presents some factors to consider in choosing computer hardware, software, and other equipment.

SUMMARY

1. There are two basic types of computers. **Analog computers** process continuous data by measuring it; **digital computers** process discrete data by counting it. Businesses use digital computers in a wide variety of applications.

2. Microprocessors are CPUs that are contained on chips. There are two kinds of microprocessors: those that drive computerized devices such as microwave ovens and those that drive computers.

3. Microcomputers are microprocessors that are fitted with an input device, an output device, and primary storage. They are often called personal computers. They are used in businesses, offices, and homes to run hundreds of software packages, including word-processing, data-management, and graphics programs, integrated software, and electronic spreadsheets.

4. The first microcomputer to gain wide acceptance in the business world was the IBM PC, which was introduced in late 1981. It was designed on an **open architecture** basis, meaning that competitors could supply hardware and software to enable the computer to meet new needs.

5. In the business world the PC XT has largely replaced the PC. The PC AT is based on a more sophisticated CPU and is several times faster than the PC for many kinds of applications. The Personal System/2 is the latest series of IBM microcomputers.

6. Many customers prefer to purchase **compatibles** (also called clones), computers made by other manufacturers that can run all or most of the software written for the IBM PC. Compatibles are also available for other popular computers.

7. There are three types of **portable computers:** pocket, or hand-held, computers; laptop computers; and transportable or "luggable" computers. As the technology of laptop computers improves, they are replacing transportables in an increasing number of applications.

8. Minicomputers are computers whose size, cost, and processing power place them between microcomputers and mainframes. Among the users of minis are small businesses, departments of large corporations, scientific laboratories, engineering firms, and educational institutions.

9. Mainframe computers are large, expensive computers that are often leased rather than purchased outright. Their processing speed is so fast that they can process millions of instructions per second (MIPS) and can be used by hundreds of users at once. Because of their size and complexity, mainframes are installed in specially prepared rooms; may be equipped with **consoles** or workstations for professional operators; are run by trained personnel; and require sophisticated input, output, and storage devices.

10. The most powerful computers are **supercomputers**, which cost $5 million or more. Their speed is measured in GFLOPS (billions of floating-point operations per second). Only a few hundred supercomputers have been sold, mostly to military and scientific institutions, although commercial use of supercomputers is increasing.

KEY TERMS

analog computer

digital computer

microprocessor

microcomputer

open architecture

compatible

portable computer

minicomputer

mainframe computer

console

supercomputer

REVIEW QUESTIONS

1. Distinguish between analog and digital computers.

2. What are microprocessors? Give an example (not mentioned in the text) of how microprocessors are used.

3. What is a microcomputer? Describe how it can be used in businesses or schools.

4. Describe the IBM PC. What is meant by open architecture? Why do some computer manufacturers choose not to use this approach?

5. What are compatibles? Why is it important for computers to be compatible with one another? Describe a situation in which compatible computers can be used.

6. What are the three categories of portable computers? How are they used?

7. What is a minicomputer and how is it used? Discuss the major differences between minicomputers and microcomputers.

8. What is a mainframe computer and how is it used? What are the special features that distinguish mainframe computers from micros and minis?

9. What is a supercomputer? Name some typical supercomputer users.

APPLICATIONS

1. Describe some of the possible applications of microprocessors in a typical day in your life. How do microprocessors make your life easier or more enjoyable?

2. Report on an article in a trade or business journal that describes a minicomputer application. Indicate why the application is well suited to a minicomputer.

3. Report on an article in a trade or business journal that describes a mainframe computer application. Indicate why the application is well suited to a mainframe.

4. Discuss the following statement: The United States will subsidize the computer industry in order to become the world leader in supercomputers.

CASE FOR DISCUSSION

Kathy Maloney is a commercial real estate agent who specializes in leasing industrial parks. She was an early participant in the computer revolution. First she bought an Apple II, on which she was able to run the pathbreaking business spreadsheet software VisiCalc. Both the Apple II and VisiCalc are obsolete now, although her husband and children still use them at home. Maloney's next machine was an IBM PC, which she upgraded with extra memory, a modem, and a hard disk. It remains her basic office computer.

Maloney does a lot of traveling, however. Her home base is in Toronto, but business takes her all over Canada. Given this situation, it seemed that a portable computer would be the logical next step. But for a long time she couldn't find one she was satisfied with. For one thing, her eyesight is not particularly good. Many of the portables had gray-on-gray displays that she could hardly read. She found some "transportable" computers that had good displays, but these were too heavy and bulky for her purposes. Finally she decided on a Gridcase. This top-of-the-line laptop computer was expensive, but it was small and light, and had by far the best display of anything in its class at the time. As she puts it, "A computer that doesn't meet my needs is too expensive no matter how little it costs."

The Gridcase is so compact that Maloney is able to use it on an airplane. On a recent sales trip, on board a morning flight to her client's city, she used her Gridcase with word-processing software to put some finishing touches on the presentation she would make. Using graphics software, she added last-minute modifications to some charts. Her plane arrived at 9:30 A.M. She took a cab from the airport to a computer rental service located near her client's office. There she used a laser printer similar to the one in her office to run off copies of her charts and data sheets.

Maloney's presentation was well received. Her client was interested and immediately wanted additional details, including some numbers that Maloney had not brought with her. She dialed her office, using the modem built into her Gridcase. This put her in touch with a large data base stored on her office machine. She retrieved the necessary items of data and displayed them for her client on the screen of the Gridcase, right there in his office.

These numbers proved to be the key to closing the deal, but the meeting ran late. Maloney missed her flight back to Toronto; she would have to return the next day. Borrowing a telephone in her client's office, she used her modem again to obtain flight data from the Official Airlines Guide. She then called a travel agent to book a morning flight and a motel.

When she reached her motel, she used the modem again. This time she dialed a local information utility. This service gave her access to information about local restaurants. After making a reservation, she used the remaining time to update her expense account and her monthly sales report. Then, just for fun, she called up some stock market information in order to decide how to invest the sales commission she had earned that day.

CASE QUESTIONS

1. What parts of Maloney's work could have been done just as well, and what parts not as well or not at all, with a transportable computer rather than a laptop model? With a minicomputer or mainframe based in her office?

2. Maloney used her computer for several different tasks during her business trip. Which of them could have been accomplished fairly easily without a computer? For which tasks was the computer very useful, or essential?

3. Given the wide variety of computers on the market, what role did considerations of ergonomics play in Maloney's choice of a computer?

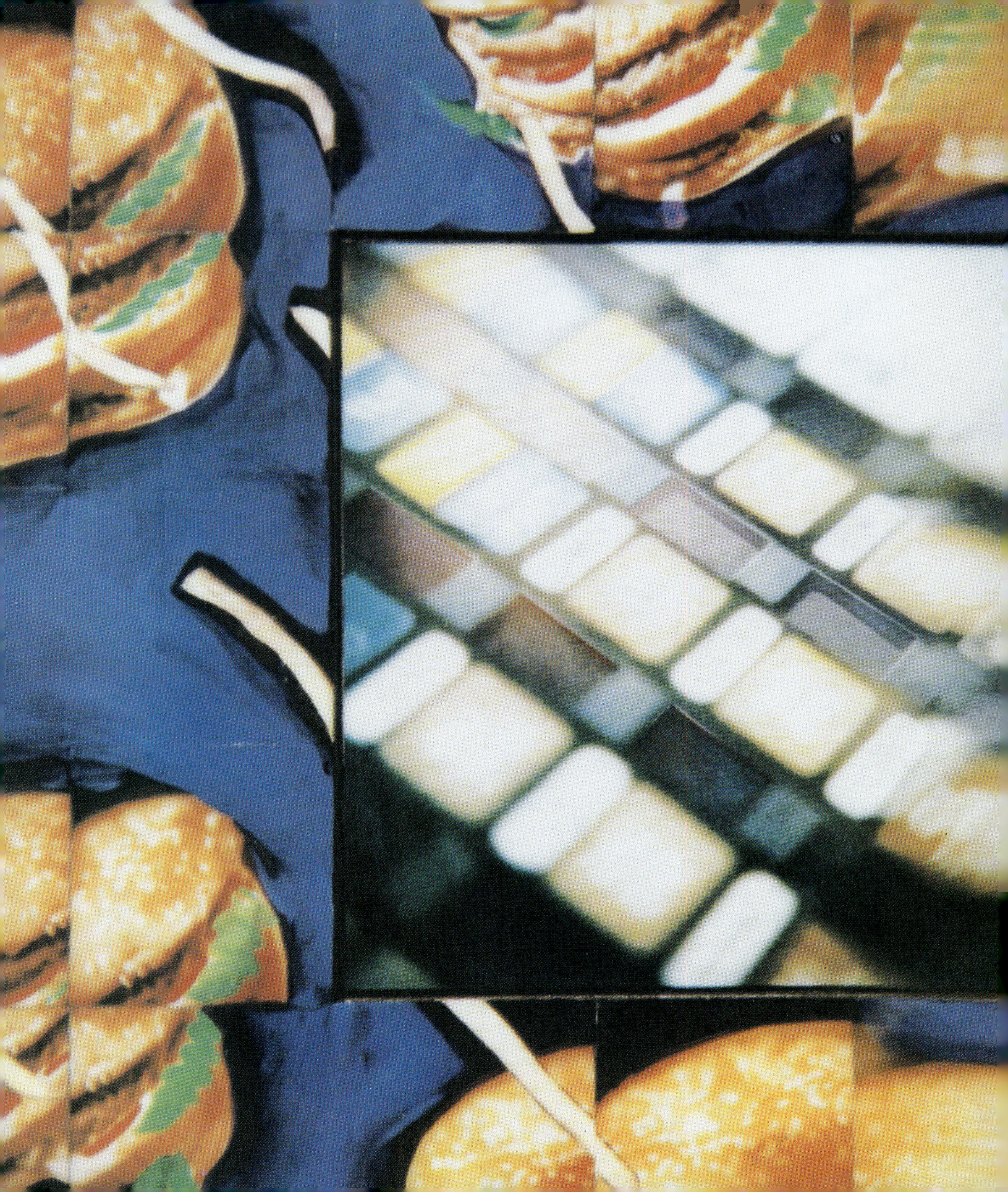

Input and Output

CHAPTER

4

The next time you stop by your local McDonald's, take a look at its computer. No, it's not in a big air-conditioned room in the basement. It's not tended by white-jacketed specialists the way the computers in comic strips are. Instead, it's right up there in front. The terminals are on the counter and the CPU is underneath. It's tended by a couple of high schoolers wearing green-and-white-striped shirts with matching visors.

While you're deciding what kind of sauce to get with your McNuggets, take a look at the keyboard on that terminal. It doesn't look at all like a typical computer keyboard. There are more than 100 keys on it, protected by a smooth plastic film that makes it easy to clean off the spilled root beer. The keys have labels like "Big Mac," "Quarter Pounder," and "Chef's Salad"—one key for every product sold by the store.

It takes less than a day to become a skilled operator of this computer. For each item ordered, the corresponding key is pushed. The price of each item appears on the terminal's two displays, one facing the operator and the other facing the customer. When the customer pays, the computer figures the change.

As each item is entered, the unit under the counter keeps track of the money that is taken in and the food that goes out. At the end of the day, the week, and the month, the store's manager has a complete report on what's been sold. The data from the computer up front later becomes input for a more complex computer system in the back, which is connected by a telephone line with McDonald's headquarters. There it becomes the basis for scheduling, inventory management, and so on. But it is the relatively simple computer up front that allows McDonald's to make its fast food really fast. It allows the stores to employ workers with little or no previous job experience. Funny-looking keyboard and all, it plays a key role in the success of this industry leader.[1]

---

[1] Information from Robin Waltner, First Assistant Manager of McDonald's in McLean, Virginia.

This chapter focuses on the input and output phases of data processing. Input and output are activities that all computers have in common, but as we will see, they can be carried out in many different ways. The specialized terminals used at McDonald's and many other stores are an example of one approach to input that is becoming more and more common. The printed reports produced by the McDonald's computer are one among many types of data output.

Some of the equipment and techniques discussed in this chapter will be familiar to you from reading Chapter 2. Others will be new. The chapter will introduce all the major input and output options, and explain how to choose the best combination of equipment for specific uses.

When you have read this chapter, you should be able to:

1. Describe the major input methods and devices and their impact on computer users.

2. Describe the major output methods and devices and their impact on computer users.

3. Make a knowledgeable choice of input and output devices for home and business microcomputers.

4. Understand and use the key terms listed at the end of the chapter.

Input

When we refer to computer input, we mean the actual data that is entered into the computer and the devices used to enter the data. Each of the different ways of entering data and the different devices involved in the input process has its own advantages and disadvantages. The choice of method and equipment depends on the particular job to be done and the resources available, including the people who will enter the data.

Data Entry

For a computer to be useful, whether in an office or factory, in a school, in a home, or anywhere else, someone must do data entry, that is, input raw data into the computer. There are two main ways of doing this: traditional data entry and source data automation.

Traditional Data Entry. The traditional way to enter data into a computer system and process it via batch processing involves many steps. Figure 4-1 presents these steps in graphic form. In step 1, the user enters data by hand on special forms known as source documents. (An example is a sales slip.) Then several similar source documents are gathered together into batches. In step 2, these documents are batched and sent to the data processing department, where data entry specialists, using workstations equipped with a keyboard, enter the data (step 3) along with special control information onto cards, disks, or tapes (step 4). In step 5, the computer processes the data on these media; the resulting information is sent back to the appropriate person or department (step 6).

The biggest drawback of traditional data entry is its slow speed. Some of the steps just described, especially collecting a batch of data, may be time-consuming. It is not uncommon for users to wait several days to receive information after supplying the input data. Any errors in filling out the source documents or inputting the data may cause further delay. Many applications, such as payroll and quarterly reports, can be scheduled so that a short delay poses no problems. But for numerous other applications, such as airline reservations and bank teller machines, such delays are undesirable or even intolerable.

Data entry
The process of inputting data into a computer.

Source document
A form that contains data for entry into a computer system.

FIGURE 4-1

Steps in Traditional Data Entry

In step 1, users enter data by hand on special forms called source documents. In step 2, these forms are batched and sent to the data processing department, where data entry specialists enter the data (step 3) onto machine-readable media (step 4). In step 5, the computer processes the data, and in step 6, the resulting information is sent to the user.

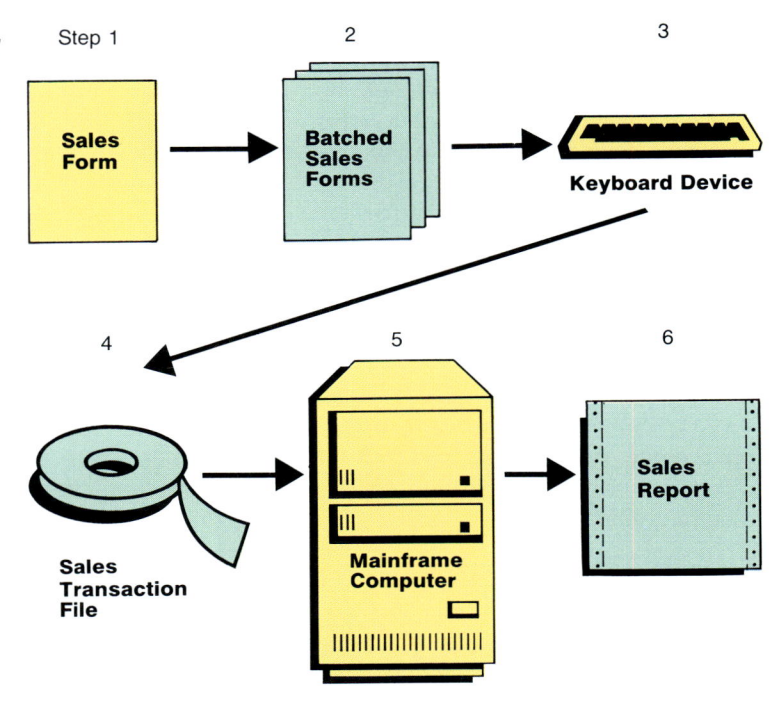

Step 1: Sales Form → 2: Batched Sales Forms → 3: Keyboard Device → 4: Sales Transaction File → 5: Mainframe Computer → 6: Sales Report

Source Data Automation. Source data automation is the use of specialized data entry equipment to collect data at the source and transmit it to the computer. It is faster and less error prone than the traditional data entry method. In many applications users enter data into the computer directly instead of relying on data entry specialists to do so. The countertop terminals used in place of conventional cash registers by McDonald's, described at the beginning of this chapter, are an example of source data automation equipment. It eliminates a step, since the data is entered only once. However, since data is entered by a person at a keyboard, typing errors may still occur.

Some source data automation equipment, described later in the chapter, eliminates data entry via the keyboard, thereby eliminating typing errors. Figure 4-2 illustrates the application of source data automation in a supermarket, where a checkout clerk enters data into the system without using a keyboard.

Source data automation
The use of specialized data entry equipment to collect data at the source and transmit it to a computer.

FIGURE 4-2

Steps in Source Data Automation

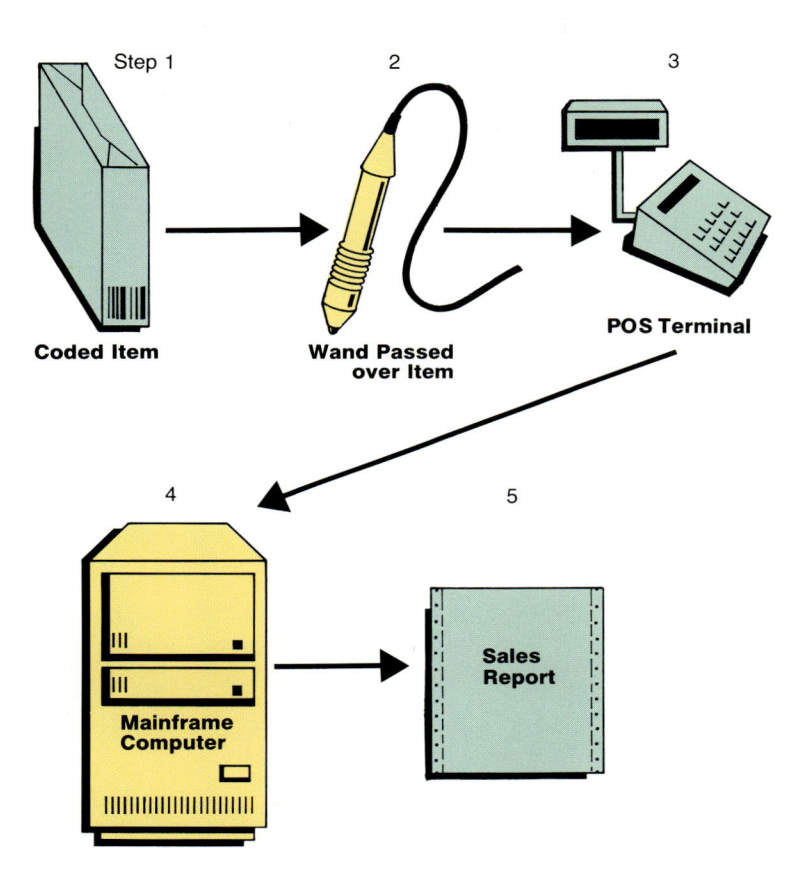

Step 1 — Coded Item
2 — Wand Passed over Item
3 — POS Terminal
4 — Mainframe Computer
5 — Sales Report

Data is entered into the system at the point where it is generated. In this example a supermarket employee passes a scanner (in the form of a wand) over an item marked with a special code. The scanner reads the code and transmits data to a point-of-sale (POS) terminal, which automatically enters it into a computer; the computer can then produce one or more sales reports.

Input Devices

Both traditional data entry and source data automation require specialized data entry devices. A wide variety of input devices are available. (See Table 4-1.) Many of these devices have been designed ergonomically, making them easier and more pleasant to work with than those available only a few

TABLE 4-1

Common Input Devices

Device	Speed	Advantages	Disadvantages	Applications
Workstation keyboard	1 – 10 cps	Familiar, visible on monitor	Requires typing, error prone	Very wide (business and home)
Key-to-tape and key-to-disk devices	5 – 20 cps	Heavy duty	Requires professional	Sizable data entry
POS terminal	Several items per minute	Reduces unit pricing, automatic inventory	Customer resistance, sometimes error prone	Retail sales
Optical character recognition devices	Several to hundreds of items per minute	Eliminates typing	May be expensive, sometimes error prone	Wide range credit cards
Magnetic ink character recognition devices	Hundreds of items per minute	Eliminates typing	Only numbers and special symbols	Banking and related industries
Mouse	Faster than keyboard where applies	Many find easy to use	Not for text entry, some models tend to "jump"	Drawings and menu selection

years ago. Selection of an appropriate input device can result in greater productivity on the part of data entry personnel.

Keyboards

Many data entry devices use a keyboard as the principal means of inputting data. But not all keyboards are equally efficient and easy to use for data entry.

QWERTY and Dvorak. The standard keyboard was designed in 1872 for the mechanical typewriters of the day. The unusual arrangement of letters, in which the first six letters spell QWERTY, as shown in Figure 4-3, was chosen specifically to slow down good typists in order to stop them from jamming the typewriter hammers.

In the early 1930s August Dvorak designed another key-

FIGURE 4-3

The QWERTY Keyboard Layout

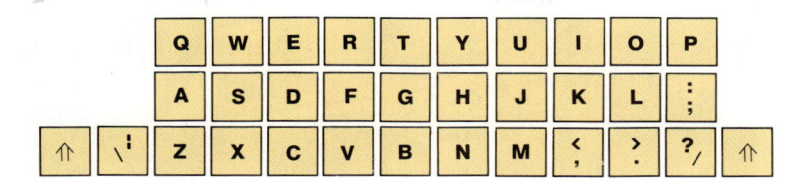

FIGURE 4-4

The Dvorak Keyboard Layout

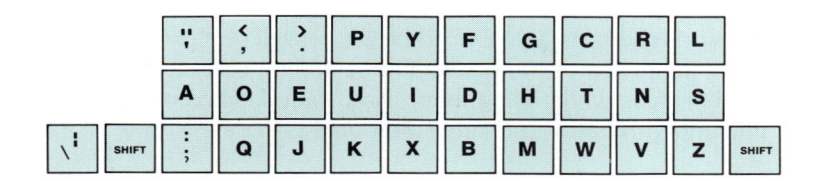

board, which bears his name. His goal was to increase typists' speed. The Dvorak keyboard, shown in Figure 4-4, contains vowels and the most commonly used consonants on the home row (the third row from the top). Over 4000 words can be typed on the home row of the Dvorak keyboard, compared to only 100 on the QWERTY.

Even though the more logical arrangement of the Dvorak keyboard leads to faster typing with less effort, and hammer jamming is no longer a problem, the QWERTY design is still in general use. The reason for this is that most people who type are used to the QWERTY layout, and learning a new layout takes time and requires retraining. In recent years, however, the Dvorak keyboard has become more popular. For example, the Apple IIc computer comes with a switch that permits the user to shift between the QWERTY and Dvorak keyboards. It is also possible to convert the keyboards of popular personal computers and even IBM Selectric typewriters from the QWERTY to the Dvorak arrangements.

Some users prefer to type with the keyboard in their lap. Ergonomically designed hardware lets users adjust the equipment to their personal preferences. (Courtesy of International Business Machines.)

Keyboard Features. Regardless of which keyboard one prefers, the keyboard selected should have a good "feel"; it should react to a light touch but not be so sensitive that characters appear when one simply rests one's fingers on the keys. Also, the keys should be far enough apart so that striking one key does not cause its neighbor to be hit as well.

Some keyboards are detachable, enabling users to hold them on their laps while using them. And some keyboards have feet that allow the user to change their angle.

Special Keys. Computer keyboards often have keys that are not found on standard typewriters. These special keys include the following:

- A *numeric keypad* that can be used to enter numbers quickly.

The left-hand side of this keyboard shows several keys, such as ESC and Control, that simplify the user's work. Users accustomed to computer keyboards may not want to return to the typewriter. (© Paul Nehrenz, The Image Bank.)

HARDWARE PART 2

- *Function keys* that are used to give commands to the computer. On many keyboards these keys are labeled F1 through F10.
- *Control (Ctrl) and Alternate (Alt) keys*, which are used in combination with other keys to give additional commands to the computer.
- *Escape (Esc) and Break keys*, which are used to cancel or change entries.
- *Delete (Del) and Insert (Ins) keys*, which are used to modify entries.

Keyboard Software. Software is available for users who wish to change the functions of certain keys. This is especially useful for people who work with more than one software package, such as one or more word-processing programs, data-base management software, and an electronic spreadsheet. Many packages assign function keys (and other special keys) to specific tasks such as underlining words. Computer programs that have a *keyboard redefinition option* enable the user to reset the function keys so that each software package uses these keys in the same way. For example, suppose that an office uses one word processor, *Computer Word*, for short memos and letters and another word processor, *Word Wonder*, for long reports and other lengthy documents. *Computer Word* uses the F5 key to underline, whereas *Word Wonder* uses the F4 key to underline and the F5 key to set the left margin. If *Word Wonder* includes a keyboard redefinition option, the user can redefine the F5 key to underline and redefine an unused key to set the left margin.

Another type of computer program that can be used to improve the keyboard is called a *keyboard enhancer*. Such programs enable users to substitute one keystroke for several others, thereby reducing typing time and errors. For example, a law office might use a keyboard enhancer to substitute "Alt-P" (i.e., pressing the "Alt" key and the "P" key at the same time) for the common legal phrase "the party of the first part." Then, instead of typing the phrase, all a user would have to do is press "Alt-P".

Terminals

For mainframes and minicomputers, much data entry is carried out at a *terminal*. Most computer terminals consist of input devices such as keyboards, output devices such as display screens, and perhaps some limited processing capabilities. Terminals can be classified according to how "smart" they are, that is, on the basis of their processing capabilities. They range from "dumb" terminals to "intelligent" terminals. The more sophisticated the terminal, the more it reduces the load on the CPU and improves system performance.

Dumb Terminals. Dumb terminals are basically keyboards attached to display screens. They are called "dumb" because they cannot do any actual data processing. They simply display the data on the screen as it is entered, enabling the user to check for accuracy and typos.

Smart Terminals. Smart terminals have some processing and storage capabilities. These capabilities are programmed into the terminal by the vendor. Those terminals that can calculate the change owed to a McDonald's customer are an example of smart terminals. Over the years smart terminals have become "smarter," meaning that more recent models have more memory and more powerful editing capabilities.

Intelligent Terminals. Intelligent terminals are equipped with a microprocessor, which increases their editing and processing capabilities substantially. An intelligent terminal can be programmed to meet the user's specific needs. Such terminals are typically used to validate data entry, that is, to make sure that data has been entered correctly.

A typical use of intelligent terminals is in an airline reservation system in which, for example, the terminals are programmed to accept only numeric flight numbers. If a ticket agent enters an invalid flight number, such as "71B" instead of "718", the terminal beeps and displays the following message on the screen:

```
Flight number entered was 71B; flight numbers are numeric only.
Please try again.
```

The terminal can also be programmed to accept only reasonable ticket prices, thereby making sure that a customer does not get billed for $10,500 for a flight from New York to Boston.

Other Data Entry Devices

Some data entry devices are operated only by data entry professionals. These devices are used to enter data from source documents onto cards, tapes, or disks, which are then used as input for a computer.

Keypunch Machines. Data may be input into a computer using the special punched cards mentioned in Chapter 2. These

In the not-so-distant past most data was entered into the computer on punched cards like those shown here. Today few applications use these cards. (© Freda Leinwand.)

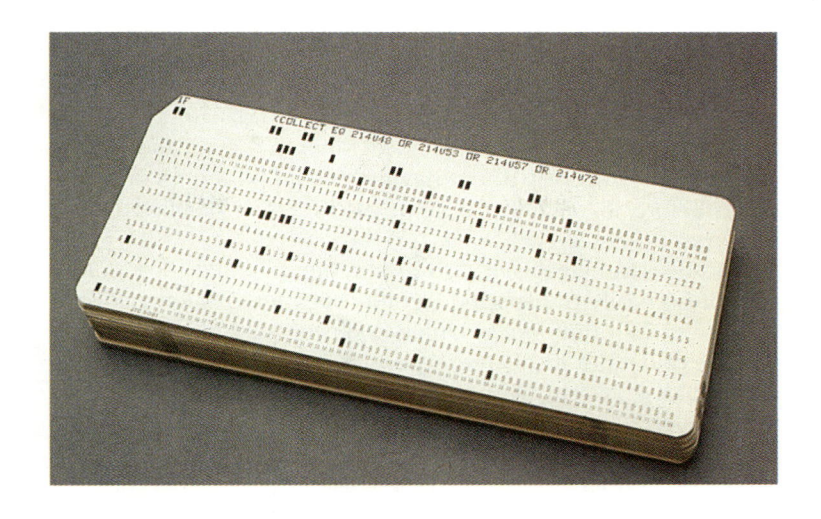

Dumb Terminal

A keyboard attached to a display screen; cannot do actual data processing.

Smart Terminal

Has some processing and storage capabilities, which have been programmed in by the vendor.

Intelligent Terminal

Equipped with a microprocessor; can be programmed to meet user's needs.

cards typically contain 80 columns and 12 rows. By pressing keys at a keypunch machine, a *keypunch operator* can either punch holes in a column or leave the column intact. The patterns formed by the holes correspond to the characters in the *Hollerith code*, which represent letters, numbers, and special characters such as !, &, +, and : . Some keypunch machines have a display that indicates the number of the next column to be punched. A machine called a *verifier* can be used to retype the same cards to make certain that the correct holes have been punched. Cards that contain errors are thrown out.

Although keypunch machines have been almost entirely replaced by more modern equipment, they are still used in some businesses and universities. For example, some utility companies use them for customer billing.

Key-to-Tape Systems. Another keyboard data entry device that was used extensively by businesses until relatively recently is the *key-to-tape system*. In such systems, as data is entered via the keyboard it is displayed on a screen, allowing immediate corrections. (Keypunch machines lack this feature.) These systems are quieter and faster than keypunch machines and offer additional information such as statistics on the operator's performance.

Key-to-tape systems have some disadvantages, however. They require a great deal of keyboarding; some models produce only small tapes or cassettes, which must be consolidated before being entered into a computer; and the tapes produced must be accessed sequentially. (Recall that sequential access means that for the system to read a particular record, it must read all of the records that come before it.)

CHAPTER 4   109   INPUT AND OUTPUT

Key-to-Disk Systems. *Key-to-disk systems* are more powerful and flexible than key-to-tape systems. The disks that they produce have more storage capacity than magnetic tapes, and data on the disks can be accessed randomly (i.e., the system can read any record without having to read all the records that come before it). In these systems also, data is displayed on a screen as it is entered.

One disadvantage of key-to-disk systems is that their output cannot be easily transported to other locations. Another disadvantage is their high price. Unless a business has a high enough volume of data to justify the expense of installing and operating a key-to-disk system, it should consider other types of data entry devices.

Key-to-Floppy Disk Systems. *Key-to-floppy disk systems* are microcomputers or similar machines that are used for data entry. They combine the random access offered by key-to-disk systems and the lower cost of key-to-tape systems. In addition, the floppy disks produced by these systems are easily transported, inexpensive, and reusable. The microcomputers used in key-to-floppy disk systems can also run software such as spreadsheets, word processors, and file management programs.

The biggest drawback of key-to-floppy disk systems is their limited storage capacity. The 360K floppy disk found on many personal computers contains much less storage space than the other systems discussed in this chapter.

Other Keyboard Systems. The keyboard data entry systems discussed so far are used mainly in offices or computer installations such as those in large corporations, small businesses, universities, and colleges. The following keyboard systems are found in other settings:
- Many banks provide *automated teller machines* that are available to any customer who has a special card. Since many customers may be unfamiliar with computers, these machines must be fairly easy to use. To deposit money, withdraw money, check a balance, and in some cases even take out a loan, all one has to do is follow the instructions, or *prompts*, that appear on the screen.
- *Factory data-collection devices* enable workers and supervisors to take inventory, read labels, and record the times a particular job begins and ends.
- Many fast-food restaurants use specially designed terminals whose keys indicate available items. For example, if you order a cheeseburger, large fries, and a cola, the employee presses keys representing these items. Your order and its cost are automatically entered into a computer.

The automated teller machine makes it possible to access banking services twenty-four hours a day. (Courtesy of Citibank.)

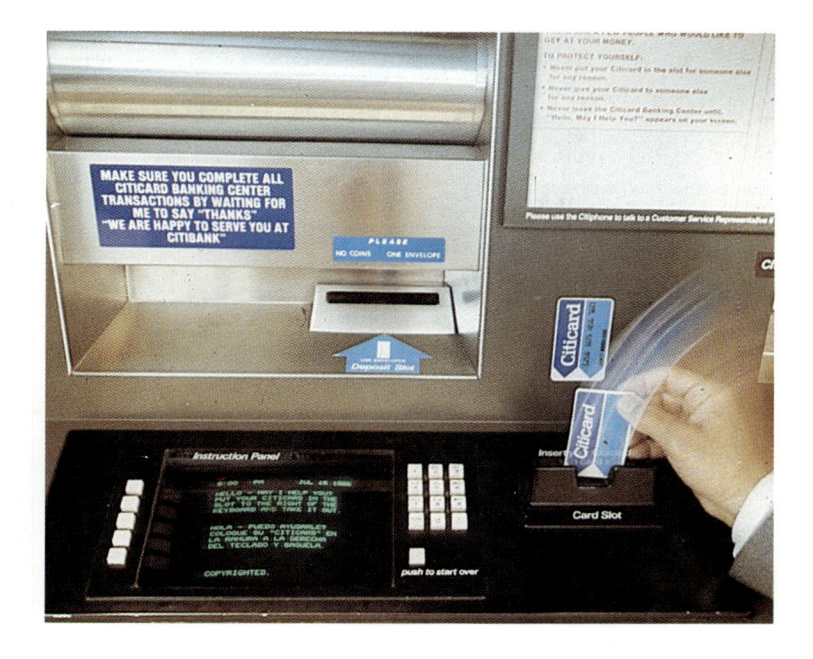

Scanners

Typing, even by experts on high-quality equipment, is still a relatively slow, error-prone method of data entry. Therefore, manufacturers have spent a lot of time and effort trying to develop input methods that bypass the keyboard. Several devices, known as *scanners*, transmit data from written or typed material directly into the computer.

Magnetic Ink Character Recognition. **Magnetic ink character recognition (MICR)** is a technique in which specialized machines read the standard set of fourteen characters—0–9 and four banking symbols—adopted by the American Bankers Association in the 1950s. Because of the limited character set it can process, MICR is restricted to processing checks and deposit slips on which data is encoded in special ink. MICR can process 2000 checks per minute. Its speed and accuracy has enabled banks to keep up with the tremendous increase in the number of checks written daily. However, because present MICR devices cannot read handwritten checks with an acceptable degree of accuracy, check amounts must be entered via a keyboard. Thus, MICR is not a fully automated system.

Optical Mark Recognition. *Optical mark recognition* is the use of special equipment known as *optical mark readers* or

Magnetic ink character recognition (MICR)
A data entry technique in which a specialized machine reads a standard set of 14 characters— 0–9 and four banking symbols.

CHAPTER 4   111   INPUT AND OUTPUT

FIGURE 4-5

Rules for Optical Character Recognition

Rule	Correct	Incorrect
1. Write big.	02834	02834
2. Close loops.	06889	06889
3. Use simple shapes.	37502	37502
4. Do not link characters.	007	007
5. Connect lines.	M4T	M4T
6. Use block print.	HELLO	Hello

mark sense readers to read documents that have been carefully marked with a special soft lead pencil, and convert the marks into computer input. The grading of multiple-choice tests is a common application of optical mark recognition. Other applications include the tabulation of marketing surveys and of census forms.

Optical Character Recognition. Optical character recognition (OCR) is a technique in which a specialized input device scans handwritten or typed characters and converts them into electronic signals that a computer can process. OCR equipment varies in cost and complexity. A word-processing service might buy an inexpensive OCR device to convert typewritten manuscripts and reports into computer-readable form before running them through the actual word processor. More expensive units can read cash register tapes, computer printouts, and even handwritten characters, provided that the user follows strict rules, as illustrated in Figure 4-5.

OCR readers enable data to be input rapidly into the computer, bypassing the slow, cumbersome step of data entry from the keyboard. However, they tend to be the opposite of user-friendly; a user who makes a slight mistake in entering the data will find the source document rejected. The limitations of optical character recognition devices are finally being overcome, however, as described in Box 4-1.

Optical character recognition (OCR)
A technique in which a specialized device is used to scan handwritten or typed characters and convert them into electronic signals that a computer can process.

This person is responding to a market survey by filling in a special form to be read by an optical mark recognition device. Schools use similar systems for multiple-choice exams. (© Lawrence Migdale, Photo Researchers.)

BOX 4-1

FRONTIERS IN TECHNOLOGY

Teaching Computers to Read

Computers are great at writing. Touch a few buttons and they spew reams of words onto sheets of paper. But putting that printed material inside another computer is hard. Computers are rotten at reading.

Engineers have been trying to teach computers to read for at least twenty-five years. But print comes in many sizes and shapes; paper varies sharply in quality; and printed material includes charts, drawings, and photographs that befuddle computers. So when someone needs to store printed information in a computer, usually the only alternative is to retype it.

Now, electronic readers are improving and may yet find a niche in libraries and offices. "Optical character recognition has always been an idea whose time never quite came. I think that's starting to change," says Howard N. Smith, president of Kurzweil Computer Products Inc., a Waltham, Massachusetts, subsidiary of Xerox Corporation, which has been in the field ten years.

Teaching the computer to convert printed images into the electronic characters it understands—that is, teaching it to "read"—is extremely difficult. Typical readers store in their memories templates of certain type fonts. When they pick up a printed pattern that matches the font in their memory, they assume that's the character. But it isn't easy. The uppercase letter O and numeral 0 look similar. So do the typewritten, lowercase letter l and the numeral 1. Moreover, the world is filled with many fonts. Even a simple business letter has a letterhead, often in several different type styles.

Makers of readers have taken several approaches to the problems. At one end, industry pioneer Recognition Equipment Corporation of Dallas makes $400,000 high-speed page readers. Recognition is best known for check and currency sorting and readers that handle signed receipts for credit card companies. Recognition's readers can be designed to read a variety of forms.

In the middle of the market are specialized office readers that read a few typewriter and computer-printer fonts. Dest Corporation of Milpitas, California, makes systems costing under $10,000. Offices that invest in these systems can save money by giving secretaries electric typewriters instead of word processors. After the first draft is done on a typewriter, it can be "read" into the word-processing system for final editing. Dest says its systems can read a page in twenty-five seconds, while a typist takes more than six minutes a page.

Palantir Corporation, a new company in Cupertino, California, recently started selling a $39,000 reader that reads almost any font in any size by recognizing the characteristics of a letter rather than by matching it to a pattern in its memory. Unlike older systems, it recognizes pictures and drawings and automatically stores them as well.

Source: William Bulkley, "Teaching Computers to Read Is Major Test for Researchers," *Wall Street Journal*, July 25, 1986, p. 23. Reprinted by permission of *The Wall Street Journal*, © Dow Jones & Company, Inc. 1986. All rights reserved.

Point-of-Sale Terminals. As mentioned earlier, fast-food restaurants use specially designed terminals to speed up customer service. Similarly, supermarkets can use optical scanners to speed up the checkout process and eliminate unit pricing. Supermarket scanners read a special product code, such as the **universal product code (UPC)**. In some systems, an employee passes a scanner or *wand* over the product; in others, the product is moved across a scanner embedded in the checkout counter. In both cases the scanner reads the code and transmits data to a sophisticated cash register known as a **point-of-sale (POS) terminal**, which automatically records the price. (Look again at Figure 4-2 to see how this works.) Depending on the sophistication of the system, inventory can be updated as the sale is made or at the end of the business day.

There are many advantages to computerizing the supermarket checkout process. Most checkout counter personnel find it easier to use a scanner than to enter data via a cash register keyboard. They also like the reduced chance of error and the virtual elimination of price checks for unmarked products. The store's owners appreciate the improvement in inventory control and the elimination of time-consuming and expensive unit pricing. Customers benefit from faster service and itemized cash receipts.

But POS terminals in supermarkets also have disadvantages. Sometimes the computerized checkout systems don't pick up the data properly, thereby causing annoying delays. Also, there is considerable customer resistance to such systems if the price is not given on each item. To overcome consumer resistance, some stores promise to give the item to the customer free of charge if the price stored in the machine is higher than the price posted on the shelf.

In spite of consumer resistance, as supermarkets, discount stores, and other firms gain experience with POS terminals they are finding benefits that were not initially exploited. As explained in Box 4-2, the POS terminal yields its greatest dividends when it becomes part of an integrated approach to retail management.

Other Input Devices and Techniques

As we have seen, scanners have both advantages and disadvantages when compared to keyboard input. In recent years, therefore, some manufacturers have devoted considerable time

Universal product code (UPC)
A standard bar code that appears on many products. This code is used with point-of-sale terminal systems.

Point-of-sale (POS) terminal
A computerized cash register.

BOX 4-2

MANAGING CHANGE

Direct Product Profitability

Often the introduction of computers into a business has ripple effects that extend to all phases of management. An example is the use of scanner-based point-of-sale terminals by supermarkets. Initially, faster checkout and daily inventory updates were seen as the main benefits of this equipment. But in a system known as *direct product-profitability analysis*, data from point-of-sale scanners is combined with data from other parts of the firm's operations to change some basic ideas about how to run a profitable supermarket. In the words of Timothy M. Hammond, senior vice-president of the Food Marketing Institute, "The industry has moved to phase 2—using the mound of scanning data to influence management."

Profit margins in the supermarket industry are extremely low. On the average, barely more than 1 percent of each dollar of sales goes to profit. This means that fine-tuning management to add a fraction of a percentage point can be crucial. The traditional guideline for supermarket managers has been the percentage of markup on each item. According to this index, certain items—house brands, for example—have long been thought of as highly profitable.

When data from scanners is combined with other data related to transportation costs, labor time devoted to stocking, shelf space used, and so on, some surprising winners and losers show up. For example, house brands no longer look as good. Their markups are high, but their turnover is low. Paper goods such as toilet paper and paper towels are losers, too—they take up too much shelf space.

On the other hand, freezer items turn out to be a winner. Their high markups and good turnover outweigh their high energy costs. Snack foods, dairy products, and magazines are also winners. The reason, revealed by direct product-profitability analysis, lies in labor savings. Manufacturers bring these items directly to the shelf, so employees' time can be used for other tasks.

According to *Supermarket News*, the key to successful direct product-profitability analysis lies in linking together data from several sources—scanners, inventory control, labor scheduling, and so on—each of which has already been computerized for its own reasons. A survey conducted by the magazine in 1986 showed that 17 percent of supermarkets already have such integrated systems and 45 percent plan to start them soon.

Still more sophisticated applications lie in the future. For example, cooperative efforts between manufacturers and retailers might determine optimal packaging, and PC-based systems might aid small grocers. The whole field of direct product-profitability analysis shows how a fairly simple innovation—scanners designed to speed up the checkout process—can have some unexpected consequences.

Sources: Gary Geipel, "At Today's Supermarkets, the Computer Is Doing It All," *Business Week*, August 11, 1986, pp. 64–65, and David Merrefield, "DPP Will Bring Net Gains Up to 2%," *Supermarket News*, February 3, 1986, p. 1.

and effort to developing input devices that do not rely on either a keyboard or a scanner. These devices make it easier for users to communicate with the computer. They include the mouse, screens that permit data entry by pointing, and systems that allow users to speak into the computer.

Mouse. Chapter 2 introduced the **mouse**, a box about the size of a tape cassette that, when stroked or rolled across a desktop, causes a highlighted area to move across a display screen. The mouse is particularly useful for choosing items from a list called a *menu*. In some systems the user need only pass the mouse over a diagram to enter it into the computer. Among the many satisfied mouse users are businesspeople who don't like to type; architects and engineers who work with technical drawings; and people who enjoy playing computer games. But like any other tool, the mouse has its drawbacks: Many models function erratically, and the user must remove a hand from the keyboard—a feature that is quite distracting to touch typists.

Pointing. Chapter 2 also discussed pointing as a nonkeyboard data entry method. Some computers, such as the Hewlett-Packard Touch-Screen, allow users to point to the screen to make selections. This technique is most effective when combined with specially designed software.

There are a variety of pointing devices besides the human finger. For more than two decades, for example, engineers, architects, draftspeople, and others have used hand-held, light-sensitive penlike devices called *light pens* to enter data. Because the tip of a light pen is much smaller than a fingertip, a light pen can sense a very precise location on the screen.

Among the advantages of pointing devices are their "natural" way of making selections and the fact that they can be used by people who cannot use other devices—by young children, for example. One disadvantage is that most people find it tiring to lift their arms and point to the screen repeatedly. Like the mouse, pointing takes a hand off the keyboard, thereby reducing the speed of data entry.

Voice Input. The data entry method that many people consider most "natural" is voice input. **Voice recognition systems** allow people to tell the computer what they want to do. In a typical application, mail sorters have both hands free to sort the mail while they communicate verbally with the computer. Such systems also make possible data entry by physically disabled people. However, because voice recognition technology is still in the early stages of development, its applications remain relatively limited.

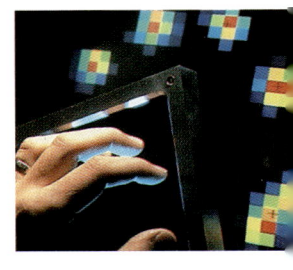

Mouse
A small object that is rolled or stroked to move a cursor and select items from a menu.

Voice recognition system
An input device that accepts and decodes human speech.

This experimental touch tablet displays color blocks to indicate the position and force of multiple finger touches. (Courtesy of AT&T Bell Laboratories.)

This designer is using a light pen to run a popular computer-aided design program called AutoCAD on a microcomputer. It is possible to create and modify the drawing with minimal use of the keyboard. (© Jerry Mason, Photo Researchers.)

HARDWARE 116 PART 2

There are two types of voice recognition devices—*speaker dependent* and *speaker independent*. Since human languages are imprecise—that is, one word may have several meanings, depending on the context—and since people's voices are as individual as their fingerprints, most voice recognition systems are speaker dependent. Speaker-dependent systems may require considerable adjustment to accommodate different speakers. Moreover, the speakers themselves must undergo extensive training before they can use speaker-dependent voice recognition systems. The computer must learn how each user pronounces different sounds, and the users must learn to speak slowly and clearly enough so that the computer can understand them.

Speaker-independent voice recognition systems can be developed to understand almost any speaker. But they are very complicated and therefore are used for applications that require a very limited vocabulary, such as sorting packages and inquiring about credit card balances.

Output

After data has been entered into a computer and processed, the computer outputs information. When we refer to output, we mean both the actual information obtained from the computer and the devices used to obtain that information. Output can take several forms. Usually it consists of text or graphics; less frequently it is in the form of film or sound. A wide variety of devices can output information in each of these forms. Examples of output include a visual display on a workstation screen, copy on paper from a printer, magnetic signals on a disk, film (microfilm or microfiche), graphics from a device called a plotter, or voices and sounds. Each of these different output methods has both advantages and disadvantages.

Since computer output comes in different forms, it can be used in different ways. For example, output in the form of disks or tape can be used as input for additional processing; output in the form of images on a screen can be used for word processing; output in the form of paper from a printer can be distributed as reports. In this section we will discuss output as a final product that is used by people. Recall from Chapter 2 that in order to be useful, output must be legible, timely, accurate, complete, concise, and relevant.

Output Devices

The two basic categories of output are alphanumeric (text) and graphic. **Alphanumeric** output consists of letters, numbers, and special characters such as commas, question marks, dollar signs, and percent signs. **Graphic** output includes pictorial representations such as bar and line graphs, charts, pictures, maps, and company logos. Various devices can be used to produce each of these forms of output.

The appropriate output device depends on what the user wants to do with the output. For example, a user who wants to send out brochures to prospective clients needs a device such as a letter-quality printer that produces high-quality **hard copy**. (*Hard copy* is permanent output such as that generated by a typewriter, as opposed to a screen display, sometimes called *soft copy*.) A user who wants to circulate a report to sales managers can use a less expensive printer. If the user wants to review the results of last week's sales meeting, a video display terminal (VDT) may be the most useful output device. But of course, there are a wide variety of VDTs to choose from. If the user has to analyze and evaluate sales data from dozens of salespeople, he or she should consider an output device that produces graphics. If the output consists of, say, several years of tax records, the appropriate output device might be one that creates information in a form that can be stored efficiently, such as microfilm. Table 4-2 shows some common output devices.

Alphanumeric
A term used to refer to data composed of letters and numbers and a few special characters.

Graphics
Data or information that is composed of pictures and diagrams.

Hard copy
Permanent output such as that generated by a printer.

Video Display Terminals

Video display terminals, also called cathode-ray tubes (CRTs) or monitors, are the most widespread type of output device. They are an integral part of most workstations, including personal computers and computer terminals. The display units of VDTs are similar to television screens, except that they are designed for close viewing and easy readability. When choosing a VDT, it is important to pay attention to ergonomic features such as screen image, screen width, and screen and image colors.

Screen Image. The screen image should be sharp, clear, and easy to read, especially for heavy users. The tails of letters

TABLE 4-2

Common Output Devices

Device	Speed	Advantages	Disadvantages	Applications
Video display terminal	10 – 400 cps	Rapid display	No hard copy, sometimes no graphics	Very wide (business and home)
Printer	Varies widely	Hard copy	Sometimes no graphics, quality varies with price	As above, desktop publishing
Plotter	Like printer	Very high precision graphics	May be expensive	Engineering, architecture, art
Computer output microfilm	Up to 500,000 cps	Very compact output	Specialized equipment and operations	Archives, banking, insurance, government
Audio response unit	Moderate, like person talking	Audible output	Often mediocre quality	Telephone jobs, supermarket checkout

such as g and y should be displayed. Another important ergonomic feature is lack of glare. Since people's eyesight and working habits vary, the screen's brightness and contrast controls are also important.

Screen Width. The width of VDT screens can vary considerably. Most screens are 10–12 inches (25–30 centimeters) square. Some older models are only 5 inches square. Typically, screens display 80 characters per line.

Screen and Image Colors. Screens can be either monochrome or full color. Monochrome screens display one color, such as amber or green characters on a single-color background, often black. Many are also capable of *reverse video*, for example, black characters on an amber background.

Full-color screens allow the user to choose both a background color and a foreground color from many alternatives. In general, text is displayed best on monochrome screens while graphic images are most striking in full color. Some systems can display sharp text and brilliant graphics simultaneously.

Cursors and Icons. A **cursor** is a special symbol highlighting an area on a VDT screen. Different systems display the cursor in different ways; common examples include a blinking underline symbol, a blinking rectangle, or an intensified line of characters. The cursor often indicates the location where text may be entered or modified.

Cursor
A special symbol that highlights an area on a screen.

A computer **icon** is a visual symbol that indicates a computer operation. For example, on the Apple Macintosh a garbage can is the icon for deleting a file. Icons are often used with a mouse; the user rolls the mouse until the arrow (a cursor) points to the garbage can. Then the user presses a button to delete the file. Many untrained users like to work with icons because they eliminate the need to memorize special commands.

Icon
A visual symbol that indicates a computer operation.

Flat-Panel Displays. At present the most popular technology used in computer monitors is a cathode-ray tube like those found in television sets. Cathode-ray tubes have several disadvantages: They tend to flicker; they give off ionizing and electromagnetic radiation, which some people believe has harmful long-term effects; and they are bulky—many are more than 6 inches thick. The latter disadvantage makes them impractical for portable computers. *Flat-panel displays,* or small, thin display screens, use a variety of new technologies to overcome the disadvantages of the cathode-ray tube. Some laptop computers use flat panel displays that are only 2 inches thick. However, the best flat panel displays are quite expensive. More reasonably priced models do not emit light but only reflect it, making them hard to read in less-than-ideal lighting conditions.

Printers

Using a screen as an output device has two major disadvantages: The output is neither permanent nor portable. Printers, on the other hand, do provide permanent, portable copy on paper (i.e., hard copy).

There are a great many types of printers, each with many different features in terms of size (commonly 80 or 132 columns), graphics capability, speed, print quality, and printing mechanism. Printers can be classified in several ways: by whether they print a character, line, or page at a time; by whether or not they actually strike the paper to create an image; or by their type quality.

Character printers, which print only one character at a time, are used with personal computers. *Line printers* or *page printers,* which print a line or page at a time, are used with minicomputers and mainframes. A typical speed for a line printer is 600 lines per minute, but some line printers work considerably faster. High-speed page printers produce 10,000 to 20,000 lines per minute, which is equivalent to several hundred pages per second, and even faster models are available. The more printing an organization does, the faster the printer it needs. Many small businesses find that a character printer or a small

FIGURE 4-6

Characteristics of a Dot-Matrix Character Printer

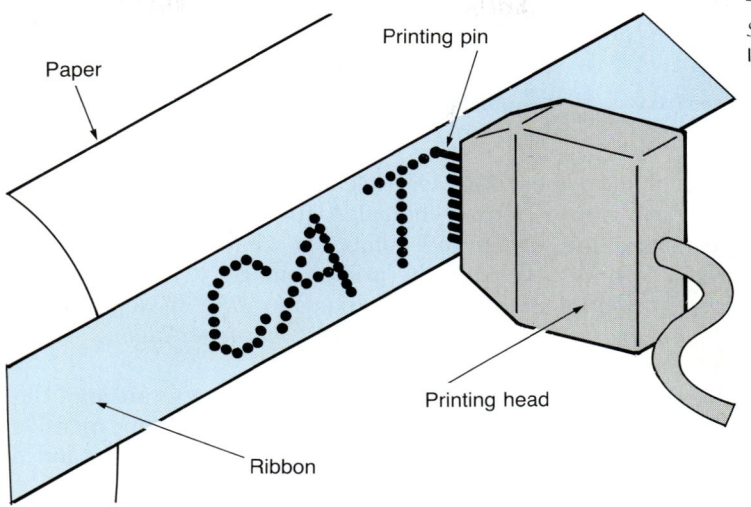

Source: Epson America, Inc.

line printer suits their requirements. Organizations such as banks and government agencies, which generate a substantial amount of paper, should consider investing in a high-speed page printer.

Impact printers, like typewriters, print by striking a printing element on an inked ribbon, thereby transferring an image to a sheet of paper. They can produce multiple copies of a document by using multipart paper containing carbons. Impact printers are noisy; in fact, the faster they are, the noisier they are. Dot-matrix printers and daisy-wheel printers are two popular categories of impact printers that are used mostly with personal computers. Line printers are impact printers used with minicomputers and mainframes.

Nonimpact printers, such as laser printers, create images on paper without actually striking it. They have fewer moving parts than impact printers have, a feature that makes them faster and quieter. But nonimpact printers cannot produce more than a single copy at a time. Page printers are nonimpact printers used with minicomputers and mainframes.

Dot-Matrix Printers. The characters printed on a **dot-matrix printer** are made up of tiny dots. The dot matrix is composed of pins, as illustrated in Figure 4-6; when the printer receives

Dot-matrix printer
A printer that forms characters when pins in a rectangular grid strike the ribbon and paper.

CHAPTER 4   INPUT AND OUTPUT

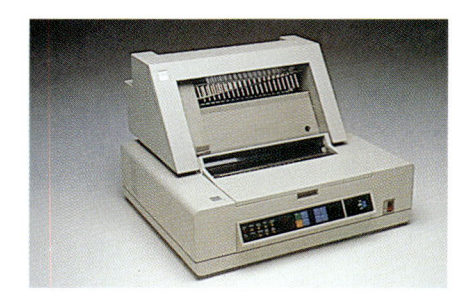

Three of the most popular printers for microcomputers are the dot-matrix printer, which can produce graphics and a variety of typefaces; the daisy-wheel printer, which can produce crisp, clear output such as business letters; and the laser printer, which combines the advantages of the other two models. [(left and center) Courtesy of Texas Instruments; (right) Courtesy of International Business Machines.]

a signal from the computer, selected pins on the matrix are pushed forward to form a character. The more pins there are on the matrix, the greater the number of characters that can be produced and the clearer the printed image. It is common for dot-matrix printers to print documents in *draft mode* at a relatively high speed and in a sharper, *near-letter-quality (NLQ) mode* at a lower speed.

Many popular, inexpensive dot-matrix printers can print different typefaces and type sizes as well as graphics. Inexpensive software enables users to prepare informal newsletters and a variety of printed material with a dot-matrix printer.

Daisy-Wheel Printers. The characters printed on a **daisy-wheel printer** are fully formed characters, not a group of dots. Since these printers produce the same quality output as a typewriter, they are often called *letter-quality printers*. The daisy wheel itself is a replaceable device that looks like the petals of a daisy and contains 100 or more characters. Because it takes time for the daisy wheel to rotate each desired character into printing position, daisy-wheel printers are much slower than comparably priced dot-matrix printers.

Daisy-wheel printers are excellent for standard business correspondence but do not offer the sophisticated features of dot-matrix printers; for example, they do not provide graphics. Moreover, it is cumbersome to print different typefaces and type sizes with a daisy-wheel printer. Instead of simply issuing a software command to the printer, the user must stop the printer and manually change the daisy wheel for each desired typeface or type size.

Laser Printers. **Laser printers** combine the advantages of dot-matrix and daisy-wheel printers. They are nonimpact printers and hence are both quiet and fast; they can print a variety of typefaces and sizes and even graphics; and they produce very high-quality copy. Laser printers are actually a special type of dot-matrix printer. The dots are so closely spaced—typically

Daisy-wheel printer
A printer that forms letter-quality characters when a removable print head strikes the ribbon and paper.

Laser printer
A printer that is driven by a laser unit.

HARDWARE 122 PART 2

90,000 per square inch—that they cannot be seen with the naked eye. Laser printers are also very fast; the models that work with microcomputers print eight or more pages a minute.

Until the mid-1980s laser printers were massive, very expensive printers that were used almost exclusively with large minicomputers and mainframes. Since then the price of the laser unit has dropped spectacularly, and desktop laser printers have become available for personal computers. One result of this phenomenon is the emergence of *desktop publishing*, in which companies produce a wide variety of professional-appearing publications, including newsletters and advertising brochures, without requiring the services of professional printers. (Desktop publishing is discussed in Chapter 14.)

Because of the relatively high costs of laser printers, many small companies or departments buy one laser printer to be shared by several users, who may also have access to other, less expensive printers. In general, laser printers for microcomputers are not built for continuous operation. For example, some manufacturers recommend that their units print no more than 3000 pages per month.

Print Buffers. Input and output devices are slow compared to the computers that drive them. Many devices, including printers, are equipped with a *buffer*, or memory, that helps bridge the gap between their speed and the computer's speed. When the user gives the command to print, the computer, working at full speed, fills the print buffer with the pages to be printed. The printer prints the contents of the buffer at its own speed. When the computer has filled the buffer, it can be used to do something else. In other words, the user does not have to wait for the printer to stop printing.

Plotters

Plotter
An output device that produces hard-copy graphics.

A **plotter** is an output device that produces hard-copy graphics. Plotters can be used to print line graphs, bar charts, circle graphs, maps, charts, and even two- and three-dimensional figures. Although plotters generally can print only straight lines, the best ones print several thousand steps per inch, thereby making it possible to produce extremely detailed output. Some plotters can produce shaded and colored figures. If the plotter is attached to a VDT, users can see their drawings before printing them.

Two types of plotters are common—*flatbed plotters* and *drum plotters*. The more expensive flatbed plotters remain stationary while one or more pens move on the page to produce the image. Drum plotters, in contrast, move while the pens move.

Plotters are typically used by computer scientists to design circuits, by engineers to prepare blueprints, by architects to design buildings, and by artists.

Computer Output Microfilm Systems

So far we have discussed output on screens and on paper. But as mentioned in Chapter 2, there is another form of output that can be obtained from a computer: film. The film can be on a roll *(microfilm)* or cut into 4 by 6 inch sheets *(microfiche)*. A **computer output microfilm (COM)** system consists of a computer that produces output and a device that reads the computer output and transforms it into microfilm reels or microfiche cards. The process can be on-line, in which case the computer transfers the documents directly to the COM unit, or off-line, in which case the computer creates magnetic tape that is later input to the COM unit.

Two advantages of COM systems are their speed and the size of their output. Their speed is measured in tens of thousands of lines per minute; the fastest models are considerably faster than page printers. At its top speed, a COM system can print a book like this one on film in only a few seconds. In addition, COM output is inexpensive to produce, transport, and store. Printed reports weighing hundreds of pounds can be put on microfilm or microfiche weighing only ounces.

The disadvantages of COM systems include the need for special equipment to read the data, the initial high cost to purchase the system, and the fact that the output cannot be updated on the spot. In addition, these systems are not suitable for organizations that constantly need printed output. COM systems are most useful for organizations that have to store huge amounts of data. Thus, insurance companies, banks, utility companies, governments, and newspapers have used COM systems for years.

Audio Response Units

Audio response units are computer peripherals that produce voices or sound. Some units, such as the telephone company systems that inform callers that "the number you have dialed has been changed . . . ," work by combining words and

Computer output microfilm (COM)
An output device that produces microfilm or microfiche.

Plotters generate large, high-quality graphic output. This marketing specialist is examining plotter output to be used in a sales presentation. (Courtesy of Hewlett-Packard.)

Audio response unit
An output device that produces sound.

HARDWARE 124 PART 2

phrases recorded by people. Others convert raw data into electronic speech. For example, the Kurzweil reading machine uses an optical scanner to convert the contents of a book into electronic signals, which are then transformed into spoken words. The main application of this machine is in reading aloud to the blind.

Audio response units have some disadvantages. A computer may not sound pleasant; it is difficult to make it sound more like a human and less like a computer. Also, most talking computer programs have very limited vocabularies. Finally, they do not produce legible hard copy.

Most businesses find that the easier it is for users to enter input and receive output that is legible, timely, accurate, complete, concise, and relevant, the greater the demands users will make on their computer system. This means that the choice of hardware for a computer system is an extremely important decision involving a careful review of both present and future needs. But computer hardware consists of other items besides input and output devices. These are discussed in the next chapter, which takes a detailed look at the central processing unit and storage systems.

Keyboard Systems
Scanners
Mouse
Pointing
Voice Recognition Systems

Input Devices

Video Display Terminals
Printers
Plotters
Computer Output Microfilm Systems
Audio Response Units

Output Devices

SUMMARY

1. Input refers to the data entered into a computer and the devices used to enter data. **Data entry** is the inputting of raw data into the computer. Traditional data entry requires specialists who enter data from **source documents** at a keyboard. More modern techniques, known as **source data automation**, allow people to enter data where it is generated. Source data automation is faster, less prone to error, and possibly cheaper.

2. The keyboard remains the most common device for entering data. The standard keyboard is called the QWERTY keyboard; many people and installations have replaced it with the Dvorak keyboard. Specially designed software, such as keyboard enhancers, and hardware, such as intelligent terminals, may increase both productivity and ease of use.

3. The traditional keypunch has been superseded by other keyboard devices, such as key-to-tape systems, key-to-disk systems, and key-to-floppy disk systems. Other keyboard systems include automated teller machines, factory data-collection devices, and customized terminals like those used in many fast-food restaurants.

4. Magnetic ink character recognition (MICR) devices are used to process checks and bank deposit slips. **Optical character recognition (OCR)** is a technique in which a specialized input device is used to scan handwritten or typed characters and convert them into electronic signals that the computer can process. The **universal product code (UPC)** is read by scanners associated with sophisticated cash registers known as **point-of-sale (POS)** terminals.

5. Three additional types of input equipment that involve neither a keyboard nor a scanner are a rolling box known as a **mouse**, special screens that allow users to select items by pointing, and **voice recognition systems**.

6. Output refers to information that is obtained from a computer and the devices used to furnish that information. Output can be either **alphanumeric** or **graphic. Hard copy** is permanent output such as that generated by a printer. Video display terminals (VDTs), also called cathode-ray tubes or monitors, are the most widespread type of output device. They may have monochrome or full-color screens, and may include such features as a symbol called a **cursor** to highlight an area, and symbols called **icons** that indicate specific operations.

7. Two common types of printers for microcomputers are **dot-matrix printers** and **daisy-wheel printers**. The former are cheaper, faster, and more flexible but do not produce as high quality output. **Laser printers** enable users to print graphics and different typefaces on the same page. Minicomputers and mainframes often run line or page printers. Many input and output devices are equipped with buffers that help bridge the gap between their speed and the computer's speed.

8. Plotters are output devices that produce hard-copy graphics. **Computer output microfilm (COM)** systems provide extremely compact output that is especially suitable for archival storage. Another type of output device is the **audio response unit**, which is used in such applications as telephone company systems that inform callers of changed numbers.

KEY TERMS

data entry

source document

source data automation

magnetic ink character recognition (MICR)

optical character recognition (OCR)

universal product code (UPC)

point-of-sale (POS) terminal

mouse

voice recognition system

alphanumeric

graphics

hard copy

cursor

icon

dot-matrix printer

daisy-wheel printer

laser printer

plotter

computer output microfilm (COM)

audio response unit

REVIEW QUESTIONS

1. Compare traditional data entry with source data automation. Give an example of how each may be used in processing school records.

2. List and explain three ergonomic features of keyboards. Describe three ways in which computer software or hardware can be used to improve the keyboard.

3. Describe three input devices that make use of the keyboard. Name a commercial application for each of these devices.

4. MICR devices, OCR devices, and POS terminals are each used in source data automation. Describe a typical application of each of these types of devices.

5. Identify and describe two input devices that rely on neither a keyboard nor a scanner. Give an example of a typical application of each device.

6. Discuss four features to look for when purchasing a video display terminal.

7. Describe dot-matrix and daisy-wheel printers. What are the advantages and disadvantages of each?

8. How does a laser printer compare with other printers for personal computers?

9. Identify and describe two output devices other than VDTs or printers. Give an example of a typical application of each device named.

APPLICATIONS

1. Summarize an article in a trade or business publication that discusses ergonomic features of computer hardware such as keyboards or monitors. How have these features increased employee productivity and satisfaction?

2. Illustrate the application of commonly used input and output devices in a college registrar's office.

3. Summarize an article in a business or trade publication that describes applications of laser printers. How are the printers used? Have they been able to eliminate the need for outside printing services?

4. Discuss the following statement: The keyboard is an obsolete data entry device.

CASE FOR DISCUSSION

What is a "secretary"? A secretary is many things, but perhaps most of all, a human input-output device.

In the nineteenth century, secretaries—or "clerks," to use the more common term at the time—wrote "output" with quill pens and took "input" as dictation with the same quill pens. A slow process.

(Culver Pictures.)

Later there were wonderful innovations. The typewriter with its QWERTY keyboard—a compromise between the desire for productivity and the limits of technology. Carbon paper. Does anyone in the Xerox age remember carbon paper?

In the modern era, input and output have gone wild with innovation. The word-processing machine. The photocopier. Soon, voice-activated word processors that take dictation, spell-check it, and send the result to a laser printer.

Clearly, the secretary is obsolete. Just as technology has claimed the jobs of harness makers, coal miners, and steelworkers, it will mean the end of the secretary. Right? Let's look at these data:

1880. The typewriter still a novelty. The first cash registers and adding machines. 5000 stenographers and typists in the United States.

1920. Addressograph machines. Ditto machines (early duplicators). Calculators that both add and subtract. 615,154 stenographers and typists in the United States.

1940. Punched-card machines. Four-function calculators. Dictaphone machines. 1,174,886 stenographers, typists, and secretaries in the United States.

1960. Magnetic tape replaces cards. Magnetic-tape "selectric" typewriters (primitive word processors). 1,464,000 secretaries in the United States.

1986. Optical character recognition. Video display terminals. Microcomputers/word processors. Photocopiers. Personal-productivity software. Early voice recognition. 4,059,000 secretaries in the United States.

Source: U.S. Department of Labor, Bureau of Labor Statistics, reported in *The Secretary*, April 1986.

CASE QUESTIONS

1. Do you agree that the secretary is a "human input-output device"?

2. In what ways do advances in data processing technology reduce the work that secretaries have to do? Why does the need for secretaries still increase?

3. What do you think will happen in the future? Will the next advance in input and output technology finally send millions of secretaries to the unemployment lines? Or will their ranks continue to grow?

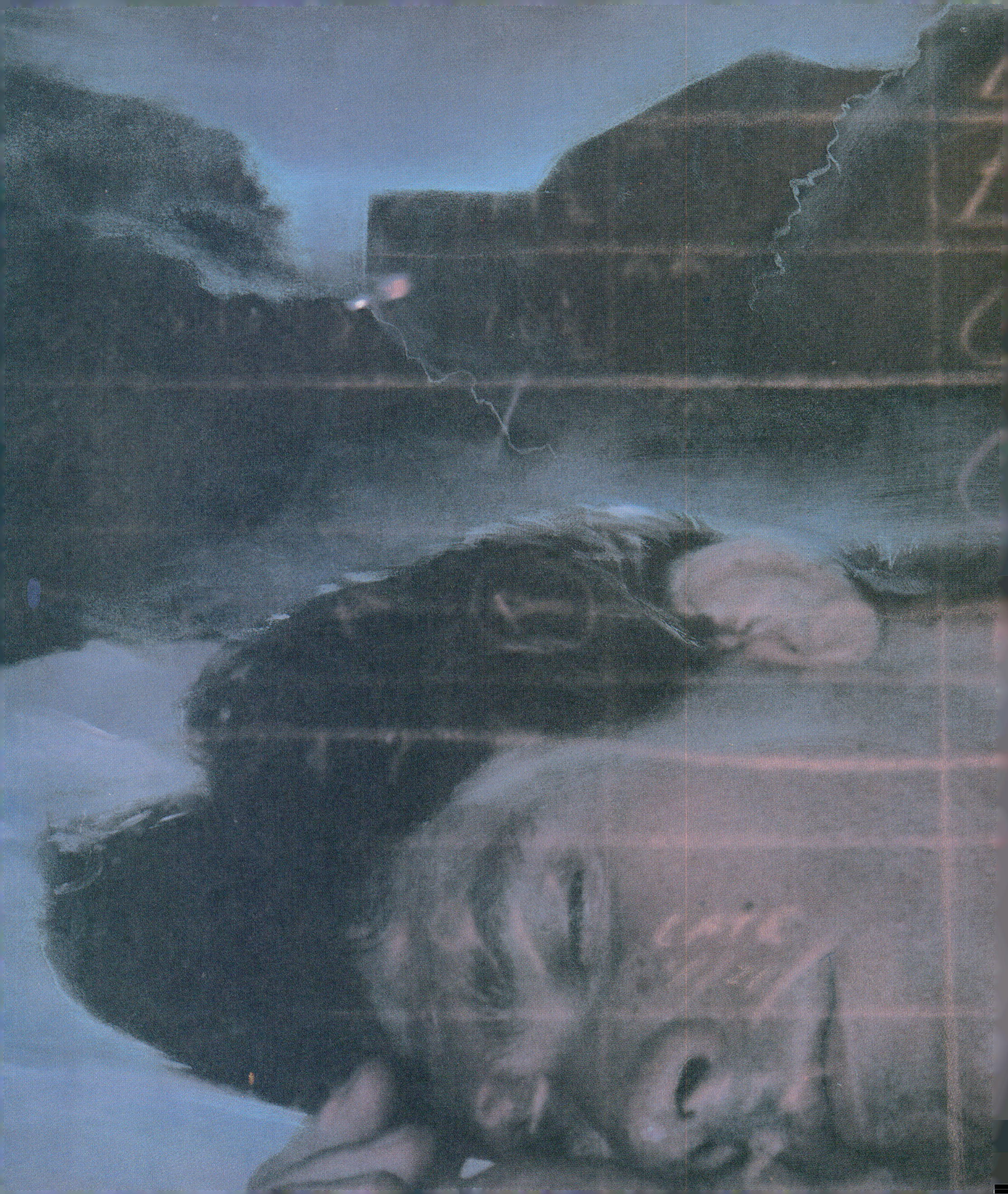

The Central Processing Unit and Storage

CHAPTER

5

George Mason University is a rapidly growing school with some 17,000 students. Located just outside Fairfax, Virginia, the campus has many lovely, modern brick buildings, plus a few that are less attractive. Central Module C, which looks like an overgrown version of a mobile home, houses the office of the registrar. Like most organizations that handle large quantities of information, the office makes heavy use of computers.

At the end of the semester, Professor Donald Ewing waits in the registrar's office to hand in the grades for his computer science class. He has entered the grades by hand on a form on which the computer has already printed out the names and ID numbers of the students enrolled in his class.

Professor Ewing's grade sheet is quickly passed to an operator seated at a video display terminal. The operator calls up the file for Ewing's class. Access to the file, which is kept on a magnetic-disk storage device attached to the university's mainframe computer, is almost instantaneous. The operator updates the file by entering the grades that Ewing has just handed in. When all the grades have been entered, the updated file replaces the earlier version without the grades. Ewing's handwritten grade sheet is then carefully filed away. If a student protests a grade, a look at the sheet will reveal whether a bad job on the final exam is to blame or whether the grade has been recorded incorrectly.

Except for the terminals used by the registrar's staff, the hardware of George Mason's computer is not trusted to the flimsy structure of Module C. Instead, it is housed in the basement of a nearby brick building. There the disk drive is humming away with the updated records of Ewing's students. But although the disk drive is a reliable machine, it is not totally safe from failure. It, and other drives like it, have been known to "crash."

The managers of the system take appropriate precautions. At the end of each day, they "back up" the contents of the disk by sequentially recording every bit of data from the disk onto a magnetic tape. That way, if the disk crashes, the data on it can be restored from the tape made the night before. Only updates done during the day would have to be entered again.[1]

---

[1] Based on information supplied by Gil Gallemore, Associate Registrar, George Mason University.

Chapter 4 discussed input and output devices, such as the video display terminal on which Professor Ewing's grades are entered and the printers on which student grade reports are produced. In this chapter, we turn our attention to two other components of the computer: its central processing unit and storage devices like the disk drives and tape drives on which George Mason's registrar keeps student records.

We saw in Chapter 2 that the CPU—the computer's brain—performs calculations and stores data temporarily while working on it. In addition to the temporary storage capacity of the CPU, virtually all computer systems have auxiliary storage devices that can handle large amounts of data and store it securely for long periods. This chapter looks not only at the storage devices themselves but also at techniques of data management that are used to organize and safeguard the contents of those devices.

When you have read this chapter, you should be able to:
1. Describe the components of the central processing unit.
2. List the major auxiliary storage devices for microcomputers and indicate their advantages and disadvantages.
3. List the major auxiliary storage devices for minicomputers and mainframes and indicate their advantages and disadvantages.
4. Describe three major methods of file organization and the advantages and disadvantages of each.
5. Understand and use the key terms listed at the end of the chapter.

The Central Processing Unit

In Chapter 2 we noted that the central processing unit (CPU) has three main parts: the control unit, the arithmetic-logic unit, and primary storage. Here we examine each of these parts in detail and then discuss the unit as a whole.

The Control Unit

All the processing that takes place in a computer is coordinated by the control unit. This unit contains an *internal clock* that ensures that all of the computer's activities are carried out as efficiently as possible. The *clock speed* (measured in millions of cycles per second, known as *megahertz* or *MHz*) is directly related to the CPU's processing capabilities. The IBM PC works at a clock speed of 4.77 MHz while the PC AT works at a clock speed of either 6 MHz or 8 MHz. Increasing the clock speed is one way of increasing a computer's performance. An increasing number of compatibles work at clock speeds of 10 MHz or 12 MHz.

The control unit also contains several temporary storage locations known as *registers*. Data and instructions are stored in the registers until the control unit commands the arithmetic-logic unit to "access" or fetch them for processing. Because the registers can be accessed at an extremely high speed, virtually all the processing that is done within the CPU takes place via the registers.

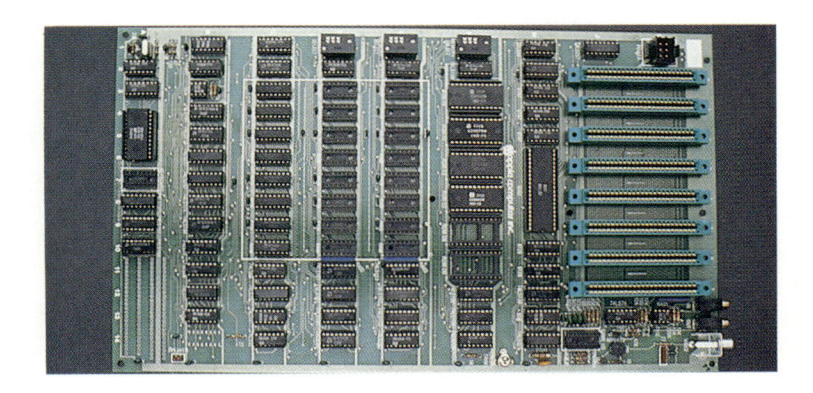

Several components of the CPU are mounted on the motherboard for the Apple II Plus computer shown here. In the event of failure, the motherboard can easily be replaced. (Courtesy of Apple Computer Inc.)

CHAPTER 5   THE CPU AND STORAGE

The Arithmetic-Logic Unit

As its name indicates, the arithmetic-logic unit (ALU) takes care of the computer's arithmetic and logic operations. **Arithmetic operations** include the familiar addition, subtraction, multiplication, and division. **Logic operations** include comparisons and tests (e.g., Is 6 larger than 9? Is L the same as P? Does the company have more vendors in the Western Region than in the Southern Region?).

Arithmetic Operations. Computers and people perform arithmetic operations in different ways. People do arithmetic using the **decimal system**, which is based on ten digits, 0 to 9. Since the decimal system is not efficient for computers, they do arithmetic using the **binary system**, which is based on only two digits, 0 and 1. Using only two digits simplifies the CPU's circuitry, enabling 0 to stand for a voltage that is off and 1 to stand for a voltage that is on. It is important to understand that a computer actually operates in terms of electrical quantities. The 0s and 1s represent binary quantities.

Logic Operations A logic operation can be thought of as a yes-or-no question whose answer serves as the basis for a particular action. People are constantly performing logic operations. For example, you are carrying out a logic operation when you ask yourself, "Do I have an eight o'clock class this morning?" If you do, you jump out of bed. If you don't, you roll over for an extra half hour of sleep.

Computers don't have to decide whether to get out of bed, but they are used for such operations as calculating a payroll. Suppose that a store's sales clerks are paid a commission, or a percentage of how much they sell, whereas the store's office staff is paid by the hour. In calculating the payroll, the computer's ALU would compare the pay category code in the record with a table of codes. The pay record for a commissioned sales clerk might have a C in this position, whereas that for a clerk paid by the hour would have an H. If the ALU found a C, it would multiply the clerk's sales for the week by the percentage commission. If it found an H, it would multiply the worker's hours by the hourly rate. In order to complete the job of calculating the payroll, the ALU would have to perform a whole series of logic and arithmetic operations of this nature.

Primary Storage

The third component of the CPU is primary storage. Primary storage is often called **memory,** but computer memory works

---

Decimal system
The commonly used number system based on the digits 0 through 9.

Binary system
A number system that contains only two digits, 0 and 1.

Arithmetic operation
An activity such as addition, subtraction, multiplication, or division that is performed by the arithmetic-logic unit of the CPU.

Logic operation
An activity such as a comparison or test that is performed by the arithmetic-logic unit of the CPU.

Memory
A part of the central processing unit in which data and programs may be stored for a short period.

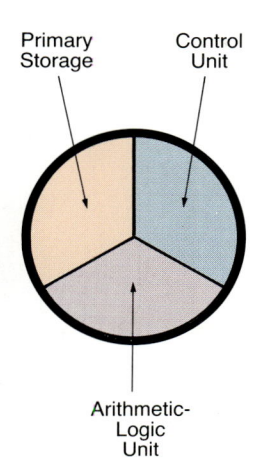

differently than human memory. When people learn something, they add that information to what they already know and theoretically can remember it for their entire life. A computer, on the other hand, has limited storage, or memory, capacity. Usually when the central processing unit receives new data, it stores it in a location that is already in use, erasing the previous contents of that location.

A CPU's primary storage is divided up into many small locations that store data for future use. In order to reuse the data, the CPU must be able to find it when it is needed. To understand how the CPU stores and finds or **accesses data**, let's compare primary storage with the safety deposit boxes available in most banks.

Bank safety deposit boxes are set up in large groups; people identify their box by a number on the front of the box. This number is, in fact, an *address* that helps people find the right safety deposit box in much the same way that a street address helps them find a particular house. The computer also identifies locations in its memory by means of **addresses**. Rather than identifying every single bit in storage by an address, the computer uses an address to identify a series of bits known as a *word*. The number of bits in a word depends on the type of computer; common values range from 8 to 64. Some computers provide for access to the individual bytes within a word.

It is important not to confuse the address of a storage device with its contents. For example, safety deposit box 104 (the one whose "address" is 104) could contain $1, or $10,000, or jewelry, or important papers. It would be a rare coincidence if safety deposit box 104 contained exactly $104. It's the same with words in computer storage: The word at storage address 104 can contain, for example, the number 72 or the name James. It would be another rare coincidence if the word at storage address 104 contained the number 104.

There are, however, some major differences between safety deposit boxes and computer memory. Safety deposit boxes have their numbers displayed clearly, whereas computer memory addresses are invisible to ordinary users. In most cases, only the computer system itself is concerned with the address of a particular item in memory.

Recall from Chapter 2 that a byte is the smallest unit of storage that concerns users; it contains one character. The chapter introduced two common abbreviations for memory size: K for 1024, often rounded to 1000, and M for 1,048,576, often rounded to 1,000,000. Most users need thousands (measured in K) or millions (measured in M) of bytes of memory for their applications. The spectacular increase in computer memory size in recent years has made it possible to run more programs

The Central Processing Unit

- Primary Storage
- Control Unit
- Arithmetic-Logic Unit

Access
The process of finding data stored in a computer system.

Address
The location of data in a computer storage medium.

simultaneously and to run programs that are more user-friendly. Most personal-productivity software requires large amounts of memory. A program like Lotus 1-2-3 takes up more memory by itself than was commonly available on mainframe computers in the mid-1970s.

There are several specific types of primary storage. The two most commonly used types are random-access memory (RAM) and read-only memory (ROM), which were defined in Chapter 2. Two other widely used types of primary storage are programmable read-only memory (PROM) and erasable programmable read-only memory (EPROM).

Random-Access Memory. The most common type of primary storage is RAM. At this writing, a set of RAM chips with 256K of memory for popular microcomputers costs about $30. Besides being inexpensive, RAM is fast. As its name indicates, it provides *random* access, meaning that the computer can access each memory location without having to read any other locations.

RAM has two serious drawbacks: It is *volatile;* that is, its contents are erased as soon as the computer's power supply is interrupted even for a short time; and it is too small to store all the information that a company or individual may need. A later section of this chapter will examine larger storage devices and show how users can combine them with RAM.

RAM is the fastest type of widely available memory for storing programs and data. Once information is placed in RAM, it can be accessed extremely rapidly. For example, a program that checks spelling and its associated dictionary can be loaded into RAM. When you want to determine whether a word ap-

These two chips are approximately the same size, but the red and gold one contains sixteen times as much memory. [(left) Courtesy of Texas Instruments; (right) Courtesy of International Business Machines.]

pearing on the monitor is spelled correctly, you can position the cursor on that word and press the appropriate function key. By the time you take your finger off the key, the program has determined whether the word can be found in its dictionary.

Read-Only Memory. The second common type of primary storage is ROM, which, unlike RAM, retains its contents even when the computer's power is turned off; in other words, it is nonvolatile. ROM's applications are limited because users and programmers cannot write on it; in other words, they cannot change it. ROM's contents are permanently encoded by the manufacturer; for example, most microcomputers come with a form of BASIC in their ROM. Increasingly, computers are being built with systems software and popular applications programs included in ROM. This feature has several advantages: The programs are always available, don't have to be "loaded in" by the user, run fast, and cannot be accidentally destroyed by a user. For example, when sports reporter Gary Pommerantz wants to write a story on his Tandy Model 200 portable laptop computer he just has to turn it on and ask for the word processor contained in ROM; he doesn't have to worry about forgetting the program when he takes his computer with him to the stadium.

Firmware. Because ROM combines aspects of hardware and software—in fact, it is software built into hardware—it is often called *firmware*. Another type of firmware, programmable read-only memory (PROM), is similar to ROM except that the purchaser must hire programming specialists to program it. When those specialists have developed a program that meets the purchaser's needs, they encode it into PROM. (The encoding process is commonly called *burning*, even though heat is not applied.) Once a program is in PROM, it cannot be accidentally destroyed by users.

A type of firmware that is similar to PROM but has the advantage of being reusable is called erasable programmable read-only memory (EPROM). Programs contained in EPROM can be erased with special equipment, thereby freeing the firmware for new programs. In addition to these existing forms of memory, engineers are constantly developing new types of memory to supplement RAM and ROM.

Codes

RAM, ROM, PROM, EPROM, and auxiliary storage (the subject of the next section) all have something in common: They contain data and information that can be represented in the

FIGURE 5-1

ASCII and EBCDIC Codes

The ASCII code has become the standard code for microcomputers. The EBCDIC code is used on medium-sized and large IBM computers.

	ASCII		EBCDIC	
Character	Bits	Decimal Value	Bits	Decimal Value
0	00110000	48	11110000	240
1	00110001	49	11110001	241
2	00110010	50	11110010	242
3	00110011	51	11110011	243
4	00110100	52	11110100	244
5	00110101	53	11110101	245
6	00110110	54	11110110	246
7	00110111	55	11110111	247
A	01000001	65	11000001	193
B	01000010	66	11000010	194
C	01000011	67	11000011	195
D	01000100	68	11000100	196
E	01000101	69	11000101	197
F	01000110	70	11000110	198
G	01000111	71	11000111	199
H	01001000	72	11001000	200

form of 0s and 1s. As noted in Chapter 2, these *bits* of data are regrouped into *bytes* or *characters* according to a code. The two most common codes are ASCII, the standard for microcomputers, and EBCDIC (see Figure 5-1), which is used on medium-sized and large IBM computers. Programs are available that convert data from ASCII to EBCDIC and vice versa. (For a more detailed discussion of codes and coding, see the appendix to this chapter.)

Considering everything the CPU does, it's remarkable that it is so small. Both the arithmetic-logic and control units of a personal computer can be placed on a single chip no larger than a fingertip. The remaining component of the CPU, primary storage, usually requires a few additional chips. The entire CPU may be smaller than a dinner plate. However, a full-fledged computer is more than a CPU; it also requires input and output devices as discussed in Chapter 4. In addition, most computer systems require extra memory, called auxiliary storage. This is discussed in the next section.

TABLE 5-1

Common Auxiliary Storage Media

Media	Capacity (in bytes)	Advantages	Disadvantages	Applications
Magnetic tape	Millions	Relatively inexpensive, easy to do backup	No random processing, relatively slow	Mostly backup and archivage for minis and mainframes
Magnetic disk	Hundreds of millions	Random access, rapid	Expensive, no automatic backups	Minis and mainframes
Floppy disk	360K to 1.2M	Inexpensive, easy for beginners	Small capacity, slow	Small personal computers
Hard disk	10M to 130M	Random access, rapid	Difficult for beginners, no automatic backup	Microcomputers in business

Storage

Because primary storage is usually too small to handle users' needs and because its contents are erased when the computer is turned off, auxiliary storage is part of almost any computer system. The amount of information that can be saved in many types of auxiliary storage is immense. However, data and instructions contained in auxiliary storage cannot be processed immediately by the CPU; they must first be transferred to primary storage. The time it takes to access data in auxiliary storage and transfer it to primary storage varies from a few milliseconds to a few seconds. This access time may seem very short, but it can be a millionfold greater than the time necessary to process the data once it has been transferred.

Storage Devices for Microcomputers

There are several popular auxiliary storage media and corresponding devices on which users can organize data for maximum accessibility. Some of these are described in the following pages; Table 5-1 presents the characteristics of the most commonly used media.

This picture illustrates diskettes produced by three different manufacturers. Floppy disks should be stored in their protective envelopes when not in use. (© Freda Leinwand.)

Floppy Disks. Floppy disks, also called diskettes or floppies, are the most popular auxiliary storage media used with business, educational, and home computer systems. Diskettes come in several sizes, including 3½, 5¼, and 8 inches in diameter, and can be either *single-sided* or *double-sided*. (In spite of their name, single-sided disks can store data on both sides; however, only one side is verified by the manufacturer to be free of defects.) They also vary in their recording density—most are either *single-density (SD)* or *double-density (DD)*. The recording density typically refers to the number of bits per inch.

A floppy disk is a piece of plastic with a magnetized coating that is permanently encased in an envelope for protection. The data on a floppy disk is stored in concentric rings called **tracks**. The tracks are divided into small areas called *sectors* that can be accessed individually. The tracks can be thought of as rings on a tree and the sectors as the segments of the rings that are formed when the tree is split lengthwise. (See Figure 5-2.)

Floppy disks for the IBM PC and compatible computers are generally double-sided and double-density, with 40 tracks per side. Each track contains 9 sectors of 512 characters each, for a total of 4608 characters. Thus, these floppy disks contain 4608 × 40 × 2, or 368,640 characters. This is commonly abbreviated as 360K and is enough storage capacity for about 180 double-spaced pages of text. Computers such as the Apple Macintosh use smaller diskettes, about 3½ inches in diameter. This newer type of diskette can hold more data; common values are 720K and 800K.

Floppy disks have several advantages: They have become a well-known technology for millions of users; they can be used for both random and sequential processing; they are small, light, and easy to store; and the prices of floppy disks and disk drives have declined dramatically in the last several years. This storage medium also has several disadvantages, however.

Track

The circular area on a magnetic disk or diskette on which data may be recorded.

FIGURE 5-2

Tracks and Sectors on a Floppy Disk

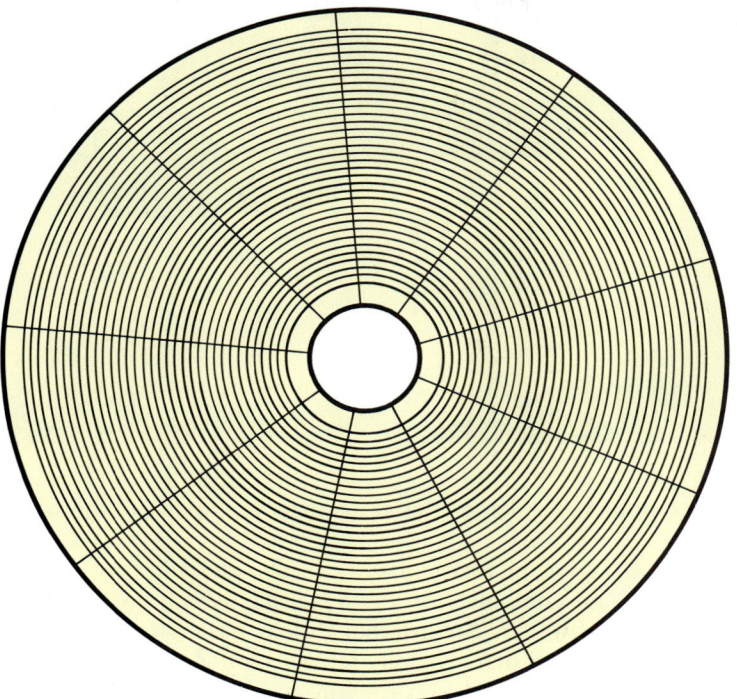

The tracks resemble rings on a tree; the sectors are the segments of the rings that are formed when the tree is split lengthwise. The use of sectors makes it easier for the system to find information on the disk.

Floppy disks are relatively slow; it may take from 75 to 600 milliseconds to find the initial location of desired data. The typical transfer rate is only 30 KB per second compared to more than 500 KB per second for some hard disks (to be discussed shortly). In addition, the storage capacity of diskettes, although adequate for most home and many office uses, is too small for many applications. Even the 1.2-MB floppy disk used with the IBM AT cannot hold the accounts receivable files for a medium-sized business, much less all of its files.

Hard Disks. Some of the disadvantages of floppy disks can be overcome by using a hard disk. Hard disks, also called fixed disks or rigid disks, are rigid metallic platters covered with a magnetized surface on which data can be recorded. Hard disks are available for computers of all sizes. The term *Winchester* is often used as a synonym for hard disk. In general, the larger

CHAPTER 5   141   THE CPU AND STORAGE

The hard disk shown here has a capacity of 20 megabytes. It is equivalent to over 50 regular floppy disks and may contain months or years of important data. (Courtesy of Apple Computer, Inc.)

These disk drives and the blue disks mounted on them are used with computers manufactured by Digital Equipment Corporation. (Courtesy of Digital Equipment Corp.)

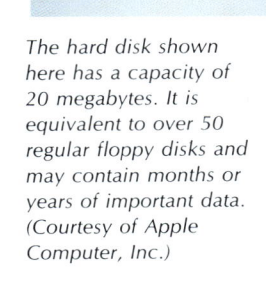

the computer, the larger, faster, and more expensive the hard disk.

Hard disks for microcomputers can be *external disks*, which sit next to the computer, or *internal disks*, which are installed inside the computer. An external disk is easier to install and repair. An internal disk typically replaces a floppy disk drive. A typical microcomputer used for business contains one floppy disk drive and one hard disk; many users prefer to have a second floppy disk drive for ease in making copies.

To visualize the storage capacity of hard disks, consider a typist who can type 60 five-letter words a minute, or almost 20,000 characters an hour. It would take this typist one thousand hours, or six months, of nonstop typing to fill a 20-MB hard disk. When we add up six months' salary plus fringe benefits and overhead, we can see that the cost of entering data on the hard disk far exceeds the purchase cost of the hard disk, which may be only a few hundred dollars.

Hard disks have the advantage of being considerably faster than floppies. A microcomputer hard disk takes about twenty to eighty milliseconds to find the location containing a specific item of data. Data is typically transferred into primary storage at rates of 100–500 KB or more per second. Hard disks also have much more storage capacity than floppy disks. A 20-MB hard disk has a storage capacity equivalent to that of about fifty floppy disks. This means that hard disk users can access a wealth of data quickly and efficiently. However, the very fact of having so much data stored in one place can be a disadvantage. A hardware failure, an operations error, or sabotage can destroy all or part of a hard disk. Consequently, the files on a hard disk must be organized very carefully. Moreover, because the hard disks themselves are rarely portable, transferring data from a hard disk to another computer requires either a lot of time or expensive equipment.

Protecting Data. Both floppy and hard disks may contain data that represents hundreds of hours of work and has a value that is often measured in thousands of dollars or more. Such data must be protected carefully. One step toward protecting data is to handle the equipment and storage media properly. (See Box 5-1.) Another way to protect programs and data is to make **backup copies**. This can be done by copying files onto a set of floppy disks reserved for this purpose. Since even a 10-MB hard disk contains the equivalent of almost thirty standard floppy disks, it is easy to see that making floppy disk backups is a time-consuming and cumbersome activity.

There are several ways to lighten the backup load. One is to copy only files that have been changed during the day. This procedure should be supplemented by a complete backup at regular intervals, perhaps once a week or once a pay period. Software is available to help users back up all or part of a hard disk to floppy disks. Another solution is to copy the material on a hard disk into a special magnetic-tape backup system. (Such systems are discussed later in the chapter.) Some organizations install two hard disks in a computer: One disk is used for processing and the other for backups. This procedure is fast and easy, but it involves some risk: If the entire computer malfunctions, both the original material and the backups may be lost.

The Bernoulli Box. There is a vast potential market for equipment that combines the storage capacity of hard disks with the portability of floppy disks. One of several products that aim to tap this market is the *Bernoulli box*, a hardware device that stores up to 20 MB of data on a removable cartridge that looks like a floppy disk. There are two versions of the Bernoulli box: a single-drive system and a double-drive system. With a double-drive system, the user has access to up to 40 MB of data. But because the cartridges are removable, a Bernoulli box system can store an almost unlimited amount of data outside of the computer itself.

A typical user of a Bernoulli box is a computerized accounting service. Each client is assigned a cartridge or cartridges containing only its own files. If they so choose, clients can keep

Backup copy
A copy of data on a file or series of files that is made to ensure continuity in case of data loss.

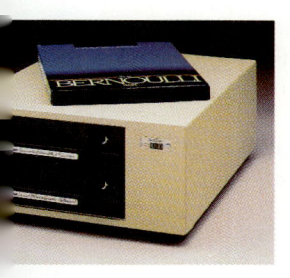

The Bernoulli box combines the advantages of hard disks and floppies. This unit contains two 10-MB cartridges, one holding accounts receivable and another holding the annual balance/income statement. (Courtesy of Iomega Corp.)

CHAPTER 5 143 THE CPU AND STORAGE

BOX 5-1

USING COMPUTERS

Be Nice to Your Storage Media

Professor Ewing is nice to his students. He prepares carefully for class, gives well-thought-out exams, and assigns grades fairly. His students think he is a great guy. But there are things that only his computer knows. Deep down, Ewing is a slob.

Ewing keeps research data, drafts of book chapters, exam questions, and much other valuable data on floppy disks. He likes floppy disks because they are inexpensive and easy to use. He has found that they also make handy coasters for his coffee cup. Ewing likes to gamble, and when he uses a floppy disk as a coaster, he is playing the odds. The odds are about 1 in 10 that the data on the disk will be lost. If the coffee is spilled and if it has cream and sugar in it, the odds are dead certain that the data will be lost.

Of course, Ewing doesn't use his most valuable data disks as coasters—only the ones that have a day's worth of hard work on them. For his really irreplaceable data, he has a neat little floppy disk storage box with a lid that closes tightly. The only thing is, he never closes the lid. He doesn't like to waste time, and closing the lid takes almost 100 milliseconds. As a result, dust, smoke particles, and humidity attack the disks. They don't get ruined right away. In fact, the effects are hard to notice at first. But last week when Ewing wanted to get back to work on his big conference paper, he popped the disk into his machine and got a message that said, "ERROR READING DISK IN DRIVE A." What the message should have said was "FATAL SMOG POISONING."

Like many people, Ewing has a number of contradictory habits. He is a smoker, but he is also a fresh-air nut, so he keeps an ashtray on his desk and the window open. His floppy disks aren't the only ones that suffer. Although Ewing doesn't know it, a few tiny smog particles have found their way through the filter that protects his computer's 20-MB hard disk drive. The pickup head of the disk drive, which reads the magnetically encoded data, floats just a few microns above the rapidly spinning disk. When the head comes upon a smog particle, it is like a car hitting a football-sized rock at 80 miles an hour.

One of these days, Ewing's hard disk is going to crash. Of course, he has carefully backed up all that data, hasn't he? Well, some of it. Yes, there's the backup for his test questions over there in the open disk file. And there's the backup for his latest journal article over there under the ashtray.

backup files in their own offices, thereby ensuring that they remain confidential.

Tape Backup Systems. A very common, easy way to back up hard disks is via *magnetic-tape backup systems*. These systems consist of tape cartridges that can hold 60 MB or more of data, a tape drive to read and write data on the cartridge; and software to facilitate the backup operation. They can be mounted inside the computer or can be placed beside it. They allow a relatively untrained operator to copy the contents of a hard disk in a few minutes. As in the case of floppy disk backups, magnetic-tape backup systems can be used to copy the entire contents of a hard disk or only selected files.

Special Storage Techniques

Auxiliary storage is slow compared to primary storage. However, primary storage is expensive compared to auxiliary storage. The challenge facing computer specialists and sophisticated users is how to optimize the use of primary and auxiliary storage in order to provide a rapid system at the lowest possible cost. Two storage techniques that can improve the productivity of a system are RAM disks and disk caching.

RAM Disks. A *RAM disk* is not an actual disk but a portion of the computer's random-access memory that is controlled by special software. Data can be stored on a RAM disk instead of on a hard disk or diskette. For example, a textbook author can begin a word-processing session by commanding the computer to copy a chapter to RAM disk. Then, because the entire chapter is in the computer's random-access memory, the author never has to wait for part of the chapter to be transferred from a floppy disk to RAM. This speeds up the writing and editing process considerably. However, the use of a RAM disk has a major drawback: It is volatile storage, not an actual disk. When the power supply to the computer is turned off or interrupted, its contents are lost. To prevent such a loss, the user should copy the contents of the RAM disk to auxiliary storage at regular intervals.

Disk Caching. *Disk caching* is a process in which selected contents of a hard disk or diskette are copied into primary storage. Whenever this data is modified, the system automatically stores the new version on the hard disk or diskette. Many users prefer disk caching over RAM disks because it offers greater data security in the event of a system failure.

Auxiliary Storage for Larger Computers

The following storage devices are used with minicomputers and mainframes. Their extensive storage capacity makes an organized procedure for backing up files an absolute necessity. In most cases users of these devices have access to a professional operations staff that is responsible for conducting regularly scheduled backups.

Magnetic Tapes. Magnetic tapes are one of the most important auxiliary storage media for minis and mainframes. A typical tape is 2400 feet (about 800 meters) long and ½ inch (about 1.2 centimeters) wide, and is mounted on a unit called a *tape drive*. Data commonly is recorded on tape at 800, 1600, or 6250 characters per inch. Because of the huge amounts of data contained on such tapes, they require special handling and care.

Most companies that use magnetic tapes need hundreds or even thousands of tapes. If a specific tape is to be located within a reasonable amount of time, the company must have detailed labeling and handling procedures. Many computer centers have *tape librarians* whose job is to categorize, store, and locate magnetic tapes.

A technique that is used with magnetic-tape systems and sometimes with magnetic-disk systems is *blocking*, or combining a group of two or more records to be read or written at a single time. (See Figure 5-3.) The use of blocking reduces the number of reads or writes and the amount of unused space (called *interblock gaps*). However, blocking involves some technical considerations, such as the possibility that not all

In the background of this picture are hundreds of magnetic tapes, each of which may contain millions of characters of data. (Courtesy of TRW Inc.)

HARDWARE 146 PART 2

FIGURE 5-3

Blocking of Records on Magnetic Tape

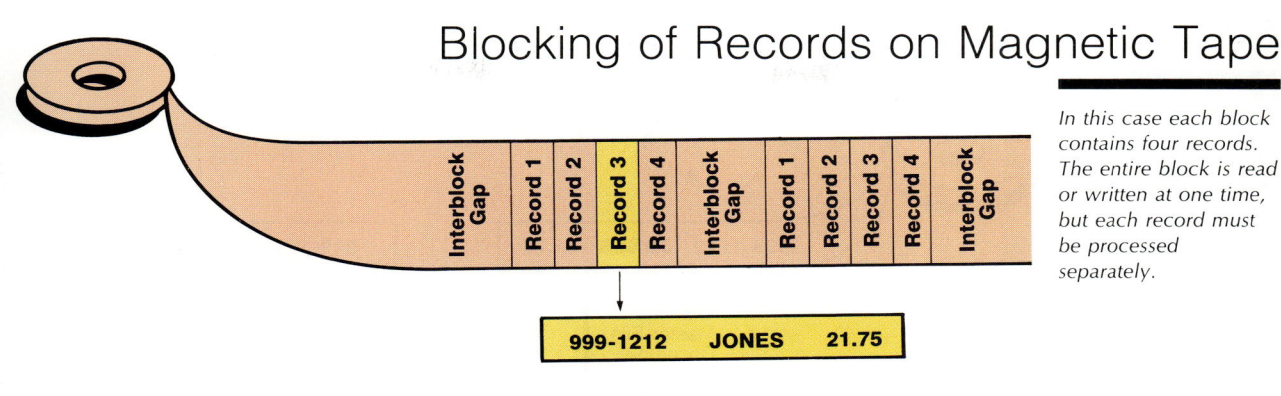

In this case each block contains four records. The entire block is read or written at one time, but each record must be processed separately.

999-1212   JONES   21.75

blocks contain the same number of records. Most of these considerations are handled by the system itself rather than by the programmer.

An example of the use of magnetic tapes is a telephone company's billing system. The company's records are stored on magnetic tape in sequential order by telephone number. To improve efficiency, the tape is organized in blocks, each of which contains four records. Thus, to process the phone bill for phone number 999-1122, the computer must find the block with that number's record in it and read it into its memory. Then the computer finds the record for phone number 999-1122 and processes it.

A major limitation of magnetic-tape storage systems is the impossibility of rewriting on a tape that is being read. Thus, a user cannot change a record on a tape without rewriting the entire tape. This means that changing or **updating** a magnetic tape requires at least three files: (1) **the old master file,** which contains the data before the changes are made; (2) **the transaction file**, which contains the changes to the data on the old master file; and (3) the **new master file**, which contains the data after the changes have been made.

As an example of the updating process, consider what takes place when a telephone company calculates and prints its telephone bills for the month of January. (See Figure 5-4.) The January phone bills are generated from two sources: the old master file, which contains customer account balances as of the end of December, and the transaction file, which contains telephone charges and credits for the month of January. The records on both files are in sequence by telephone number. The computer reads the data in the old master file into its memory

Updating
The process through which data on a master file is modified to reflect changed conditions such as customer payments or purchases.

Old master file
The file that contains basic data for a computer application before an update is carried out.

Transaction file
A file that contains changes to be made in a master file.

New master file
The file that contains basic data for a computer application after an update has been carried out.

CHAPTER 5   THE CPU AND STORAGE

FIGURE 5-4

Sequential Update

In this telephone billing application the old master file is updated (modified) once a month to take into account the transactions of the month, such as payments and charges. The updated tape is called the new master file. This example illustrates updating of the December old master file with the January transactions to produce the January new master file.

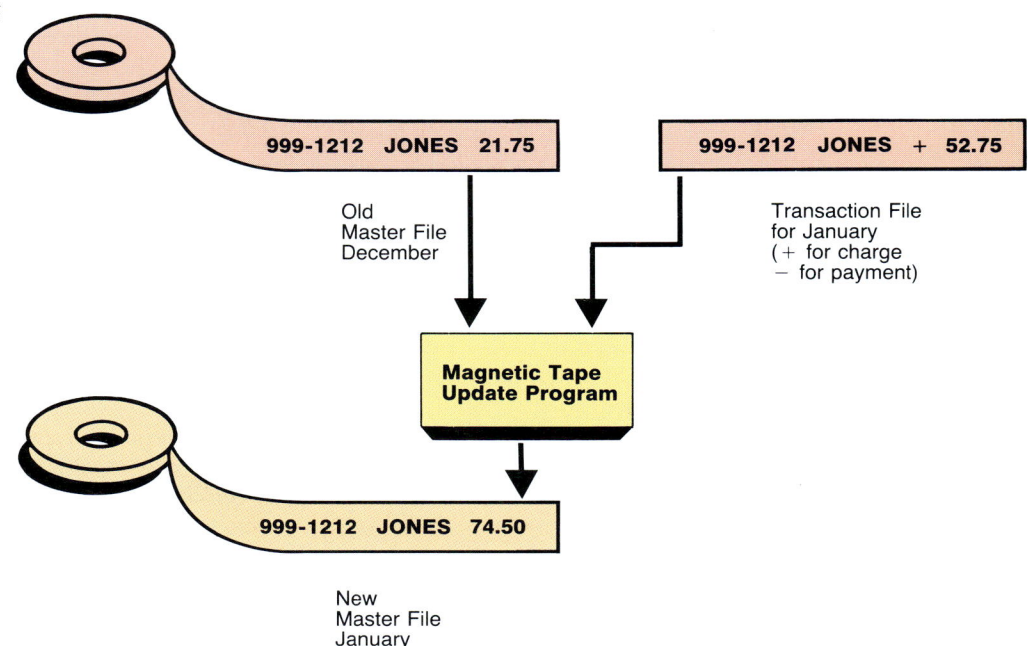

Old Master File December: 999-1212 JONES 21.75

Transaction File for January (+ for charge − for payment): 999-1212 JONES + 52.75

Magnetic Tape Update Program

New Master File January: 999-1212 JONES 74.50

and then updates it according to the data in the transaction file. The updated data is written on a new master file containing customer account balances as of the end of January. The records on the new master file are also in sequence by telephone number. A special program reads this new master file and prints the telephone bills for the month of January. At the end of February, this new master file becomes the old master file; it will be processed against the transaction file consisting of telephone charges and credits for the month of February to create the new master file for the end of February. This updating process is repeated each month. The result of the process is three *generations* of magnetic tapes, often known as grandfather, father, and son.

A major advantage of the magnetic-tape updating process is that the old master files serve as backups. If something goes wrong with the new master file for the month of February, it can be recreated from the old master file for the month of January and the transaction file for the month of February.

Magnetic tapes have other advantages as well. Not only do they store a large quantity of data in a small space, but they are inexpensive and can be erased and used again. They are durable, and with proper handling they can be accessed frequently and last for years. Moreover, records on magnetic tape can be of any length.

Magnetic tapes have some disadvantages, however. As noted earlier, they are limited to sequential processing: To access a specific record, the user must access all preceding records. In addition, as we will see shortly, processing of magnetic tapes is slow compared to processing of magnetic disks. And finally, the tapes are susceptible to damage from dust, humidity, smoke particles, and temperature extremes.

Magnetic Disks. Magnetic disks are the main auxiliary storage media for minicomputers and mainframes. Magnetic disks are similar to the floppy disks and hard disks used with microcomputers, but they are larger and faster and store more data. Some older models contain removable units, but the trend is toward fixed disks, since the data stored on fixed disks is always available. Moreover, because fixed disks are sealed in an airtight case with their access mechanism, they are better protected and tend to last longer than removable disks. The storage capacity of magnetic disks varies widely, but a capacity of 800 MB per disk drive unit is not uncommon.

A typical magnetic disk is composed of one or a few *platters* that look like phonograph records. The disk spins continuously at a speed of about 3600 revolutions per minute, and data can be recorded on both sides, or *surfaces*, of each platter, except that no data is recorded on the very top and very bottom surfaces of the disk.

The *disk drive* (see Figure 5-5) reads and writes data with a comblike access mechanism that typically contains an access arm and one read/write head for each recording surface of a platter. Several disk packs may be mounted on one disk drive. Like floppy disks, the read/write heads are designed to avoid touching the platter surfaces.

All magnetic disks have the capability for both random and sequential processing. Users describe the record they want in natural terms (e.g., "flight #615 on June 30th"). The software translates this record into a physical location on the disk (e.g., record number 51 on track 17 of recording surface 12). Then the system must access the disk. In the case of random access, the read/write heads move as a unit until they are positioned over track 17. Then the head associated with recording surface 12 is switched on. Finally the head accesses record number 51. The entire process takes less time to do than to describe.

CHAPTER 5   149   THE CPU AND STORAGE

FIGURE 5-5

Accessing Data on a Magnetic Disk

This process requires three operations: moving the read/write heads to the appropriate track, choosing the read/write head for the desired platter, and waiting for the data on the rotating disk to come near the selected read/write head. Source: Adapted from Marilyn Bohl, Introduction to IBM Direct Access Storage Devices (Chicago: Science Research Associates, 1981).

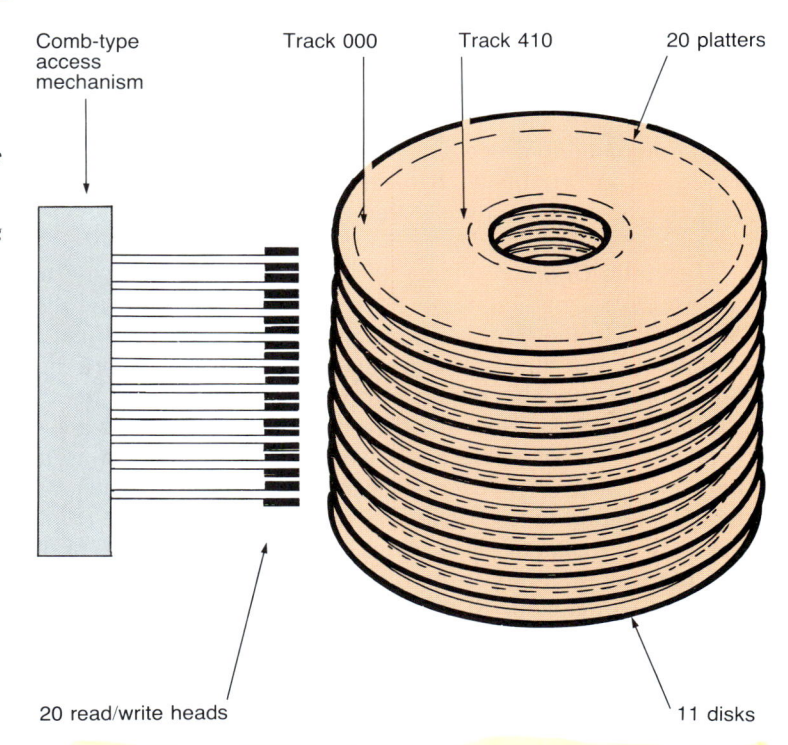

Comb-type access mechanism

Track 000

Track 410

20 platters

20 read/write heads

11 disks

A *cylinder* consists of all the data tracks that can be accessed without moving the read/write heads, for example, all track 9s on the entire disk. To improve the speed of operations, sequential files on magnetic disks are often organized in cylinders. (See Figure 5-6.) To illustrate this method, let's assume that we have a file requiring two tracks. The first part of the file is on track 9 of recording surface 6. The second part of the file is on track 9 of recording surface 7. After the access arm has been placed on track 9, the disk drive reads the entire file without moving the access arm.

Contrast placing data in cylinders to the more "natural" method in which the data is placed on tracks 9 and 10 of recording surface 6. To read the entire file, the access arm must be moved twice: first to track 9 and then to track 10. Moving the access arm is the most time-consuming part of a read or write operation. Consequently, data should be placed in cylinders to save time when processing magnetic disks sequentially.

FIGURE 5-6

Cylinders on a Magnetic Disk

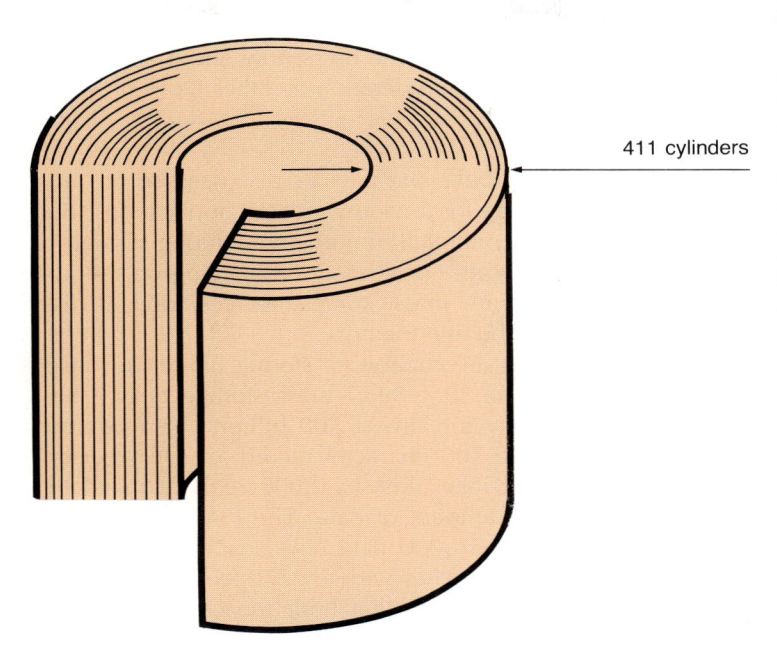

411 cylinders

All data on a cylinder can be accessed without moving the read/write heads. Source: Adapted from Marilyn Bohl, *Introduction to IBM Direct Access Storage Devices* (Chicago: Science Research Associates, 1981).

Modern computer systems take the responsibility for organizing the data into cylinders when appropriate.

Magnetic disks are very fast; it may take only twenty milliseconds to find a record on a disk. Unlike magnetic tapes, magnetic disks can be modified without having to rewrite the entire contents of the disk. The hardware and software for disk systems usually is more expensive than that for tape systems. Also, disk systems do not provide backup as readily as tape systems do. When a record on a disk is modified, the old data is lost forever unless a copy was made previously. Magnetic disks are also more sensitive to mechanical failure than magnetic tapes and more vulnerable to breaches of security.

In sum, magnetic disks and magnetic tapes each have advantages and disadvantages. Although many minicomputers and mainframe computer systems use a combination of these auxiliary storage media, increasingly the processing itself is performed with disks, while the use of tapes is limited to file backup and archives. The system used by the registrar of George Mason University, described at the beginning of this chapter, is a case in point. For daily operations, student grade records are kept on disk. This allows quick random access and permits a few or many records at a time to be updated in any order. However, the disk is vulnerable to failure. Thus, each night the data is backed up on tape. Some information that is not used every day is also kept on tape. As flexible as the combination of disk and tape is, some users now and in the future will have to give serious consideration to other types of auxiliary storage devices.

Other Storage Devices. The devices discussed so far provide fast, reliable storage for a wide variety of applications. But storage technology is continually improving. Among advanced devices that may be worth considering, depending on the application in question, are mass storage devices, optical disk storage, and magnetic bubble memory.

Mass storage devices are capable of storing billions of characters. For example, an IBM 3850 mass storage device has enough storage capacity for almost 500 billion characters, or enough room to store a 100-character record for every person on the earth. It would take almost 50,000 reels of magnetic tape to store the same amount of data. The IBM unit is composed of approximately 10,000 data cells, each containing a spool of magnetic tape 3 inches wide by 770 feet long. Data is accessed by a mechanical arm that finds the correct cell, removes the spool of tape and unwinds it, and transfers the data to a separate magnetic disk where it is processed.

The disadvantage of mass storage devices is that they are slow compared to magnetic disks. The time from the initial request for data to the moment the data is processed may be as long as 15 seconds; in contrast, data stored on a disk is usually available in a fraction of a second. Thus, mass storage devices are generally used when storage requirements are huge and time is not a critical factor. Typical users of these devices are government agencies such as the Internal Revenue Service and the Social Security Administration and commercial users such as banks and insurance companies.

Optical disk storage media have a huge storage capacity. For example, a 12-inch optical disk, which has dozens of times the storage capacity of a magnetic disk, could store the entire contents of the *Encyclopedia Britannica*. Information is written on optical disks by a powerful laser beam that produces a pattern of bits on the surface of the disk. The information stored on an optical disk can consist of images or voices as well as characters. Because most commercial optical disk systems don't allow users to modify information once it has been written, optical disks are generally used for archival storage or to store refer-

Storage Devices for Microcomputers

Floppy Disk
Hard Disk
Bernoulli Box
Tape Backup System

Storage Devices for Larger Computers

Magnetic Tape
Magnetic Disk
Mass Storage Device
Optical Disk
Magnetic Bubble Memory

Optical disks are an increasingly popular storage medium. As their price decreases, they may largely replace traditional storage media such as magnetic tape and disks. (© Don McCoy, Rainbow.)

Bubble memory is used in special storage applications such as portable computers and industrial equipment. This particular memory has been magnified 3000 times. (Courtesy of AT&T Bell Laboratories.)

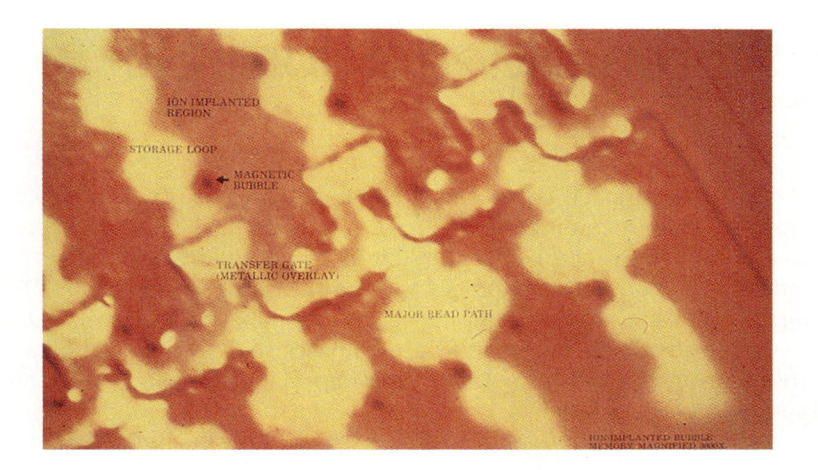

ence materials. However, optical disks are now becoming available to owners of personal computers. (See Box 5-2.)

A *magnetic bubble memory* is a chip containing microscopic bubbles that are used for memory and auxiliary storage. Unlike RAM, this form of memory retains its contents even after the computer has been turned off. A bubble memory can store up to 3 million characters per square inch. And because it has no moving parts, it is shock resistant and requires very little power. However, this technology is expensive and is largely limited to special applications such as portable computers and industrial environments, where its distinctive qualities compensate for its high cost.

File Organization

Throughout this chapter we have emphasized the importance of choosing the appropriate auxiliary storage device for specific user needs. But it is just as important to organize the data being stored. In other words, users need to know what storage equipment is best suited to their needs and how to use that equipment to store data. This section describes three traditional approaches to file organization. Each of them requires the use of a special field to identify each record in the file. This is known

BOX 5-2

FRONTIERS IN TECHNOLOGY

Optical Storage Media for PCs

The same 4.7-inch compact disks that have revolutionized audio recording are beginning to have an impact on the personal-computer market as desktop mass storage devices. Compact disks are an optical storage device that records digital data in the form of microscopic pits etched in a spiral on a plastic surface. A laser beam just 1 micron wide is scattered by the pits and reflected by the flat "lands" between them, enabling the encoded information to be read. Because information recorded on the most common form of compact disks can be read but not erased, this approach to storing data is known as CD-ROM, for Compact Disk/Read-Only Memory. A single CD-ROM disk can store 550 MB, the equivalent of 1500 floppy disks or 200,000 pages.

The drives used to read compact disks use the same basic technology as their audio counterparts. The drives are available as add-on units that sit beside a personal computer, and also as units that can be inserted in the computer to replace an existing floppy disk drive. The main difference between audio and data recording on compact disks is the degree of precision required in recording the data and reading it back. Losing one bit of data in the middle of a Beethoven symphony creates a distortion that is too tiny for even the most polished ear to detect. But a single error in a data processing application could snowball into a $1000 error on a client's tax return or a failed scientific experiment. Through the use of special techniques, it is possible to hold the error rate to as little as one undetected wrong bit in 2 quadrillion disks.

The first applications of CD-ROM will give personal-computer users access to huge data bases such as financial data bases, patent information, books in print and other library data, medical and drug references, and so on. Previously these large data bases have been available to PC users only via on-line information services that link the user's PC to a host mainframe via telephone lines. CD-ROM has the potential to greatly reduce the cost of access to these data bases.

Not only can CD-ROM store large data bases, it permits them to be manipulated in many useful ways. For example, a disk that contains abstracts of engineering articles could be searched for all abstracts containing the words "optical," "storage," and "data." This is possible because the huge storage capacity of CD-ROM means that the disks have room for a full text inversion—an index showing the location of every word in the entire recorded text.

Further advances are on the horizon. One is the CD-WORM ("write once, read many times"). This technique allows the user to write data on the disk, but not to erase it. Erasable disks are also in the development stage. Researchers are also attempting to overcome one of the present disadvantages of CD-ROM: access times and data transfer rates that are inferior to those of today's magnetic hard disks.

Source: Jeffrey Bairstow, "CD-ROM: Mass Storage for the Mass Market," *High Technology*, October 1986, pp. 44–51.

Key field
A field that identifies each record in a file.

Sequential file
A file whose records must be accessed in order, starting with the first record on the file.

Sorting
The process of arranging data in a useful sequence.

as the **key field**, or *key*. (Recall from Chapter 3 that a field is a contiguous group of characters that has a meaning. A collection of related fields is a record, and a collection of related records is a file.)

Sequential Files

The simplest way to organize files is sequentially. **Sequential files** consist of records that are stored in a particular order, usually in the order in which they were originally created. For example, suppose that we are considering at a company's payroll records, which are stored in order by employee number (the key field). If the highest current employee number is 1234, the next person hired would be assigned a higher number, perhaps 1235, and his or her records would be stored under that number. When employees leave the company their numbers usually are not reassigned. Over time some numbers will be "missing" in much the same way that some baseball players' jacket numbers are "missing" after they have retired.

Updating this payroll file is very similar to the process of updating telephone bills discussed earlier. The updated payroll file is used to generate a paycheck file whose records contain information that will appear on the employees' paychecks. Although the payroll file is based on employee numbers, the paychecks themselves should be printed in an order related to the employees' location within the company to facilitate distribution. This means that records on both the paycheck file and the payroll file should also contain a special field that indicates each employee's location. Records on the paycheck file are sorted, that is, placed in order by employee location, before the paychecks are printed.

As has been noted several times, before processing a given record on a sequential file, the computer must access all records that precede it on the file. This is not usually a problem in processing a payroll file. Employees are paid periodically, and during each pay period there is ample time to collect a group of transactions, sort them, update the old master file, and verify the new master file and paycheck file before printing and distributing the paychecks. You will recall from Chapter 2 that this type of system is known as a batch-processing system. In general, sequential files are used with batch processing, producing reports at regular, scheduled intervals.

Sequential processing is rarely suitable for on-line systems such as over-the-phone airline reservation systems. It is inefficient to access all records with a flight number lower than the one requested, and customers are not willing to wait until the

CHAPTER 5 155 THE CPU AND STORAGE

next morning for information on flight availability. But when the user can wait, sequential processing has several advantages: It can be used with relatively inexpensive storage devices such as magnetic tapes; it creates generations of files, thereby facilitating the production of backups; and it is easy to understand and program.

A disadvantage of sequential processing is that transactions must be sorted beforehand. This can be a problem for heavy users, since it can tie up the computer for long periods. Also, data on sequential files may not be current because of the time it takes to accumulate batches of transactions and run the update program. And finally, information is available only on a periodic basis, not on demand.

In spite of these disadvantages, sequential processing meets many business needs. For example, an airline company may use it to calculate statistics on how many seats are unoccupied on each of its flights. But when customers want to reserve seats or the airline's managers want instant data on seat availability to use in planning a new marketing campaign, they need a different kind of file organization. One type of file that provides for instant information retrieval is the random-access file.

Random-Access Files

Random-access files, also called **direct-access files**, allow the computer to process a record without first having to process all of the preceding records. Such a file would, for example, allow the computer to look up the availability of seats on flight 615 to Cleveland without having to read flight numbers 1–614.

In order to process direct-access records, the computer system must include an auxiliary storage device that *supports* (i.e., provides for) direct access. Both floppy and magnetic disk drives support direct-access files; magnetic tapes do not. In addition, computer specialists must set up the system so that it can translate a request such as "flight number" 615 to a disk address, or location, such as record number 51 on track 17 of recording surface 12.

As an example of the processing of a direct-access file, consider a university that has a file composed of student records. The key field in these records is the student number, which can range from 1000000 to 9999999. It might be simple to assign student number 1211267 to recording surface 12, track 112, and record number 67. But student number 7866612 cannot be similarly assigned if recording surface 78 or track 666 does not exist. Furthermore, assigning addresses in this way would re-

Random-access file
A file in which any record can be processed without processing all preceding records or accessing an index. Also called direct-access file.

FIGURE 5-7a

Hashing a Record for a Random-Access File

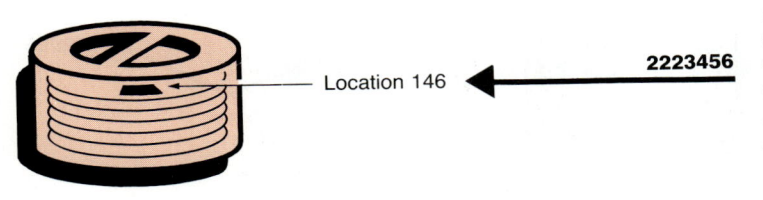

Location 146 ← 2223456

In this example the computer uses a simple calculation to determine that record number 2223456 should be placed in location 146. If this location is empty, the computer assigns record number 2223456 to it.

quire exactly 9 million locations, or one for each possible student number. Clearly this is wasteful no matter how many students there are. In practice it is rarely feasible to translate the key field directly into a disk address. It is necessary to apply a method that *transforms* record keys into disk addresses in such a way that any record can be found rapidly.

Hashing. The process of transforming the key to a disk address is known as *hashing*. Among the commonly used hashing methods is the *division/remainder method*, in which the key is divided by a given number and the remainder is then used to determine the disk address of the record. This method works best when the record key is divided by a *prime number*, that is, a number that can be divided evenly only by itself and 1.

To see how hashing could be used in the university example given earlier, suppose there is enough room on the disk for a file made up of 1000 records. (See Figure 5-7a.) To assign locations to the records, the record key is divided by the largest prime number less than 1000, which is 997. The remainder is the *relative record location*, that is, the location of the record relative to the beginning of the file. For example, if we divide record number 2223456 by 997, the result is 2230 with a remainder of 146. This indicates that student number 2223456 is to go in relative location 146; in other words, it will be found 146 locations past the beginning of the file.

There are some problems associated with hashing, however. (See Figure 5-7b.) For example, when student number 5002095 is hashed using the method just described, the remainder is 146; therefore, this record should go in relative location 146. But another record, student number 2223456, is already in that location. This is called a *collision*. The records for students 2223456 and 5002095 are *synonyms*. In such a situation, student record 5002095 can be assigned to the next available location, perhaps 147. The more locations in a file are filled, the

CHAPTER 5   157   THE CPU AND STORAGE

FIGURE 5-7b

A Synonym on a Random-Access File

In this example the computer determines that record number 5002095 should be placed in location 146. However, another record already occupies this location. The two records are synonyms, and a collision has occurred.

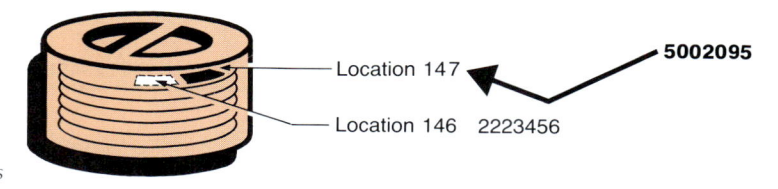

Location 147 ← 5002095
Location 146 2223456

greater the chance of collisions. To keep synonyms to a reasonable level, users who hash records should not fill a file to more than 80 percent of its capacity.

Like sequential files, direct-access files may require sorting. For instance, when the time comes to process students' grades at the end of the semester, it would take a long time to look for each student record individually. It is much more efficient to sort the records by student number and then process them sequentially.

Advantages and Disadvantages. As the name implies, direct access allows the user to access records directly, without having to access preceding records. This makes applications such as over-the-phone airline reservations possible. In addition, many applications do not require the sorting of transactions before processing. On the other hand, direct-access files require fairly expensive storage devices and control software, and the files require extra space to reduce the problem of synonyms. The system does not provide for backups as readily as sequential processing does, and processing of random-access files for sequential applications requires sorting and may be less efficient than using sequential files themselves.

Indexed-Sequential Files

Another type of file, **indexed-sequential files,** attempts to combine the best aspects of the systems just described. Like records on sequential files, records on indexed-sequential files are stored and can be accessed sequentially. And like records on random-access files, records on indexed-sequential files can be accessed randomly according to their key fields. These files require magnetic disks or diskettes and may include magnetic

Indexed-sequential file
A type of file whose records can be accessed rapidly via a series of indexes.

FIGURE 5-8

Accessing Data on an Indexed-Sequential File

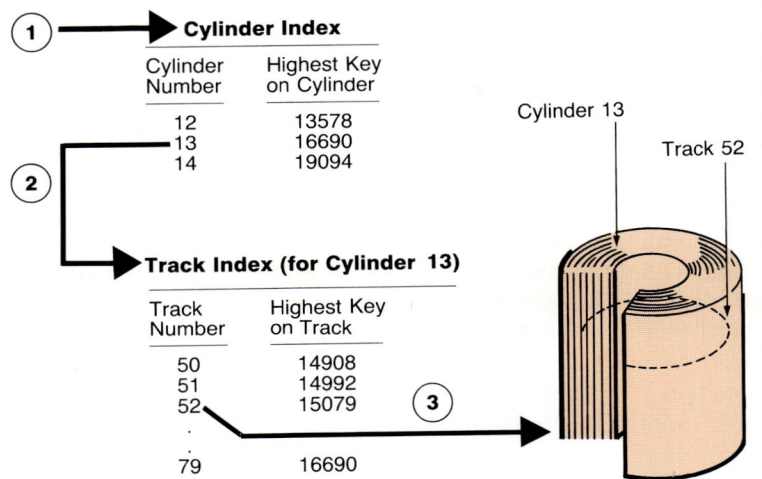

① ▶ **Cylinder Index**

Cylinder Number	Highest Key on Cylinder
12	13578
13	16690
14	19094

② ▶ **Track Index (for Cylinder 13)**

Track Number	Highest Key on Track
50	14908
51	14992
52	15079
.	
79	16690

Cylinder 13
Track 52

③

To access record number 15000, the computer (1) reads the cylinder index to determine that the record will be on cylinder 13. Then (2) it reads the track index for cylinder 13 to determine that the record will be found on track 52. Finally (3) it reads track 52 to find the record.

tapes for backup purposes. Indexed-sequential files are available on mainframe computers, minicomputers, and some microcomputers.

To get an idea of how indexed-sequential files are accessed, consider how you would find an article entitled "Computers" in an encyclopedia. First you would look at the spine of each volume of the encyclopedia. This is actually an index of the contents of that volume. Volume 1 may cover subjects from A to Battlewagons, Volume 2, subjects from Battlewagons to Cows, and so on. Perhaps the article on computers is in Volume 2. Next you would look in the index to Volume 2 to find the page on which the article starts. Finally, you would turn to the correct page and look for the article. This method obviously is much quicker than reading or even scanning every article in the encyclopedia.

The computer finds a desired record in an indexed-sequential file in much the same way that you would find the "Computer" article in an encyclopedia. It consults a series of *indexes*, one after another, until it homes in on the requested record's location. (See Figure 5-8.) This method is much faster than having the computer read an entire file sequentially. However, it is usually slower than finding the record by random access.

Systems that support indexed-sequential files often provide special features such as the one used in a company that issues

CHAPTER 5   159   THE CPU AND STORAGE

vendor numbers depending on the vendor's state of residence: Vendors 01000 to 01999 reside in California, vendors 02000 to 02999 in Oregon, and so on. When the company decides to produce a report for all vendors east of the Mississippi, it supplies the first vendor number desired, in this case 22001, and the computer finds all the other appropriate records in sequence.

Indexed-sequential files have the advantage of providing both sequential and direct access. They usually require less space than random-access files. Their disadvantages are that they require fairly expensive storage devices and control software; usually perform sequential processing less rapidly and efficiently than sequential files; and perform random processing less rapidly and efficiently than random-access files.

Sequential files, random-access files, and indexed-sequential files are the major traditional types of file organization. However, there are many other ways in which files can be organized to meet a company's needs. Chapter 10, "Data-Base Concepts," presents an entirely new way of organizing data to meet sophisticated processing needs.

Appendix: Inside the Computer

In this appendix we will focus on three aspects of the internal workings of a computer: (1) how processing actually takes place, (2) the codes used to store data and instructions, and (3) the numbering systems used to process numerical items.

Processing

As noted in the chapter, the central processing unit contains several storage locations known as registers. Because their contents can be accessed very rapidly, almost all processing takes place via the registers. The number, size, characteristics, and names of the registers vary from one type of computer to another.

The CPU also contains primary storage. For purposes of illustration, primary storage can be divided into four areas: input

FIGURE 5A-1

Data Flow

Data flows from an input device through the central processing unit to an output device. Because primary storage is limited, data is often stored temporarily on auxiliary storage devices such as diskettes.

storage area, program storage area, working storage area, and output storage area. The relative size and location of these areas are not fixed but vary according to program requirements.

Data Flow. Data originates at the input devices. (See Figure 5A-1.) The control unit transfers the data into the input storage area of primary storage. When it is needed for processing, the data is transferred into the registers of the arithmetic-logic unit. Because the storage capacity of the registers is quite limited, data is placed in the working storage area of primary storage. But since the working storage area is also limited, some of the data may also be placed on auxiliary storage devices such as diskettes. Data from either the working storage area or the registers is moved into the output storage area in preparation for printing or display.

Instruction Flow. Instructions also enter the computer via an input device such as a keyboard. (See Figure 5A-2.) First they go into the input storage area; from there they are transferred

CHAPTER 5   161   THE CPU AND STORAGE

FIGURE 5A-2

Instruction Flow

Instructions flow from an input device through the central processing unit to an output device. Typically the instructions do not actually go into the arithmetic-logic unit but are decoded by the control unit, which then initiates processing of the data in the registers associated with the arithmetic-logic unit.

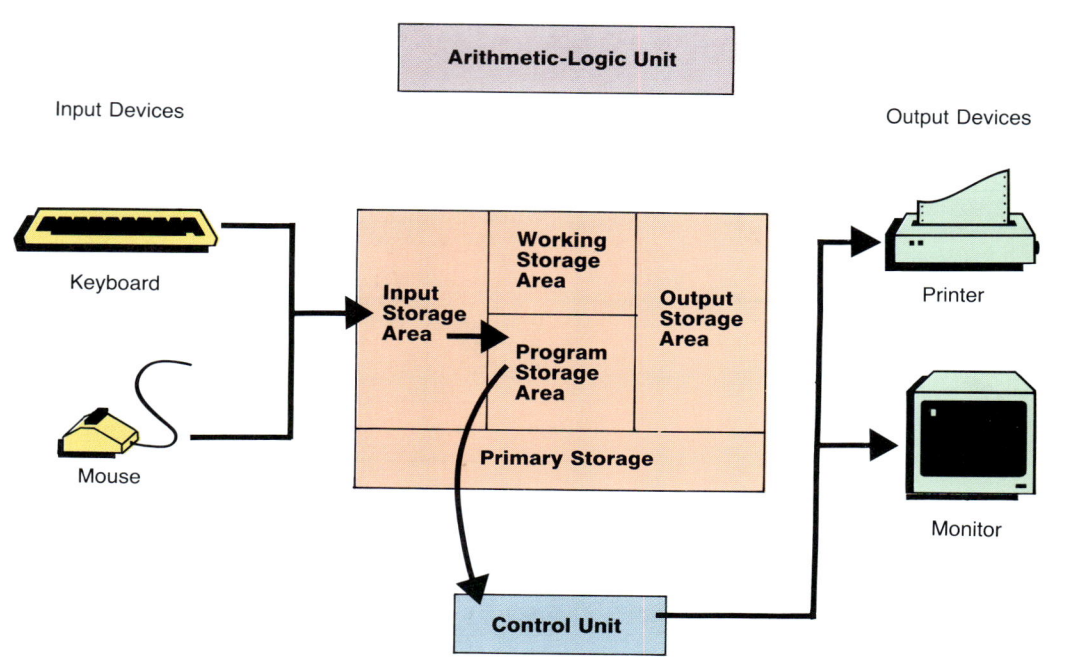

into the program storage area. The control unit decodes instructions one by one and commands the arithmetic-logic unit to carry out each instruction. It is only at this point that the data is actually processed.

Command Flow. Instruction processing is composed of two parts: the *instruction cycle* (*I-cycle*) and the *execution cycle* (*E-cycle*). In the instruction cycle the control unit gets the desired instruction from primary storage. The instruction is carried out during the execution cycle.

Command flow can be illustrated by an example in which the computer is instructed to add a bonus to a salary. The instruction cycle is composed of the following steps:

1. The control unit uses a register known as the *program counter* to get the next instruction (the addition instruction) from primary storage. The program counter is then updated to point to the instruction following the addition instruction.

2. The control unit determines what kind of instruction will be

HARDWARE 162 PART 2

executed, in this case an addition instruction. We can think of an instruction as an imperative sentence such as "Add Bonus to Salary." This step decomposes the instruction into a verb (Add) and one or more objects (Bonus and Salary).

3. The control unit places the addresses (not the contents) of the objects (Bonus and Salary) into the *address registers*.

The execution cycle is composed of the following steps:

1. The control unit uses the address registers to access the values of Bonus and Salary from primary storage and places those values in the storage registers.

2. The control unit commands the arithmetic-logic unit to carry out the addition as indicated in the instruction register.

3. The arithmetic-logic unit carries out (executes) the addition.

4. The control unit transfers the calculated sum from the arithmetic-logic unit to another register called the *accumulator*.

The program then returns to the first step of the I-cycle for the next instruction, perhaps saving the sum for future reference.

Codes for Storing Data

We noted in the chapter that the two most widely used codes for storing data in primary and secondary storage are ASCII and EBCDIC. (See Figure 5-1.) These two codes express a single character in an 8-bit byte. Because 8 bits are used for a single character, each code can be used to produce up to 256 different characters. Many of the items in the ASCII code are standard, but some are not. For example, IBM uses a happy face and an inverse happy face on the monochrome monitor (but not on the printer). The extra codes are often useful for producing graphics.

Many programs encode data in their own standard form. For example, a popular word-processing program, MultiMate, stores data on a diskette or hard disk in its own format. The complete MultiMate package includes a program that enables users to convert documents written in MultiMate's format into ASCII or vice versa. This feature is especially useful in an office that contains several types of computer hardware and software.

Most users will not consider changing their present software if it would mean reentering large amounts of data. Software manufacturers therefore need to provide a relatively painless means of converting files created by their most popular competitors. In fact, the internal storage codes used by Lotus 1-2-3 and VisiCalc have practically become industry standards.

Numbering Systems

Several different numbering systems are used to process data in a computer. Of these, the most widely used are the decimal system, the binary system, and the hexadecimal system.

The Decimal System. The familiar decimal system is based on the number 10, probably because our ancestors counted on their fingers. In this system there are ten basic symbols: 0 through 9. To express a number greater than 9, it is necessary to use two or more symbols. For example, the decimal number 11 means 1 times 10 plus 1 times 1. Because there are ten symbols, each digit has ten times the magnitude of the one to the right of it. The decimal system is not the most practical system for processing numbers in a computer.

The Binary System. The binary system is based on the number 2. In this system there are two basic symbols, 0 and 1, which can be represented in computer storage by the presence or absence of a current or voltage. To express a number greater than 1, it is necessary to use two or more symbols. For example, the binary number 11 means 1 times 2 plus 1 times 1 (i.e., the decimal number 3). Because there are two symbols, each digit has two times the magnitude of the one to the right of it. Arithmetic operations in the binary system follow special rules that are easily handled by computer circuitry. However, the binary system has a major drawback: Even medium-sized numbers require several figures, and because they contain only 0s and 1s they are hard to read. For example, the decimal number 100 is expressed as 1100100 in the binary system. The decimal number 4000 requires eleven 0s and 1s.

The Hexadecimal System. The hexadecimal system is based on the number 16. In this system there are sixteen basic symbols: the numbers 0 through 9 and the letters A (10) through F (15). Thus, the decimal number 14 is expressed as E in the hexadecimal system. To express a number greater than 15, it is necessary to use two or more symbols. For example, the hexadecimal number 11 means 1 times 16 plus 1 times 1 (i.e., the decimal number 17). Because there are sixteen symbols, each digit has sixteen times the magnitude of the one to the right of it. Although this system uses unfamiliar symbols, it has the advantage of being quite compact. For example, the decimal number 4000 requires only three digits; it is expressed as FA0. Many electronic calculators can be used for hexadecimal calculations and can quickly convert numbers to and from this system.

SUMMARY

1. The central processing unit (CPU) is the brain of the computer. It is composed of the control unit, the arithmetic-logic unit, and primary storage. The control unit controls the arithmetic-logic unit and primary storage and coordinates all processing in the computer system. The control unit contains an internal clock and several temporary storage locations called registers.

2. The arithmetic-logic unit takes care of **arithmetic operations** (addition, subtraction, multiplication, and division) and **logic operations** such as comparisons and tests. Computers do not perform arithmetic using the familiar **decimal system** but instead use the **binary system**, in which two digits, 0 and 1, represent the electrical quantities actually in storage.

3. Primary storage, also called **memory**, stores data and programs for a short period. Memory capacity is measured in K (thousands) and M (millions) of bytes or characters. Before reading or writing the contents of primary storage the computer must **access** them via an internal **address**. The most common types of primary storage are random-access memory (RAM) and read-only memory (ROM). Other types of primary storage include programmable read-only memory (PROM) and erasable programmable read-only memory (EPROM).

4. The contents of both primary and auxiliary storage are coded. Two popular codes are ASCII, the standard for microcomputers, and EBCDIC, which is used on large and medium-sized IBM computers. Special programs permit conversion between one code and another.

5. Auxiliary storage is part of almost any computer system because primary storage is usually too small to handle a user's needs; moreover, its contents are erased when the computer is turned off. The major auxiliary storage devices for microcomputers are floppy disks and faster, more powerful hard disks. Data is stored on these devices in concentric rings called **tracks**. The Bernouilli box is one of several products that combine the portability of floppy disks with the greater storage capacity of hard disks. Several techniques are available for making **backup copies** of valuable programs and data.

6. Magnetic tapes are an important auxiliary storage media for minicomputers and mainframes. They contain vast amounts of data. Magnetic tapes offer only sequential access, and the user cannot change a record on a tape without rewriting the entire tape. **Updating** a magnetic tape requires at least three files: the **old master file**, the **transaction file**, and the **new master file**.

7. Another auxiliary storage medium for minicomputers and mainframes is magnetic disks. These are similar to floppy disks or hard disks for microcomputers but are larger and faster and store more data. Magnetic disks provide both sequential and random access.

8. Research and development efforts in storage technology are continuously seeking to bring new technologies to market. De-

SUMMARY
CONTINUED

vices that may meet special storage needs include mass storage units, optical disks, and magnetic bubble memory.

9. A **key field** is a special field that identifies each record in a file. **Sequential files** consist of records that are in order by key field. These records are usually stored in the order in which they were originally created. It is common to **sort** sequential files to meet diverse processing needs.

10. **Random-access files** or **direct-access files** allow the computer to process a record without first processing all of the preceding records. Computer specialists set up these files so that the software can translate a user request into an address on the disk.

11. **Indexed-sequential files** attempt to combine the best features of sequential and random-access files. They permit both sequential and random access.

KEY TERMS

arithmetic operation

logic operation

decimal system

binary system

memory

access

address

track

backup copy

updating

old master file

transaction file

new master file

key field

sequential file

sorting

random-access file

direct-access file

indexed-sequential file

REVIEW QUESTIONS

1. What is the CPU? List its parts and their functions. Describe the number system used by the computer.

2. Describe the most common types of primary storage and their characteristics.

3. Name the two most widely used codes for the contents of storage and the types of computers to which they apply.

4. Why is auxiliary storage necessary? What are the two major types of storage devices for microcomputers? List the advantages and disadvantages of each.

5. What is the major sequential-storage device for minicomputers and mainframes? List its advantages and disadvantages.

6. What is blocking? Why is it used?

7. Describe the process of updating a magnetic tape.

8. What is the major direct-access storage device for minicomputers and mainframes? List its advantages and disadvantages.

9. List three other direct-access storage devices for minicomputers and mainframes. Name an application for each of these devices.

10. List the three major types of file organization. When is each type appropriate? What are the advantages and disadvantages of each?

APPLICATIONS

1. Interview a person who uses a microcomputer at home or at work. Describe the computer's auxiliary storage devices and how the user interacts with them.

2. List the major types of computer auxiliary storage. For each type, describe appropriate applications for your college. Justify each choice.

3. List the major types of file organization. For each type, describe appropriate applications for your college. Justify each choice.

4. Discuss the following statement: Computer users need not be concerned with the devices used to store data, since this is a concern of technicians.

CASE FOR DISCUSSION

Linda Ho is a lawyer who operates a small practice in Pasadena, California. Her specialty is patents and trademarks.

Ho's office is on the second floor over a real estate agency. On a clear day she can see the mountains from her window. At 7:30 A.M. one clear Monday morning Ho comes into her office, pours herself a cup of coffee, and sits down at her desk. She turns on her Compaq computer.

The computer has been programmed so that the first thing it does is retrieve a daily calendar that has been stored on its hard disk. Looking at the calendar, Ho is reminded that she has a lunch appointment with a client who wants to discuss a complex trademark infringement case. Also, she sees that some important papers have to be filed with a state office no later than 5:00 that afternoon. Not so bad. The schedule leaves her most of the day to do research on a big case that she is just starting. The case concerns patents in the area of biotechnology—a rapidly developing field of law in which Ho is thinking of specializing.

To begin her research, Ho slips a small silvery disk into her CD-ROM drive, thereby giving instant access to more than 100,000 pages of patent law cases and citations. It would take days to sift through all of that material in the library. Using her computer, Ho enters certain key words, beginning with "biotechnology." The computer consults an index and finds all the cases in which that term, and the others she has entered, are mentioned. Within minutes she has identified several previous court cases that appear to be relevant to the work she is now doing.

The cases she has identified total about twenty pages. She instructs her computer to print them out at draft speed on her dot-matrix printer. Despite her enthusiasm for the "electronic office," Ho, like many computer users, finds it easier to read long documents from paper than directly from the computer screen. Just before lunch Ho's secretary comes in with some correspondence that he has prepared, following instructions that Ho gave the day before. In the case of these short documents, paper is dispensed with. The secretary hands Ho a floppy disk that he has prepared on his own computer using a word-processing program. Before leaving to meet her client for lunch, Ho slips the disk into the floppy disk drive of her own machine and calls the letters up onto the screen. There are no major problems. She corrects the spelling of a client's name and changes a few other words here and there. She adds a last-minute idea to one of the letters. She then hands the disk back to her secretary, who will print an original of each letter for her signature. An extra copy of each letter will be stored on paper in the office file.

After a lunch in a downtown restaurant, Ho returns to the office. Before continuing her research on the biotechnology case, she calls up the file containing information on the case of the client with whom she had lunch. Consulting notes she made in the restaurant on the back of an envelope, she updates certain information in the file. Some major court dates have been changed, so she also enters these using the daily calendar program. She then throws the envelope into the wastebasket.

Before leaving, Ho signs the letters written earlier in the day and verifies that her secretary has filed the required documents on schedule. Her last task before leaving is the same each day. She inserts a special tape cartridge into the drive of a unit that sits on the desk beside the computer. In response to a few instructions, the computer downloads the entire 10-MB contents of her hard disk onto the cartridge. She locks the cartridge in the office safe before walking out the door.

CASE QUESTIONS

1. Why does Ho store her daily calendar on the hard disk of her computer rather than using a floppy disk, a RAM disk, or a CD-ROM disk?

2. If Ho did not have a CD-ROM drive for her computer, what would be the most practical alternative?

3. Why does Ho's secretary use floppy disks for preparing correspondence?

4. Why does Ho download the contents of her hard disk to tape each night before going home?

5. Ho's office is not a "paperless" office. Three uses of paper documents are mentioned. Why is paper still used in each case?

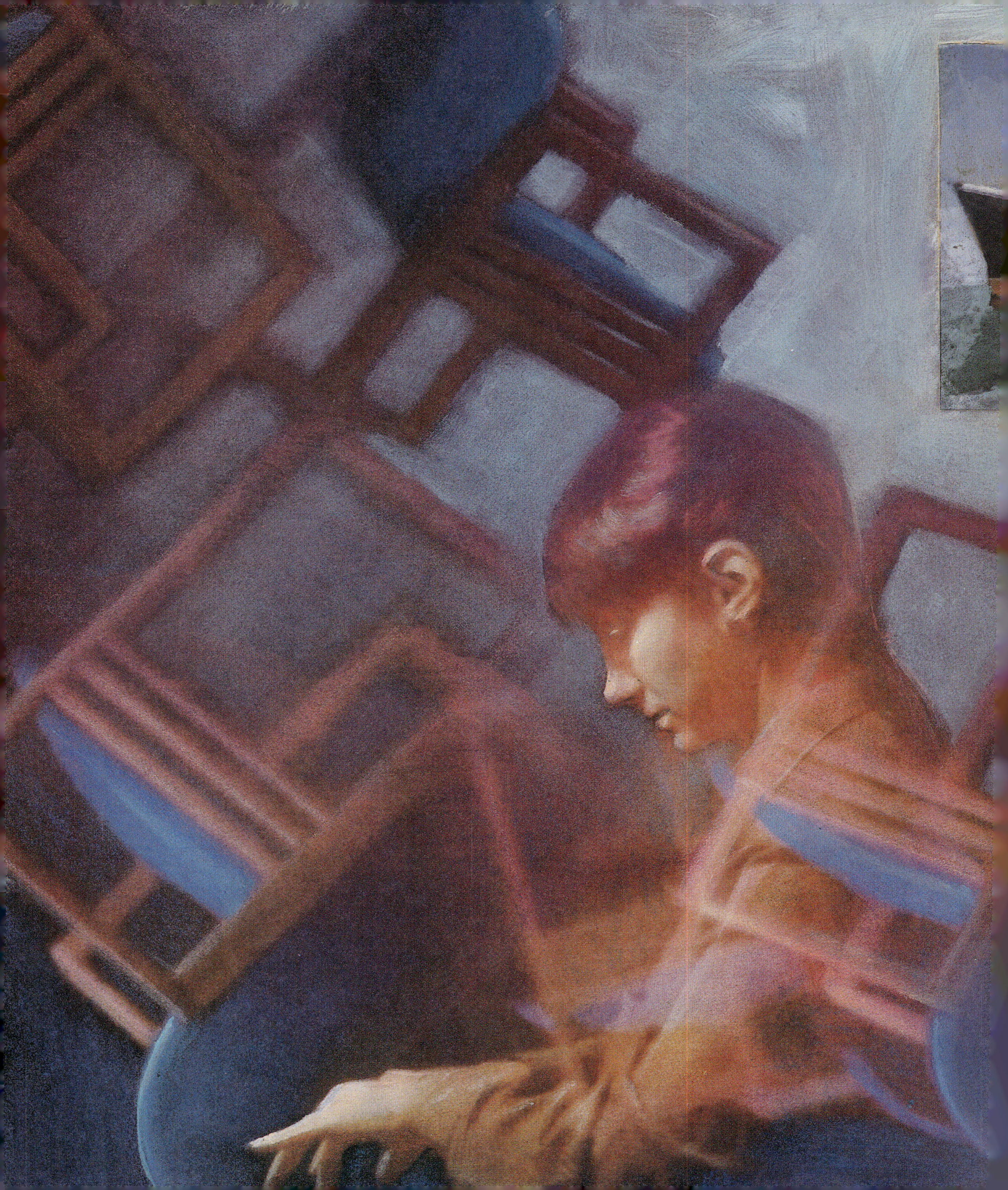

Data Communication

CHAPTER 6

ABC Shipping Brokers is a company in New York City that solves transportation problems for its clients. It has several branch offices in the city. In one of them, an agent, Jim White, is talking to a customer, Jennifer Rohrbach.

Rohrbach is the president of a firm that designs ergonomic office furniture for computer users. The furniture is built on contract by manufacturers in several locations and sold to customers throughout the world. Right now Rohrbach needs to ship a container of furniture by sea from a factory in Raleigh, North Carolina, to a customer in Liverpool, England. What port should the container be trucked to? How much will the shipping cost? When will the furniture arrive? Rohrbach needs to know all these things in order to confirm the deal.

White has worked for ABC for a number of years. In response to a request like this, he used to consult printed shipping schedules and tariff tables. The customer could come back and get a confirmation the next day, after it had been verified that all the space on that ship had not yet been sold, that the tariffs hadn't changed, and so on. Now, instead, he enters the request into the microcomputer on his desk and waits for it to be processed.

But how is White's computer able to give him the information that there is still space available at the quoted rate? How can White be sure that an agent in another ABC office hasn't just sold the last available space? White's microcomputer is able to handle this problem because it is linked by telephone line to the minicomputer in ABC's main office. That computer stores a data base that is maintained up to the minute, twenty-four hours a day.

In just a few seconds, the reply comes back. The furniture should be trucked to Norfolk, Virginia. It will go on the Liberian-registered freighter *Ocean Challenger* and will arrive in Liverpool on June 25. The total shipping cost is within a limit that is agreeable to both Rohrbach and her customer. The deal is closed on the spot.

Chapters 3, 4, and 5 discussed the different types of computers and the physical components of a computer system that enable it to accept, store, and process data and output information. This chapter presents another component of many individual and business computer systems: data communication. The process through which Jim White exchanged data with the minicomputer in ABC's main office is an example of data communication. We will look at other applications of data communication in business and home settings and at the hardware and software used in various settings.

When you have read this chapter, you should be able to:

1. Describe what data communication does, how it is used, and where it is used.
2. Define information utilities and discuss their applications in businesses and homes.
3. Use the basic terminology of data communication.
4. Name and describe the equipment used in data communication.
5. Differentiate among the major network configurations and suppliers.
6. Describe teleprocessing and discuss how it is used in business.
7. Describe distributed data processing and list its applications in business.
8. List the essential features of local area networks, compare them to multiuser systems, and describe the advantages of each.
9. Understand and use the key terms listed at the end of the chapter.

Data Communication Systems

Data communication
The transmission of data, information, and programs from one location to another.

Message
Data that is sent from a transmitter to a receiver, including the user's transaction and control information for the data communication system.

The lifeblood of business is information. As businesses become more widely dispersed, their growth and survival depend increasingly on information flowing rapidly and effortlessly from one branch of the company to another. Equally important to modern businesses is the flow of information to and from external sources such as customers. The transmission of data, information, and programs is called **data communication** or **telecommunication**. Data communication systems typically involve both transmission and processing of data.

Computerized data communication systems enable users to obtain the up-to-date data, information, and programs they need to do their work. These systems consist of the following components:

1. The *source* of data, which can be a person or a collection of data known as a *data bank*.
2. The *transmitter*, which is a computer or a video display terminal that sends the data in the form of a **message** from the source to the receiver.
3. The *channel*, which is the path over which the data travels from the source to the receiver.
4. The *receiver*, which is the computer or terminal that captures the data after it has been transmitted.
5. The *destination*, which is the person who eventually uses the data.

In the case of ABC Shipping Brokers, Jim White used his computer to inquire about available ships and rates. Here, the five components are as follows (see Figure 6-1a):

1. Jim White, who translates the customer's request into a form the computer can handle, is the *source*.
2. The *transmitter* is White's personal computer.
3. The *channel* is the telephone line that links White's branch office with ABC's main office.
4. The *receiver* is the minicomputer in the head office that decodes the message received and checks for shipping availability.

FIGURE 6-1

Components of Data Communication Systems

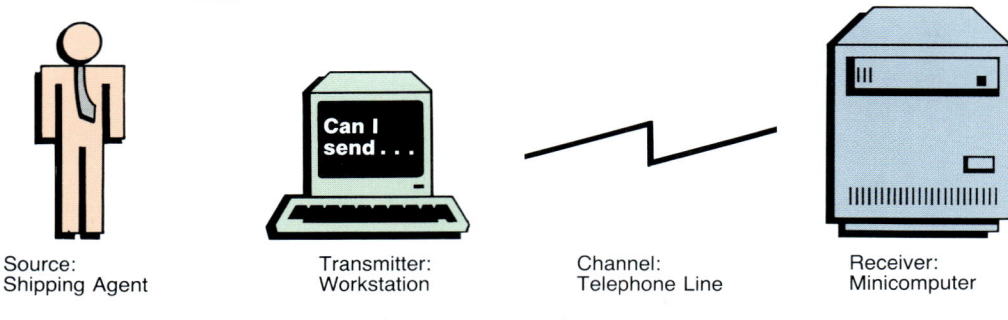

Source: Shipping Agent | Transmitter: Workstation | Channel: Telephone Line | Receiver: Minicomputer

(a) The customer's initial request

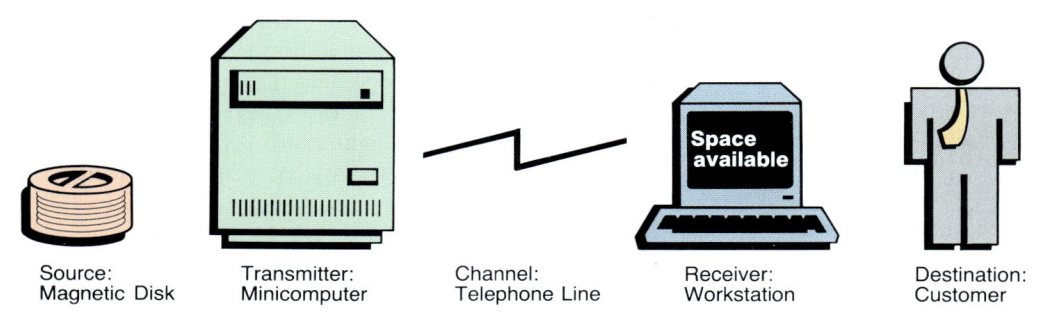

Source: Magnetic Disk | Transmitter: Minicomputer | Channel: Telephone Line | Receiver: Workstation | Destination: Customer

(b) The return message

5. The *destination*, in this case nonhuman, is the data base stored on the minicomputer, which is consulted and updated as a result of the request.

White's message, as is often the case with telecommunication, prompts a return message. For the return message, the components are as follows (see Figure 6-1b):
1. The data bank in the head office is now the *source*.
2. The *transmitter* is the minicomputer.
3. The *channel* is the telephone line, as before.
4. The *receiver* is White's personal computer.
5. The *destination* is Rohrbach, the customer who made the initial request to ship the furniture.

It should be clear from this example that the different components of a data communication system are not fixed but depend on the direction and the precise nature of the communication. Before looking at the details of how data communication systems are put together, let's look at some of their applications.

Data Communication Applications

A frequently asked question is, "When do you want it?" Often the answer is "Yesterday!" Data communication cannot furnish the answer yesterday, but it can furnish the answer so fast that it has replaced batch processing for most business uses. Without data communication, many developments, such as the "automated office" to be discussed in Chapter 14, simply would not exist. Data communication has also become an important aspect of the home-computer market. In fact, most of the computer applications discussed in the rest of this book involve data communication.

Data communication may be used externally, in which case the communication is with an outside agency, or it may be used internally, in which case all communication takes place within the organization. A major external application of data communication is information utilities.

Information Utilities

Information utilities, sometimes called *information services*, are collections of specialized information that are available on a fee basis to subscribers via personal computers or computer terminals equipped for telecommunication. Users receive the information via a local or long-distance telephone call. The following are a few examples of what businesses can obtain from information utilities:

- Financial information such as stock, bond, and commodity quotations; Dow Jones stock market averages and news reports; Dun & Bradstreet Index; Standard & Poor's Index.
- Information about airline and train schedules, availability of hotel and motel lodgings, car rental agencies.
- Computer conferencing, which enables people in many different locations to hold a conference without leaving their desks; some of these utilities provide a record of each participant's contributions.

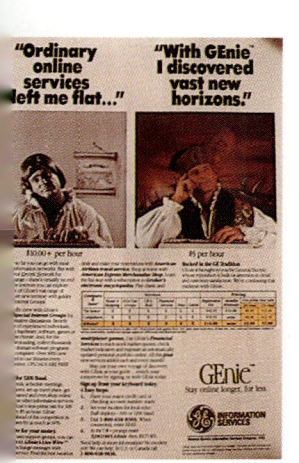

GEnie, a division of General Electric, is a popular supplier of information services to both individuals and corporations. (© Chris Pullo.)

Information utility
A collection of specialized information that is available on a fee basis to subscribers via personal computers or computer terminals.

CHAPTER 6 175 DATA COMMUNICATION

- Specialized information sources, including LEXIS for lawyers and AMA/NET for doctors.
- Economic data banks containing information provided by the government or by private institutions.

Dow Jones News/Retrieval, operated by the publishers of *The Wall Street Journal*, is one of the most versatile of the business-oriented information utilities. (See Box 6-1.) But individuals as well as businesses can benefit from the use of information utilities. Many of the services just listed, such as financial information and travel information, can also be accessed by individuals from their home computers. In fact, personal uses of information utilities are a major application of home computers. The following are some examples of information utilities that are often used by individuals:

- Electronic funds transfer, which allows subscribers to make financial transactions from their home computers.
- Electronic conferencing, which enables people to get together with others who share their interests; this is similar to computer conferencing. An example is BIX (BYTE Information Exchange), which allows subscribers to hold discussions with other microcomputer users.
- Electronic shopping, which enables subscribers to examine a catalog and purchase merchandise without leaving home; some electronic shopping services offer discounts.
- Research data banks, which can help students prepare term papers; they are available twenty-four hours a day, seven days a week.
- Entertainment services, such as games, movie and theatre reviews and schedules, ticket ordering services, and restaurant guides.

Internal Uses

Within a company or organization, data communication is used to transfer data, programs, and information from the point where they originate to the point where they are processed or used. As companies expand their operations geographically, internal data communication becomes even more important.

Data communication systems link one or more computers and their peripheral equipment, including storage devices and a variety of workstations. The data communication system may connect equipment within a single building or throughout the world. Even though such systems are usually on-line, offering rapid, sometimes instantaneous, response, they may also be off-line, offering a deferred response at the user's convenience. Both on-line and off-line systems involve a wide variety of special software and specialized communication equipment.

BOX 6-1

USING COMPUTERS

Dow Jones News/Retrieval

The Wall Street Journal, published by Dow Jones & Co., has been a leading business tool for more than 100 years. It began as a newsletter providing up-to-the-minute stories on financial markets for a handful of readers. Clerks copied the news by hand using carbon paper to make ten copies at a time. Runners then rushed the newsletter to offices in New York's financial district.

Technologies have changed, but *The Wall Street Journal* is still the leader in up-to-the-minute business news. It is now a fat newspaper with nationwide same-day distribution. In fact, the very size and frequency of this publication creates a problem for its users. How do you find that important story that was published last week or last month—the one that you didn't realize was so important at the time? It's somewhere in that stack of *Wall Street Journals* in the corner, isn't it? Or was it in the one you left on the subway last Wednesday?

If the personal computer on your desk has a modem and you are a subscriber to Dow Jones News/Retrieval, your problem is quickly solved. In response to a few keystrokes, your communication software automatically dials the number of the Dow Jones service and you are connected. The story you wanted had something to do with Diamond Shamrock, a company whose stock interests you. To search for the latest story on Diamond Shamrock, you simply type

```
//DJNEWS
.DIA 01
```

and the headline of the most recent story will be printed on your screen:

```
DIAMOND SHAMROCK AGREES TO
CLEAN UP NEW JERSEY TOXIC SITE
```

If you have forgotten that DIA is the abbreviation for Diamond Shamrock, you consult an index. If the headline tells you that this is the story you wanted, you can then call up the full story.

What if you have forgotten what company the story was about? Instead you just remember that there was a story about dioxin pollution in New Jersey that might affect your investment decision. No problem. Instead of //DJNEWS, you type //TEXT, and you have access to the "free text search" facility of Dow Jones News/Retrieval. You enter the key words DIOXIN and NEW JERSEY. You are then given the headline of the most recent story in which both of those words are mentioned. It is the story about Diamond Shamrock, and it does not matter that the word "dioxin" wasn't mentioned in the headline. Dow Jones's mainframe computer, to which your personal computer is now connected, has no problem sifting through every word of thousands of articles to find the one you are looking for.

There are lots of other things you can do with Dow Jones News/Retrieval besides look up headlines. You can get stock and bond price quotes, financial data, a weekly economic survey, a weather report, or even a movie review.

No doubt carbon paper was a technological marvel in its day. But this is even better.

Basic Data Communication Concepts

Although businesses and individuals can use data communication systems without knowing anything about data communication terminology and equipment, they can do so more efficiently and effectively if they are familiar with some basic concepts. This section discusses some of those concepts and provides an overview of the software that can be used to improve a data communication system.

A key factor in any data communication system is the speed of data transmission. This speed varies greatly, depending on the system's components. It can be measured in bits per second, commonly called **baud**. A rule of thumb states that 10 baud are equivalent to approximately one character per second. Thus, 300 baud are equivalent to about thirty characters per second. At this rate it takes about one minute to fill a computer screen, a slow speed for many applications.

Baud
The speed at which data is transmitted in a data communication system.

Communication Channels

Communication channels, also called links, lines, or circuits, provide the connection between the transmitter and the receiver. Communication channels differ in many aspects, including cost, speed, distance covered, reliability, noise, and security. Designers of data communication systems can choose from a wide variety of channels, including telegraph and Telex, telephone lines, coaxial cables, fiber optics, and microwave and satellite transmission. Many data communication systems combine two or more different types of channels. As data communication systems grow, designers may add new channels based on modern technology without discarding existing channels. In fact, many data communication systems are not fully computerized and rely on communication channels such as telegraph lines for some data transmission.

Telegraph Lines. The first communication channels, tele-

This user is composing a message on a microcomputer to be sent to a client by Telex. (Courtesy of RCA Corp.)

graph lines, enabled messages to be sent across the United States over one hundred years ago. Because of their slow speed by today's standards, they are better adapted to sending birthday greetings than they are to transmitting computer data. The nationwide Telex service provided by Western Union is a noncomputerized form of data communication that is used by businesses and individuals. Sending a Telex is an inexpensive, rapid way of confirming an order. Unlike the telephone, it provides a written record of the transaction.

Telephone Lines. Telephone systems may include any of the communication channels discussed in the following paragraphs. At present, the most common component of telephone systems is the familiar copper wire telephone line. In fact, the term *line* is often used to refer to any kind of communication channel and does not necessarily imply the presence of telephone lines.

There are several advantages to using the telephone for data communication. One is that it is extremely accessible—there are over 500 million telephones in the world, any two of which could be used to communicate with each other. In many countries telephone service is fast and reliable. And because the telephone system has been in existence for so long, a large portion of its capital cost has been recovered, making it a relatively inexpensive way to communicate.

Despite the many advantages of using the telephone system for data communication, it is not an ideal system. Its main disadvantages stem from the fact that the telephone was designed and developed for voice transmission, which is quite different from data transmission. For one thing, voice transmission does not require the same speed as data transmission. Another difference is that when there is poor transmission, telephone listeners automatically correct messages on the basis of their context, much as they do in face-to-face conversation. In a data communication system, that is not possible. If 1 bit of information is missing, it may be necessary to repeat the entire transmission.

Another disadvantage of using telephone lines for data transmission is that the quality and speed of standard telephone lines, also known as *dial-up lines*, are not suited to all users' needs. Many dial-up lines cannot transmit data at speeds exceeding 2400 baud without generating numerous errors. Users who transmit data between two points several hours per day on a regular basis can probably save money by leasing *dedicated lines*, which can transmit 9600 bits per second or more. Dedicated lines have been specially prepared, or *conditioned*, to reduce background noise and may also be conditioned to increase their transmission speed.

Both dial-up and dedicated lines are *voice-grade lines*, which means that neither is ideal for transmitting data. *Digital lines* are designed for data transmission. They transmit data at speeds of up to 56K bits per second and have a low error rate. However, they are considerably more expensive than voice-grade lines and are not available in all locations.

Coaxial Cables. Data can also be sent over *coaxial cables*. These cables are composed of a copper conductor surrounded by insulation, which itself is surrounded by a tube-shaped metal conductor. A large coaxial cable may transmit over 100,000 telephone conversations at a time without any appreciable amount of crosstalk (i.e., interference by neighboring conversations). Crosstalk is annoying in telephone conversations; it is unacceptable in data communication. Coaxial cable tends to be costly, however. Organizations commonly use coaxial cable to connect computers and workstations in buildings that are within a radius of a few miles.

Fiber Optics. Another technology that is used for data transmission is fiber optics cables. A *fiber optics cable* contains strands of glass that are thinner than human hair. A ½-inch fiber optics cable can replace a 6-inch coaxial cable. At present, fiber optics systems can transmit nearly 1 billion bits per second, or the equivalent of more than 15,000 ordinary telephone lines, over 25 miles without requiring signal amplification. In comparison, coaxial cables can transmit one-tenth that amount of data only a few miles before signal amplification is required.

Fiber optics cables offer several advantages as a data-trans-

A stylized image is transmitted through a coherent fiber optics bundle. A single fiber optics cable like the one shown here can replace 15,000 or more ordinary telephone lines. [(left) © C. Falco, Photo Researchers; (right) © Bill Pierce, Rainbow.]

mitting channel. One of these is price. In 1977, 1 meter of fiber optics cable cost $3.50; by 1985, the price had dropped to $0.25. During the same period the price of the 24-gauge copper wire commonly used in coaxial cable increased. Another advantage of fiber optics cable is that signals transmitted by this means cannot be tapped. This makes fiber optics ideal for military uses. In general, it is too expensive to replace existing cable systems with fiber optics, but many new systems are using this technology. It has been estimated that by 1990 more than one-quarter of all intracity transmissions in the United States will take place via fiber optics channels.

Microwave Transmission. A method of data transmission that eliminates the need for wires or cables is *microwave trans-*

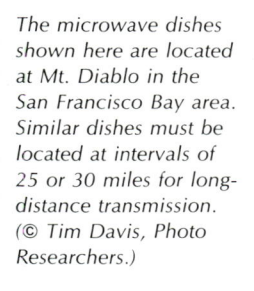

The microwave dishes shown here are located at Mt. Diablo in the San Francisco Bay area. Similar dishes must be located at intervals of 25 or 30 miles for long-distance transmission. (© Tim Davis, Photo Researchers.)

CHAPTER 6   181   DATA COMMUNICATION

This television communications satellite rises from the cargo bay of the Earth-orbiting shuttle Discovery. (Courtesy of National Aeronautics and Space Administration.)

mission. Microwave signals, a form of radio waves, travel in straight lines. Because of the barriers created by mountains and the curvature of the earth, terrestrial microwave stations must be within 25 or 30 miles of each other. Repeater stations retransmit data over longer distances. Microwave signals are rapid, but the need for repeater stations places constraints on their use.

Satellites. One way of eliminating the need for repeater stations is to use *communications satellites*. These satellites orbit the earth once a day and therefore appear to be stationary, eliminating the need for tracking. Cable television is the major user of commercial communications satellites. Because of the distance of the satellites from the earth (about 22,300 miles), it takes about one-half second to send a signal to a satellite and back. This amount of delay makes satellites unsuitable for certain applications.

Communication Terminology

Like any other discipline, data communication has its own language and terminology. Here we will discuss three aspects of communication—direction of transmission, protocols, and types of transmission signals—and define the most important terms in each.

Simplex Channel
(Source → Receiver)

Half-duplex Channel
(Source ↔ Receiver)

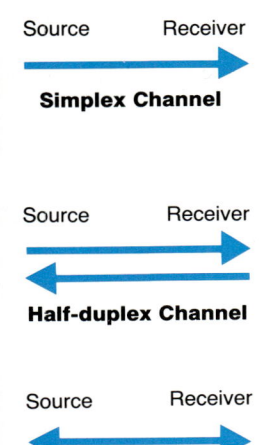

Full-duplex Channel
(Source ↔ Receiver)

Direction of Transmission. Communication media are classified on the basis of their ability to transmit in different directions. *Simplex channels* transmit a signal in only one direction. Radio stations transmit over simplex channels; listeners cannot communicate with the station by retransmitting radio waves. The line that connects an input device to a central computer may be a simplex channel.

Half-duplex channels transmit a signal in either of two directions, but only one at a time. A conversation between two people, as long as they don't interrupt each other, illustrates the half-duplex mode of communicating. First one person talks while the other listens; then they reverse roles. Dialogs between mainframe computers and terminals or between two microcomputers often take this form.

Full-duplex channels transmit signals in two directions at the same time in much the same way that a two-way street carries traffic in both directions simultaneously. Another example of full-duplex transmission is a conversation between two people who are both talking at the same time. Full-duplex transmission is faster than half-duplex transmission because it eliminates the delay that occurs when the direction of transmission is reversed. Full-duplex transmission is often used when two minicomputers or two mainframe computer systems communicate.

Protocols. Data communication involves transmitting data and programs among computers, terminals, and other equipment. For communication to be effective and efficient, the sending device and the receiving device must work together. A *protocol* is a set of procedures that are used to regulate the transfer of data between communication devices. Protocols include many functions, such as error detection and transmission, line and message control, and identification procedures. Major manufacturers of communication equipment provide their own protocols. The adoption of a standard protocol makes a communication system easier to organize and modify and usually increases its efficiency.

In this section we consider two important aspects of communication protocols: how the connection between the message receiver and the transmitter is initiated and how the message is transmitted. *Polling* is the method by which each communication device is asked, in a predetermined sequence, whether it has a message to transmit. If so, the polling operation is suspended during transmission. *Contention* is the method by which communication devices ask for a line for data communication. If two devices make their request at the same time, neither obtains the right to transmit and they each must make the request again.

FIGURE 6-2

Analog and Digital Signals

(a) Analog signals, similar in form to radio waves, can be readily transmitted over a wide variety of channels.

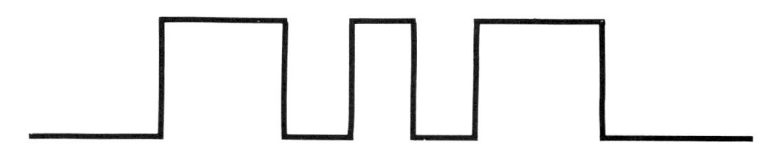

(b) Digital signals are present in computers and workstations. They cannot be readily transmitted over most channels.

Asynchronous Transmission

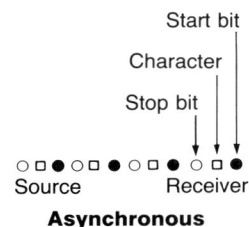

Start bit
Character
Stop bit

Source — Receiver

Synchronous Transmission

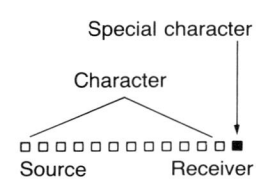

Special character
Character

Source — Receiver

Asynchronous transmission refers to communication in which the data is transmitted one character at a time between a sender and a receiver that are not synchronized with each other. It is often called *start-stop transmission* because the character that is transmitted is preceded by a *start bit* and terminated by one or two *stop bits*. Asynchronous transmission was the first type of transmission available and consequently is often used in older systems. Most dumb terminals use this transmission method, as do many smart or intelligent terminals and even microcomputers.

Synchronous transmission refers to communication in which the data is transmitted in blocks of characters between a sender and a receiver that are synchronized with each other. The message is preceded by one or more special characters whose function is to synchronize the sender and the receiver. Once these two units are synchronized, the message transmitted can be quite long. Synchronous transmission is faster than asynchronous transmission because it is continuous instead of starting and stopping for every character. However, it requires relatively expensive equipment such as a clock for synchronization and a buffer to collect a block of characters prior to transmission. It is used with some terminals and microcomputers as well as with other communication devices.

Type of Signals Transmitted. There are two basic types of signals in data communication systems. *Analog signals* are continous waves like those produced by the human voice. (See Figure 6-2a.) They are easily transmitted over long distances via standard telephone lines or the other communication channels described earlier. In contrast, *digital signals* are not continuous waves but take on a few, usually two, distinct states, which can be referred to as 0 and 1. (See Figure 6-2b.) Computers and terminals generate and process digital signals. Digital signals can be transmitted over short distances through special cables, but they do not lend themselves readily to transmission over longer distances by standard telephone lines or most other communication channels. They may, however, be transmitted over digital telephone lines, and digital lines are often used in telephone networks along with traditional telephone lines.

Communication Equipment and Software

Reliable, confidential, and cost-effective data communication requires other hardware and software besides communication channels. This section examines some of the hardware that is commonly used in data communication systems.

Modems. Many data communication systems make use of devices called **modems**. The word *modem* stands for *modulation-demodulation*. *Modulation* is the process of transforming a digital signal into an analog signal, and *demodulation* is the reverse process. Thus, at one end of the transmission a modem transforms the digital signals used in a computer or terminal into analog signals like those used in most communication channels. At the other end of the transmission, another modem transforms the analog signals back into digital signals.

The majority of modems are attached or built into a personal computer or terminal and plug directly into a standard telephone outlet. These are often called *direct-connect modems*. The speed of modems varies; those used with microcomputers typically process 300, 1200, or 2400 bits per second. At 1200 bits per second, it takes about fifteen seconds to fill a computer screen; at 2400 bits per second, this time is cut in half. The speed of a modem is important, since the faster the modem, the faster the transmission, and the faster the transmission, the lower the long-distance telephone charges. However, a high modem speed is not very useful if the available telephone lines cannot handle high-speed transmission. High-quality modems automatically reduce their transmission speed if available lines

This modem converts digital signals generated by a computer or terminal into analog signals for long-distance transmission. At the other end of the line, another modem makes the reverse conversion. (Courtesy of International Business Machines.)

Modem
A device that converts an analog signal into a digital signal or vice versa. The word modem is an abbreviation of modulation-demodulation.

CHAPTER 6   185   DATA COMMUNICATION

An acoustic coupler like the one shown here enables employees on the road to send data to the head office from a telephone booth. (Courtesy of Tandy Corp.)

are unable to handle high-speed transmission or if there is a slower modem at the receiving end of the line.

Modems for microcomputers have become more sophisticated in recent years. Features that once were optional have become standard for a wide variety of models. Among those features are auto-dial, in which the user types the phone number at the computer and the modem does the actual dialing, and auto-answer, in which the modem answers the phone and collects data automatically. Modems also offer users the ability to diagnose malfunctions in the sending or receiving modem or in the line, and the ability to monitor the call while it is in progress.

A special type of modem, called an *acoustic coupler*, enables users to attach a computer terminal or portable computer to a telephone receiver. They furnish virtually instant access to data communication wherever a telephone is handy. For example, with an acoustic coupler a salesperson on the road can use the nearest telephone to transmit data on the day's sales to a computer in the head office. The disadvantage of acoustic couplers is that they don't provide as good a connection as the more common direct-connect modems.

Communications Controllers. Another hardware device that is often used in data communication systems is a *communications controller*, a device that coordinates a group of terminals or microcomputers. A communications controller lets each workstation supply input to the computer in turn. It then transmits the output generated by the computer to the appropriate device or devices. The use of communications controllers can reduce line costs considerably.

Multiplexers and Concentrators. *Multiplexers* are devices that combine signals from several low-speed lines and then transmit the combined signal over a high-speed line. At the other end of the transmission, another multiplexer separates the combined signal into its original components. The single high-speed line usually costs less than the low-speed lines that it replaces.

Concentrators are intelligent multiplexers, which means that they can be programmed to perform a wide variety of message-handling activities, such as checking for transmission errors, modifying a message's transmission speed, and converting messages from one code to another. For example, a concentrator can convert a message coded in ASCII, which is used extensively with microcomputers, to EBCDIC, which is used mostly with larger IBM computers. Unlike multiplexers, which are used in pairs, concentrators are used one at a time. However, because of the rapid development of both multiplexers and concentrators the two terms are often used interchangeably.

To get an idea of how concentrators can improve a data communication system, consider the case of ABC Shipping Brokers, the company introduced earlier in the chapter. When ABC purchased a competitor, Allied Shipping Brokers of Philadelphia, it decided to centralize computer operations in the New York office. This involved merging data from the two operations and upgrading the minicomputer in the head office. It also meant choosing data communication equipment, including the communication channels that would be used to transmit data between Philadelphia and New York.

ABC could connect a 1200 bit per second line from each of its four Philadelphia offices to the head office in New York. But its line costs would be reduced if it used a single 4800 bit per second telephone line to link a multiplexer in the head office with another multiplexer in one of the Philadelphia offices. Then it could use short, fairly inexpensive lines to connect all the Philadelphia offices to the Philadelphia multiplexer. Another option would be to use a single concentrator instead of a pair of multiplexers. Because a concentrator can process messages and store them in case of overflow, its use might enable ABC to link its New York and Philadelphia offices with a 2400 bit per second line, thereby reducing line costs even further.

Front-End Processors. *Front-end processors*, also called *front-ends*, are computers that relieve the central processor of all communication tasks, thereby freeing it for data processing. Among the many functions of front-end processors are the following:

1. Assigning a serial number to each message and stamping it with the time and date of handling.
2. Compensating for differences in message speed and code between the sending and receiving devices.
3. Editing messages.

This Wang VS300 superminicomputer is being used as a front-end processor to relieve the central computer of all communication tasks. (Courtesy of Wang, Inc.)

4. Keeping a record or *log* of all messages that will be used for audit purposes.
5. Determining alternative routes for message transmission if a line is not functioning or is overloaded.
6. Polling workstations to determine whether they have a message to transmit or are ready to receive a message.

Multiplexers, concentrators, and front-end processors are used to increase productivity and decrease communication costs. Data communication specialists must carefully weigh both technical and financial considerations in deciding whether such equipment can meet their needs. An essential element in this decision is the likelihood of increased use of data communication within the organization in the future. It is common for data communication systems to grow faster than expected, since users frequently think of new applications for the system once they have become familiar with its capabilities.

Data Communication Software. Special software is required to handle telecommunication functions effectively. Because many types of telecommunication equipment are programmable, several of the functions described earlier, such as code conversion, may actually be performed by software. Other software functions include coordinating and scheduling the processes that occur within the telecommunication system, detecting transmission errors and correcting them or requesting retransmission, editing messages (e.g., making sure that numeric fields contain only numeric data), decoding messages and sending them to the proper destination, answering incoming calls and dialing outgoing calls, and gathering statistics on system performance. The software that performs these various functions may be located within the main computer, but in recent years the trend has been to locate it in the front-end processor, concentrator, communications controller, or modem.

Networks

Computer network
A data communication system that links computer systems and their workstations.

Computer networks are data communication systems that link computer systems and their workstations. Such networks enable users to share access to information such as airline flight availability and checking account balances and to update common files such as ticket reservations and passbook deposits and withdrawals. Some networks span the globe; others cover a relatively small area, perhaps 1 mile or less.

Many computer networks are born when a business outgrows its original minicomputer or mainframe. Often the company buys a compatible computer from the same manufacturer that supplied the first computer. As soon as two computers are available, users may seek to integrate them, thereby creating a network. Another reason for the creation of networks is the increasing business use of personal computers. When personal computers were first installed, their users tended to work independently, running their own personal-productivity programs and accessing their own files. But before long many users realized that they would be better off sharing programs and data with other users within the organization. Often the result was the creation of networks that include several microcomputers and perhaps one or more minicomputers or mainframes. In many organizations today, the mainframe network and the microcomputer network are connected and function as a unit.

Network Configurations

Computers of any size can be networked with each other; in fact, it is quite usual for networks to contain computers of different sizes. Networks also contain many kinds of software, communication equipment, and communication channels. This means that setting up a network is a complex process that requires careful study. Not only must the appropriate components be selected, but they need to be linked together in the way that will best meet the organization's data communication and data processing needs. Although each network has its own unique

FIGURE 6-3

A Star Network

The system's most powerful computer is at the center of the star.

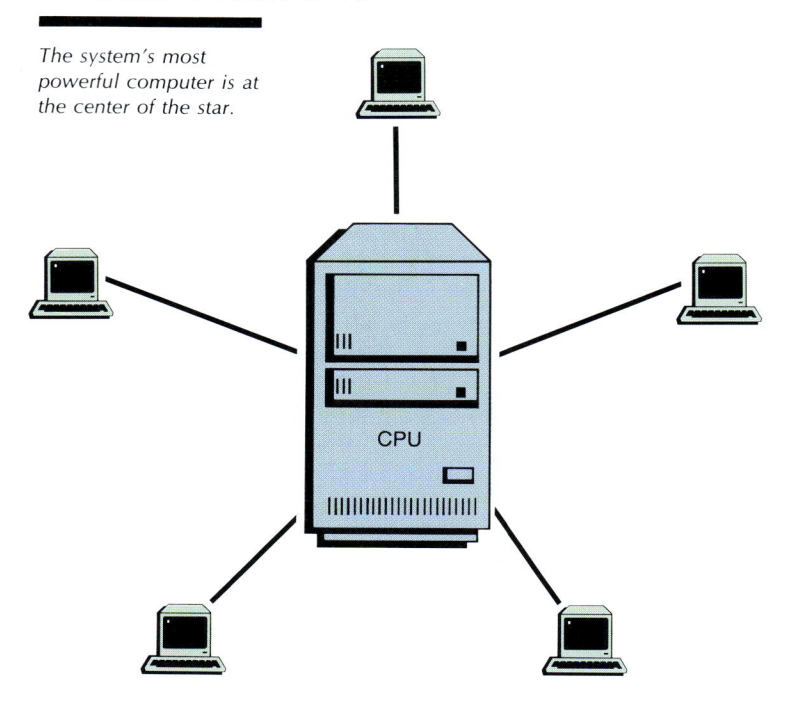

characteristics, network configurations can be classified into four general categories, depending on the physical arrangement of equipment in the system. Those categories are star networks, ring networks, bus networks, and hierarchical networks.

Star Networks. A network system in which the computers are arranged in a star pattern, such as the one in Figure 6-3, is called a *star network*. At the center of the star is the system's most powerful computer, and radiating out from the center are its less powerful computers or workstations. In a star network, all messages must pass through the central computer. A typical user of a star network is a centralized banking operation whose branches do not process data but send it to the central computer for processing.

Star networks are easy to expand; in most cases installing a link from the central computer to a new location does not interrupt service. But they have the disadvantage of relying on a single computer. If the central computer ceases to function, the

FIGURE 6-4

A Ring Network

All the computers in a ring network usually have approximately the same processing power.

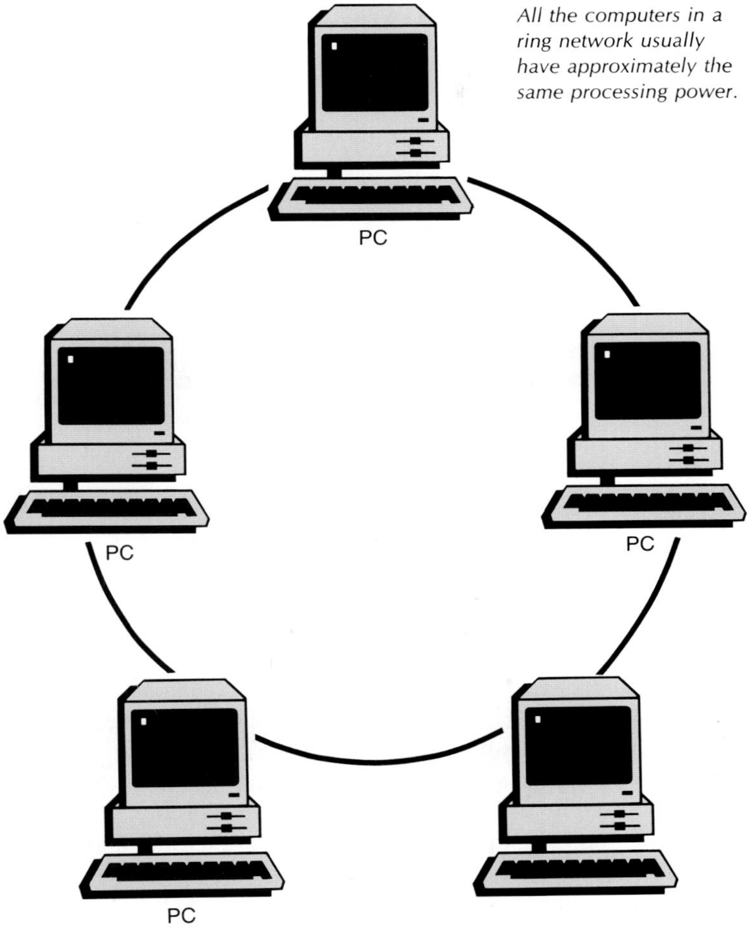

entire system is disrupted. Moreover, the line costs of star networks tend to be high.

Ring Networks. When computers are arranged in a circle as shown in Figure 6-4, the system is known as a *ring network*. Usually all of the computers in a ring network have approximately the same processing power. Because the failure of a single component can paralyze the entire ring, most ring networks are set up so that they can bypass a disabled unit if necessary.

CHAPTER 6 191 DATA COMMUNICATION

FIGURE 6-5

A Bus Network

In a bus network, all signals are sent to all of the devices in the network.

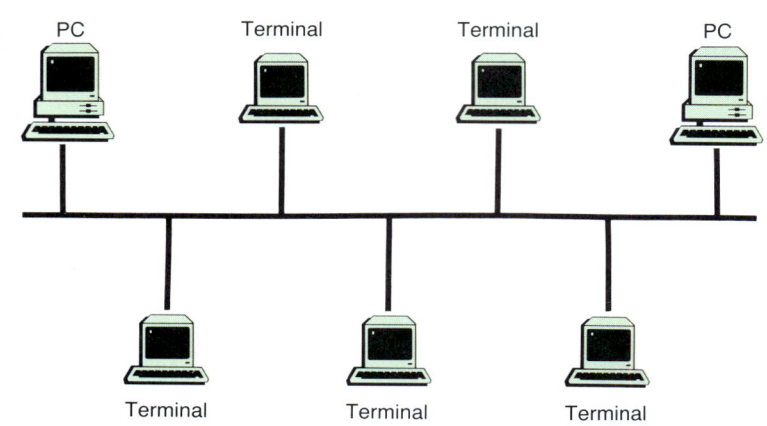

Ring networks may have lower line costs than star networks. However, the addition of a new computer to the system takes the network out of service because it breaks the ring. Also, each unit in the network passes on all transmissions, creating the need for special provisions to ensure security and confidentiality of data.

Bus Networks. Figure 6-5 illustrates *bus networks*, which are composed of a single full-duplex line connected to two or more computers. In a bus network, all signals go to all attached devices, thereby increasing the system's reliability. Bus networks are more flexible than ring or star networks and are a popular configuration for small network systems. They require less cable or telephone line than other types of networks. However, they are subject to interference due to signal reflection if the workstations are placed too near each other, and it is difficult to perform maintenance tasks while the system is in use.

Hierarchical Networks. A network system that is composed of several layers of computers is called a *hierarchical network*. In this type of network, a powerful central computer is attached to one or more smaller computers, each of which is attached to several microcomputers or terminals. (See Figure 6-6.) Some hierarchical networks are combinations of ring and star networks.

FIGURE 6-6

A Hierarchical Network

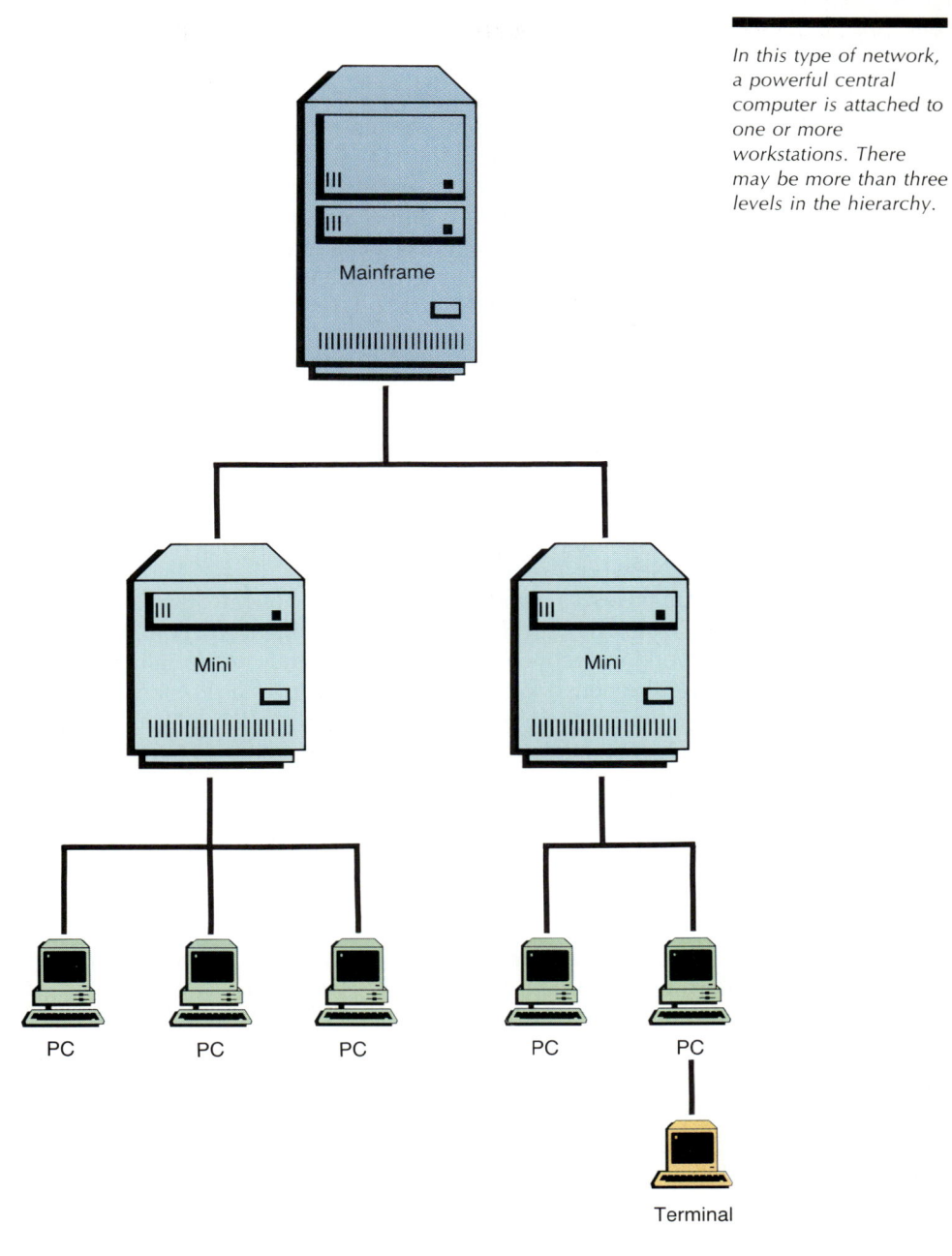

In this type of network, a powerful central computer is attached to one or more workstations. There may be more than three levels in the hierarchy.

CHAPTER 6   193   DATA COMMUNICATION

Network Suppliers

Once an organization has selected a configuration for its network, it has to decide on a supplier. There are three basic types of network suppliers: private networks, vendor networks, and value-added networks.

Private Networks. A *private network* is custom designed for a particular organization. Private networks typically contain a variety of equipment supplied by different manufacturers. Private networks have two main advantages: They are designed to handle the specific needs of the organization, and they are relatively secure, since other organizations cannot have direct access to them. On the other hand, they are expensive, and it is difficult and time-consuming for the organization to supervise their design and implementation.

Vendor Networks. A company can also choose to install a *vendor network*, a network that is put together by an outside organization. The vendor furnishes everything needed except the transmission lines, which are supplied by another source such as the telephone company. Most mainframe and minicomputer manufacturers supply vendor networks such as IBM's Systems Network Architecture (SNA).

Purchasing a vendor network has several advantages. The user can benefit from the vendor's experience in computing and networking technology. Security is likely to remain high because the network is not shared. If there is a problem, the user has only one party to contact, and the vendor is likely to maintain a long-term commitment to upgrading network components while maintaining their compatability. This approach also has some disadvantages, though: The cost can be quite high; the vendor is unlikely to use a competitor's components even if they are better suited to the user's needs; and the vendor may have more control over the network than the user.

Value-Added Networks. Some vendors lease communication lines and then "add value" to them, for example, by improving their speed and error-detection capability or providing data processing and storage services. The resulting networks are called *value-added networks*. Since the company pays only for services actually used, value-added networks are relatively inexpensive. Another advantage is that they support data communication between one company and another. But because resources are shared with outsiders, security can be a problem. And, as in the case of vendor networks, users do not have control of the network.

Teleprocessing

Teleprocessing
A data communication system in which only one computer processes applications programs.

A **teleprocessing** system is a data communication system in which only one computer processes application programs. (See Figure 6-7.) Most teleprocessing systems include computerized devices such as front-end processors to handle the system's communication needs; this equipment frees the central computer for the actual processing of data. Strictly speaking, teleprocessing systems that contain only one computer should not be considered networks; however, because teleprocessing systems and networks share many characteristics, teleprocessing systems are classified as star networks.

Teleprocessing systems were developed in the 1960s to meet the needs of businesses that had to send information back and forth among different locations. Although other kinds of data communication systems have been developed in the ensuing years, teleprocessing remains an important method of data processing and communication in many organizations.

Types of Systems. There are several types of teleprocessing systems, each serving a particular user need. *Remote batch systems* enable people to enter data and programs at their convenience. The data is then processed according to a predetermined schedule and returned to the user later for correction, if necessary. Users still have to wait for the results of the processing, but the waiting time is much less than would be the case if the information were sent through the mail. A typical use of a remote batch system is to prepare the payroll for a company with many branches.

On-line query systems are used to obtain answers within a few seconds to questions such as, "How many first-class seats are available for flight 136 to Chicago?" With these systems, a marketing manager can quickly obtain information on product sales for use in making such decisions as whether to launch a new product line. Many on-line query systems are user-friendly and allow users to ask questions themselves, without the aid of computer specialists.

On-line transaction systems are teleprocessing systems whose users can update files by entering a *transaction* such as, "Reserve two first-class seats on flight 136 to Chicago." The update transaction must be entered in a standard form. Unlike queries, update transactions actually change the data in the system; therefore, processing updates is more complicated than processing queries. For example, if only one seat is left on flight 136 to Chicago and two transactions attempt to reserve it, the system must determine which transaction has priority and assign the seat accordingly, rejecting the second transaction.

FIGURE 6-7

Teleprocessing

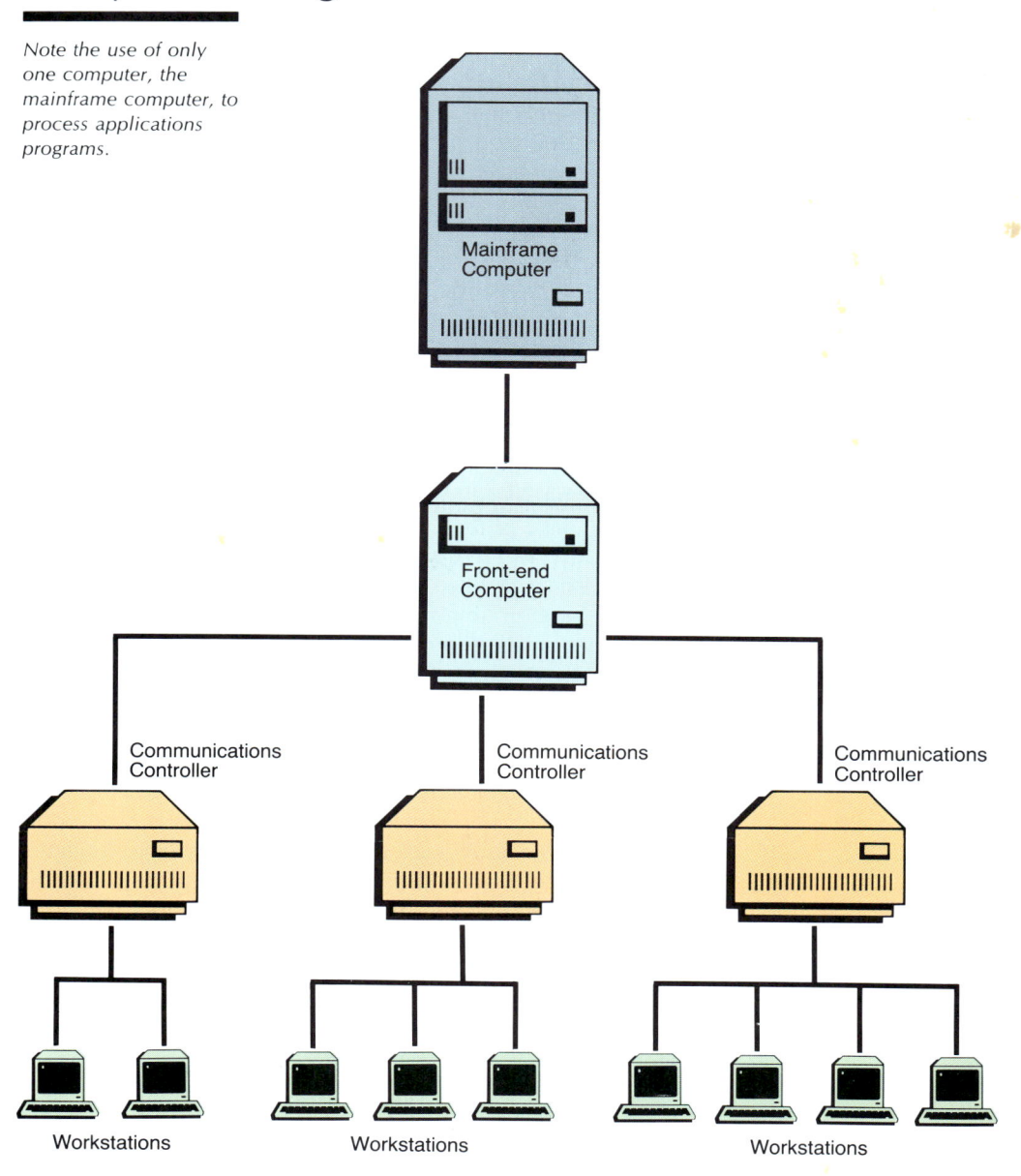

Note the use of only one computer, the mainframe computer, to process applications programs.

On-line program development systems enable programmers to develop and test programs at a workstation. With these systems, programmers can see almost instantly whether or not their programs are correct. On-line program development systems require greater processing power and more sophisticated software than the batch-processing facilities that have traditionally been used for program development. But the increased productivity made possible by such a system usually makes up for its higher cost.

Time-Sharing. Companies commonly access a teleprocessing system via a cost-saving method known as **time-sharing**. With time-sharing, many users share a teleprocessing system or network. Each user is charged only for the resources, such as processing time or magnetic-disk file storage, that he or she actually uses. The value of time-sharing results from its fast *response time*, that is, the time it takes for the computer to begin to reply to a user's request; that time is often less than one second. Depending on the system's processing power and workload, each of its dozens or hundreds of users may have the impression that the system is working for him or her alone.

Backup and Recovery. Successful teleprocessing requires specific procedures for *backup* and *recovery*, that is, restarting a system after it has failed. One reason such procedures are necessary is that it is virtually impossible to repeat the exact sequence of events that caused a system to fail. As an illustration of this problem, consider a bank's teleprocessing system that failed just at the moment that a customer was making a deposit. If a teller wrongly assumed that the system had failed *before* the deposit was made, the customer would be credited with the same deposit twice. On the other hand, if the teller wrongly assumed that the system had failed *after* the deposit was made, the customer would not be credited with the deposit even though he or she had actually deposited funds. To simplify recovery procedures, many teleprocessing systems stamp each transaction with the date, the time of day, a serial transaction number, and the addresses of the message's source and destination.

Security. In the days before teleprocessing, security was less of a problem than it is today. Users had to present their requests for information to computer specialists, who then submitted the requests to the computer. Since teleprocessing tends to make the company's information resources readily available to users, strict security measures are needed to protect "sensitive" information. One such measure is the use of **passwords**, or individ-

---

Time-sharing

A processing method in which large numbers of users share a tele-processing system or network, with each user charged only for the resources that are actually used.

Password

A code that permits a user to access a computer system.

ual access codes, that allow only authorized users to access the system. Another popular technique is *data encryption*, in which data is scrambled according to a secret code before being transmitted. Both of these techniques are widely used in all kinds of computer systems, although neither is foolproof.

Distributed Data Processing

In contrast to teleprocessing, a data communication system in which more than one computer processes users' applications programs is a **distributed data processing (DDP)** system. A DDP system can be a ring, star, or hierarchical network. Such systems typically include minicomputers and microcomputers but may combine computers of all sizes. Each distributed data processing system is unique, since it is designed to meet an organization's specific needs.

Figure 6-8 illustrates a manufacturing company's DDP. In this hierarchical network there are one or more microcomputers at each of the firm's branch offices and plants, a minicomputer at each of its four regional offices, and a mainframe computer at its head office. The microcomputers process data at each of the branch offices and plants, prepare reports for their personnel, and send summary data to the minicomputer in the regional office. Each minicomputer processes the summary data from the branch offices and plants along with other data generated in the regional office, prepares reports for personnel in the regional office, and sends a summary of this data to the mainframe computer in the head office. The mainframe computer processes the summary data received from the regional offices along with other data generated in the head office and prepares reports for the head office personnel. Data also flows in the other direction, from the head office to the branch offices and from the branch offices to the local offices and plants.

Compared with teleprocessing, DDP can be less expensive since each location processes data on the spot and transmits only summary data to the next level of the hierarchy. This reduces the costs of communication lines and other equipment. Another potential advantage of DDP compared to teleprocessing is that users have greater control over the data processing function. For example, DDP users can determine how the local workstation will be run and purchase additional equipment if necessary.

A significant factor in the decision to install a DDP system is the issue of program standardization. Users generally want their applications programs to run the same way on every workstation in the system. One way to achieve program standardiza-

> **Distributed data processing (DDP)**
> *A data communication system in which more than one computer is used to process applications programs.*

FIGURE 6-8

Distributed Data Processing System for a Manufacturing Company

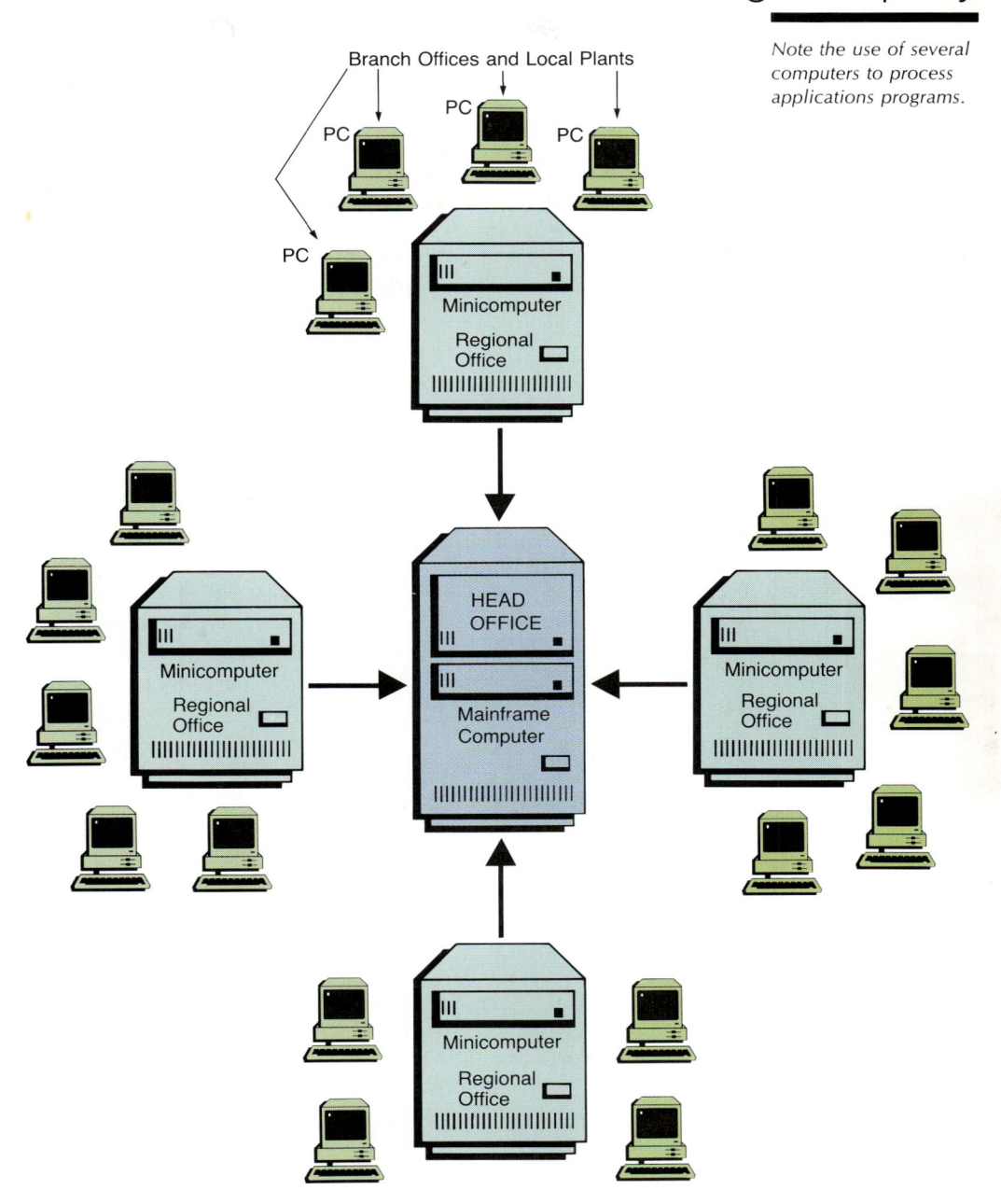

Note the use of several computers to process applications programs.

CHAPTER 6 199 DATA COMMUNICATION

tion is to send applications programs from the central computer over communication lines to the regional and local computers, a process known as *downloading*. However, given the variety of equipment used in DDP systems, it is not always possible for all computers in the system to use the same programs. Also, DDP applications programs may be too complicated for the average user in a local office. But since most companies cannot afford to post technical personnel in their local offices, such personnel are usually found only at the central location.

Clearly, it is in the organization's best interest to make its DDP system as foolproof as possible, as well as to train users to deal with the kinds of problems that may arise in such a system. Users need to be given unambiguous instructions about what to do and whom to notify if the system ceases to function. In addition, a system will run more efficiently if it is developed with an eye toward possible future needs.

Local Area Networks

Distributed data processing systems continue to pose a challenge to computer personnel and users in the late 1980s. In fact, one type of DDP, the **local area network (LAN)**, is one of the most dynamic fields of data communication. Almost from the day personal computers became popular there was a demand for ways to link them with computers of all sizes, but especially with other personal computers and with mainframes. This job is more difficult than it seems, partly because companies usually purchase many different kinds of personal computers. A local area network can coordinate widely different computer systems.

Local area networks are telecommunication networks that cover a geographically limited area, usually less than 1 or 2 miles. A typical LAN connects personal-computer systems and other equipment such as television sets, copying machines, and building alarms within an office building or among a series of buildings such as those on a university campus. As in the case of conventional networks, different LAN hardware configurations meet different needs; common configurations for LANs include star, ring, and bus networks.

Local area networks require high-speed transmission lines that enable personal-computer users to send files that may be thousands of characters long to one or more other personal computers. Coaxial cable, which can transmit data at speeds of up to 100 million bits per second, has been the standard for LANs. Recently, fiber optics cable has also come into use in this application. (See Box 6-2.) Because of the LAN's rapid

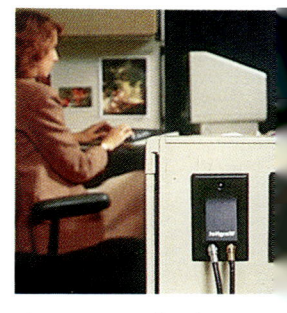

Local area network (LAN)
A data communication network that covers a geographically limited area, often connecting microcomputers, peripheral devices, and other office machines.

The Wang Net local area network enables users within a radius of a mile or two to share computer hardware and software. (Courtesy of Wang, Inc.)

BOX 6-2

FRONTIERS IN TECHNOLOGY

Fiber Optics for Local Area Networks

Many of the initial applications of fiber optics technology have been for long-distance communication. Work is even under way on an undersea system that will link the United States to France and the United Kingdom, replacing satellite transmission channels for both voice and data communication. But now fiber optics are beginning to find applications on a much smaller scale, in local area networks (LANs) that link computers within a single building. So-called campus networks are also being installed using fiber optics to link a group of adjoining buildings. Examples can be found at Rockefeller Center in New York and at the campuses of Stanford University and the University of Pittsburg.

Sheer speed and capacity are useful in LANs just as they are in long-distance communication. For example, firms that use computer-aided design and computer-aided manufacturing (CAD/CAM) may need to transmit huge volumes of data between departments or to computerized machine tools on the factory floor. But there are other advantages that often are even more important. One is the immunity from electrical interference that fiber optics enjoys. For example, Manhattan's World Trade Center is being wired with fiber optics cable because rooftop antennas that collect microwave and video transmissions could interfere with computer terminals connected by coaxial cable. Security from eavesdropping is a second key advantage of fiber optics.

Up to this point, LANs have turned to fiber optics technology only when these aspects of communication quality have outweighed the higher cost. In LAN applications, it is not the cost of the cable itself that is crucial, but the cost of the devices needed to link them to the individual microcomputers and mainframe computers that make up the network. Costs are coming down, however. For example, optical transceivers will soon be available for a fraction of the price of the separate devices formerly used to transmit and receive optical signals.

Items as mundane as cable connectors and couplers have raised the price of fiber optics in LAN applications. A coaxial cable connector can be bought for a few cents at any electronics store. But the hair-thin fibers of glass that carry optical signals must be lined up precisely if an adequate connection is to be made. Moderately priced connectors that automatically attain the required degree of precision are only now reaching the market.

Some observers worry that firms will have a hard time finding uses for the huge transmission capacities of fiber optics. Others, such as Jon Silber, manager of marketing research at Kessler Marketing Intelligence, a firm that specializes in fiber optics, believes that this will not be a problem. Silber points to the huge demand on transmission capacity that is made by such growing applications as computer graphics, CAD/CAM, picture phones, and other forms of video. In these applications, the advantages of fiber optics over copper wire come to the fore.

Source: Martin Pyykkonen, "Networking with Light," *High Technology*, February 1986, pp. 25–31.

speed, several users can share expensive equipment, such as laser printers, that a single personal-computer user might not be able to justify or afford.

Multiuser Systems

Sometimes the objective of sharing data and resources can be met by a company's regular computer system without additional equipment. For example, one way to share an expensive printer is to buy a simple "A-B" switch that allows two neighboring computers to access it. When all the computers in an office or other work environment are the same model or compatibles, data can be transferred from one to another by being copied onto a floppy disk. In addition, certain kinds of software can "translate" information from one computer system to another.

Another way in which users within a company can share data and resources is with a multiuser system. *Multiuser systems* are composed of a large microcomputer or a small minicomputer and several dumb terminals. They are used in many offices, especially where employees tend to run the same applications. The advantages of multiuser systems relative to LANs are as follows:

- It is generally less costly to add dumb terminals to a multiuser system than to add microcomputers to a local area network.
- Multiuser systems come from a single vendor, whereas LANs are usually composed of computers and equipment from several different manufacturers. This means that only one

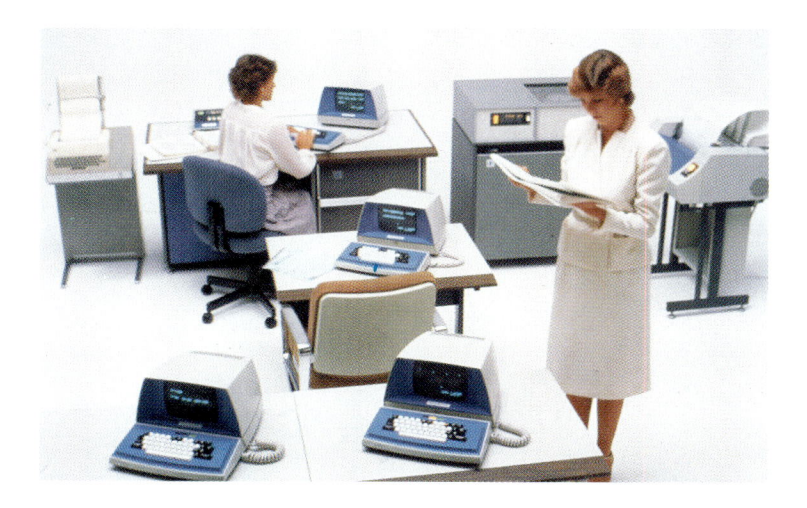

Multiuser systems are a feasible alternative to local area networks for many applications.

company needs to be contacted when a problem arises in a multiuser system, whereas LAN users might have to contact several companies.
- Multiuser systems are available in complete form, ready to be demonstrated and installed. Many LANs are not available off-the-shelf but are custom made. In such cases users cannot see ahead of time what they are purchasing.
- Multiuser systems offer homogeneous software and hardware, which means that users can work at any available workstation. In a LAN, by contrast, only certain programs work on certain computers, and users may have to wait for a particular computer to become available.
- Data integrity is easier to achieve in multiuser systems than in a LAN. Because the data on multiuser systems is centralized, it is easier to institute and carry out backup procedures.
- Because the workstations in a multiuser system are dumb terminals without disk drives, users cannot carry home floppy disks that contain confidential information.

This is not to say that there is no reason to invest in a LAN instead of a multiuser system. LANs offer the following advantages to users:
- Personal-productivity software is more readily available for LANs than for multiuser systems. Even when such software is available on multiuser systems, it tends to be less sophisticated and harder to use.
- The variety of software and hardware available on a local area network is far greater than that available on a multiuser system.
- Many LANs run around the clock, offering users considerable flexibility in choosing working conditions and hours.
- The failure of a LAN workstation is less critical than the failure of a multiuser system's central processor, because it is often possible to add a microcomputer to a LAN without having to shut down the rest of the network.

It should be clear from the variety of advantages offered by both LANs and multiuser systems that choosing between them is not a simple matter. The needs of the user in terms of cost, flexibility, software sophistication, and other factors must be kept in mind. Indeed, software may be more important than hardware—hardware alone cannot solve users' problems. The nature and importance of software are discussed in detail in the next four chapters.

SUMMARY

1. Data communication, also called **telecommunication**, is the transmission of data, information, or programs from one location to another. Computerized data communication involves a source of data and a transmitter that sends a **message** from the source over a channel to a receiver.

2. Data communication may be used externally or internally. A major external use of data communication is **information utilities**, or collections of specialized information that are available on a fee basis to subscribers.

3. The speed of data transmission is measured in bits per second, or **baud.** Communication channels include telegraph, Telex, and telephone lines; fiber optics cables; and microwave and satellite transmission. The most widely used communication channel is the telephone system. Communication channels may be simplex, half-duplex, or full-duplex.

4. Two types of signals are present in data communication systems. Analog signals are continous waves that are easily transmitted over long distances via communication channels. Digital signals combine 0s and 1s and are used to process data within a computer.

5. The most widely used communication equipment is the **modem**, a device that converts digital signals into analog signals and vice versa. Other communication devices are used to reduce line costs; they include communications controllers, multiplexers, and concentrators. Front-end processors are used to reduce the communication load on the central processor.

6. A **computer network** is a data communication system that links computer systems and their workstations. Common network configurations are the star, ring, bus, and hierarchical configurations. Network suppliers include private networks, vendor networks, and value-added networks.

7. A **teleprocessing** system is a type of network in which only one computer processes applications programs; others may handle communication. There are four main types of teleprocessing systems: remote batch systems, on-line query systems, on-line transaction systems, and on-line program development systems. Many teleprocessing systems provide **time-sharing**, which can give dozens or hundreds of users access to the central computer at the same time.

8. Distributed data processing (DDP) is the use of more than one computer to process applications programs. DDP systems may be less expensive than teleprocessing systems and provide users with greater control over the data processing function, but they are more difficult to organize and standardize.

9. Local area networks (LANs) are data communication networks that cover a geographically limited area. They can include personal computers and peripherals as well as a wide variety of office machines, all connected by high-speed lines owned by the user company. A set of large microcomputers or small minicomputers connected with dumb terminals is known as a multiuser system. Because LANs offer personal-productivity programs, they are often chosen in preference to multiuser systems.

KEY TERMS

data communication

telecommunication

message

information utility

baud

modem

computer network

teleprocessing

time-sharing

password

distributed data processing (DDP)

local area network (LAN)

REVIEW QUESTIONS

1. What is data communication? What are its components?

2. What are four typical information utilities. List several business and home applications of information utilities.

3. What do communication channels do? Describe and compare four types of channels.

4. Define the following terms: *protocol*, *polling*, *contention*, *asynchronous transmission*, and *synchronous transmission*.

5. Distinguish between analog and digital signals.

6. What does a modem do? Describe three other types of communication equipment, giving the advantages of each.

7. What is a computer network? Describe the most common network configurations and the advantages of each.

8. Define teleprocessing and compare the four main types of teleprocessing systems. Give an example of how each could be used.

9. Describe and give an example of distributed data processing. How does it differ from teleprocessing?

10. Describe and give examples of a local area network and a multiuser system.

11. Compare LANs to multiuser systems, giving the advantages of each.

APPLICATIONS

1. Report on a microcomputer user with access to other computers via data communication. Describe what each of the two computers does.

2. Talk to someone who has a home computer equipped with a modem.

3. Interview a user of a local area network. Describe what the user does with the LAN and whether it meets his or her needs.

4. Discuss the following statement: Data communication is an unnecessary luxury for most businesses.

CASE FOR DISCUSSION

Ralph is head of marketing management at a medium-sized auto parts maker in Columbus, Indiana. Several years ago all of the product managers, salespeople, financial managers, and others in his company got personal computers. The company was careful about compatibility in selecting hardware and software. People working on related projects can exchange data by passing floppy disks around, but it is hard to keep the data on the disks up-to-date as they are passed from one user to another. Sometimes it is also possible to arrange to have data from the firm's mainframe computer backed up on floppy disks, but the data processing department may take two or three days to do this. Ralph has complained about these problems to the head of the company and has suggested that a local area network could be set up to link the PCs to one another and to the mainframe. His boss asks him to look into the matter. To get some ideas, he arranges to have lunch with Jan, a consultant specializing in LANs. Here is part of their conversation:

JAN: You'd better start by telling me what you expect to be able to do with a LAN that you can't do now.
RALPH: The first thing, I think, is data sharing. We have worked out a very good order-entry and order-tracking system, and more and more people are using it all the time. People are entering orders, changing orders, checking stocks of various items, and so forth. Disks are all over the place. Halfway through a telephone session with a client, you realize you're working with an out-of-date version of the data base and you've just sold something that's out of stock. Then there's the matter of getting data out of the mainframe. The data processing department doesn't always seem to take our PCs seriously as part of their computing resources. I think we could operate more efficiently if we were able to communicate directly.
JAN: Those are both legitimate reasons to want to network. If you don't mind, though, I'll play devil's advocate a little. For example, you realize that one of the main appeals of personal computers in the first place was to free the user from the central control of a data processing department. Are you prepared to go back under central control?

RALPH: I hadn't thought of it that way, but I suppose it is something we'd have to put up with to get the benefits. Anyway, if I wanted to do something on my own—work on a spreadsheet, say—I could still unplug from the network, couldn't I?

JAN: If the network was designed the right way, yes. But privacy and security are big issues in networking. That's one of the reasons my clients find that they need a consultant like me to help set things up and train their people in how to use it.

RALPH: I guess what you're saying is that networks don't just come in a box, ready for you to plug in. What else do you do other than advise on security issues?

JAN: Well, we find that a lot of people underestimate the amount of tinkering and fiddling a network needs. And the tinkering isn't only with hardware. There are utility programs to write, backup procedures to work out, no end of things. When you get right down to it, a network doesn't make administrative duties go away or eliminate the need for planning. That's why my services are in demand.

RALPH: So when you add the cost of your work to the cost of the hardware and software that needs to be bought, how much is it all going to cost?

JAN: There is a rule of thumb that networking shouldn't cost more than 15 percent of the cost of the system as a whole, but that's a very optimistic figure. There are lots of hidden costs that push it over that. One of those costs is my time, at $120 an hour. By the time I've customized menus, converted programs, and handled a whole lot of other details, I'd say my average bill was about $15,000—and that's on top of the basic costs for hardware and software.

RALPH: Hmm. I'm glad I talked to you for the price of a lunch before I brought you in at $120 an hour!

JAN: Well, remember, I was just being devil's advocate. Sometimes the gains in efficiency from a network are so great that they'll pay off the cost in six months.

Source: Based on ideas from Robert Luhn, "The Organization LAN," *PC World*, February 1985, pp. 72–80.

CASE QUESTIONS

1. After lunch Ralph goes back to his office and gets out a yellow pad. He draws a line down the middle. On the left, he writes "reasons to network." On the right, he writes "reasons not to network." Fill in the two columns for him.

2. Using the yellow pad lists as a basis, write a short note to the boss with your recommendations.

P

ART 3

Software

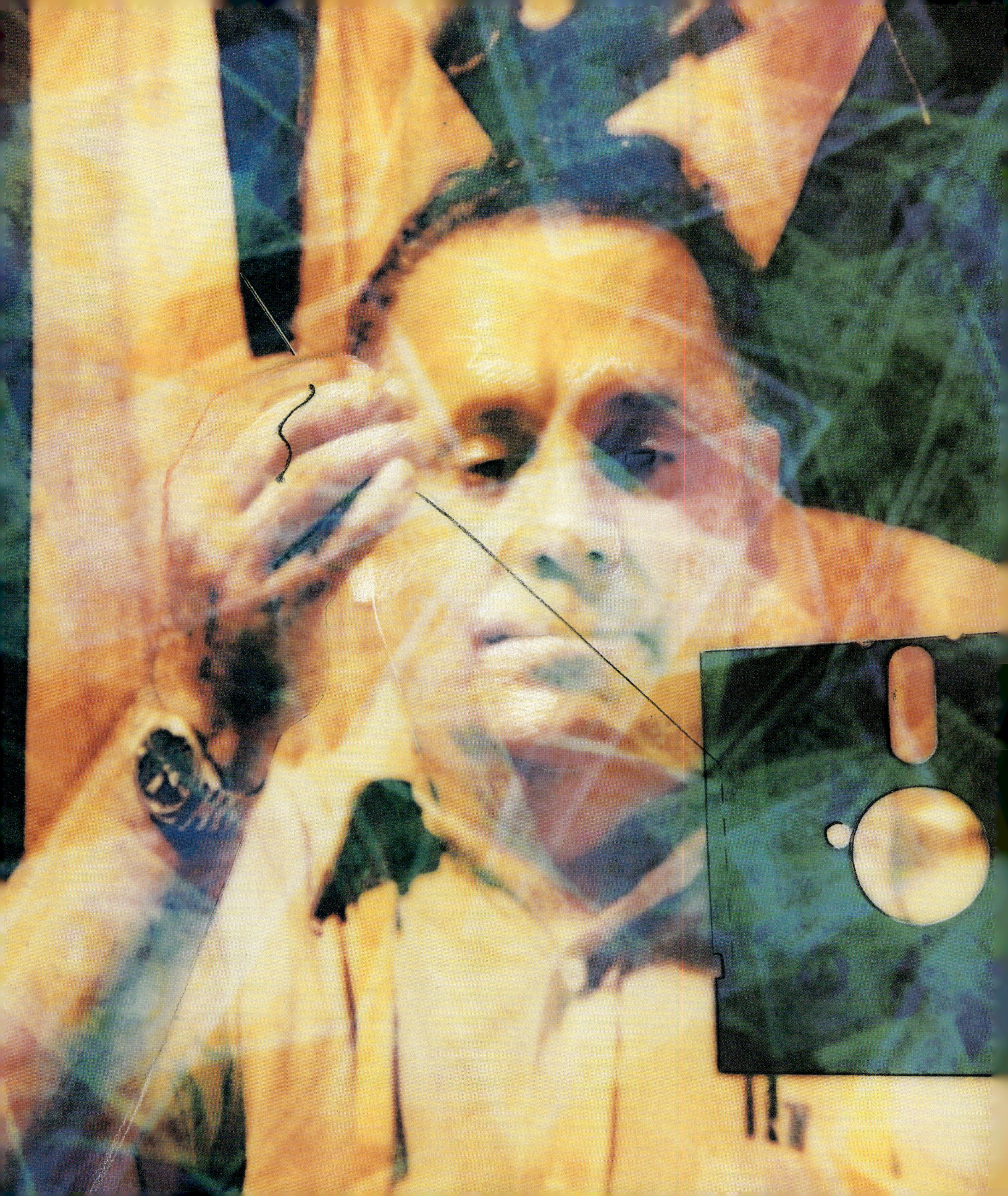

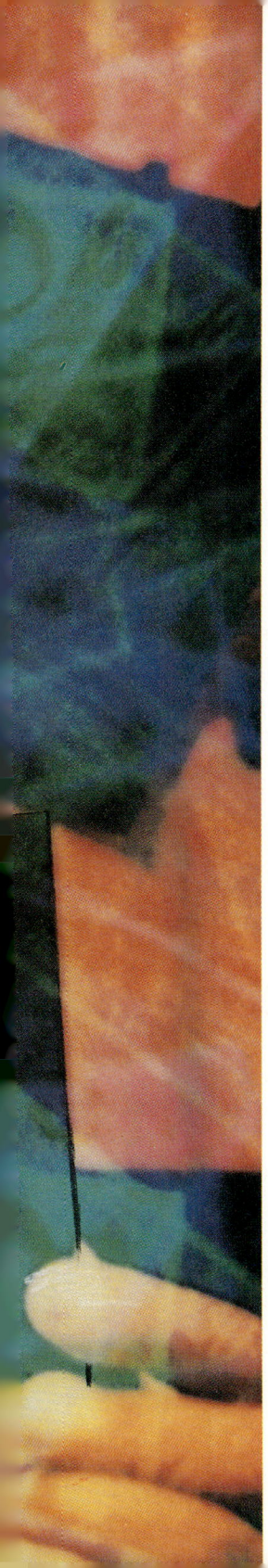

Programming: Process, Tools, Techniques

CHAPTER

7

"I never knew there was so much to running your own business! Orders are pouring in, but the more work we do, the more things get out of control. Little things keep nickel-and-diming away the profit I ought to be making by now."

The speaker was Jim Ryan, head of Acme Manufacturing. He was talking to Georgia Rimaldi, formerly his boss at a big machine tool company in the Midwest. When the big company had had trouble with overseas suppliers of simple plastic parts, such as control knobs, Ryan had seen an opportunity. Rimaldi had said, "Go for it—and keep in touch. You're going to make mistakes, and you won't be able to help us unless you let me help you."

Because he was closer than the overseas suppliers, Ryan could make sure his parts always arrived on time. Because he knew the big firm's needs, the parts he supplied were always suited to their applications. But Ryan's background in manufacturing didn't help him with all aspects of running a small business.

"Let me give you an example," he said. "Every day the mail comes full of bills from suppliers. Some are $20 for glue and tape, others are $10,000 for basic materials. Sometimes the big ones get paid late and we miss a big discount because my people got behind paying the little bills. Sometimes they pay early, and that puts a strain on our cash flow. Sometimes we end up sending five little checks to the same supplier because the invoices didn't all come in the mail together. It seems like I'm always out on the factory floor trouble-shooting, and I haven't had time to organize the office work the way it should be."

"I'd say straightening out those accounts payable was a job for a computer," replied Rimaldi.

"Yeah, I've got a computer, too, and a good guy to run it. He does a good job on our billing, but he says our payables problem doesn't really fit any of his packaged software. So that part of the job is still being done by hand."

"Well," said Rimaldi, "our experience is that packaged software can never cover every job there is to be done, either in a large company or in a small one. We've got a programmer who does some freelance work. She might be able to help you out. It seems to me that the job won't be so hard if a simple, structured approach is used."

Hardware, discussed in Part 2, is an essential part of all computer systems. Hardware alone, however, cannot straighten out Acme Manufacturing's accounts payable problem. Without software, hardware is no more than a collection of electronic circuits, disk drives, printers, and the like. In this part of the book, therefore, we turn to software.

This chapter describes the procedures and techniques used in writing computer programs, using Acme's accounts payable problem as a case in point. Five phases of computer programming are illustrated. The chapter then discusses some tools and techniques that can enhance a programmer's productivity and facilitate communication between programmers and users.

When you have read this chapter, you should be able to:

1. Explain why it is important for business professionals to know about programming.

2. Identify the role of computer professionals and business professionals in the program development process.

3. List and describe the five phases of the program development process.

4. Discuss the importance of structured programming, including its impact on the five phases of the programming process.

5. Describe the diagraming techniques used in the programming process.

6. Understand and use the key terms listed at the end of the chapter.

The Program Development Process

Although many inexpensive, easy-to-use software packages are available, it is still necessary for future business professionals to know about programming. For one thing, packaged software often doesn't meet the specific needs of a business. Hence, businesses spend billions of dollars each year to develop software to help solve their problems. That software is developed by programmers. At the very least, therefore, business professionals must be able to communicate with programmers, specify what is needed, and make sure that the final product meets their needs.

There are additional benefits to knowing both the theory and the practice of computer programming. As we will see in this chapter, the program development process requires organization, attention to detail, perseverance, and logical thinking—all qualities that are valuable in the business world. Furthermore, business professionals are increasingly likely to use personal-

This photograph illustrates only a few of the tens of thousands of software packages available. In spite of the number and variety of software packages on the market, business and other users often must contract for custom software to meet their needs.

productivity software such as electronic spreadsheets and file- or data-base management programs. A good understanding of the programming process enhances the user's ability to make the most of such software.

The programming process has often been compared to building a house. Both the programming process and the house-building process can be completed successfully and efficiently only if everyone involved follows a plan, always taking care to devote the appropriate amount of effort to each of many phases. In both kinds of projects, the first phase is to set objectives in the light of constraints such as the amount of money and time available to complete the project. After objectives have been defined, work proceeds on the preparation of more detailed specifications—the diagrams that represent the program to be developed, which can be compared to blueprints that depict the future house. Once those involved in the project are sure that the diagrams or blueprints describe a feasible solution to the objectives (within the given constraints), it is time to begin the actual construction.

During the construction phase it is necessary to test for errors. The earlier an error is found, either in the programming process or in the house construction process, the less expensive it is to repair. After the programmer and the builder have tested their respective products and are reasonably sure that they are free from serious errors and meet the objectives set earlier, the products are transferred to new owners—to the appropriate business department or the home buyer.

In practice, no matter how well the product has been tested, the new owner will inevitably be faced with errors. Neither a computer program nor a house is ever completely finished. Both require constant maintenance and upgrading to meet future needs. But with proper attention to planning, design, construction, and maintenance, both can provide major benefits to their owners.

Programmers and Systems Analysts

Just as it takes a variety of skilled personnel to build a house, it takes a variety of personnel, both technical and nontechnical, to carry out the programming process. Programmers are responsible for implementing a computerized solution to an organization's needs. They communicate with the computer via one or more specialized "languages" that direct the computer to perform calculations efficiently and rapidly. But a computerized solution is meaningless if it fails to meet the user's needs.

This programmer is in the final steps of preparing a sales analysis program for a medium-sized textile business. The programming field offers many opportunities for handicapped workers. (© Freda Leinwand.)

Because programmers are computer specialists and not business specialists, they are often aided by systems analysts who combine technical knowledge with practical experience and communication skills. The need for systems analysts and their precise role in the program development process depends on the scope of the project and its future impact on users. Chapter 12 investigates the system development process, a lengthy, complex process that has a greater impact on the way people work than the program development process. This chapter examines a programming project with a relatively modest goal, one that does not threaten to create substantial changes within the organization. In cases such as this, a systems analyst may not be required; a senior programmer with solid business experience can often replace the analyst.

Other technical personnel who may be required to make the program perform adequately include the computer operator, who is responsible for the actual running of the computer, and data control personnel, who are responsible for supplying the computer system with data and recording the results of computer processing. It is essential for users to be represented in the program development process. In fact, excluding users from this process is likely to result in a program that does not meet their needs.

Steps in the Programming Process

The programming process consists of five steps:
1. Defining the problem
2. Designing the solution

An essential element in the success of any programming project is a series of meetings between users and technical personnel to iron out problems and make sure that users' needs are being met. (© Frank Siteman, Rainbow.)

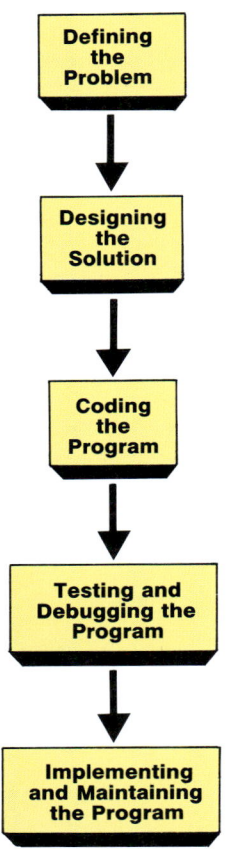

The Program Development Process

- Defining the Problem
- Designing the Solution
- Coding the Program
- Testing and Debugging the Program
- Implementing and Maintaining the Program

3. Coding the program
4. Testing and debugging the program
5. Implementing and maintaining the program

Each of these steps will be defined and illustrated in this section. The rest of the chapter will explore the programming tools and techniques associated with each step.

Defining the Problem. The most critical step in the programming process is defining the problem to be solved. Since users often do not know exactly what they want the computer to accomplish for them, computer programmers and systems analysts are expected to help them specify a goal, such as scheduling payment of the company's bills or calculating the minimum number of items to keep in inventory. The more precise the goal, the easier it is for programmers to focus their efforts on helping the user achieve it. An early, precise definition of the problem to be solved reduces the chance of disappointments and misunderstandings later.

Once the problem to be solved has been defined in detail, the computer specialists estimate the program's cost and the time needed to write it and put it into service. If necessary, they work with users to scale down the solution to meet budgetary and other constraints.

To better understand the problem definition step of the programming process, consider the initial meeting between Jim Ryan of Acme Manufacturing and Esther Smythe, the freelance programmer. Ryan, you will recall, intends to use the computer to help schedule the payment of Acme's bills. He tells Smythe that he wants to improve Acme's cash flow by paying all bills on the last day possible without incurring any late payment charges. In order to define the problem to be solved in clear terms, Smythe asks specific questions such as what daily volume of bills is to be paid, whether Ryan wants the computer to produce the actual checks or only to suggest which checks are to be written, and how people will use the output reports. Smythe also draws sketches of output reports, which Ryan modifies to suit his specifications.

Because the definition of the problem is so fundamental to the program's success and because errors and misunderstandings are so frequent, this initial phase includes written **documentation**, which in this case consists of a report stating the agreed-upon problem definition, a description of the desired output, and a detailed list of the inputs required to yield the eventual output. It also includes a preliminary estimate of the cost, personnel, and computer resources necessary to produce the solution, and a tentative schedule indicating when the solution will be available. In defining the problem, Smythe and Ryan consult with people in Acme's accounts payable department. Once all the parties involved are satisfied, the design phase of programming can begin.

Designing the Solution. After the users and computer specialists have jointly determined what the problem is, it is necessary to decide how the problem will be solved. If the report prepared in phase 1 is unclear, inconsistent, or incomplete, the computer specialists and users must meet again to clarify the problem. Finally the programmer begins to design the solution by developing an algorithm.

An **algorithm** is a set of well-defined rules for solving a problem in a finite number of steps. In computer terms, it is the set of processing steps required to transform inputs into output. A recipe is an algorithm; it lists the detailed steps necessary to transform ingredients such as flour, butter, sugar, and eggs (input) into a cake (output). Programmers are often tempted to start coding a program before completing the algorithm. This is just as dangerous as starting to bake a cake without first making sure all the ingredients are available.

The first step in designing the solution is to determine the desired output and design its format. The output that Ryan wants is a report suggesting which of Acme's bills should be paid on which date, together with a list of available discounts. Next the input is considered. In this case the input includes Acme's existing accounts payable master file, data on suppliers' discount policies, a daily indication of the company's cash reserve, and the bank rate for short-term loans.

Many tools are available to help programmers prepare algo-

Documentation
A detailed written description of a program or a system.

Algorithm
A set of well-defined rules for solving a problem in a finite number of steps.

Pseudocode

An informal language that is used to express algorithms in a natural fashion. The word pseudocode is often used to refer to the document itself as well as to the language in which it is expressed.

rithms. Among these is **pseudocode, an informal language that is used to represent the details of a computer program**. Smythe uses pseudocode and other tools (discussed in detail in the next section) to describe the algorithm that will serve as the foundation for the program she is developing. Here is an early version of the algorithm expressed in pseudocode. (Smythe's comments or questions are placed between asterisks.)

Create table of supplier discount policies	* not all suppliers give discounts *
Read accounts payable master file	* AP83-02 *
Loop while there are bills to process	* usually about fifty bills*
Find supplier on table	* what if cannot find? *
	* how often is the table changed ? *
Calculate and store discount	* on total bill or ? *
Read accounts payable master file	* keep reading *
Endloop	
Sort bills to pay	* what if several bills from one supplier? *
	* with the same date? on different dates? *
Print report discounts available	
Print report bills to pay	* totals? *

    * Note: Ryan said something about the daily interest rate. Perhaps if we have to borrow money it may be less costly to forgo the discount and pay the bill later—must look into this. *

    As programmers develop algorithms and design solutions, they inevitably discover that some details and information are missing, incomplete, or in error. In such cases they return to the user for clarification. Programmers are not expected to decide business policy or to know all the specifics of a business application; they are expected to ask the user for such information and to design the solution and write algorithms accordingly, making relevant suggestions when necessary.

    As Smythe writes the algorithm for Acme's accounts payable discount program, she might have to ask application-related questions such as whether the discount is on the entire bill or only on the basic charge, exclusive of freight and tax. Or she might need information such as the source of input data, what data is currently available, how often the program or programs will be run, and how much computer time and additional resources each processing run will require. Some of these questions are of a technical nature; others should be directed to Ryan and to the users for whom the program is being designed.

    The completed pseudocode and the answers to the additional questions asked by the programmer provide the basis for a *solution design report. This report also includes updated projections of costs and a revised schedule.* Because of the technical nature of some material, it is advisable to include a nontechnical summary for the benefit of the managers who will approve or reject the solution design report. When the report has been approved, work proceeds on the next step, coding.

Coding the Program. Pseudocode is an informal language that is used in designing a program; it cannot be input to a computer. Before the program can be input, it must be coded. Coding is the process of expressing an algorithm in a form that the computer can understand, that is, in a special computer language such as COBOL, FORTRAN, or BASIC. If the algorithm has been written in a fairly detailed pseudocode, this step is relatively straightforward. The programmer translates the solution design into instructions in the programming language, filling in any information that was omitted during the previous step. (A sufficiently detailed pseudocode can be translated into almost any programming language. The choice of an appropriate programming language is discussed in the next chapter.)

Translating pseudocode into a programming language requires a thorough knowledge of that language. For example, the pseudocode statement

Read accounts payable master file

is translated into several COBOL instructions, one of which might be

```
READ ACCOUNTS-PAY-MASTER-FILE
     AT END MOVE 'YES' TO END-FLAG.
```

Because these highly technical instructions depend on the specific programming language chosen and are not part of the business problem to be solved, they normally are not included in the pseudocode.

Let's return to the Acme Manufacturing example to see how coding works in a business situation. Smythe, the programmer who designed the accounts payable program, will be helped in this phase by Leo MacKay, a computer systems major who often works with her.

MacKay codes the program in COBOL, one of the most commonly used programming languages for mainframe computers, following the specifications in Smythe's pseudocode. The result is a set of instructions. The program is fairly long, so MacKay enters it into a terminal with the aid of an *editor,* or software similar to a word processor that is used in creating and modifying computer programs. (Some programmers use word processors for this task.) When the program is complete, he enters a command that sends it to the central computer. The computer then translates the program from COBOL into a form that it can process, that is, into binary form. This translation process may involve several steps. The COBOL instruction

Coding
The process of translating an algorithm into a computer language such as COBOL, FORTRAN, or BASIC. The word code *is often used to refer to the finished program.*

CHAPTER 7 **219** PROGRAMMING

```
READ ACCOUNTS-PAY-MASTER-FILE
    AT END MOVE "YES' TO END-FLAG.
```

would be translated into a form such as

```
0111100010010100100010101010001100
0000111001010010001110000100100 0
```

etc.

Since businesses' needs are always changing, programs must be designed and written so that they can be easily modified. It is disruptive, as well as financially unfeasible, to rewrite a program from scratch whenever a change is required. In addition, it is common for several programmers to work on a program, and it is not unusual for different people to design the program, code it, and modify it. Thus, programs must be coded in a form that is easy to read and understand by any experienced programmer who is familiar with the language being used.

Testing and Debugging the Program. The overwhelming majority of programs do not work properly the first time they are run, and even apparently correct programs may contain errors. At this point the next step, testing and debugging, begins. **Testing** is the process of determining whether a program contains errors that prevent it from doing what it was intended to do. **Debugging** is the process of finding those errors, which are known as *bugs*. The length and difficulty of this step should not be underestimated; in many cases it takes longer for a programmer to test and debug a program than to code it.

There are three types of bugs: syntax errors, logic errors, and run-time errors. *Syntax errors* are mistakes in spelling, punctuation, spacing, word usage, and other coding rules that prevent the translation process from being carried out successfully. For example, because of a typographical error, MacKay entered the word RED instead of READ. As a result, instead of producing a list of discounts, the computer generated an *error message*:

```
* unknown verb
```

MacKay made another syntax error when he forgot a hyphen in REPORT-BILLS-TO-PAY. This generated the error message

```
* unknown identifier
```

When all syntax errors have been corrected, the translation process can be completed and the resulting program will run, perhaps to completion. However, the program may still contain certain other errors. A *logic error* occurs when an instruction commands the computer to do something different from what is really intended. For example, a logic error occurs when a

Testing
The process of determining whether a program contains errors that prevent it from doing what it was intended to do.

Debugging
The process of finding bugs, or errors, that prevent a program from doing what it is supposed to do.

This programmer is checking a thirty-eight-page printout in an effort to determine which instruction caused a run-time error. (© Robert J. Witkowski, The Image Bank.)

programmer incorrectly codes a formula with a minus sign instead of a plus sign. In this case the computer has no trouble carrying out the calculation, but the result will be incorrect. Some logic errors are easy to locate; others can take days or even weeks to find. A *run-time error* prevents the program from running to completion. For example, when it expects to read a number it might read a character such as B, which it cannot process. Run-time errors also may be hard to find. Therefore, it is essential to test a program exhaustively before it is put into service. It is necessary to develop a set of test data (e.g., billing dates and amounts) that can be used in testing the program for logic and run-time errors.

We return to Acme Manufacturing to see how MacKay tested and debugged his program to find an error that could have important consequences. Because Acme's suppliers have different discount policies, MacKay spent a considerable amount of time testing cases involving different suppliers. The documentation indicated that XYZ Distributors offers discounts of 2 percent for bills of up to $10,000.00 and 2.5 percent for bills of $10,000.00 and above if they are paid within ten days. During a test run for this supplier, however, a bill of $10,000.00 was discounted by $200.00 instead of $250.00. MacKay reread the supplier's discount specifications and proceeded to verify the way the program carried out this calculation. He used an editor to scan the program, looking for the value 10000.00. (The program will not contain the value $10,000.00.) The editor located the value 10000.00 in the following instruction:

```
IF NET-AMOUNT GREATER THAN 10000.00
    DISC-RATE = 0.025
ELSE
    DISC-RATE = 0.02.
```

We can translate this COBOL instruction into English as follows: If the bill to be paid is greater than 10000.00 ($10,000.00), the discount rate is 0.025 (2.5 percent); otherwise the discount rate is 0.02 (2 percent). This instruction is not a correct rendition of the supplier's discount policy: For a $10,000.00 bill, the COBOL program as it stands calculates a 2 percent discount whereas the supplier offers a 2.5 percent discount.

Once MacKay had found the error, he corrected the instruction to read as follows:

```
IF NET-AMOUNT GREATER THAN 10000.00
OR NET-AMOUNT EQUAL TO 10000.00
    DISC-RATE = 0.025
ELSE
    DISC-RATE = 0.02.
```

Before rerunning the program, he checked to be sure that the program did not contain the same or similar errors in other instructions. To do this he commanded the editor to find every occurrence of the word GREATER and, as an added precaution, every occurrence of the word LESS. At each occurrence of these words he determined whether a change was necessary.

To speed the testing and debugging process, many programmers use a type of software known as a *debugging package*. With a debugging package, the programmer can stop the program at any point, enter test data, and see the effects immediately. Many debugging packages permit the programmer to obtain a complete list of the program's instructions in the order in which they were executed. In essence, debugging packages allow the programmer to run the program in slow motion. For example, MacKay can stop the program when it reaches the discount calculation, enter the value 10000.00 (and other values such as the supplier's name or number), restart the program, and stop it once again when it outputs the discount amount.

As in other steps of the programming process, adequate documentation of the testing and debugging phase of program development is extremely important. It is necessary to record test results and program changes so that programmers who work on the program at a later date will understand in detail what it does and why it was written in its present form. In the absence of accurate, readable documentation, programmers who must modify the program are likely to make the same or similar errors as were made previously; this wastes both programmer time and computer processing time.

Implementing and Maintaining the Program. Once a program has been tested and found to be error-free, it can be *implemented* or put into service. The program is then ready for the final step: maintenance.

Some details of program performance cannot be known precisely until the program is actually used. For example, until MacKay sees his discount program in use, he cannot determine precisely how long it takes to run and what resources, such as magnetic-disk usage and computer paper, it requires. Also, when many people start using a program, it will be tested in ways that the programmer never imagined. Users' needs change, and new bugs surface. **Program maintenance** is the process of revising the program to meet new requirements and correct any bugs that users find.

Shortly after Acme Manufacturing started using the discount program, Ryan and MacKay met to discuss Acme's revised re-

Program maintenance
The process of revising a program to meet new requirements and eliminate bugs.

quirements and the bugs that users had discovered. One user, for example, had found that the program did not take leap years into account. The user was unable to enter any bills dated February 29. MacKay corrected this problem quickly, but he didn't stop there. Like any good programmer, when faced with an error he looked beyond the immediate symptoms. For example, he surmised that if the program would not accept any input dated February 29 it probably would not count February 29 when calculating the ten days for payment. He tested this hypothesis and, after determining the exact nature of the problem, corrected it. He wrote a special program segment designed to process calendar dates for leap years and made it available, along with the appropriate documentation, to the other programmers in the computer services department.

The other facet of program maintenance is writing modifications to meet user requests. These requests are an indication of user satisfaction with the program; if users found the program inadequate for their needs, it is highly unlikely that they would ask for program modifications. Instead, they would request a new program and perhaps a new programmer. In the case of the Acme discount program, Ryan wanted the computer to accompany every proposed discount with a list of other bills from the same supplier. Armed with this list, accounts payable personnel could decide to send a single check to the supplier and save the time and money involved in writing several checks, even if this meant paying some bills earlier than necessary.

To get a better idea of how a program is modified, let us suppose that supplier PDQ, which offers a 2 percent discount on all bills paid within ten days, has sent Acme the following bills: invoice no. 13528 dated March 1 for $12,527.89 and invoice number 13634 dated March 9 for $78.13. The present version of Acme's accounts payable discount program indicates that invoice number 13528 may be paid on or before March 11 to obtain the discount and that invoice no. 13634 may be paid on or before March 19 to obtain the discount. The program does not relate these two bills from the same supplier. It would be advantageous for Acme to pay both bills on March 11 and save the cost of writing and processing an additional check. But the accounts payable personnel do not have the time to figure this out; on March 11 they issue a check for $12,277.34 ($12,527.89 minus the discount), and on March 19 they issue a check for $76.57 ($78.13 minus the discount).

Ryan has asked MacKay to modify the discount program so that accounts payable personnel will know about all bills from a given supplier. MacKay makes the necessary changes in the program to produce the following report segment:

```
         Suggested bills to pay    Date March 11
Supplier   PDQ Dist.
    INV. #       AMOUNT TO PAY      DISC.          BILL. DATE
    13528        $12,277.34         $250.55        3/01/XX
    13634        $     76.57        $  1.56        3/09/XX
    TOTAL        $12,353.91         $252.11
```

    The programmer should follow the standard programming process when making changes, whether to correct errors or to meet additional user requests. It is important to clarify objectives and write appropriate pseudocode before coding any program changes and retesting the modified program with the complete test data. If these procedures are not followed, the results are unlikely to be fully satisfactory to the user.

    Some changes are too substantial to be made within the framework of the original program. For example, suppose Ryan asks MacKay for graphic output, since the senior managers want to be able to see discount statistics quickly and easily. Instead of changing the COBOL program, MacKay may suggest that Acme use a communication program to transfer the results of the accounts payable program from the mainframe computer to a microcomputer, where they will be further processed to generate and display graphics. In this case personal-productivity software such as Lotus 1-2-3 will be used to supplement rather than replace the COBOL program.

Programming Tools and Techniques

    A wide variety of tools and techniques can increase the productivity of programmers and facilitate communication between users and computer professionals. Many of these tools and techniques can be used in more than one stage of the program development process. For example, we have already examined pseudocode, a tool that is used in all stages of program development except the initial step, problem definition. This section introduces structured programming, a technique that applies to programming in general, and then presents several tools and techniques that can be used in the various steps of the program development process.

Structured Programming

Structured programming
A technique for designing and writing programs that divides programs into logical, readily identifiable modules.

Structured programming is a technique for designing and writing programs that divides a program into logical, readily identifiable components called *modules*. A structured program will enter each module only at the beginning and leave it only at the end. When the techniques of structured programming are applied correctly, the resultant program is easier to design, code, and maintain than a program developed by traditional methods.

Structured programming arose in response to the need to reduce the time and expense involved in writing, debugging, and maintaining programs. Maintenance is an especially important concern, since most business programs require frequent alterations to meet changing needs; moreover, programmers tend to change jobs often. It was discovered that programmers' productivity could be improved if they restricted their coding to only a few basic building blocks or structures (to be discussed later in the chapter). Some programmers think of structure in artistic terms, as Box 7-1 illustrates.

To get an idea of the potential value of structured programming, consider the following simplified example of a common programming error. The first version is written in an unstructured manner. It does not calculate the discount rate immediately after determining the net amount; instead it skips to another part of the program to carry out the calculation. Both the first version and the second version furnish the same results for the same test data. But few organizations would accept the first version, which is considerably harder to understand and modify. For example, it would be easy for the programmer writing the first version to forget the instruction GO TO WRITE-ROUTINE., in which case the discount rate would always be set at 0.02, regardless of the amount of the bill.

(1)

```
        IF NET-AMOUNT GREATER THAN 10000.00
        OR NET-AMOUNT EQUAL TO 10000.00
              GO TO CALC-BIG-NET
        ELSE
              GO TO CALC-SMALL-NET.
CALC-BIG-NET.
        DISC-RATE = 0.025.
        GO TO WRITE-ROUTINE.
CALC-SMALL-NET.
        DISC-RATE = 0.02.
WRITE-ROUTINE.
```

BOX 7-1

USING COMPUTERS

A Programming Superstar Talks About Balance and Elegance

If programming had a hall of fame, C. Wayne Ratliff would be in it. He is the creator of dBASE II, a popular data-base management program. In this interview Ratliff talks with Susan Lammers, editor-in-chief of Microsoft Press.

LAMMERS: *What is it about programming that satisfies you?*
RATLIFF: I like the high-tech aspect of being able to create something and have it appear on the screen. If you write a program well, it's very elegant; it sings, it's well built. I enjoy it from an engineering point of view, just like a well-built car, a well-built bridge, a well-built building. Everything about it seems in balance, tuned.
LAMMERS: *Would you elaborate on this feeling for balance and elegance?*
RATLIFF: Balance takes many forms. The code should be crisp and concise. You should be able to explain any module in one sentence, and statements should be in alphabetical order, if possible. Indentations shouldn't go off the edge of the paper at any point. The program shouldn't have one huge "if" and a tiny "else." Balance should be everywhere.

LAMMERS: *When you write code, does it come out balanced the first time or do you make a lot of changes?*
RATLIFF: I do a lot of changing. There's an analogy between writing code and sculpting a clay figure. You start with a lump of clay and then scrape away, add more clay, then scrape again. Every now and then you decide a leg doesn't look right, so you tear it off and put a new one on. That's a lot of interaction.

The ideal program module should be a page long. If it grows beyond a page, I have to decide what I'm trying to accomplish—how many separate things am I working on? Should they be broken into separate modules? Part of the elegance, and the balance, is that at a certain level, in this layer-cake hierarchy of a program, all the modules should be about the same weight and the same size, perform the same duty, and have the same functionality.
LAMMERS: *How does balance help a program?*
RATLIFF: The program becomes maintainable. When you have good balance, it's as though you've discovered some basic underlying principle and implemented it.

Source: From *Programmers at Work.* Reprinted by permission of Microsoft Press. Copyright © 1986 by Microsoft Press. All rights reserved.

```
                       (2)
          IF NET-AMOUNT GREATER THAN 10000.00
          OR NET-AMOUNT EQUAL TO 10000.00
                DISC-RATE = 0.025
          ELSE
                DISC-RATE = 0.02.
          WRITE-ROUTINE.
```

Structured programming should always be employed, whether by a single programmer or a *programming team*, a group of programmers and support personnel who work together to transform an algorithm into a computerized solution. A chief programmer is responsible for dividing the work among team members, coordinating their activities, and making sure that they all follow the same set of standards. The chief programmer divides the program into modules and usually writes the main module and assures that all modules are coordinated. The remaining modules may be divided among the other team members.

In the remainder of this chapter, we will reexamine the five steps of the programming process to see how structured programming can be used to make the process more efficient. In discussing each step we will also explore some of the tools and techniques used by programmers to carry out that step.

Defining the Problem

In the problem definition stage, computer specialists and users meet to determine the exact nature of the problem. This step includes the division of the problem to be solved into modules. It is documented by means of diagrams and forms that illustrate and clarify the output that the user desires as well as the input and processing necessary to produce the desired output. This documentation will continue to serve both the programmer and the user throughout the programming process.

Top-down design
A technique in which a large problem is subdivided into modules and each module, which represents a specific aspect of the problem, is broken down into smaller modules.

Top-Down Design. **Top-down design**, an essential part of structured programming, is a technique in which a large problem is subdivided into modules and each module, which represents a specific aspect of the problem, is broken down into smaller modules. In this way the overall structure of the program, including the way the modules interact, is determined before any of the modules are coded. In the case of Acme Manufacturing's accounts payable program, the program could be subdivided into four modules: the main module, which controls the entire program; an input module, which obtains and edits input data; a calculations module, which determines available

CHAPTER 7   227   PROGRAMMING

FIGURE 7-1

A Printer Spacing Chart

(printer spacing chart form with handwritten sample)

```
LIST OF BILLS TO PAY
SUPPLIER  XXXXXXXXXXXXXX
INV. #    AMT. TO PAY    DISC.     DATE OF BILL
99999     $99,999.99     $999.99   99/99/99
99999     $99,999.99     $999.99   99/99/99

TOTAL     $99,999.99
```

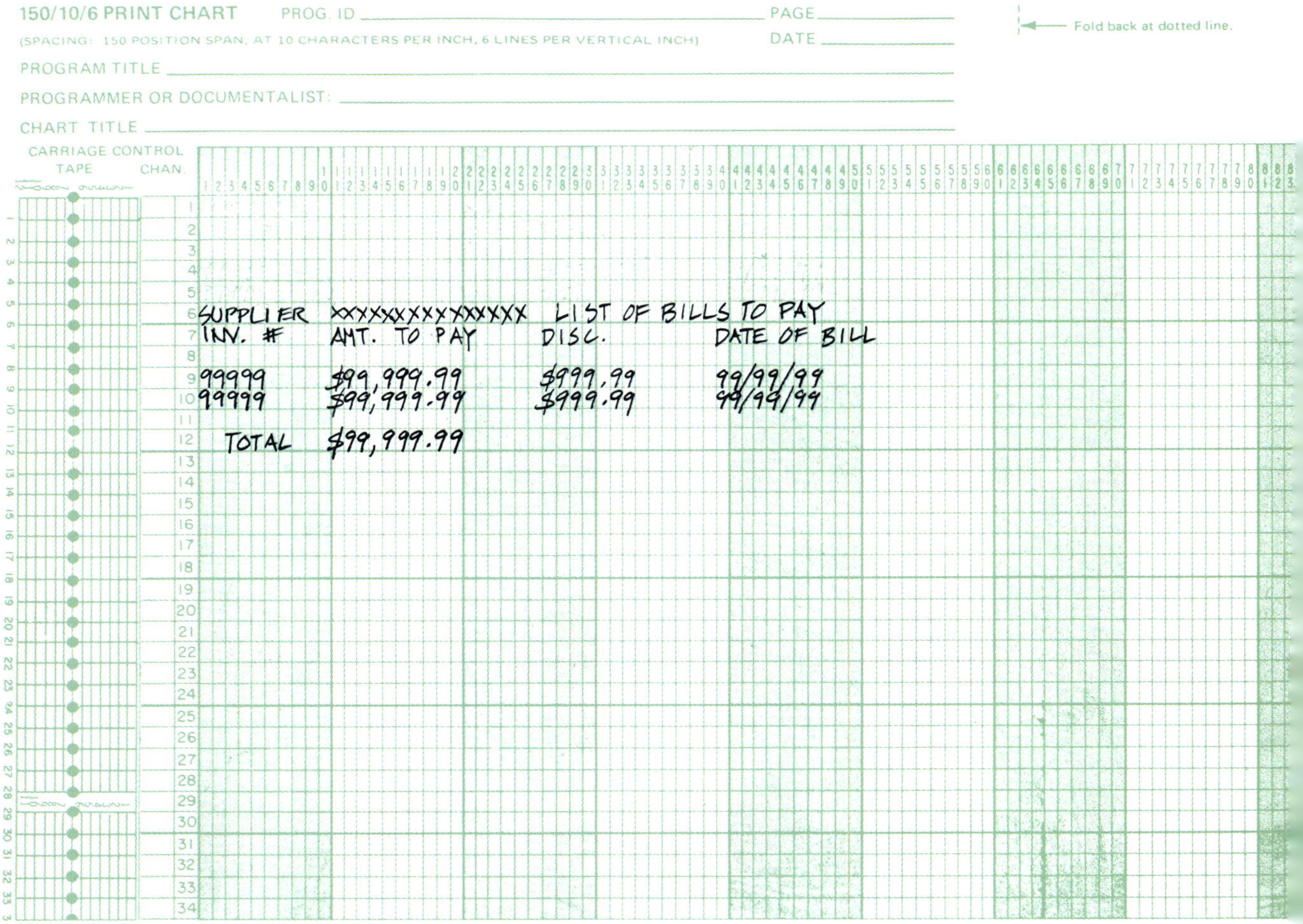

discounts; and an output module, which prints the reports produced by the program. Depending on the size of the project, different programmers could be assigned to each of the different modules.

The traditional documentation tools used in this stage include printer spacing charts, record layout forms, and screen layout forms. Let's take a brief look at each of these tools.

Printer Spacing Chart. A *printer spacing chart* illustrates the format of the reports to be generated by the program. Program-

FIGURE 7-2

A Record Layout Form

Date	Application		Form Number
\multicolumn{4}{c}{Record Layout Form}

Program Name A/P Discount	Program Number 214	Programmer MacKay, L.
Record Name	File Name	File Number

Field		Size	Type	Field Name	Remarks
From	To				
1	8	8	N	Supplier Number	
9	22	14	A	Supplier Name	
23	47	25	A	Supplier Address	
Approved by			Date		

mers and users can review the chart and change it if necessary before the algorithm is developed or the program is coded. The chart contains identifying information such as program ID and title, programmer's name, report title, date, and page. The blank chart has numbered lines and columns and is divided into boxes. Headings and titles are filled in, but actual data is represented by Xs in the case of alphanumeric or special characters and 9s in the case of numeric characters. Figure 7-1 illustrates a printer spacing chart for the discount list that is to be prepared for the accounts payable department of Acme Manufacturing.

Record Layout Form. A *record layout form* shows the format in which data is stored in the computer, for example, the number of bytes reserved for the supplier's name and address. It also indicates the type of data (i.e., numeric or alphanumeric) and the placement of the decimal point where applicable. Users usually do not review this form, but it is essential to the programming process. An example is shown in Figure 7-2.

FIGURE 7-3

A Screen Layout Form

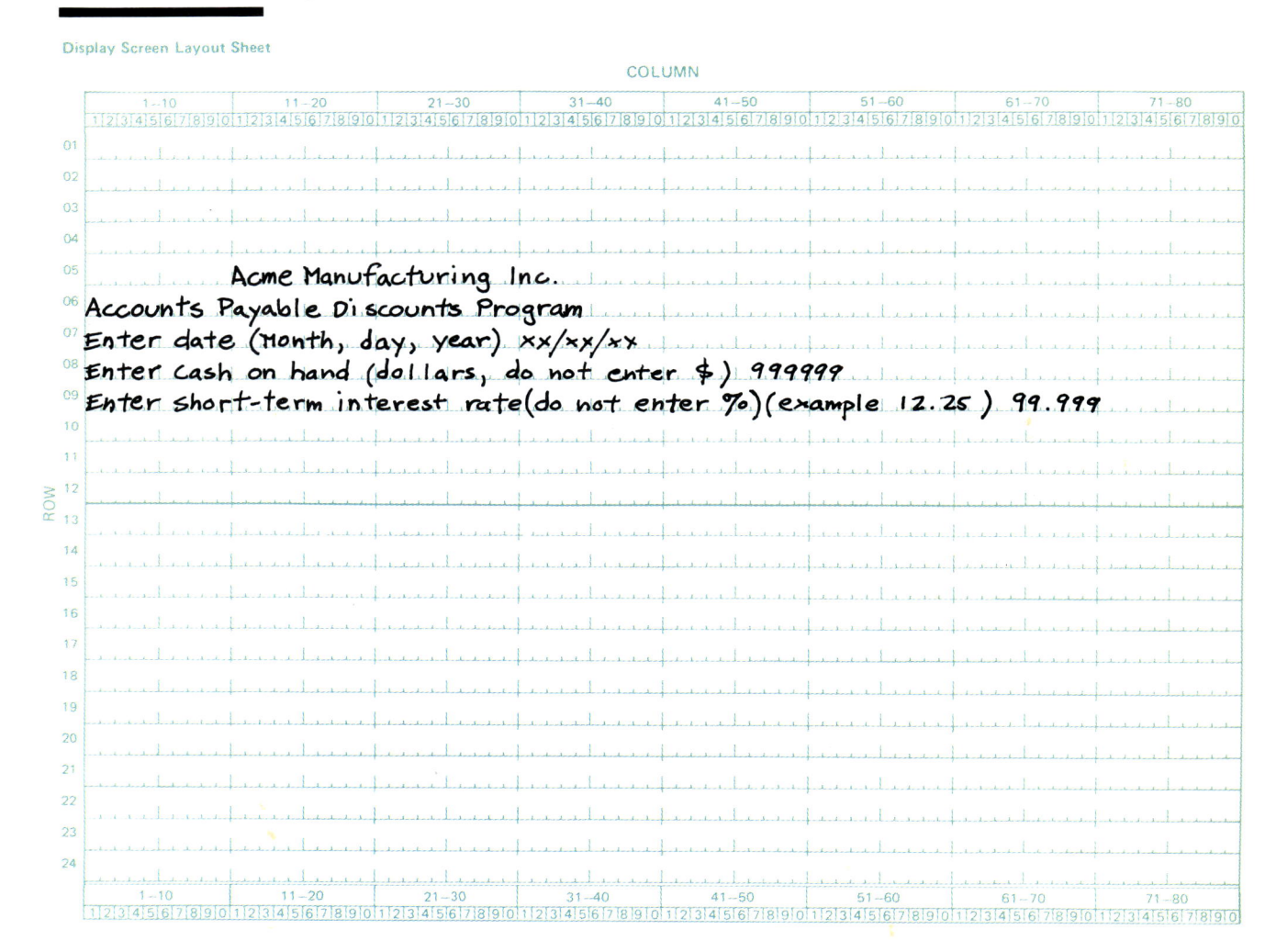

Display Screen Layout Sheet

```
Acme Manufacturing Inc.
Accounts Payable Discounts Program
Enter date (month, day, year) xx/xx/xx
Enter cash on hand (dollars, do not enter $) 999999
Enter short-term interest rate (do not enter %)(example 12.25) 99.999
```

Screen Layout Form. *Screen layout forms show users an example of each type of computer screen display that might appear during the execution of the program.* They typically distinguish between computer-generated data and data entered by users. An example of a screen layout form is shown in Figure 7-3.

Designing the Solution

The initial top-down design and the forms just described provide documentation of the problem definition stage of the programming process. They are used in the next stage, designing the solution. Top-down design plays a major role in this stage also.

Top-Down Design. In the solution design stage most of the modules that were identified during the problem definition stage are broken down into smaller modules. For example, the calculations module of the Acme discount program is divided into one module that determines the supplier's policy on discounts and another that calculates the available discount. The output module is subdivided into separate modules for each report to be produced.

Structure Charts. Structure charts, which look like the organization charts representing relationships within a company, are graphic representations of a program's modules and their interrelationships. Each module is represented by a rectangle containing a brief description of its function. The structure chart is organized into levels, with the top level corresponding to the overall problem; the next level corresponding to the main input, processing, and output modules; and the third level corresponding to more detailed modules. Figure 7-4 shows how the modules in a structure chart for Acme's discount program might look.

Pseudocode. Structure charts present a general picture; the specific details of the way in which the computer will carry out a program are furnished by other diagrams. Among these are pseudocode and flowcharts.

As noted earlier in the chapter, pseudocode is an informal language that is used to represent the essentials of a computer program. It is, in effect, a compromise between English and a programming language. The exact nature of a pseudocode may vary: Some users prefer a general pseudocode that presents an overview of the program, whereas others want the pseudocode to resemble the programming language as closely as possible and represent the program in more detail. An important feature of pseudocode is that it can be created and modified with a word processor. However, pseudocode is often supplemented and sometimes replaced by diagrams such as flowcharts. Figure 7-5 presents an overview of Acme's discount program in pseudocode.

Structure chart
A graphic representation of a program's modules and their interrelationships.

FIGURE 7-4

A Structure Chart for an Accounts Payable Program

Depending on the algorithm, it may be advisable to include an additional level of detail.

```
                    Program
                    Accounts Payable
                    Discounts
           ┌───────────┼───────────┐
         Input    Processing    Output
```

- Read Table of Suppliers' Discount Policies
- Read Daily Interest Rate
- Read Accounts Payable Master File
- Calculate and Store Discount
- Sort Bills to Pay
- Print Report Discounts Available
- Print Report Bills to Pay

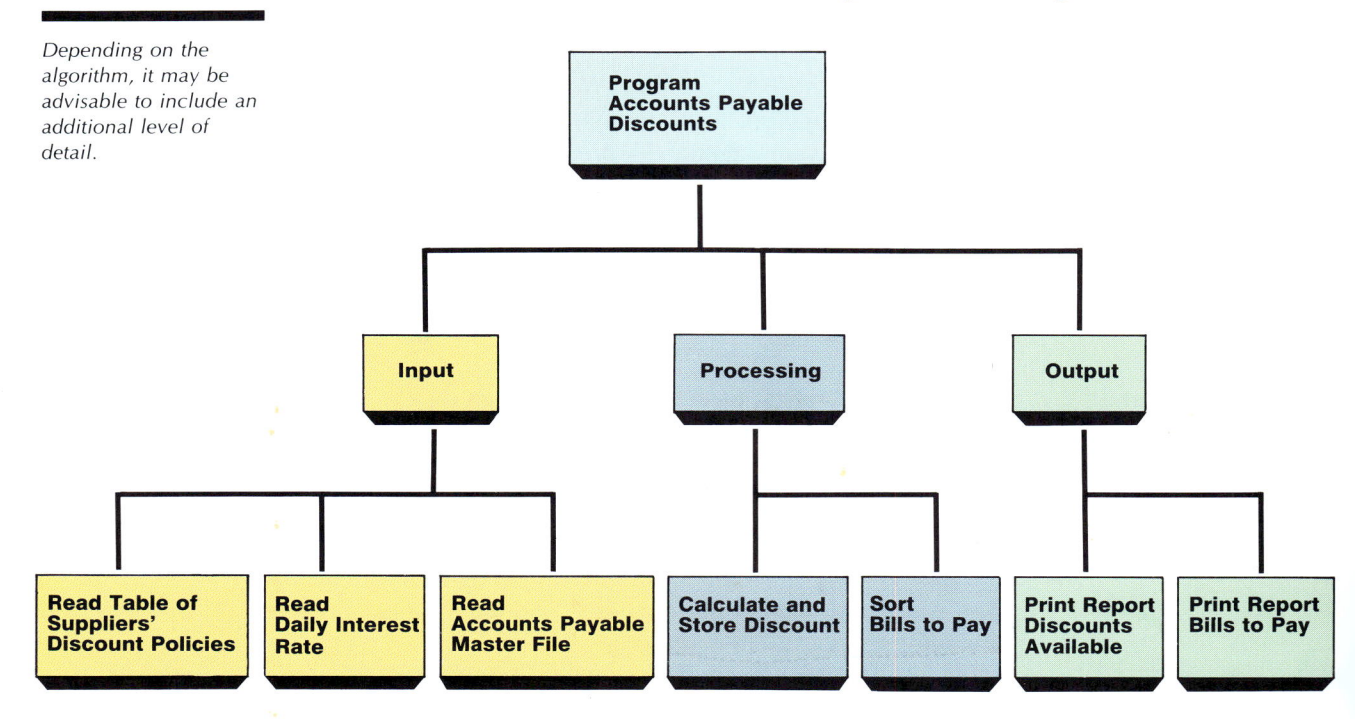

FIGURE 7-5

Pseudocode for an Accounts Payable Discount Program

Pseudocode can be written in greater detail, depending on documentation needs.

```
Read Table of Suppliers' Discount Policies
Read Daily Interest Rate
Read Accounts Payable Master File
While More Bills to Process
    Calculate and Store Discount
    Read Accounts Payable Master File
End While
Sort Bills to Pay
Print Report Discounts Available
Print Report Bills to Pay
```

Flowchart templates are often used to draw neat flowcharts during the solution design phase of the programming process. (© Freda Leinwand.)

Flowchart

A diagram using standard symbols that expresses the relationships among processing activities within a program.

Flowcharts. **Flowcharts,** sometimes called *program flowcharts,* are visual diagrams that illustrate the essential elements of a program. Figure 7-6 is a flowchart that presents an overview of Acme's discount program; it uses the standard flowchart symbols illustrated in Figure 7-7. Pseudocode and flowcharts can each be used to express the contents of individual boxes in structure charts, as shown in Figure 7-4.

Structured Walkthrough. Before the solution design is presented to management, it is subjected to a process known as a *structured walkthrough.* In a structured walkthrough the designer presents (or "walks through") the design to a group of colleagues, who review it for errors, clarity, and conformity to organizational standards. There are two reasons for performing a structured walkthrough: (1) Team members often find errors in a program design that the designer overlooked, and (2) a design that has been reviewed by a team will be easier to modify than one that has been developed in isolation. If the original designer leaves the project, another team member can modify the program if it needs to be changed.

Coding the Program

Structure charts, pseudocode, and flowcharts are intermediate tools that help software specialists design a solution to a problem after it has been defined. After one or more of these tools has been used to rough out the solution, the next step is coding the program.

CHAPTER 7   233   PROGRAMMING

FIGURE 7-6

Flowchart for an Accounts Payable Discount Program

This flowchart shows the relationship among the different activities in the program. Note that the rectangle is drawn with a pair of vertical lines. It represents a process that can be shown in a more detailed flowchart. A programmer would refer to the detailed flowcharts before coding the program.

- Begin
- Read Table of Suppliers' Discount Policies
- Read Daily Interest Rate
- Read Accounts Payable Master File
- More Bills to Process?
  - N → Sort Bills to Pay → Print Report Discounts Available → Print Report Bills to Pay → End
  - Y → Calculate and Store Discount → (loop back to Read Accounts Payable Master File)

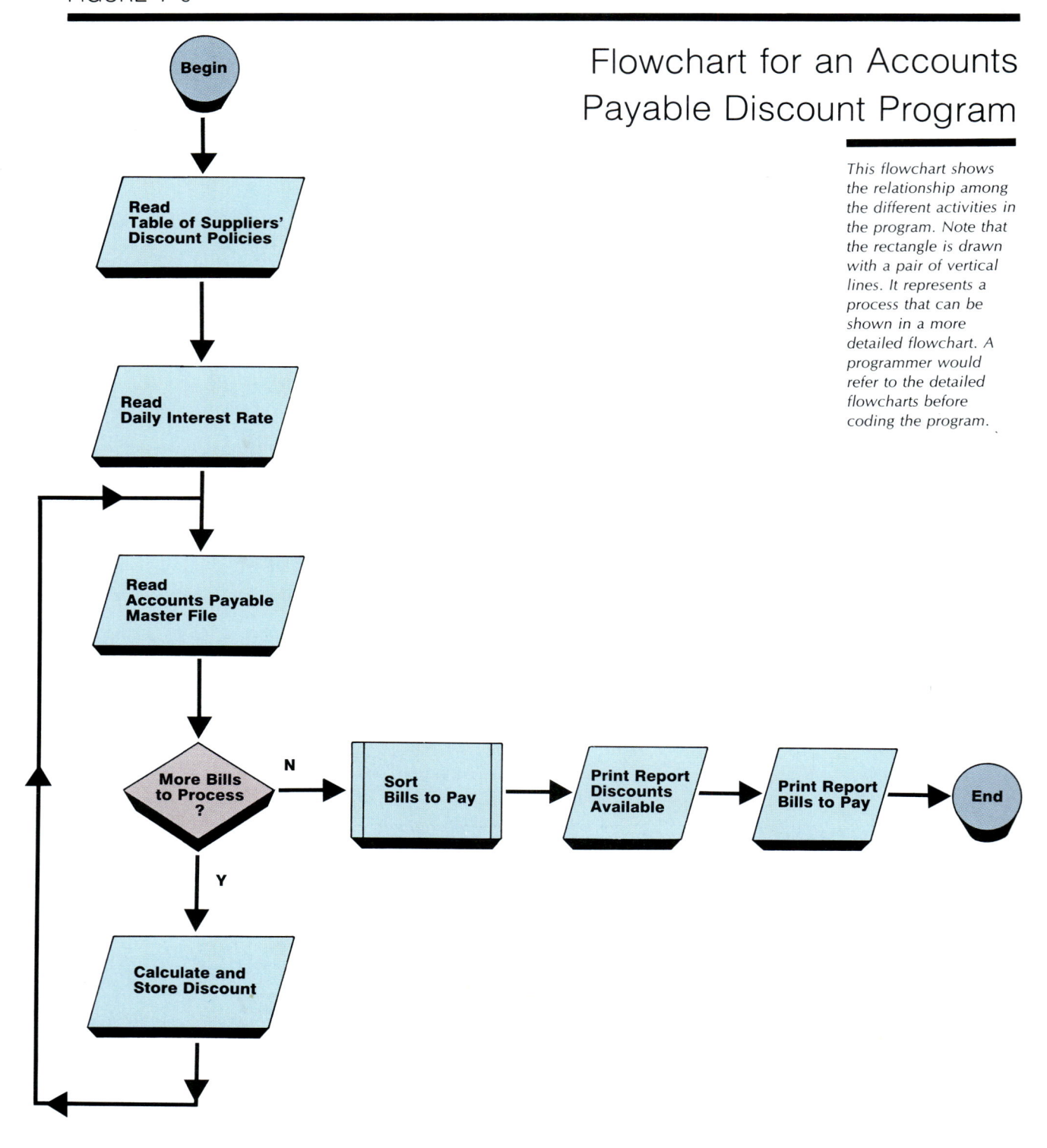

FIGURE 7-7

Standard Flowcharting Symbols

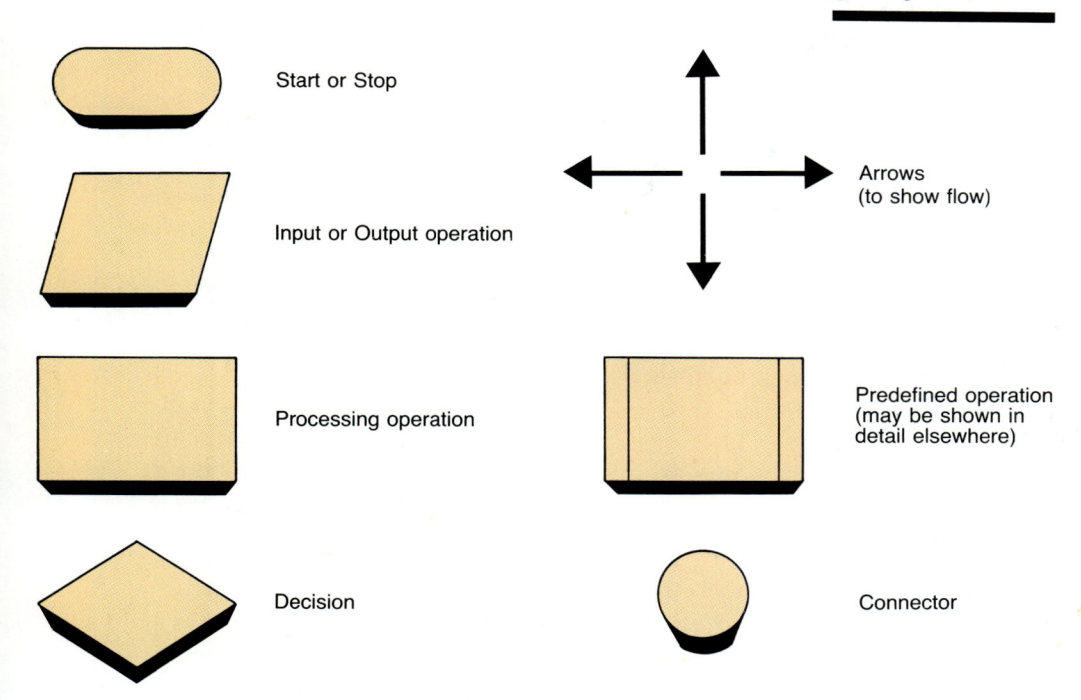

Start or Stop

Input or Output operation

Processing operation

Decision

Arrows (to show flow)

Predefined operation (may be shown in detail elsewhere)

Connector

Sometimes the coding phase of software creation can be partially automated. (See Box 7-2.) For the most part, however, the coding is done line by line by a skilled programmer working with an editor or perhaps simply a yellow pad. Automated or not, the job of coding a program is greatly aided if the previous steps have been guided by the philosophy of structured programming. Applications of the structure concept to the coding phase include the use of certain basic structures, restriction or elimination of the GO TO statement, limitation of the size of modules, and application of the programming team concept.

Basic structures

The programming structures necessary for coding a structured program, including the sequential structure, the selection structure, the looping structure, and often the case structure.

Basic Structures. It has been proved mathematically that all algorithms used in computer programs can be expressed as combinations of a few **basic structures**: sequential structure, selection structure, and looping structure. It has also been shown that programmer performance can be substantially improved if programs are designed and coded using these three structures and an additional one known as the case structure. Let's take a brief look at each of these structures.

CHAPTER 7 235 PROGRAMMING

BOX 7-2

FRONTIERS IN TECHNOLOGY

Programs That Help Programmers Program

Programmers are finally joining clerical workers, engineers, accountants, and managers in the ranks of people whose productivity is being increased by computers. A new generation of software is enabling them to produce big chunks of high-quality prefabricated computer code as much as 100 times faster than is possible using the traditional yellow-pad approach.

In traditional software development, a systems analyst, working with the end-user, defines a problem and designs a solution. The analyst's pseudocode or flowchart is then turned over to a programmer. The programmer translates the solution design into hundreds or thousands of lines of code written in a language such as COBOL. Often as few as 20 lines of code may be a good day's work for a programmer.

This is where a tool known as a COBOL generator comes in. These mainframe-based software packages can produce up to 2000 lines of code a day in response to very general instructions. In effect, they read pseudocode and write COBOL.

Up to now, COBOL generators have been able to code only about 80 percent of a typical progam. The prefabricated chunks produced by the generator still have to be stitched together by hand and customized to a particular application. However, products are beginning to reach the market that provide the capability to generate entire programs automatically when design has been completed.

Powerful as they are, COBOL generators have some drawbacks. For one thing, programmers are faced with the job of modifying and maintaining code that they did not write themselves. Also, when modifications are needed, programmers must choose between writing them by hand or modifying the original pseudocode and regenerating the entire program. The latter choice uses the full power of the generator, but it risks losing earlier hand-made modifications. Finally, because the generators do not give progammers the freedom to use all the high-precision tricks that a language like COBOL can do, the resulting programs may not run as efficiently as those written by hand.

Coding typically represents about 15 percent of the cost of the whole application, which includes everything from problem definition to maintenance. Care must be taken to ensure that savings realized in the coding phase are not offset by inefficiencies elsewhere. Still, as products are improved, generators for COBOL and other leading languages are sure to become widely used.

Source: David H. Freedman, "Programming Without Tears," *High Technology,* April 1986, pp. 38–45.

Sequential Structure

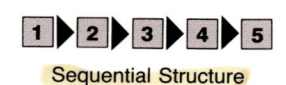

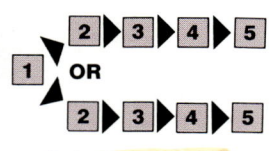

Selection Structure

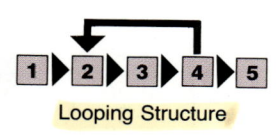

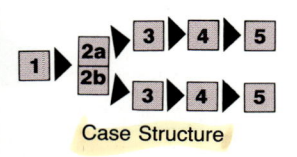

Looping Structure

Case Structure

Basic Structures

The *sequential structure* is the simplest basic programming structure. In this structure, modules or instructions are processed in order, one after the other. In the Acme program, an example of sequential structure would be

Read Table of Suppliers' Discount Policies
Read Daily Interest Rate
Read Accounts Payable Master File

(Figure 7-8 illustrates this sequential structure in pseudocode and flowchart form.) Note that although the sequential structure appears in almost all programs, there are few programs that can be created using *only* the sequential structure.

The *selection structure* is used when there is a choice between two possibilities. For example, in Figure 7-9 the selection structure is used to determine whether a given bill is less than $10 000.00 and then to calculate the appropriate discount. In structured programming, the divergent paths in a selection structure reconverge before processing continues. The selection structure is important because it allows different processing functions to be performed in response to different situations.

The *looping structure* is used to repeat a series of activities until a *condition* is met—for example, until there are no more records to process. Figure 7-10 illustrates the looping structure for Acme's discount program. [Many programming languages allow the looping structure to be expressed as follows: A series of activities is repeated while (as long as) a condition is met.] The looping structure is important because it allows the computer to process a series of items.

Although any program can be constructed from a combination of the three structures just described, the *case structure* is frequently used to simplify processing. It works in much the same way as a switching station in a railroad yard: It shunts items into different groups. In the Acme discount program, the case structure could be used to separate bills below $500.00 from those between $500.00 and $999.99, those between $1000.00 and $1999.99, and so on. Once the bills have been separated, they can be processed using an appropriate combination of the basic programming structures—including, on occasion, one or more additional case structures.

The GO TO Instruction. The *GO TO instruction* allows programmers to *branch*, that is, to skip from one part of a program to another. For example, upon encountering a negative invoice number a program could branch to a special module that processes errors. This may seem like a useful tool, but in the late 1960s some computer scientists realized that excessive use of

FIGURE 7-8

Sequential Structure

(a) Pseudocode illustrating sequential structure for an accounts payable program. (b) Flowchart illustrating sequential structure for an accounts payable program.

Read Table of Suppliers' Discount Policies
Read Daily Interest Rate
Read Accounts Payable Master File

(a)

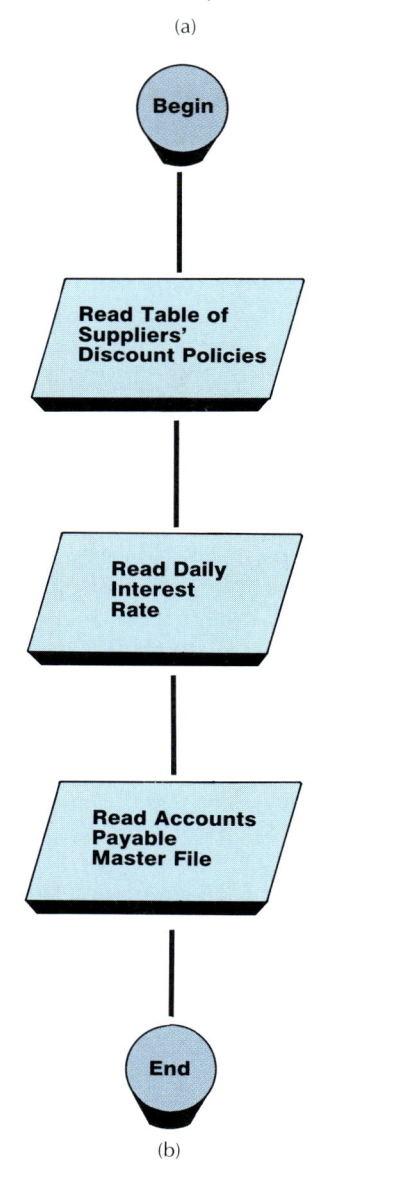

```
                    Begin
                      │
                      ▼
         ┌──────────────────────┐
         │ Read Table of        │
         │ Suppliers'           │
         │ Discount Policies    │
         └──────────────────────┘
                      │
                      ▼
         ┌──────────────────────┐
         │ Read Daily           │
         │ Interest             │
         │ Rate                 │
         └──────────────────────┘
                      │
                      ▼
         ┌──────────────────────┐
         │ Read Accounts        │
         │ Payable              │
         │ Master File          │
         └──────────────────────┘
                      │
                      ▼
                     End
```

(b)

FIGURE 7-9

Selection Structure

If Bill under $10,000 then
    Calculate Smaller Discount
Else
    Calculate Larger Discount

(a)

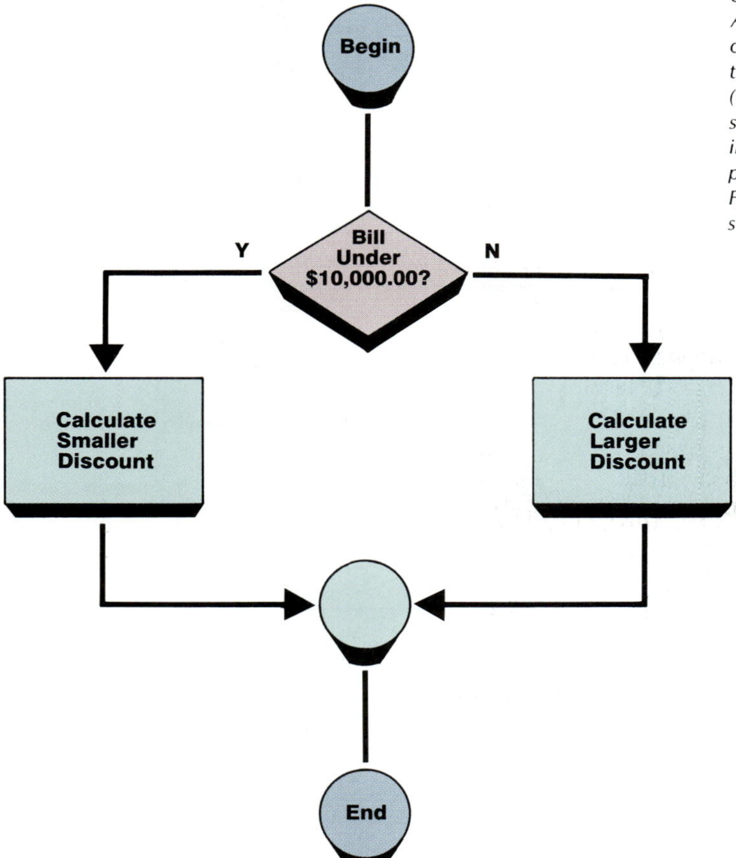

(a) Pseudocode illustrating selection structure for an accounts payable program. The selection separates the two paths corresponding to different discounts. After the appropriate discount is applied, the two paths converge (End if). This selection structure did not appear in the main pseudocode. (b) Flowchart illustrating selection structure.

(b)

FIGURE 7-10

Looping Structure

(a) Pseudocode illustrating looping structure for an accounts payable program. The first Read is used to start the repetitive processing with a bill to process. In this looping structure repetitive processing continues while (as long as) there are more bills to process. (b) Flowchart illustrating looping structure.

```
Read Accounts Payable Master File
While More Bills to Process
        Calculate and Store Discount
        Read Accounts Payable Master File
End While
Summary Activities
```
(a)

(b)

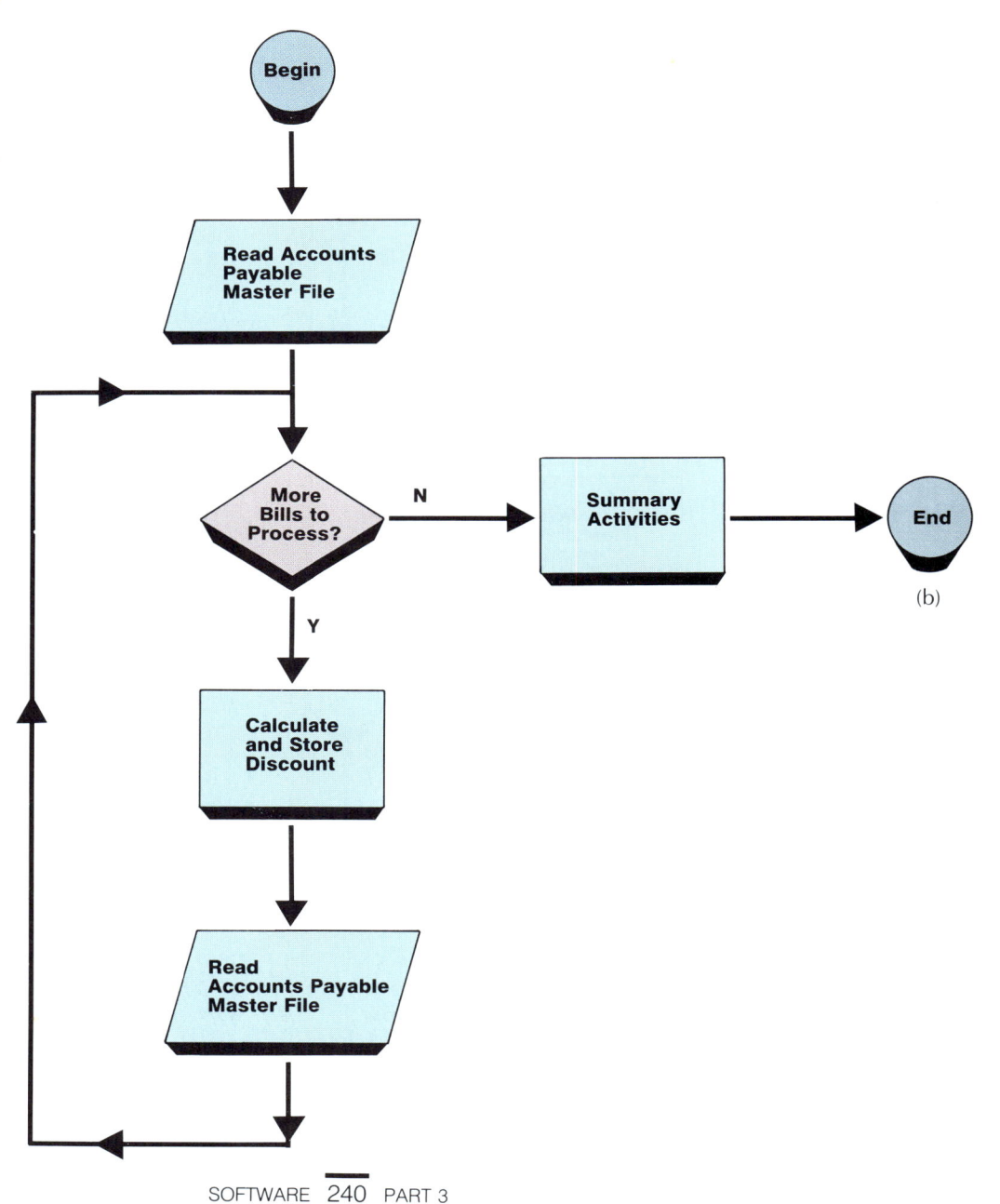

SOFTWARE 240 PART 3

GO TO instructions could make it difficult to find bugs or make changes in a program. We saw in the example at the beginning of this section how a few unnecessary GO TO instructions complicated a short program segment and increased the possibility of error. Often programmers have had to rewrite programs that used too many GO TO instructions because they could not understand them well enough to modify them.

Programs in which GO TO instructions are prevalent are known as *spaghetti programs* because trying to trace a single instruction in such a program is like trying to isolate a strand of spaghetti on a plate. Moreover, in much the same way that removing a single strand of spaghetti will move many other strands, modifying one instruction in a spaghetti program will affect other instructions. In practice, it is very hard to maintain spaghetti programs because the programmer can never be sure that the desired change will not affect the program in unanticipated ways.

In structured programs, on the other hand, instructions are relatively easy to locate and changes can be made in one part without altering the rest of the program. This is because the program was coded as separate, manageable modules corresponding to the modules on the structure chart. Also, many organizations establish a maximum module length equal to the length of a sheet of computer printout—about 60 lines—so that programmers can see the code for an entire module at once.

Testing and Debugging the Program

The use of structured programming and associated techniques such as top-down design in earlier stages of the programming process simplifies the testing and debugging stage: Modules can be tested as they are completed rather than after the entire program has been coded, and when bugs are found, only a small portion of the program has to be checked. It is a lot easier to find an error that is known to be located in a 50-line module than one that could be anywhere in a 500-line program.

Desk-Checking. The first step in testing a program is called *desk-checking*. In this process the programmer reads each instruction and determines how the computer would process it. If MacKay had desk-checked the Acme program, he might have caught the bug described earlier without having to run the program on the computer. Once the programmer has desk-

Bugbusters is one of many debugging packages designed to help eliminate program bugs. [© Chris Pullo; (inset) © Hans Pfletschinger, Peter Arnold.]

checked the program, it goes through a review process similar to the structured walkthrough described earlier. To obtain the maximum benefit from this activity, the programmer and other members of the programming team should interact in accordance with the principles of egoless programming.

Egoless Programming. *Egoless programming* is an approach in which all members of the programming team are free to criticize each other's program design and coding efforts. In other words, the programmer's ego is not involved in the program and suggestions are welcomed rather than challenged. Egoless programming is a reflection of the fact that the program belongs to whoever is paying for it, not to the programmer. However, because programmers are human, it is not always easy to put egoless programming into practice. Some companies attempt to alleviate this problem by excluding from the review process anyone who could influence the programmer's salary and promotion prospects.

Egoless programming, structured walkthroughs, and the programming team are related approaches that are all intended to change the programming process from an individual effort to a team effort. Businesses and other organizations use these techniques because they cannot afford to have programmers think of programs as their own private property or to have programs that are understood by only one individual who could leave the company at any time.

Implementing and Maintaining the Program

A program has no value until it is implemented, and once it has been implemented it must be maintained. The use of structured programs and careful documentation of each step in the programming process are the two main ways of ensuring easy program maintenance. It is important to remember that programs are often maintained by programmers who did not write the original program. Designing and coding a program according to the principles of structured programming enables different programmers to update and debug it as necessary. And thorough documentation provides programmers with a standard for comparison if a module needs to be changed.

This chapter has set forth the basic processes and techniques used in writing computer programs. Early in the chapter we noted that computer programs are written in special languages known as programming languages. Chapter 8 examines several computer languages, emphasizing the modern, easy-to-use languages known as fourth-generation programming languages. Chapter 9 goes on to explore several personal-productivity software packages, while Chapter 10 discusses data-base management systems and the programming languages associated with these systems.

SUMMARY

1. Computer programmers transform the needs of a business into a computerized solution. They are often aided by systems analysts, people who combine technical knowledge with practical experience and communication skills.

2. The program development process is composed of five steps: defining the problem, designing the solution, coding the program, testing and debugging the program, and implementing and maintaining the program.

3. Since users often do not know exactly what they want the computer to accomplish for them, programmers and systems analysts may help them establish their goal. This step includes written **documentation**: a report stating the problem; a description of the desired output; a detailed list of the necessary inputs; a preliminary estimate of the cost, personnel, and computer resources required; and a tentative schedule.

4. The programmer begins to design the solution by developing an **algorithm**, a set of rules for solving a problem in a finite number of steps. A key tool for preparing algorithms is **pseudocode**, an informal language that is used to represent the details of a computer program.

5. Coding a program is the process of translating an algorithm into a computer language such as COBOL, FORTRAN, or BASIC.

6. Testing is the process of determining whether a program contains errors; **debugging** is the process of finding those errors or bugs. Syntax errors are mistakes in spelling, punctuation, spacing, word usage, and other coding rules. Logic errors occur when an instruction commands the computer to do something different from what was really intended. Run-time errors prevent the program from running to completion.

7. Program maintenance consists of revising the program to meet new requirements and correct any bugs that users find.

8. Structured programming is a technique for designing and writing programs that divides programs into logical, readily identifiable modules. Structured programming is often done by a programming team.

9. A key aspect of structured programming is **top-down design**, in which the problem to be solved is broken down into modules. It makes use of a variety of tools such as printer spacing charts, record layout forms, and screen layout forms.

10. In designing the solution, top-down design is used to divide the modules into smaller modules. This step makes use of **structure charts**, which are graphic representations of a program's modules and their interrelationships. Diagrams called **flowcharts** may be used to represent processing steps within a given module. The solution design is reviewed by peers in a process known as a structured walkthrough.

11. All algorithms used in computer programs can be expressed through some combination of a few **basic structures**: the sequential structure, the selection structure, the looping structure, and the case structure.

12. In the testing and debugging stage, the programmer desk-checks the program, reading each instruction and processing it as the computer would. Programming teams typically review each member's work, looking for errors in both design and coding; this process is known as egoless programming.

KEY TERMS

documentation

algorithm

pseudocode

coding

testing

debugging

program maintenance

structured programming

top-down design

structure chart

flowchart

basic structures

REVIEW QUESTIONS

1. Given the fact that many excellent software packages are available, why do people still write programs?

2. Identify and describe the different computer specialists involved in the programming process. Why is it important for the user to be involved in the programming process?

3. List the five steps of the programming process. Compare them to the steps in building a house or some similar project.

4. Describe the work done by computer specialists and users during the problem definition stage of programming.

5. Identify the work done by computer specialists and users in designing the solution to a problem. List four questions to be answered in the documentation for this stage.

6. What does the programmer do during the coding step? Why is it important to create a detailed pseudocode before beginning this step?

7. Describe the testing and debugging processes. What is the difference between a syntax error and a logic error?

8. Why are documentation and program maintenance so important?

9. What is structured programming? What are its advantages compared with the traditional approach to programming.

10. What is top-down design? How does it affect the programming process?

11. Illustrate the three basic types of structures that can be used to express an algorithm.

12. Describe the problems that may result from excessive use of the GO TO instruction.

APPLICATIONS

1. Interview a programmer or programming student and ask to be allowed to examine the diagrams he or she uses in preparing a typical program. Find out how he or she feels about various kinds of diagrams and structured programming in general.

2. Draw a flowchart or write pseudocode to illustrate your activities for an hour after you awaken. Identify the three basic types of structures if they are present.

3. Draw a structure chart of this chapter.

4. Discuss the following statement: Given human nature, egoless programming is impossible to put into practice.

CASE FOR DISCUSSION

Over a century ago a new technology—the railroad—brought prosperity to the town of Randolph, Vermont. Signs of that prosperity remain in a quiet street lined with spacious Victorian houses and shaded by spreading sugar maples. But today most trains pass through Randolph without stopping.

Walking some of these streets whose appearance has hardly changed since the railroad age, the casual visitor might think that the town of Randolph has been frozen in time. This impression would be wrong, however. If one steps inside the offices of Randolph National Bank, Vermont Castings, or many other businesses, one finds computers everywhere doing the same jobs they would do in a big city.

Computers have brought change to the town government of Randolph as well. In 1982 the town bought a computer system for use by its school administrators. At that time the most urgent need was to computerize budget and payroll work. The system served that purpose adequately, but it has become obsolete in some respects. Now school superintendant Roger Bourassa wants to acquire an improved system that will serve the Randolph schools and also those of neighboring Braintree and Brookfield.

What Bourassa wants is an integrated system for budget, staff, and student records management. This new system would continue to do the budget and payroll work of the old system, but it would add other functions as well. For example, it would allow centralized processing of purchase requests. Purchase orders for everything from desks to chalk originate in the various schools of Randolph and the neighboring towns. With the new system, these could be entered on a terminal at each school and automatically transmitted to the central office. If several schools ordered chalk at the same time, for example, the school could place a consolidated order with the supplier and save some money.

In addition, the new system would give the central office quick access to student records, including grade and attendance records. Attendance records would be typed on school terminals and instantly transferred to the central office.

Principal Stephen Metcalf notes that the system could also be used to improve communications with parents. Mailings could be made to parents of children participating in certain special programs. The computer would also notify the central office of children with attendance problems. An administrator could then contact the parents to discuss the problem.

Superintendant Bourassa has proposed spending $86,000 on the system. This sum would include $25,000 for software and would also cover the cost of equipping each school with terminals and printers.

You are the president of Upper Valley Systems, Inc., a small software company located in nearby Bethel, Vermont. You would like to bid on the software phase of the new system that Bourassa wants to buy for the Randolph school system. On the basis of your experience with similar jobs in the past, you think you can work within the $25,000 budget, but you will need more information about the school system's requirements before you can be sure of this.

Write a short initial letter to Superintendant Bourassa introducing yourself and your firm.

Source: Sandy Cooch, "Time to Computerize, Says Bourassa," *White River Valley Herald* (Randolph, Vermont), November 27, 1986, p. 1.

CASE QUESTIONS

Your letter should

1. Outline the information you will need to obtain in order to do the job.

2. Describe the capabilities of your firm.

3. List the services you can offer.

Past experience has taught you that the five-step program development process provides a useful framework for communicating with clients and helping them communicate their needs to you. Structure your letter in such a way that it touches briefly on each of those five steps as it applies to the problem faced by the Randolph school system.

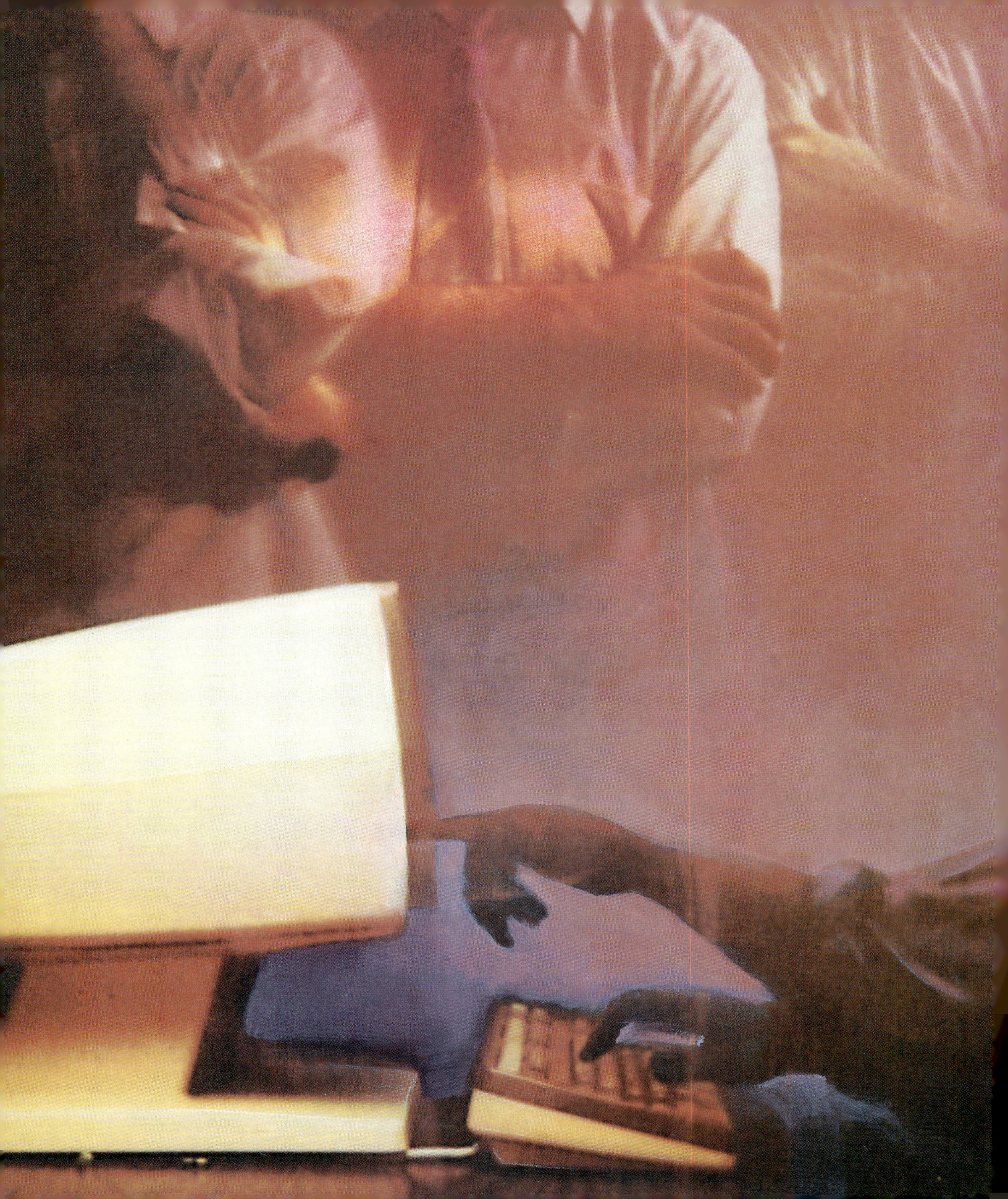

Programming Languages and Operating Systems

CHAPTER

8

It's a bright February day. The bare branches of oak trees cast sharp shadows on the campus of Linfield College. Winter sun is a rare thing in rainy Oregon, but freshman Larry Halvorsen can't enjoy it. He has economics homework to do.

He enters the department's computer lab, located on the second floor of a building that formerly housed the chemistry department. Although he is not very familiar with computers, he doesn't need to be for this assignment. He turns on the IBM PC on the table in front of him. First the computer's PC-DOS operating system must be loaded. Halvorsen doesn't have any idea what PC-DOS really is, but that is no problem. He only needs to follow a few simple instructions. Next he takes a floppy disk labeled *Econograph* from his notebook and inserts it in the disk drive. He types the word ECON, and the screen lights up with a computer-aided instruction package for introductory economics.

Halvorsen presses a key to choose today's assignment—aggregate supply and demand—from a menu presented on the screen. As he works through the assignment, questions appear, right answers are rewarded, wrong answers are corrected, and animated graphs dance across the screen. It's as close to a painless way to learn economics as there is. In fact, if *Econograph* were bigger and better, with more graphs and more lessons, Halvorsen would be happy to spend more afternoons in the computer lab.

On the same February afternoon, the sun is lower in the sky on the campus of the University of Delaware. John Bergman sits in his office, also working on *Econograph*. Bergman is not learning economics, however, and his *Econograph* screen does not show the pretty graphics. Instead, it shows line after line of computer code. Bergman is the programmer who wrote *Econograph*, working with his colleagues Charles Link and Jeff Miller. He has taken the program apart and is tinkering with its innards, much as a mechanic might disassemble an engine in search of a way to improve its performance. Bergman's work won't be done in time to help Halvorsen, but by next fall the souped-up version of *Econograph* will be available. Next year's students will be a step closer to the ideal of economics without tears.

Chapter 7 provided a first look at the process of programming that lies behind every computer application, from learning economics to launching a communications satellite. This chapter focuses on one aspect of software—the special computer languages in which programs are written. The various levels of programming languages—low-level languages, high-level languages, and very-high-level languages—are introduced. Specific languages are described, including Pascal, the language that John Bergman chose to write *Econograph*. The chapter also discusses the software that controls the computer's operations, that is, the operating system. It examines the basic functions and specific features of an operating system and shows how even a nontechnical user like Larry Halvorsen can use the operating system to perform specific tasks.

When you have read this chapter you should be able to:
1. Describe what a programming language is and what it does.
2. Distinguish among machine languages, assembly languages, and high-level programming languages.
3. Identify the major high-level programming languages and discuss their applications.
4. Discuss advantages and disadvantages of very-high-level programming languages compared to high-level languages.
5. Describe the functions and features of operating systems.
6. Discuss how users interact with the operating system of a computer.
7. Understand and use the key terms at the end of the chapter.

Programming Languages

Programming languages
Specialized languages that enable people to prepare computer programs.

Programs like the Acme Manufacturing discount program described in Chapter 7 are written in **programming languages**. These are specialized languages that enable people to write programs that can be run on a computer. A wide variety of programming languages are available. Some of those languages, such as FORTRAN, are used mostly for scientific and engineering applications, while others, such as COBOL, are used mostly for commerical applications. Several programming languages are easy enough that nonspecialists can start programming within hours of their first lesson; others are used almost exclusively by specialists and only after considerable training.

In spite of their great variety, programming languages have many traits in common. They are all similar to human languages in that communication is done via a type of sentence known as an *instruction* that contains a verb and an object. Like human languages, programming languages follow rules of grammar or syntax. For example, a COBOL instruction might read as follows:

```
WRITE REPORT-BILLS-TO-PAY.
```

In this instruction, WRITE is the verb and REPORT-BILLS-TO-PAY is the object.

In all programming languages, instructions are written in a *source code*. The source code is entered into the computer, which translates it into a form that it can process, known as *object code*. When the program is run, the computer uses the object code to process data.

The following example illustrates the relationship among the source code, the object code, the raw data, and the information produced:

```
WRITE REPORT-BILLS-TO-PAY.        (Source code)
011100100101010010101001001010    (Object code)
110010101010010101111110001011
PDQ Manu. 13528 12277.34 250.55 March 1    (Raw Data)
```

```
Suggested bills to pay      Date     March 11

Supplier   PDQ Dist.

Inv. #   Amount to pay      Discount
13528    $12,277.34         $250.55
(Information generated when the object
    code executes and processes the data)
```

Most of the programming languages that are used today can be classified into one of three levels: low-level languages, high-level languages, and very-high-level languages. Each succeeding level represents a major improvement in terms of ease of use and programming features provided.

Low-Level Programming Languages

Low-level programming languages are programming languages that force the programmer to code instructions in considerable detail. Programs written in these languages are usually closely related to the way in which the computer actually carries out operations, and as a result they tend to be highly computer dependent. When the company changes computers, it is usually necessary to rewrite programs that have been written in low-level languages.

There are two basic types of low-level languages: machine languages and assembly languages. In this section we will take a brief look at machine languages and then go on to discuss assembly languages, which are in widespread use for some applications.

Machine Languages. The first programming languages, which were coded in 0s and 1s, were called **machine languages** or first-generation programming languages. In Acme Manufacturing's discount program, an instruction to calculate the net amount on a $500 purchase, given the amount, the tax, and the freight, might look something like this if it were written in machine language:

```
10111000001010100001001111100011
00101010000011000000000100001010
00101010000011000000001000000111
10100010001100000000110010011100
```

Obviously, there are many problems with instructions like these. A main disadvantage for users is that the program bears no resemblance to the design specifications. The disadvantages

Machine language
A programming language that is composed entirely of 0s and 1s. The computer itself can respond only to machine language.

for programmers are that it is difficult to avoid transcription errors and omissions and equally difficult to locate any errors that are made. Today few programmers write machine-language programs. If they need to write programs that are closely associated with the way the computer actually carries out operations, they may use assembly languages.

Assembly Languages. For more than thirty years programmers have coded their programs in languages that resemble English, beginning with assembly languages (also called second-generation programming languages). These languages allow programmers to replace the 0s and 1s of machine languages with letters and symbols. For example, an assembly-language program segment for the preceding calculation might take the following form:

```
MOV AL, AMOUNT
SUB AL, FREIGHT
SUB AL, TAXES
MOV NETAMT, AL
```

These instructions resemble imperative sentences in English, with verbs like MOV (move) and SUB (subtract) and nouns like AMOUNT and NETAMT (net amount). (AL is a register that is used for temporary storage.)

Even though programmers can use English-like languages, computers cannot recognize anything other than electronic impulses expressed as 0s and 1s. Program instructions therefore have to be translated into a form that can be processed by computers. The more English-like a programming language is, the more sophisticated this translation process has to be. The translation process is carried out by a language translation program, a type of systems software.

Programs that translate assembly language into machine code are called assemblers. They enable programmers to use a name like AMOUNT instead of numbers like 0001, thereby saving time, reducing errors, and making the program easier for the programmer to modify. Assemblers produce a source code listing, an object code listing, and error messages to help document and test programs. They may include debugging packages that make it easier for programmers to test and debug programs.

Assembly language is certainly more readable than machine language, but it is not an ideal programming language. The source code of programs written in assembly language is illegible to users. Programmers must keep track of the contents of the various storage areas in the computer, a difficult task; moreover, traditional assembly languages are machine dependent—that is, a different assembly language is needed for each type

---

Assembly languages
Programming languages that allow the programmer to use letters and symbols to replace the 0s and 1s of machine language.

Assembler
A program that translates assembly-language programs into machine language.

of computer. For example, an assembly-language program written for the IBM PC will not run on an IBM mainframe computer without special software. This last drawback is particularly serious for companies that use a variety of computers, and it has led to the development of several assembly languages that can run on different computers.

An important advantage of assembly languages is that assembly-language programs may run very rapidly. In addition, any type of program a user wants can be written in an assembly language. The language is customized to a particular series of computers and therefore can take advantage of special features of the computer such as graphics.

Despite the advantages of assembly languages and their vast improvement over machine languages, they have some distinct limitations. Users and managers are unable to read assembly-language programs and are dependent on programmers to modify them. Most programmers dislike working with such programs because writing and modifying them is a time-consuming, painstaking process. For these reasons, the next level of programming languages, which are known as high-level languages, was developed.

High-Level Programming Languages

High-level programming languages, also called third-generation programming languages, resemble English and mathematical notation to a much greater degree than assembly languages do, enabling programmers to communicate with computers more easily and permitting nonprogrammers to read the programs in many situations. There are many high-level languages, each of which was developed to help solve a particular type of problem. In recent years, however, the boundaries among the different high-level programming languages have become blurred. New versions of existing languages combine the best features of different languages. For example, new versions of BASIC incorporate features that were formerly the exclusive domain of Pascal.

High-level languages have the following characteristics:
1. They allow programmers to concentrate on the problem to be solved rather than on the computer's internal operations. For example, programmers need not be concerned with where items are stored in memory.
2. One high-level-language instruction can correspond to many machine-language instructions. For example, the COBOL instruction

High-level languages
Programming languages that resemble English or mathematical notation and permit more natural communication between the programmer and the computer than assembly languages do.

```
SUBTRACT TAXES, FREIGHT FROM AMOUNT GIVING NET-AMOUNT
```
may be translated into the assembly-language instructions
```
MOV   AL, AMOUNT
SUB   AL, FREIGHT
SUB   AL, TAXES
MOV   NETAMT, AL
```

Since it has been shown that programmers tend to write the same number of instructions per day regardless of the complexity of the programming language, high-level-language programmers get more done in a day than assembly-language programmers do.

3. It is easier to apply the principles and techniques of structured programming with high-level languages than with low-level languages.

4. There are many testing and debugging features in high-level languages that increase programmers' productivity and eliminate tedious tasks. Some high-level languages have a built-in editor or word processor, which can speed up coding and debugging considerably.

5. Most high-level languages are standardized to some extent, making it possible to use the same program on several types of computers. For example, the COBOL program written for Acme's accounts payable department could be run with minor modifications on mainframes, minicomputers, or powerful personal computers.

6. Users can read some high-level-language programs, a feature that enables them to compare the program to their specifications.

Translating High-Level Languages. Like assembly languages, high-level languages need to be translated into machine language. Assemblers translate assembly languages into machine code; similarly, **interpreters** and **compilers** translate high-level languages into machine code so that the computer can recognize the instructions. The main difference between interpreters and compilers is that interpreters translate one instruction at a time, performing the operation if possible, whereas compilers translate an entire program into machine code before performing any operations. Here is an example. The BASIC program

```
10 PRINT 10 * 10
20 PRINT 10 * 20
30 END
```

would produce the following results:

```
100
200
```

Interpreter
A program that translates a high-level language program one instruction at a time, executing it if possible.

Compiler
A program that translates an entire high-level language program into machine language before attempting to perform any operations.

CHAPTER 8 255 PROGRAMMING LANGUAGES

whether it was interpreted or compiled. However, if we modify this program to introduce a syntax error in the second instruction, we can see the difference between these two translation methods. The interpreted BASIC program

```
10 PRINT 10 * 10
20 PRNT 10 * 20
30 END
```

would produce the following results:

```
100
Syntax error in line 20.
```

The first instruction is interpreted and, because it is without error, executed immediately. The second instruction is interpreted, and because PRNT is not recognized, an error message is produced.

The compiled BASIC program

```
10 PRINT 10 * 10
20 PRNT 10 * 20
30 END
```

would produce the following results:

```
Syntax error in line 20.
```

The compiler translates the entire program before executing a single instruction. Because line 20 contains an error, the computer does not execute any instructions.

Because the interpreter checks and carries out each instruction individually, the programmer can see its effect immediately. When debugging an interpreted program, the programmer can determine exactly what the program is doing by entering one or more instructions and rerunning the program. A disadvantage of interpreters is that they do not produce object code. This means that the computer must translate the program into machine code one line at a time each time it is run. If a line is executed 100 times, it is translated 100 times. Therefore, interpreters are much slower than compilers and assemblers for running most programs.

Compilers, on the other hand, allow the programmer or user to insert an entire program (or program segment) and then give the command to compile it. The computer compiles the program and generates object code. If the program compiles without any errors, the programmer or user gives a command to run the (compiled) object code. A major advantage of compilers is that once a program has been compiled and its object code produced, tested, and debugged, the object code can be simply rerun with new data. In other words, the source code does not

**FORTRAN
(FORmula
TRANslator)**
*A high-level
programming
language that was
developed primarily
to enable scientists
and engineers to
express problems in
mathematical
formulas.*

**COBOL (COmmon
Business Oriented
Language)**
*The most widely
used programming
language for
commercial and
administrative
applications on
mainframe
computers.*

have to be translated each time the program is run. This makes compiled languages faster to execute than interpreted languages.

FORTRAN. Over the years literally hundreds of high-level programming languages have been developed. In the rest of this section we will examine several of the more important ones, beginning with the first major high-level language, FORTRAN. **FORTRAN** (*FORmula TRANslator*) was released by IBM in 1957 primarily for use by scientists and engineers. The language is specifically geared to mathematical formulas. FORTRAN caused a minor revolution in the computer world: Many FORTRAN users found that they were able to write their own programs rather than have professional programmers write them. This was important because programmers rarely had sufficient scientific or engineering knowledge to fully understand the users' needs and translate them into computer language.

Since FORTRAN was introduced before the advent of structured programming, many FORTRAN programs are difficult to read and modify. The nature of many scientific and engineering programs is such that once they have been debugged and run properly, they need little or no updating. Nevertheless, since its inception FORTRAN has undergone numerous revisions. In the late 1970s FORTRAN 77, which contains many features of structured programming, was introduced. FORTRAN is now available for computers of all types, but it is still used mostly for scientific and engineering applications. Figure 8-1 illustrates a FORTRAN program that calculates the true annual rate of interest for a loan.

COBOL. **COBOL** (*COmmon Business Oriented Language*) was conceived in 1959 at a U.S. Department of Defense meeting. The goal of the meeting, which included representatives

The Pentagon is the headquarters of the U.S. Department of Defense, the world's largest computer user. The Defense Department was a major force in the development of two programming languages, COBOL and Ada.

FIGURE 8-1

A FORTRAN Program

```
00100C This program calculates the true rate of interest
00110C List of variables
00120C    PAYYR    Payments per year
00130C    FINCHR   Total finance charges
00140C    AMOUNT   Amount financed
00150C    NUMPAY   Total number of payments
00160C    ANRATE   Annual interest rate
00200     REAL    FINCHR,AMOUNT,ANRATE
00210     INTEGER   PAYYR,NUMPAY
00220     PAYYR  = 12
00230     FINCHR = 600.00
00240     AMOUNT = 3000.00
00250     NUMPAY = 36
00300     ANRATE = 2 * PAYYR * FINCHR * 100 / (AMOUNT * (NUMPAY+1))
00310     PRINT, ' For a loan with'
00320     PRINT, PAYYR, ' Payments per year'
00330     PRINT, FINCHR, ' Total finance charges'
00340     PRINT, AMOUNT, ' Amount financed'
00350     PRINT, NUMPAY, ' Total number of payments'
00360     PRINT, ' The annual interest rate (%) is ', ANRATE
00370     STOP
00380     END
```

This program calculates the true annual rate of interest (about 12.97 percent) for a loan of $3000.00 repaid at $100.00 per month for three years.

from private industry, government users, and computer manufacturers, was to establish a common programming language for business and related applications. The committee achieved its goals with COBOL, which soon became the most widely used business programming language for mainframe computers.

The following features have enabled COBOL to remain successful as a business programming language for about thirty years:

1. *Standard.* From its inception, COBOL has been standardized to a large degree. Thus, it is possible for a company to change computers without having to rewrite its COBOL applications from scratch.

2. *Readable.* Because COBOL resembles English, COBOL programs are fairly legible, reducing the amount of documentation needed and facilitating maintenance.

3. *Adaptable.* COBOL is a flexible language in that it has evolved as users' needs have changed. Since its inception it has undergone many changes, for example, gaining the ability to process indexed-sequential and random-access files instead of only sequential files as originally designed.

4. *Structured.* Because COBOL was developed before the invention of structured programming, it does not take full advantage of this technique. However, it is possible to write reasonably well-structured programs in COBOL.

The last two decades have seen many attempts to replace COBOL. However, it will undoubtedly remain an important programming language for commercial applications, especially since many companies have invested a great deal of money and time in COBOL programs and programmers. Figure 8-2 illustrates a COBOL program that calculates the true annual rate of interest for a loan.

BASIC. In 1964 two Dartmouth College professors, John Kemeny and Thomas Kurtz, invented **BASIC** (*B*eginner's *A*ll-purpose *S*ymbolic *I*nstruction *C*ode). Their goal was to enable students to use the computer. Today BASIC is the most popular programming language. Virtually every personal and home computer can run BASIC. However, there is no single, widely accepted version of BASIC, as there is in the case of COBOL. Instead, different manufacturers offer different versions or dia-

BASIC (*Beginner's All-purpose Symbolic Instruction Code*)
A programming language that was invented in 1964 for the purpose of enabling students to use the computer.

The BASIC programming language was developed at Dartmouth College in Hanover, New Hampshire, by John Kemeny (right) and Thomas Kurtz in 1964. More recently Kemeny and Kurtz produced a version of BASIC known as True BASIC to meet the programming challenges of the 1980s and 1990s. [(left) Courtesy of True Basic Inc.; (right) Courtesy of Dartmouth College.]

FIGURE 8-2

A COBOL Program

This program calculates the true annual rate of interest (about 12.97 percent) for a loan of $3000.00 repaid at $100.00 per month for three years.

```
001000 IDENTIFICATION DIVISION.
001010 PROGRAM-ID. INTEREST.
001020 AUTHOR. LEVI REISS.
001030 DATE-WRITTEN. MARCH 31, 1988
001040 DATA-COMPILED. APRIL 4,1988
001050
001060 ENVIRONMENT DIVISION.
001070 CONFIGURATION SECTION.
001080 SOURCE-COMPUTER. CYBER-170.
001090 OBJECT-COMPUTER. CYBER-170.
001100
001200 DATA DIVISION.
001210 WORKING-STORAGE SECTION.
001220 01   INTEREST-DATA.
001230      05   PAYMENTS-PER-YEAR        PICTURE 99.
001240      05   TOTAL-FINANCE-CHARGES    PICTURE 999.99.
001250      05   AMOUNT-FINANCED          PICTURE 9999.99.
001260      05   NUMBER-OF-PAYMENTS       PICTURE 99.
001270      05   ANNUAL-INTEREST-RATE     PICTURE 99.999.
001280
001500 PROCEDURE DIVISION.
001510 BEGIN.
001520     MOVE 12 TO PAYMENTS-PER-YEAR.
001530     MOVE 600.00 TO TOTAL-FINANCE-CHARGES.
001540     MOVE 3000.00 TO AMOUNT-FINANCED.
001550     MOVE 36 TO NUMBER-OF-PAYMENTS.
001560     COMPUTE ANNUAL-INTEREST-RATE = 2 * PAYMENTS-PER-YEAR
001570        * TOTAL-FINANCE-CHARGES * 100
001580        / (AMOUNT-FINANCED * (NUMBER-OF-PAYMENTS + 1)).
001590     DISPLAY   " For a loan with".
001600     DISPLAY   PAYMENTS-PER-YEAR " Payments per year".
001610     DISPLAY   TOTAL-FINANCE-CHARGES " Total finance charges".
001620     DISPLAY   AMOUNT-FINANCED " Amount financed".
001630     DISPLAY   NUMBER-OF-PAYMENTS " Total number of payments".
001640     DISPLAY   " The annual interest rate (%) is ".
001650     DISPLAY   ANNUAL-INTEREST-RATE.
001660     STOP RUN.
```

FIGURE 8-3

This program calculates the true annual rate of interest (about 12.97 percent) for a loan of $3000.00 repaid at $100.00 per month for three years.

A BASIC Program

```
010 REM Program to calculate
020 REM The annual interest rate
030 REM List of variables
040 REM   P   Payments per year
050 REM   C   Total finance charges
060 REM   F   Amount financed
070 REM   N   Number of payments
080 REM   R   Annual interest rate
090 LET P = 12
100 LET C = 600.00
110 LET F = 3000.00
120 LET N = 36
130 LET R = 2 * P * C * 100 / (F * (N + 1))
140 PRINT " For a loan with"
150 PRINT, P, " Payments per year"
160 PRINT, C, " Total finance charges"
170 PRINT, F, " Amount financed"
180 PRINT, N, " Total number of payments"
190 PRINT, " The annual interest rate (%) is ", ANRATE
999 END
```

lects. The differences among these versions are usually minor, so that once one has learned one version of BASIC it is relatively easy to learn the other versions.

Originally, BASIC was not a structured programming language, but many newer versions enable users to write structured programs. BASIC is taught in many schools and is used by many people to program home computers. The appendix at the end of this book presents an introduction to BASIC programming. Figure 8-3 illustrates a BASIC program that calculates the true annual rate of interest for a loan.

PL/I (Programming Language I)

A high-level programming language developed by IBM in the mid-1960s. It includes features of COBOL, FORTRAN, and assembly languages.

PL/I. PL/I (Programming Language I) was invented by IBM in the mid-1960s to replace COBOL, FORTRAN, and assembly language; it includes features of all three of those languages. There are a number of advantages to combining the best features of several programming languages in a single all-purpose

FIGURE 8-4

A PL/I Program

This program segment illustrates the calculation of overtime pay for a series of employees who are paid at the rate of time and a half for all hours worked over thirty-five.

```
OVT: PROCEDURE OPTIONS(MAIN);
DECLARE (RATE, HOURS, OVERTIME) FIXED DECIMAL;
GET LIST (RATE, HOURS);
DO WHILE (HOURS > 0);
    IF HOURS <= 35 THEN OVERTIME = 0;
        ELSE OVERTIME = 1.5 * RATE * (HOURS - 35);
    PUT EDIT (RATE, HOURS, OVERTIME) (F(15,3));
    PUT SKIP;
END;
END OVTPL1;
```

language. For example, as modern businesses place increased emphasis on mathematical and statistical techniques, many business programmers need the capacity for more powerful mathematical calculations than can readily be performed with COBOL. At the same time, many scientists and engineers need a programming language that provides greater file-handling ability than FORTRAN does. For both groups, PL/I may be the best programming language.

Because it combines the features of several languages, PL/I is a very extensive language. However, beginners can start to write programs in PL/I by learning only the features that they need. As they become more experienced, they can learn additional features and use them to master more complex problems. PL/I can also be used to write structured programs. It runs mostly on IBM mainframe computers. Figure 8-4 illustrates a PL/I program segment that calculates overtime pay for a series of employees.

Pascal. Pascal takes its name from Blaise Pascal, the seventeenth-century French mathematician who invented the adding machine. It was developed by the Swiss mathematician Niklaus Wirth in 1971. It was the first programming language to be designed since the advent of structured programming; in fact, Pas-

Pascal
The first programming language to be designed after the development of structured programming, whose concepts it incorporates.

FIGURE 8-5

A Pascal Program

```
PROGRAM INTERESTRATE(INPUT, OUTPUT);
  VAR
    FINCHR,AMOUNT,ANRATE : REAL;
    PAYYR,NUMPAY : INTEGER;
(* List of variables *)
(*      PAYYR    Payments per year *)
(*      FINCHR   Total finance charges *)
(*      AMOUNT   Amount financed *)
(*      NUMPAY   Total number of payments *)
(*      ANRATE   Annual interest rate *)
  PAYYR  := 12;
  FINCHR := 600.00;
  AMOUNT := 3000.00;
  NUMPAY := 36;
  ANRATE := 2 * PAYYR * FINCHR * 100/(AMOUNT*(NUMPAY+1));
  WRITELN(' For a loan with');
  WRITELN(PAYYR, ' Payments per year');
  WRITELN(FINCHR, ' Total finance charges');
  WRITELN(AMOUNT, ' Amount financed');
  WRITELN(NUMPAY, ' Total number of payments');
  WRITELN(' The annual interest rate (%) is ', ANRATE)
END.
```

This program calculates the true annual rate of interest (about 12.97 percent) for a loan of $3000.00 repaid at $100.00 per month for three years.

cal was devised for the purpose of teaching structured programming concepts. In the past few years it has become the second most commonly used language for the teaching of programming.

At present Pascal is not widely used for commercial projects. But as more people with experience using Pascal enter the labor force, it could come into increasing use for solving problems both in business and in science and engineering. Figure 8-5 illustrates a Pascal program that calculates the true annual rate of interest for a loan.

C. In 1972 Dennis Ritchie of Bell Laboratories invented the programming language **C**. A key feature of C is *portability*: Programs written in C can be easily moved to another computer.

C
A hybrid language that combines many features of high-level languages with the power of assembly languages.

FIGURE 8-6

A C Program

This short C program, when run at a workstation, asks the person to enter his or her name and then greets the person.

```
main()
{
char*name
 printf("What is your
 name?");
 scanf)"%s",name);
 printf("Hi,%s\n",name);
}
```

Portability is particularly important for companies that use several different computers, and for software manufacturers that want to be able to develop programs that can be used on a wide range of computers. Among the numerous software packages written in C is the highly popular dBASE III.

C is a hybrid language; it combines features of both high-level languages and assembly languages. C is particularly well suited to structured programming. Also, C programs are easier to write and debug than assembly-language programs. At this writing, therefore, C is probably the fastest-growing programming language, but because of its sophisticated nature, it is not an appropriate tool for teaching computer programming. Its use in standard business applications is still fairly limited. Figure 8-6 illustrates a small C program.

Ada. In 1975 the U.S. Department of Defense held an international competition for the development of a new universal programming language. The competition lasted several years and drew a multitude of submissions. The winner was a French project headed by Jean Ichbiah. The language itself was named for the world's first programmer, Lady Ada Lovelace.

Ada is based on Pascal but can do much more. One of its key features is its ability to perform several activities simultaneously, which makes it particularly useful for industrial and military applications. However, Ada is not easy to learn or implement. As of 1986 there still was no complete Ada compiler for personal computers. The language is limited largely to use

Lady Ada Lovelace was the world's first programmer and a collaborator in the design of the first computer. The Ada programming language was named in her honor. (Culver Pictures.)

FIGURE 8-7

An Ada Package

This program segment is used to validate a date entered; for example, that the day is in the range of 1 to 31.

```
PACKAGE CALENDAR IS
  TYPE TIME IS
    RECORD
      YEAR: INTEGER RANGE 1901..1999;
      MONTH: INTEGER RANGE 1..12;
      DAY: INTEGER RANGE 1..31;
    END RECORD;
  FUNCTION CLOCK RETURN TIME;
  FUNCTION "+"(A: TIME; B: DURATION) RETURN TIME;
  FUNCTION "+"(A: DURATION; B: TIME) RETURN TIME;
  FUNCTION "-"(A: TIME; B: DURATION) RETURN TIME;
  FUNCTION "-"(A: TIME; B: TIME) RETURN DURATION;
END CALENDAR;
```

on mainframe computers by the Department of Defense. Figure 8-7 illustrates an Ada package, a feature that is useful for dividing programs into smaller modules or segments.

ALGOL. *ALGOL (ALGOrithmic Language)* was the first major programming language to be designed by a committee and the first international programming language. The initial version of ALGOL was released in 1958. Many of the features of ALGOL, such as the use of procedures (see Figure 8-8), have been carried into other programming languages such as Pascal, C, and Ada. Although ALGOL is not used extensively for commercial applications in North America, it remains a popular programming language in Europe.

APL. In the 1950s Ken Iverson of Harvard University invented *APL (A Programming Language)* as a tool for applied mathematics; subsequently it was applied to computer programming. APL is an extremely concise language: An entire program might take only one or two lines of code. Since APL requires a special keyboard because of its unusual symbols, it generally is not used for business applications such as payroll

FIGURE 8-8

An ALGOL Procedure

This program segment is used to calculate the largest and smallest elements of an array.

```
PROCEDURE MAXANDMIN (A, R, C, BIG, LITTLE); VALUE R,C;
   REAL ARRAY A; INTEGER R, C; REAL BIG, LITTLE;
     BEGIN REAL MAX, MIN; INTEGER I, J
       MAX := MIN := A[1,1];
       FOR J := 1 STEP 1 UNTIL C DO
          FOR I := 1 STEP 1 UNTIL R DO
             IF A[I,J] > MAX THEN MAX := A[I,J] ELSE
             IF A[I,J] < MIN THEN MIN := A[I,J];
             BIG := MAX; LITTLE := MIN
     END
```

and billing. It is better suited to applications that require sophisticated mathematical techniques, such as statistical analysis. Figure 8-9 illustrates a small but useful APL program.

RPG. *RPG (Report Program Generator)* was first marketed by IBM in 1964 with the goal of convincing small businesses to move their data processing applications from punched-card machines to small computers. It represents an unsuccessful attempt to create a programming language that managers could use without the help of computer programmers. But even though very few managers use RPG today, it remains an easy language for programmers to learn, partly because of its limited processing capabilities. RPG can be used on small IBM mainframes and minicomputers. Many small businesses continue to use RPG because it meets their needs; as their needs expand, however, they may consider other solutions.

The Programming Dilemma. The development of high-level programming languages and their use in business have greatly changed the ways in which many businesses operate. Many of the changes have been positive; however, there are some negative aspects as well. In the early 1980s the famous computer industry analyst and author James Martin coined the phrase "the programming dilemma" to refer to the problems that arise from using high-level programming languages to cre-

FIGURE 8-9

An APL Program Segment

```
      ∇SUM
[1]  'THE SUM OF THE INTEGERS FROM 1 TO 100 IS'; +/ι100
```

This program segment calculates and prints the sum of the integers from 1 to 100.

ate and modify information systems. By their very nature, high-level programming languages contribute to the following aspects of the programming dilemma:

1. Many computer solutions are expensive and take an excessively long time—often years—to develop. For many applications, a proposed solution destined to come into use three or four years later is no solution at all.

2. Many programs are highly complex; their length is often measured in thousands of instructions. A system may contain dozens of interrelated programs and hundreds of thousands of instructions. Coding, testing, and debugging these programs may require several person-years, and it is difficult to modify the programs to meet changing requirements.

3. There is a shortage of experienced computer programmers and systems analysts. A related problem is that programmers spend 60 to 80 percent of their time maintaining current systems and programs rather than developing new ones. These constraints frequently result in substantial backlogs in applications programming. Some users may have to wait for several years to have their problems placed on the agenda of the computer services department.

During the past several years there have been numerous efforts to reduce or eliminate the programming dilemma. A major step in this direction is to apply a new type of programming language: a very-high-level programming language that, in theory, represents as great an advance over high-level languages as high-level languages did over assembly languages.

Very-High-Level Programming Languages

Very-high-level programming languages, also called *nonprocedural programming languages* or *fourth-generation programming languages*, date back to the mid-1970s. Today there are many fourth-generation languages. The characteristic that distinguishes them from high-level programming languages is that they enable people to specify *what* they want the computer to do rather than *how* the computer should do it. In other words, fourth-generation languages provide a more natural way for people to communicate with the computer, thereby reducing the programming dilemma in two distinct but complementary ways: (1) Programmers can concentrate on the problem to be solved rather than on the syntax of the programming language, and (2) users can obtain information from the computer without having to rely on computer specialists. Fourth-generation programming languages can be classified into four categories: query languages, application generators, code generators, and natural languages.

> **Very-high-level programming languages**
> *Programming languages that allow people to specify* what *they want a computer to do rather than* how *the computer should do it.*

Query Languages. *Query languages* are very-high-level programming languages that enable users to obtain information from a data base by asking questions or queries. After a relatively short training period, users are able to formulate their own queries without the aid of computer specialists. In the late 1980s a few dozen query languages were available, including *ADASCRIPT+*, a query language associated with a popular mainframe data-base management system, ADABAS. The following lines are written in *ADASCRIPT+*:

```
FIND PERSONNEL WITH NAME = ALEXANDER AND AGE = 30 THRU 45
     CONTROL ON NAME AND ACCUM SALARY
DISPLAY FIRST-NAME NAME AGE SEX SALARY.
```

The answer to the query depends on the contents of the data base. The following is an example:

	LAST-NAME	AGE	SEX	SALARY
HENRY	ALEXANDER	30	M	$ 22,500
HOLLY	ALEXANDER	40	F	$ 36,000
CHARLIE	ALEXANDER	33	M	$ 20,960
HELEN	ALEXANDER	42	F	$ 25,000
	4*			$104,460
END OF REPORT		4 RECORDS FOUND		

This example illustrates the ability of query languages to select records that meet predetermined criteria, such as name and age. Another feature of query languages is the ability to sort selected information from the data base, for example, to list all employees with the same job title in order by salary.

Most users could learn to write queries like those shown here in only a few hours, whereas professional programmers would have to write hundreds of lines of code in COBOL or another high-level language to get the same information. The advantage of using query languages is that users can write their own programs for simple applications, thus avoiding long delays in obtaining programs and freeing programmers from small but time-consuming tasks so they can work on large, more complicated programs using high-level languages. Box 8-1 discusses one application of a very-high-level query language.

Application Generators. An *application generator* enables users or programmers to produce a complete application such as an accounts payable, inventory, or payroll program. There are dozens of application generators on the market, mostly for mainframe computers. The user creates the application by engaging in a dialog with the application generator. For example:

```
What is the name of the input file? Acct-pay file
Do you want to sort the Acct-pay input file (Yes/No)? Yes
On what field do you want to sort the Acct-pay input file?
Account-number
Do you want to sort the Acct-pay input file on other fields in
addition to the Account-number (Yes/No)? Yes
On what other field besides the Account-number do you want to
sort the Acct-pay input file? Invoice-date
```

The dialog continues until enough information has been entered for the computer to generate the program or programs.

A common feature of application generators is *screen painting*, in which users can tell the computer, in nontechnical language, what screens they would like to see as output. Here is an example:

```
                    ACCOUNTS PAYABLE PROGRAM
            ACCOUNT NUMBER DEFINITION SCREEN            (APS-17/B)

ACCOUNT NUMBER    999999
NAME              XXXXXXXXXXXXXXXXXXXXXXXXXXXXXXXXXXXX
ADDRESS           XXXXXXXXXXXXXXXXXXXXXXXXXXXXXXXXXXXX
                  XXXXXXXXXXXXXXXXXXXXXXXXXXXXXXXXXXXX

PHONE             (999) 999-9999
CONTACT           XXXXXXXXXXXXXXXXXXXXXXXXXXXXXXXXXXXX
```

BOX 8-1

MANAGING
CHANGE

Cost-Justifying a Very-High-Level Language

Very-high-level languages can bring many benefits to businesses, but they are likely to come with a price tag of six figures or more. A data processing manager therefore must not only identify the technical benefits of a new software system but also balance those benefits against the costs. A proposal containing both the technical advantages of the system and its cost-justification can then be prepared for the scrutiny of other managers outside the data processing department.

As an example of the cost-justification process, consider the search for a new corporation-wide information tool for Meridian Bancorp of Reading, Pennsylvania. Meridian is the fifth-largest bank holding company in Pennsylvania. Primary responsibility for selection and cost-justification of the new system lay with Gary Rossell, vice-president for data processing.

Rossell began by identifying a product that would meet the firm's technical specifications. The choice on technical grounds was Nomad 2, a fourth-generation database management system (DBMS) developed and marketed by D&B Computing Services. Only after the selection was made did the cost-justification phase begin.

"We always separate selection from justification," says Rossell, "to ensure that we do not come up with a system that, although it fits the budget, might be merely the best choice among a group of second-rate products or one that does not have all the necessary features for our organization's needs. Any other kind of planning would be a bit like deciding you could afford to spend only $6000 on a new automobile before deciding that you really needed a passenger van that could hold eight people in relative comfort.

"Naturally, if we could not cost-justify our choice, we would have to turn to the three R's: regroup, reassess, and, possibly, reselect. The inability to cost-justify would definitely make us reexamine our selection decision in depth."

Cost-justification, Rossell adds, requires a completely different mental set than that required for identifying technical criteria and setting goals. Even so, it is much easier once one becomes familiar with the product's capabilities.

In Meridian's case, Rossell identified four areas of potential cost-justification. The first was the reduced cost of developing new applications of the DBMS. An analysis of the coding process for a typical application showed that 80 percent of the coding time was devoted to routine tasks such as developing screens. Nomad 2 could take over many of these functions and could be operated by less expert, and hence lower-salaried, personnel. Expert programmers could then concentrate on the remaining 20 percent of the coding process that involved logic unique to the application.

A second area consisted of savings outside of application development. These included reduction of purchases of time-sharing services, in-house handling of jobs that were previously done by service bureaus and contract programmers, and avoidance of purchases of add-on software that would be needed for the existing system if Nomad 2 were not acquired.

In addition, Rossell's report to management outlined several other savings. These were items that were harder to put a dollar amount on, but that Rossell felt were nonetheless significant. Examples included reducing the number of jobs that are never requested because users have given up on trying to get what they want from the old system, and meeting the demands of personal-computer users who are outgrowing the capabilities of their desktop machines.

Rossell submitted two separate cost-justification estimates based on these three areas, each of which proved the ability of the new system to pay for itself. Meanwhile, he and his staff continued to work on identifying the fourth cost-justification area: new business opportunities that the new system might create.

Source: Copyright 1985 by CW Communications/Inc., Framingham, MA 01701—Reprinted from Gary G. Rossell, "So You Have Chosen Your 4GL—Now Can You Cost-Justify It?" *Computerworld Focus*, September 18, 1985, pp. 35–36.

Programming Languages

- Query Languages
- Application Generators
- Code Generators
- Natural Languages

Very-High-Level Languages

- FORTRAN
- COBOL
- BASIC
- PL/I
- Pascal
- C
- Ada
- APL
- RPG

High-Level Languages

- Machine Languages
- Assembly Languages

Low-Level Languages

The program converts this information into a program segment that will display the required screen.

The programs produced by some application generators are in high-level programming languages such as COBOL or BASIC. This means that programmers and systems analysts can take the source code and tailor it to an organization's specific needs. The drawback of this procedure is that the organization's technical staff, rather than the software vendor, is responsible for the application. This defeats the purpose of purchasing an application generator. However, if an organization intends to customize the source code generated by the application generator, it can purchase a related product, a code generator, to make the task easier.

Code Generators. A *code generator* is a very-high-level language that is used to produce portable COBOL or other high-level-language programs for specific applications such as accounts payable, inventory, or payroll. As described in Chapter 7, code generators are tools that enhance the productivity of programmers. They can work alongside existing programs written in COBOL or, on occasion, in other languages. Code generators may use existing COBOL programs as input; in fact, some code generators are specifically designed to change unstructured COBOL programs into structured COBOL programs. Unlike most application generators, code generators are meant to be used by computer specialists.

Natural Languages. *Natural languages*, which are currently being developed, are an extension of query languages. They enable users to type or speak into a computer in everyday speech. Some natural languages understand only a limited vocabulary that can be spoken by anyone; others can be "trained" to recognize a particular individual's voice and to understand many more words.

The development of natural languages promises to bring the power of the computer to the handicapped and other users with special needs. When people can communicate with the computer without having to learn a special programming language, their productivity will increase enormously. No longer will it be necessary for a manager to stop in the middle of a dialog with the computer to look for a co-worker or a manual to explain a message that has appeared on the screen or to find the correct form in which to enter an instruction.

Some software packages can be purchased with a *natural language interface*, which enables the user to employ everyday language in giving instructions to the computer. For example, R:base 5000, a popular data-base management program for the

IBM PC, can be purchased with a natural language interface called Clout. When the user enters a word that Clout does not recognize, it asks a series of questions to find out the word's meaning and then adds the word to its dictionary. Suppose, for example, that a user enters the following sentence:

> Give the name of all the slackers and their sales by product in the Northern Region.

First the program decomposes the sentence and finds that it can understand everything except the word *slackers*. It then asks,

> What do you mean by slackers?

The user replies,

> A slacker is a vendor who has sold less than $5000 in the last month and less than $15000 in the last quarter.

The system now has enough information to answer the original request and produces the required list of vendors. It then asks,

> I understand that a slacker is a vendor who has sold less than $5000 in the last month and less than $15000 in the last quarter. Do you want me to add the word slacker to my dictionary?

If the user responds yes, the program will henceforth "understand" the words *slacker* and *slackers*.

Disadvantages of Very-High-Level Languages. Very-high-level languages are easier to use and more like English than high-level languages. In addition, each fourth-generation language has certain specific advantages. However, these very advantages give rise to some disadvantages. Among them are the following:

1. *Hardware requirements*. Programs written in fourth-generation languages often use two to five times the CPU time and disk storage space as similar programs written in high-level languages such as COBOL or PL/I. As users become accustomed to receiving information whenever they need it, they tend to increase the number of requests for information they make, thereby placing further demands on the existing hardware.

2. *Processing limitations*. In many cases the computer-generated code of a fourth-generation language will not fully meet an organization's processing needs. This disadvantage can be overcome if the language allows some modules to be written in a high-level programming language such as COBOL or FORTRAN.

3. *Lack of standardization*. Unlike the case for high-level programming languages, there is no widely accepted standard for fourth-generation programming languages. This lack of standardization makes it difficult to use the same applications on different computer systems. COBOL and FORTRAN specialists are usually available, but it may be difficult for an organization to find specialists in a particular fourth-generation language.

4. *Inefficient programming.* Because users generally are not technically oriented, they may not phrase their queries correctly or efficiently. For example, they may ask questions in such a way that they direct the computer to read and reread the same file needlessly, or they may mistakenly ask for information that they already have. In addition, users may formulate queries that cost more to process than the value of the information generated.

Very-high-level languages do not represent an automatic solution to the programming dilemma, but they are a beginning. Organizations are increasingly using these languages to help reduce the programming dilemma both in developing new applications and in maintaining existing ones.

Selecting a Programming Language

Given the wide variety of programming languages available, it is not always easy to select the most appropriate language for a particular individual or business need. There are, however, some criteria that should be kept in mind when deciding which language is best suited to a specific application.

1. *Programming application.* In general, commercial applications require extensive file-handling capabilities such as are available with COBOL, while scientific and mathematical applications need superior mathematical processing facilities such as are available with FORTRAN. However, these facilities may be offered by other languages such as PL/I and C. Also, an increasing number of business applications call for extensive mathematical or statistical manipulation and other techniques such as graphics.

2. *Performance objective.* Although several different languages can be used for the same purpose, each language is best suited to specific tasks. If a program must make full use of special hardware features (e.g., sophisticated graphics), assembly languages should be considered because they permit direct control over the computer's internal operations. If speed is a major concern, C or assembly languages are appropriate.

If the main objective is to develop the application very quickly, fourth-generation programming languages should be considered. Fourth-generation languages are needed if users are to be furnished with a "programming" capability.

3. *Language availability*. Language availability refers not only to the availability of the software and hardware to run a language, but also to the availability of people who are qualified to write programs in that language. Since the advent of personal computers, it has become possible to obtain a wide variety of programming languages at a relatively low cost. However, obtaining qualified programmers is more difficult. It can take several months to bring a computer programmer to a reasonable level of proficiency in a new programming language. Organizations would be well advised to maintain training programs to ensure that skilled programmers are available when they are needed.

4. *Portability*. If an organization has a variety of computer equipment and wants to be able to run the application on all of that equipment, portable languages such as C and, to a lesser extent, Pascal should be considered.

5. *Maintenance*. If the application is expected to undergo extensive maintenance, as is typical of most business applications, ease of maintenance is a major consideration. This means that the language chosen should support structured programming and provide for clear documentation.

6. *Programmers and users*. In many ways an organization's staff is the most important factor in deciding which programming language to use. If the programmers are highly skilled in assembly language, for example, they may program just as quickly and efficiently as COBOL programmers and it would be inefficient to retrain them to use high-level languages. It is also necessary to consider the kind of user who will be interacting with the system. Some users will refuse to apply any query language at all, while others, given appropriate training, will quickly start developing their own small applications.

7. *Programmer preference*. The final consideration in the choice of a language is programmer preference. Programmers tend to have a favorite language or languages in which their productivity is substantially higher than in other languages. Although programmers do not make the final decision on which programming language to use for a particular application, their opinions are important.

In choosing a language for a particular application, some of the considerations listed here may be critical while others do not matter much. Box 8-2 presents an actual case study in the choice of a language. In this case performance and mainte-

BOX 8-2

USING COMPUTERS

Choosing a Language for *Econograph*

When economists Charles Link and Jeff Miller wanted to design a computer-aided instruction package for economics, they asked expert programmer John Bergman to join the team. After several meetings at which they discussed the type of package they wanted to produce, Link, Miller, and Bergman agreed on the outlines of a program. As the proposal took shape, Bergman pondered the problem of what language to use. Should the program be written in assembly language? In a compiled or interpreted version of the popular BASIC? In structured Pascal? In lightning-fast C?

Bergman looked at the requirements. First of all, the project was a big one. The final version of *Econograph* would include some 10,000 lines of code. Writing such a large program in assembly language would be extremely tedious. Also, for the program to fit on no more than two floppy disks, a compiled language would have to be used. The common forms of BASIC, which are interpreted rather than compiled, would be too bulky.

More than anything, the size of the project made a structured approach to programming imperative. The program would have to be broken down into manageable, uniform, well-organized units to permit efficient debugging and maintenance. It is not impossible to write structured programs in BASIC, but that language was not designed with structured programming in mind. The need for structure narrowed Bergman's choices to C and Pascal.

Each of these has its advantages. One advantage of C is the speed of the compiled program. But for this application speed was not critical. The pace of progress through an *Econograph* study session is set by the user, not the machine. In some cases Bergman would actually need to reduce the speed of the program.

Programs written in Pascal tend not to run as fast as programs written in C, but they take up less room. This was critical for the *Econograph* project, which had to be limited to two disks. Pascal also had some other advantages. It has excellent input-output tools, especially for graphics. And Pascal allows the use of *overlays*—a technique in which chunks of the program stay on the disk most of the time, to be called into active memory only as needed. Heavy use of overlays would be needed to meet another requirement imposed by the publisher, namely, ability to run the program on a PC with as little as 128K of memory.

Pascal didn't offer quite everything. For example, it does not permit a technique called linking, which allows sections of a program to be stitched together after they have been compiled. It also places a limit on the quantity of code that can be compiled at one time. Bergman was able to find ways around these drawbacks, however. The final choice, then, was Pascal.

nance were key considerations, with programmer preference also playing a role.

Whatever programming language is chosen, both programmers and users will have to communicate with the computer. They do this via an operating system, the subject of the final section of this chapter.

Operating Systems

Operating system
Systems software that supervises the input, output, storage, and processing functions of a computer system.

An **operating system** is systems software that supervises the input, output, storage, and processing functions of a computer system. Every computer has an operating system. When the computer is turned on, the operating system must be activated. This is often done automatically but may sometimes require that the user insert a floppy disk containing the operating system. The system then continues to operate until the user turns the computer off. Some functions of the operating system are internal and are not at all evident to the user; others are controlled by the user. In addition, some functions and features of operating systems are common to all computers, while others are specific to certain types of computers.

Types of Operating Systems

Operating systems are concerned with the inner workings of the computer and therefore are different for different types of computers. In general, mainframe computers and supercomputers use *proprietary operating systems,* that is, systems that are specifically designed for a particular family of computers. Many minicomputers use the standardized operating system UNIX, which is discussed later in the chapter. Although a number of microcomputers, such as the Apple Macintosh, use proprietary operating systems, many others use operating systems that have become industry standards. Among these are CP/M, which is still used on many smaller microcomputers; PC-DOS, which is used on the IBM family of personal computers and some compatibles; and the closely related MS-DOS, which is used on other compatibles.

Programs and associated data may have to be modified or *converted* to some extent when they are transferred from one computer to another that uses a different operating system. In contrast, moving programs and data from one computer to another with the same operating system may require no conversion whatsoever. The user simply moves the diskette to the other computer. This feature helps explain the popularity of standard operating systems.

Functions of Operating Systems

The operating system can be viewed as the interface between the computer's hardware and its applications software, that is, the program that produces results for the user. It is typical to divide the functions of the operating system into three categories: job management, resource management, and data management.

Job Management. Efficient operation of mainframes and minicomputers involves coordinating dozens or even hundreds of jobs that are being performed at the same time. A key function of the operating system is to make certain that all of these jobs get done as fast as possible and that the computer is never idle. The operating system's *job management* function initiates, monitors, and terminates the processing of each job.

As an example of job management, consider the different functions of the operating system for a minicomputer in The Longmann's Insurance Company. For simplicity, we consider only two users: George Morison, a typist who is using a word-processing program to enter the text of new insurance policies, and Jan Kurlancz, an insurance agent who is using a statistical package to analyze policy rates. Each user is sitting at a workstation. Morison turns on his computer and, at the request of the operating system, enters a password. Job management verifies the password and starts Morison's word-processing program. A second or two later the process is repeated for Kurlancz. Job management reads the users' commands and passes on their requests to resource management and data management (to be described shortly). When Kurlancz indicates that she wants to sign off, job management terminates her job and calculates the amount that her department will be charged for computer services.

Resource Management. A computer system includes a variety of resources, such as primary storage, input and output devices, and CPU processing time. Another function of the operating system, called *resource management*, is to allocate these resources to various jobs so that work gets done as quickly and efficiently as possible. When notified by job management, resource management allocates time on the central

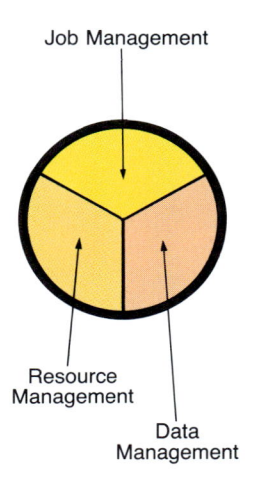

Operating System Functions

processing unit, first to one user and then to another. Again at the request of job management, resource management allocates access to the hard disk to a particular user. Thus, if both Morison and Kurlancz request data from the hard disk at the same time, one of them will have to wait for a brief interval, probably less than a second.

Data Management. The *data management* function of the operating system handles the inputting and outputting of data as well as its storage and retrieval. A key function of data management is to relate the *logical data* as seen by the user to the *physical data* that is actually contained on the storage device—in this case, the hard disk. Kurlancz, for example, describes the data that she works with as policy rates. She has been told that these rates are available in the file POL88A. She is not concerned with the actual location of this particular file on the hard disk. Data management must convert her request for file POL88A to the appropriate physical location on the hard disk before Kurlancz can make use of this data.

Operating System Commands

The job, resource, and data management functions of the operating system are all internal, and users generally are not aware of them. In addition, when the computer is turned on, the operating system may automatically perform certain internal functions that enable it to display the date and time and check how much memory is available in the computer.

There are, however, certain aspects of the operating system with which users do interact. In the case of personal computers, users give *commands* to the operating system when they want the computer to perform certain tasks. For example, there are commands to make copies of diskettes, check how much memory is available on a diskette, list the files on a diskette, and delete files. Additional commands enable the user to erase files, sort files in a specific order (e.g., by date), and make backup copies of files. On minicomputers and mainframes, users interact with the operating system via what is called job control language (to be discussed shortly).

User Interaction on a PC. There are technical aspects of operating systems that need not concern users. On the other hand, users who are familiar with the nontechnical aspects of a computer's operating system can use the computer and its programs much more efficiently. This will become clear in the following example.

The user is inserting a diskette to activate the operating system of a Texas Instruments microcomputer. (Courtesy of Texas Instruments.)

Claudia King just began a data processing course. She has been instructed to copy a file from her teacher's master diskette onto her own diskette. King is working on an IBM PC that has two floppy disk drives and uses the most common operating system, PC-DOS or DOS (short for *Disk Operating System*).

King inserts a diskette containing the operating system into the left-hand drive, turns on the computer, and the operating system begins working immediately. After completing its opening routines, it displays a prompt, A>, on the screen, which means that it's ready for King to type a command. (The A means that the operating system expects the user to work with disk drive A.)

Before a file can be copied onto a blank diskette, the diskette has to be initialized, or prepared to receive data; this process is called *formatting*. At the A> prompt, she types the command, or instruction, that tells the operating system to format the blank disk:

```
format B:
```

When the formatting is done, the operating system will display a message like the following:

```
Formatting...Format complete

     362496 bytes total disk space
     362496 bytes available on disk

Format another (Y_N)?
```

King types an N to indicate that she does not want to format another diskette. When she has done so, the A> prompt appears again.

Now King removes the diskette containing DOS from drive A and replaces it with the master diskette containing the file to be copied. King wants to copy the file TEACH.BAS, a BASIC program that her teacher has written. At the A> prompt, King types the command

```
COPY TEACH.BAS B:
```

This tells the operating system to copy the file from the diskette in drive A onto the one in drive B.

If the command is typed correctly, the file can be copied in a matter of seconds, depending on its size. After King gives the command, all she has to do is wait for the message

```
1 File(s) copied
```

which tells her that the copy has been made.

Although the copy procedure may seem simple to the user, this command causes the operating system to carry out many activities. Before it can copy the file, the operating system has to make sure the syntax of the command is correct; even a slight error can lead to unexpected results or inability to carry out the command. For example, if King typed COPY TEACH.BAS B, accidentally omitting the colon after the B, the operating system would respond with an error message.

The operating system also checks to see if there is already a file named TEACH.BAS on the diskette in drive B. If there is, the system copies the file from the diskette in drive A onto the TEACH.BAS file in drive B, erasing the original TEACH.BAS file on the diskette in B. Clearly, therefore, it is extremely important to check file names and diskettes carefully before entering the copy command. The operating system provides a command, DIR, that enables the user to obtain a *directory* or list of the files on a diskette.

The operating system makes sure there is enough room for the TEACH.BAS file on the diskette in drive B. Since King is using a new diskette, there will be room; however, users often copy files onto diskettes that already contain files. If there is not enough room, the operating system displays a message like the following:

```
Insufficient disk space
    0 File(s) copied
```

The system also checks to make sure the disk drive door is closed. If it's not, it displays an appropriate message. And it checks to see if the diskette in drive B can be written on. Users often place a small tab on the slot in the diskette to prevent accidental erasing of files.

Most operating systems will check on these and other things

Once the operating system of this Tandy 1000 microcomputer has been activated, the user can choose among several applications. (Courtesy of Tandy Corp.)

before carrying out a user's command, but different systems handle the information in different ways. For example, some operating systems inform users that they are attempting to copy a file onto a diskette that already contains a file with the same name, whereas other systems, such as DOS, do not.

One reason for the popularity of Lotus 1-2-3 and many other personal-productivity software packages is that they allow the user to employ operating system functions without leaving the program. They may also provide services that complement the operating system. For example, Lotus 1-2-3 informs the user of a possible overwrite of the file.

Several popular personal computers have very different operating systems. For example, users of the Apple Macintosh do not have to deal with commands like copy and delete. Instead, with the aid of a mouse (see Chapter 2), they can move the cursor to select the picture or icon that corresponds to what they want to do. To delete a file, they position the cursor on the appropriate icon. Many users, particularly those who do not like to type, prefer this way of interacting with the computer.

User Interaction on Minicomputers and Mainframes. Typically, from the user's point of view the differences between working with microcomputer operating systems and the operating systems of minicomputers and mainframes are not very great. With appropriate training, users can work with either type of system. There are, however, some differences between the ways in which users interact with the operating systems of these two categories of computers. For example, many minicomputer and mainframe operating systems require the use of specialized languages known as *job control language*. Following are a few lines of a widely used job control language:

```
//JOB117     JOB      (3984,444),    LEVI REISS, CLASS=A
//LKED       EXEC     PGM=IEWL,COND=(12,LE,FORT)
```

Because the coding of job control language commands is more difficult than coding in most high-level programming languages, the preparation and testing of such commands is not done by users but is assigned to programmers.

Another difference between the operating systems of large and medium-sized computers and those of microcomputers is that the former restrict access to users who have passwords; this restriction does not usually apply to microcomputer users. While a large proportion of microcomputer users work with floppy disks, users of minicomputers and mainframes work with magnetic disks and tapes that may not be removed from the computer center. Also, microcomputer users operate relatively independently. For example, they must back up their own files, whereas users of larger computers can rely on the services of computer professionals for file backup. As minicomputers increasingly must compete with microcomputers for business applications, the differences between these types of computers, including their operating systems, will continue to decrease.

Special Features of Operating Systems

There are standard functions that all operating systems perform, as discussed earlier. In addition, there are special features that have been available on large computers for more than twenty years and are available on many of the more powerful microcomputers. These features include multiprogramming, multiprocessing, and virtual storage.

Multiprogramming. The earliest computers were able to perform only a single activity at any one time. For example, whenever a card reader had to input a card, the entire computer system waited for the operation to be completed. Today's computers, which may handle complex programs and dozens or even hundreds of programs at once, have to be able to perform many activities simultaneously. The operating system makes this possible through *multiprogramming*, the ability of a single central processing unit to carry out more than one instruction at what appears to be the same time. Time-consuming operations such as input and output may be initiated by the central processing unit, which can proceed to another program while the original operation is completed automatically. Since even a relatively slow input or output operation is rapid by human standards, it looks as if the computer is running two or more programs at once.

Multiprocessing. Some companies have computer networks in which the computers are in geographically dispersed locations, whereas others have two or more computers at the same location. There is a growing tendency for a single computer to contain more than one central processing unit. In each of these cases the operating system is used for *multiprocessing*. Multiprocessing is the ability of a computer system with more than one CPU to run two or more instructions at the same time. Thus, for example, if a company outgrows its mainframe computer, it can purchase another processor that works in tandem with the first one. The operating system then allocates jobs to either of the two processors.

Virtual Storage. In order for a computer to execute an instruction, the instruction must be in primary storage. Because the size of primary storage is always limited compared to the capacity of secondary storage, these two types of storage must be combined to allow larger programs to run. *Virtual storage* is an operating system function that enables a computer to run programs that cannot fit in available primary storage. When an instruction to execute is not found in primary storage, the virtual-storage function automatically "makes room" for it and transfers it into primary storage. Transferring instructions one at a time would be very inefficient, so the operating system transfers a portion of the program stored on disk.

Virtual storage enables programmers to write extensive programs without worrying about the availability of primary storage. However, it is not without disadvantages. It is quite complicated for the operating system to decide when and what to transfer from primary storage to disk and vice versa. This difficulty is increased for computers running numerous programs at the same time. Virtual-storage capabilities increase the size of the operating system and cause it to run more slowly. Moreover, transferring instructions back and forth between primary and secondary storage takes time. In spite of these drawbacks, however, most mainframe and minicomputer operating systems have virtual-storage capabilities.

Standardization

Business users have always had a strong interest in the standardization of computer hardware and software. When the time comes to upgrade their hardware or acquire additional software, they want to be able to choose the most suitable product without having to worry about whether the hardware and software will work together. As mentioned earlier, traditionally the operating systems for mainframes and minicomputers were proprietary. This meant that changing the hardware required changing the operating system and, therefore, modifying the software or even re-creating it from scratch. While mainframe computer manufacturers could afford to spend the millions of dollars necessary to develop their own operating systems, such a choice was clearly impossible for most microcomputer manufacturers. Many adopted the popular CP/M (Control *Program* for *Microcomputers*) operating system. In 1981, however, IBM introduced its PC, and its immediate and overwhelming popularity caused its operating system, PC-DOS, to become the de facto industry standard, along with the quite similar MS-DOS.

UNIX. Clearly it would be advantageous to combine the standardization of microcomputer operating systems with the ability of mainframe computer operating systems to serve large numbers of users simultaneously. Several operating systems have been designed with these goals in mind. The most widely used of these is UNIX, which was developed about 1970 at AT&T's Bell Laboratories. UNIX can run on computers ranging in size from supercomputers to large microcomputers. UNIX often serves as the operating system for computer networks of all sizes. For years UNIX was restricted largely to technical applications, but in recent years it has found a place in numerous business applications. It remains to be seen whether UNIX will achieve the degree of popularity for commercial applications that it has already earned in technical applications.

This chapter has described what programming is, what kinds of programming languages are available and when each should be used, and what a computer's operating system is. However, these are not the aspects of data processing that will concern you most—unless you decide to become a computer specialist. Chapter 9 examines how people actually use computers. It discusses several software applications that are useful in business and other environments and how personal-productivity software is used to carry out these applications efficiently.

The UNIX operating system and the hardware required to run it are stored on a motherboard that can be inserted in AT&T microcomputers. (Courtesy of AT&T.)

SUMMARY

1. **Programming languages** are specialized languages that enable people to prepare computer programs. The first programming languages, which were coded in 0s and 1s, were low-level languages called **machine languages**.

2. **Assembly languages** allow the programmer to use letters and symbols to replace 0s and 1s. Programs that translate assembly-language programs into machine language are known as **assemblers**.

3. **High-level programming languages** resemble English or mathematical notation and permit more natural communication between the programmer and the computer. They also make it easier to apply the principles and techniques of structured programming.

4. There are two basic types of translation programs: interpreters and compilers. **Interpreters** translate the program one instruction at a time, performing the operation if possible. An interpreted program must be translated from scratch each time it is run. **Compilers** translate the entire program into machine language before attempting to perform any operations.

5. **FORTRAN** (FORmula TRANslator) was developed primarily to enable scientists and engineers to express mathematical formulas. **COBOL** (COmmon Business Oriented Language) is the most widely used programming language for commercial and administrative applications on mainframe computers. **BASIC** (Beginner's All-purpose Symbolic Instruction Code) was designed to enable students to use the computer. **PL/I** (Programming Language I) was invented by IBM and includes features of COBOL, FORTRAN, and assembly language.

6. **Pascal** was the first programming language to be designed after the introduction of structured programming, whose concepts it incorporates. **C** is a hybrid language, combining features of several high-level languages with the power found in assembly languages. Other high-level programming languages include Ada, ALGOL, APL, and RPG.

7. **Very-high-level programming languages** allow people to specify *what* they want the computer to do rather than *how* the computer should do it. These languages can be classified into several categories: query languages, application generators, code generators, and natural languages. The disadvantages of very-high-level languages include hardware requirements, processing limitations, lack of standardization, and inefficient programming.

8. An **operating system** is systems software that supervises the input, output, storage, and processing functions of a computer system. Many microcomputers use IBM's PC-DOS operating system.

9. Although operating systems vary greatly, they all share certain basic functions: job management, resource management, and data management. Additional features include multiprogramming, the ability of a single central processing unit to carry out more than one instruction at what seems to be the same time; multiprocessing, the ability of a computer system with more than one processor to run two or more instructions at the same time; and virtual storage, a method by which the operating system allows the computer to run programs that do not fit in available primary storage.

KEY TERMS

programming language

machine language

assembly language

assembler

high-level programming language

interpreter

compiler

FORTRAN

COBOL

BASIC

PL/I

Pascal

C

very-high-level programming language

operating system

REVIEW QUESTIONS

1. What are programming languages? What language is used by the computer itself? Why aren't programs written in this language very often?

2. How do assembly languages differ from machine languages? List some of the things that an assembler does.

3. Define high-level programming languages. What are the advantages of high-level languages compared to assembly languages? What are their disadvantages?

4. Name and describe the two types of translation programs for high-level programming languages. Distinguish between them from the programmer's point of view.

5. Describe the following high-level languages, indicating how they could be used: FORTRAN, COBOL, BASIC, PL/I, Pascal, C, Ada, ALGOL, APL, RPG.

6. Compare and contrast very-high-level programming languages and high-level programming languages.

7. Name the criteria for selecting a programming language. In your opinion, which two are the most important? Justify your choices.

8. What is the purpose of an operating system? Describe briefly how a user interacts with a microcomputer operating system to copy a file. (Identify both the computer and the operating system used.)

9. What are the three basic functions of an operating system? What are some of the special features of operating systems? Which of these features are important to business users?

APPLICATIONS

1. Discuss the differences between two dialects of BASIC as described in advertisements.

2. Interview a student who has used more than one programming language. Which one does the student prefer and why?

3. Describe the features offered by a very-high-level programming language as presented in an ad. Find an article about an application using that language. Compare the application with the claims made in the advertisement.

4. Discuss the following statement: The programming dilemma will remain even if very-high-level programming languages are used.

CASE FOR DISCUSSION

The East Virginia Highway Authority (EVHA) had computer problems. The problem was with the COBOL-based software that was used to process applications for drivers' licenses, vehicle registrations, titles, and so on.

One problem was that the system, which had been modified repeatedly over the years, had become difficult to maintain. Modifications of the system that were needed in order to comply with new laws or to overcome errors took months.

Also, the system was not very user-friendly. The users included thousands of clerks in neigborhood EVHA offices, some of whom had little familiarity with computers and many of whom worked only part-time. They had to memorize many codes and abbreviations in order to process applications, and when they made mistakes, the error messages displayed on the screen were often confusing or uninformative.

In 1987 a new director was appointed to head the EVHA. He was determined to solve the problem once and for all. His dramatic move was to convert the entire system from COBOL to NATLANG, a natural language interface that allowed clerks to address their computers in ordinary English.

For example, suppose an applicant named Janet Johnson Downey wanted a license plate with her initials on it. Before the plate could be issued, the clerk processing the application would have to check to see if anyone was already using the desired letters by typing

```
>VANSRCH JJD/CUR
```

to find out if anyone currently had the plate JJD. Any mistake—say, an extra space beween "VANSRCH" and "JJD"—would produce a message that said

```
SYNTAX ERROR 1038
```

Unless the user had memorized a long list of error codes, a bulky printed manual would have to be consulted to find out that error 1038 meant an extra space.

With NATLANG, after the applicant's name and address were entered, the clerk and the computer would enter into a dialog something like this:

```
Operator:  CAN WE GIVE THIS LADY A PLATE
           WITH HER INITIALS?
Computer:  DO YOU MEAN IS THE VANITY PLATE
           JJD CURRENTLY IN USE?
Operator:  YES
Computer:  THE PLATE JJD IS CURRENTLY IN
           USE BY JOHN J DILLWATTER OF
           213 FALLS ROAD, LITTLETOWN EV.
Operator:  WHAT CAN WE GIVE HER THAT IS
           CLOSE TO JJD?
Computer:  THE FOLLOWING VARIATIONS ARE
           AVAILABLE: JJD 1; JD; J-J-D
Operator:  OK, LETS GO WITH J-J-D
Computer:  REQUEST PROCESSED. VANITY
           PLATE J-J-D IS NOW ASSIGNED TO
           JANET JOHNSON DOWNEY OF 311
           MAPLE STREET, HENRIETTA EV.
```

In a test at one local office, everyone loved NATLANG. Clerical personnel liked the flexibility and user-friendliness of the system. Supervisors noted a dramatic drop in the time needed to train operators. Applicants were pleased with the quicker, more accurate service. On the basis of this test, NATLANG was put on-line throughout the state in June 1987.

The result was a total disaster. The system's hardware, which could process VANSRCH JJD/CUR in a couple of microseconds, took ten times as long to process CAN WE GIVE THIS LADY A PLATE WITH HER INITIALS. Ten times a couple of microseconds was still pretty fast—as long as only one local office was using the system. However, when a thousand users got on the system at once, the tenfold increase in processing time vastly overloaded the system's capacity. The response time for each instruction stretched to several minutes. Lines at local offices stretched out the door and across the street. Applicants' patience stretched to the breaking point and then snapped.

At one local office, applicants who had waited for several hours started throwing chairs and ashtrays when EVHA employees tried to close the office for the day without having served everyone in line. The whole EVHA system had to be shut down for a week while the old COBOL system was resurrected.

CASE QUESTIONS

1. What aspects of the programming dilemma are illustrated by this case?

2. How does the case illustrate the strengths and weaknesses of very-high-level languages?

3. What actions could the EVHA have taken, short of the natural language interface, to solve its initial software problems?

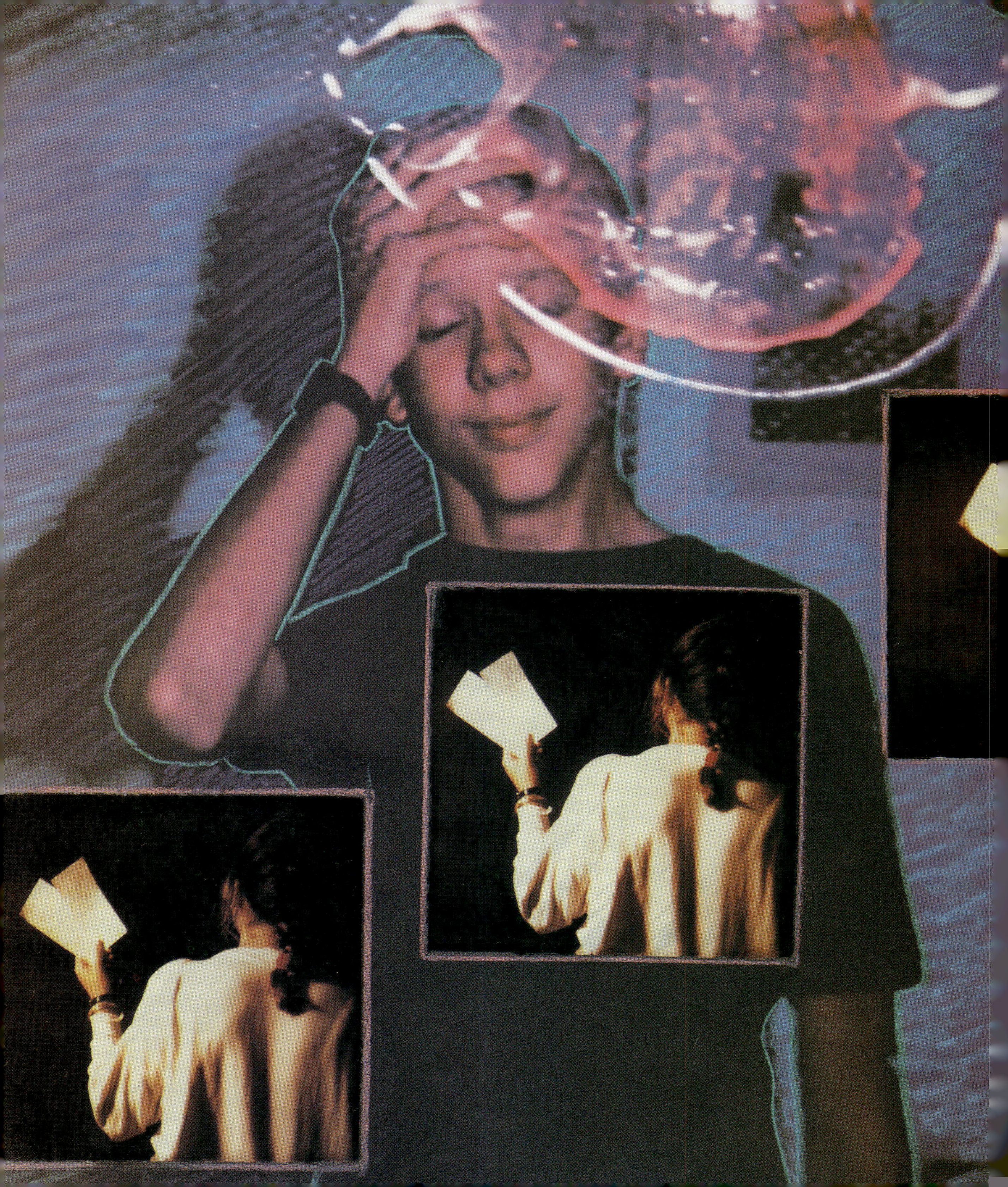

Personal-Productivity Software

CHAPTER 9

A brass plaque on the door of a second-floor office announces John E. Bilodeau, D.D.S., M.S., Orthodontics. Inside the office two people are seated at computer screens. One of them, Nina Giaime, is calling up records from a data base. She has requested a listing of all patients who have started treatment this week. The computer finds 9 of them among the 2117 active patients. Giaime transfers to a word-processing function. She then instructs the system to print welcoming letters to each of the nine people on the list.

Meanwhile Vincent, a tall, sandy-haired teenager, walks somewhat sheepishly to the front desk. "I lost my retainer," he says in a low voice. "Dr. Bilodeau says he'll have a new one by Thursday. How much is it going to cost?" Vincent is thinking about the stupid way in which he lost the retainer. He was eating lunch at McDonald's. He set the retainer down in the plastic box that his McDLT came in. By the time he finished he had forgotten all about it. He threw the box out, retainer and all. Now he is wondering whether his parents will make him pay for it.

Jean Inson, Bilodeau's other assistant, types Vincent's name on a keyboard. A chart appears on a computer screen in front of her. Inson moves the cursor to a field labeled "procedure" and types in 183, the code for a lost retainer. The "payments" column at the right of the screen flashes $85.

"That is going to be $85," she says. "Can you bring a check with you when you come to pick it up?"

"Yes," replies Vincent, thinking of how many hours of bagging groceries it will take to earn $85.

Inson taps a few more keys and the screen changes. A brightly colored grid appears, representing a page in an appointment calendar. "What time would you like to come in Thursday? We have a 2:00 or a 4:15."

"4:15, I guess," says Vincent.

With a few more keystrokes Inson enters the 4:15 appointment. A cell in the chart changes colors to indicate that it is filled. On a corner of the desk a printer beeps to life and spits out two ticket-sized slips of paper. "Here's your appointment slip, and this other one is a record of your visit for the attendance office at school."

Chapters 7 and 8 discussed programming, progamming languages, and operating systems, which are used mostly by programmers and systems analysts to develop applications for users. This chapter looks at another category of software: the personal-productivity software that managers and other users employ to keep records, write and edit documents, and develop budgets.

Three of the most widely used personal-productivity applications—data-base management, word processing, and electronic spreadsheets—will be explored here. The Orthotrac software used by Dr. Bilodeau to manage his orthodontic practice is an example of personal-productivity software. It combines data-base management and word-processing functions. We will see many other applications of this kind of software at various points in this chapter.

When you have read this chapter, you should be able to:
1. State the advantages of data-base management programs compared to traditional record keeping.
2. List the major functions of data-base management programs.
3. State the advantages of word processing on a computer compared to typing on a typewriter.
4. List the major functions of word-processing programs.
5. State the advantages of electronic spreadsheets compared to processing worksheets with a calculator.
6. List the major functions of electronic spreadsheets.
7. Understand and use the key terms listed at the end of the chapter.

Data-Base Management Programs

The first type of personal-productivity software to be explored in this chapter is data-base management programs. You will recall from Chapter 2 that such programs allow users to develop and modify files of data and extract information in various ways. In this section our focus will be on data-base management programs for microcomputers. Chapter 10 discusses related software for minicomputers and mainframes.

File Management versus Data-Base Management

All businesses, whether they are computerized or not, use files of data. For example, an orthodontist's office like Dr. Bil-

This user is modifing a marketing data base with the aid of a light pen. Data-base management programs enable users with limited training to create and modify data bases. (© Dick Luria, Photo Researchers.)

CHAPTER 9   293   PERSONAL-PRODUCTIVITY SOFTWARE

BOX 9-1

MANAGING CHANGE

When to Computerize a Data Base

Dr. John Bilodeau is a big fan of Orthotrac, the software package that he uses to manage his orthodontic practice. Before Orthotrac, Bilodeau says, it was not uncommon actually to lose patients. A six- or eight-year-old child might be referred for possible treatment by a local dentist. Bilodeau would examine the patient and advise yearly follow-up consultations with treatment to begin, say, at age ten. If the patient missed the follow-up appointments, the file might lie idle in a drawer for months or even years. The pressure of day-to-day work rarely allowed time to have an assistant search through more than 2000 files to find patients who were, say, more than thirty days overdue for consultations. With Orthotrac, such searches can be made routinely.

Of course, the system has its costs. There was an initial price tag of more than $40,000, plus a hefty annual maintenance fee. And there was an extended period of confusion while everyone in the office was learning to use the new system. But to Bilodeau the benefits, in terms of building the practice and improving customer service, are well worth the costs.

A few miles away, Bilodeau's friend and racquetball partner Fred Dibbs runs his orthodontic practice without a computer. Dibbs has met with Orthotrac sales representatives, but he has decided, for the time being at least, not to buy. In his view, the benefits of the system do not justify its costs.

A visit to Dibbs's office shows that the absence of a computer does not mean the absence of a data-base management system. Dibbs's system is based on paper, not electronics. A variety of customized paper forms save time and improve the accuracy of record keeping. Indexing and tabbing of paper files speed record retrieval. A special call-back book is kept and reviewed periodically to avoid losing patients who miss appointments or fail to schedule them.

Yes, says Dibbs, there would be some improvement in service to patients with a computerized system, but the improvement would not be dramatic. A computerized system would be a convenience, nice to have, but not essential. Dibbs also sees some hidden costs of computerization. For example, he has experienced considerable turnover among his staff. The job of training new staff members to use the system would be a constant problem.

Who is right? Probably each has made the right decision for a given situation and management style. Bilodeau runs a larger practice and sees the computer as a tool to be used in building it aggressively. Dibbs's practice is smaller, and he is content to keep it that way. Also, Bilodeau was interested in computers before he bought the Orthotrac system. To him, the job of computerizing his practice was an application of familiar principles. Dibbs has nothing against computers, but they hold no special magic for him. At some point elements in the cost-benefit equation may change, and then Dibbs will computerize. But not yet.

odeau's must have files containing personal data about patients, data about procedures used to treat various conditions, and financial data. Many firms manage these files using paper records, but increasingly computers are used even in small businesses. (See Box 9-1.)

When files consist of paper records stored in drawers, even fairly simple tasks can require a search through an entire file. For example, suppose Dr. Bilodeau wanted a list of all patients who had lost their retainers within the past year. With a paper filing system, each patient's folder would have to be pulled one at a time and examined to see if a retainer had been lost. This process could take hours and therefore would not be done unless absolutely necessary. With the computerized system, the file can be searched within minutes.

A *file-management program* allows individual files to be searched and sorted, but it does not enable the user to process two or more files simultaneously. This kind of processing requires a more sophisticated product: a **data-base management program**. Such a program enables the user to set up and process a data base—a set of related files—on a computer. The user thereby gains a great deal of flexibility in extracting information from the files. For example, the patient records in the doctor's data base can be entered chronologically but retrieved in different ways, such as by patient number or by similarity in a specific trait (e.g., all patients who have had whooping cough or all patients over age 65). Data in one or several records or in an entire file can be changed easily. It is also relatively easy to create additional files when needed.

To illustrate how data-base management programs work, we will set up and process a data base using a specific program, dBASE III. (The original program, dBASE II, has been upgraded by Ashton Tate, its developer, first to dBASE III and then to dBASE III Plus. With only a few minor changes, the example presented here will work on both of these other versions.) With a few changes, this application will work on other data-base management programs.

In the course of developing this book, one of the authors decided to start collecting product information by sending in the reader response cards found in many technical magazines. (See Figure 9-1.) A data-base management program was initially used to keep track of which responses had been received and which had not. Over time more data was added to the data base and several types of information were extracted from it. Many businesses use file-management and data-base management programs in a similar fashion to keep track of their correspondence.

Data-base management program

A program that is designed to store, retrieve, and manipulate data from one or more files.

FIGURE 9-1

Reader Response Cards

By filling out a single card as illustrated at the bottom of this figure, readers of technical magazines can obtain extensive product information.

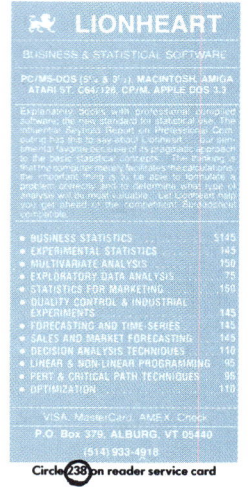

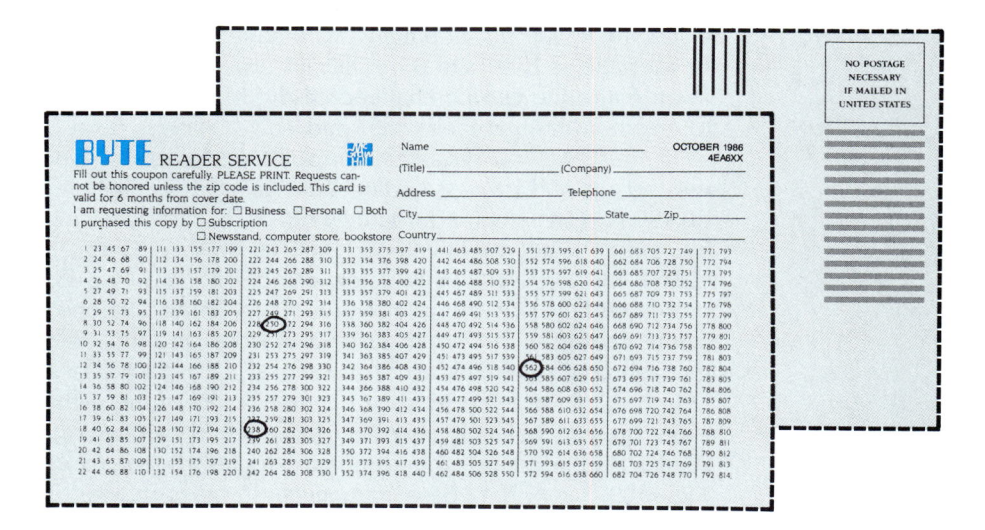

Mechanics of Data-Base Management Programs

Before setting up our data base, let's briefly review the data hierarchy described in Chapter 2: bit, byte, field, record, file, and data base. You will recall that the bit is the basic unit of data and that bytes are represented by characters, that is, letters, numbers, and special symbols such as commas and question marks. Fields are groups of related characters; a record is several related fields; a file is a group of related records; and a data base is a group of related files.

For the product advertisement data base, the fields are as follows:

Source (e.g., technical magazine)
Issue
Page
Product (name)
Application (of product)
Chapter (i.e., relevant chapter of text)
Has information been received from the manufacturer?
Number of pages of information received

In our example, the record is the group of fields for each advertisement, the file is the collection of records for all the advertisements, and the data base is the collection of all the files for this application. When we begin working with this application, the data base consists of a single file called ADS. Later, when the need arises, we create additional files that will be part of the same data base. For example, we might create one file per chapter—ADS1, ADS2, and so on. The relationships among the parts of a data base are shown in Figure 9-2.

The advertisement information file, called ADS, contains one record for each advertisement. These records are created in the order in which the advertisements are read (later they can be sorted in various ways to meet different needs). Each record contains the fields listed earlier and, for the dBASE III program, are identified as follows:

Field 1	SOURCE	Magazine in which advertisement appeared
Field 2	ISSUE	Magazine's cover date
Field 3	PAGE	Page number on which advertisement appeared
Field 4	PRODUCT	Name of the product
Field 5	APPLIC	Product's principal application
Field 6	CHAPTER	Indicates relevant chapter of text
Field 7	RECV	Indicates whether a reply has been received
Field 8	REMARKS	Additional remarks, such as product's cost

The data base can now be set up using dBASE III.

FIGURE 9-2

The Parts of a Data Base

As the user works with the application, he or she may add more files to the data base.

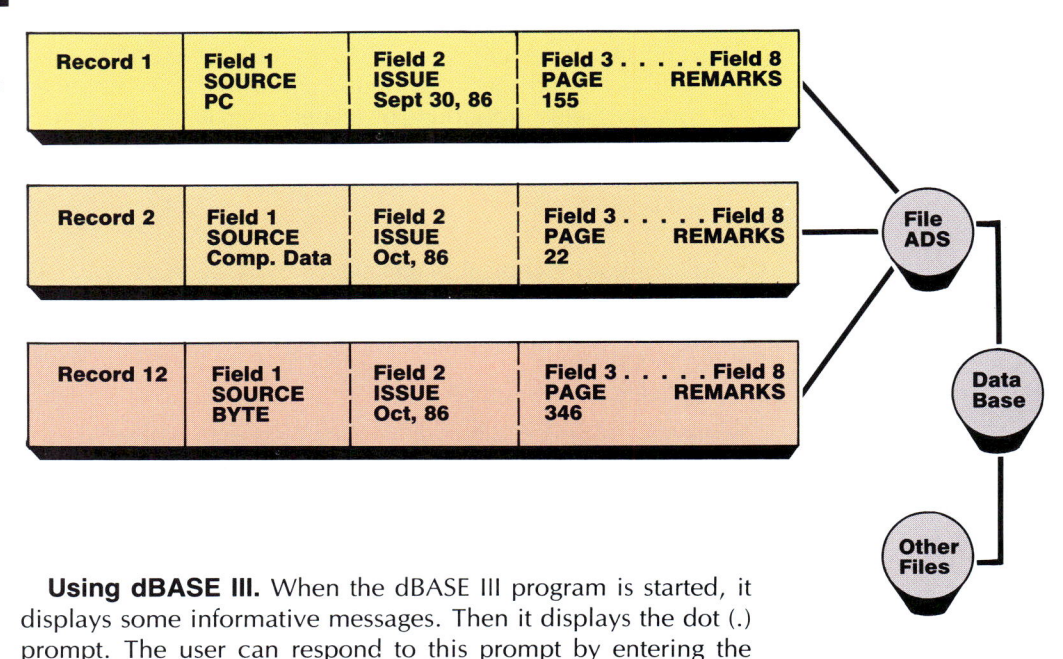

| Record 1 | Field 1
SOURCE
PC | Field 2
ISSUE
Sept 30, 86 | Field 3 . . . . . Field 8
PAGE   REMARKS
155 |

| Record 2 | Field 1
SOURCE
Comp. Data | Field 2
ISSUE
Oct, 86 | Field 3 . . . . . Field 8
PAGE   REMARKS
22 |

| Record 12 | Field 1
SOURCE
BYTE | Field 2
ISSUE
Oct, 86 | Field 3 . . . . . Field 8
PAGE   REMARKS
346 |

File ADS
Data Base
Other Files

Using dBASE III. When the dBASE III program is started, it displays some informative messages. Then it displays the dot (.) prompt. The user can respond to this prompt by entering the following:

    CREATE

to which the computer responds:

    Enter the name of the new file

to which the user responds:

    B:ADS

The dialog continues, with the computer supplying screens prompting the user for information about field name, type, width, and position of the decimal point, where applicable.

Entering the Record Structure. Before creating a file, the user must supply the program with a *record structure* that specifies certain basic information about each field in a given record. (Each record in a particular file has the same record structure.) The system enters the field number, and the user enters information for each field. In our example, this is done as follows:

SOFTWARE 298 PART 3

FIGURE 9-3

A Record Structure

```
. DISPLAY STRUCTURE
Structure for data base : B:ADS.DBF
Number of data records  :      12
Date of last update     : 05/01/87
Field   Field name   Type         Width   Dec
    1   SOURCE       Character      10
    2   ISSUE        Character      10
    3   PAGE         Numeric         3
    4   PRODUCT      Character      12
    5   APPLIC       Character      10
    6   CHAPTER      Numeric         2
    7   RECV         Logical         1
    8   REMARKS      Character       5
** Total **                         54
```

1. FIELD NAME is the name of the field, such as SOURCE, ISSUE, PAGE, and PRODUCT in the file ADS.

2. TYPE indicates the nature of the bytes in the field. *Character fields* contain any combination of letters and numbers; examples from ADS are SOURCE and REMARKS. *Numeric fields* contain only numbers and are generally used for fields in which numeric calculations will be done. In the ADS file, PAGE and CHAPTER are numeric fields. Because PAGE is a numeric field, the system will reject a page number such as 12A. *Logical fields* allow for one of two possibilities: true or false (or yes or no). ADS has one logical field, RECV, whose value indicates whether or not a reply has been received from the manufacturer.

3. WIDTH tells the program the maximum length each character and numeric field will be. (It knows that the length of a logical field is one character.)

4. DECIMAL PLACES are used with numeric fields to indicate the number of digits after the decimal point.

Figure 9-3 shows the dBASE III record structure for the eight fields in the ADS file.

FIGURE 9-4

A Box for Data Entry

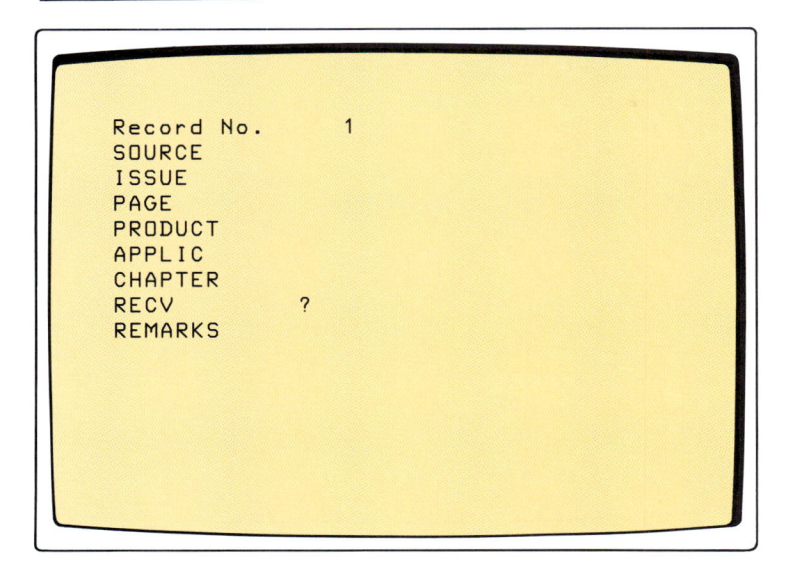

```
Record No.      1
SOURCE
ISSUE
PAGE
PRODUCT
APPLIC
CHAPTER
RECV            ?
REMARKS
```

Choosing Field Names and Widths. Field names and widths should be easy to recognize without using an excessive amount of space. (Many programs limit field names to eight characters, but the width can be considerably greater.) If the width for SOURCE is only four characters, the abbreviation for *PC Magazine* might be PCMA; five characters might give PCMAG, a much more recognizable name. But a width of five would be too short for *Personal Computing* (PERSO). PERCOMPU, which requires a width of eight characters, is much better.

Entering Data. When the record structure has been entered, dBASE III is ready to receive specific data for the fields for each record in the ADS file. The program displays a data entry box for the first and each succeeding record. As shown in Figure 9-4, this box contains the record number, the name of each field, and space in which to insert the data for the field. Note the use of the question mark (?) in the logical field. Figure 9-5 shows the first record for the ADS file with the fields filled in.

FIGURE 9-5

Data for One Record

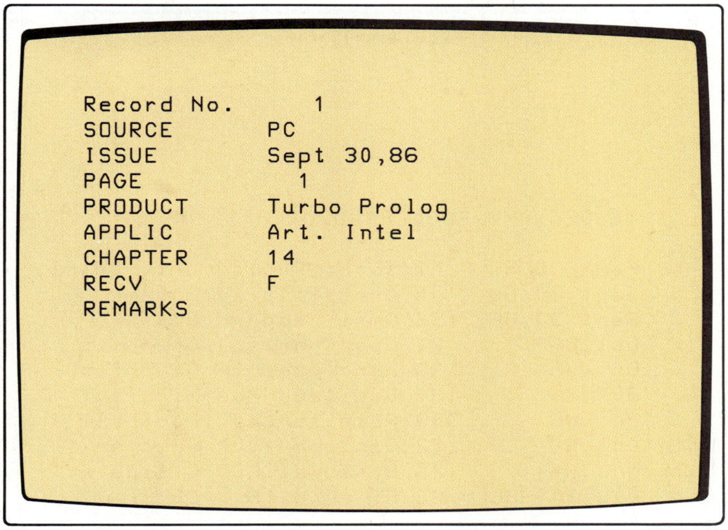

```
Record No.      1
SOURCE          PC
ISSUE           Sept 30,86
PAGE            1
PRODUCT         Turbo Prolog
APPLIC          Art. Intel
CHAPTER         14
RECV            F
REMARKS
```

Displaying and Printing Data. After the data just described has been entered, the program can display the record on the screen. A user-friendly aspect of data-base management programs is that they stop after displaying a full screen of data to allow the user to verify the data before continuing. However, screen images are temporary, and the user often needs a hard copy of the data base. Such a copy is obtained by printing the record. Figure 9-6 shows a printout of the data for the ADS file. The data is in raw form; that is, it is printed out as it was entered, without any additional explanatory information.

Editing Data. After the fields in a record have been entered, the program permits the user to make changes, for example, to correct errors, to update the record to reflect changed conditions (e.g., receiving the requested information from the manufacturer), and to add information (e.g., the cost of the product). Most data-base management programs include a simple word processor that allows the user to insert or delete characters.

FIGURE 9-6

Contents of a File in Raw Form

```
. DISPLAY ALL
Record#   SOURCE       ISSUE         PAGE PRODUCT       APPLIC       CHAPTER RECV REMARKS

      1   PC           Sept 30,86       1 Turbo Prolog  Art. Intel        14  .F.
      2   PC           Sept 30,86       3 Crosstalk XV  Modem              6  .F.
      3   PC           Sept 30,86     155 Omni-reader   OCR                4  .F.
      4   BYTE         Oct,86          34 EnerCharts    Graphics          11  .F.
      5   BYTE         Oct,86         138 Herc Graph P  Graphics          11  .F.
      6   BYTE         Oct,86         161 Logitech Mod  Modula-2           8  .F.
      7   BYTE         Oct,86         346 Pointspread   Football          16  .F.
      8   Comp. Data   Oct,86          22 Genicom 1000  Printer            4  .F.
      9   Comp. Data   Oct,86          23 Honeywell IO  Office Aut        14  .F.
     10   CW Focus     Aug 20, 86      22 FilePro 16    DBMS              10  .F.
Press any key to continue...
Record#   SOURCE       ISSUE         PAGE PRODUCT       APPLIC       CHAPTER RECV REMARKS

     11   BYTE         Aug, 86        183 CompuServe    Info. Serv         6  .F.
     12   CW Focus     July 9, 86      37 SCdraw        Graphics          11  .F.
```

Producing Reports. After the records have been edited, they can be reviewed on the screen and printed out. The printouts will show the data in raw form, as illustrated in Figure 9-6. Since data in this form is difficult to read, data-base management programs can produce more understandable reports, such as the one shown in Figure 9-7. Such customized reports are produced by filling in the blanks as illustrated in Figure 9-8. The program saves the answers to the questions in a *report form* that can be reused to produce the same types of reports with different data or modified to produce different reports.

FIGURE 9-7

A Customized Report

```
. REPORT
Enter report file name:B:RPTADS
     Page No.       1
05/01/87
                              Advertisement Report

     MAG.          ISSUE         PAGE PRODUCT        APPLICATION CHAP RECV REM.

     PC            Sept 30,86       1 Turbo Prolog   Art. Intel   14  .F.
     PC            Sept 30,86       3 Crosstalk XV   Modem         6  .F.
     PC            Sept 30,86     155 Omni-reader    OCR           4  .F.
     BYTE          Oct,86          34 EnerCharts     Graphics     11  .F.
     BYTE          Oct,86         138 Herc Graph P   Graphics     11  .F.
     BYTE          Oct,86         161 Logitech Mod   Modula-2      8  .F.
     BYTE          Oct,86         346 Pointspread    Football     16  .F.
     Comp. Data    Oct,86          22 Genicom 1000   Printer       4  .F.
     Comp. Data    Oct,86          23 Honeywell IO   Office Aut   14  .F.
     CW Focus      Aug 20,86       22 FilePro 16     DBMS         10  .F.
     BYTE          Aug,86         183 CompuServe     Info. Serv    6  .F.
     CW Focus      July 9,86       37 SCdraw         Graphics     11  .F.
```

With many products, including dBASE III, it is easy to modify the report forms.

Sorting Files. One of the main advantages of computerized data bases over traditional office filing systems is that records in a data base can be entered in a given order and sorted and printed out in a different order. For example, the records in the ADS file shown in Figure 9-6 can be sorted and displayed as shown in Figure 9-9.

FIGURE 9-8

Preparing a Report

The user prepares a report by filling in the blanks that appear on the screen.

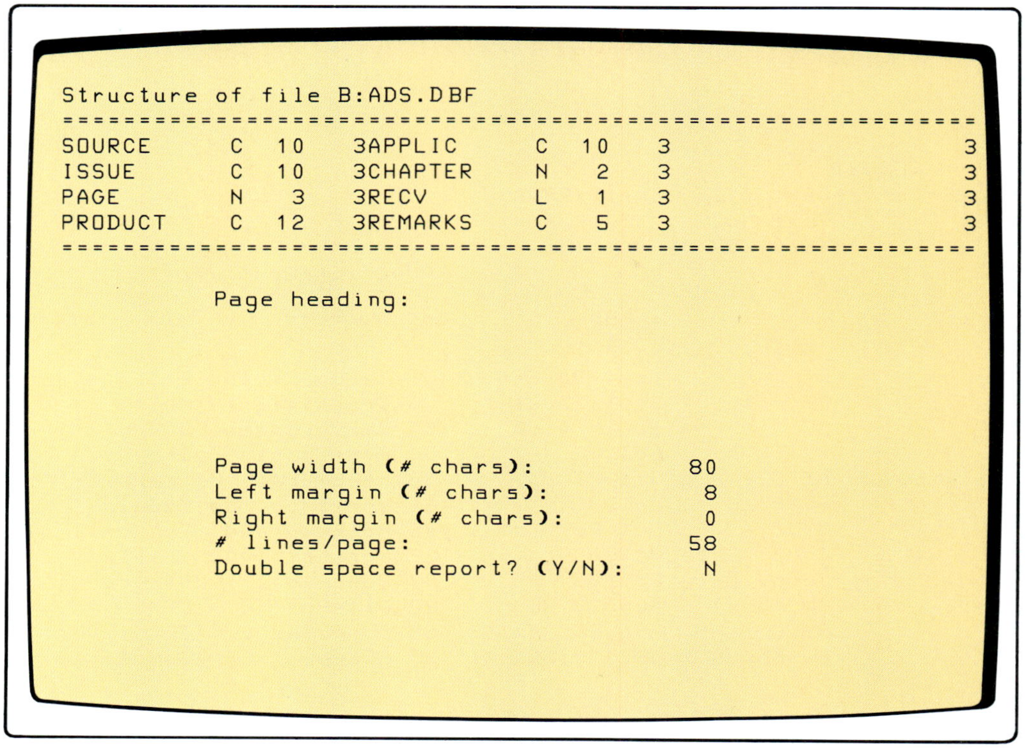

```
Structure of file B:ADS.DBF
================================================================
SOURCE      C   10     3APPLIC      C   10    3              3
ISSUE       C   10     3CHAPTER     N    2    3              3
PAGE        N    3     3RECV        L    1    3              3
PRODUCT     C   12     3REMARKS     C    5    3              3
================================================================

          Page heading:




          Page width (# chars):           80
          Left margin (# chars):           8
          Right margin (# chars):          0
          # lines/page:                   58
          Double space report? (Y/N):      N
```

Performing Arithmetic. In addition to setting up and editing records and producing reports, file and data-base management programs can be used to perform arithmetic functions. Examples include adding 1 to a chapter number if a new chapter is inserted, or adding the amount of a new invoice to a customer's current bill.

Extracting Records. Whether a business is using a traditional filing system or a computerized one, files often become too large and cumbersome to be used efficiently. The business may then decide to divide a large file into several smaller ones. In the ADS example, the original file contained all the product inquiries from all the magazines. After data had been collected

FIGURE 9-9

Sorting a File

```
. USE B:ADS
. SORT ON CHAPTER TO B:ADSRT
  100% Sorted            12 Records sorted
. USE B:ADSRT
. DISPLAY ALL
Record#   SOURCE        ISSUE         PAGE  PRODUCT        APPLIC      CHAPTER  RECV REMARKS

      1   PC            Sept 30,86    155   Omni-reader    OCR              4   .F.
      2   Comp. Data    Oct,86         22   Genicom 1000   Printer          4   .F.
      3   BYTE          Aug,86        183   CompuServe     Info. Serv       6   .F.
      4   PC            Sept 30,86      3   Crosstalk XV   Modem            6   .F.
      5   BYTE          Oct,86        161   Logitech Mod   Modula-2         8   .F.
      6   CW Focus      Aug 20,86      22   FilePro 16     DBMS            10   .F.
    BYTE          Oct,86        138   Herc Graph P   Graphics        11   .F.
      8   BYTE          Oct,86         34   EnerCharts     Graphics        11   .F.
      9   CW Focus      July 9,86      37   SCdraw         Graphics        11   .F.
     10   PC            Sept 30,86      1   Turbo Prolog   Art. Intel      14   .F.
Press any key to continue...
Record #  SOURCE        ISSUE         PAGE  PRODUCT        APPLIC      CHAPTER  RECV REMARKS

     11   Comp. Data    Oct,86         23   Honeywell IO   Office Aut      14   .F.
     12   BYTE          Oct,86        346   Pointspread    Football        16   .F.
```

This file has been sorted and listed by relevant chapter.

for several months, the original file had to be divided into several smaller files.

The process of selecting specific records within a file is known as *extracting* (or *selecting*) *records*. This process may be used to create a smaller file or to produce a report containing only certain records. Successful record selection requires familiarity with the data-base program and the contents of the file.

FIGURE 9-10

Extracting a File

```
. USE B:ADS

. COPY TO B:ADS14 FOR CHAPTER = 14
      2 records copied
. USE B:ADS14
. REPORT
Enter report file name:B:RPTADS
       Page No.      1
       05/01/87
                               Advertisement Report

       MAG.         ISSUE         PAGE PRODUCT        APPLICATION CHAP RECV REM.

       PC           Sept 30,86       1 Turbo Prolog   Art Intel     14  .F.
       Comp. Data   Oct,86          23 Honeywell IO   Office Aut    14  .F.
```

In the case of the ADS file, several approaches were considered. A separate file could have been created for each magazine; for each issue of each magazine; or for each type of application (i.e., printers, monitors, word-processing programs, data-base management programs, etc.). Some approaches would create too many small files, which would be just as difficult to use as one large file. Creating a file for each magazine might be the most appropriate choice for entering data in the records but might not be the best choice for using the information and producing reports. In this case the user decided to divide the original file into a set of files containing information relevant to each chapter of this book; thus, all the records that applied to each chapter became a separate file. For example, the records for Chapter 14 became the new file ADS14, and a report for ADS14 was produced as shown in Figure 9-10.

Modifying Record Structures. Like traditional filing systems, computerized data bases are organized before the system is actually used. Therefore, it is not surprising that after a while users discover more efficient ways to organize the system. In addition, the uses of the data base may change over time, requiring changes in its structure. A computerized data-base system makes it easy to enter and correct data, create files from existing files (as was done for the file ADS14), and modify the record structure.

Soon after the record structure for the ADS file was set up, the author found that many products applied to two chapters. For example, the product Omni-reader, an optical character reader, applied to Chapter 4, "Input and Output," as well as to Chapter 14, "The Automated Office." Therefore, a new field, APPL2ND, needed to be added to the record structure. With dBASE III, adding a new field or otherwise modifying a record structure is a straightforward process. This has a very important consequence: Users need not be entirely sure how to set up an application before beginning to derive the benefits of computerization. They can make needed changes as they go along, without having to rewrite the application from scratch.

In this section we have mentioned only a few of the capabilities of data-base management programs. For example, many such programs offer sophisticated programming facilities. The next chapter examines the similar but more powerful data-base software used on minicomputers and mainframes. Here we turn to another category of personal-productivity software: word processing.

Word Processing

Word processing *The use of a computer program to enter text, modify its content and appearance, and print it.*

Word processing is the use of a computer program to enter text, modify its content and appearance, and print it. In the 1960s, computer-like machines whose function was limited to word processing, called *dedicated word processors*, appeared.

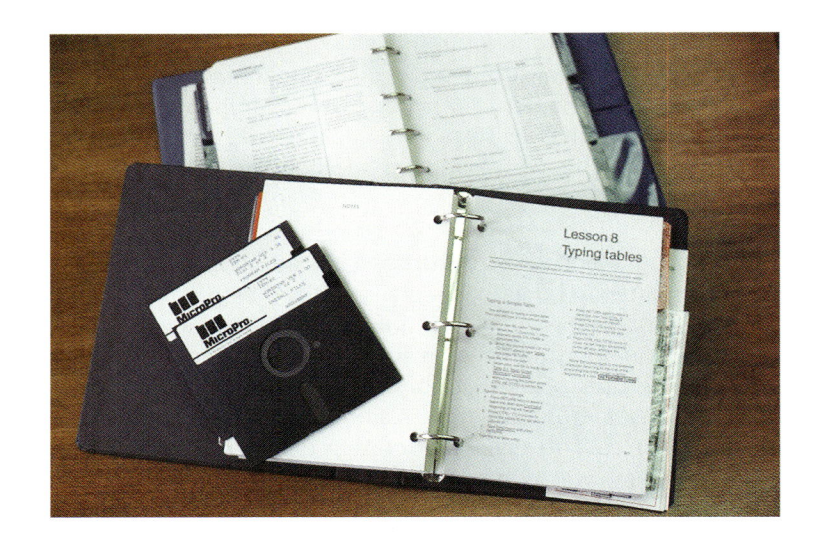

This picture shows a well-known word-processing package, WordStar. Purchasers of this package obtain program disks along with extensive documentation and training materials. (© Erin Calmes.)

Dedicated word processors are computer-like machines whose function is basically limited to word processing. Note the extensive keyboard, which contains numerous special keys to increase user productivity. (© David W. Hamilton, The Image Bank.)

In the 1970s, personal computers that could handle many functions, including word processing, became increasingly popular, and the term *word processor* came into widespread use. Today this term is used to refer both to word-processing software and to the hardware on which it is run. Although some form of word processing can be done on almost any computer, this chapter focuses on personal computers.

Many types and levels of word-processing programs exist, ranging from programs for first-time users to programs for professional writers and secretaries. All such programs can be used to save time and increase efficiency. A student can use a word processor to enter and correct parts of a term paper, retyping only changed material rather than having to retype the entire paper. Businesses also can increase productivity through word processing. For example, Dr. Bilodeau's assistant, Nina Giaime, uses a word-processing program to prepare letters to patients who are beginning treatment or to the parents of patients who are not brushing their teeth properly. These and many other form letters can be prepared without being typed repeatedly and can be customized for each patient.

Using Word-Processing Programs

Word-processing programs enable people to focus on what they want to say rather than on the mechanics of writing, rewriting, and editing. Once they master the program, certain operations become almost automatic. Examples include inserting, deleting, changing, and moving text; changing aspects of format, such as margins, line spacing, and type size; and underlining and boldfacing.

When a word processor is used, text is displayed on a monitor as it is being entered, enabling the user to make changes and corrections before printing out a copy. Thus, rather than typing, then inserting and deleting text with pencil; retyping, making additional changes with pencil, marking sections of text to be moved, and then physically moving them; retyping with different margins; and ending up with a page like the one in Figure 9-11—only to realize that it contains a typo and must be retyped again—the word processor user can make changes on the monitor and print out a clean, easy-to-read copy like that shown in Figure 9-12. A key advantage of word processing is that if a final copy from a word processor contains a typo, the user can simply correct the typo and print out a new page.

Mechanics of Word Processing

The process of producing and editing documents is similar for most word-processing programs. Basically, it involves dealing with two separate factors: *content,* or the text and illustrations themselves, and *format,* or the way the content is presented. Format includes such factors as margins, spacing, and type size. To see how the fundamental features of most word-processing programs work, consider Lincoln's Gettysburg Address. A copy of its content, produced with a popular word-processing program, MultiMate, is presented here exactly as it

FIGURE 9-11

Producing a Document with a Typewriter

    Now we are engaged in a great ^civil^ war, testing ~~if~~ ^whether^ that nation or any nation so conceived and so dedicated can (endure long). It is altogether fitting and proper that we should ^We are^ meet on a great battle⊃ f~~ei~~ild of that war. We ha~~ev~~ come to dedicate a portion of that field, as a final resting-place for those who here gave their lives that that nation might be alive.

(a) Original version.

↳ do this

    Now we are engaged in a great civil war, testing whether that nation or any nation so conceived and so dedicated can long endure. We are met on a great battlefield of that war. We haev come to dedicate a portion of that field, as a final resting-place for those who here gave their lives that that nation might live. It is altogether fitting and proper that we should do this.

(b) Corrected version.

was delivered at the dedication of the military cemetery at Gettysburg, Pennsylvania, on November 19, 1863. (In the absence of special formatting commands, other word processors would produce a somewhat different-looking version of this speech.)

    Fourscore and seven years ago our fathers brought forth on this continent a new nation, conceived in liberty and dedicated to the proposition that all men are created equal.
    Now we are engaged in a great civil war testing whether that nation or any nation so conceived and so dedicated can long endure. We are met on a great battlefield of that war. We have come to dedicate a portion of that field, as a final resting-place for those who here gave their lives that that nation might live. It is altogether fitting and proper that we should do this. But in a larger sense, we cannot dedicate--we cannot consecrate--we cannot hallow--this ground. The brave men, living and

FIGURE 9-12

Producing a Document with a Word Processor

    Now we are engaged in a great ^civil^ war, testing ~~if~~ ^whether^ that nation or any nation so conceived and so dedicated can endure long. (It is altogether fitting and proper that we should meet on a great battlefield of that war. We have come to dedicate a portion of that field, as a final resting-place for those who here gave their lives that that nation might ~~be~~ live.

(a) Original version. → do this

    Now we are engaged in a great civil war, testing whether that nation or any nation so conceived and so dedicated can long endure. We are met on a great battlefield of that war. We have come to dedicate a portion of that field, as a final resting-place for those who here gave their lives that that nation might live. It is altogether fitting and proper that we should do this.

(b) Corrected version. The use of a word processor makes it possible to correct errors without retyping the text each time an error is noticed.

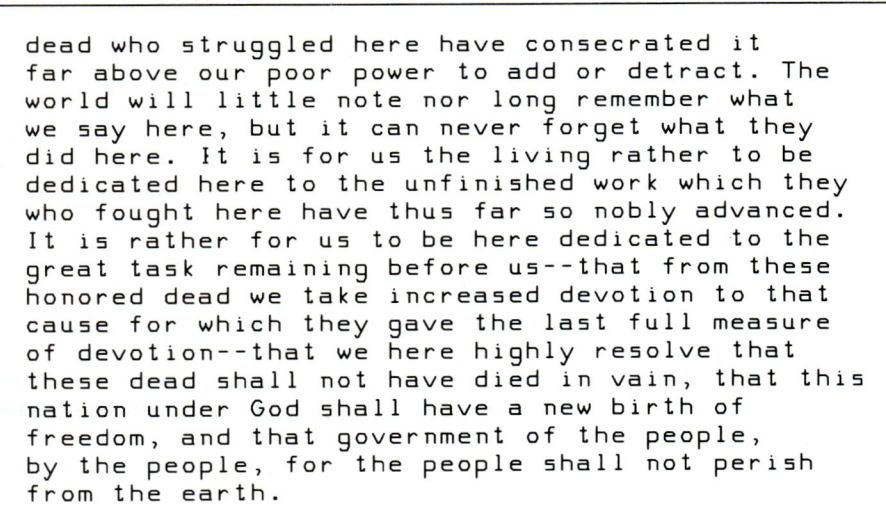

Abraham Lincoln, fourteenth President of the United States and author of the Gettysburg Address. (Culver Pictures.)

dead who struggled here have consecrated it far above our poor power to add or detract. The world will little note nor long remember what we say here, but it can never forget what they did here. It is for us the living rather to be dedicated here to the unfinished work which they who fought here have thus far so nobly advanced. It is rather for us to be here dedicated to the great task remaining before us--that from these honored dead we take increased devotion to that cause for which they gave the last full measure of devotion--that we here highly resolve that these dead shall not have died in vain, that this nation under God shall have a new birth of freedom, and that government of the people, by the people, for the people shall not perish from the earth.

    To enter a document like the Gettysburg Address onto a word processor, the user must learn some basic word-processing functions. Although these functions are essentially the same for all word-processing programs, they are carried out in different ways by different programs. Once a user has mastered one program, however, it is not difficut to learn others.

FIGURE 9-13

WordStar Control Panel

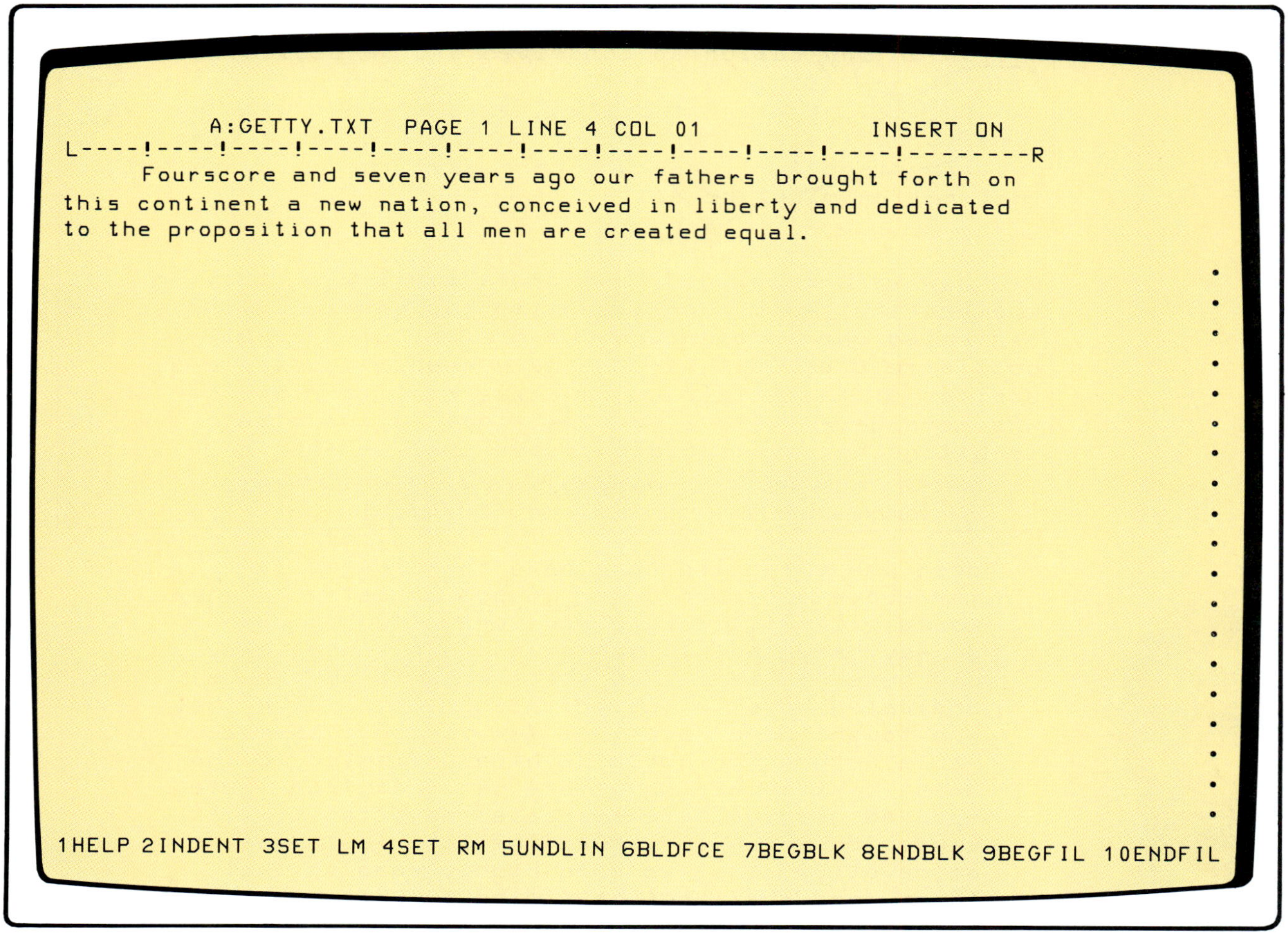

```
            A:GETTY.TXT   PAGE 1 LINE 4 COL 01              INSERT ON
L----!----!----!----!----!----!----!----!----!----!--------R
        Fourscore and seven years ago our fathers brought forth on
this continent a new nation, conceived in liberty and dedicated
to the proposition that all men are created equal.


















1HELP 2INDENT 3SET LM 4SET RM 5UNDLIN 6BLDFCE 7BEGBLK 8ENDBLK 9BEGFIL 10ENDFIL
```

The top line presents some basic information about the document being processed, including the name, page, line, and column position of the cursor.

The bottom line indicates the function keys used with this product on the IBM PC (highlighted on the monitor). For example, F1 is pressed to obtain a Help screen.

The Control Panel. A word processor displays one or more lines at either the top or the bottom of the monitor that serve as a *control panel*. The function of this display is similar to that of a car's dashboard display, that is, to make sure basic information is readily available at all times. A control panel for a widely used word-processing program, WordStar, is shown in Figure 9-13. It indicates the name of the document and the page, line, and column number where the cursor is positioned. When the cursor is moved, this information changes automatically. Some control panels also provide *help screens*; an example is presented in Figure 9-14.

Entering Text. Entering text with a word processor is similar to using a typewriter, except that word processors have extra features that make entering and changing text easier, more efficient, and less time-consuming. One such feature, mentioned earlier, is that a word processor enables the user to see the text on a monitor and make changes before printing out the document. Another feature, called *word wrap*, eliminates the need to enter carriage returns except at the end of each paragraph. Word wrap automatically positions words on a line and moves those that don't fit to the next line.

Inserting Text. Unlike typewriters, which usually require the user to retype an entire line or page when inserting text, word processors make this operation very easy to carry out. With many programs the user need only position the cursor at the point where text is to be added, perhaps strike the insert or Ins key, and then type the desired text. The word processor takes care of all the "overhead," such as positioning the remaining text and handling margins. Even when the word processor requires the use of a few commands to handle insertions, this procedure is much easier and less frustrating than retyping a page. Some word processors make the inserted text easier to see by highlighting it.

Deleting Text. All word processors allow the user to delete unwanted portions of text and reorganize the remaining text. Deleting a single character usually involves pressing the delete or Del key. Deleting several characters or a *block* of text requires a series of keystrokes. Many word processors highlight the block to be deleted in order to reduce the potential for error. Some word processors go even further: They provide an "undo" **command** that "rolls back" the effect of the last command entered. This command is especially helpful if the user has accidentally deleted several pages of text.

The enter, change, insert, and delete functions are the basics

Command
A precise statement or set of keystrokes that instructs a software package to perform a particular operation.

FIGURE 9-14

WordStar Help Screens

WordStar provides different levels of help at the user's request. In this context a level of 0 is no help at all (providing experienced

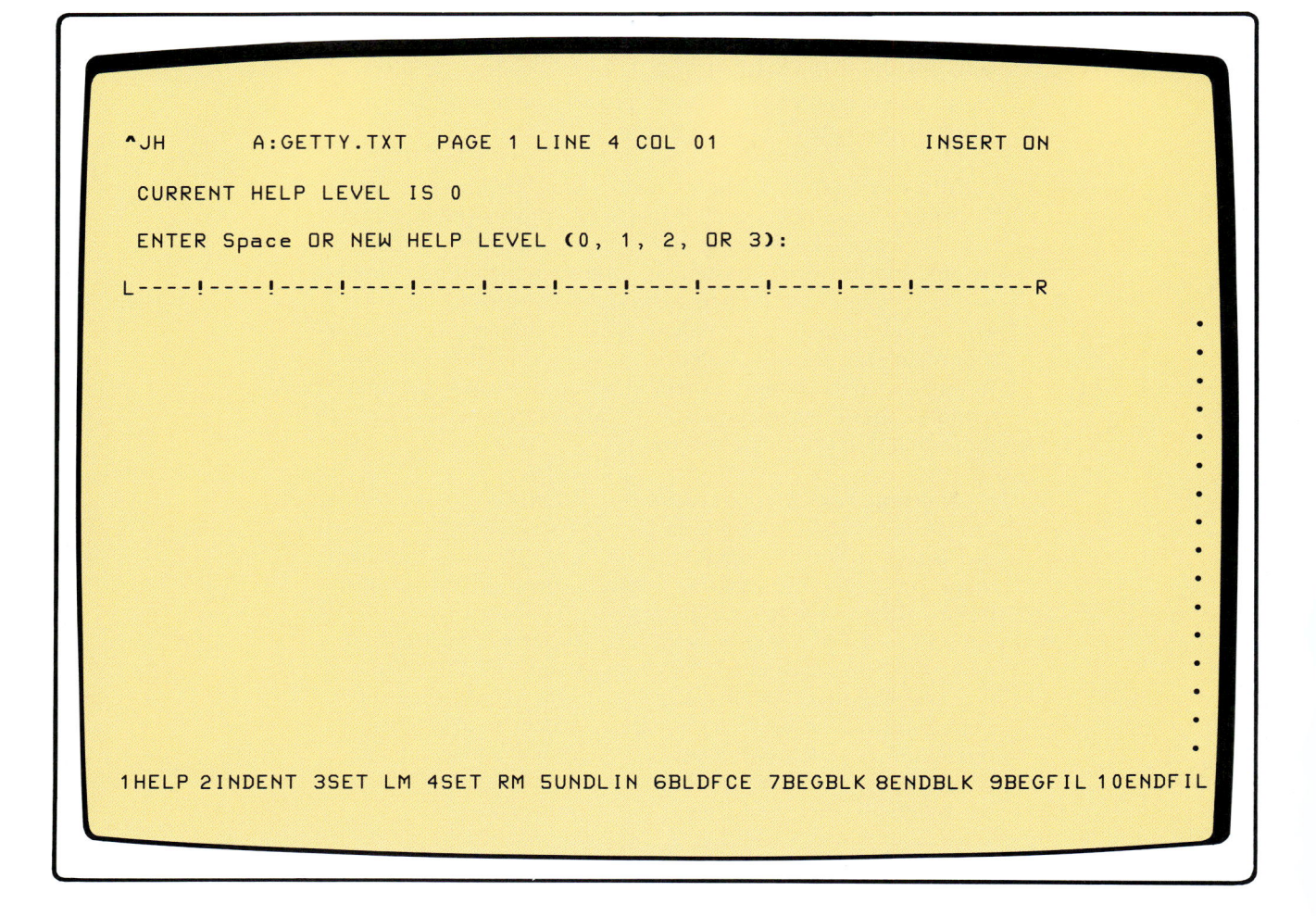

```
^JH        A:GETTY.TXT    PAGE 1 LINE 4 COL 01                    INSERT ON
 CURRENT HELP LEVEL IS 0
 ENTER Space OR NEW HELP LEVEL (0, 1, 2, OR 3):
L----!----!----!----!----!----!----!----!----!----!--------R
                                                                           •
                                                                           •
                                                                           •
                                                                           •
                                                                           •
                                                                           •
                                                                           •
                                                                           •
                                                                           •
                                                                           •
                                                                           •
                                                                           •
                                                                           •
                                                                           •
 1HELP 2INDENT 3SET LM 4SET RM 5UNDLIN 6BLDFCE 7BEGBLK 8ENDBLK 9BEGFIL 10ENDFIL
```

of word processing. But word processors can do much more. For example, they can move text from one place to another, copy text so that it appears in several places, look for a word or group of words and replace it with another one, and underline or boldface parts of a text.

Changing Text. Although it is always possible to change text by first deleting the unwanted text and then inserting the

users with a maximum working area on the monitor). The example below shows a help screen at the maximum level of 3.

```
              A:GETTY.TXT  PAGE 1 LINE 4 COL 01        INSERT ON
                       < < <   M A I N   M E N U   > >
>
      --Cursor Movement--    ! -Delete- ! -Miscellaneous-  ! -Other Menus--
  ^S char left  ^D char right !^G char  ! ^I Tab   ^B Reform ! (from Main only)
  ^A word left  ^F word right !DEL chr lf!^V INSERT ON/OFF   !^J Help   ^K Block
  ^E line  up   ^X line down  !^T word rt!^L Find/Replce again!^Q Quick  ^P Print
         --Scrolling--        !^Y line   !RETURN End paragraph!^O Onscreen
  ^Z line down  ^W line up    !          ! ^N Insert a RETURN !
  ^C screen up  ^R screen down!          ! ^U Stop a command  !
  L----!----!----!----!----!----!----!----!----!----!----!--------R




  1HELP 2INDENT 3SET LM 4SET RM 5UNDLIN 6BLDFCE 7BEGBLK 8ENDBLK 9BEGFIL 10ENDFIL
```

changes (or vice versa), most word processors allow the user to type the new text directly over the old. This is illustrated in Figure 9-15, in which the incorrectly spelled word *Fourcsore* is corrected.

Moving and Copying a Block. These two operations allow the user to reorganize text rapidly. Although the mechanics of moving a block differ from one word processor to another, the basic principle is the same. The user identifies a block of text

FIGURE 9-15

Correcting an Error with a Word Processor

These three images show the steps in correcting an error by typing over it. In (a) the user notices the error; in (b) the user positions the cursor at the point of the error; and in (c) the user types over the error.

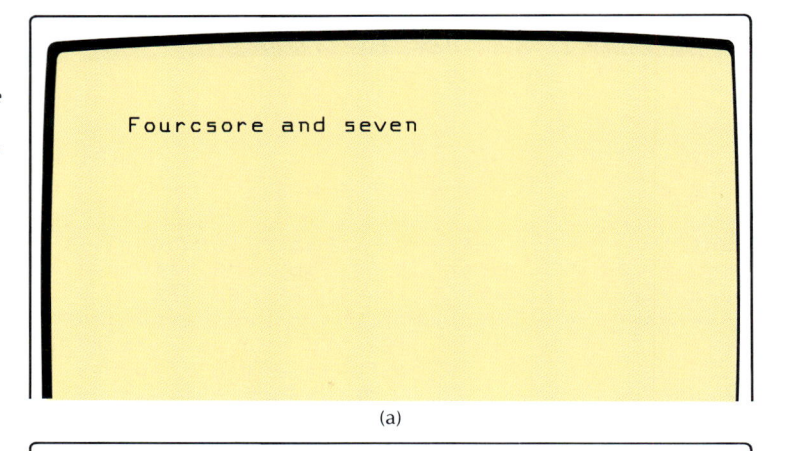

Fourcsore and seven

(a)

Four<u>c</u>sore and seven

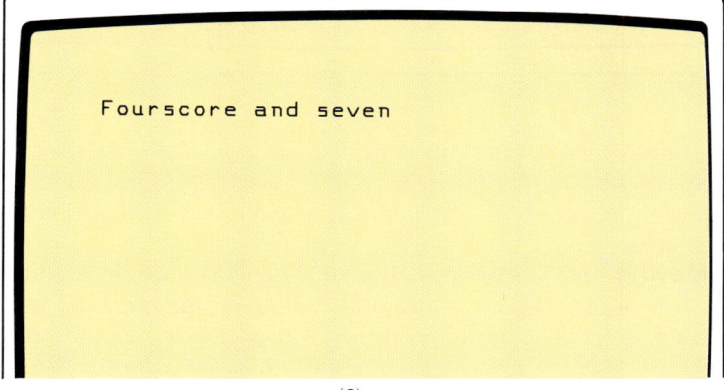

(b)

Fourscore and seven

(c)

SOFTWARE 316 PART 3

to be moved and its new location. Thus, suppose the first sentence of the Gettysburg Address had been written as follows:

```
Fourscore and seven years ago our fathers
brought forth on this continent a new nation,
dedicated to the proposition that all men are
created equal and conceived in liberty.
```

If the phrase *conceived in liberty* is moved to a position directly after the comma and some minor adjustments are made, such as moving *and* to its proper location, the sentence reads as Lincoln delivered it:

```
Fourscore and seven years ago our fathers
brought forth on this continent a new nation,
conceived in liberty and dedicated to the
proposition that all men are created equal.
```

Sometimes the user wants to copy a block to a new location rather than move it. In other words, the block appears in both the old and new locations. This operation is done with the copy command, which is usually quite similar to the move command. The copy command is often used in business and other applications. For example, several paragraphs appearing in a contract could be copied to a technical appendix where they can be discussed in detail.

String
A collection of characters.

Finding and Replacing Strings. A **string** is a collection of characters; for example, the word *computer* is a string of eight characters, the phone number 555-1212 is a string of eight characters, and the address 17 Maple Lane is a string of thirteen characters (spaces within the string are counted). Word-processing programs enable users to find a specified string and, if desired, replace it with another string. This command is called *find and replace* or *search and replace*.

The find-and-replace operation is complicated because of the number of available options. For example, in the simplest case we could ask the word processor to replace all occurrences of the string *personal computer* with the string *microcomputer*. With some word processors, several operations would be necessary to make such a substitution. Depending on the sophistication of the program, a given number of occurrences of a string can be replaced automatically, or the program can stop at each occurrence and ask the user whether it should be replaced or not.

There are many ways in which this operation can be used to make routine business chores easier and less time-consuming. For example, if it was discovered that a client's name had been misspelled throughout a series of correspondence, the name

CHAPTER 9 317 PERSONAL-PRODUCTIVITY SOFTWARE

could easily be found and replaced at every point where it occurred. Or if a very long phrase, such as "the party of the first part and the party of the second part" (used in legal documents), was to appear in a document many times, a special symbol such as @ could be entered. Then a search and replace could be carried out to insert the entire phrase wherever it should appear.

Underlining and Boldfacing Text. In addition to adding, deleting, moving, copying, finding, and replacing text, word processors can highlight text, for example, by underlining or boldfacing it. The word *microcomputer* in the preceding discussion was underlined to make it stand out. Highlighting mechanisms differ from one word processor to another, but most word-processing programs offer some mechanism for highlighting.

On some word processors, the monitor displays the code for the special effect, rather than the effect itself. For example, to boldface text using WordStar, users press the F6 key to mark the beginning and end of the text that is to be boldfaced. Rather than seeing the text appear in darker type on the screen, users see special characters at the beginning and end of the selected text. When the text is printed, it appears in bold type and the special characters are not printed.

Other word processors have a feature called WYSIWYG, for "What you see is what you get." With these programs, the text appears on the screen as it will appear on paper. This feature helps the user avoid annoying errors such as forgetting to enter the code to mark the end of the text to appear in boldface—an error that can cause dozens of pages to be printed incorrectly. Some programs use a combination of codes and WYSIWYG.

Additional Features

In addition to the basic word-processing features used for writing, rewriting, and editing, there are other features that can help users prepare more accurate and better-written documents. These include spelling checkers, thesaurus programs, and grammar/style checkers. These features may be built into a word processor or may take the form of a separate program that is used along with a word processor (and other personal-productivity software).

Spelling Checkers. *Spelling checkers* are programs that find typographical errors or misspellings in a text. They look up each word in their dictionary and let the user know if there is no match. A spelling checker can find a misspelling such as *mispelling* for *misspelling*, but it cannot find a typographical error such as *bat* for *tab* or *dew* for *wed* since all four of these words appear in its dictionary.

When the spelling checker finds an "error," it gives the user several options: The word can be accepted as is, retyped correctly, or added to the user's auxiliary dictionary. For example, the word *flexitime* may not be present in the standard dictionary, but a personnel director will probably want to add it to his or her auxiliary dictionary when writing a report on the feasibility of flexitime. Many vendors of spelling checkers offer specialized dictionaries to accompany their software. For example, an orthodontist might appreciate a dictionary of dental items, whereas a systems analyst would require an entirely different dictionary.

This book was written with the aid of a spelling checker called Turbo Lightning. Each time a word was typed, Turbo Lightning checked it against a dictionary in its memory; if it could not find the word, it emitted a beep. The word was then checked against a bigger dictionary stored on disk, corrected if it was wrong, added to the dictionary if it was going to be used often, or left as it was if it was correct but was not wanted in the dictionary. (The latter option is often used for proper names.)

The word processor that was used to write this text, Multi-Mate, also has a built-in dictionary. It can be used to check a portion of a document or an entire document at one time. After the text is typed, the user gives MultiMate the command to spell check. The program then checks all of the words, showing a count of how many were not found in the dictionary. At the end of the spell check, the user can deal with each of these words individually.

On-Line Thesaurus. An *on-line thesaurus* helps users choose words with similar meanings. The user types a word and enters the command to use the thesaurus. The on-line thesaurus then displays a set of synonyms on the screen. Some spelling checkers contain an on-line thesaurus as well as a dictionary.

An on-line thesaurus can help users write better term papers, business letters, reports, ad copy, and so on. For example, suppose a copy writer is preparing copy for a direct-mail piece that includes a series of questions to which the answer is "right." Using Turbo Lightning, the copy writer could find twenty-five adjectives, eleven nouns, and twelve adverbs to use as synonyms for *right*.

Grammar and Style Checkers. In addition to programs that find typos and spelling errors and programs that suggest synonyms, there are programs that check grammar. They help the user avoid errors of punctuation, subject and verb agreement, and the like. More sophisticated programs check style, for example, overuse of the passive voice, sexist terminology, and excessive repetition of words or expressions.

Style checkers can be helpful, but they must be used carefully. For example, consider the third sentence in the second paragraph of Lincoln's Gettysburg Address:

```
We have come to dedicate a portion of that
field, as a final resting place for those who here
gave their lives that that nation might live.
```

A style checker will report that this sentence contains twenty-seven words and the word *that* occurs three times, for a frequency of about 11 percent. It will probably suggest that the word is overused. Moreover, the program will undoubtedly signal the occurrence of two *that*s in succession toward the end of the sentence—an example of sloppy writing. A sophisticated style checker might even compose a letter to Mr. Lincoln suggesting that he take a remedial writing course.

Mail Merge Programs. Businesses and other organizations often generate large volumes of form letters that can best be handled by word-processing and related programs. For example, a charitable organization might want to write individualized letters thanking contributors for their donations. Those letters can be created with the aid of a word processor and then merged with a list of addresses using a *mail merge* program. The use of such a program reduces the error rate and increases employee productivity. Mail merge programs are often accompanied by file-management programs that can be used to keep the organization's mailing list up to date.

Electronic Spreadsheets

A *spreadsheet* is simply a chart with rows and columns of numbers and descriptive words. The following is an example of a simple spreadsheet:

Grades for Intro to DP Class

	Ex. #1	Ex. #2	Midterm	Ex. #3	Ex. #4	Final exam
Jones, J	8	9	77	10	9	89
Gordon, A	9	10	89	9	7	78
Lee, HL	9	9	74	7	6	70
Ng, N	8	10	87	10	10	97

For centuries spreadsheets have been used for record keeping and financial analysis in a wide variety of applications, including business, science, engineering, and personal finances.

A typical spreadsheet application is maintaining a budget, whether for an individual, a household, a small business, a department of a corporation, or the corporation itself. Generally, spreadsheets are used for two kinds of budgets: those that describe past and present financial activities and those that attempt to forecast the future. Forecasts are particularly difficult to create and maintain, since financial information related to individuals and businesses changes constantly. Moreover, as soon as one assumption changes, many of the calculations must be redone, a tedious and time-consuming process. For example, suppose that an accountant worked out a five-year sales forecast for a small business as follows:

Allied Widget Corp. Sales Forecast (thousands of dollars)

	Year I	Year II	Year III	Year IV	Year V
Product A	300	330	363	399	439
Product B	200	240	288	346	381
Product C	100	130	169	220	286
Product D	50	100	200	300	450

If a competing company came out with a revolutionary new product while management was reviewing the plan the company would naturally want to change many items in its forecast spreadsheet, thereby causing the accountant many additional hours of work. Even a simple addition error could require the accountant to spend hours recalculating the spreadsheet data.

In 1977 Dan Bricklin, an MBA student at the Harvard School of Business, and Robert Frankston, a student at the Massachusetts Institute of Technology, joined forces to develop a computer program that would do spreadsheet calculations. In 1979 they marketed the first **electronic spreadsheet**, VisiCalc (short for Visible Calculator). It was the kind of success that most people only dream about: This one program completely changed the nature of the microcomputer market.

Before VisiCalc appeared, businesses had shown little interest in microcomputers. But within a few months, as word of

Electronic spreadsheet

A program that converts a computer monitor into part of a worksheet, to be used in calculations such as budgeting and financial analysis.

Dan Bricklin (left) and Bob Frankston developed VisiCalc, the "most significant contribution to the microcomputer industry in 1979." Although VisiCalc is no longer sold, its development was a milestone in the history of microcomputer software. (Courtesy of Software Arts, Inc.)

VisiCalc's usefulness spread, business sales of microcomputers increased dramatically. Today Lotus 1-2-3, a successor to VisiCalc that can handle data management and graphics in addition to spreadsheets, is the world's most popular personal-productivity software.

Using Electronic Spreadsheets

Electronic spreadsheets caused a revolutionary change in business procedures. In a period of less than ten years, almost all types of businesses began using computers to do their spreadsheets. Past, current, and future budgets and other financial information are now entered and stored on disks instead of in ledger books. In addition to budgets, the uses of electronic spreadsheets for businesses of all sizes include sales forecasts, inventory management, production scheduling, and statistical analysis.

Figure 9-16 shows projected budgets for Allied Widget that were produced using Lotus 1-2-3.

Mechanics of Electronic Spreadsheets

To understand electronic spreadsheets, consider the case of a student budget such as Karen Chan's budget for January, February, and March. Before anything can be done on the computer, all of the relevant data must be gathered. Chan's data includes her fixed expenses:

Tuition: $960 in January
Books and supplies: $225 in January
Rent: $225 per month
Heat and utilities: $125 per month

FIGURE 9-16

Budget for Allied Widget

```
                              Allied    Widget
                    Balance   Sheet     (Figures in \1000)

Year ending Dec. 31    1988    1989      1990 (proj.)

Current Assets
        Cash           1500    2000      2000
        Accounts Rec. 20000   22000     24000
        Inventory     17500   21000     25000

Total Current Assets  39000   45000     51000

Fixed Assets
        Land          10000   10000     10000
        Plant         20000   18000     16200
        Equipment     45000   50000     54000

Total Fixed Assets    75000   78000     80200

TOTAL ASSETS         114000  123000    131200

Current Liabilities
        Accounts Payable  12000  13500  15000
        Salaries Payable   8000   9500  11000
        Taxes Payable      6000   7500   7500
        Short-term Loans Payable
                          15000   5000   4300

Total Current Liabilities 41000  35500  37800

Long-term Debt
        Bond Issues       20000  29500  29000
        Term Loans        10000   9500   8500

Total Long-term Debt      30000  39000  37500

TOTAL LIABILITIES         71000  74500  75300

NET WORTH
        Common Stock      32500  35000  38500
        Retained Earnings 10500  13500  17400

TOTAL NET WORTH           43000  48500  55900

TOTAL LIABIL. AND NET WORTH 114000 123000 131200
```

and her variable expenses:

Food: $150 per month
Clothing: $50 per month
Entertainment: $65 per month

To convert this data into an electronic spreadsheet, Chan begins by loading Lotus 1-2-3 into her computer's memory. After she has followed a few initial instructions, the screen displays an empty worksheet. (In the discussion of spreadsheets, the term *worksheet* refers to the spreadsheet form, whether blank or filled in for a specific application; the term *spreadsheet* refers to the program that is used to create and modify the worksheet.)

Worksheet and Control Panel Screen. The computer screen for an electronic spreadsheet has two parts: the worksheet and the control panel. These are shown in Figure 9-17 for Lotus 1-2-3. A worksheet is a grid of rows and columns. Because the worksheet is so large—some products permit more than 2048 rows and 256 columns—the user can see only a small part of it at any one time. Each row is identified by a number, and each column is identified by a letter (A–Z) or pair of letters (such as AA or AD). Columns and rows intersect to form *cells*; each cell is initially nine characters wide, but its width can be changed. Cells are identified by column and row, for example, A1, A2, B1, B2, AA1, AB23; the column (letter) designation always comes first.

Lotus's *control panel* consists of the three lines at the top of the screen that contain information about the worksheet. (Other spreadsheets provide different control panels.) The upper left-hand corner of the first line of the control panel indicates the *active cell*, that is, the highlighted location on the worksheet that is ready to receive data. In Figure 9-17 the active cell is A1. Depending on the program used, there are several ways to change the active cell and "navigate" through the worksheet. The upper right-hand corner of the first line indicates the *mode* the program is in; Figure 9-17 shows that it is in the READY mode, which means that it is ready to receive data. Other examples of modes are HELP and MENU. In the MENU mode, the second line of the control panel displays choices from a menu, and the third line describes the highlighted menu choice.

Worksheet Cells. When a worksheet is in the READY mode, it is ready to accept one of the following items:
- A *label* (or *string*), which is the spreadsheet's word for text. Labels are used for identification and explanatory purposes.
- A *value*, which is a number or formula used in calculations.
- A *command*, which tells the spreadsheet to perform some operation, such as blanking out all or part of the screen.

FIGURE 9-17

Empty Worksheet and Control Panel for Lotus 1-2-3

```
A1:                                                              READY

        A         B         C         D         E         F         G         H
 1
 2
 3
 4
 5
 6
 7
 8
 9
10
11
12
13
14
15
16
17
18
19
20
```

Entering Labels. Labels generally start with a letter, which is followed by a combination of letters, numbers, and special symbols, including $, %, and #. Each spreadsheet has its own rules for specifying labels; for example, some require that the entry be prefixed with a special character such as ' or ". Labels are generally entered for column and row headings.

Chan's budget can now be entered into the computer. First, Chan enters a label for the worksheet title. In cells D1 to H1 she enters *Budget for First Q*; one word is entered per cell.

CHAPTER 9 325 PERSONAL-PRODUCTIVITY SOFTWARE

Then she enters labels for column heads: in cell C2, *January*; in cell D2, *February*; and in cell E2, *March*. Next, she enters the row labels in cells A3 to A20. The first row label, *Fixed expenses* in cell A3, is fourteen characters wide, including the space. In fact, most of the row labels in column A are wider than the standard nine characters and flow into column B. Most spreadsheets permit users to increase or decrease the column width if they so desire. This feature helps users produce professional-looking worksheets.

Chan finishes entering the labels in column A. The worksheet for her budget with column and row labels is shown in Figure 9-18.

Entering Numbers. Chan can now enter numerical amounts in her worksheet. Spreadsheets have special rules for entering numbers:

1. When entering numbers like 12,000, do not enter the comma.
2. When entering dollar amounts, do not enter the dollar sign.
3. Enter the decimal point when a number has a decimal part, such as 25.15 or 0.50.
4. Percent signs may be entered (note that the spreadsheet will read 100% as 1, 50% as 0.5, and 25% as 0.25).

Figure 9-19 shows Chan's worksheet with amounts entered for fixed and variable expenses for January to March. The totals are not filled in. Instead of using a calculator to determine the totals and then inserting them, Chan can let the spreadsheet do the calculations automatically by entering formulas in the cells for the totals.

Entering Formulas. Spreadsheets also have rules about how to enter formulas in cells:

1. With many spreadsheets, a formula must begin with an arithmetic operator, such as + or −.
2. A formula usually expresses a calculation in terms of cells, such as A1 or B2, *not* in terms of the numbers in the cells.

To obtain a total of her fixed expenses, Chan would have to add up the numbers in cells C5, C6, C7, and C8. Therefore, in cell C10 (total fixed expenses) she enters the spreadsheet formula +C5+C6+C7+C8. The formula is displayed in the control panel, not the cell; when she presses the RETURN (or ENTER) key, the number 1535 appears in the cell. The spreadsheet has automatically performed the calculation and displayed the answer in the cell. Chan similarly enters the appropriate formulas in the cells for total fixed expenses, total variable expenses, and total expenses, pressing the RETURN key after entering each formula and seeing the results displayed almost

FIGURE 9-18

Setting Up a Spreadsheet Worksheet

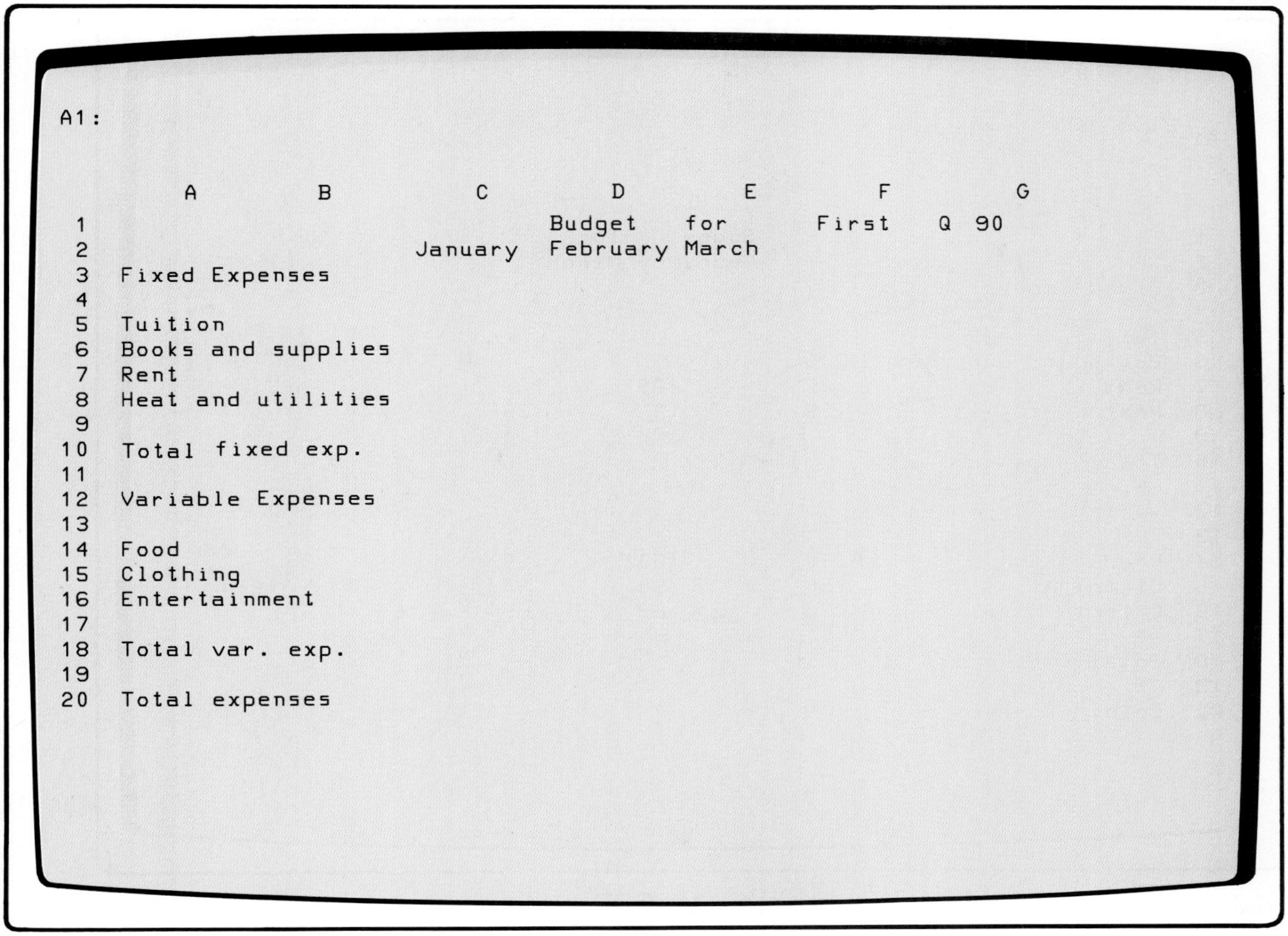

```
A1:

         A         B         C         D         E         F         G
 1                                    Budget    for       First     Q 90
 2                           January  February  March
 3   Fixed Expenses
 4
 5   Tuition
 6   Books and supplies
 7   Rent
 8   Heat and utilities
 9
10   Total fixed exp.
11
12   Variable Expenses
13
14   Food
15   Clothing
16   Entertainment
17
18   Total var. exp.
19
20   Total expenses
```

A student budget showing column and row headings and cell identifiers. In this and the remaining figures in the chapter, Column H has been removed for the sake of simplicity.

instantaneously. Figure 9-20 shows Chan's worksheet with the totals entered.

The ability to process formulas is an integral part of any electronic spreadsheet. The use of formulas enables users to see the effects of changes in data very rapidly. For example, suppose that Chan decided to purchase study guides for two of her courses, thereby increasing the amount for books and supplies from $225.00 to $245.00. When she enters the amount 245.00

FIGURE 9-19

A Worksheet with Values Entered

```
A1:

         A          B           C          D         E         F         G
  1                                     Budget    for       First    Q 90
  2                              January February March
  3   Fixed Expenses
  4
  5   Tuition                      960
  6   Books and supplies           225
  7   Rent                         225        225       225
  8   Heat and utilities           125        125       125
  9
 10   Total fixed exp.
 11
 12   Variable Expenses
 13
 14   Food                         150        150       150
 15   Clothing                      50         50        50
 16   Entertainment                 65         65        65
 17
 18   Total var. exp.
 19
 20   Total expenses
```

Student budget showing amounts for individual items

in cell C6, the spreadsheet automatically recalculates the formula in C10, producing a revised total of 1555. If instead of entering the formula at C10 she calculated her total fixed expenses either manually or with an electronic calculator, she would have to redo the calculation to account for the higher amount spent on books and supplies.

Using Functions. Entering formulas in cells and letting the spreadsheet do the calculations is certainly faster than doing

FIGURE 9-20

A Worksheet with Totals

	A	B	C	D	E	F	G
1				Budget	for	First	Q 90
2			January	February	March	Total	1st Q
3	Fixed Expenses						
4							
5	Tuition		960			960	
6	Books and supplies		225			225	
7	Rent		225	225	225	675	
8	Heat and utilities		125	125	125	375	
9							
10	Total fixed exp.		1535	350	350	2235	
11							
12	Variable Expenses						
13							
14	Food		150	150	150	450	
15	Clothing		50	50	50	150	
16	Entertainment		65	65	65	195	
17							
18	Total var. exp.		265	265	265	795	
19							
20	Total expenses		1800	615	615	3030	

The spreadsheet program uses formulas entered by the student to calculate total expenses for this budget.

them by hand or with a calculator. However, spreadsheets provide an additional, often more efficient way to do calculations: by using functions.

A *function* can be thought of as a formula that has been written by the programmer who created the spreadsheet. Most spreadsheets provide dozens of functions that can be used for business, scientific, engineering, and other applications. Some examples of functions in Lotus 1-2-3 are @SUM(A1..A25), which adds up the amounts in cells A1 to A25; @PMT, which calculates a loan payment; and @AVG(A1..A25), which calculates the average of the amounts in cells A1 to A25.

As with amounts and formulas, there are rules for using functions:

1. In Lotus 1-2-3, all functions begin with the @ sign.
2. Two dots (..) are used to indicate a range.

Instead of entering the formula +C5+C6+C7+C8 in cell C10, Chan can enter the function @SUM(C5..C8). The spreadsheet will automatically add the values in all the cells in the range from C5 to C8. Functions are extremely useful, since they can replace long, complicated formulas. They enable an untrained user to take advantage of advanced financial, statistical, and mathematical calculations by following a few simple rules.

Correcting Errors. If the user makes an error when entering data into cells and notices it before pressing RETURN, he or she can correct it by erasing the characters one by one, using the BACK SPACE key. If, however, the error is not noticed until after the RETURN key has been pressed, the simple word processor that is a part of most spreadsheet programs can be used to correct the mistake. It is extremely important to check all entries in the worksheet, especially formulas and functions. A seemingly minor error can have major consequences.

Giving Commands. When users want a spreadsheet program to do something, such as change the width of a column or save data, they must enter a command. (A command is simply an instruction to the spreadsheet to carry out a specific action.) Spreadsheets have specific rules about how to enter commands. For example, in Lotus 1-2-3 a command must be preceded by the forward slash (/).

The Copy Command. When a user is working with budgets and other financial reports, the same data and formulas often appear in different parts of a worksheet. The copy, or replicate, command lets users copy data or formulas from one part of a worksheet to another. The Lotus copy command allows the user to copy data from a column or row to one or more other columns or rows. Chan could take advantage of this command by entering only the data for January and copying it for February and March, taking care not to copy the amounts for tuition and for books and supplies, which apply only to January.

Printing Worksheets. A disadvantage of the monitor screen for displaying worksheets is its size, which is often limited to 25 lines and 80 characters per line. Even relatively small worksheets are too large to be displayed on the screen in their entirety. Users therefore may print a worksheet several times during the development process, as well as the final version. Programs are available that allow users to print long worksheets horizontally as well as vertically.

When Chan wants to print her worksheet, she enters the command /P. She then has the option of saving her worksheet on a special print file. (This is useful when the printer is unavailable.) She chooses to print and indicates the range of her worksheet to be printed by entering A1..G20.

Saving Worksheets. When the user works on a worksheet, it is in primary storage. If the user wants to keep a permanent copy, it must be saved to a file on a disk. To save her worksheet, Chan enters Lotus's File Save command followed by the disk drive in which the file will be saved (B) and the name of the file (BUDGET), as follows:

```
/File Save B:BUDGET
```

After Chan has saved her file, she can erase the worksheet from primary storage. When she wants to use it again, she will have to load it back in. If she already has a file named BUDGET on the diskette in drive B, the system will check with her before canceling the previous version. In this way the system can prevent the user from losing hours of work.

Erasing and Retrieving Worksheets. When a user is finished with a worksheet and has printed and saved it on a disk (if desired), he or she can erase it from primary storage. In addition, before starting to work on a new worksheet, the user should erase the previous worksheet from primary storage. The spreadsheet command to erase worksheets is generally Erase or Zap. (Before actually erasing a worksheet most programs ask the user for a confirmation of the command.)

After a file has been saved on a disk and erased from primary storage, the user must load it back into storage to work on it. The Lotus 1-2-3 command for this is Retrieve. It is important to be aware that the Retrieve command erases any file currently in primary storage before it loads the one requested.

Inserting Rows and Columns. After a basic worksheet has been completed, the user may discover categories and items to add to it, making it necessary to insert additional columns and rows. Spreadsheets include an insert command that enables the user to "open up the worksheet" in order to add more rows and columns. When a new row is added, all the rows beneath it move down one row; when a new column is added, all the columns to the right of it move to the right. Electronic spreadsheets automatically adjust formulas when necessary. For example, if Chan decided to insert blank lines to separate her expense categories, the totals would remain unchanged, but the spreadsheet would modify the formulas that are used to calculate the totals.

Suppose Chan decides to buy a car and wants to add its expenses to her budget. Under fixed expenses she will add *Car loan* and under variable expenses, *Gas and oil*—thereby adding two new rows to her worksheet. She begins by moving the cursor to row 8 and inserting a new row below it; then she enters the label *Car loan* in column A and the value of 150 in columns C through E for January through March. She makes a similar change for her monthly *Gas and oil* expenses of 70. The revised worksheet is shown in Figure 9-21.

Asking What If? Questions. In order to pay for her car, Chan needs to take a part-time job. She has been offered two jobs—one in a fast-food restaurant and the other in a clothing store. Both pay $300 a month. "What if I took the fast-food job?" she wonders. "My food expenses would be lower. But if I took the clothing store job my clothing bills would be reduced. On the other hand, my food expenses would be higher since I would have to eat out more." Chan can use her worksheet to help her determine which job offer to accept.

The ability of electronic spreadsheets to recalculate formulas automatically enables managers and others to use them to answer *What if? questions*. The user can set up a worksheet, including initial values and formulas; ask *what* would happen to the budget *if* one value were increased by a certain percentage, *if* another value were decreased, *if* one were increased and two were decreased, or any other combination of changes; and see the effects of the changes almost immediately.

To help her decide which job to take, Chan sets up two worksheets based on the one in Figure 9-20, but with several changes:

1. A row for income has been added.
2. Amounts for January to March income and their totals have been inserted.
3. A row for total net expenses has been added.
4. The formula for total net expenses has been inserted in the cell for January and copied into the cells for February, March, and First Quarter Total.
5. All the figures added to the worksheet have been placed in the appropriate format.

FIGURE 9-21

Revised Worksheet

	A	B	C	D	E	F	G
1				Budget	for	First	Q 90
2			January	February	March	Total 1st Q	
3	Fixed Expenses						
4							
5	Tuition		960			960	
6	Books and supplies		225			225	
7	Rent		225	225	225	675	
8	Heat and utilities		125	125	125	375	
9	Car loan		150	150	150	450	
10							
11	Total fixed exp.		1685	500	500	2685	
12							
13	Variable Expenses						
14							
15	Food		150	150	150	450	
16	Clothing		50	50	50	150	
17	Entertainment		65	65	65	195	
18	Gas and oil		70	70	70	210	
19							
20	Total var. exp.		335	335	335	1005	
	Total expenses		2020	835	835	3690	

In the fast-food job worksheet shown in Figure 9-22, Chan has reduced her food expenses by 20 percent because of a meal allowance. In the clothing store job worksheet shown in Figure 9-23, she has reduced her clothing expenses by 30 percent and increased her food expenses by $20 a month. Once she set it up correctly, the electronic spreadsheet automatically changed her totals so that she could see the effects of each job on her total expenses and total net expenses.

FIGURE 9-22

Chan's Fast-Food Job Worksheet

Fast-food job	January	Budget February	for March	First Total 1st Q	Q 90
Income	300.00	300.00	300.00	900.00	
Fixed Expenses					
Tuition	960.00			960.00	
Books and supplies	225.00			225.00	
Rent	225.00	225.00	225.00	675.00	
Heat and utilities	125.00	125.00	125.00	375.00	
Car loan	150.00	150.00	150.00	450.00	
Total fixed exp.	1685.00	500.00	500.00	2685.00	
Variable Expenses					
Food	120.00	120.00	120.00	360.00	
Clothing	50.00	50.00	50.00	150.00	
Entertainment	65.00	65.00	65.00	195.00	
Gas and oil	70.00	70.00	70.00	210.00	
Total var. exp.	305.00	305.00	305.00	915.00	
Total expenses	1990.00	805.00	805.00	3600.00	
Total net expenses	1690.00	505.00	505.00	2700.00	

Here and in Figure 9-23, the column letters and row numbers have been removed for the sake of simplicity.

The example of Karen Chan's budget illustrates in a simplified form how electronic spreadsheets are used by businesses and organizations to present data and help managers make decisions. Chan could have compared the economic aspects of the fast-food and clothing store jobs without the aid of her computer. But when a manager must take into consideration variations in and interactions among hundreds or even thousands of factors, electronic spreadsheets become a necessity.

In coming years the ability to manipulate worksheets will be

FIGURE 9-23

Chan's Clothing Store Job Worksheet

Clothing store job	Budget	for	First	Q 90
	January	February	March	Total 1st Q
Income	300.00	300.00	300.00	900.00
Fixed Expenses				
Tuition	960.00			960.00
Books and supplies	225.00			225.00
Rent	225.00	225.00	225.00	675.00
Heat and utilities	125.00	125.00	125.00	375.00
Car loan	150.00	150.00	150.00	450.00
Total fixed exp.	1685.00	500.00	500.00	2685.00
Variable Expenses				
Food	170.00	170.00	170.00	510.00
Clothing	35.00	35.00	35.00	105.00
Entertainment	65.00	65.00	65.00	195.00
Gas and oil	70.00	70.00	70.00	210.00
Total var. exp.	340.00	340.00	340.00	1020.00
Total expenses	2025.00	840.00	840.00	3705.00
Total net expenses	1725.00	540.00	540.00	2805.00

as much a prerequisite for managerial success as the ability to communicate clearly. Familiarity with word-processing and data-base management programs is also essential for prospective managers. Fortunately, the job of managers who need to use several different types of personal-productivity software is being made easier by a movement toward integration of different applications. Current directions in integration—an active frontier in personal-productivity software—are described in Box 9-2.

BOX 9-2

FRONTIERS IN TECHNOLOGY

Integrating Personal-Productivity Software

You are the brand manager for Kyss lipstick, which is marketed by a large cosmetics company. It is almost lunch time, and you are rushing to get a presentation ready for a 2:00 P.M. meeting. You have hammered out most of what you need to say using the word-processing package on your personal computer. To complete the report, you need a graph showing recent and projected sales of Kyss. But the data on sales for recent years resides in your data-base management program. Once you have retrieved the data, you will need to make some "what if?" projections using your spreadsheet. When you have the projections, you will switch to a graphics program to prepare a chart for your presentation, then zip back to the word processor to write up a ringing conclusion to your report.

For the next two hours, you hop madly from one program to another, shuffling files, making ASCII conversions, reformatting, editing, sometimes scribbling data from one application onto a yellow pad and reentering it via the keyboard when you reach your destination. As the clock strikes 2, you rip the last page of your report out of the printer and sprint down the corridor to your meeting. Sweaty and flustered, you make a mess of your presentation. My friend, you need integration!

Integration is the ability to share data among applications programs. It is the top priority for managers buying personal-productivity software today. Full integration has three facets. The first is *data compatibility*—the ability of one program to read files written by another, and to use them without extensive editing. The second is *concurrency*—the ability to pull up a function, such as a spreadsheet, without leaving another function, such as a word processor. The third element is *command consistency*—the ability to use similar instructions to move around menus and issue commands in a variety of applications programs.

As yet, there is no such thing as complete integration. Software suppliers are working on the problem, however, and several partial solutions are already available. These include the following:

- **Integrating environments.** An integrating environment is a program that allows the user to call up one applications program while another is being run, to snip needed data from it, and then take the data back to the original program to be used as needed. This is often accomplished through the use of "windows." Windows are areas of the screen that show one application while other areas of the screen show another.
- **Multifunction packages.** A multifunction package is an applications program that combines several functions. The idea of integration was popularized by Lotus 1-2-3, which added simple graphics and data management functions to the spreadsheet that is the package's central feature. More recent multifunction packages offer a greater range of functions, such as combining full word-processing capabilities with spreadsheet, graphics, and data-base management.
- **Product families.** These are separate applications programs—word processing, spreadsheet, and so on—that offer common file formats but not concurrent processing.

Full integration of personal-computer software is technologically within reach but is not yet a market reality. One stumbling block is the individualism of personal-computer users, who develop loyalty to certain software packages with quirks that defy full integration. Another is the PC-DOS operating system, which was designed before integration was seen as a pressing need. However, future versions of the personal computer's operating system may come with built-in integration capabilities.

SUMMARY

1. Data-base management programs are designed to store, retrieve, and manipulate data from one or more files. With a few easily learned commands, users of programs such as dBASE III can create the structure for records in a file; enter, display, print, and edit data; sort a file; extract records; and perform arithmetic. Additional commands allow users to modify structures and to work with more than one file at a given time.

2. Word processing is the use of a computer program to enter text, modify its content and appearance, and print it. Word processors are computers or similar devices that are used to perform word processing.

3. By means of simple **commands**, users of word processors can enter, insert, delete, and change text. Additional commands allow the user to move text from one point to another, find and replace a collection of characters known as a **string**, and provide for boldface printing and underlining.

4. Many word processors offer a feature known as WYSIWYG (What you see is what you get), in which the user can preview on the monitor an exact image of the document to be printed. Other features accompanying word processors include spelling checkers, on-line thesaurus programs, the ability to check grammar and style, and mail merge programs.

5. Spreadsheets are rows and columns of numbers and descriptive words. For centuries spreadsheets have been used for record keeping and analysis in a wide variety of applications including business, administration, science, and engineering. An **electronic spreadsheet** is a program that converts a computer monitor into part of a worksheet, to be used in calculations such as budgeting and financial analysis.

6. A few simple commands allow users of electronic spreadsheets such as Lotus 1-2-3 to enter data into a worksheet, correct errors, reformat the worksheet, enter functions, copy data from one area of the worksheet to another, save, retrieve, and modify the worksheet.

7. The ability of electronic spreadsheets to recalculate formulas automatically and rapidly enables managers and others to use them to answer What if? questions, seeing what would happen in a given situation if one or more items were changed.

KEY TERMS

data-base management program

word processing

command

string

electronic spreadsheet

REVIEW QUESTIONS

1. What are data-base management programs? How can they increase productivity?

2. Describe how a typical data-base management program performs each of the following:
- create the structure for records in a file
- enter data
- display data
- print data
- edit data
- sort a file
- extract records

3. What is word processing? Describe how users can benefit from it.

4. Describe how a typical word-processing program performs each of the following:
- insert text
- delete text
- change text
- substitute one string for another
- provide for boldface printing and underlining

5. Have you seen a word processor that offers WYSIWYG? What is the advantage of this feature? Can you think of any disadvantages?

6. List three additional programs that increase the power and flexibility of word-processing programs. What are their advantages and limitations?

7. What are spreadsheets? Describe a spreadsheet application that you have used. What are electronic spreadsheets?

8. Describe how a typical electronic spreadsheet performs each of the following:
- enter numbers
- enter labels
- enter formulas
- use functions

APPLICATIONS

1. Interview someone who uses a file-management or data-base management program. What are the applications for which the program is used? Describe the advantages and disadvantages of carrying out these tasks with the aid of a computer program instead of manually.

2. Interview someone who uses a word-processing program. Answer the same questions as in application 1.

3. Interview someone who uses an electronic spreadsheet. Answer the same questions as in application 1.

4. Discuss the following statement: Mastery of word processing is a necessity for anyone who wants to be a professional writer.

CASE FOR DISCUSSION

When Bob Williams ended up in the hospital following a car accident caused by his vehicle's faulty braking system, he sued the manufacturer. His lawsuit was based on similar complaints made by other owners of that particular model. Williams's willingness to settle out of court for $3 million presented the manufacturer's attorneys with an immediate decision: Should they settle with the plaintiff at a known cost or take the case to trial in the hope of winning a lesser award or a possible acquittal?

Lawsuits that raise the same questions are faced by attorneys every day. The area is known as litigation risk analysis, and the Washington, D.C., law firm of Wilmer, Cutler, and Pickering has turned to Lotus 1-2-3 for help in assessing the implications of various legal strategies for damage awards. The analysis techniques that this firm uses can be extended to virtually any field in which sequential decisions can lead to a variety of conclusions.

Litigation risk analysis entails the examination of a number of lawsuit scenarios. In cases such as the one described, several outcomes are possible. The plaintiff may be willing to forgo the inconvenience of a trial and settle out of court for a certain sum. If the case does go to trial, a jury may rule in favor of one side or the other based on the particular facts presented. A judge may disallow certain evidence, and damage settlement amounts may be influenced by precedents. For attorneys plotting legal strategies, it is crucial to know the chances of a case going in any given direction.

The intricacies of many cases make risk analysis complex, especially when the process involves hundreds of decisions, each of which has an impact on others. These decisions can be laid out in a series of possible scenarios or paths, collectively called a decision tree. Prior to the advent of personal computers and spreadsheets, litigation risk analysis was performed in one of two ways: tediously on paper or instinctually in an attorney's head. The former was time-consuming and often inaccurate; the latter depended heavily on intuition and memory. By plotting a risk-analysis model with a computer and spreadsheet, however, you eliminate many of the tedious aspects of the paper-and-pencil method while you inject a measure of objectivity into the process. In addition, using a spreadsheet for risk analysis allows both attorney and client to see quickly the ramifications of various legal maneuvers.

The chart on the next two pages shows a decision tree representing the case of Bob Williams vs. United Motors Corporation. Each branch of the tree represents a decision or event that can take place in the course of the case. The percentage figures below each scenario show estimated probability. Serially multiplying the percentage values along each path gives the overall probability of that course of events. The sum of the probabilities of all the paths is 100 percent. Column P shows the Lotus 1-2-3 formulas used to carry out the multiplications along each path.

Source: Edward Jones, "Risk Analysis With 1-2-3," *Lotus*, July 1985, pp. 65–67. Copyright © 1985 Lotus Publishing Corporation. Used with permission. All rights reserved.

CASE QUESTIONS

1. In what sense does the use of an electronic spreadsheet increase the personal productivity of an attorney in a case like the one described? Is the quantity of the attorney's output increased? The quality? Is the resulting decision really more "objective," or is it still based on intuition? Discuss.

2. Suppose that the judge decides not to allow Williams to submit a certain item of evidence. Without this evidence, you estimate that the likelihood of the jury's finding negligence falls to 50 percent. Show how changing the probabilities in column F affects

CASE QUESTIONS

the probabilities in column N. If you have Lotus 1-2-3 or a similar spreadsheet, reconstruct the worksheet shown in the chart and use it to answer this question. If not, carry out the required calculations by hand.

3. The "expected loss" from a given scenario is the loss from that scenario (column N) multiplied by the probability of the scenario (column O). For example, the expected loss from the first scenario (high award with punitive damage) is $5,500,000.00 × 0.36, or $1,980,000. You should accept the offer of an out-of-court settlement if the sum of the expected losses from all scenarios

CASE FOR DISCUSSION

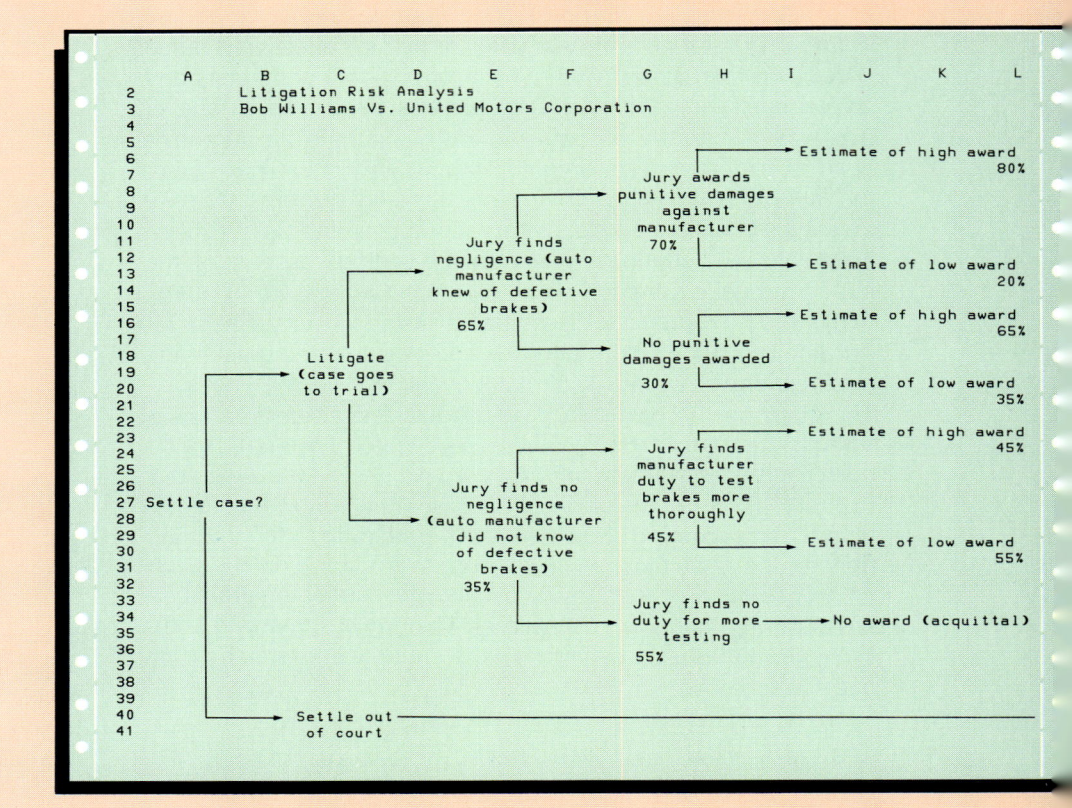

```
           A    B        C         D         E         F           G              H           I         J          K          L
  2             Litigation Risk Analysis
  3             Bob Williams Vs. United Motors Corporation
  4
  5                                                                                                         ─────► Estimate of high award
  6                                                                                                                                   80%
  7                                                                                      Jury awards
  8                                                                                   punitive damages
  9                                                                                        against
 10                                                                                      manufacturer
 11                                                                    Jury finds           70%
 12                                                                   negligence (auto                      ─────► Estimate of low award
 13                                                                    manufacturer                                                    20%
 14                                                                   knew of defective
 15                                                                       brakes)                           ─────► Estimate of high award
 16                                                                         65%                                                        65%
 17                                                                                      No punitive
 18                                          Litigate                                   damages awarded
 19                                         (case goes                                        30%           ─────► Estimate of low award
 20                                          to trial)                                                                                 35%
 21
 22                                                                                                         ─────► Estimate of high award
 23                                                                                      Jury finds                                    45%
 24                                                                                      manufacturer
 25                                                                    Jury finds no     duty to test
 26                                                                    negligence        brakes more
 27             Settle case?                                          (auto manufacturer thoroughly
 28                                                                    did not know           45%           ─────► Estimate of low award
 29                                                                    of defective                                                    55%
 30                                                                      brakes)
 31                                                                        35%
 32
 33                                                                                      Jury finds no
 34                                                                                     duty for more ─────► No award (acquittal)
 35                                                                                        testing
 36                                                                                          55%
 37
 38
 39
 40                         ─────► Settle out
 41                                 of court
```

CASE QUESTIONS

involving going to court exceeds $3 million. Using your reconstructed worksheet or working by hand, add a column Q that shows the expected losses. Sum the column. Should you accept the offer of settlement?

4. At each branch in the decision tree, the probabilities must sum to 100 percent. For example, in column F the probability of finding no negligence must be 100 percent minus the probability of finding negligence. How could this fact be used in setting up the worksheet so that when a pair of probabilities is changed, only one figure needs to be entered?

	M	N	O	P
2			Probability	Formulas
3	Punitive amount:	$2,500,000.00	of this	for
4	Compensatory amount:	$3,000,000.00	scenario	column O
5	======================			
6	Total amount:	$5,500,000.00	36%	+F17*I13*L9
7				
8				
9				
10	Punitive amount:	$1,000,000.00		
11	Compensatory amount:	$1,500,000.00		
12	======================			
13	Total amount:	$2,500,000.00	9%	$F17*I13*L15
14				
15				
16	Total amount:	$3,000,000.00	13%	+F17*I21*L18
17				
18				
19				
20	Total amount:	$1,500,000.00	7%	+F17*I21*L23
21				
22				
23	Total amount:	$2,500,000.00	7%	+F33*I30*L26
24				
30	Total amount:	$500,000.00	9%	+F33*I30*L31
35	Total amount:	$0.00	19%	+F33*I36
36			======================	
37			100%	@SUM(O9..O34)
41	Settlement amount:	$3,000,000.00		

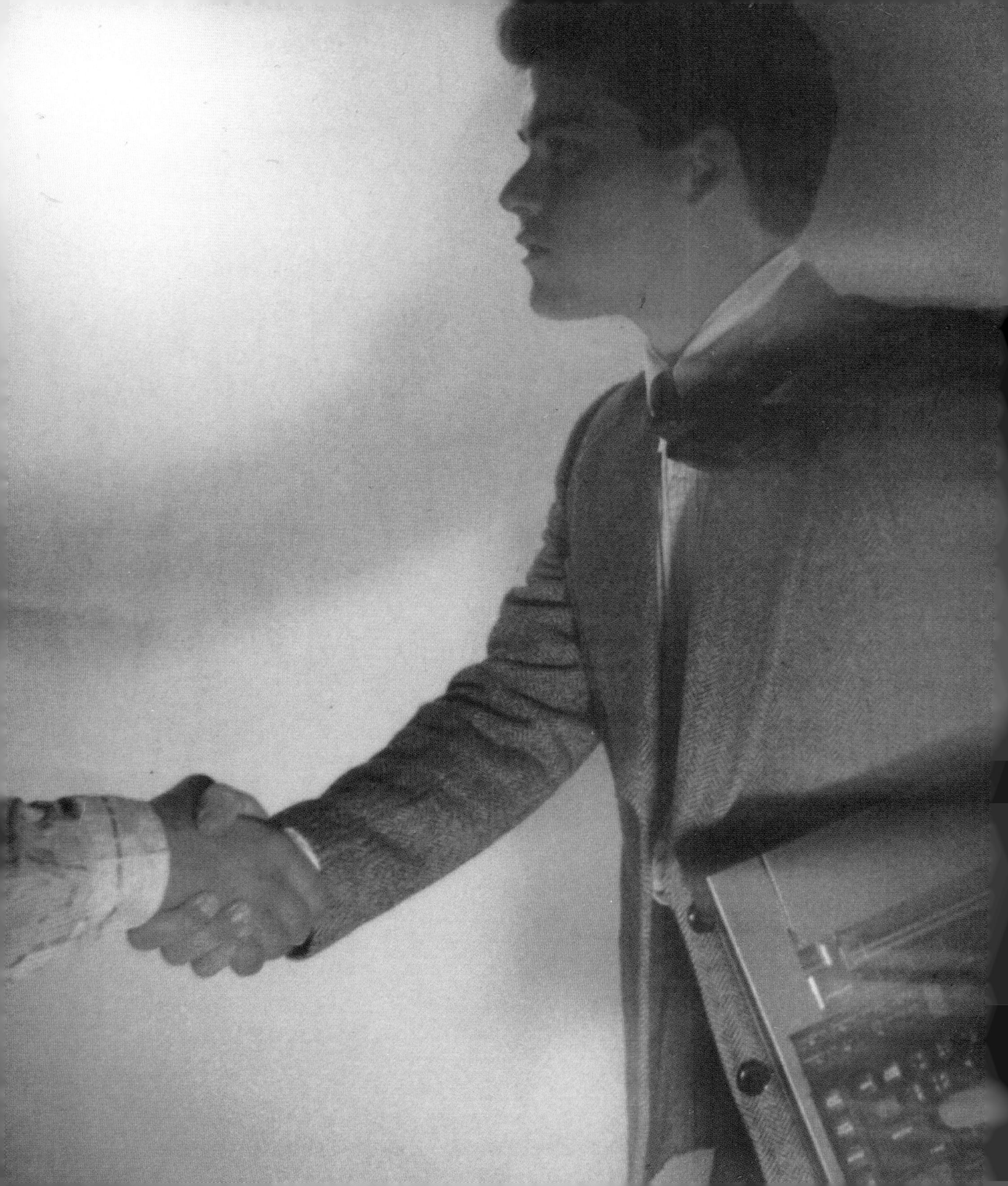

File-Processing and Data-Base Systems

CHAPTER

10

"One thing a salesperson hates is to be surprised by questions about scheduled shipments that haven't arrived," says Russell Sprague. Sprague is director of commercial information systems for Monsanto Polymer Products. Monsanto's salespeople do not have that problem. Before they call on a customer, they use a computer terminal to ask for an order status report that summarizes all the customer's bookings and shipments. If any orders are not being filled on schedule, the report includes an explanation. This puts the salesperson in a better position to explain to a customer what has happened and what is being done about it.

Salespeople are assured of the latest data because the On-line Automated Commercial Information System (OACIS) is hooked into Monsanto's automated order-billing system. As new orders come in and shipments go out, the data base is updated constantly. Thus, salespeople can get data on everything that occurred up to 6:00 P.M. the previous day.

The order status report is not the only sales aid that OACIS has to offer. For example, before making a call, salespeople may request data on specific products that the customer bought in the current month, the previous month, and the year to date. To help determine what products to emphasize, Monsanto salespeople can also ask OACIS for a report comparing their sales forecasts for the customer with the amount of various products already purchased in the current period.

Sprague stresses that the system was designed to be "as user-friendly as possible." This goal has been achieved because "the sales force, to a large extent, designed the system." For half a year Sprague and his staff toured district offices, asking salespeople what information they felt would be most helpful in their jobs and how they would like to have the information presented.

Field sales managers, for their part, insisted that the system be limited to information retrieval. They did not want salespeople to be able to manipulate or alter data. To accomplish this, the system was built around "read-only" terminals built by Digital Equipment Corporation.

The system turned out to be so popular that salespeople soon wanted to take the terminals home. Portable terminals allow salespeople to keep in touch even when extensive traveling keeps them away from home most of the time.[1]

---

[1] "A Daily Dose of Data for Monsanto Salespeople," *Sales and Marketing Management*, December 9, 1985, p. 70.

Chapter 9 discussed data-base management programs as one of the three most important kinds of personal-productivity software. The chapter focused on data-base management programs for microcomputers. This chapter continues the discussion of data-base management by exploring systems that are used on larger computers. Monsanto's OACIS is an example of such a system. Because it is linked directly to the company's mainframe-based automated order-billing system, it provides information that is far more complete and timely than would be possible if each salesperson maintained a separate personal-computer data base.

This chapter begins by looking at traditional methods of processing data in files. The three file organizations presented in Chapter 5 are reviewed and two others are introduced. Then some drawbacks of traditional processing are given, leading to a presentation of a more sophisticated way to manage data: using data-base management systems. The fundamentals of data-base management systems, the people associated with them, the special types of programming language used with them, and the data models on which they are based are described. The advantages and disadvantages of data-base management systems are discussed, and guidelines for selecting and installing a system are presented.

When you have read this chapter, you should be able to:

1. Discuss traditional file-processing systems and compare and contrast file-processing and data-base management systems.
2. Identify the roles of the people associated with a data-base management system.
3. Discuss and compare the programming languages associated with data-base management systems.
4. Describe the purpose and contents of a data dictionary.
5. Compare and contrast the three data models.
6. Write elementary queries using structured query language.
7. List the advantages and disadvantages of using a data-base management system.
8. Describe the criteria for selecting a data-base management system.
9. Understand and use the key terms listed at the end of the chapter.

File-Processing Systems

You will recall from Chapter 2 that all the data in a computer is organized in a hierarchy that consists of bits, bytes (or characters), fields, records, files, and data bases. (See Figure 10-1.) The specific way in which the data is structured within the data hierarchy depends on the organization's information-processing objectives. Chapter 5 also presented three basic types of file organization, which will be reviewed here. Together with the two additional types that will be introduced in this chapter, they represent commonly used methods of processing data, namely, **file-processing systems.**

File-processing system
A computerized system consisting of files that are designed and organized to meet specific needs, such as accounting, sales, and marketing applications.

A file-processing system is a computerized system consisting of programs and files that are designed and organized to meet specific needs, such as accounting, sales, and marketing applications. For example, in a particular company the accounting file may store data to the nearest cent, the sales file to the nearest dollar, and the marketing file to the nearest $1000. In such a system, data is not a centralized resource but can readily be used only for the specific application for which it was set up. If the company wanted to use the data for another purpose, such as an advertising campaign, it would have to set up a new file.

File-processing systems can be batch or interactive systems and can run on computers of all sizes, including microcomputers, minicomputers, and mainframes. Any of the file organizations discussed in this chapter can be used with a file-processing system.

Types of File Organization

Chapter 5 presented three basic types of file organization: sequential, random-access (also called direct-access), and indexed-sequential. Each type has both advantages and disadvantages and is most suitable for certain user needs.

Sequential Files. Sequentially organized files can be used with relatively inexpensive storage devices. Sequential files pro-

FIGURE 10-1

The Data Hierarchy

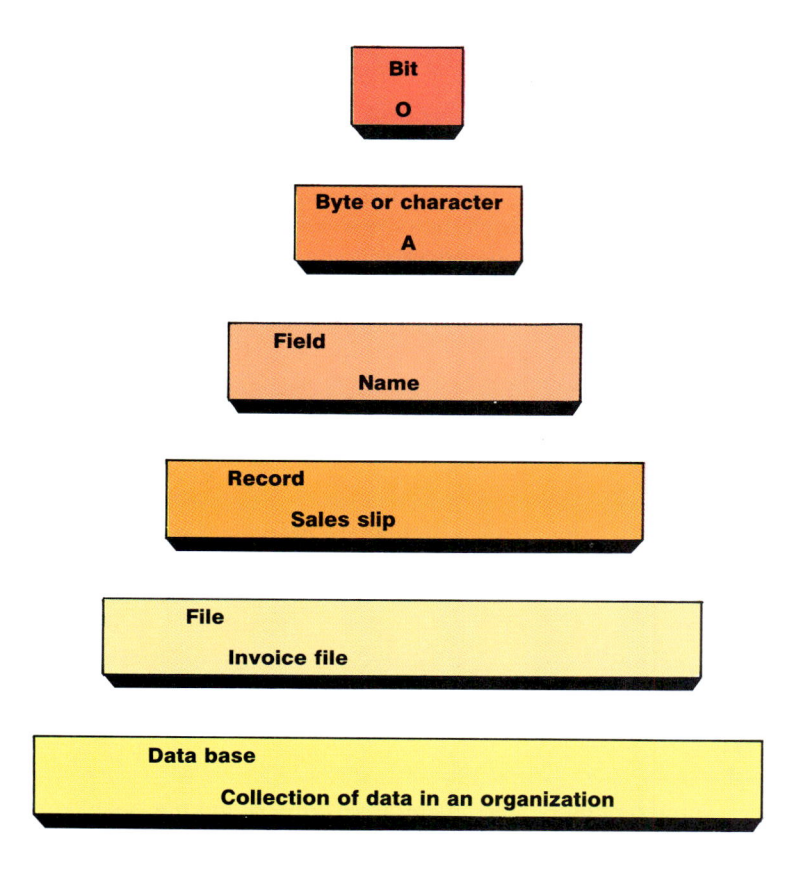

Bit
O

Byte or character
A

Field
Name

Record
Sales slip

File
Invoice file

Data base
Collection of data in an organization

duce backup copies readily. On the other hand, these files may require sorting, and in order for one record to be processed, all the preceding records must be processed. Also, since users commonly process a group of change requests or transactions at once, information on a sequential file may not be timely. In general, sequential files are well adapted for scheduled, periodic batch processing such as a weekly or biweekly payroll, but rarely furnish up-to-the-minute information and are not satisfactory for answering unscheduled requests such as: Is employee number 17825 covered by Worker's Compensation? or How much overtime did the Production Department incur last week?

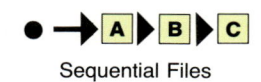

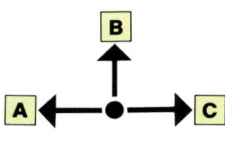

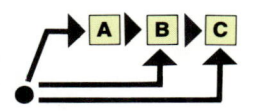

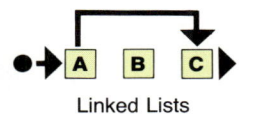

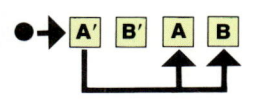

Types of File Organization
- Sequential Files
- Random-Access Files
- Indexed Sequential Files
- Linked Lists
- Inverted Files

Random-Access Files. Random-access (or direct-access) files allow a record to be processed without first requiring all previous records to be processed. In addition, many applications involving random-access files do not require sorting, and several records can be updated with one transaction. However, random-access files require relatively expensive magnetic-disk storage and use extra space to avoid an excessive number of synonyms (i.e., several records "colliding" in storage as described in Chapter 5). Moreover, they require special backup procedures, and sorting is necessary to prepare sequential reports. Proper use of random-access files permits questions like those just mentioned to be answered in a few seconds. A common application of direct-access files is an airline reservation system.

Indexed-Sequential Files. Indexed-sequential files represent a compromise between sequential and random-access files. They allow files to be accessed both randomly and sequentially. Unlike the two methods just described, indexed-sequential files readily furnish sequential reports starting in the middle of the file, such as a payroll report listing all employees whose employee number is greater than 1000. They do not, however, perform sequential processing as efficiently as sequential files, nor can they perform random processing as efficiently as random-access files. Indexed-sequential files are used by many businesses for such applications as accounting and inventory management, in which both (sequential) reports and (random) queries are frequently encountered.

Although these three types of file organization can handle many business needs, there are numerous situations for which they are inadequate. Two additional ways to organize files—linked lists and inverted files—are used for other types of data-handling requirements.

Linked Lists. A file on a magnetic disk can be organized as a *linked list*. In a linked list, records that share a common value (such as engineer) for a specific field (such as job title) are linked together via a special field known as a *pointer*. To see how linked lists work, suppose the personnel department of Roadworks, Inc., is interested in rapidly accessing the records for all the engineers in the company. In this application the pointer points to the next record with the same job title.

As shown in Figure 10-2, the first engineer on the file is employee number 12593. Its pointer field indicates that the next engineer is employee number 24671, the next one is 39145, and the last one is 18999. The pointer field of the last engineer on the file contains a special value, perhaps 99999, which in-

FIGURE 10-2

A Linked List

The first engineer on this file is employee number 12593, whose record contains a pointer field of 24671, which points to the next engineer on the file. The next engineer on this file is employee number 24671, whose record contains a pointer field of 39145, which points to the next engineer on the file. In a similar way the record for the engineer whose employee number is 39145 points to the record for engineer 18999. The final engineer on this file is employee number 18999, whose record contains a pointer field of 99999, which indicates that there are no additional engineers on this file.

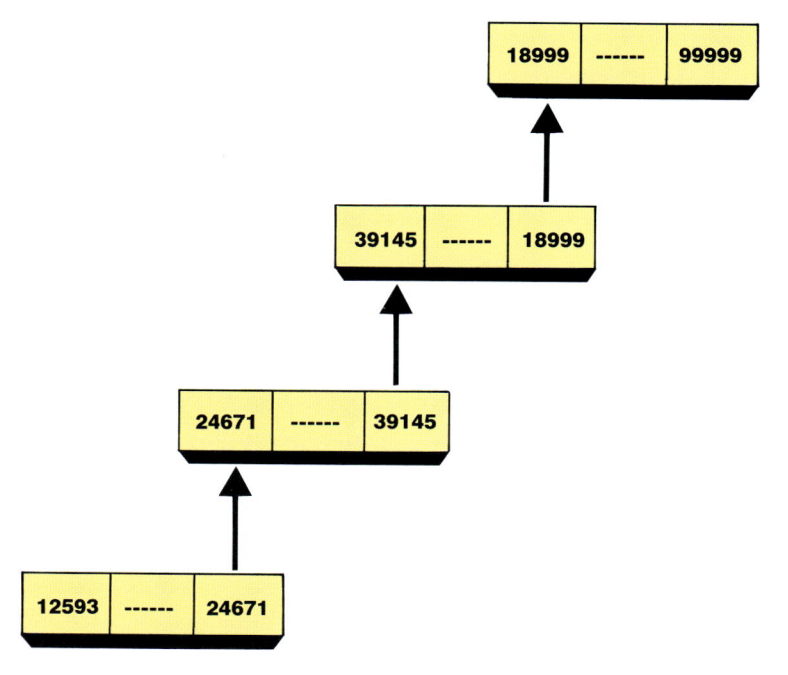

dicates that it is the last one. The program that prints the personnel report first finds employee number 12593 and then follows the pointers one by one to locate all engineers on the file.

The method of following the pointers on a linked list is a lot faster than reading every record in a file to see which ones represent the desired records. However, the pointer fields occupy considerable space on the file, and fairly sophisticated programming is required to maintain linked lists when adding and deleting records. Moreover, linked lists can be used only if they have been set up before a user makes a request for information. In our example, because there are no pointers associated with the age field it would be necessary to read all the records in the file to list employees age 63 and over.

Inverted Files. Another method of file organization is known as *inverted files*. Each record in an inverted file is an index indicating the address of records on the original file that share a particular characteristic, such as the same job title. Road-

FIGURE 10-3

A Direct-Access File and an Inverted File

39145	Engineer	---------
29451	Receptionist	---------
24671	Engineer	---------
20113	Programmer	---------
34414	Receptionist	---------
12841	Programmer	---------
12593	Engineer	---------

Receptionist	34414	29451	
Programmer	12841	20113	
Engineer	12593	24671	39145

The inverted file is created from the direct-access file by regrouping all the secondary keys with the same value of a given field, in this case the job title. The first record on this file contains the employee numbers of all the engineers. This record is useful for accessing all the engineers rapidly.

works' direct-access employee file (Figure 10-3a) can be used to generate an inverted file (Figure 10-3b). The inverted file enables the computer to locate records for all the engineers much more quickly than is possible via a traditional direct-access or indexed-sequential file. In many cases alphanumeric fields such as *engineer* are coded numerically.

The existence of several inverted files simplifies the processing of requests. For example, Roadworks' personnel department could easily get a list of all engineers who speak French in order to fill a position in Paris from within the organization. However, inverted files may require considerable storage space and are difficult to implement and maintain.

Drawbacks of Traditional File Processing

Each of the types of file organization that we have discussed is suitable for specific types of processing and has some unique advantages. But because all of these approaches are associated with traditional file processing, they share certain drawbacks. For one thing, applications programmers must know the specific file to which a record belongs and the size and arrangement of the fields within the record. In the Roadworks example, the applications programmer must know the name and size of the job title field and the type of file organization used.

Another drawback of traditional file processing is the extreme difficulty of processing data from more than one file at a time without writing a program for that purpose. For example, suppose that Roadworks' personnel department wants to know which of the engineers who speak French will be available during the next forty-five days. The project files that indicate assignments have been created to meet the specific needs of the engineering departments. Therefore, it is highly unlikely that they will define or process data in precisely the same fashion as the personnel files. An applications programmer would have to produce a special program to read and process the project files and the personnel file or files in order to select acceptable candidates.

Most organizations require more than forty-five days for a program to be assigned, designed, written, tested, debugged, and put into service. In situations like this one, a personnel agent might obtain the list of engineers by running a single computer program and then telephone the possible candidates to see whether they speak French and are available for the Paris position. This partially automated process is time-consuming and error prone. Moreover, although the personnel agent can telephone a dozen candidates, the same cannot be said about a marketing department faced with comparing information in 1200 surveys with client information on an existing file in order to develop an advertising campaign.

Still another disadvantage of traditional file-processing systems is that they rarely make it easy for users to obtain responses to unforeseen requests. In an age in which managers want full, rapid access to data of all kinds, such systems are insufficient. Thus, although in many organizations file-processing systems continue to meet scheduled, predictable needs such as payroll and basic accounting applications, they must usually be supplemented or replaced by data-base management systems if managers are to receive the timely information that they need to remain competitive.

Data-Base Management Systems

Data bases and data-base management systems are techniques for organizing and processing data that have extended

Data-base management system (DBMS)

The software that controls the creation, maintenance, and use of a data base.

and to a large extent replaced traditional files and file-processing systems in many organizations. A data base is a collection of data that has been organized to permit ready access by both technical personnel and end-users. A **data-base management system (DBMS)** is the software that controls the creation, maintenance, and use of a data-base.

Users can think of a data base as an integrated collection of files and a data-base management system as a sophisticated tool for extracting data from the data base. Instead of storing data in fragmented files that are directly useful for only one or a few programs, data bases store data in such a way that it can be used by a wide variety of programs. For example, the same data can be accessed and processed by payroll programs, personnel programs, and accounting programs. The data in a data base can even be accessed in response to requests that were not foreseen when the data base was originally set up. For example, given a query language (see Chapter 8), the user can obtain a list of all engineers who speak French and are available for relocation, or all employees who are sixty-three years old or over. They can obtain the desired information if the relevant data is contained in the data base, without having to worry about how the data is stored.

Data-base management systems come in all sizes, depending on the size of the data base and the nature of the problems that it is designed to solve. At one extreme, organizations such as banks and insurance companies use data-base management systems (DBMSs) that can generate reports for hundreds or even thousands of users; they rely on computer specialists to keep the system running and add new features requested by users. At the other extreme, many individuals use a form of DBMS on their personal computers to help them organize their family budgets, write business correspondence, and perform other tasks as illustrated in Chapter 9. A link between the large data bases maintained on mainframe computers and the personal-productivity applications of personal computers is provided by on-line data-base services like the one described in Box 6-1.

Some important features of DBMSs are the different categories of personnel who use the data base; the three types of programming languages associated with a DBMS; the data dictionary, which contains information about the elements in an organization's data base; and the general models in which data is organized for a DBMS. We will see that these features are interrelated; for example, different types of programming languages serve different categories of personnel ranging from managers with ad hoc requests for information to data-base specialists.

DBMS Personnel

There are three categories of personnel who interact with a DBMS. The first consists of technical specialists; they include systems programmers and the data-base administrator (to be described shortly). These specialists design the data base and are responsible for keeping it up to date and making sure it performs efficiently. The second category consists of applications programmers, who write programs to process the data base in response to end-users' needs. Applications programmers have to understand how a data base is organized, and although they need not know the details of how the DBMS actually finds the data in the data base, they do have to know how to command the system to carry out this operation. The third category is composed of users who, with the aid of query languages, obtain information from the data base.

A DBMS and its specialists are similar to a library and its reference librarian. Just as people can go to the librarian to help them find a specific book in a reference library, they go to a data-base specialist to help them access specific data from a data base. The applications programmer writes programs that work somewhat like a librarian who analyzes users' requests and finds the desired books faster than users themselves would by searching in the card catalog. The data-base administrator and systems programmer are similar to the library director and technical specialists, who do not interact with the average library user but are responsible for organizing the library and the card catalog so that books and other reference materials can be located rapidly.

The Data-Base Administrator. The **data-base administrator (DBA)** is the person or group that is responsible for designing, installing, and controlling the data base, as well as for administering it. The DBA therefore needs superior technical and administrative skills, and sizable data bases require a sizable DBA group. Technically, the DBA must set up the data base in such a way as to satisfy users' requirements while at the same time meeting stringent technical standards. Administratively, the DBA is responsible for enforcing data definition standards throughout an organization. This can be extremely difficult when traditional file-processing methods, which usually define data in a wide variety of ways, are replaced by a data-base management system. In such situations the DBA must convince some departments to change the way they define and handle data that they consider to be their own private domain.

Data-base administrator (DBA)
The person or group that is responsible for designing, installing, and controlling a data base.

DBMS Programming Languages We noted in Chapter 8

that different programming languages are suited to different programming needs and hence serve different categories of personnel. In general, each of the categories of people who work with data-base management systems works with a specific type of programming language. The data-base administrator and systems programmer use a programming language that serves to set up the data base and define the relationships among the various kinds of data it contains. Such a language is known as a data definition language and is too detailed for the purposes of end-users and applications programmers.

Data Definition Language. Data-base management systems are concerned with logical and physical data. You will recall from Chapter 8 that logical data is what is seen by the user (e.g., flight number 615), whereas physical data is the actual contents of the storage device (e.g., the data located at record number 51 on track 17 of recording surface 12). The *data definition language (DDL)* is used by data-base specialists such as systems programmers and data-base administrators to describe how data is organized in the data base. In effect, it is used to relate the physical and logical data to each other.

The complete description of the way in which data is organized on the data base is the *schema*. It may take months for a team of specialists to set up the schema to meet an organization's data-base processing objectives. But neither the end-users nor the applications programmers are concerned with the schema or the data definition language. The tools they use to extract information from the data base are much easier to work with.

Data Manipulation Language. The *data manipulation language (DML)* is the language used by applications programmers to retrieve and modify data within a data base. Many data manipulation languages are extensions of common programming languages such as COBOL. With the aid of a DML, COBOL programmers can perform such operations as finding the next engineer in the data base. The programmer need not know in detail how the data-base management system actually finds a specific item of data, but he or she must know how to command the system to carry out this operation.

Applications programmers do not deal with the data base as a whole but only with a section of it defined in a *subschema*, or part of the schema, that is pertinent to a specific application. As far as they are concerned, the subschema describes the data base. If, for instance, the subschema does not include the data item containing salary figures, the applications programmer would have no way of knowing how to access this information.

Query Language. The third category of programming languages associated with DBMS is *query languages*. These languages are a type of fourth-generation or very-high-level programming language. They enable end-users to extract information from a data base without having to be a programmer or consult a specialist. Query languages vary widely and can be highly dependent on the type of system used. Later in the chapter we will see how a popular query language known as structured query language can be used to set up and obtain information from a sample data base.

The Data Dictionary

The **data dictionary** is an organized collection of information about all the data elements or data items (e.g., job title) within the data base, including the name, size, and type of the data element, the relationship of the data element to other data elements in the data base, and what values (e.g., engineer) the data elements can have. The data dictionary requires that data definitions within an organization be standardized, and to maximize its effectiveness it should be on-line and accessible to the data-base administrator, systems and applications programmers, and sophisticated end-users. In contrast to file processing, in which each type of data item is defined in each file in which it is used, all items in the data base are defined once in the data dictionary. (The term *self-defining* is sometimes used in referring to data dictionaries.)

As an example of a data dictionary, consider the following typical entries for the element or data item Hourly Rate of Pay:
1. The name and definition of the data item—in this example, Hourly Rate of Pay. This information can be accompanied by abbreviations used for different programming languages, such as HOURLY-RATE-OF-PAY in COBOL and HRTPAY in FORTRAN.
2. A list of all programs and subschemas that use the data item HOURLY-RATE-OF-PAY and those that use HRTPAY.
3. Aliases, or synonyms, used for the data item. Perhaps one department refers to this data item as the Hourly Pay Rate. The dictionary will contain all such aliases and be able to use the same data item regardless of the name used by a particular department.
4. Related data elements. The data dictionary will, for example, relate the data item Fringe Benefits, used by the cost-accounting group, with Hourly Rate of Pay.
5. The size and type of the data item. The dictionary would

Data dictionary
An organized collection of information about all the data elements within a data base.

contain the information that the hourly rate of pay is numeric and includes a maximum of 2 digits before the decimal point and 2 digits following the decimal point (e.g., allowable values are 11.25 and 7.00 but not 6.127 and 102.4).

6. Range of legal values. The range of values for Hourly Rate of Pay might be 4.00 to 31.50. Any value outside this range will be rejected.

The data dictionary should also include the following supplementary information:

7. A list of all record names and the data items contained in each record. (This corresponds largely to the record layout mentioned in Chapter 7.) This list may be accompanied by passwords associated with the record or the field so that only people with security clearance can access this part of the data dictionary.

8. A list of the report names and the fields in each report. This list can also have associated passwords and require security clearance.

Data dictionaries are excellent tools for helping an organization administer and maintain its data base. For example, suppose all employees at Universe Airlines had hourly rates of pay with only 2 digits after the decimal point, such as 9.25, and the data element in the data dictionary was defined accordingly. Also suppose that a new contract has just been signed and that some employees will now be receiving an hourly rate of pay of 9.745. The data definition of Hourly Rate of Pay will have to be changed to accommodate an additional digit after the decimal point.

If Universe Airlines does not have a data dictionary, it will be necessary to examine literally hundreds of programs that might process the hourly rate of pay, and to change this data element to accommodate the extra digit. This cumbersome process will take an inordinate amount of time and inevitably lead to errors and inconsistent results. If Universe Airlines has a data dictionary, however, the dictionary can be scanned, either manually or by computer, to determine which programs need to be modified. In many cases these modifications need be made only via the data dictionary.

There are numerous DBMS software packages on the market, each of which has unique features that may render it suitable for an organization's specific needs. Businesses cannot afford the time or effort to evaluate all of these packages. There are, however, several ways to classify data-base management systems. One classification is by the size of computer the DBMS is designed to serve; another is by the type of data model the business uses.

Data Models

There are three basic models for organizing and processing data in data bases: hierarchical, network, and relational. These models are concerned with the logical organization of the data. The way in which a DBMS manipulates data items is determined by the data model on which it is based.

Choosing the appropriate model makes it easier to construct a DBMS that meets the organization's needs easily and efficiently. We will see that some models respond to end-user inquiries more readily than others. However, because of the number of evaluation factors involved, such a model is not necessarily the most appropriate one in a particular business situation.

The Hierarchical Model. The **hierarchical model** for data bases is one in which each data record can have one or more subordinate data records. This model is also known as a *tree* because of its resemblance to an upside-down tree. The three programming languages mentioned earlier are all used with the hierarchical model. In general, users do not query a hierarchical data base themselves but depend on an applications programmer to formulate their queries.

The hierarchical model is similar to the hierarchy of managers in an organization. An essential aspect of a hierarchical organization is that no individual reports to more than one superior; the same requirement holds true for hierarchical data models.

Figure 10-4 illustrates the hierarchical data model for a data base that contains information on teachers. Each teacher is described in a record that is not dependent on any other record in the data base. It is known as the *root*, and in this example it is identified by employee number. The root records also contain other information, such as employee name and rank.

Each first-level root record can have one or more second-level subordinate records. In the figure, these subordinate records correspond to a particular semester and are identified by the year and season. These subordinate records contain information that is specific to the given semester for the given teacher, including number of classes assigned and auxiliary duties such as membership on committees.

Each subordinate record can also have one or more subordinate records. They contain information that is specific to the first-level subordinate record and the root record. In our example, the class record contains information that is specific to the given course for the given semester for the given teacher. Class records are identified by course number and section number

Hierarchical model
A data model in which each data record can have one or more subordinate data records.

FIGURE 10-4

Records Organized According to the Hierarchical Model

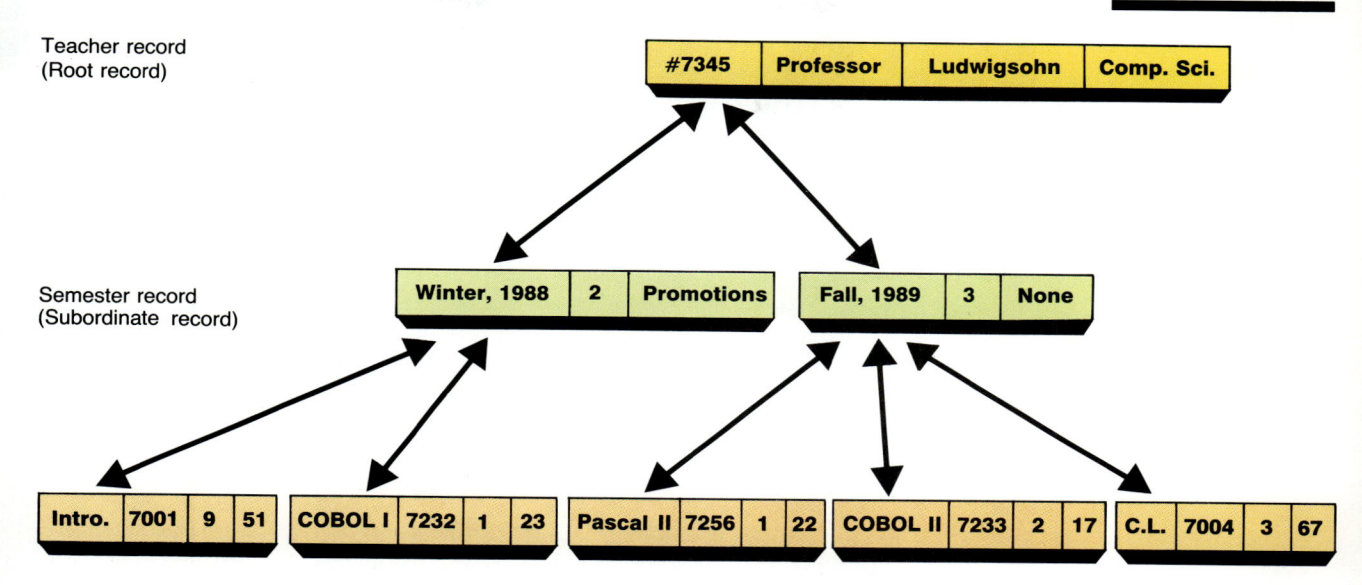

Teacher record (Root record): #7345 | Professor | Ludwigsohn | Comp. Sci.

Semester record (Subordinate record): Winter, 1988 | 2 | Promotions — Fall, 1989 | 3 | None

Class record (Subordinate record): Intro. | 7001 | 9 | 51 — COBOL I | 7232 | 1 | 23 — Pascal II | 7256 | 1 | 22 — COBOL II | 7233 | 2 | 17 — C.L. | 7004 | 3 | 67

The hierarchical model resembles an upside-down tree. In this example the teacher record is the root; there is one teacher at the base of the tree whose record contains the ID number, the rank, the family name, and the department. Each teacher record may be associated with one or more semester records containing the semester identification, the number of courses taught, and memberships on committees. Each semester record may be associated with one or more class records containing the course name, course number, section number, and the number of students.

and can include course name, number of students, and so on. Hierarchical data bases allow for almost any number of levels of subordinate records.

Because the data about teachers is organized in a data base, it can be processed and accessed in numerous ways. For example, suppose the college wants to determine whether there is any correlation between a teacher's rank and the percentage of students who fail that teacher's course. The computer begins by reading a given teacher's record and ascertaining his or her rank. It then accesses each semester record for that teacher and finally each class record, from which it obtains the number of students and number of failures for the given teacher. It repeats this process for each teacher and compares the tabulated results. The data in the teacher data base can also be used for more traditional reports such as student grades and teacher assignments.

In business applications, many data relationships take a hierarchical form. For example, the manufacture of a finished product can be broken down into assemblies, each of which can be further broken down into subassemblies. But not all relationships lend themselves to a hierarchical model. In a col-

CHAPTER 10 359 FILE-PROCESSING AND DATA-BASE SYSTEMS

Relationships among parts, subassemblies, and assemblies— such as a piston, an automobile engine, and the finished automobile—can be readily expressed in a hierarchical data base. Data about parts is contained in third-level subordinate records, data about subassemblies in second-level subordinate records, and data about assemblies in first-level root records. [(top left) © Al Satterwhite, The Image Bank; (top right) © Dick Luria, Photo Researchers; (bottom) Courtesy of Hewlett-Packard.]

lege, for instance, each student takes several courses and each course has many students; thus, each record and subordinate record is associated with more than one higher-level record. Data bases like the one consisting of students and courses lend themselves more readily to the network model.

SOFTWARE 360 PART 3

FIGURE 10-5

Records Organized According to the Network Model

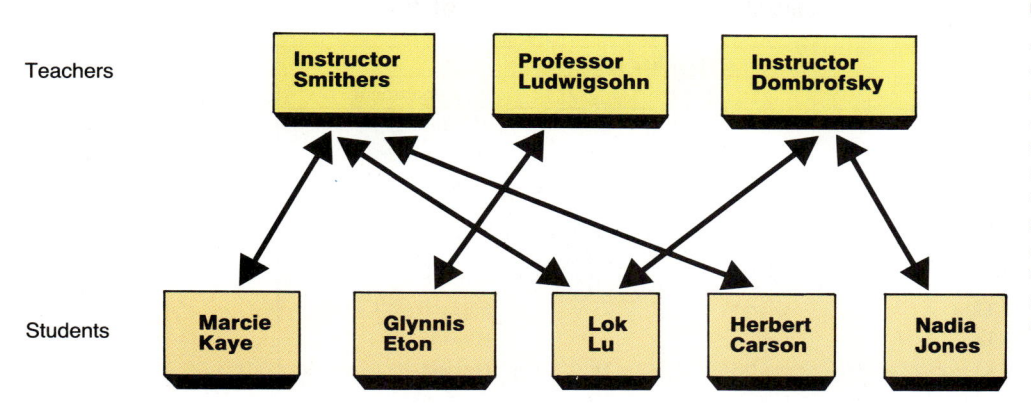

Teachers: Instructor Smithers, Professor Ludwigsohn, Instructor Dombrofsky

Students: Marcie Kaye, Glynnis Eton, Lok Lu, Herbert Carson, Nadia Jones

In the network model a record such as the record for Instructor Smithers can have several subordinate records (Kaye, Lu, and Carson), and a record such as the record for Lu can be subordinate to several records (Smithers and Dombrofsky).

Network model
A data model in which data records can have one or more subordinate data records and can themselves be subordinate to one or more data records.

The Network Model. The **network model** is one in which each data record can have one or more subordinate records and can itself be subordinate to one or more data records. An example of a network relationship is the one between teachers and students. As illustrated in Figure 10-5, each teacher can have several students and, at the same time, each student can have several teachers. With the network model it is possible to access any record in the data base starting from any other record. For example, to find the names of students who have the same teachers as Lok Lu, we would follow the arrow to Lu's teachers—Smithers and Dombrofsky—and then follow the arrow from each of them to their respective students, Marcie Kaye and Herbert Carson in the case of Instructor Smithers and Nadia Jones in the case of Professor Dombrofsky.

The network model was the basis for the first widely used data-base management system, Integrated Data Store, which was developed in the early 1960s at General Electric. Beginning in the early 1970s, the Conference on Data System Languages, commonly known as CODASYL, published a series of language specifications for data-base management systems that follow the network model. Among the important packages based on the CODASYL specifications are IDS/II (Integrated Data Store/II) from Honeywell Information Systems and IDMS (Integrated Data Management System) from Cullinet. Commercial DBMSs do not follow the CODASYL specifications completely, and although competing network DBMSs share more

FIGURE 10-6

A Relational Model

The relational model consists of a series of tables relating the various data elements. The relationships of the data within the tables are often intuitive.

Teacher Table		
Name	Rank	Department
Ludwigsohn	Professor	Computer Science
Smithers	Instructor	Chemistry
Dombrofsky	Instructor	Slavic languages

Student Table			
Family name	First name	Age	Permanent Residence
Kaye	Marcie	19	Alabama
Eton	Glynnis	26	England
Lu	Lok	22	Nevada
Carson	Herbert	18	Nevada
Jones	Nadia	17	California

similarities than hierarchical or relational products, network DBMSs are not standardized.

Typical applications of network DBMSs include order processing, accounting, and payroll. These applications tend to have the following characteristics: a sizable data base containing perhaps millions of records; thousands of transactions per day; hundreds of on-line users who access the data base at the same time; and complex transactions, each of which may access and update many data items. If the data base is properly organized, a network DBMS can process applications rapidly and efficiently. However, once the structure of a network data base has been implemented, it is difficult to modify it. Therefore, another data model—the relational model—should be considered for applications whose structure is likely to change often.

The Relational Model. The **relational model** is based on *tables*, or two-dimensional collections of data, organized in rows and columns, that represent the relationships among the data items. Figure 10-6 shows two examples of tables—a teacher table and a student table. The columns (also known as *attributes*) contain the properties of the items, such as name, rank, and department for the teacher table and family name, first name, age, and permanent residence for the student table. The rows (also known as *tuples*) contain the values for each column, such as the name, rank, and department for each teacher

Relational model
A data model composed of tables that represent the relationships among the data items.

SOFTWARE 362 PART 3

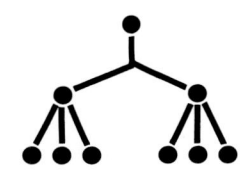

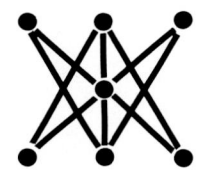

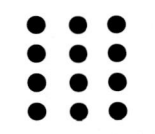

Hierarchical Model

Network Model

Relational Model

Data Models

and the family name, first name, age, and permanent residence for each student. We will see in the next section how a user can define and manipulate a data base similar to the one illustrated in Figure 10-6.

Relational data-base management systems tend to be used for small personal and departmental data bases; generally they are too slow to be useful for large-scale activities such as billings or payroll. A company's major data bases usually use the network or hierarchical models. The relational model is particularly useful in cases in which the relationships among the data items cannot be predicted. For example, a personnel officer using a relational data base could obtain a list of all employees who meet any combination of criteria as long as the data exists in the data base. With a relational data base it is as easy to obtain a list of all engineers who speak French, are single or childless, have been with the company at least four years, and are not over fifty years old, as it is to obtain a list of all engineers. The relative ease with which relational data bases may be queried has made them increasingly popular with both users and computer professionals, who spend less time helping users compose queries and thus are freed to perform work that users are unable to do themselves.

Data-base management systems that are based on the relational model have some serious drawbacks, however. First, they are not cost-effective for large applications. As mentioned earlier, they may run very slowly, particularly when accessing large data bases. Second, for maximum performance the data in the tables must be carefully organized in a process known as *normalization*. For these and other reasons, relational systems have not yet proven themselves in commercial settings for major applications. As both hardware and software technologies advance, an increasing proportion of new applications will undoubtedly make use of relational systems. Box 10-1 explores efforts to overcome one major barrier to wider use of relational data bases.

Figure 10-6 presents a clearer picture of the teacher and student data and its interrelationships than either Figure 10-4 or Figure 10-5. Unlike the hierarchical and network models, the relational model does not use a separate data manipulation language; data manipulation is done with a query language.

Structured Query Language

Now that the features of data bases have been presented and discussed, let's consider an example of how to use a query language to set up and access a relational data base containing

BOX 10-1

MANAGING CHANGE

Overcoming the Conversion Barrier

The theoretical advantages of relational data-base management systems have drawn much attention, and the technology is now entering the mainstream of commercial data processing. As in many cases, however, a promising change in technology poses significant management problems. In this case the problem is how to make the transition to a relational DBMS without disrupting the daily work of the organization.

A firm with a well-developed hierarchical or network DBMS will have hundreds or even thousands of applications based on the existing system. Many organizations cannot interrupt their daily routines long enough for a complete rewrite of these applications. Also, new applications written with the relational DBMS in mind may have to operate using data generated by old applications.

Relational systems are potentially superior in terms of ease of use, flexibility, and greater productivity in application development. But in managing the conversion to a relational DBMS, the manager must balance the gains in productivity resulting from implementation of the relational system against the costs of conversion, including both the cost of rewrites and the cost of disrupted work flow. Ultimately, the market will accept relational DBMSs only if this conversion problem can be solved in a satisfactory way.

One approach to the conversion problem is known as *migration software*. Migration software sidesteps the need to rewrite applications by allowing old applications to run on the new data base. It functions as a sort of buffer that makes the new data base look like the old one so that old applications programs "think" nothing has changed.

Some relational-DBMS enthusiasts find migration software hopelessly inelegant because it does not allow users to tap the full potential of the new relational structure. They have compared the use of migration software to serving a fine wine in Styrofoam cups. However, even though migration software is not the crystal goblet that the purists would prefer, it permits essential business functions to continue with a minimum of disruption during the transition to the new data base.

In addition to keeping old applications running, migration software can be used to automate the conversion of the data base itself. Migration software can use straightforward rules to remap the old hierarchical structure into the new tabular format of the relational DBMS.

Although avoiding disruption is the focus of migration software in the short run, the long-run goal is, of course, increased productivity. This will be accomplished as applications are extended to make full use of relational tools. But today data processing managers are not willing to tolerate huge disruptions of ongoing operations as the price of implementing a new technology, no matter how theoretically elegant it may be.

Source: Stephen Gerrard, "A Pragmatic Response to Relational Rules," *Computerworld*, January 27, 1986, pp. 61–66.

Informix SQL is one of several commercially available products that offer users features that augment the standard SQL. (© Chris Pullo.)

employee information. Recall that query languages are fourth-generation DBMS languages that can be used by nonspecialists to extract information from a data base. They are typically used with the relational data model. *Structured query language (SQL)* is a commercially available query language that was originally designed for mainframe computers but is now available for mainframes, minicomputers, and microcomputers. Since SQL handles more functions than traditional query languages, it can meet many of the needs of end-users, applications programmers, systems programmers, and data-base administrators.

Creating the Table.[1] Like many products associated with relational data bases, SQL uses the term *table* to mean a two-

---

[1]This example is adapted from training materials published by Oracle Corp., a leading marketer of SQL software.

dimensional collection of data organized in rows and columns. These tables must be defined and loaded with data before the data base can be accessed. There are two tables in the example: a department table (DEPT) and an employee table (EMP). The following command creates the department table:

```
CREATE TABLE DEPT (DEPTNO    NUMBER(2),
                   DNAME     CHAR(14),
                   LOC       CHAR(13));
```

This command tells the computer to create a table DEPT with a numeric field DEPTNO (department number) that is a maximum of 2 digits wide; a character field DNAME (department name) that is a maximum of fourteen characters wide; and a character field LOC (location) that is a maximum of thirteen characters wide.

The employee table is created with the following command:

```
CREATE TABLE EMP (EMPNO    NUMBER (4) NOT NULL,
                  ENAME    CHAR(10),
                  JOB      CHAR(9),
                  SAL      NUMBER (7,2),
                  COMM     NUMBER (7,2),
                  DEPTNO   NUMBER (2));
```

This command tells the computer to create a table EMP with a numeric field EMPNO that is a maximum of 4 digits wide and must be present (when the NOT NULL specification is coded, it becomes impossible to enter an employee whose employee number is not given). This field is to be followed by a character field ENAME (employee name) that is a maximum of ten characters wide, a character field JOB (job title) that is a maximum of nine characters wide, numeric fields SAL (salary) and COMM (commission) that are a maximum of 7 digits wide, two of which are to the right of the decimal point, and a numeric field DEPTNO (department number) that is a maximum of 2 digits wide.

Loading the Table. Once a table has been created, rows of data can be entered into it. The following is a simple command for entering data:

```
INSERT INTO DEPT
VALUES (30, 'SALES', 'CHICAGO');
```

This command tells the computer to insert into the DEPT table a row of data containing the department number 30, the department name SALES, and the location CHICAGO. In a similar way we can insert the first row in the EMP table as follows:

```
INSERT INTO EMP
VALUES (7369, 'JONES', 'CLERK', 800.00,, 20);
```

FIGURE 10-7

A Table Used with Structured Query Language

DEPT TABLE		
DEPTNO	DNAME	LOC
10	ACCOUNTING	NEW YORK
20	RESEARCH	DALLAS
30	SALES	CHICAGO
40	OPERATIONS	BOSTON

This table expresses the relationships among the department numbers, the department names, and the locations for the DEPT table.

FIGURE 10-8

A Table Used with Structured Query Language

EMP TABLE					
EMPNO	ENAME	JOB	SAL	COMM	DEPTNO
7369	JONES	CLERK	800.00		20
7499	ALLEN	VENDOR	1,600.00	300.00	30
7521	WARD	VENDOR	1,250.00	500.00	30
7566	SMITH	MANAGER	2,975.00		20
7654	MARTIN	VENDOR	1,250.00	1,400.00	30
7698	BLAKE	MANAGER	2,850.00		30
7782	CLARK	MANAGER	2,450.00		10
7788	SCOTT	ANALYST	3,000.00		20
7839	KING	PRESIDENT	5,000.00		10
7844	TURNER	VENDOR	1,500.00	0.00	30
7876	ADAMS	CLERK	1,100.00		20
7900	JAMES	CLERK	950.00		30
7902	FORD	ANALYST	3,000.00		20
7934	MILLER	CLERK	1,300.00		10

Figures 10-7 and 10-8 show the DEPT and EMP tables after the initial data has been loaded.

Querying the Table. Once tables have been created and loaded with data, they can be queried. Querying a table means finding specific information in the table. To query the data base

This table expresses the relationships among the employee numbers, the employee names, the job titles, the salaries, and the department numbers for the EMP table.

for all the data from the DEPT table, we would use the command

```
SELECT     DEPTNO,DNAME,LOC
FROM       DEPT;
```

which means find and list the DEPTNO (department number), DNAME (department name), and LOC (location) of records in the DEPT (department) table. In answer to the query, the data base will give the following information:

```
DEPTNO DNAME      LOC
------ -----      ---
    10 ACCOUNTING NEW YORK
    20 RESEARCH   DALLAS
    30 SALES      CHICAGO
    40 OPERATIONS BOSTON
```

A simpler way to ask a data base for *all* of the data in a specific table is by using the asterisk (*), which indicates all columns in the table. Using the asterisk, the query can be rewritten as follows:

```
SELECT     *
FROM       DEPT;
```

The data base will give the same response whether all data elements are queried by name or an asterisk is used.

Not all users will need all of the data in a table. The SELECT command can be used to query specific information. To select only two columns of information, DEPTNO and DNAME, from the DEPT table, we would use the command

```
SELECT     DNAME,DEPTNO
FROM       DEPT;
```

The results follow:

```
DEPTNO DNAME
------ -----
    10 ACCOUNTING
    20 RESEARCH
    30 SALES
    40 OPERATIONS
```

To select specific rows, such as employees who belong to department number 10, we would use the command

```
SELECT     EMPNO,ENAME,JOB,DEPTNO
FROM       EMP
WHERE      DEPTNO = 10;
```

The result would be as follows:

```
EMPNO  ENAME   JOB         DEPTNO
-----  -----   ---         ------
 7782  CLARK   MANAGER         10
 7839  KING    PRESIDENT       10
 7934  MILLER  CLERK           10
```

More Complicated Queries. The SEARCH command can also help users look for data that fits more than one condition (e.g., someone who is an employee, a manager, *and* in department number 10); for data that fits alternative conditions (e.g., someone who is an employee, a manager, *or* in department number 10); or for data that fits all items in a range (e.g., all employee numbers between 7300 and 7600). For example:

```
SELECT EMPNO,ENAME,DEPTNO
FROM EMP
WHERE EMPNO BETWEEN 7300 AND 7600
   AND DEPTNO = 30;
```

The result would be as follows:

```
EMPNO  ENAME  DEPTNO
-----  -----  ------
 7499  ALLEN      30
 7521  WARD       30
```

Sorting the Result of a Query. SQL also enables users to sort data. For example, all employees in DEPTNO 30 can be sorted in ascending order of SAL, as follows:

```
SELECT    SAL,JOB,ENAME
FROM      EMP
WHERE     DEPTNO = 30
ORDER  BY  SAL;
```

The result would be as follows:

```
     SAL  JOB      ENAME
     ---  ---      -----
  950.00  CLERK    JAMES
1,250.00  VENDOR   WARD
1,250.00  VENDOR   MARTIN
1,500.00  VENDOR   TURNER
1,600.00  VENDOR   ALLEN
2,850.00  MANAGER  BLAKE
```

Querying More Than One Table. A key feature of both data-base management programs and data-base management systems is their ability to process records from more than one source at a time. For example, suppose a user wants to know where employee ALLEN works. The fields ENAME and LOC are needed, but they are in two different tables: ENAME is in EMP table and LOC is in DEPT table. The field DEPTNO is in both tables. In a file management program, two queries are needed. First the EMP table is queried to find ALLEN's DEPTNO:

```
SELECT    ENAME,DEPTNO
FROM      EMP
WHERE     ENAME = 'ALLEN';
```

The result of this first query is

```
ENAME  DEPTNO
-----  ------
ALLEN     30
```

Next, using the DEPTNO, the DEPT table is queried to find ALLEN's LOC:

```
SELECT    LOC
FROM      DEPT
WHERE     DEPTNO = 30;
```

The result of the second query is

```
LOC
---
CHICAGO
```

In a DBMS, ALLEN's LOC can be accessed from the EMP and DEPT tables as follows:

```
SELECT    ENAME,LOC
FROM      EMP, DEPT
WHERE     ENAME = 'ALLEN'
AND       EMP.DEPTNO = DEPT.DEPTNO;
```

This single query lists information if two conditions are true: The ENAME is equal to ALLEN and the DEPTNO in the EMP table is equal to the DEPTNO in the DEPT table. The results are the same as those obtained using two separate queries.

Creating a Report. In addition to accessing data in various ways, SQLs can be used to create reports—in other words, to present the results of one or more queries in an easy-to-read form that may be embellished with identifying information. Although we will not examine the commands used to produce this report, it is worth noting that the SQL program that creates a report is only eleven lines long and can readily be learned by managers and other users. (The COBOL program required to produce such a report might contain a few hundred lines of code and could be written only by COBOL programmers.)

The commands for this SQL report are as shown on page 371.

FIGURE 10-9

An SQL Report

```
Mon Sep 5              ACME WIDGET                 page 1
                     PERSONNEL REPORT
               EMPLOYEE                  MONTHLY
DEPARTMENT     NAME         JOB          SALARY
----------     --------     ----         ----------
ACCOUNTING     KING         PRESIDENT    $5,000.00
               CLARK        MANAGER      $2,450.00
               MILLER       CLERK        $1,300.00
**********                                ----------
                                         $8,750.00

RESEARCH       SCOTT        ANALYST      $3,000.00
               FORD         ANALYST      $3,000.00
               SMITH        MANAGER      $2,975.00
               ADAMS        CLERK        $1,100.00
               JONES        CLERK          $800.00
**********                                ----------
                                        $10,875.00

SALES          BLAKE        MANAGER      $2,850.00
               ALLEN        VENDOR       $1,600.00
               TURNER       VENDOR       $1,500.00
               WARD         VENDOR       $1,250.00
               MARTIN       VENDOR       $1,250.00
               JAMES        CLERK          $950.00
**********                                ----------
                                         $9,400.00
                - Company Confidential -
```

```
COLUMN   DNAME   HEADING    'DEPARTMENT'
COLUMN   ENAME   HEADING    'EMPLOYEE|NAME'
COLUMN   JOB     HEADING    'JOB'
COLUMN   SAL     HEADING    'MONTHLY|SALARY'    FORMAT $99,999.99
BREAK ON DNAME SKIP 1
COMPUTE SUM OF SAL ON DNAME
TTITLE   'ACME WIDGET||PERSONNEL REPORT'
BTITLE   '- Company Confidential -'
SELECT   DNAME,ENAME,JOB,SAL
FROM     EMP,DEPT
WHERE    EMP.DEPTNO = DEPT.DEPTNO
ORDER    BY   DNAME,SAL, DESC;
```

An example is shown in Figure 10-9.

Advantages of Data-Base Management Systems

The information needs of individuals and businesses can vary greatly. For some applications, file-processing systems are adequate, whereas for others data-base management systems are necessary. Data-base management systems have several advantages, including the following:

1. *Data duplication is reduced.* Traditional file-processing systems contain the same data item in many different files. Data-base management systems reduce this duplication of data, and many data items are present in only one location. When a data item appears in more than one location it may have different values at the same time. For example, suppose that both the payroll file and the personnel file contain employee department numbers. Whenever an employee changes departments, both of these files must be updated. But it is unrealistic to assume that every time an employee changes departments the two files will be updated simultaneously. For at least a short time the two files will contain different data. If during this time the files are accessed to generate reports, the reports may contain contradictory information. If the firm has a DBMS, the employee's department number can be changed once and all future reports will contain the correct information.

2. *Flexibility is increased.* The data in a DBMS is the property of the organization rather than of a particular department. Therefore, authorized users can access any information they need, either by themselves (using a query language such as SQL) or with the help of a specialist, regardless of which department originally furnished the data.

3. *Data is independent of the programs that access it.* Independent data means that applications programmers do not have to reconcile different definitions of data, such as the payroll department's definition of the hourly rate of pay, which does not include fringe benefits, and the accounting department's definition, which includes those benefits. Moreover, programs do not need to be changed when data formats are changed.

4. *Data security can be enhanced.* A DBMS can screen requests to access data and refuse to supply data to individuals who lack proper authorization. Furthermore, it can be set up so that certain people can access certain information, depending on their authorization code. A well-designed DBMS also keeps track of every attempt to access any sensitive data. In contrast, traditional file-processing systems usually allow or deny access to an entire file rather than to specific data, and they rarely keep track of attempts to access files.

5. *Division of labor is encouraged.* With a DBMS, selected personnel are responsible for data handling for the entire company, in contrast to the traditional system in which programmers set up their own data files and write programs to process only those files. DBMS personnel become experts in defining data and organizing it for efficient access, thereby freeing programmers to concentrate on specific applications.

Disadvantages of Data-Base Management Systems

Although they have many advantages, data-base management systems also have several disadvantages compared to file-processing systems. Not all of these disadvantages apply in every situation, but they should be considered when an organization plans to install a DBMS.

1. *A DBMS is expensive.* The DBMS software package may cost over $100,000 for mainframe computers and about $10,000 for minicomputers. (Microcomputer products are less expensive but are also considerably less powerful.) The cost of the software package itself usually represents only a fraction of the system's total cost.

2. *Specialized personnel are needed.* A high level of skill is necessary to initiate and administer data bases, and people with these skills are in short supply. Applications programmers who know DBMS are also needed, and they also tend to be in short supply. Consequently, these specialists command relatively high salaries. In addition, all personnel who interact with the data base must be trained—another source of expense for the firm that installs a DBMS.

3. *Traditional boundaries are crossed.* In general, managers do not like to relinquish control over resources that have traditionally been their responsibility, including data. But with a DBMS all data is centralized and can be accessed by people in different departments. For example, although payroll and accounting data becomes the property of the organization as a whole, the payroll and accounting departments may still believe that their definition of a specific data item, such as the hourly rate of pay, is the only reasonable one. In such cases the data-base administrator decides on the definition of the data item.

4. *More hardware resources are needed.* It would seem that because redundancy is reduced by a DBMS, data storage requirements are also reduced. But in reality extra space is needed for the indexes and pointers that enable users to access data located anywhere in the data base. Also, backing up key portions of the data base requires additional storage. Many organizations have seen their storage requirements more than double after they have converted to a DBMS. The problem is especially acute for a relational DBMS, in which the potential for better performance is purchased at the price of even greater demands on hardware. However, as Box 10-2 explains, new types of hardware are becoming available to meet the challenge.

5. *A DBMS cannot be reversed.* Once a data-base management system has been installed, it is almost impossible to return to the original file management system.

Technical Challenges

The installation of a DBMS entails several technical challenges. For example, in an increasing number of systems the mainframe or minicomputer DMBS must work in conjunction with microcomputers. Coordinating the systems is a major concern of network designers. For the different systems to work together, it must be possible to *upload* the data from microcomputers to the mainframe data base and to *download* it from the data base to the microcomputers. Other technical problems include the need to maintain *security* (i.e., to ensure that users can download only data for which they have authorization) and *data integrity* (i.e., to verify that data is correct before adding it to the data base). Related to data integrity is the need to make sure that only one user at a time can update the data.

Selecting a DBMS

Because of the large number of data-base management systems available, each with its own potential advantages and disadvantages, selecting a system is a lengthy, difficult process. To simplify the choice, purchasers can adopt a two-step approach: First choose a data model that will best meet the user's needs and then choose a specific DBMS software package based on the selected model. For example, if an organization has a massive investment in COBOL programs and programmers, it is likely that it will choose a DBMS based on the hierarchical or network model, which can work with COBOL. On the other hand, if end-users within the organization must be able to write their own queries, the organization should consider a relational DBMS.

BOX 10-2

FRONTIERS IN TECHNOLOGY

Special Hardware Helps Meet the Relational-DBMS Challenge

New York's Citibank is an aggressive contender in the increasingly competitive financial-service business. To enhance the effectiveness of its management and marketing, Citibank decided to develop an integrated data base of customer information. The new system takes a "customer portfolio approach" that allows the bank to serve a customer as an individual rather than as a collection of accounts.

Even without the new data base, however, the bank's IBM hardware was under heavy pressure from growing transaction-processing demands. By 1986 its computers were already processing some 250 transactions per second from automatic-teller machines during peak periods. As use of the machines spread, that figure was doubling every two years.

According to Jim Umberger, vice president of data-base operations for Citibank, the only way to meet the needs of transaction processing plus the new customer portfolio system would be to divide the bank's data base among many machines. But that would defeat the purpose of integration.

The solution: three DCB/1012 data-base machines from Teradata Corporation of Los Angeles. Data-base machines are specialized hardware that execute relational data-base management systems. They connect to mainframes, minis, or even microcomputers to handle storage and retrieval functions while the host machine is left to process applications.

By eliminating the need to use the limited CPU of the host computer for the huge storage and retrieval demands of a relational DBMS, the data-base machines greatly increase the speed at which applications can run. Best of all, data-base machines typically cost less than host machines of comparable power and often can eliminate the need to buy additional hosts.

Data-base machines are still a tiny part of the computer market, but if relational DBMSs really prove to be the wave of the future, this market segment will grow. Data-base machines represent another instance in which small start-up companies have achieved success by solving a problem to which giant IBM offers no solution.

Source: Lee Sigler, "Relating to Database Machines," *Datamation*, April 1, 1986, pp. 83–89. Copyright © Cahners Publishing Company.

CHAPTER 10   375   FILE-PROCESSING AND DATA-BASE SYSTEMS

FIGURE 10-10

Worksheet for Selecting a DBMS

This worksheet can readily be processed with an electronic spreadsheet such as Lotus 1-2-3. The completed worksheet should be kept as part of the documentation for the product selection.

Selection Criteria	Weight (1 to 10)	Product's Score (1 to 10)		
		I	II	III
User interface	8			
Data types	4			
Data structures	5			
Data manipulation	5			
Performance	9			
Data dictionary	7			
DBA tools	7			
Other	4			

Because there are so many factors to consider before deciding on a DBMS, it is a good idea to set up an evaluation table in which each product being considered is rated according to a set of criteria that have been chosen and given relative weights depending on the purchaser's needs. Figure 10-10 shows an evaluation table for selecting a DBMS. The selection criteria include the following factors.

User Interface. Ideally, untrained users should be able to formulate their own queries for a DBMS. Relational data-base management systems rank high in this regard. Also, user needs must be considered and products evaluated for special features such as graphics.

Data Types. The different types of data elements that can be processed by the DBMS must be considered, especially in relation to the needs of technical specialists. For example, some organizations require special characters such as the British pound symbol. It is also important to take into account the product's limits, such as the maximum number of characters allowed for a single field.

Data Structures. The DBMS must provide a wide range of ways in which the data elements can be structured. A relational DBMS provides the widest possible range. However, if the application requires a relatively unchanging set of relationships among the data items (e.g., processing a standard payroll), it is a good idea to consider the greater efficiency made possible by the hierarchical and network models.

Data Manipulation. Closely related to the way in which data is structured is the way in which it is manipulated. You will recall that a relational DBMS uses a single language to serve as both a query language and a data manipulation language. The use of such a language simplifies matters for applications programmers who are called upon to compose queries for users who are unable to write their own. On the other hand, a combined programming language may not be best suited for two widely divergent purposes. And in many cases organizations want to convert their COBOL or other high-level-language file-processing programs into programs that can process the data base. This requires a traditional data manipulation language that is an extension of a file-processing language such as COBOL.

Performance. The organization needs to establish a minimum acceptable level of DBMS performance, such as the number of transactions per second that the system must carry out, and set limits on the system's capacity—for example, the maximum number of records allowed in the data base and the maximum size of each record. These limits must be determined in the light of the projected future growth of the data base.

Data Dictionary. Although almost all DBMS provide a data dictionary, these dictionaries are not equally flexible. Many people feel that the data dictionary should itself be a small data base that can be accessed by all personnel.

Other Features. Many DBMSs provide such tools as software that can be used in designing the data base, programs that help load data from the original files onto the data base, monitors to measure the performance of the data base, programs that can be used to reorganize the data base, and routines that enable the data-base administrator to restart the system after it has stopped. Other important considerations in the selection of a data-base management system are security, vendor support, documentation, and the ability of the DBMS to interface with other software. For many organizations a key feature is the ability to upload and download data to microcomputers.

Installing a Data-Base Management System

The installation of a DBMS is a lengthy process that requires a skilled team and user cooperation. The process usually consists of the following steps.

Installing the Software. The first step is to install the software package, along with additional hardware if necessary. Generally the vendor helps install mainframe and microcomputer DBMSs. It's important to keep a detailed record of installation procedures so that the process can be repeated in the event of a system failure.

Customizing the System. When a company purchases a DBMS, the system usually must be customized to meet the organization's specific needs. This step may include such activities as allocating the proper amount of storage to internal tables and buffers. Most modern DBMS can be fine-tuned by the database administrator or systems programmers. The tuning process originally takes place with test data; when test data has yielded satisfactory results, *live data* (i.e., data from actual applications) is loaded into the data base and testing is continued. As more and more data is added to the system, additional problems appear and are solved.

Furnishing Documentation and Training. The documentation provided by the vendor of a DBMS usually is either too general or too technical to meet an organization's needs. Therefore, the people responsible for the DBMS must provide documentation, as well as training, for all users of the system. The training should begin before the system is installed. As the DBMS is used, people will find new applications and new users will be added, thereby increasing the need for continued training.

Evaluating and Auditing the System. Once a data-base management system is fully functioning, it must be evaluated in relation to the company's objectives (e.g., providing requested information in a reasonable amount of time). Most sophisticated DBMSs make it possible for technical personnel to determine the precise steps followed by the system when it is responding to a given request. This information enables them to fine-tune the system and to reorganize the data base if necessary.

We have seen in this chapter two very divergent methods of organizing and processing data. The first method, traditional file processing, treats data as belonging to a specific department such as payroll or accounting. It may meet users' needs for scheduled, predictable applications such as processing a payroll or basic accounting applications. The more sophisticated data-base management systems treat data as a resource for the entire organization and are useful for meeting information needs that cross departmental boundaries. The value of such systems will become even clearer in Part 4.

SUMMARY

1. A **file-processing system** is a computerized system consisting of files that are designed and organized to meet specific needs such as accounting, sales, and marketing applications. In file-processing systems data is not a centralized resource but is used only for a specific application.

2. The three most important types of file organization are sequential, random-access (also called direct-access), and indexed-sequential. Other traditional types of file organization include the linked list, in which records that share a field value such as department or job title are linked together by pointers, and the inverted file. Each record in an inverted file is an index indicating the address of records on the original file that share a particular characteristic.

3. All of the types of file organization described in this chapter are associated with traditional file processing and thus share certain drawbacks: Applications programmers must know the specific file to which the record belongs; it is extremely difficult to process data from more than one file at a time without writing a program for that purpose; and file-processing systems rarely make it easy for users to obtain responses to unforeseen requests.

4. A data base is a collection of data within an enterprise that has been organized to permit ready access both by technical people and by end-users. A **data-base management system (DBMS)** is the software that controls the creation, maintenance, and use of a data base.

5. There are three categories of personnel who interact with data-base management systems: trained specialists, who design the data base and are responsible for keeping it up to date and making sure it performs efficiently; applications programmers, who write programs to process the data base; and users, who obtain information from the data base with the aid of query languages. The **data-base administrator (DBA)** is the person or group responsible for designing, installing, and controlling the data base.

6. Each of the categories of people who work with a DBMS uses a specific type of programming language. The data definition language is used by data-base specialists such as systems programmers and DBAs to describe how data is organized in the data base. The data manipulation language is used by applications programmers to retrieve and modify data. Query languages enable end-users to extract information from a data base without the aid of a specialist.

7. A **data dictionary** is an organized collection of information about all the data elements in a data base. For each data item, it contains such information as the name of the item, a list of programs that use it, and related data items. For maximum effectiveness, data dictionaries should be on-line and accessible to the DBA, systems and applications programmers, and sophisticated users.

8. There are three fundamental models for organizing and processing data bases: hierarchical, network, and relational. A **hierar-**

SUMMARY CONTINUED

chical model is one in which each data record may have one or more subordinate data records. This model is also known as a tree because it resembles an upside-down tree. A **network model** is one in which each data record can have one or more subordinate data records and itself be subordinate to one or more data records. A **relational model** is based on tables, or two-dimensional collections of data, organized in rows and columns, that represent relationships among the data items.

9. Structured query language (SQL) is a widely used query language for relational DBMSs. It is available from different vendors for a wide range of mainframes, minicomputers, and microcomputers and allows nontechnical users to create tables, insert data, query data from one or more tables, sort the result of a query, and create reports.

10. Data-base management systems have several advantages over file-processing systems: Data duplication is reduced; flexibility is increased; data is independent of the programs that access it; data security can be enhanced; and division of labor is encouraged. On the other hand, DBMSs are expensive, require specialized personnel, cross traditional boundaries within an organization, almost inevitably require more hardware resources, and, because they replace file structures, cannot be reversed.

11. Selecting a DBMS is a lengthy, difficult process. To simplify this process, it is recommended that purchasers follow a two-step approach: First choose the data model and then choose the particular product.

12. Installing a DBMS is a lengthy process that requires a skilled team and user cooperation. The steps involved include installing the software, customizing the system, furnishing documentation and training, and evaluating and auditing the system.

KEY TERMS

file-processing system

data-base management system (DBMS)

data-base administrator (DBA)

data dictionary

hierarchical model

network model

relational model

REVIEW QUESTIONS

1. Define and give an example of a file-processing system.

2. Briefly describe the three most important types of file organization. Also describe two additional types and indicate a potential application for each. What do all of these types of file organization have in common?

3. Identify possible drawbacks of file-processing systems. In what types of applications can these systems be used profitably in spite of their drawbacks?

4. Distinguish between a data base and a data-base management system. How does a DBMS differ from a file-processing system?

5. Describe the three categories of personnel who work with data-base management systems and identify the type of programming language that each uses.

6. What is a data dictionary? What does it contain?

7. What is a data model? Identify the three basic data models. Give an application for each.

8. What does SQL stand for? Describe how users can apply an SQL to help solve their problems.

9. Identify the advantages and disadvantages of data-base management systems compared with file-processing systems. In your opinion, which of these advantages and disadvantages are most important and why?

10. Outline the steps in the selection of a data-base management system. Why should future DBMS users be interested in this process?

11. Outline the steps in the implementation of a data-base management system. Why should future DBMS users be interested in this process?

APPLICATIONS

1. Collect articles describing uses of query languages by nontechnical personnel. How are these users applying query languages?

2. Collect advertisements for several commercial database management systems. Which data models do these products use? What advantages are claimed for these products.

3. Report on advances in computer hardware that are expected to influence DBMSs. Describe why and how they affect software.

4. Discuss the following statement: Database management systems have made file-processing systems obsolete.

CASE FOR DISCUSSION

According to the most recent in-house survey of General Electric Company's 84,000 salaried employees, more than 15,000—or almost one out of five—spend most of their time doing some kind of work with computers. Lacking common data on this vast pool of talent—data showing what they do, where they do it, their job histories, and their career aspirations—GE faces a personnel problem that is common to large, decentralized companies: Qualified full-time staff are often overlooked while high-level technical positions are routinely filled with outside candidates or temporary contractors.

"How do you put your arms around a company like GE if you're one individual among thousands?" asks GE manpower executive Helen Klein. "It can get awfully frustrating."

An end to such frustration may be near with the advent of the Computing People Project, a comprehensive personnel placement program that will eventually make accessible (for a PC workstation) both a list of company-wide job openings and an up-to-date inventory of computer personnel. The project, which was begun in 1984, has generated strong interest among initial participants. According to Klein, who is the project's chief architect, GE stands to save millions in training costs and other expenses related to hiring people from outside the company. Equally important are the dividends in increased productivity and competitiveness that are expected to result from improving the environment for the career development of GE's computer people.

Upon completion of the merger with RCA that was announced last December, GE will rise from ninth to seventh on the list of the nation's largest industrial companies. The Computing People Project reflects the important role that people with computing skills will increasingly play at the company. People with computing skills are found in all of GE's corporate "functions"—engineering, marketing, finance, and manufacturing—and in all of its twenty or more component businesses, which include lighting, aircraft engines, household appliances, and consumer electronics.

Moreover, according to Michael Duesing, manager of computing personnel development, "computing" people comprise the only segment of GE's work force that is actually growing, at about a 12.5 percent annual rate. They are "a valuable, in-demand resource," he says.

Indeed, the project was designed in part as a response to career frustrations voiced by GE's computer professionals. Under the "protocols" of the current placement system, managers must notify their representative in employee relations when they have job openings. The employee relations person is also informed when an individual has been made "available" by his or her manager—that is, free to seek a position elsewhere in the company. The next step is to "get on the telephone and call whomever they know within the company," says Duesing.

In-house surveys showed that computing people were eager for promotional opportunities and more career guidance. They were also more willing to leave the company to get them; computer personnel had a turnover rate 20 percent higher than the company average.

The centerpiece of the system is relatively simple, both in its technology and in practice. First, mainframe-resident data bases are created for computing personnel and for computing jobs that need filling. Next, personal-computer workstations are made available to employee relations representatives, allowing them to post job vacancies electronically while simultaneously searching the candidate files for people with closely matching skills. Candidate lists generated in this fashion will be turned over to the manager who will do the interviewing and hiring. Duesing clams that under this approach, no suitable candidates will be overlooked, no matter where they work at GE.

Source: Jeffrey L. Craig, "GE's Electronic Corporate Ladder," *Datamation*, April 15, 1986, pp. 117–120. Copyright © Cahners Publishing Company.

CASE QUESTIONS

1. Managing means "getting things done through people." How does this case illustrate the value of a DBMS as a management tool?

2. You are a GE executive. Your department needs a programmer with at least two years of experience with COBOL. Your budget allows $28,000 per year for this position. Describe the query that you would make to find out whether any candidates are available within GE.

3. Show how a data definition language, a data manipulation language, and a query language would be employed by the Computing People Project.

COMPUTERS:

Computers and Government

Computers have transformed the way the nation is governed, from Washington D.C. to the county sheriff's office. The influence of computers on government begins in the electoral process. Candidates use computers to help manage their campaigns and to tally the results of political polls. In one experimental technique, members of an audience listening to a political speech or viewing a campaign commercial can push a button on a handheld device to register their reactions automatically. On election day, news media using computers to record the results of exit polls can sometimes determine the outcome of a contest before all the votes have been cast.

Between elections, computers help in the day-to-day work of government. Engineers use computers to design civic improvement projects and to estimate their costs. Agents of the extension service of the U.S. Department of Agriculture use computers to analyze soil samples. State troopers can use computers mounted on the dashboards of their patrol cars to check the license plate numbers of cars that they suspect may be stolen.

National defense accounts for some of the most intensive use of computers. Today's jet fighters are virtually computers with wings.

(© Alvis Upitis, The Image Bank.)

(© C. L. Chryslin, The Image Bank.)

THE IMPACT

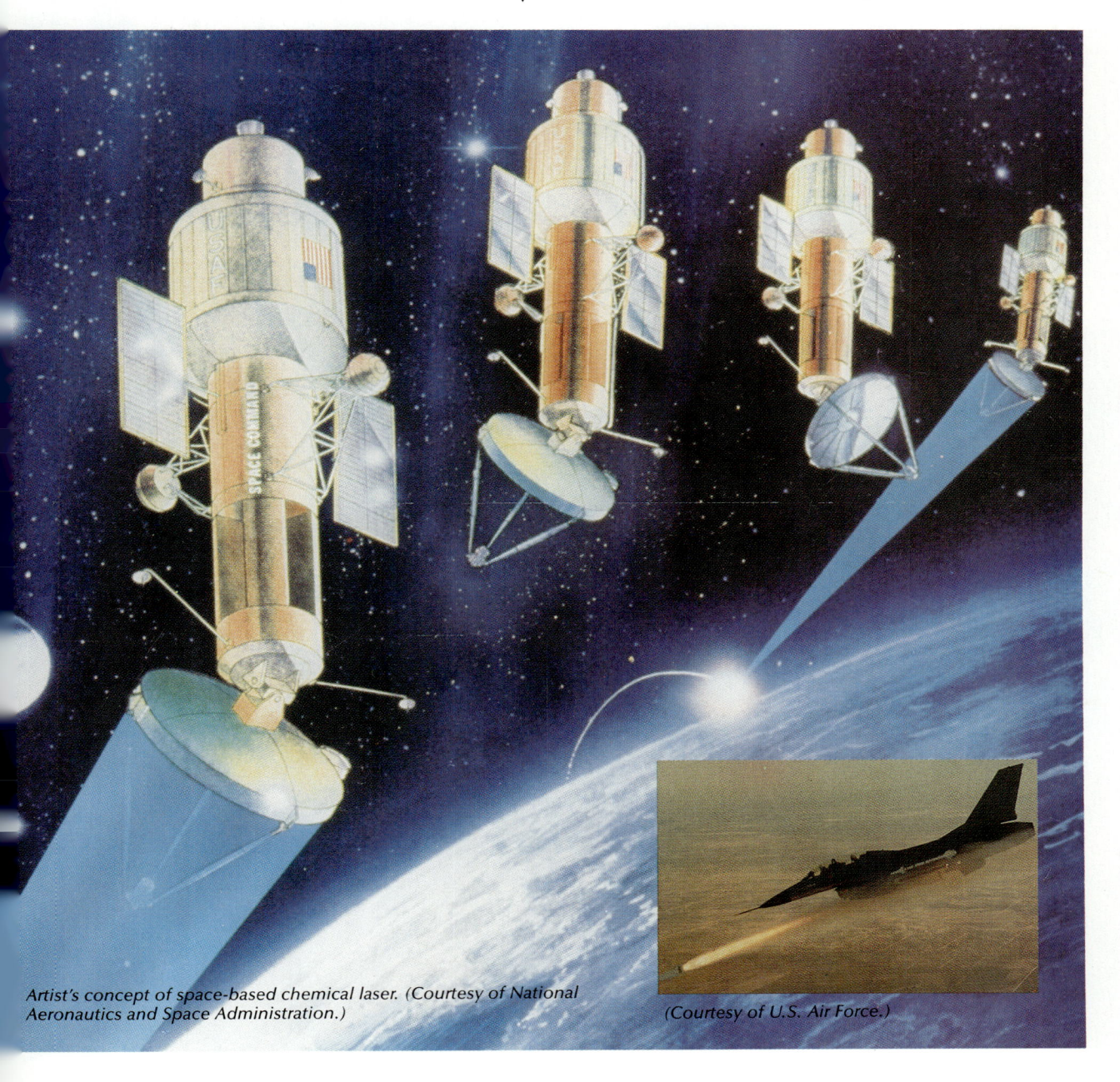

Artist's concept of space-based chemical laser. (Courtesy of National Aeronautics and Space Administration.)

(Courtesy of U.S. Air Force.)

(© Chuck O'Rear, Woodfin Camp.)

Computer-aided geological research. (© Hank Morgan, Photo Researchers.)

But even these amazing machines are nothing compared to the "Star Wars" technology that is on the drawing boards. Tasks such as aiming a chemical laser in outer space to intercept and destroy an intercontinental missile pose some of the greatest challenges ever for designers of computer hardware and software.

Among the potential negative consequences of the computerization of government services and operations are massive invasions of privacy. The existence of extensive data bases could enable totalitarian regimes to monitor and interfere in the private lives of citizens. A knowledgeable, concerned public is essential to ensure that government expands its use of computers without infringing on the rights of individuals.

Engineers checking the feasibility and cost of a civic improvement project. (© Tom Hollyman, Photo Researchers.)

(Opposite) Computer-controlled traffic. (© Chuck Fishman, Woodfin Camp.)

Bus dispatcher. (© Roger Miller, The Image Bank.)

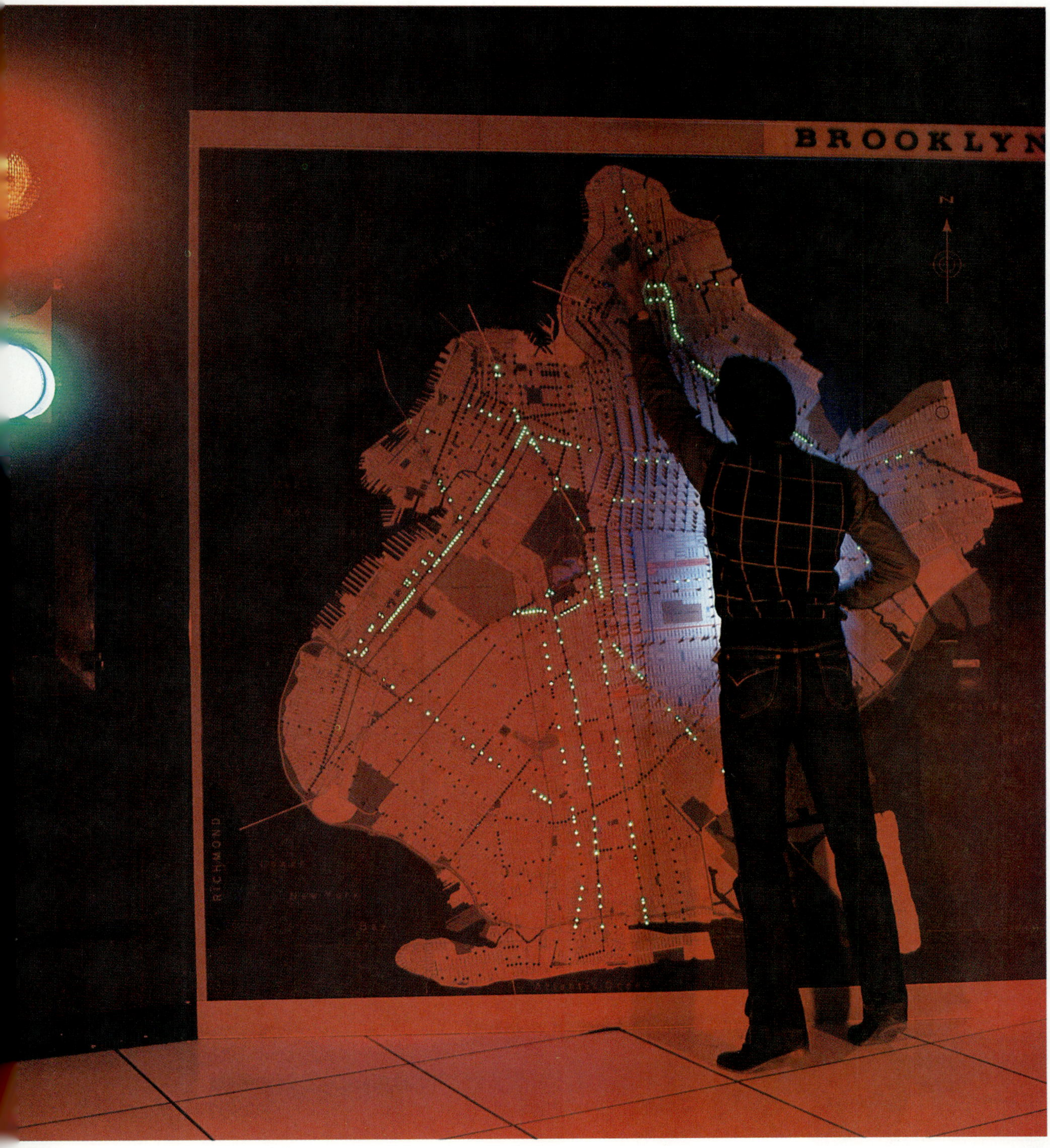
BROOKLYN
N
RICHMOND

Computers and Education

From kindergarten to graduate school, computers are becoming an increasingly important part of the teaching and learning process.

Computers are used in teaching every subject. The computer screen can be used to solve math problems, to perform language drills, to create works of art—even, believe it or not, to dissect a frog. Computer simulations are especially useful in teaching subjects like anatomy and dance.

Computers are an important aid to testing. By freeing instructors from the routine work of scoring exams and recording grades, they make more time available for the creative aspects of teaching.

Computers are especially helpful in teaching handicapped students. They are good training aids and can be programmed to suit individual needs. Unlike human teachers, they are available around the clock and will not become impatient

In the nation's universities, the use of computers as an aid to research is no longer confined to engineering and science departments. For example, scholars at the University of California at Irvine have compiled a "word bank" of classical Greek literature containing more than 60,000 cross-referenced entries. Another innovative use of computers in higher education is the Electronic University Network, which delivers courses and degree programs via microcomputers.

Diagram of a typical dicotyledonous flowering plant. (Courtesy of Reed College.)

(© Steve Niedorf, The Image Bank.)

(© Mark Perlman, Black Star.)

A children's dance class taught with the aid of computers. (© Lawrence Migdale, Photo Researchers.)

(© Mark Tuschman, Phototake.)

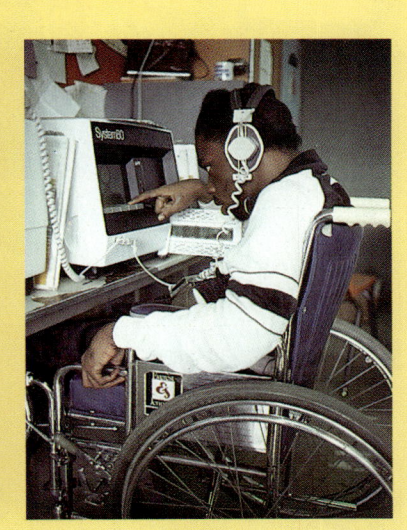

(© Blair Seitz, Photo Researchers.)

Computers and Work

Government officials, fighter pilots, and teachers are not the only people whose work is aided by computers. Hundreds of occupations have been transformed by the use of computers.

For example, the job of setting switches in a railroad yard used to be performed manually, outdoors, in all kinds of weather. Now it is performed electronically by an operator sitting at a computer console in a central control tower.

Steelmaking is another occupation that has been extensively computerized. Electronic devices permit greater precision in process control, thereby cutting waste and improving product quality.

In the world of finance, computers are everywhere. They make it possible for hundreds of millions of shares of stock to be traded each day, and they link financial centers around the world to form a global 24-hour market.

(© Marc Anderson.)

(© Dick Luria, Photo Researchers.)

This chef uses a small computer to maintain inventory. *(© Will McIntyre, Photo Researchers.)*

(© Angel Franco, Woodfin Camp.)

Ford Motor Company uses computers in training auto mechanics. *(© Jacques M. Chenet, Woodfin Camp.)*

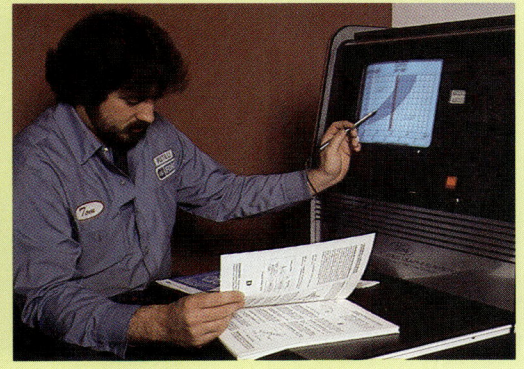

(© Dan McCoy, Rainbow.)

Even occupations that depend largely on the skills of individuals—like those of chef, farmer, or auto mechanic—can benefit from the use of computers for record keeping, inventory management, and other clerical tasks.

Computerization has brought new problems to the workplace as well as new possibilities. When too little attention is given to ergonometric factors, computer use can lead to fatigue and eyestrain. Improving the fit of people and computers is one of the major challenges of managing change in today's workplace.

(Courtesy of International Business Machines.)

(© Chuck O'Rear, Woodfin Camp.)

(© Sepp Seitz, Woodfin Camp.)

Computers and Leisure

When people leave their jobs, they do not leave their computers behind. Games ranging from chess to Trivial Pursuit have been issued in computer versions. They provide a partner who is always willing to play, never cheats, and won't berate you for making the wrong move. Some computer games offer different levels of performance and are accompanied by dazzling graphics and sound.

The impact of computers on leisure activities ranges far beyond computer games and video arcades, however. Would you like to see a movie? The movie you see is likely to contain computer-generated special effects and to have been filmed and edited with the aid of computers. If you would prefer something more traditional—a Shakespeare play, perhaps—you may be surprised to find that theatrical lighting has been revolutionized by computerized systems that enhance the subtlety and precision of stage lighting. Perhaps you will even view the movie or the play in

(© Richard Hutchings, Photo Researchers.)

the company of someone you met through a computerized dating service.

If you want to get away from the urban scene, computers may follow you to the wilderness. Park rangers use them to keep track of both people and wildlife in national parks. And the modern, lightweight gear that makes your wilderness experience more comfortable could not have been designed or manufactured without the aid of computers.

DATING SVCS • 525
Call Us First! Very Reasonable
Guaranteed results. All Ages.
Free Brochure. 718-698-5353
PROFESSIONAL DATING SERVICE

Catholic Singles?
Join Catholic Singles Dating Project
Brochure 212-365-4417/201-794-1515

CLASSICAL MUSIC LOVERS' Exchange
Nationwide link between
unattached music lovers. Write:
CMLE, Box 10, Pelham, NY 10922

COMPUTER MATCH
Call 24 hr tape, full info.: (718)877-6340

FIELD'S 212-913-3232
Friendship, Love & Happiness
Free Consultation & Booklet
Open 7 days — All ages — Est. 1920
42 E. 41 St. Rm. 1200 NYC 10017

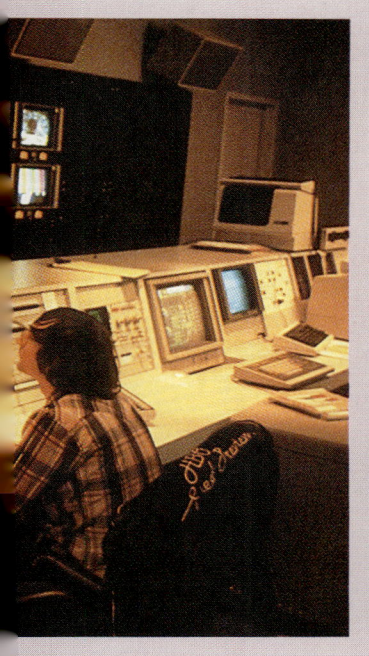

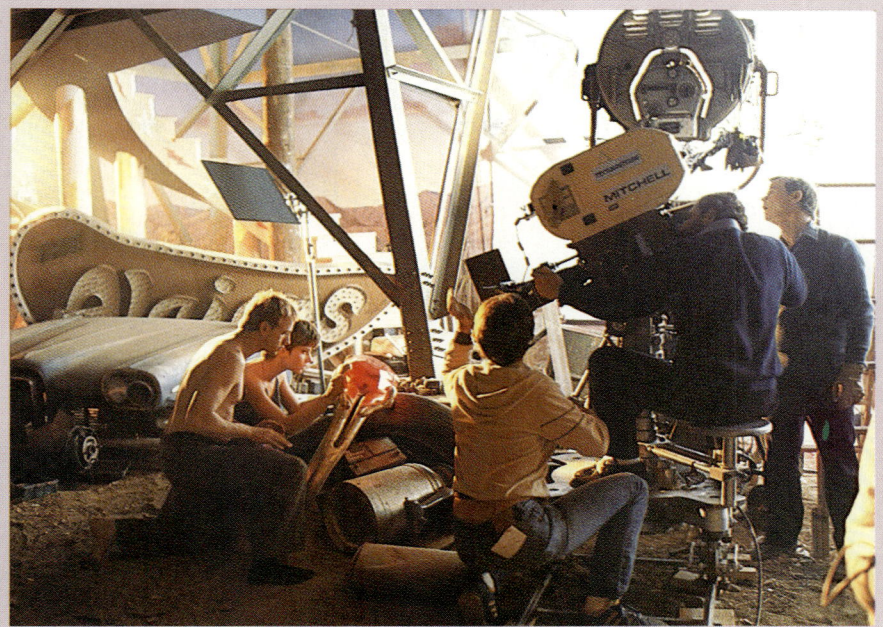

Filming "One From the Heart." (© Peter Sorel, Sygma.)

(© Richard Hutchings, Photo Researchers.)

(Far left) © John Blaustein, Woodfin Camp.)

(Left) Creating special effects for "American Werewolf." (© Bob Willoughby, Sygma.)

Computers and Sports

Professional sports is big business today, and like other businesses, it is heavily computerized. Teams use computers to track prospects beginning as early as junior high school. Coaches use computers to plan game strategies. Stadiums use electronic scoreboards to communicate with the fans. And the control room for broadcasting the Superbowl to those who cannot attend looks as complex as the command center of a modern aircraft carrier.

The results of judging in competitions such as gymnastics and ice skating are tallied by computer. Some sports fans may remember that a computer program had to be upgraded during the 1976 Olympics in order to register Nadia Comaneci's perfect 10.0 scores in gymnastics.

Participants in amateur sports benefit from computers, too. The weekend tennis player can use the same high-tech, computer-designed racquet that Martina Navratilova uses. Joggers can use computer simulations to improve their performance. Simulations are also used in sports medicine—for example, to help orthopedists treat wrenched backs and sprained ankles resulting from a weekend volleyball game.

The National Football League's Instant Replay Center. (© Ricardo Alberto Salas.)

Broadcasting Super Bowl XVIII. (Focus on Sports.)

(Focus on Sports.)

(Above) Skater Debi Thomas awaits her scores for technical merit and artistic impression. (Focus on Sports.)

(Above right) Several judges rate the performance of a figure skater. (Focus on Sports.)

(Right) Bo Jackson was drafted by the Kansas City Royals after playing on their farm team, the Chicks. (Focus on Sports.)

(Courtesy of Essential Sports Products, Ltd.)

(© Y. Arthus Vandystadt, Photo Researchers.) (© Chuck O'Rear, Woodfin Camp.)

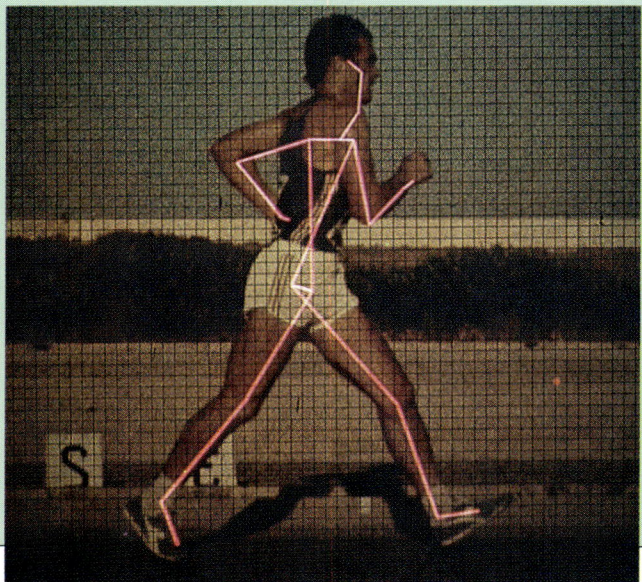

Computers and Health Care

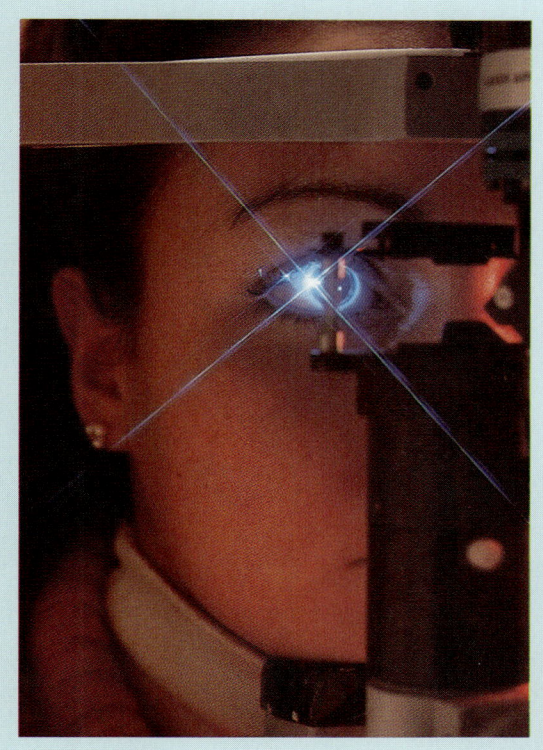

(© Mel DiGiacomo, The Image Bank.)

(© Will/Deni McIntyre, Photo Researchers.)

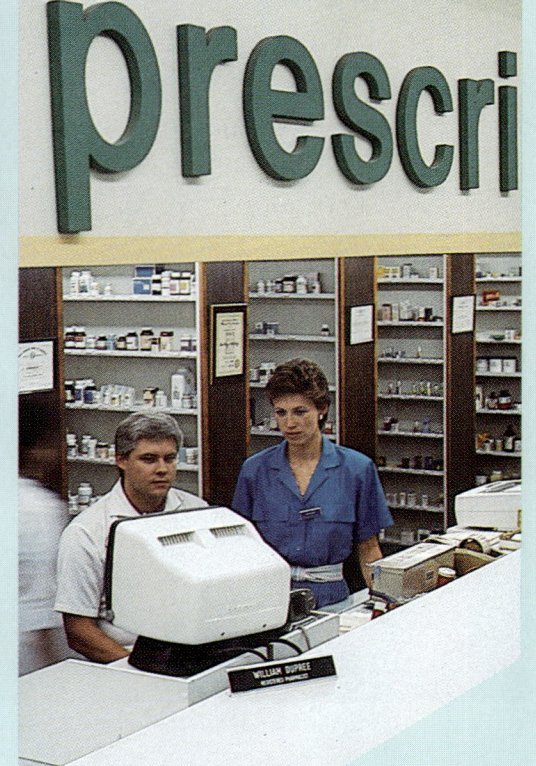

In health care, computers often make the difference between life and death. Surgeons use computers to enhance the precision of their operations. Computers monitor the vital signs of patients in intensive care. Computerized equipment administers radiation to kill cancer cells while leaving surrounding tissue unharmed.

Computerized equipment is used to evaluate x-rays and other medical tests. But in many instances traditional x-rays are being replaced by computer axial tomography (CAT scans), in which the computer takes x-rays of thousands of cross-sectional "slices" of the patient's body and combines them to create a three-dimensional picture.

Rehabilitation and physical-therapy programs often use computerized systems to provide feedback to patients, and pharmacists use computers to keep track of prescriptions and check on possible drug interactions.

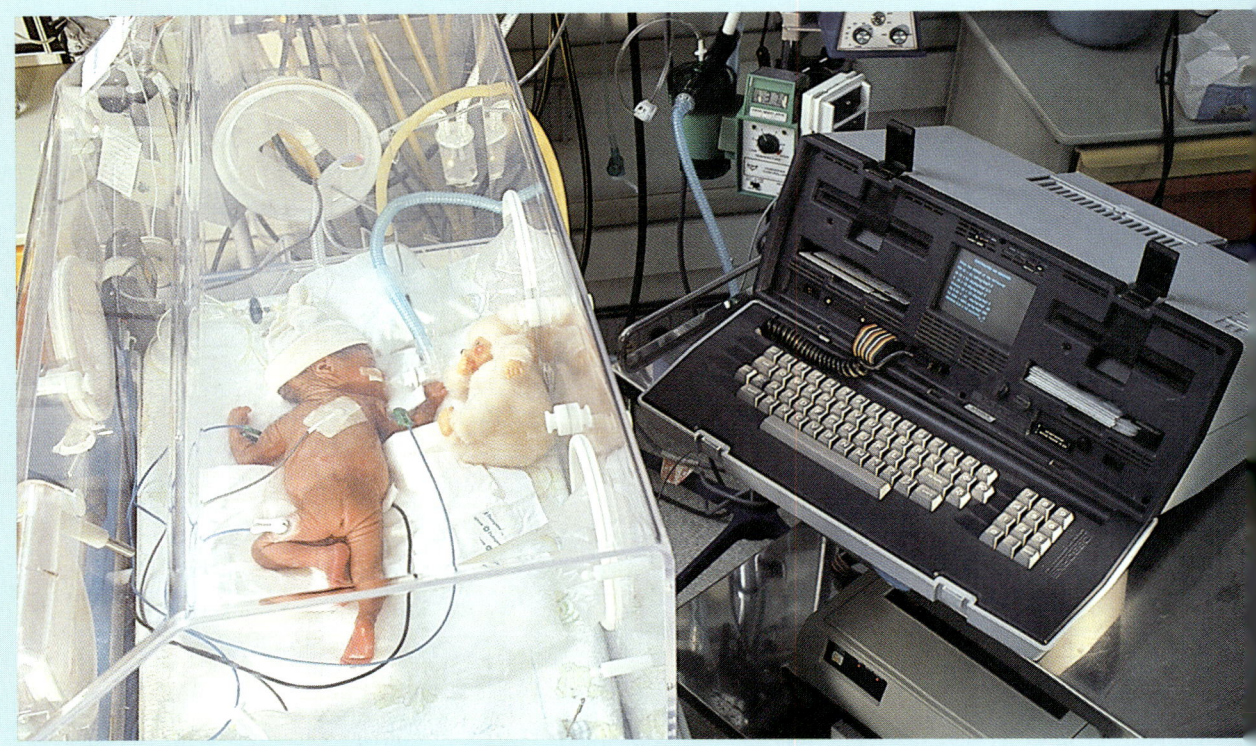

(© Jim Balog, Black Star.)

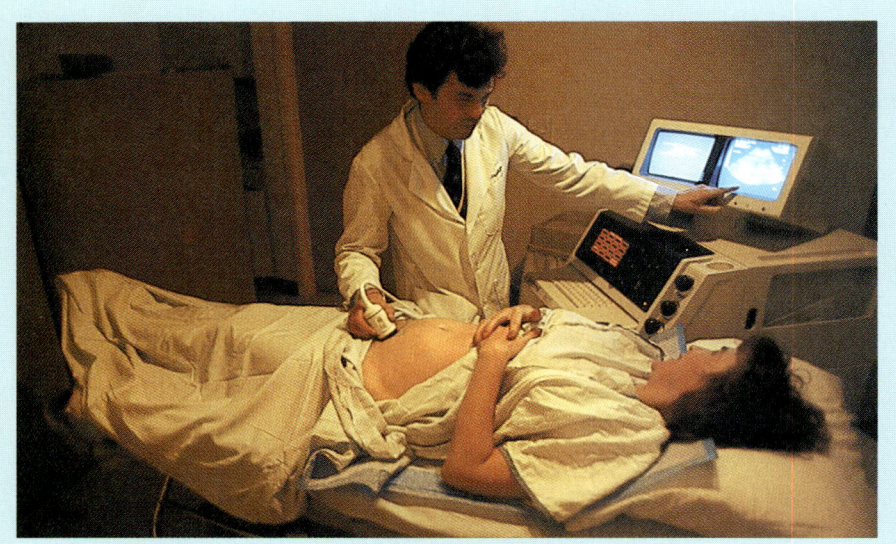

Fetal imaging on ultra-sound. (© John Ficara, Woodfin Camp.)

Designing a heart valve. (© Alvis, The Image Bank.)

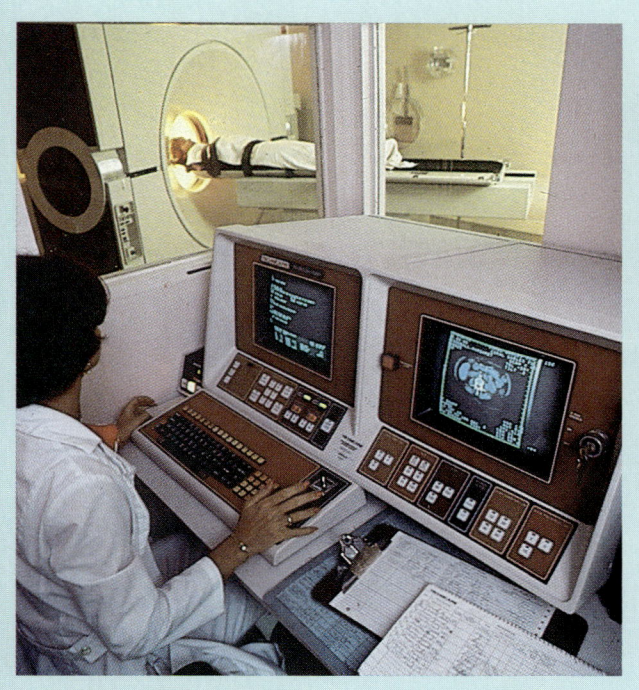

This outdoor tricycle uses a computerized electrical stimulation-feedback system to cause paralyzed muscles to pedal the tricycle. (Courtesy of Wright State University.)

(© Larry Mulvehill, Photo Researchers.)

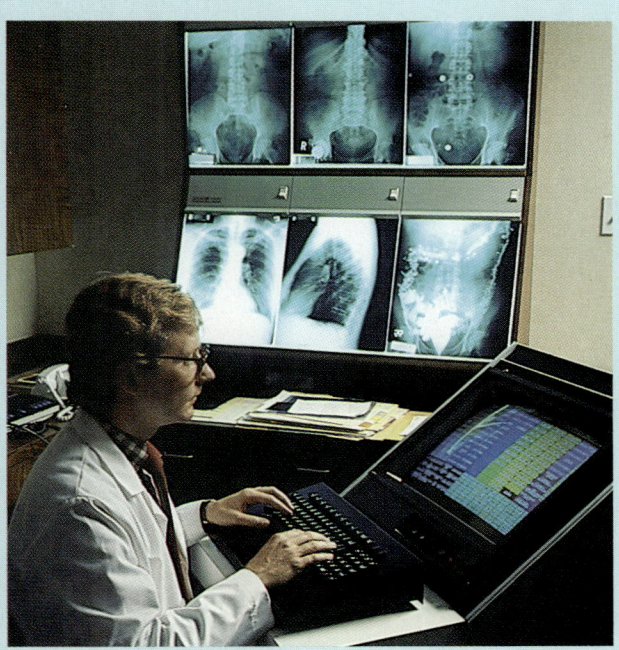

Computers play a key role in medical research as well. Computers track epidemics. They make it possible to identify the exact structure of a virus so that a vaccine can be created. And statistical studies help identify factors in diet and the environment that pose potential health hazards. But none of this technology is cheap. In some cases, computers are responsibile for increasing the cost of health care even while they increase its quality.

(© Ravi Arya, Black Star.)

401

Computers and Design

The process of design is a search for the beautiful and the functional. Designers in many areas have found computers an invaluable aid to creativity. In fact, it's safe to say that computers are the key tool in designing the world we live in.

Computer-assisted design makes it possible to picture a shoe, a car, a building, or even a computer chip on a screen, and to rotate it for viewing from every direction. The result: a more comfortable shoe, a more economical car, a more beautiful building, and new kinds of chips.

(© Joseph Nettis, Photo Researchers.)

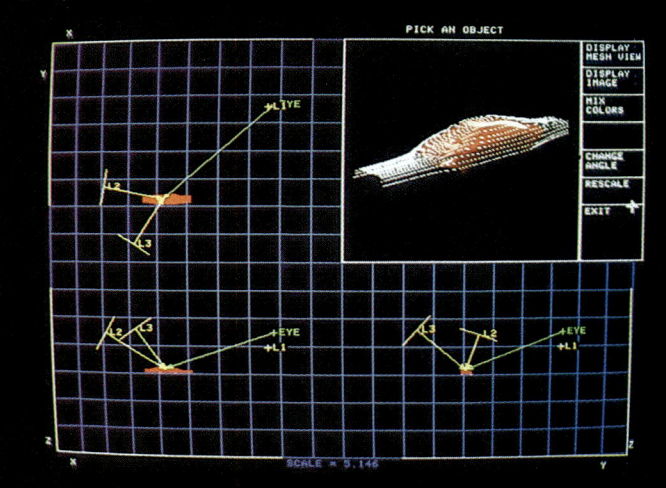

(© Hank Morgan, Rainbow.)

(© Jerry Mason, Photo Researchers.)

This layout designer is using a computer system to design an integrated-circuit chip. *(© Gregory Heisler, The Image Bank.)*

This wiring diagram was produced using a CAD system. (Courtesy of Kliegl Bros. Lighting.)

(© Charles Mahaux, The Image Bank.)

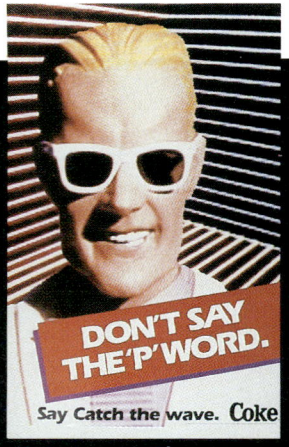

(© Jacques M. Chenet, Woodfin Camp.)

Combining graphics with animation creates some spectacular results. An example is the TV character Max Hedroom, who is entirely computer-generated, including his voice.

Computer graphics offers endless possibilities for self-expression. Some form of computer graphics is available on almost every computer system. Architects, artists, engineers, businesspeople, and students are among the many users who are enjoying this new way of displaying their creativity.

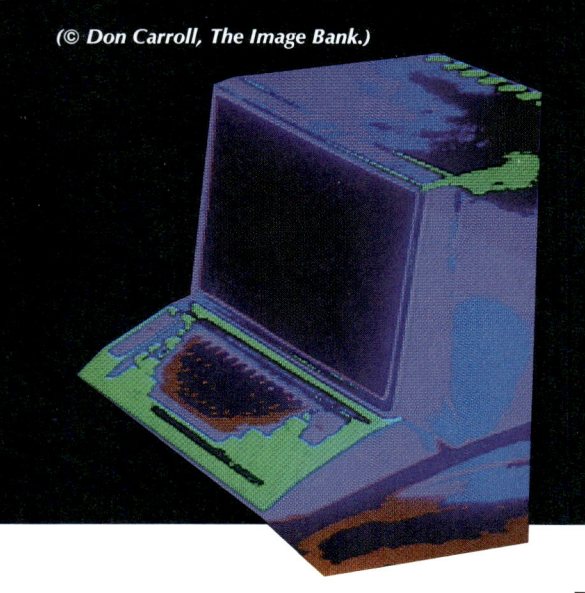

(© A. Pasieka, The Image Bank.)

(© Don Carroll, The Image Bank.)

(© Laurence M. Gartel, The Image Bank.)

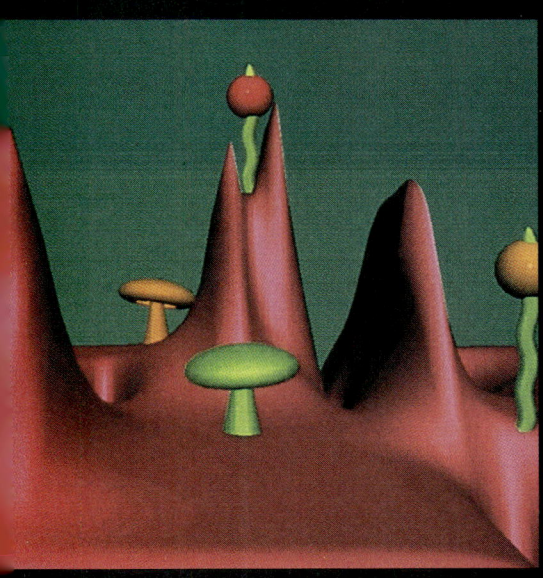

(© Melvin Prueitt, Photo Researchers.)

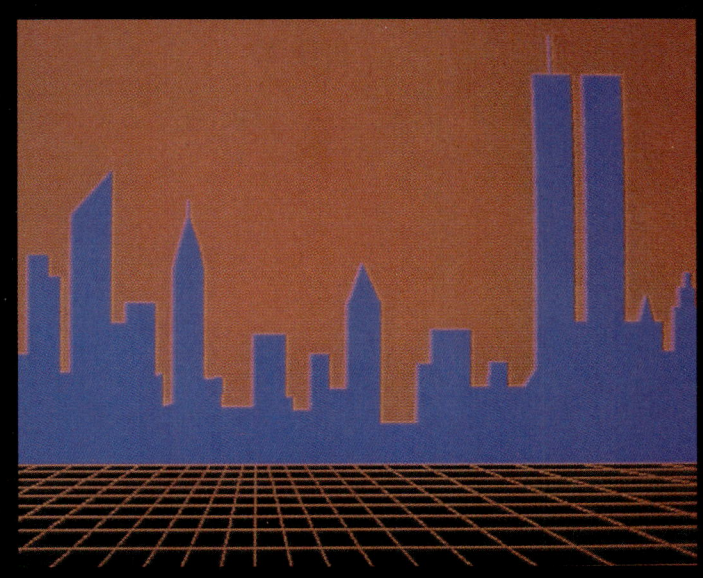

(© Robert Kristofik, The Image Bank.)

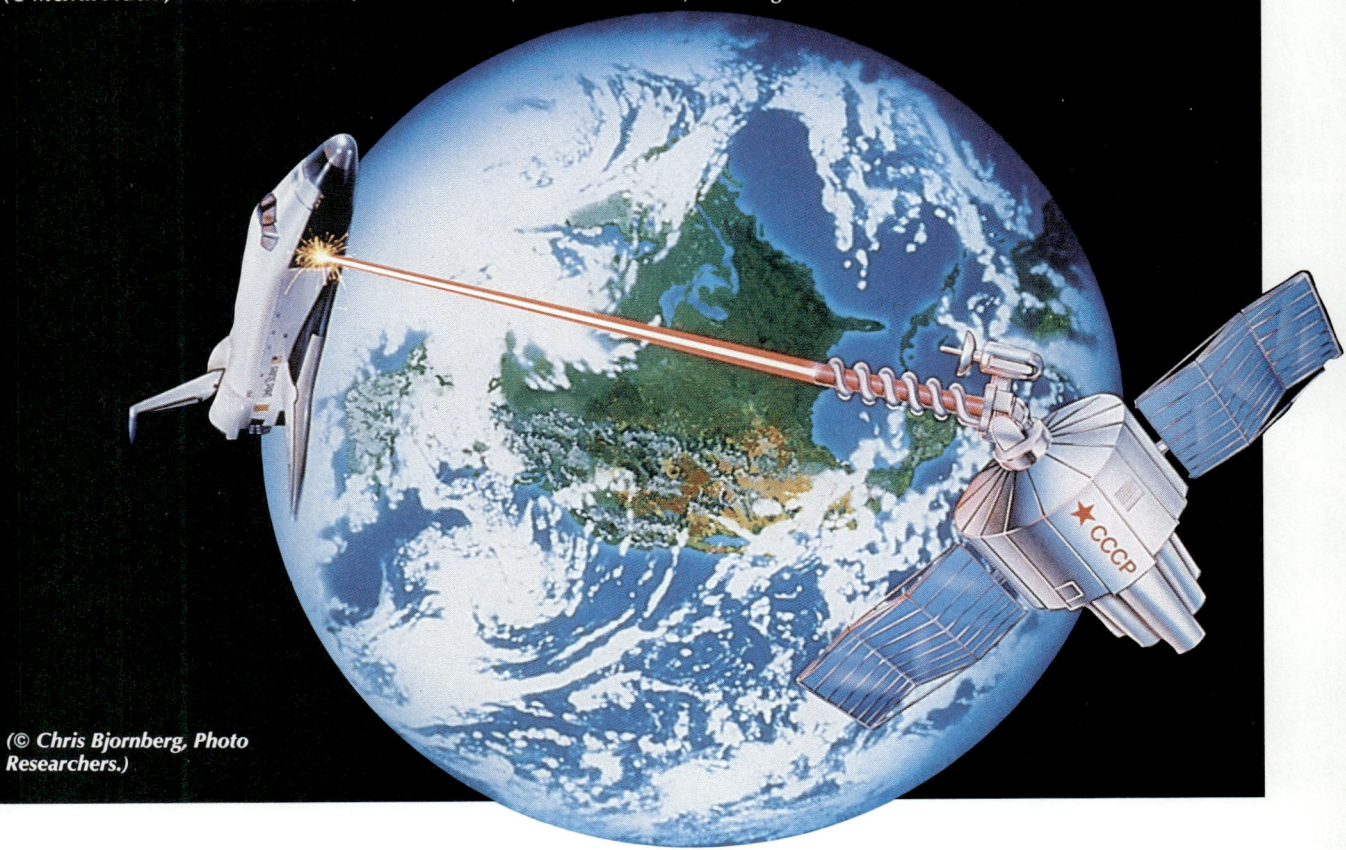

(© Chris Bjornberg, Photo Researchers.)

P

PART 4

People and Systems

Introduction to Business Systems

CHAPTER

11

Philip Cavavetta buys merchandise for his Boston-area drugstores from two wholesalers. One of them, McKesson Corporation of San Francisco, is getting more of his business these days. Why? "Their computer system is so good," he says.

Not long ago salespeople from McKesson, like those from other wholesalers, would drop by Cavavetta's Econo Drug Marts to take orders for cough syrup, aspirin, penicillin, and Valium. When the store ran short between salespeople's visits, clerks would read new orders over the phone to tape recorders at McKesson's warehouse.

Today a clerk in Cavavetta's stores walks the aisles once a week with a McKesson-supplied computer in hand. If the store is low on, say, cough syrup, the clerk waves a scanner over a McKesson-provided label stuck to the shelf. The computer takes note and, when the clerk is finished, transmits the order to McKesson.

At first glance it appears that McKesson has simply automated a costly, labor-intensive chore. But far more has happened: McKesson's computers not only dispatch the orders to a warehouse but also tell Cavavetta each month how profitable each of his departments is and print price stickers that add in the precise profit margin that he has selected.

Other McKesson computer services keep tabs on prescription-drug use by drugstore customers, check to be sure no one is taking medicines that shouldn't be taken simultaneously, and bill insurers for subscribers' medicines.

If Cavavetta buys from his alternative supplier, a regional wholesaler, he gets none of that. And if he wants to switch to a McKesson competitor with a similar computer service, he will have to relabel his shelves and learn another computer system.

A decade ago McKesson's drugstore distribution system was doing so poorly that the company considered ditching it. Back then, 800 salespeople sold about $915 million in merchandise to independent drugstores. Last year, 375 salespeople sold $3 billion worth, and drugstore distribution is now McKesson's biggest business.[1]

---

[1]David Wessel, "Computer Finds Role in Buying and Selling, Reshaping Business," *Wall Street Journal*, March 18, 1987, p. 1.

This part of the book explores various ways in which hardware, software, and people are linked together to create computer information systems. It consists of five chapters. Chapter 11 presents an introduction to business subsystems and the computer information systems that meet their needs. The system development process and applications of information systems for different levels of personnel and in various contexts are discussed in Chapters 12–15.

This chapter begins by focusing on the differences between personal and organizational applications of computers. The notion of a system is discussed in detail, beginning with a stereo system and continuing with computer information systems and business subsystems. A personal computer might take care of a simple application like checking inventory on the shelf of an individual store, but the other services that McKesson provides require a computer *system*. This chapter discusses the notion of a computer system in detail and goes on to describe three types of computer information systems. The chapter concludes with a discussion of the objectives, features, and outputs of representative business information systems, namely, accounting, inventory, and sales analysis.

When you have read this chapter you should be able to:
1. Discuss the differences between personal and organizational applications of computers.
2. State the key characteristics of systems.
3. Compare and contrast the three levels of computer information systems.
4. Describe some typical business subsystems.
5. Discuss three ways in which computer information systems can aid businesses and other organizations.
6. Present the key characteristics of common information systems for accounting, inventory, and sales.

Personal versus Organizational Applications

People who want to use computers to keep records, process words and numbers, and obtain information to solve specific problems often can benefit from personal-productivity software that they apply themselves, as we saw in Chapter 9. In other cases, however, users must rely on computer specialists to furnish the programs and systems necessary to get the job done. To better understand what such specialists do and why they are necessary, let's take a closer look at some of the most important differences between personal and organizational applications of computers.

Personal Applications

Personal applications usually serve a single user. Such applications tend to have several characteristics in common: They are interactive, use small data bases, have moderate security requirements, have a short implementation time, and do not require the services of specialists.

Interactive. Most users of personal applications engage in a constant dialog with the computer. Applications such as word processing and electronic spreadsheets owe their existence to the ability of the computer to respond almost instantaneously to the user's input.

Small Data Bases. Users of personal applications tend to work with a relatively small data base, often consisting of a few thousand records or less. The records themselves may be downloaded to the user's microcomputer from a corporate data base. For example, an executive sales manager considering a new commission plan need not access every vendor record in the corporate data base. Instead, he or she may use software that selects sample records at random. Since these data bases are accessed by relatively few people, the software need not provide a means of allowing dozens of users to access the data base at the same time.

Moderate Security Requirements. It is unlikely that the information used in personal applications would be of interest to many people besides the individual user. Moreover, it is fairly easy to prevent the uploading of data from the user's microcomputer to the corporate data base.

Short Implementation Time. Once a user knows how to work with a personal-productivity program, it is easy to begin applying it to specific problems. In the example mentioned earlier, if the sales manager uses a data-base management program to create and analyze vendor records but forgets to include the date-of-hire field, this can easily be added later. A growing number of organizations have the hardware, software, and communication technology required to transfer files from their mainframe computers to microcomputers. This also reduces the time needed to implement personal applications.

Low Need for Specialists. Because of the relative simplicity of personal applications and their fairly straightforward hardware and software requirements, such applications often can be developed by users themselves. Additional applications can be developed with a moderate amount of assistance from computer specialists, often computer programmers as in the case of the accounts payable program discussed in Chapter 7.

Organizational Applications

Organizational applications of computers are designed to meet the needs of many people within the organization. In contrast to personal applications, they tend to be noninteractive, use large data bases, have stringent security requirements, take a long time to implement, and require the services of technical personnel.

Noninteractive. Batch processing is still the preferred way of handling many of an organization's basic applications. For example, companies that send out thousands of bills per month will regroup these bills to achieve maximum processing efficiency and minimum error. Once the data has been entered into the computer and processed, it may undergo interactive processing. For example, in response to a telephone inquiry, a billing clerk could inform a customer of the balance due on his

Personal Applications

Interactive
Small Data Bases
Moderate Security Requirements
Short Implementation Time
Low Need for Specialists

Organizational Applications

Noninteractive
Large Data Bases
Stringent Security Requirements
Long Implementation Time
Technical Personnel Required

Characteristics of Computer Applications

or her account. In more sophisticated systems a manager could query the computer about the percentage of bills due for more than thirty days.

Large Data Bases. The data bases of many organizations can be measured in billions or trillions of bytes. Such data bases far exceed the storage capacity of microcomputer hard disks and are contained in mainframe systems. The software required to manage such data bases, described in Chapter 10, also goes far beyond the limits of microcomputer data-base management programs. The data-base management systems that serve organizational users are a far cry from personal-productivity programs, even when they share some of the same features. For example, a mainframe data-base management system must devise a way for dozens of people to access the data base simultaneously without interfering with each other and without having to wait an unacceptably long time.

Stringent Security Requirements. The central data base is among the most important resources of an organization. If billing records are destroyed, for example, the company's survival is threatened. Therefore, every program that accesses the organizational data base must be examined carefully to ensure that no illegal access is attempted. Because of the importance of the data base, it is necessary to develop and enforce detailed backup procedures to prevent loss of data as a result of human error, sabotage, or natural disasters.

Long Implementation Time. Because of their complexity, organizational applications usually take months or even years to implement. This is especially frustrating in the ever-changing environment of business, in which the conditions prevailing when an application is first considered may no longer apply by the time the application is implemented. In many cases the organization's personnel also change before the new application is implemented.

Technical Personnel Required. Because of the characteristics described, most organizational applications require one or more technical people in both the development and implementation phases. This almost inevitably leads to conflicts as people whose backgrounds and experience differ widely are forced to work together and make compromises. Personalities clash and misunderstandings are frequent. The organization can reduce the likelihood that such problems will arise by carefully following the steps in the system development process, which are described in Chapter 12.

Systems

Throughout this book the word *system* occurs with great frequency. It is impossible to understand and appreciate what a computer can do both for individuals and for organizations without having a clear idea of what a system is. Therefore, let's take a brief detour and describe a system that everyone has used at one time or another—a stereo system. (See Figure 11-1.)

All systems have the following characteristics:
1. They have a goal or goals.
2. They operate according to well-defined procedures.
3. They are composed of parts that must be coordinated and can themselves be considered small systems.
4. They provide feedback.

In addition, most systems exist to benefit people and constantly interact with them. Stereo systems illustrate the general principles of systems as follows:
1. A stereo system has a goal—the proper reproduction of music.
2. The system is operated according to specific procedures.

Modern stereo systems are often computerized to provide greater flexibility, higher performance, and ease of use. (Courtesy of Magnavox.)

FIGURE 11-1

Basic System Characteristics

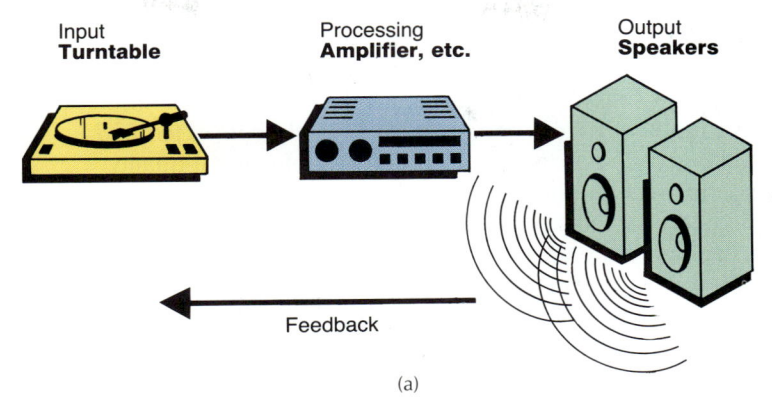

Input
Turntable

Processing
Amplifier, etc.

Output
Speakers

Feedback

(a)

(a) A stereo system is a classic example of a system. It has a goal, operates according to specific procedures, is composed of coordinated parts, and provides feedback. (b) A computer information system also has a goal, operates according to specific procedures, is composed of coordinated parts, and provides feedback.

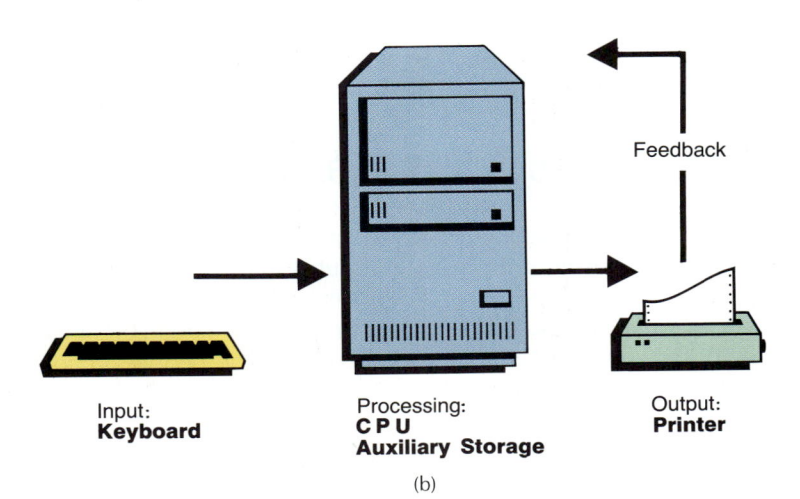

Feedback

Input:
Keyboard

Processing:
C P U
Auxiliary Storage

Output:
Printer

(b)

For example, when you got your first stereo you had to be sure you knew how to turn it on, adjust the bass and treble, and place records on it. Whenever you listen to your system, you have to take into account whether the sound will disturb others, and adjust the volume accordingly.

3. A stereo system is composed of parts that must be coordinated and properly balanced to meet its goal. It includes a turntable, an amplifier, and two or more speakers. These parts must be compatible and must be connected correctly. It is pointless to get a sophisticated amplifier if you have poor-quality speakers.

4. A stereo system's parts can themselves be considered small systems, or *subsystems*. The speakers, for example, are subsystems. Each speaker has a goal, namely, the output of high-quality sound. There are operating procedures for speakers, and their volume may have a limit determined by other people at home or in a nearby house or apartment. The speaker is composed of parts such as the woofer (which produces low-frequency sounds) and the tweeter (which produces high-frequency sounds). These parts are chosen according to a goal and must be properly connected and balanced. If your goal is to produce professional-quality sound, you will need professional-quality components.

5. Stereo systems provide *feedback*, that is, a means by which to compare the system's actual output to the desired output and make any necessary corrections. Examples of feedback from a stereo system are hearing music and then increasing the treble or the bass for a better sound, and having your next-door neighbor ask you to lower the sound.

6. Finally, as is the case with most systems, a stereo system has a human element. The goal of the system is to produce good music for people to listen to and enjoy. The system can meet this goal only if people interact with it constantly.

Businesses as Systems

Now that we understand the general concept of systems, we can look at business systems, computer information systems, and how they are interrelated. A business itself can be considered a system: It has a goal, procedures, coordinated parts that are subsystems (see Figure 11-2), feedback, and people. In addition to being a system, a business uses systems, called information systems. Each business subsystem, such as accounting or sales, may use one or several computer information systems to meet its goals as well as the goals of the business as a whole. To see how all of these subsystems fit together, we will introduce the different levels of computer information systems, describe some typical business subsystems, and see how information systems are applied to the subsystems of a business.

Computer Information Systems

Computer information systems are typically divided into three basic categories based on the information needs they serve: operations information systems, management information systems, and decision support systems. These systems are used by oper-

FIGURE 11-2

A Small-Business Subsystem

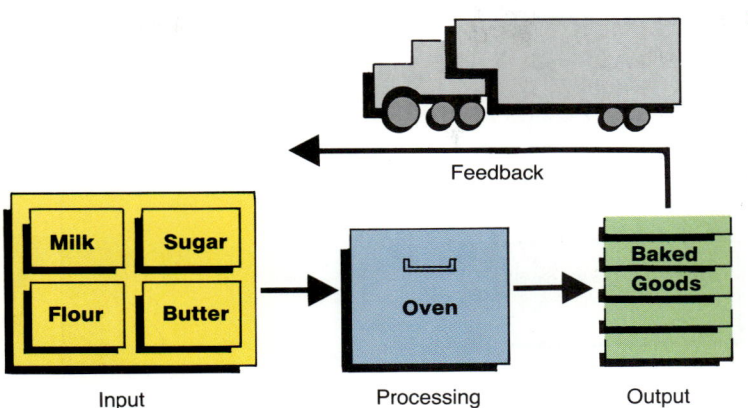

This diagram represents one subsystem of a bakery, the subsystem that prepares goods for sale. Other subsystems purchase new materials, take orders for baked goods, and so forth. All of these subsystems must be coordinated if the business is to meet its goals.

Input — Milk, Sugar, Flour, Butter
Processing — Oven
Output — Baked Goods
Feedback

---

ations personnel and the three levels of management—supervisory, middle, and top managers. In general, less sophisticated information systems are used by personnel at lower levels. Each of these systems is introduced briefly here and discussed further in Chapter 13.

Operations Information Systems. *Operations information systems*, also called *data processing systems*, are designed to automate clerical work and help supervisory managers make routine decisions. These computer systems closely parallel the clerical systems that they automate and therefore tend to be the first information systems developed in a company.

Operations information systems produce three general types of output (see Figure 11-3):

1. Business documents such as paychecks, invoices, and purchase orders, which are similar to the documents produced by noncomputerized clerical systems.

2. Lists and summaries of business documents suitable for verifying information and for future reference. Occasionally middle managers refer to these lists and summaries when performing their controlling function.

3. Computerized versions of business documents and the corresponding lists and summaries. This information provides the data for the management information systems and decision support systems to be discussed shortly. In practical terms, such information is unavailable with manual systems.

FIGURE 11-3

Three Types of Data Processing Outputs

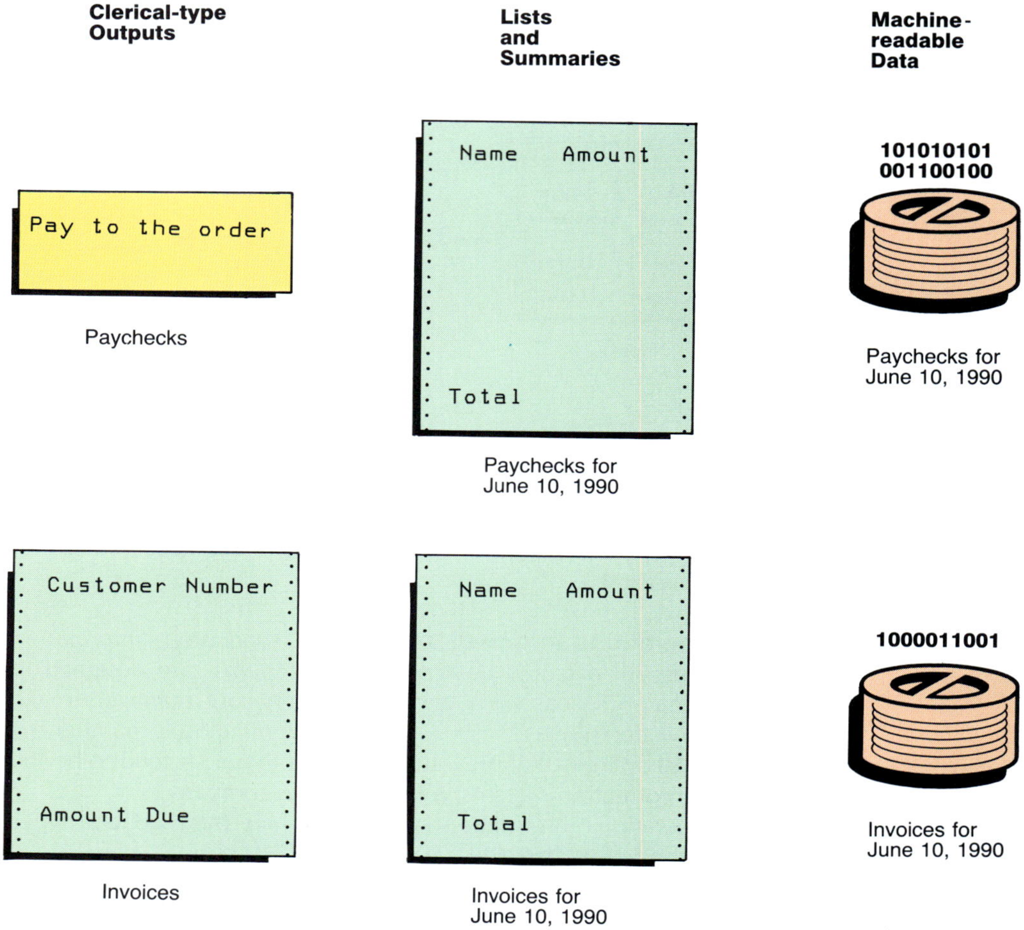

Clerical-type Outputs	Lists and Summaries	Machine-readable Data
Paychecks	Paychecks for June 10, 1990	Paychecks for June 10, 1990
Invoices	Invoices for June 10, 1990	Invoices for June 10, 1990

Management Information Systems. *Management information systems (MIS)* provide managers with information on a scheduled basis. These systems integrate, consolidate, and summarize the information generated by operations information systems. For example, a middle manager who is responsible for developing a sample budget for a new product line will access an MIS to gather production, sales, inventory, and other information generated by several different operations information systems. He or she will integrate and process this information,

FIGURE 11-4

Business Subsystems

Marketing	Finance and Accounting	Production	Research and Development	Human Resources	Computer Services
Define customer needs	Obtain needed funds	Make goods	Develop new products	Employee relations	Create information systems
Meet those needs	Process financial information	Put together the service	Research new products	Hiring Training	Maintain information systems

interpret the results, and come up with a budget or perhaps a set of alternative budgets. In addition to such areas as budgeting and planning, computers are also increasingly important for middle managers in production tasks. (See Box 11-1.)

Decision Support Systems. *Decision support systems (DSS) are used by managers in making certain kinds of decisions. Whereas an MIS serves large numbers of managers, a DSS may be designed to help a single executive solve a specific problem. For example, a DSS can be used to help top management decide whether to go ahead with a new product line. It processes the same data as the MIS, plus additional data such as sales figures for competing products. It performs statistical analyses and allows the user to engage in a dialog with the system.*

Business Subsystems

Since a business is a system, it has a goal, namely, to make goods or provide services at a profit. A business is usually divided into subsystems (commonly called departments) that are designed to help it meet its goal. (See Figure 11-4.) Each of the subsystems needs its own data and information, which it can obtain from the information systems discussed earlier.

BOX 11-1

MANAGING CHANGE

The Middle Manager in the Factory of the Future

Production efficiencies made possible by advancing technologies such as computer-assisted drafting and robotics seem capable of reducing work in process to the point where the middle management function in the factory, as we know it today, becomes obsolete.

But this scenario is excessively grim. It is more likely that there will be a substantial reshaping of the middle management function, rather than its disappearance. Examples:

1. Labor Reporting/Attendance

Manual: Information is collected via punched cards or labor tickets and transferred manually onto payroll sheets. This requires 25 to 30 percent of middle management's time.

Automated: Information is collected through CRT terminals on the shop floor and connected to the company computer. Basic payroll responsibility shifts to accounting. This would require only 4 percent of management's time each week.

2. Expediting

Manual: Ubiquitous "hot lists" and notebooks are carried throughout the plant to determine specific bottlenecks and pinpoint requirements. This typically requires about 20 percent of a middle manager's time.

Automated: On-line reporting systems will enable the manager to expedite shop orders on the computer. CRTs located throughout the plant will allow the manager to communicate with other sections of the factory electronically. This would require only about 8 percent of a supervisor's time.

3. Inventory Control/Materials Handling

Manual: Placing materials in a warehouse requires finding available space by trial and error. Overseeing the labor-intensive movement of materials from the raw-materials stockroom to the work center is a time-consuming process requiring 8 percent of a manager's time each week.

Automated: Computers can track work in process automatically. In addition, the amount of handling needed to complete a product part will be calculated, and the overall production schedule can be predicted with greater accuracy. This will require only 2 percent of a manager's time.

4. Quality Control

Manual: Product quality currently is treated almost as a by-product of the manufacturing process. The quality-control function now utilizes only about 5 percent of management's time.

Automated: With computerized quality reports for each employee and statistical process controls, the manager will be able to access and analyze data to identify and examine problems in product quality. The middle manager can use quality-control data as a decision-making tool instead of reacting to crises in the production process. About 15 percent of the manager's time would be available for this function in the future, and should result in a more efficient production process and greater productivity.

5. Employee Relations

Manual: Owing to continuing pressure on management to "get the product out the door," training and motivating employees often is minimized. Currently, managers spend only about 4 percent of their time on this function weekly.

Automated: Computerization will free managers to become more people-oriented. In addition, communications will be facilitated by data-base systems that can be accessed from the shop floor. Employee communications will account for approximately 25 percent of the manager's time.

6. Maintenance

Manual: As products are introduced or retired, the manager must coordinate this change. Tool maintenance and contingency plans in the event of breakdowns need to be planned and calculated carefully. This now requires about 7 percent of the manager's time.

Automated: Maintenance records for all tools used in production can be stored in computerized systems. By maintaining such information on the computer, together with information on requirements, managers can readily locate specific tools and analyze remaining useful life. This will minimize breakdowns and relevant time to repair machines.

Conclusions

In order to negotiate the transition from a semiautomated plant environment to the fully automated factory of the future, middle managers must use the time freed by computerization to address, on a more sophisticated level than ever before, critical questions of product quality and employee motivation—questions that have been underaddressed as a result of the time pressures under the older production methods.

Source: Adapted, by permission of the publisher, from "Will Middle Managers Work in the 'Factory of the Future'?" Joel C. Polakoff, *Management Review*, January 1987, pp. 50–51, © 1987 American Management Assoc., New York. All rights reserved.

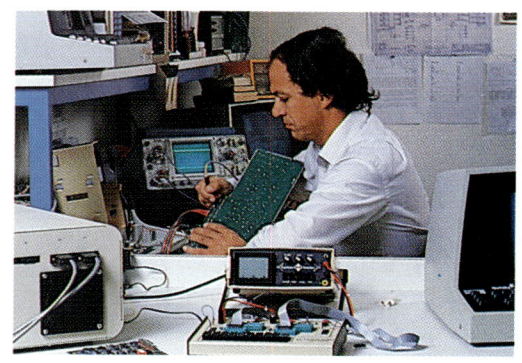

The personnel, marketing, research and development, accounting, and production departments of a business all benefit from computer information systems. The personnel director reviews job descriptions with a prospective employee. Marketing personnel use computer reports to discuss advertising strategy for a new product. In the research and development department, a technician conducts a series of tests of a proposed product. In the accounting office, an employee enters billing data. Production personnel may use computer systems to gather statistics on items manufactured and the number and type manufacturing errors. (© Michal Heron, Woodfin Camp; © Don McCoy, Rainbow; © Lawrence Migdale, Photo Researchers; © Joel Gordon; Courtesy of Hewlett-Packard.)

Typical Business Subsystems

Each business has its own unique characteristics and needs and, hence, its own subsystems, or departments. There are, however, certain business functions that are common to most businesses. Typical business subsystems (departments) include marketing, finance and accounting, production, research and development, human resources, and computer services. In this section we will illustrate the role that each of these subsystems can play with respect to a manufacturing firm's new product line.

Marketing. *Marketing* is the process of determining potential customers' needs and then channeling goods or services into meeting those needs. The McKesson computer system described at the beginning of the chapter is an example of one that focuses on the marketing subsystem. Marketing activities include defining customer needs; setting prices for goods and services; advertising (i.e., informing customers about the availability of goods and services); assuring product delivery; and providing customer service. The marketing department is responsible for informing both present and potential customers about the new product line.

Finance and Accounting. *Finance* is the process of obtaining needed funds and putting them to use in order to meet the goals of the firm. For example, the finance department raises the money to manufacture and launch the new product line. *Accounting* is the process of obtaining, processing, and communicating financial information. For example, the accounting department can tell us whether the new product line is making a profit and, if so, how much.

Production. *Production* is the physical process of making the goods or putting together the service. It includes purchasing raw materials, scheduling, and controlling inventory. Production is responsible for the actual production and distribution of the new product line.

Research and Development. *Research and development*, or *R&D*, is responsible for developing new products and improving existing ones. Since the business world is constantly changing, this subsystem plays a crucial role in meeting a firm's goals. R&D helps develop the new product line and does research for an even newer product line that will be the eventual successor to the one that was just launched.

Human Resources. *Human resources*, or *personnel*, is the business subsystem that is responsible for employee relations, including hiring, providing orientation, training, appraising performance, and managing career paths. Human resources is the group that helps determine whether the company needs new workers and managers to handle the new product line, and if so, hires them and arranges for their training.

Computer Services. *Computer services*, also called the *data processing department*, is responsible for creating and maintaining the organization's computer information systems. Computer specialists employed by the computer services department would work with users from other departments to help create the information systems used by the company in its efforts to produce and sell the new product line.

In recent years many organizations have changed the name of their computer services department to Management Information Systems Department. This new name reflects the increased role of MIS in the department's work. Also, the title of the department head has often been upgraded. (See Box 11-2.)

Computer Information Systems in Business

Each of the various business subsystems can benefit from computer information systems in several ways: (1) They get information from computer systems that are specifically designed for their subsystems. (2) They exchange data and information with other business subsystems. (3) They take advantage of computer information systems that provide data and information to all levels of management, transcending departmental boundaries.

BOX 11-2

MANAGING CHANGE

What's in a Name?

The issue of corporate titles has recently gained importance for managers of management information systems in the race with traditional managers for status within an organization.

Titles trace an upward spiral as the role of corporate computing expands. The first corporate computing managers often had the title of "DP manager," reflecting the dominant function of their departments—data processing. The DP manager evolved into the "director of management information systems" as the concept of corporate computing evolved.

Most recently, MIS has been shortened to "information systems" and encompasses more than traditional computing functions. The vice-president or director of information systems is now responsible for such things as telecommunication, electronic publishing, and desktop computing. In fact, the concept of information systems is so broad that it can accommodate almost anything in an era that has already been dubbed The Information Age.

All the names for the computing function are still in widespread use. A scan of the titles of members of a national organization of corporate computing managers reveals the following:

- Executive vice-president of technology and communications
- Vice-president of computer operations
- Director of DP and information systems
- Manager of DP
- Vice-president of communications and DP
- Director of computer systems
- Manager of information systems and communications services
- Vice-president of information management
- Director of information facilities
- Vice-president of MIS
- Vice-chairman

All of these titles refer to the top computer management post in a major corporation.

While executives may privately chuckle at the importance placed on titles, they are also highly attuned to the career implications involved in even the most innocuous-sounding title changes. They know that if Romeo and Juliet's last names had been different, the outcome of the play would also have been different.

Source: Alan Radding, "MIS Asks, 'What's in a Name,'" *Computerworld*, April 13, 1987, p. 77. Copyright 1987 by CW Publishing Inc., Framingham, MA 01201

Marketing Information Systems. Marketing information systems collect, process, and present information on which marketing decisions are based. They help businesspeople determine marketing strategy and tactics and carry out marketing campaigns. Typical components of marketing information systems are the following:

- **Marketing accounting systems,** which inform managers about the sales and profitability of individual products, as well as about credit sales and inventory.
- **Marketing intelligence systems,** which inform managers about the external marketplace; for example, who is selling what and how successful they are in terms of market share and profitability.
- **Marketing research systems,** which are used to obtain information to solve specific marketing problems such as product potential and advertising impact.

Top-level marketing managers also use decision support systems to help them set marketing strategy and decide how to carry out marketing campaigns.

Accounting Information Systems. *Accounting information systems* can be divided into two general categories: managerial systems and financial systems.

- Managerial systems provide information to a company's managers. They are used for marketing, budgeting, cost control, pricing, and labor contract negotiations.
- Financial systems supply information about a business to outsiders such as the government and stockholders. They are used to produce financial statements, tax returns, and reports to regulatory agencies like the Securities and Exchange Commission.

Production Information Systems. *Production information systems* start with the purchasing and receiving of raw materials, continue with production scheduling and quality control, and terminate with inventory and shipping. Increasingly these systems also include *robot control systems, computer-aided design systems*, and *computer-aided manufacturing systems*.

Research and Development Information Systems. *Research and development information systems* are concerned with what is as well as what could be. They are used to calculate "what if?" scenarios, such as the profit that will be generated if a new product line achieves a 5 percent, 10 percent, or 25 percent market share.

Decision support systems help research and development business subsystems decide which products and services to continue producing and which ones to abandon.

Human Resources Information Systems. *Human resources information systems* are used to provide information on current and future personnel. Traditional personnel information systems produce payrolls, maintain personnel records, and analyze labor costs. More sophisticated systems also provide training and development analysis, employee skills inventories, and personnel requirements forecasting.

Computer Services Information Systems. As noted earlier, the computer services department creates information systems. Like any other department, however, it needs information to meet its goals. *Computer services information systems* help the computer services department determine whether it is meeting its goals. These systems include reports describing projects undertaken, targeted and actual dates of completion, and targeted and actual personnel requirements and costs for each project.

Information systems specifically designed for different business subsystems can provide significant benefits to the business as a whole. However, there are other ways in which computer information systems aid businesses. One is by making it easier for various departments to exchange data and information with other departments. (See Figure 11-5.) For example, the data that is input to the production department comes from orders generated by the marketing and sales department, and the information that is output from the production department is sent along to the accounting department to generate bills, or in the case of returns, customer credits.

Another way computer information systems benefit businesses is by providing data and information vertically to all levels of management. (See Figure 11-6.) Information from each subsystem is used to help top managers make major decisions such as whether to drop or expand a new product line.

Commonly Used Computer Information Systems

The most commonly used computer information systems include systems designed for accounting, inventory, and sales ap-

FIGURE 11-5

Horizontal Exchange of Data

This figure illustrates the exchange of data that takes place as a customer's order moves through the company.

Department	Sales	Production	Accounting
Document	Order →	Work Order →	Invoice
Data	Order # Customer # Customer name Item Order date Vendor	Work order # Customer # Customer name Item Order date Vendor Order #	Invoice # Customer # Customer name Item Order date Vendor Order # Work order #

plications. Although our discussion will focus on business applications, many of these systems can also be used by nonprofit organizations. For example, nonprofit organizations must account for their financial activities even though their goal is not to make a profit. In many cases they may also modify information systems designed for commercial inventory and sales applications.

The information systems described in this section are simplified models of a very complex reality. As you will recall from the discussion at the beginning of the chapter, organizational applications take a long time, usually several months, if not years, to be developed and implemented by a team of computer specialists and users.

Accounting Systems

Accounting systems are at the heart of most organizations' computer information systems. In many organizations accounting applications were the first computer systems to be implemented. Several aspects of operations information systems for the accounting department resemble traditional clerical and control operations.

Accounts Receivable. Modern businesses function on credit. Many customers are unwilling to purchase goods or services from a company that will not extend credit. A business that extends credit to its customers must control two related

FIGURE 11-6

Vertical Exchange of Data

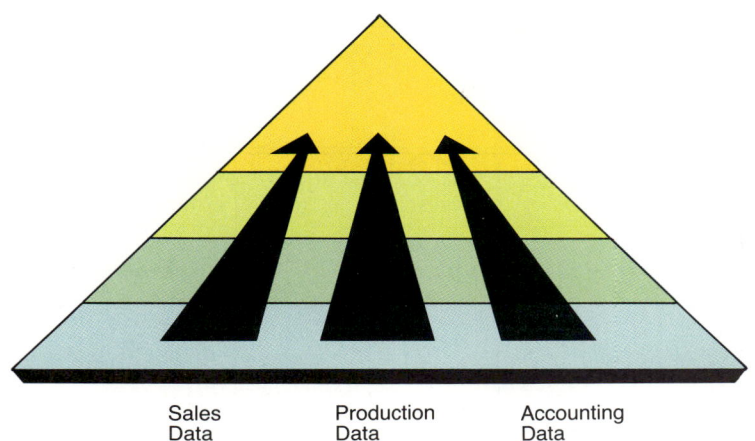

Data from each of the business subsystems may be transferred vertically to managers of the same or other subsystems. This transfer often involves summary data and is carried out by a management information system.

Sales Data | Production Data | Accounting Data

functions: the extension or denial of credit to particular clients and the collection of money owed to it. The latter function is the domain of the accounts receivable department. For decades many such departments have been using computers to help them carry out this task.

The basic objective of accounts receivable information systems is to achieve rapid payment of bills by customers. This objective can be met by producing accurate, legible statements on a regular basis, usually monthly. A secondary objective of these information systems is to inform management of the firm's overall credit situation as well as the credit picture for individual clients. A well-functioning system will increase the speed with which money is collected and reduce the number of bad debts.

There is no single standard type of accounts receivable system. Businesses can choose from a variety of systems, depending on their specific needs. Of course, the more sophisticated the system, the more money it will cost, the more time it will take to purchase or develop, and the greater the chance of error. The basic features of accounts receivable systems include the following:

1. The ability to apply cash on-line. This feature brings the customer's credit record up to date, enabling him or her to obtain further credit more rapidly.

2. The ability for the customer to direct payment to specific items rather than to the total unpaid balance. This feature is

FIGURE 11-7

An Aged Accounts Receivable (Overdue Bills) Report

Acme Manufacturing
Aged Accounts Receivable Report

July 17, 19XX

Amount due

Client Number	Client Name	0-30 days	31-60 days	61-90 days	over 90 days	Total due
188973	Golden Distributors	198.35	84.75	1779.19	122.52	2184.81
199187	Wabash Industries	0	535.00	0	0	535.00
292920	Beller Supplies	2000.19	214.75	0	0	2214.94
Total		2198.54	834.50	1779.19	122.52	4932.75
Number		3	4	1	1	9
Average		732.85	208.63	1779.19	122.52	548.31

particularly important when disputed items are included in the balance due.

3. The ability to enter adjustments for items such as payments, purchases, and interest charges.

4. The ability to handle different discount policies. For example, the company may offer varying discounts to customers who purchase different quantities of merchandise or pay their bills by a certain date.

5. The ability to interface with other systems, such as credit and general ledger.

Systems also differ widely in the reports they produce. Among the types of reports generated by accounts receivable systems are the following:

1. Aged accounts receivable reports. (See Figure 11-7.) ("Aging" accounts is the process of grouping accounts according to their due dates.)

2. Customer statements with dunning messages.

3. Daily business reports, including start-of-day and end-of-day totals, gross and net sales, cash receipts, and discounts.

4. Customer lists and mailing labels by territory, by industry, by vendor, and so forth.
5. Sales analysis reports by vendor, customer, and territory.

Payroll. The basic objectives of a payroll information system are the following:
1. To prepare accurate, timely paychecks for employees.
2. To collect and transfer mandatory deductions such as federal and state taxes.
3. To collect and transfer optional deductions such as employee savings plans and stock benefits.
4. To keep accurate records of sick leave and vacation credits. In addition, many organizations extend their payroll systems to provide information on labor costs and productivity.

For some organizations, meeting payroll objectives is a complicated process because of union contracts, sales commission plans, letters of agreement defining compensation and benefits for nonunion employees, and governmental regulations. It is not surprising that many organizations do not handle their payroll in-house but send it to an outside service for processing.

Among the characteristics of typical payroll systems are the following:
1. The ability to process different types of pay, including hourly, piecework, commission, and salaried employees, with or without overtime provisions. Many systems provide for direct deposit of checks.
2. The ability to perform automated calculations of federal, state, and local taxes.
3. The ability to perform automated calculations of deductions such as health insurance, savings bond purchases, union and professional association dues, and various fringe benefits.
4. The ability to apportion payroll costs to different accounts according to criteria defined by the user. For example, during a specific period a system could charge 30 percent of an employee's gross pay and fringe benefits to project A, 62 percent to project B, and 8 percent to general overhead.
5. The ability to perform automated check reconciliation, that is, to make sure that all checks have been cashed for the correct amount.

The payroll system produces a variety of reports, including payroll checks and stubs, reports for government agencies, check registers, and overtime reports.

Other Accounting Systems. Other accounting systems include *accounts payable*, whose objective is to pay the organization's bills at the latest date possible, taking into consideration any discounts offered for early payment; *fixed assets*, which handles data on the depreciation of fixed assets (such as machinery) for tax, financial reporting, and insurance purposes; and *general ledger*, whose objective is to consolidate all financial data within the firm and generate monthly and annual financial statements such as income statements and balance sheets. Many of these accounting systems usually are present in nonprofit organizations as well as in businesses. Regardless of the type of organization, it is necessary for the accounting information system to be integrated with the organization's other information systems.

Inventory Control and Management Systems

Inventory, meaning a stock of finished goods on hand and ready for shipment, is a necessity in most firms for two reasons: (1) to permit the firm to ship goods when they are ordered and (2) to make it possible to manufacture goods at times other than the time of sale. Inventory costs are high. They include interest charges on the unsold goods, storage costs, and an allowance for spoilage and pilferage. However, many firms could not do business without maintaining a certain level of inventory. Everything else being equal, customers will order from a company that can ship goods from stock rather than one that takes several weeks to produce or buy the item in question. Moreover, it is inefficient for a company to produce a single item on demand rather than manufacturing a series of items ahead of time.

It is difficult to calculate the optimum level of inventory. When parts of a product must be ordered from a supplier, the variables that enter into this calculation include the demand for the finished product, the purchase order cost, the cost per unit, the inventory carrying cost, and the time it takes the supplier to furnish the item. Similar calculations are required for in-house production. In addition, the cost of "stockouts," that is, not having an item in stock, must be estimated. Other factors that influence buying patterns include the state of the economy and the impact of the company's advertising campaigns.

Computers can perform the large volume of calculations necessary to manage a sizable inventory. They can provide useful reports, thereby freeing personnel from many of the day-to-day details involved in controlling and managing inventories. These individuals can then devote their efforts to analyzing existing inventory management policies and procedures and to developing new ones if necessary.

Computerized inventory management systems perform the following functions:

1. Maintain a cost history for all items based on purchases and the cost of preparing an order.
2. Process receipts of inventory, including item number, quantity ordered, quantity received, vendor number, and purchase order number.
3. Automatically reorder items, generating purchase orders based on criteria defined by the user.
4. Prepare and process cancellations for items that have been ordered but not received.
5. Reassign order quantities on the basis of changed demand, unit cost, purchase order, and inventory carrying cost.

The reports produced by inventory management systems include a daily listing of all inventory activity, including receipts, returns, and purchases; a list of suggested items to order and the appropriate quantities; a list indicating the amounts of all items in stock; a comparison of calculated inventory with physical inventory (i.e., the amount actually in stock); and a picking list, that is, a list of items to be removed from stock and assembled into orders.

Sales Analysis Systems

Sales analysis systems have three basic objectives: to produce commission statements, to determine the profitability of individual products and product lines, and to aid specialists in analyzing markets and forecasting sales. They perform the following functions:

1. Provide sales data by vendor, customer number, item number, territory, selling price, discount, and so forth.
2. Calculate current-period (e.g., week, month, or quarter) and year-to-date amounts and comparable figures for past periods.
3. Compare actual and budgeted data and analyze any differences between them.
4. Provide for a thirteen-period fiscal year if required.

A sales analysis system provides a variety of reports, including daily summaries of sales activity by territory, vendor, customer, and item; analyses of sales by each vendor and their contribution to profits; analyses of sales to each customer and their contribution to profits; and reports on vendor commissions.

With this brief description of computer information systems used by businesses, we conclude our introduction to information systems. In the next chapter we will examine the process of creating and maintaining such systems, that is, the system development life cycle.

SUMMARY

1. Personal applications of computers usually serve a single user. They tend to be interactive, use small data bases, have moderate security requirements, have a short implementation time and not require the services of specialists. Organizational applications serve many users and tend to have noninteractive aspects, use large data bases, have stringent security requirements, take a long time to implement, and require the services of technical personnel.

2. All systems have a goal or goals; operate according to well-defined procedures; are composed of parts that must be coordinated and can themselves be considered small systems; and provide feedback. In addition, most systems exist to benefit people and constantly interact with them.

3. There are three basic categories of computer information systems: operations information systems, management information systems, and decision support systems. In general, less sophisticated information systems are used by personnel at lower levels of the management hierarchy.

4. A business is usually divided into subsystems (commonly called departments). Among these are marketing, finance, accounting, production, research and development, and human resources or personnel. The computer services or data processing department is responsible for creating and maintaining computer information systems for all departments in the organization.

5. The various subsystems of a business benefit from computer information systems in three main ways: (a) They get information from computer systems that are specifically designed to meet their needs. (b) They exchange data and information with other business subsystems. (c) They can take advantage of computer information systems that provide data and information to all levels of management, transcending departmental boundaries.

6. The basic objective of an accounts receivable information system is to achieve rapid payment of bills by customers. A secondary objective is to inform management of the company's overall credit situation as well as the credit picture for individual customers. A payroll information system prepares paychecks for employees, collects and transfers mandatory and optional deductions, and keeps records of sick leave and vacation credits.

7. Computers can perform the large volume of calculations necessary to manage a sizable inventory, thereby freeing inventory personnel to analyze inventory management policies and procedures.

8. Sales analysis systems have three basic objectives: to produce commission statements, to determine the profitability of individual products and product lines, and to aid specialists in analyzing markets and forecasting sales.

REVIEW QUESTIONS

1. Compare and contrast personal and organizational applications of computers. Describe the role of users and specialists in each case.

2. Define the term *system* and describe a system with which you are familiar. Identify the components of the system.

3. Compare and contrast the three levels of information systems. How are they related to the levels of management?

4. Describe the basic objectives of each of the following business subsystems: marketing, finance and accounting, production, research and development, human resources, and computer services.

5. List the major ways in which business subsystems can benefit from computer information systems.

6. Describe the basic objectives of computer information systems for a firm's marketing, finance and accounting, production, research and development, human resources, and computer services departments.

7. Describe the main features of accounts receivable information systems.

8. Describe the main features of payroll systems.

9. Describe the main features of inventory management and control systems.

10. Describe the main features of sales analysis information systems.

APPLICATIONS

1. Report on the use of computers in an accounts receivable information system, using either interviews or articles in trade or business publications. What is the role of microcomputers, if any, in this system?

2. Report on the use of computers in an inventory management and control system.

3. Report on the use of computers in a business information system other than one discussed in the text.

4. Report on the use of computers in an application for a nonprofit organization. Compare this application with a business application.

CASE FOR DISCUSSION

Sometime within the next ten years or so, a Nebraska farmer will switch on his TV set and settle back for the evening while his new assistant tends the weeds on the back forty. Chugging down rows of crops, the assistant—a computerized, radar-controlled vehicle fitted with a machine vision system, a pump, and a few gallons of herbicide—will stop briefly at a clump of vegetation to analyze its shape and complexity. If the image is substantially different from that of crops stored in the computer's memory, a signal will go out to the pump and a preset burst of liquid will be delivered to the doomed plant.

The automated weed killer is just one example of the "smart machines" that may be working on some American farms by the end of this decade. These systems, called *prescription farming*, aim to boost the productivity of U.S. agriculture and reverse declines in its international competitiveness. Also included are irrigation and fertilization based on networks of computers and sensors. Robotized harvesters, automated animal-control devices, and food-handling and food-processing equipment are nearing trials.

"The challenge now is to develop these machines, which consider every variable as you go down the field and make the necessary adjustments," says James Anderson, dean of agriculture at Michigan State University (East Lansing) and past president of the American Society of Agricultural Engineers.

The notion of fully automated farms—in which robotic tractors traverse fields day and night, in good weather and bad, sensing variations in field conditions and automatically correcting for them—is not as fanciful as it sounds. "The technology is here," says Ralph Nave, national program leader for energy and engineering at the U.S. Department of Agriculture's Agricultural Research Service (ARS—Beltsville, Md.). "Being able to accurately locate the tractor or combine in the field is probably five years away."

Much of the technology focuses on controlling one of the most important of all farm resources: water. Using new methods of measuring water and turning it on and off only as needed, prescription farming could dramatically reduce water consumption and make every drop count, especially in areas where water is steadily being diverted to urban populations. And by extending water-sensing techniques to fertilizer control, smart farm machines could protect the supply of drinking water by limiting the amount of fertilizers used, thereby preventing residues from accumulating in the groundwater.

Conventional irrigation-monitoring systems use timers or measures of water flow—indirect indicators of the amount of moisture in the soil. Moisture must then be calculated using estimates of average rates of evaporation and transpiration. Whenever actual rates differ from the average, the wrong amount of water is delivered.

A sensor-based system for monitoring soil moisture has been developed by Richard Miller, a professor of electrical engineering at the University of Central Florida (Orlando). Miller compares the sensor and its associated electronics, computer, and controls to a home heating system. "You set your thermostat and the system controls the temperature of your house," he says. "Our computer checks the soil moisture through a sensor and controls the irrigation system to keep the soil moisture in a preset range. It has the potential to do the same thing with fertilizer."

Source: Paul Raeburn, "Automating America's Heartland," *High Technology*, December 1985, pp. 48–55.

CASE QUESTIONS

1. Consider a fully automated farm. Describe each of the four characteristics of a system as applied to the farm.

2. Now consider one of the machines used for prescription farming, such as the automated weed-killing vehicle or an automated watering machine. Can you identify each of the four characteristics of a system for this subsystem alone? Are there subsystems of this subsystem as well? If so, comment on them.

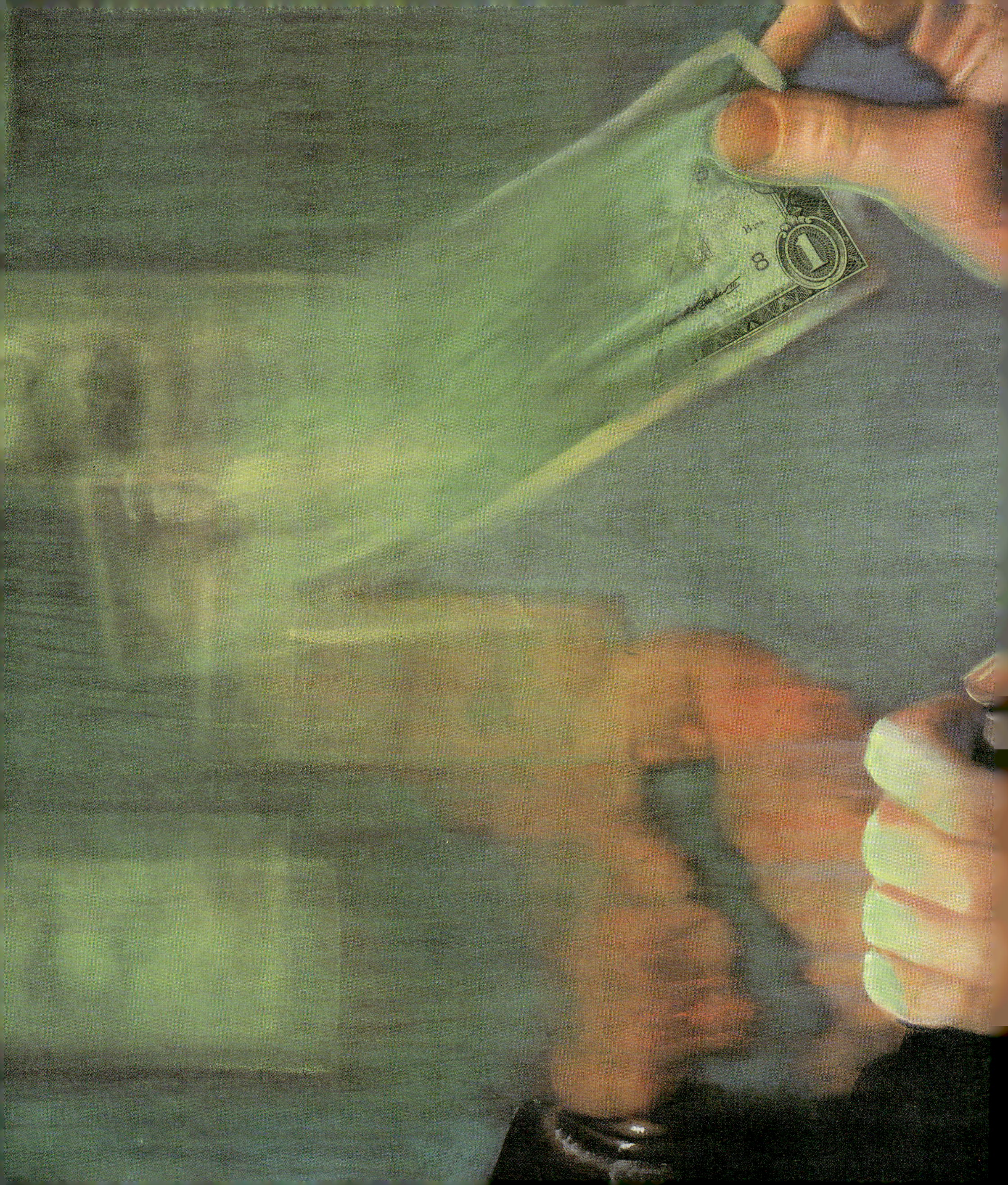

Management and Systems Analysis

CHAPTER

12

"Gamma missile inbound four o'clock high!" squawks a synthesized voice. The starship pilot immediately identifies the threat on the computer display in front of her: a flashing red blip that is rapidly growing larger.

What to do? There are two options: (1) Fire an interceptor missile. Probability of success, 70 percent. (2) Take evasive action in the form of a dive into hyperspace. The gamma missile, which lacks hyperspace drive, cannot follow. But a dive into hyperspace will take the pilot out of action for several precious minutes.

The flashing blip grows larger. "Estimated impact three seconds . . . two seconds . . . one second . . ." continues the synthesized voice, emotionlessly. The starship is in trouble. The pilot fires an interceptor missile. Too late!

"Fatal error. Game over. Would you like to play again?" says the toneless voice.

"No," types Lisette Morin, the pilot. It's a good game, but too much like real life. Her department is in as much trouble as the imaginary starfighter.

Morin is assistant director of accounts receivable for PDQ Distributors, a distributor of arcade games, home video games, and other electronic entertainment items. The company is a big one, but it hasn't been big very long. That's part of the problem. It started out just five years before in one corner of a basement. Now it is a major player in the market for video games, but some of its internal operations still reflect its informal origins.

The accounts receivable department is one of the trouble spots. In recent months it has been taking an average of three days to prepare and mail an invoice once an item has been shipped. Also, billing clerks have fallen behind in locating customers' credit limits and payment histories. This creates a dilemma for Morin. Often she must decide how to handle an account without adequate information. Should she fire a defensive missile by denying credit but, in doing so, risk losing the account? Or should she take a dive into hyperspace, extending credit without knowing the customer's past payment performance?

Morin has considered improving the computer programs used in processing accounts receivable, but she knows that the trouble is more than a programming problem. The only solution seems to be to develop a whole new payments system.

On her way back from lunch, she runs into Rene Howarth, the credit manager. "Rene," she says, "I've got a preliminary systems request form ready to go to the computer services department. Let's put it through this afternoon."

The world of business is constantly changing, and companies, like starship pilots, must react quickly if they are to survive. PDQ's problem in managing change is typical of companies that start out small and grow quickly. PDQ has found that the information systems that help a firm meet its objectives must develop and change as the company does. If a company is not yet computerized, the appropriate next step may be to install a computer system; if it already has such a system, management should probably consider new ways of applying the existing system or an upgraded system.

Information systems are both an agent of change and a tool for harnessing change. This chapter examines information systems and describes how systems analysts deal with the need to change those systems as an organization changes. The system development life cycle is explored and is compared to the program development process presented in Chapter 7.

When you have read this chapter you should be able to:

1. Describe the effect of change on organizations and their information systems.
2. Identify the personnel involved in the development and maintenance of computer systems.
3. Discribe the phases of the system development life cycle, indicating the personnel and tools involved in each phase.
4. Understand and use the key terms listed at the end of the chapter.

Systems and Change

Modern societies are faced with an unprecedented degree of change. Changes are occurring in many area simultaneously; technological, economic, social, and political changes combine to create an extremely challenging environment for businesses and other organizations. This is having an enormous impact on businesses in general and their computer information systems in particular. To succeed, businesses and their computer information systems must keep up with and adjust to the changes in their environment and, when possible, anticipate and prepare for them.

A Brief Review

As we saw in Chapter 11, a system is a collection of interrelated parts that work together to meet specified objectives. All systems share certain properties: They have a goal; they operate according to well-defined procedures; they are composed of parts that must be coordinated and may themselves be considered subsystems; they provide feedback. In addition, people are an integral element of most systems.

Businesses rely on a variety of systems, including operations information, management information, and decision support systems, to meet their daily needs and set and evaluate their short- and long-term goals. Each of these systems also plays a role in enabling the business to meet its major objective: making a profit. This goal can be attained only if the various subsystems of the business, such as marketing, finance and accounting, and production, work together in the interests of the company, adjusting to change and, whenever possible, planning ahead. The system that enables these various subsystems to work together efficiently and effectively is the information system.

System Personnel

Systems consist of many interrelated parts and as such involve many people who perform different but interrelated tasks. Similarly, the program development process discussed in Chapter 7 involves different people who carry out different but related functions. The many groups of people who deal with computer systems include the systems analyst, users and management, computer programmers, and other computer personnel.

The Systems Analyst. The systems analyst is the computer specialist who is responsible for analyzing the business subsystem and developing the computer information system. He or she serves as a liaison between users, who work with the system, and programmers, who develop programs that process data at the request of users. A systems analyst may or may not know how to program but must be familiar with computers and with the business application for which the system is being designed.

Systems analysts are agents of change. Part of their job is to help convince management that a proposed system makes sense and to obtain the cooperation of all of the system's potential users, including those who are staunchly opposed to a computerized environment or see no need to change the existing system. During the first stages of system development, the analyst is responsible for explaining to users what the computer can or cannot do for them and for helping them make choices within the framework of the organization's special constraints and requirements.

This systems analyst is meeting with programmers to make sure that they understand her instructions for preparing a new information system. She also confers with users on a regular basis to ensure that their needs will be met by the new system. (© Freda Leinwand.)

Users and Managers. Chapter 2 introduced several categories of computer users, ranging from people who have no direct contact with the computer system, such as a client telephoning a travel agent to reserve airline seats, to sophisticated microcomputer users, sometimes called power users. This chapter focuses on the middle range of users, including managers and operations personnel such as clerks and vendors.

Managers play an important role in system development. At each stage in the system development process they decide whether to accept the system as recommended, to modify it, or to cancel the project. Their support can make the difference between success and failure for a project. Experience has shown that the higher the level of management that actively supports a system development project and the more visible that support, the greater the project's chances of success.

Computer Programmers. Computer programmers are not business specialists, but programmers who are familiar with a particular business specialty tend to produce better programs and more productive systems than those who lack relevant experience. For example, a programmer who has worked on several accounts payable systems can contribute valuable ideas during the development of such systems. He or she may recognize incomplete or incorrect specifications, thereby saving the organization time and money.

Other Personnel. In addition to systems analysts, users, and programmers, other types of personnel may interact with computer systems. Operations personnel within a user's department include clerks and vendors. Other computer specialists who

A field engineer inserts a new circuit board in an IBM computer. Within a minute the computer will be running again. (Courtesy of International Business Machines.)

CHAPTER 12   443   MANAGEMENT AND SYSTEMS ANALYSIS

may be required for an information system to function efficiently include computer operators (to run the computer), field engineers (to repair hardware), librarians (to keep track of magnetic disks and tapes), and other personnel (to keep track of the system's output and distribute it to users).

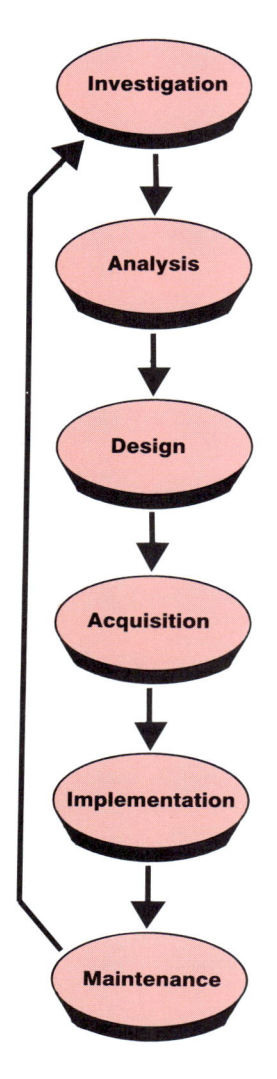

The System Development Life Cycle

The **system development life cycle** is the set of activities required to produce an information system. It is an ongoing process in which the system is created, grows, matures, and eventually outlives its usefulness and ceases to exist. The system development life cycle is often divided into six steps, as follows:

1. *Investigation.* Systems analysts and users work together to define the problem to be solved and determine whether a solution is feasible given such constraints as budget, personnel, and development time.

2. *Analysis.* Systems analysts and users collect data on how the business subsystem and the existing information system actually work. This data is analyzed to determine where change is needed.

3. *Design.* In this step, systems analysts and users determine how to build the new or revised information system. The participants decide on the hardware and software required to construct the information system, and they produce the initial programming specifications.

4. *Acquisitions.* The approved hardware and software are acquired, or programs are developed in-house.

5. *Implementation.* The information system is put into use. This phase involves testing the programs and the way they fit into people's operating environment.

6. *Maintenance.* Like program maintenance, system maintenance is an ongoing process; it includes both correcting errors and modifying the information system to meet user needs.

The System Development Life Cycle

System development life cycle
A set of activities whose goal is to produce an information system.

PEOPLE AND SYSTEMS 444 PART 4

At some point, however, the system no longer meets user needs adequately and must be replaced. Then the system development life cycle begins again. Note that few systems are ever developed in order, from step 1 to step 6. Analysts and users often return to previous activities and phases to change or complete information.

In many ways the system development life cycle is similar to the program development process discussed in Chapter 7. Both require a multidisciplinary team, including computer specialists and users, and both consist of similar stages extending from problem definition to product maintenance. The main difference between them lies in the scope of the problem to be solved. The program development process may be used when the problem to be solved does not change the basic flow of work within a department. We saw an example of this in Chapter 7 when Acme's accounts payable department requested a program that would aid in determining which bills to pay on certain dates. In contrast, when the problem to be solved involves major changes in the way work is performed, the program development process is usually insufficient. In such cases it may be necessary to combine hardware, software, and personnel to create an information system.

Although there is some disagreement regarding the specific stages of the system development life cycle, many organizations follow the six stages listed and described here.

System Investigation

System investigation

The stage of the system development life cycle that consists of defining the problem to be solved and determining whether a feasible solution exists.

System investigation consists of two activities: defining the problem and determining whether a feasible solution exists, given such constrains as budget, personnel, and time. These activities are carried out jointly by systems analysts and users. This initial stage ends with a report stating the problem and the feasibility of attempting to solve it with available resources.

Defining the Problem. Defining the problem is the most important activity in the system development life cycle. The future success of the system requires that the systems analyst and user develop a clear statement of the problem and the objectives and scope of the proposed solution. An investment of time at this point can pay off handsomely in later stages. It must be kept in mind that although the managers of the client organization are aware that there is a problem before the systems analyst is called in, they may have only a hazy idea of what the problem is. Box 12-1 describes a typical case.

BOX 12-1

MANAGING CHANGE

Help! Our Network Is Out of Control

In a fast-changing business, a system that seems to be working can quickly develop problems. This happened to Eastern Financial Group (EFG), a large multistate financial institution with headquarters in Philadelphia. The problem reached Bill Glikbarg, an IBM systems analyst, in the form of a not very specific cry for help: "Our network is out of control." And it was not a small network, either. It consisted of some 15,000 terminals in offices scattered over half a dozen states up and down the Eastern Seaboard.

In what way was it out of control? EFG's managers were not quite sure. They just knew that there were complaints—that things didn't work, didn't get fixed when they didn't work, and so on. The initial contact led to a three-month system investigation effort that involved interviews with about fifty operations managers, planning managers, designers, and engineers who ran the EFG network.

One of the first things Glikbarg's team found was that EFG's engineers and designers were so busy putting out fires that they never had time to think about the network as a whole. "Four more terminals, quick, in the Elizabeth, New Jersey, office." "We can't access the data base we need for a big report that's due Friday." That sort of thing.

One problem was that the system had grown at such a speed and in such a way that the people running it had lost track of who had what equipment where. In would come a seemingly simple request from a user—"my terminal is broken." But what kind of terminal? What is it hooked up to? What kind of software? What part of it is broken? It had become increasingly difficult for the people responsible for fixing things to get answers to basic questions like these.

Glikbarg found that EFG had twenty-five "help stations" that users could call when they wanted something fixed. Responsibility was divided among them in such a way that a call to Station 1 would get a response like, "Oh, I see. You'll have to call Station 14 on that one." Station 14 would pass the problem to Station 5, Station 5 to Station 19, and so on. For each station the user would have to go through a long explanation of what the equipment was, where it was, what the software was, and what the problem was.

Working closely with EFG's managers, Glikbarg and his fellow IBM analysts developed a system investigation report, or "system architecture study," as IBM calls it. This report laid out the requirements for the new system. For example, in the case of the help station aspect of the problem, several requirements were formulated:

- Each user station should have a code number. When the user gives the code number to the help station operator, the operator should immediately be able to call up on a screen the location, equipment type, and so on.
- If the first station contacted can't fix the problem, that station operator should be able to transfer the call to the appropriate station without disconnecting.
- The first station contacted should always be responsible for following up the call. For example, the day after a call, the station should call the user back to say, "Yesterday I transferred you to Station 10. Did they solve your problem?"
- The help station system should include an artificial intelligence capability to handle routine problems. With the computer using voice synthesis and the user responding via the touch-tone pad on a telephone, simple problems could be handled in a question-and-answer format. If the problem could not be solved in this way, it would at least be better defined and routed to the appropriate human help station operator.

The help station problem was just one of many that were covered in IBM's system architecture study. Because it would not be reasonable to try to fix everything at once, the document included a system of priorities. The priorities were based on "business cases" that estimated the payback period for investments in various aspects of the system. For example, it might be estimated that the $100,000 spent to enable help station operators to switch calls directly to other stations would pay for itself in nine months in terms of time saved by users. The investment in the artificial intelligence capability might take fifteen months to pay for itself. Both were worth doing, but the call-switching problem was worth solving first.

The report was accepted by the client and became the basis for a phased design and implementation program. At that point the problem passed out of Glikbarg's hands. It was not long before another client was on the phone. "We need some terminals. Can you help?"

The Feasibility Study. When the problem has been defined to the satisfaction of all concerned, a **feasibility study** is carried out to determine whether a particular problem can be solved with the resources available. Typically, the study considers several potential solutions to the stated problem and concentrates on the most promising ones.

To determine whether a project is feasible, it is necessary to weigh several related aspects: financial, technical, temporal, and human. Businesses usually cannot consider a proposed system that does not make financial sense. If the project is expected to cost more than the additional revenue it is likely to generate, it is usually terminated without further ado.

The technical feasibility of a project refers to whether it can be accomplished given the hardware, software, and computer personnnel that an organization has or can acquire. If, for example, the proposed solution includes a local area network or requires an experienced C-language programmer and those facilities or personnel are not available, the solution must be modified or rejected.

Temporal feasibility refers to whether the system can be completed within the allotted time frame. For example, ninety days is not enough time for an organization to develop its own accounts receivable system but may be enough for it to select, purchase, and install a commercial accounts receivable package, especially if little or no modification is required.

The final feasibility consideration is the human one. There is no point in developing a system that cannot be run by the available operations personnel after a suitable training period. It may take the programmer longer to create a more user-friendly system, but the extra cost in terms of programming time will be offset by higher user productivity.

The System Investigation Report. The problem definition and associated feasibility study culminate in the production of a report summarizing the system investigation stage. Although the specific contents of the report depend on the nature and scope of the project, it typically contains the following types of information:

1. A detailed statement of the objectives and scope of the project. This statement is phrased in business rather than technical terms and includes quantitative measures, such as costs in terms of both time and money, to enable people to determine whether the objectives have been met when the system is put into service.

2. The names and functions of all personnel assigned to the project and a request that they be authorized to contact other employees when necessary to obtain information.

Feasibility study
A study that determines whether or not a particular problem can be solved with the resources allocated by management.

3. A brief description of the business subsystem, its present information system, the changes to be made, and the expected impact of those changes.
4. An evaluation of the feasibility of the proposed solutions, including their financial, technical, and human aspects.
5. A list of policy questions that the system team is unable to answer, with a request that management supply the answers.
6. A timetable for the proposed system, including dates for the proposed steps in the project.

This report (as well as the other reports in the system development life cycle) is sent to management for approval. On the basis of the report, a decision is reached regarding whether the organization will proceed with the project, modify it, or terminate it.

System Investigation: An Example. To see how the system development life cycle functions in business, let's look at the case of PDQ Distributors, which was introduced at the beginning of the chapter. PDQ's problem, we saw, was an inadequate accounts receivable system. Lisette Morin, assistant director of accounts receivable, filed a preliminary systems request form. (See Figure 12-1.) The project was assigned to Senior Systems Analyst Barclay Rosser.

Next, Rosser, Morin, and Rene Howarth, the credit manager, met to define the problem—the first stage of the system development life cycle. The first thing they did was to translate the vague goal of speeding up the invoicing process into quantitative terms of having 90 percent of invoices mailed to customers within one working day of receiving the necessary forms. In a similar manner they formulated the goal of getting information to the credit department on time as follows: The credit department will be able to respond to 95 percent of clients' inquiries regarding availability of credit by accessing the new system.

Then the team examined the feasibility of different solutions according to financial, technical, temporal, and human criteria. They rejected any solution that required a new computer because of budget constraints, and they rejected any solution that was based on a data-base management system because all personnel with data-base experience had been assigned to long-term projects. After eliminating the clearly unfeasible solutions, they compared the feasible solutions to determine which one was best.

For example, they examined two ways in which the credit department could obtain information about clients: (1) It could access printed reports created by a batch-processing system, or (2) it could make inquiries from a workstation using an on-line system. The first solution would be quicker to implement and

FIGURE 12-1

Request for System Services

```
                    PDQ DISTRIBUTORS
              Preliminary Systems Request Form

From:     Morin, Lisette
Title:    Assistant Director of Accounts Receivable
Date:     February 15, 19XX

Subject:  We request that someone from the Computer Services Department
          investigate the possibility of examining the situation in our
          department: problems noted are excessive time to process bills
          and insufficient information for credit purposes.
```

would cost less, but it had the disadvantage of not providing up-to-date information. Although an on-line system would not have this drawback, the team decided that such a system would be too expensive for PDQ to implement.

The PDQ team conducted a *cost-benefit analysis* to determine whether the proposed solution would best meet the company's needs. First it determined the *tangible costs* to the company, that is, the direct costs of developing and operating the system:

	First Year	Second Year	Third Year
System development	$21,000		
Training	$5,200	$2,400	$1,200
System maintenance		$11,000	$12,100
Additional operating costs	$4,000	$4,400	$4,800

Next it determined the *tangible benefits*, that is, the direct financial benefits that would come from the new computerized system. One tangible benefit, accelerating PDQ's cash flow, would result from sending out bills two days earlier than before. At a 12 percent annual rate of interest it cost .12/365, or .0329 percent, to borrow money for a single day. Shortening the bill collection time by two days would save the company $658 for every $1 million billed each year, a substantial saving for a company billing over $13 million a year.

A System Investigation Report

```
New Accounts Receivable System
Report prepared by Rosser, B
Senior Systems Analyst, Computer Services
Date: March 15, 1989

Statement of objectives: Design and implement a new computer
information system for A/R that will (1) enable 90 percent of
invoices to be mailed to customers within 1 working day of
receiving the request for invoice and (2) enable the Credit
Department to respond to 95 percent of clients' telephone
inquiries concerning available credit.

Associated personnel
Rosser, Barclay: Senior Systems Analyst, Computer Services
Morin, Lisette: Assistant Director of Accounts Receivable
Howarth, Rene: Credit Manager

The above request permission to contact other personnel in
Accounts Receivable, Credit, and other departments during
working hours to obtain necessary information related to the
proposed system.
```

The *intangible costs and benefits* (that is, those for which a monetary value could not be allocated or assigned) were considered next. The team realized that initial employee dissatisfaction would lower productivity. During a meeting of the system study team, Howarth remarked that a properly designed training program could substantially reduce employee dissatisfaction and that the resultant intangible costs could be kept to a minimum. Rosser agreed, but commented that extended training requires careful explanation to higher management.

Rosser used an electronic spreadsheet to prepare the cost-benefit analysis. After examining the problem definition and the feasibility study, the manager of the accounting department recommended that the report be accepted, but asked that the team make an effort to cut costs and identify additional areas of possible benefit. Figure 12-2 shows part of the system investigation report presented to PDQ's management.

Systems Analysis

During the second stage of the system development life cycle, **systems analysis**, the systems analyst, aided by users and operations personnel, determines how the existing information system functions in order to design and develop the new system. This stage involves gathering and analyzing data using a variety of tools and diagrams. It culminates in a report that describes the present system and expands on information in the feasibility study report. If the systems analysis report is accepted by management, the project moves on to the next stage of the system development life cycle, systems design.

Gathering Data. The first step of systems analysis is gathering data on the existing information system—that is, learning about the organization, the people, and the work. Analysts typically begin to gather data by consulting written documentation, such as organization charts and procedure manuals. Ultimately, though, they need the cooperation of users and management for verification, clarification, and undocumented information.

An *organization chart* (see Figure 12-3), which resembles the hierarchy chart discussed in Chapter 7, illustrates the reporting relationships within an organization and shows the division of work, the type of work performed by each individual, the management hierarchy, and the way related jobs are grouped into departments. Like most documentation, it must be current to be useful and shows only the formal organization of the company.

Procedure manuals, also called *standards manuals*, describe how such activities as preparing a bill or shipping a package are to be carried out. Each department should have its own procedure manuals, which are used in training new employees and are available for reference by experienced employees. To be effective, such manuals must be updated promptly to reflect any change in procedures.

After obtaining an initial overview of the present system from written material, the analyst consults with the users and operations personnel by means of interviews and questionnaires. The analyst is trying to get a picture of the organization's informal structure in order to determine how the existing system really operates.

During interviews, analysts confirm their understanding of the written documentation and obtain insights into how operations are actually carried out and managed and what changes are desired. For example, the systems analyst might ask a clerk in the credit department how many requests for credit he or she receives per day or the approximate average amount of credit

Systems analysis
The stage of the system development life cycle in which the systems analyst, in conjunction with users, determines how the existing information system functions in order to design and develop a new system.

FIGURE 12-3

An Organization Chart

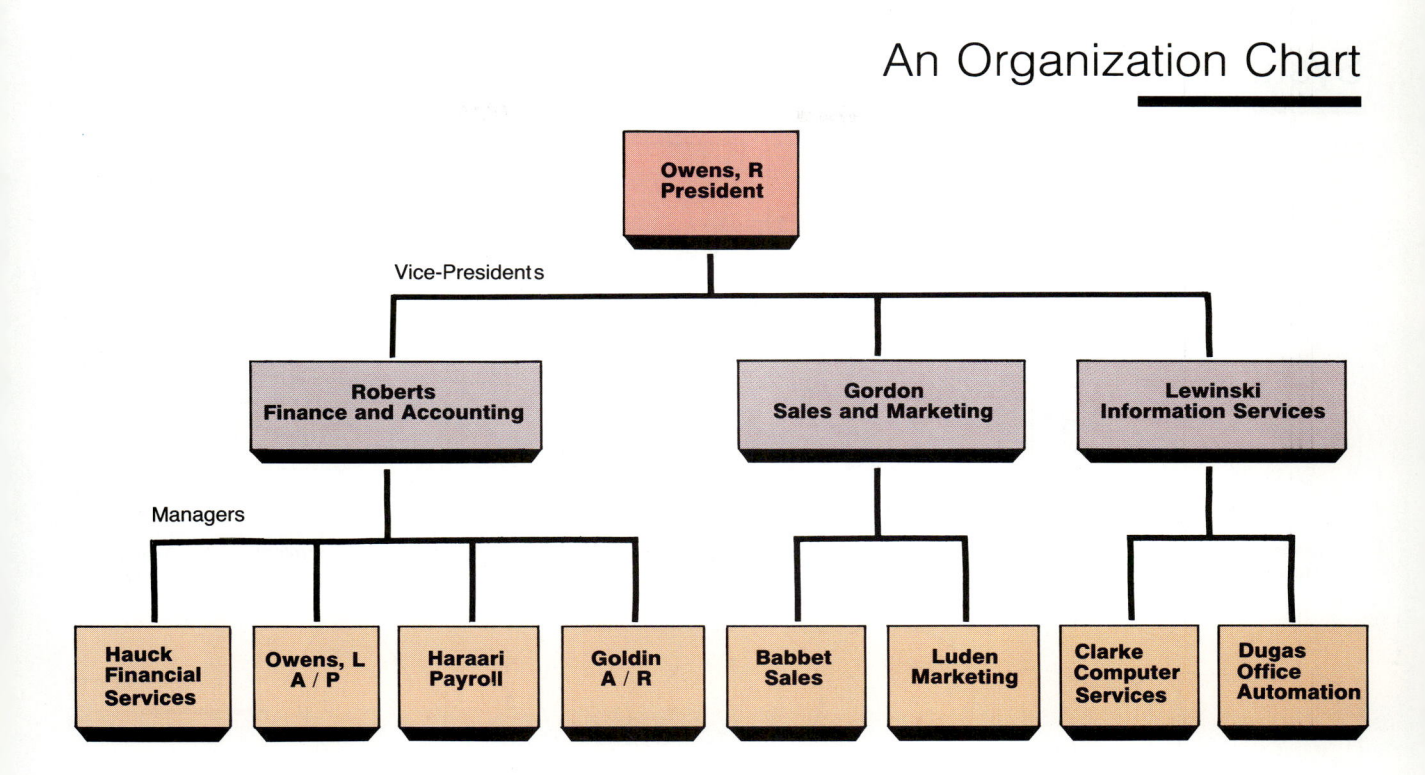

```
                        Owens, R
                        President
                           |
        Vice-Presidents
     _____|_____
    |                      |                      |
  Roberts               Gordon                Lewinski
Finance and         Sales and            Information
Accounting          Marketing              Services
    |                      |                      |
Managers
 ___|_____   ___|___         ___|___
|       |       |      |  |       |       |       |
Hauck  Owens,L Haraari Goldin Babbet Luden Clarke  Dugas
Financial A/P  Payroll A/R   Sales Marketing Computer Office
Services                                    Services Automation
```

requested. The analyst might ask a manager in the accounts receivable department about turnover among billing clerks. Questionnaires, which are often used to supplement interviews, solicit specific information from respondents. Analysts often distribute trial questionnaires to a limited number of participants before producing the final version. In our example, Rosser prepared a short questionnaire for selected clients that included the following questions:

1. How often do you purchase from PDQ Distributors?
2. What is the amount of your average purchase?
3. Do you purchase on credit? If so, what is your credit limit?
4. How long does it take to get your credit approved?
5. How satisfied are you with the way your credit applications are handled at PDQ Distributors?
6. What suggestions can you make concerning the way credit is handled at PDQ Distributors?

Other data-gathering techniques include observation and work sampling. In *observation*, the systems analyst or other spe-

FIGURE 12-4

System Flowcharting Symbols

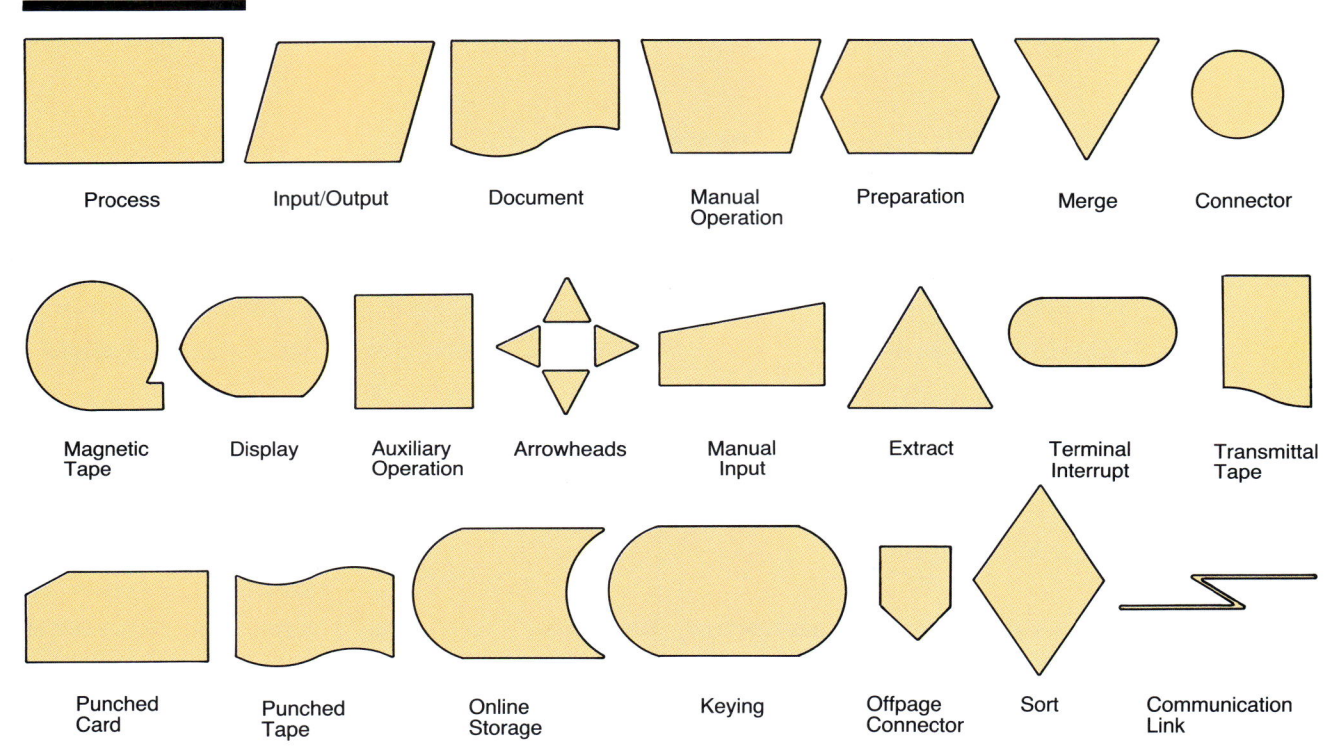

| Process | Input/Output | Document | Manual Operation | Preparation | Merge | Connector |

| Magnetic Tape | Display | Auxiliary Operation | Arrowheads | Manual Input | Extract | Terminal Interrupt | Transmittal Tape |

| Punched Card | Punched Tape | Online Storage | Keying | Offpage Connector | Sort | Communication Link |

These symbols are the standard defined by IBM. By combining several symbols it is possible to depict other items.

cialist (e.g., an industrial engineer) watches an operation such as producing a bill or preparing a package for shipment. In *work sampling*, representative transactions are selected for study. For example, the analyst might choose fifty invoices at random and gather statistics on the time it takes to complete and mail the invoices and the rate of error in preparing them. These statistics are used to evaluate the managers and operations personnel assigned to the system as well as the system itself.

Presenting and Analyzing Data. Once the data has been gathered, it has to be presented in a form that will allow it be validated and analyzed. The purpose of the data analysis step is to review the data and determine what is relevant to the users' needs. For example, samples of output are reviewed in order to ascertain which existing reports, if any, are not cur-

FIGURE 12-5

A System Flowchart

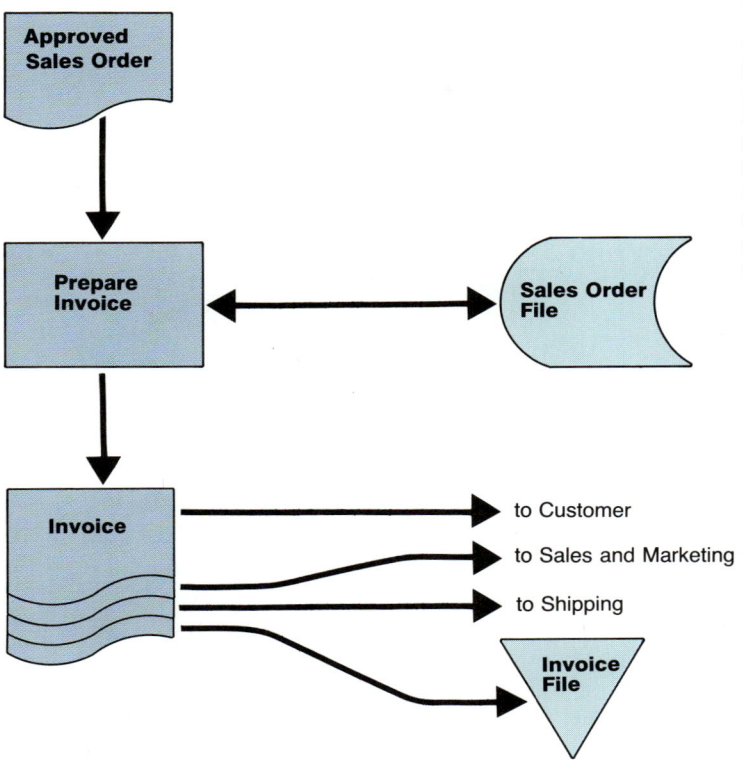

This flowchart segment illustrates the processing of an approved sales order at PDQ Distributors. Note the different symbols for the Sales Order File on magnetic disk and the manual Invoice File (stored in a filing cabinet).

rently used and whether any reports can be modified to facilitate their use by managers and operations personnel.

Among the diagrams used to present the data are flowcharts, data flow diagrams, and grid charts. *System flowcharts* represent the general flow of information and major processing steps within a system. As shown in Figure 12-4, they use some of the symbols used in program flowcharts, as well as other symbols that represent input and output devices and processing activities. Figure 12-5 is part of a system flowchart illustrating the processing of an approved sales order by the accounts receivable department.

System flowcharts are often criticized because they are difficult to prepare and modify, are not computerized, and do not express the concepts of structured programming and system de-

CHAPTER 12 455 MANAGEMENT AND SYSTEMS ANALYSIS

FIGURE 12-6

Data Flow Diagram Symbols

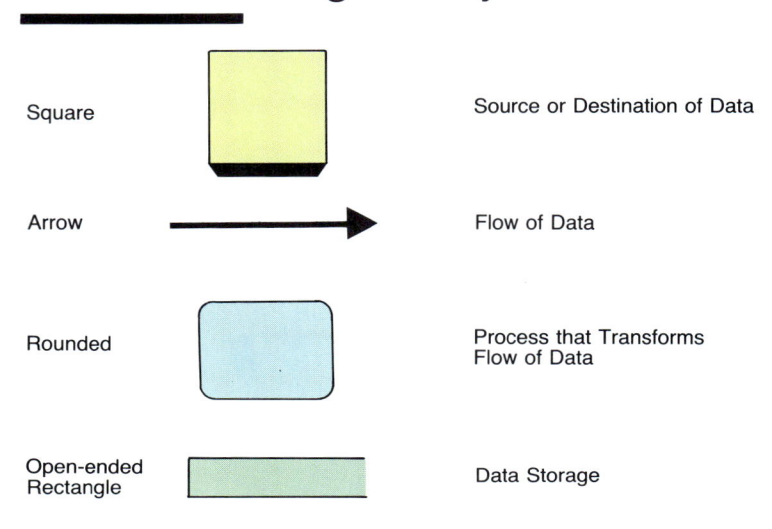

Symbol	Name	Meaning
Square		Source or Destination of Data
Arrow	→	Flow of Data
Rounded		Process that Transforms Flow of Data
Open-ended Rectangle		Data Storage

velopment. However, they do serve as a vehicle for communication between computer specialists and users and are used in many organizations.

Data flow diagrams are used by systems analysts to study the relationships among the elements of the existing information system. Using the four symbols shown in Figure 12-6, such diagrams show where the data comes from and goes to, the processes that transform the data, and the locations in which the data is stored. Data flow diagrams indicate *logical* details, such as what happens when a bill is sent or a payment is received, not *physical* details, such as whether a file is stored on magnetic tape or magnetic disk. (You will recall from Chapter 7 that one of the key features of the structured approach is that it delineates the logical interrelationships among activities within a program or system.)

Another useful diagram for analyzing and presenting results is the *grid chart*. Such a chart shows the relationships among elements in a business system; for example, the grid chart in Figure 12-7 shows which reports are used by different departments. Another use of grid charts is to provide a picture of which computer programs and which departments are using particular files. This information may be especially useful if a company decides to integrate an application into an existing data base.

FIGURE 12-7

A Grid Chart

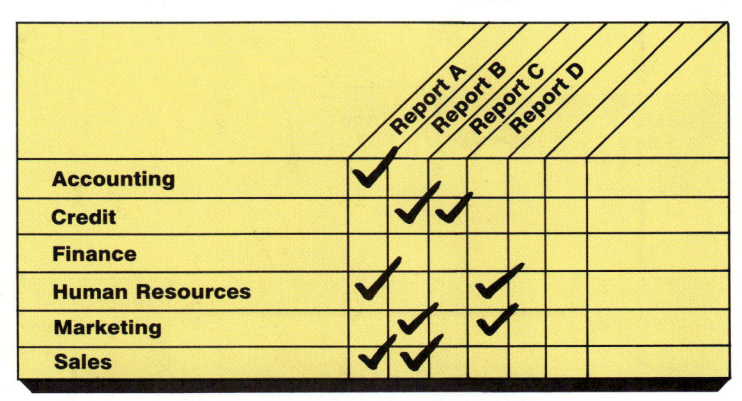

This type of diagram can show which departments receive which reports. Other grid charts are used to show relationships such as between programs and files or between departments and programs.

	Report A	Report B	Report C	Report D		
Accounting	✓					
Credit		✓	✓			
Finance						
Human Resources	✓		✓			
Marketing		✓	✓			
Sales	✓	✓				

The Systems Analysis Report. The gathering, presentation, and analysis of data culminates in a report that typically contains the following information:
- A restatement of the problem, with changes that reflect the data analysis.
- A model of the existing information system, describing its business objectives, main processing functions and operations, and personnel.
- Difficulties associated with the existing system.
- An indication of how the existing system interfaces with other business subsystems and information systems.
- A transcript of all interviews and a summary of questionnaire results.
- A preliminary cost-benefit analysis of the proposed system.
- An updated calendar for development of the proposed system.
- A technical appendix, which includes the diagrams produced during the systems analysis stage and a preliminary list of input, output, processing, storage, and other requirements.

Systems Analysis at PDQ Manufacturing. PDQ's systems analyst, Barclay Rosser, began the systems analysis stage by reviewing the documentation prepared by the previous systems team. Rosser noted that the system flowcharts showing operations in the credit department were missing or out of date. Figure 12-8 illustrates the interface between the accounts receivable and credit departments.

FIGURE 12-8

A System Flowchart

This is a simplified example of a system flowchart representing the present billing system at PDQ Distributors, produced during systems analysis. Note the use of different symbols for manual and computerized files.

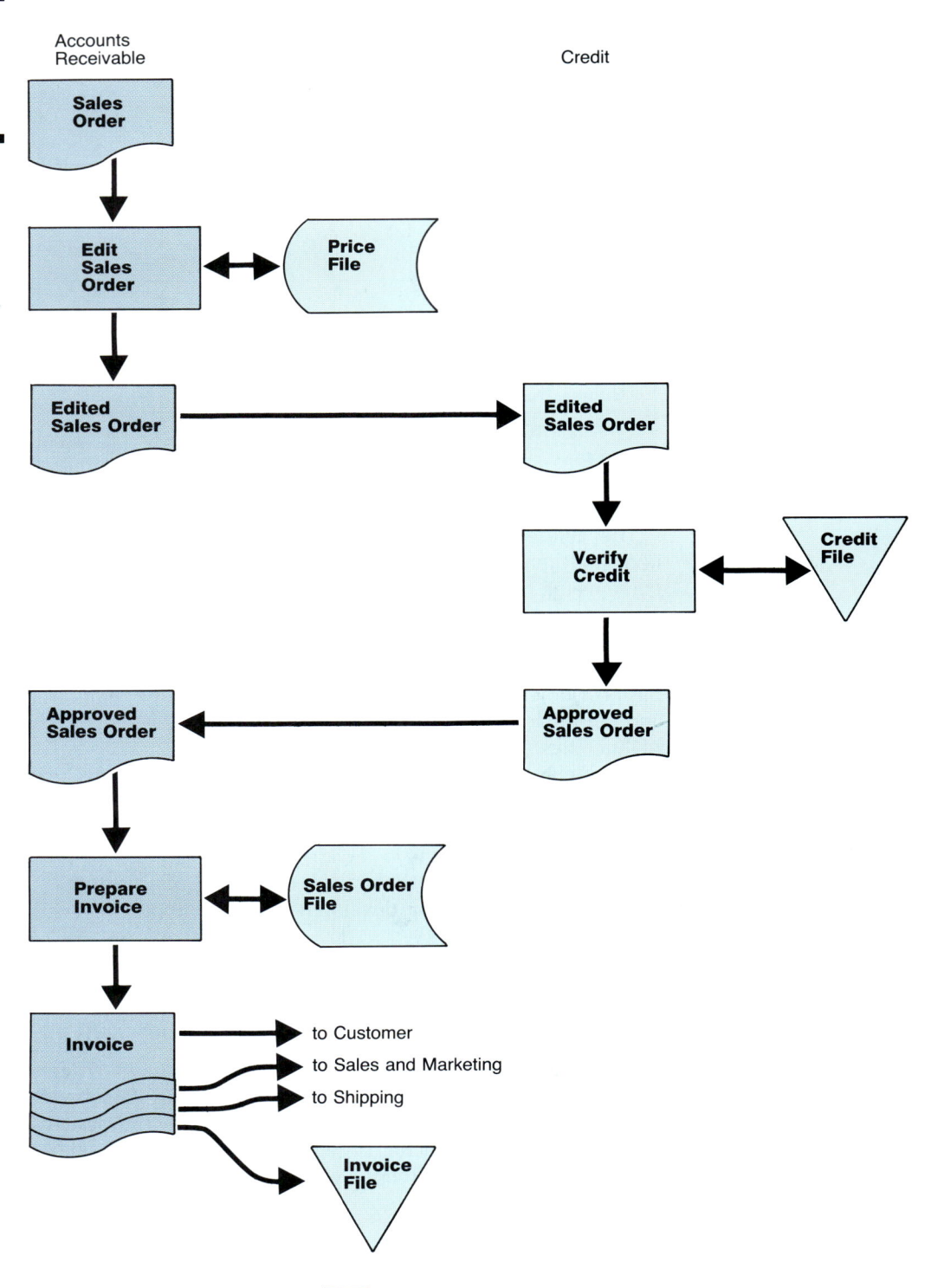

Accounts Receivable

Sales Order → Edit Sales Order ↔ Price File

Edit Sales Order → Edited Sales Order → Edited Sales Order (Credit)

Credit

Edited Sales Order → Verify Credit ↔ Credit File → Approved Sales Order → Approved Sales Order (Accounts Receivable) → Prepare Invoice ↔ Sales Order File → Invoice

Invoice:
- to Customer
- to Sales and Marketing
- to Shipping
- Invoice File

PEOPLE AND SYSTEMS 458 PART 4

After receiving permission from Morin and Howarth, Rosser spent several hours just observing how people in the accounts receivable and credit departments carried out their work; he then interviewed them. He also consulted trade journals to familiarize himself with how other companies were developing accounts receivable systems, and he collected literature on accounts receivable systems using personal computers.

Rosser then prepared sketches of the data flow diagrams in Figure 12-9 and reviewed them with Morin and Howarth. He also prepared detailed grid charts for all the reports, files, and programs in the system. These would be used in describing PDQ's traditional file-processing system and, eventually, in putting the firm's important applications into its data-base management system.

Finally, Rosser realized that the feasibility study had underestimated the time it would take to develop the system. He calculated that system development costs would be 40 percent higher than the initial estimates. After considerable discussion and a warning against further cost increases, management accepted the systems analysis report. The team immediately began working on the system design.

System Design

System design
The stage of the system development life cycle in which the hardware and software components of the new system are specified in detail.

System design is the third stage of the system development life cycle. In this stage the hardware and software components of the new information system are specified in detail. The systems analyst, working in conjunction with the user, determines the equipment necessary for input, output, storage, and communication, and produces the initial specifications for all the programs that will be included in the system. This stage is terminated by the system design report. If the system design report is accepted by management, the project moves on to the next stage of the system development life cycle, system acquisition.

As the system design progresses, users gain a better idea of what the new system will look like. They begin to request different or additional system functions. At first the analyst attempts to comply with the users' requests, but at some point it becomes impossible to make the changes requested and still meet schedule and budget constraints. At this point the analyst *freezes* the design. Any subsequent requests are handled during the system maintenance stage.

The system design stage is related to the solution design stage of the programming process; in both cases the goal is to produce a sufficiently detailed design to enable programmers to write one or more programs that will meet users' needs. How-

FIGURE 12-9

A Data Flow Diagram

This is a simplified example of a data flow diagram representing the present billing system at PDQ Distributors, produced during systems analysis. Note that there is no indication of whether a file is manual or computerized.

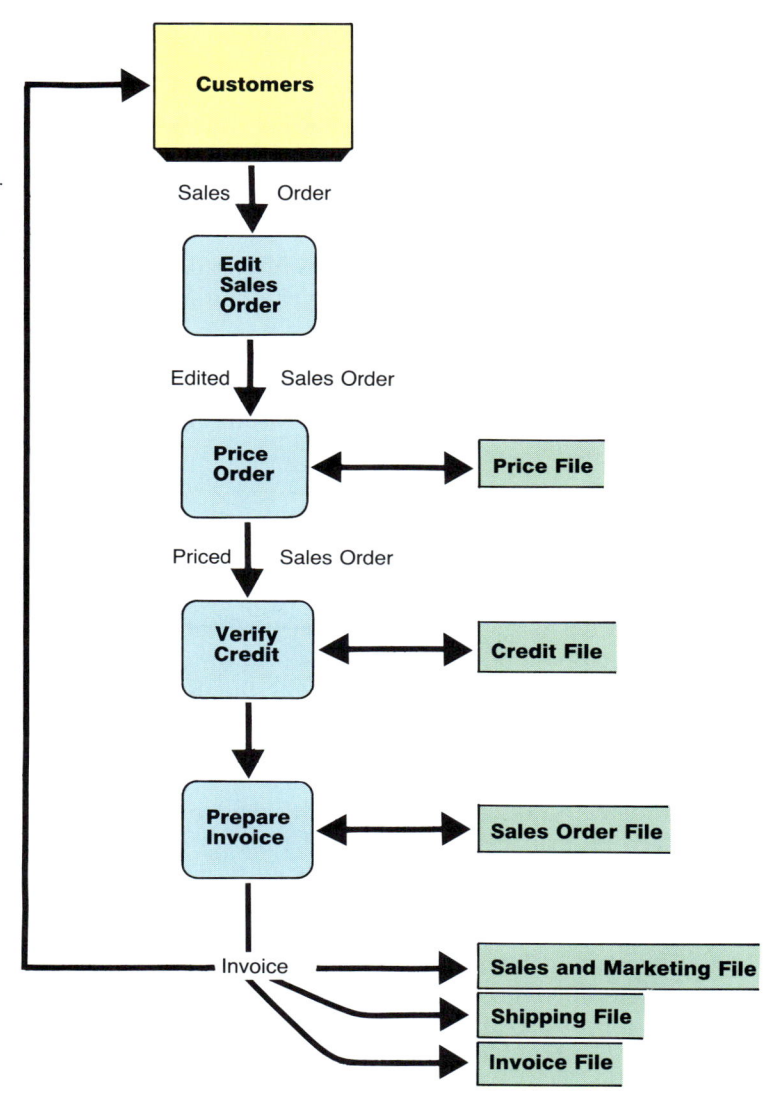

- Customers → Sales Order → Edit Sales Order
- Edit Sales Order → Edited Sales Order → Price Order ↔ Price File
- Price Order → Priced Sales Order → Verify Credit ↔ Credit File
- Verify Credit → Prepare Invoice ↔ Sales Order File
- Prepare Invoice → Invoice → Customers
- Invoice → Sales and Marketing File
- Invoice → Shipping File
- Invoice → Invoice File

PEOPLE AND SYSTEMS 460 PART 4

ever, system design is more complicated than program design: It is composed of many programs that must be coordinated, and since the new system will change the ways in which people work, the system design process must take human factors into consideration.

System design can be broken down into five components: output design, input design, processing design, file design, and system testing design. The first four components are concerned with establishing an appropriate combination of hardware and software, and the final component ensures that the programs will perform as specified. This stage concludes with a system design report.

Output Design. Because for most users the output *is* the system—that is, the part of the system that is supposed to supply them with the information they need—the system design process typically begins with the output design. The systems analyst prepares samples of every report that will be furnished by the system, together with an indication of the frequency of each. The output design also indicates which reports will be hard copy and who will receive them.

Input Design. After determining the system output, the analyst works on the input design, that is, the method of data entry. The input design should provide the user with a sample of every dialog that is likely to occur between the user and the computer; such dialogs either supply data to the computer or request the computer to take action. If menus are used, the input design should provide an example of each menu. It should also indicate the anticipated volume of data to be entered.

Ergonomic considerations play a major role in this step, too. The systems analyst must ascertain who will be entering data into the system and attempt to adapt the system to the ways in which they work, rather than forcing the users to adapt to the system. In many instances it is recommended that the analyst consider source automation devices, which were discussed in Chapter 4.

The input design also indicates the type of processing (on-line or batch), the hardware device on which data will be entered (e.g., via a microcomputer or terminal), and who is authorized to provide the data. In addition, it supplies programmers with specifications for every data item and field that is part of the input.

There are a variety of tools that can be used to show users the proposed input design. The screen layout form described in

Chapter 7, for example, illustrates the prompts that appear on the screen and some possible responses.

Processing Design. The processing design stage takes into consideration two aspects of the system: the structure on which the system is based and the manual processing that is part of the system. Because the system team is designing an entire system, with many components and programs, it is essential to use the structured methodology, including techniques and diagrams such as top-down design and structure charts. (See Chapter 7.) This involves "decomposing" the proposed information system into subsystems, each of which is served by one or more programs, and determining how these programs will interact. The next step is to develop the program algorithms that will convert the user's inputs into the desired outputs. A key feature of the structured methodology is that the system is decomposed *before* being designed in detail.

Almost all systems include manual processing, such as filling out forms, telephoning the client, or reading the system documentation to determine what to do in unusual cases. Without a properly organized manual system, the most sophisticated automated system will not function properly. In the processing design step the analyst describes the manual processing, using tools such as data flow diagrams and system flowcharts. The potential users review these diagrams and suggest changes.

File Design. The file design consists of a detailed description of all files associated with the system—for example, the transaction and master files for the accounts receivable system at PDQ Distributors. Systems analysts consult with users to establish how data is to be stored, the required frequency of access, and the required response time. They include the following information in the file design description:
- The name, type, and format of all data items to be stored.
- How items are organized into records, files, and, on occasion, data bases.
- Inquiry and update procedures for the files (e.g., whether each individual file can be processed on-line or only by batch processing).
- The data access privileges of each user, such as who has the right to read and update a given file.
- Documentation of the information in a data dictionary.

The traditional record layout forms described in Chapter 7, together with the data dictionary approach described in Chapter 10, are used to document this step.

System Testing Design. Although programs cannot be tested until they have been written or purchased, it is recommended that planning tests and developing test data begin once the output, input, processing, and file designs are well under way. Because users, particularly operations personnel, know the application best, they can suggest special conditions to test for. An associated activity is the design of *file conversion programs*, or programs that convert files running on the old system to run on the new system. A user representative should be present in both the system testing design and file conversion design steps.

The System Design Report. The output, input, processing, file, and system testing steps culminate in the system design report, which serves as a summary of the system design stage. This report typically contains the following information:
- A nontechnical summary of the output, input, processing, file, and system testing designs, including the relevant controls (e.g., a list of who is authorized to access each file in the proposed system).
- A statement of the proposed solution's financial, technical, and human aspects—in other words, how much it will cost, what resources are required and what benefits are expected, and how it will affect the way people perform their work.
- An updated schedule for developing of the proposed system.
- A technical appendix, which includes the diagrams developed during the system design phase. This will be the programmer's key tool in developing and testing the programs.

System Design at PDQ Distributors. Barclay Rosser began the system design stage of the system development life cycle by reviewing the systems analysis report. Working with a user, he then developed samples of the screens that were to be part of the new system. When the screen designs were approved, they became part of the system design report. (See Figure 12-10.)

After completing the processing design and sketching the basics of the file design, the team determined that the file access method should be sequential. Rosser then completed the tentative data dictionary, which was stored on a microcomputer hard disk.

Next Rosser worked with Len Maddox, the programmer, to develop test data and design file conversion programs and procedures for testing the system. Finally, the system design report was put together and accepted by management, and the team was ready to proceed with the next stage, system acquisition.

FIGURE 12-10

Part of a Data Entry Screen

```
       Column
                  1    1    2    2    3    3    4    4    5    5
             1    5    0    5    0    5    0    5    0    5    5
       Row
       1



       5              PDQ Distributors
                Billing System
                Date (Month, day, year)  XX/XX/XX
                Client number  999999
                Client name (Last name first) XXXXXXXXXXXXXXXXX
       10
                Enter data for each line item.
                Enter two carriage returns after the last line item.
                Enter N in the tax area if the item is not taxable.

                Product     Description              Quantity    Unit   Total  Tax
                Number                                           Cost   Cost
```

Users of this system enter data at the screen. The computer automatically calculates the tax and totals.

TABLE 12-1

Advantages of Software Acquisition Options

Package	In-House Development	Software Development House
Lower cost	May meet needs best	Custom product
Available immediately	Most control	Expert staff
Established product	Meets organization's standards	

System Acquisition

System acquisition *ABBR*

System acquisition is the fourth stage of the system development life cycle. In this stage the approved hardware and software are acquired or custom programs are developed, following the program development process described in Chapter 7.

This stage involves a choice among three possibilities: The company must decide whether to purchase existing software or to have software created within the organization or by an outside organization. Table 12-1 summarizes the advantages of each of these options.

Depending on what software will be used, additional hardware may be needed. The system acquisition phase ends with a report summarizing its activities and recommendations.

Purchasing Ready-Made Software Packages. If ready-made software, known as software packages or off-the-shelf software, meets an organization's needs as documented in the system design report, it is advantageous to purchase such software, since it is readily available and less expensive than custom-made software. An organization that decides to purchase off-the-shelf software must choose among an enormous variety of packages. For example, there are more than 70,000 software packages available for the IBM PC, including hundreds of general accounting packages. It is therefore recommended that prospective software package purchasers adhere to a procedure like the following:

1. Use the system design report to identify the characteristics that any acceptable software package must meet. Keep in mind that it is unlikely that any available package corresponds exactly to the specifications set out in the system design report, and even if one does, it may not be the best choice because of high cost and difficulty of use.

System acquisition
The stage of the system development life cycle in which the approved hardware and software are acquired or custom programs are developed.

FIGURE 12-11

Package Selection Criteria

Data expressed in this figure can be processed by an electronic spreadsheet such as Lotus 1-2-3.

Selection Criteria	Weight (1 to 10)	Product's Score (1 to 10)			
		I	II	III	IV
Meets design specs.	10	8	9	8	6
Vendor reputation	8	8	7	7	5
Cost	7	3	4	3	7
Performance	8	6	7	6	7
Ease of customization	6	2	4	5	5
Documentation	7	6	5	5	3
Maintenance	8	5	7	6	4
Other	6	8	9	7	9
Weighted Total		355	399	360	342

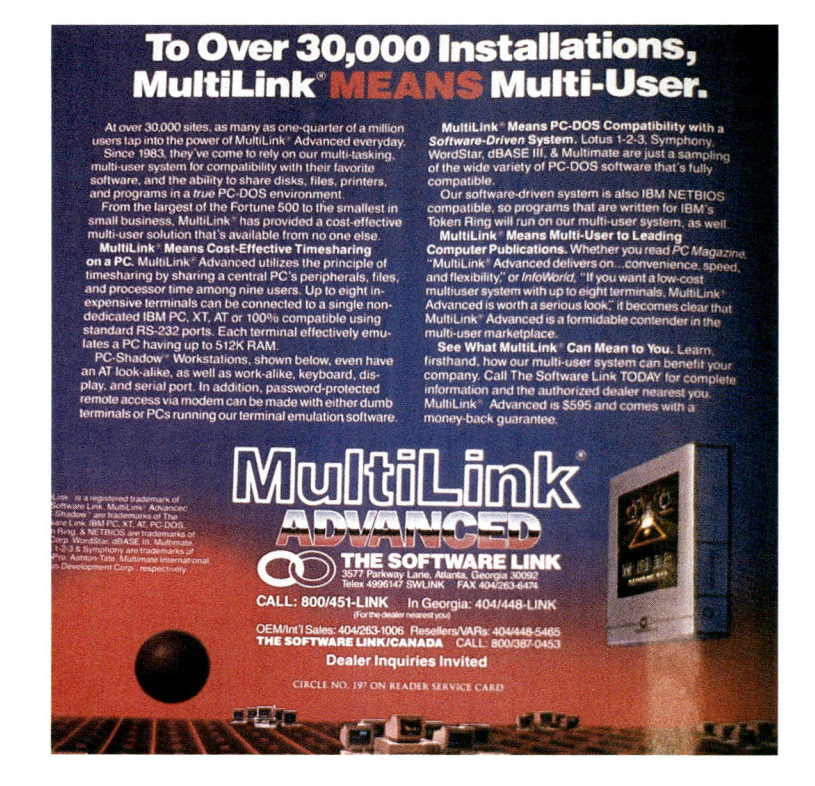

Thousands of software packages like this data communication package compete for user acceptance. This particular product has been sold to more than 30,000 installations. (© Chris Pullo.)

2. Specify the criteria to be used in selecting a package, and assign to each criterion a weight that indicates its relative importance, as shown in Figure 12-11. An electronic spreadsheet can be used to process package evaluation data and present tentative selections to management.

3. Prepare a *request for proposal* stating the organization's software needs, and submit it to potential vendors such as software development houses, the vendor of hardware used in the installation, and firms that specialize in finding appropriate software for clients.

4. Collect and evaluate the proposals from potential vendors using the weighted criteria developed in step 2. Perform a preliminary evaluation to select the most appropriate packages. Then examine each of these in greater detail and make the final selection.

5. Negotiate a contract with the vendor. Specify in writing the vendor's obligations for training, installation, and maintenance.

Developing Custom Software. Ready-made software does not always meet a purchaser's needs. For example, many organizations handle their accounts receivable in unique ways, and they need a customized accounts receivable package. It may be possible to alter existing software packages to meet an organization's specific needs, and in fact many packages provide for a degree of customization. For example, an accounts receivable package might allow users to choose the size and range of account numbers, thereby enabling them to use their present account numbers rather than being forced to change them. However, if a purchaser needs customization that goes beyond the choices offered by the package, the alterations may cost more than the original package. Furthermore, it is usually impossible for purchasers to make the alterations themselves. Therefore, a company may decide to have software custom designed for its specific needs.

Once a company decides to acquire custom software, it must also decide whether to develop the software itself or contract with a software development house for the work. If the company chooses the latter course, it must go through an evaluation procedure similar to that described for purchasing software packages. Because custom software cannot be demonstrated in advance, the experience and reputation of the software development house are important factors in this evaluation. Furthermore, a member of the systems team must be given responsibility for ensuring that the development is done on time and according to the specifications in the system design report.

Purchasing Hardware. The new software may require different or additional hardware. It is essential to determine what hardware will be needed for other proposed systems within the organization in the foreseeable future. In addition, the compatibility of the new hardware with existing and future systems must be considered.

The System Acquisition Report. The system acquisition report, which summarizes the system acquisition stage, includes the following information:
- A restatement of the problem with changes that reflect the system acquisition stage.
- A recommendation regarding which method of system acquisition to use and the reasons for the choice. If necessary, a detailed cost-benefit analysis of the various options is included.
- A statement of the proposed solution's financial, technical, and human aspects.
- An updated schedule for development of the proposed system, including dates for the remaining steps.
- If the organization has chosen to develop its own programs, an appendix containing programming documentation, which is an extension of the programming specifications developed in the system design stage.

System Acquisition at PDQ. After a preliminary review of the available software packages, the team members at PDQ were unable to discover any software that met the accounts receivable and credit departments' specific needs. And because of PDQ's financial situation, they could not use a software development house to write a custom program. Therefore, they decided to ask programmer Len Maddox to develop the software in-house.

In many respects, Maddox's experiences in writing the programs for PDQ's new accounts receivable system were similar to those of Leo MacKay, who wrote the accounts payable program for Acme discussed in Chapter 7. Working from the pseudocode and other program documentation presented in the system design report, Maddox coded the programs in COBOL. As the coding proceeded, he tested the programs, recorded the test results, and updated the pseudocode and other documentation. Because there were several interrelated programs, the programming effort was considerably more involved than was true for the accounts receivable program. On the other hand, Maddox's greater experience in using the structured methodology and structured programming techniques made it possible for him to finish the programs on time and within budget limits.

System Implementation

System implementation
The stage of the system development life cycle in which the system is actually put into service.

In the fifth phase, **system implementation**, the information system is actually put into service. The programs are tested to see how they fit into the users' operating environment, and the users receive training and documentation so that they can work with the new system.

System implementation consists of three steps: testing the completed system, training the people who will use the system, and converting from the old system to the new one. This stage ends with a postimplementation review of the system.

Testing. Testing actually begins during earlier stages—testing procedures and test data are developed during the system design phase, and programs are tested as they are developed. During the implementation stage, programs are tested to determine whether they work together properly and to find out how they handle erroneous data. The more programs in the system and the more people interacting with the system, the greater the possibility of system errors and the more extensive the testing required. In complex systems it can be difficult to correct an error in one program without adversely affecting other programs in the system.

A common example of an error that can prevent two programs from working together occurs when the first program supplies an invoice number, a customer number, and the amount due to a second program, which expects to receive this data in a different order. Even if each program works correctly when taken separately, the two programs cannot work together.

Training. At the same time that the system is being tested, users and computer personnel, such as console operators, undergo training. In general, the more a system is expected to alter the way people work, the more extensive the training should be. Training methods include individual training, workshops, and computer-aided training or tutorial programs.

Individual training, also called *one-on-one training*, can be personalized to meet employees' specific needs, but it is time-consuming and expensive for large groups. Workshops or classroom training can be an effective method if users have access to a workstation. It allows users to compare their experiences, but it may intimidate some users. Tutorial programs are generally available only for commercial software packages such as Lotus 1-2-3. The better tutorials allow users to proceed at their own pace and thus offer some of the advantages of one-on-one training at a lower cost. In some cases system development includes developing special tutorial programs for new users.

Computer training sessions enable future users to become familiar with software at their own pace. (Courtesy of International Business Machines.)

Conversion. During conversion, the new system actually replaces the existing one. Typically, this step involves two activities: converting the files and installing the new system. During file conversion, the file conversion programs are completed and tested. All files, whether manual or computerized, are verified for accuracy and timeliness and any necessary changes are made. Then the data contained in manual files is entered into the computer.

Because the company continues to operate while file conversion is taking place, each file must be updated. It is typical to set a cutoff date after which only the converted files will be updated.

Once the system has been adequately tested and training and file conversion are well under way, the system can be installed. The new system replaces the old one and becomes the property of the users rather than that of the system development team. However, testing and training must continue even after the system has been installed.

There are several approaches to system installation; the one chosen depends on an organization's needs and personnel. In the approach known as *abrupt cutover*, also called *crash conversion*, on a given date the old system is replaced by the new one and ceases to exist. The advantages of this approach are its simplicity and the lack of transition costs. On the other hand, it requires detailed planning and nerves of steel. Abrupt cutover is often used to change accounting practices at the end of a fiscal year.

If the *parallel operation* approach is chosen, there is a transition period during which data is processed by both the old system and the new one. The advantage of this approach is that if problems arise, the old system can process the data while the problems are being solved. However, parallel operation involves additional expenses due to duplication. This method is often used when a company is converting from a manual to an automated system.

Another approach to system installation is *pilot testing*, in which only one department or location carries out the conversion initially. Pilot testing offers the advantage of enabling the organization to discover problems and solve them before fully implementing the system. The disadvantage of this approach is that different parts of a company use different information systems and processing methods, and the pilot installation may not accurately reflect the system in its entirety. Another disadvantage is that pilot testing tends to require more time than the other conversion methods. It is often used in a multibranch company, in which the conversion takes place fully, but in only one branch at a time.

Postimplementation Review. During the *postimplementation review*, people who were not part of the system development team determine how well the system meets the objectives that were defined during the system investigation stage and modified during the subsequent stages. They establish the extent to which the system procedures are actually followed, and they evaluate the role of the new system in the operations of the departments for which it was designed. An important aspect of the postimplementation review is a cost-benefit analysis of the system in its final form.

System Implementation at PDQ. Rosser began the system implementation stage with file conversion. There were several training sessions and three postimplementation reviews: one soon after the system was installed, one six months later, and a final one a year after system installation. Although the costs were higher than projected, the benefits more than made up for the increased costs. The users clearly were satisfied with the new system.

Requests for modifications in the system were added to the requests that had been frozen during the system design stage. The team then began the final stage in the system development life cycle, system maintenance.

System Maintenance

System maintenance

The stage of the system development life cycle that consists of correcting errors and modifying the information system to meet users' needs.

System maintenance, the sixth and final stage of the system development life cycle, is an ongoing process that includes correcting errors and modifying the information system to meet users' needs. It is a major activity in most computer installations, often requiring over 50 percent of analysts' and programmers' time and effort. In this stage the analyst and the user follow an abbreviated form of the system development life cycle

TABLE 12-2

Dos and Don'ts of System Development

Do	Don't
1. Familiarize programmers as thoroughly as possible with the technical concepts inherent in the systems that they are developing.	1. Copy a system exactly as it was implemented in another organization.
2. Make programmers feel like part of the user or technical group for which the system is being developed.	2. Have a vendor design the system for you.
3. Choose DP subsystem leaders who are skilled both in the subject matter at hand and in system development.	3. Forget to ask users for their input when designing the system.
4. As they work, encourage programmers to talk directly to people who understand the technical aspects of what is being coded.	4. Tell management that you can have the system designed, installed, and up-and-running in six weeks.
5. Schedule regular (not necessarily frequent) meetings of DP subsystem leaders and managers.	5. Forget to plan for conversion of your manual files to the automated systems.
6. Schedule regular reviews at which users and informed advisors check on system development progress. Make sure programmers attend.	6. Implement all planned applications simultaneously.
7. Avoid making programmers wait for the final specification decisions. Take a position, begin coding even if on a tentative basis, and make sure the ability to change is coded into the system.	7. Pick hardware and software that has the capacity to handle today's volume of records and number of users but cannot handle more.
8. Anticipate all potential problems and errors as thoroughly as possible. Build switchable fixes into the software.	8. Put all that big computer equipment down in the basement near the utility closet and boiler.
9. Manage change. Accept valuable design changes that reject those that are spurious, unsupported, or unnecessary.	9. Keep the records automation system and the documents away from the users.
10. Use and strictly enforce modern programming techniques of top-down design, modularity, structural coding, and thorough documentation.	10. Forget to develop any conventions, formats, or guidelines for entering data in the records.

Source: Adapted from Joel S. Zimmerman, "The Right Stuff," *Datamation,* January 15, 1986, p. 78, and Bonnie Canning, "Record Automation: 25 Guaranteed Ways to Fail," *Administrative Management,* December 1986, p. 14.

to identify new system requirements or existing requirements that are not being met, analyze them in light of the new system, and design and implement a solution. The programmer will then update any programs that need to be modified. If the systems analyst has used the top-down approach and if the programmer has used the structured methodology, the time required to correct programming errors can be reduced sharply. (Table 12-2 lists some of the dos and don'ts of effective system development.)

System Maintenance at PDQ. At PDQ, Rosser was besieged with requests for changes. He met with Howarth, Morin, Maddox, and a member of the postimplementation review team to group these requests in a logical order and decide which changes to make immediately, which to reject, and which to implement in the next version of the system. For, as an experienced systems analyst, Rosser knew that no system lasts forever. As Box 12-2 indicates, trying to prolong the life of an obsolescent system—even one that has done its job well—may mean excessive maintenance costs and loss of strategic opportunities for the organization as a whole.

Prototyping

We have seen that the system development process requires many steps, some of which are tedious and cumbersome. Moreover, several years can elapse before the system is actually installed, and as a result of poor communication between users and systems analysts the final system may turn out to be quite different from what the user desired. The use of *prototypes*, or small working models of the system, can speed the system development process and increase the probability that users will be satisfied.

Prototype development often includes the use of tools such as screen painting (see Chapter 7) and application generators (see Chapter 8). With the aid of these tools, systems analysts may be able to develop a prototype of a system in a short time. Users can "see" a model of the new system and suggest modifications. Because they can understand a prototype more readily than a set of technical documents, they can participate more fully in the development of the system.

In this chapter we have examined the process of developing a computer information system and identified the role of users and computer specialists in that process. We examined the six-stage system development life cycle, focusing on the tools used and the interaction between users and computer specialists in each stage. Chapter 13, "Management Support and Expert Systems," explores the types of computer information systems that serve different levels of personnel, ranging from transaction-processing systems to executive information systems.

BOX 12-2

MANAGING CHANGE

When to Throw Your System Away

Computers are often described as agents of change. They change the way an organization does its work: Orders are filled faster, salespeople are better informed, and so on. They also change the way an organization needs to think. But in this respect not all parts of the organization change at the same rate, and problems can arise as a result. Nick Doggett, a systems analyst with USAir, tells the following story to illustrate this point.

In 1984 a certain large company—call it Westex—acquired a computer system for management support staff. The system, which was the state of the art at the time, consisted of an IBM PC on each worker's desk, equipped with 256K of memory and two floppy disk drives. With the aid of off-the-shelf personal-productivity software like Lotus 1-2-3 and WordStar, the PCs greatly improved the quality and timeliness of the reports on which the company's management based its decisions. The managers could now keep track of which customers were satisfied and which were not; which regional sales groups were most productive; and so on. The system was acquired on the assumption that it would pay back its initial cost in 2½ years. That assumption was fully borne out by experience.

Now it is 1988. The system is four years old, has long since paid for itself, and is no longer the state of the art. Its maintenance costs are substantial, both in terms of the bill submitted by the firm that keeps the hardware running and in terms of the cost of paying users to learn and operate the system, paying the people who train them, and so on. There is new hardware and software on the market that can run circles around the existing system. For example, there's a Compaq machine based on a speedy 386 chip, with 1 MB of RAM, an internal 40-MB hard disk, and graphics capability. There is integrated personal-productivity software that would eliminate the time-consuming task of moving data among incompatible word-processing, spreadsheet, and graphics programs. There are local area networks that can serve as an alternative to standalone machines. And all this can be acquired for about the same cost as the system Westex bought in 1984.

A proposal for a new system is submitted. It, too, will pay for itself in 2½ years. The quality and timeliness of reports will again take a great leap forward. Competitors are already using this type of system.

But when the answer to the proposal comes back from Westex's finance department, it's no. Personal computers are office equipment. On the corporation's books office equipment has a seven-year life. It is depreciated over a seven-year cycle. There are still three years to go before the PCs will be fully written off. They can't just be thrown away. After all, they still work. So the PCs live on, with system maintenance costs rising to 70 percent of life-cycle system costs.

What is the moral of the story? To Doggett, it is that all parts of the organization, including finance, must change their thinking when computers come onto the scene. In this case, depreciation concepts that were developed for electric typewriters should not be applied to computers. Too little emphasis is placed on *opportunity costs*. Opportunity costs mean costs measured in terms of lost opportunities to keep up with the competition, lost opportunities to use highly paid people to perform creative tasks rather than shuffle files from WordStar to Lotus, and lost opportunities to produce better-quality, higher-impact reports.

For some applications, says Doggett, we may be entering an era of throwaway systems. Sometimes excessive maintenance costs may point to failure in the analysis, design, or acquisition phases. But they may also simply mean that an organization is holding onto an obsolete system too long. Conservative thinking—"If it ain't broke, don't fix it"—sometimes makes sense, but in the fast-moving world of computers, this is not always true.

SUMMARY

1. A system is a collection of interrelated parts that work together to meet common objectives. Systems have a goal; operate according to well-defined procedures; are composed of parts that can themselves be considered subsystems and must be coordinated; provide feedback; and include people as an integral element. The system that enables the subsystems of a business—marketing, finance and accounting, production, research and development, and human resources—to work together successfully is the information system.

2. Systems include people at various levels who do different but interrelated tasks. The systems analyst serves as a liaison between users, who work with computer information systems, and programmers, who develop programs that process the data input by users. At each stage of the system development process, management decides whether to accept the system as recommended, modify it, or cancel the project. Other computer specialists that may be required for the information system to function efficiently include computer operators, librarians, and field engineers.

3. The **system development life cycle** consists of six stages: investigation, analysis, design, acquisition, implementation, and maintenance. The first stage, **system investigation**, consists of two activities: defining the problem to be solved and determining whether a feasible solution exists within constraints such as budget, personnel, and time. A **feasibility study** is done to determine whether a particular problem can be solved with available resources.

4. During the second stage of the system development life cycle, **systems analysis**, the systems analyst, aided by users and operations personnel, determines how the existing information system functions in order to design and develop the new system. This entails gathering data on the existing system, presenting and analyzing the data, and preparing a report summarizing the systems analysis stage.

5. In the **system design** stage the hardware and software components of the new information system are determined. Initial specifications are developed for all the programs that will be included in the system.

6. System acquisition is the fourth stage of the system development life cycle. During this stage the approved hardware and software are acquired or custom programs are developed.

7. In the fifth stage, **system implementation**, the information system is actually put into service. Implementation consists of three steps: testing the completed system, training the personnel who will use the system, and converting from the old system to the new one. During the postimplementation review, people who were not part of the system development team determine how well the system meets the organization's objectives.

8. System maintenance, the sixth and final phase of the system development life cycle, is an ongoing process that includes correcting errors and modifying the information system to meet users' needs. It is a major activity in most computer installations, often requiring over 50 percent of the time of analysts and programmers.

KEY TERMS

system development life cycle

system investigation

feasibility study

systems analysis

system design

system acquisition

system implementation

system maintenance

REVIEW QUESTIONS

1. Compare the various types of personnel involved in setting up and operating an information system. What is the advantage of the user having a working knowledge of computers? What is the advantage of the programmer having a working knowledge of the business application for which the new system is being developed?

2. Define the system development life cycle and briefly describe each of its stages.

3. Compare the system development life cycle with the program development process. Under what conditions is each process appropriate?

4. Discuss the activities and personnel involved in the system investigation stage. List the criteria for determining the feasibility of a proposed solution.

5. Discuss the activities and personnel involved in the systems analysis stage. Why is it necessary to analyze a system that is slated to be replaced?

6. Discuss the activities and personnel involved in the system design stage.

7. Discuss the activities and personnel involved in the system acquisition stage, and describe the software evaluation process.

8. Discuss the activities and personnel involved in the system implementation stage. Compare and contrast three methods of converting from an old system to a new one.

9. Discuss the activities and personnel involved in the system maintenance stage. What can be done during the earlier stages to improve the efficiency of analysts and programmers in this stage?

APPLICATIONS

1. What skills must a systems analyst have in order to obtain full cooperation from users? How are these skills different from those of a computer programmer?

2. What problems might secretaries encounter when they begin interacting with computers? What can systems analysts do to reduce the impact of these problems?

3. To what extent will programmers interact with users? What can programmers do to improve their interaction with users?

4. Discuss the following statement: Because of its many steps, the system development life cycle is hopelessly unwieldy.

CASE FOR DISCUSSION

Marie Reynolds received a B.A. from South State University in 1967. She was an excellent student. In a freshman survey course, she made her first acquaintance with Plato and Aristotle. Determined to pursue interesting ideas wherever the trail led, she ended up majoring in classics. But her classics major never led to a career. She spent the next twenty years putting her husband through law school and raising three children.

When friends asked her why she didn't work, she always knew what to say. "Work! I put in more hours a week than you do. I'm planner, manager, and chief executive officer of a very busy and very successful small business."

But the year her youngest son was a senior in college, she began to suffer the first symptoms of "empty-nest syndrome." What was she going to do for the next twenty years? She toyed with the idea of getting a graduate degree in classics, but what would she do with that? The idea of a career in teaching had no charm for her at this stage in her life. It was time, she thought, to look for a job.

Reynolds tried making up a resume, but after she had filled in her name and address she didn't know what to write next. For lack of anything else, she went to work as a checkout clerk in a local discount store, and after six months she got a raise to $4 per hour. Her feet were sore from standing all day, the pay was lousy, and she quit. Next she tried a stint as a waitress. She earned more, and the job was a bit more interesting than her work in the store, but it meant that she often had to work in the few evening hours when her husband was home.

She did learn a few things from her work experience, though. First, she learned that when she worked 40 hours a week outside the home it was very hard to keep her house as clean as she had before. Second, she learned that even if her lawyer-husband would be happy to pay the bill, it is very hard to find a good housekeeper. Some of the housekeepers she hired were good, but they didn't stay on the job. Some put in the hours requested, but they didn't get much work done. Others kept running the electric bill through the laundry or putting sterling silver candlesticks through the dishwasher.

"Housekeeping is a job I know inside out," Reynolds said to

herself one day. "It's a job that needs management. I'll bet I could hire the same people, and with a little planning, organization, leadership, and control I could double their productivity. If they got more work done and did things the way people really want them done, I know I would have no trouble finding clients who would be happy to pay a premium rate for their services."

On the basis of this reasoning, she started her own business, Rent-A-Mop. She hired three other women at $6 per hour. The four of them, all dressed in white sweatsuits with a big red mop emblem, would descend on a client's house and go at it as a team. One of them would start with the laundry. Another would head for the dishes. The third would tackle the floors—vacuuming, waxing, whatever was needed. The fourth would take on windows and ovens. In half a day they would get as much work done as most conventional housekeepers do in a week. For this Reynolds charged $150, and everyone told her it was a bargain.

She was right in thinking that her services would be in demand. Her list of clients grew by leaps and bounds. Soon she had two teams, then five, then a company van, then a full-time office manager—and then things started going wrong. Appointments were missed. Bills went unpaid. Supplies would run out and have to be replaced on an emergency basis at supermarket prices rather than at wholesale prices. Reynold's teams washed windows for customers who wanted floors waxed, and they waxed the floor where the customer wanted the oven cleaned. "I'm losing control of this thing," she confided to a friend one evening. "I've let it grow too fast, and now I'm in over my head."

"Why don't you get a computer to help you with bill paying and scheduling?" the friend suggested.

"But I don't know how to use a computer."

"Don't worry about that," said the friend. "I'm a systems analyst. My job is to show people how they can use computers to help solve their problems. I tell you what. I'll help you solve your problem if you'll help me solve mine. My house is a mess and my housekeeper just quit."

CASE QUESTIONS

You are Reynolds's friend. Play the role of systems analyst.

1. Outline the services you will offer in terms of the six steps of the system development life cycle.

2. Write your choice of a system investigation report, a systems analysis report, a system design report, or a request for a proposal (directed to a retail hardware/software vendor).

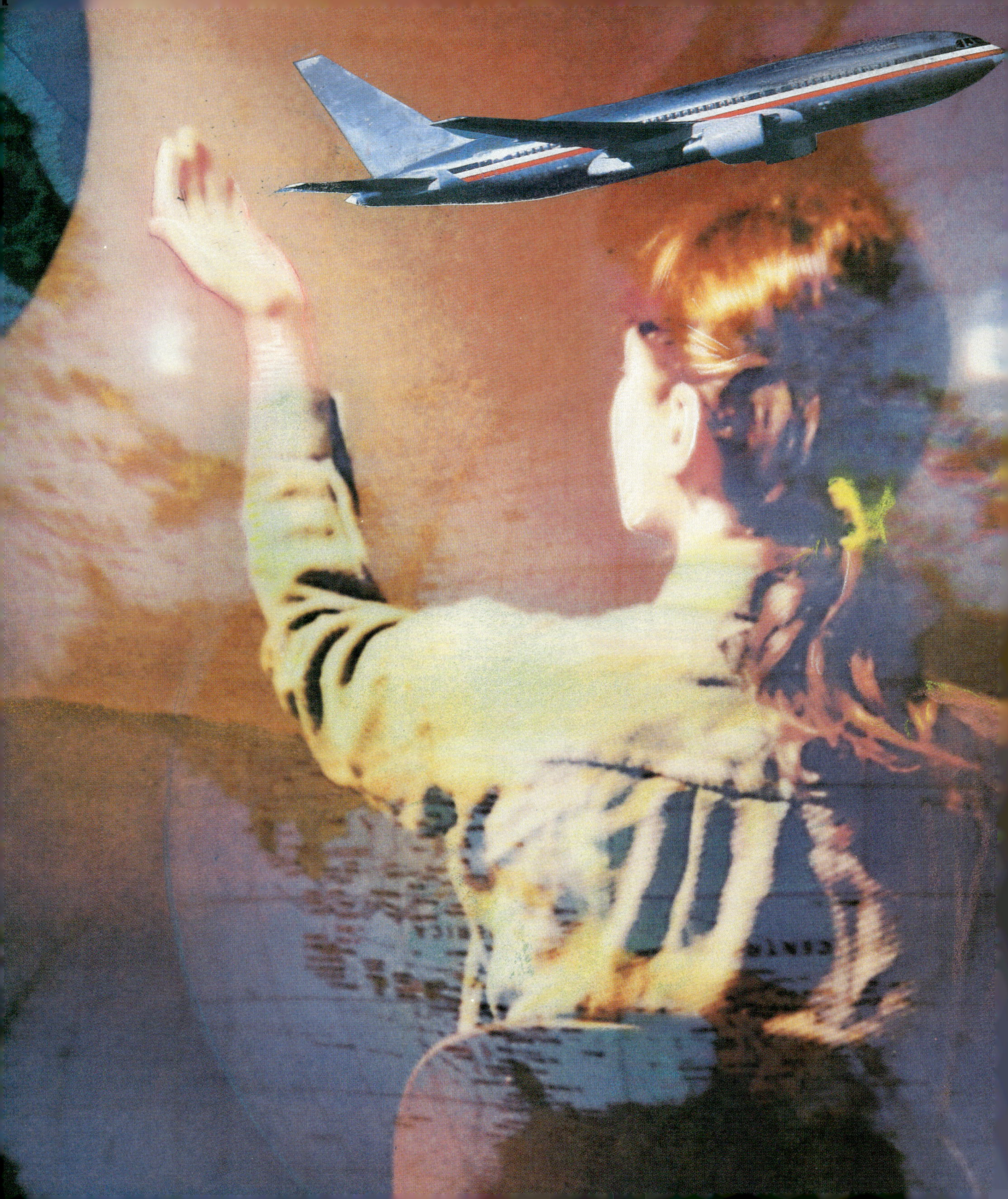

Management Support and Expert Systems

CHAPTER

13

Great Falls Travel occupies a pleasant office in a colonial-style shopping center off a main road. One whole wall is taken up by a map that bears the title "A New and ACCVRAT Map of the World Drawne according to ye Truest Descriptions and Best Observations that have beene made by English or Strangers." A sharp contrast to the dragons and sailing ships that decorate this antique chart is provided by the very modern-looking video display terminals sitting on the desk of each of Great Falls Travel's agents.

Agent Judy Prince is at one of the desks, beginning her day's work. Her computer screen displays a queue, or list, of thirty-two things that she needs to do today. The first item is, "Check the status of the Savins' flight to Amsterdam. Is it still wait listed?" Calling up additional data to the screen, Prince sees that the flight is now confirmed. She will call the Savins to let them know.

Just then the phone rings. "Great Falls Travel," Prince answers. "Martha's Vineyard on the eighth? Let me see what's available."

At the stroke of a key, the queue disappears and is replaced by a table of flights to Martha's Vineyard. "Would you like to leave from National Airport or Dulles? . . . Dulles then. . . . We're showing a New York Air flight at 11:30 via LaGuardia, getting in at 2:29. The fare is $119 each way. There's a $99 fare, but it's showing not available on that day. Shall I pick up the 11:30 flight? . . . How many are going?"

Prince makes a few more keystrokes, and the screen changes again. Now she begins to fill in the blanks on a Passenger Name Record, or PNR in travel-agent jargon. She types the name "Parker N Mrs." The computer responds with the message "Format error." Prince retypes the name correctly—Parker/N Mrs. Because Mrs. Nancy Parker is a regular customer, her address, telephone number, credit card number, and other data are already on file. The computer adds that information to the PNR automatically. Prince completes the PNR by entering the flight number and date in their proper locations.

Prince then makes one more keystroke, and the message "Transaction completed" appears on the screen. Instantly the whine of a high-speed printer can be heard from a back room, and in a few seconds the printer spits out a ticket. A second printer then goes to work printing an itinerary. When the itinerary is done, a third machine prints a boarding pass.

This chapter discusses a variety of computer information systems. It begins with the systems used by operations personnel like Judy Prince and their supervisors. Other systems to be discussed include management information systems, which supply information on a scheduled basis for use in tactical planning and control, and decision support and executive information systems, which provide information on demand for use in strategic planning. All of these information systems could be developed according to the system development life cycle discussed in Chapter 12, or they could be produced, at least in part, by users with the aid of an information center, also discussed in this chapter.

When you have read this chapter you should be able to:
1. Describe the information systems pyramid and the different levels of management it serves.
2. Discuss operations information systems and explain the relevance of batch-processing and on-line transaction-processing systems.
3. Explain the relationship between management information systems and operations information systems.
4. Compare and contrast decision support systems and management information systems.
5. Discuss expert systems, including their benefits and drawbacks.
6. Describe an information center.
7. Understand and use the key terms listed at the end of the chapter.

Operations Information Systems

Operations information system (OIS)
A computer system that enables an organization to process files or data bases and produce documents that keep track of employees, customers, goods and services, cash, buildings and equipment, and the like.

Figure 13-1 presents a graphic representation of the relationships among the three main types of information systems and the various levels of management. Such a diagram is often called an *information systems pyramid*. At the lowest level of the pyramid are **operations information systems (OIS)**, also known as data processing systems. These systems enable operations personnel to process files or data bases and produce documents that keep track of employees, customers, goods and services, cash, buildings, equipment, and so on. Such systems are often clerical in nature; for example, they are used to record the sale of a boat or a screwdriver, calculate an employee's overtime pay, or figure out depreciation on machinery. The data that is processed and generated by operations information systems, known as *production data*, serves as the starting point for more sophisticated systems that provide information for different levels of management and technical personnel.

Operations information systems collect, process, and store data, using different processing methods depending on the user's information needs and available resources. Traditional systems, such as some payrolls, may be based on batch processing. (See Chapter 2.) On-line systems require more expensive hardware and more sophisticated software but offer faster response times, often a few seconds or less. One type of operations information system that has gained widespread popularity in recent years is the on-line transaction-processing system described in the next section.

On-line transaction-processing system (OLTPS)
A computer information system in which several users can make inquiries and updates of a shared data base at the same time.

On-Line Transaction-Processing Systems

On-line transaction-processing systems (OLTPS) are systems in which several users can make inquiries or updates of a shared data base at the same time. For example, airline reser-

FIGURE 13-1

The Information Systems Pyramid

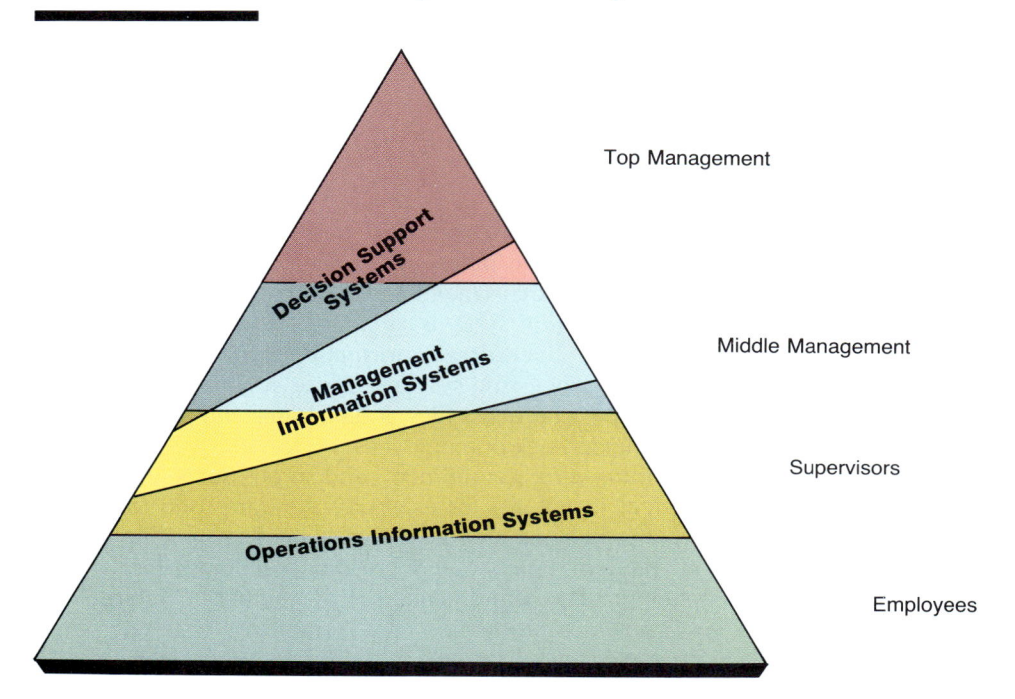

(Pyramid diagram showing, from top to bottom: Decision Support Systems — Top Management; Management Information Systems — Middle Management; Operations Information Systems — Supervisors; base — Employees)

vation agents may access such a system to inquire about seat availability and reserve seats. Because the agents are on-line to the data base that contains data on seat availability, their transactions may be processed within a few seconds.

On-line transaction-processing systems are composed of one or more mainframes or minicomputers, assorted data communication hardware and software (see Chapter 6), and a varying number of users, often several hundred. Unlike some other data communication systems, they generally serve technically unsophisticated users such as travel agents and airline reservation personnel. Since the system is interactive, users expect the system to respond to their input instantaneously.

The basic measure of an OLTP system's performance is the number of transactions that can be processed per second—some businesses are asking for systems that can handle more than 1000 transactions per second. It is estimated that by 1990, 70 percent of all new business computer systems will include on-line transaction-processing capabilities.

FIGURE 13-2

An On-Line Transaction-Processing System

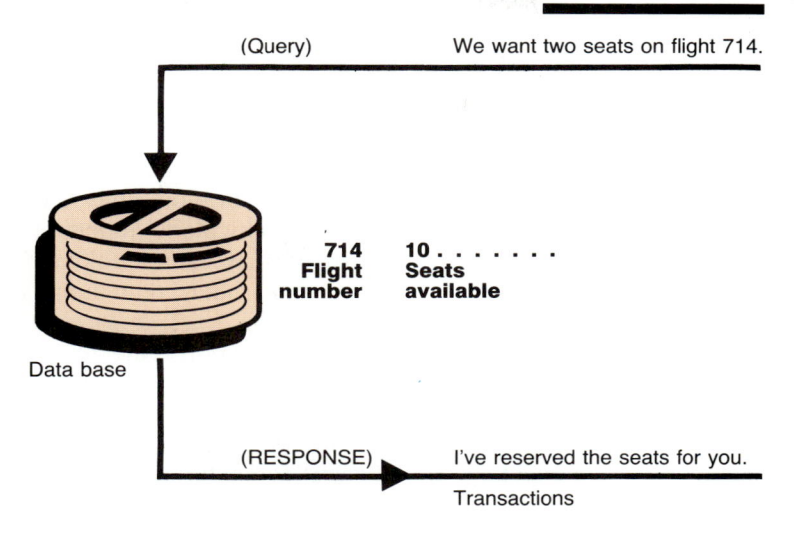

(Query) — We want two seats on flight 714.

Data base

714 Flight number | 10 . . . . Seats available

(RESPONSE) — I've reserved the seats for you.

Transactions

In many ways airline reservation systems are typical of on-line transaction-processing systems. To begin with, they are large-scale systems; for example, even the relatively small TWA airline reservation system uses an IBM mainframe that is connected to about 150 300-MB disk drives (the equivalent of almost 150,000 diskettes) and supports 12,000 terminals. They are used by hundreds of TWA reservation agents serving customers at the same time, as illustrated in Figure 13-2. In peak periods the system processes over 200 messages per second.

This airline reservation agent at O'Hare Airport is able to service customer requests within a few seconds by using an on-line reservation system. (© Jeff Lowenthal, Woodfin Camp.)

CHAPTER 13   MANAGEMENT SUPPORT AND EXPERT SYSTEMS

On-line transaction-processing systems handle major business activities and therefore must be available around the clock. Furthermore, once an OLTP system has been installed, it is usually impossible to replace it with manual processing, even temporarily. Therefore, these systems have to be extremely reliable.

Special Features. Many minicomputer-based systems include specially designed hardware and software components that keep OLTP systems running even if one or more units fail. This feature, known as *fault-tolerance*, is particularly important for manufacturing and military systems that cannot tolerate even a few seconds of computer *down time*, that is, time during which the computer is not available for use.

Another safety feature provided by many systems is the ability to keep track of each transaction as it takes place and, if necessary, roll back (or erase) its effect. For example, if an agent at an airline reservation terminal is in the process of reserving a seat when the connection to the central computer and its associated data base is severed, the system can determine whether or not the transaction was completed. If the transaction was completed, the system adjusts the number of seats available for the given flight. If it was not, the system "rolls back" the incomplete transaction and notifies the agent, who then reenters it.

OLTP systems must solve the problem known as *concurrent update*. Concurrent update occurs when two or more transactions try to update a data base at the same time. For example, suppose there are ten seats left on flight 714 to Chicago, as shown in Figure 13-3. When the first travel agent reserves a seat on this flight, he or she will see ten available seats. After the reservation is made, there will be nine seats available. If another travel agent reserves a seat at the same time, that agent will also see ten seats available. And after the second reservation the data base will also show nine seats available rather than the correct number, eight. This error can result in overbooking of the flight.

Since airlines overbook seats to compensate for "no shows," airline reservation systems may not be disturbed by the concurrent update problem. But other industries, such as banking, require on-line transaction-processing systems that will not permit any imprecision in furnishing information.

In some systems the concurrent update problem is eliminated by "locking" the record, that is, refusing to give a second transaction access to a record as long as the first transaction is in the process of updating the same record.

FIGURE 13-3

Concurrent Update

First travel agent reserves one seat on Flight 714; when transaction is completed, nine seats remain.

Second travel agent reserves one seat on Flight 714 at the same time; when transaction is completed, nine seats remain according to the file. However, only eight seats remain on the flight.

714 Flight number — 10 . . . . Seats available

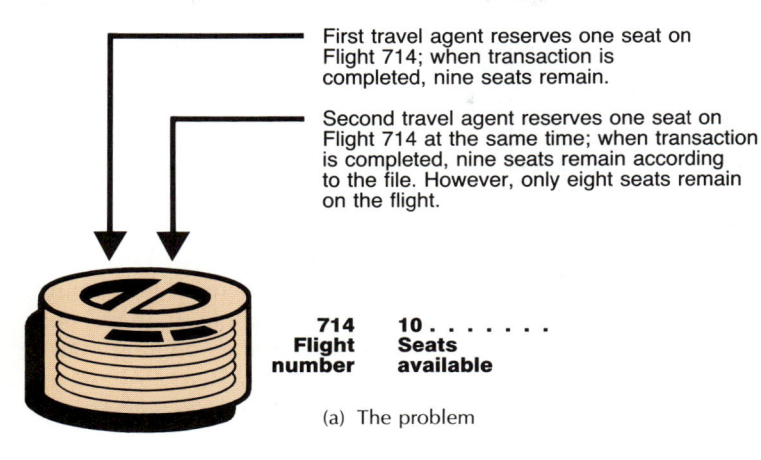

(a) The problem

Concurrent update is a potential problem with on-line transaction-processing systems. If two transactions attempt to update the same data at the same time, each transaction ignores the effect of the other, leading to inconsistent data, as shown in (a). One possible solution is to suspend the second transaction until the first transaction has been completely processed, as shown in (b).

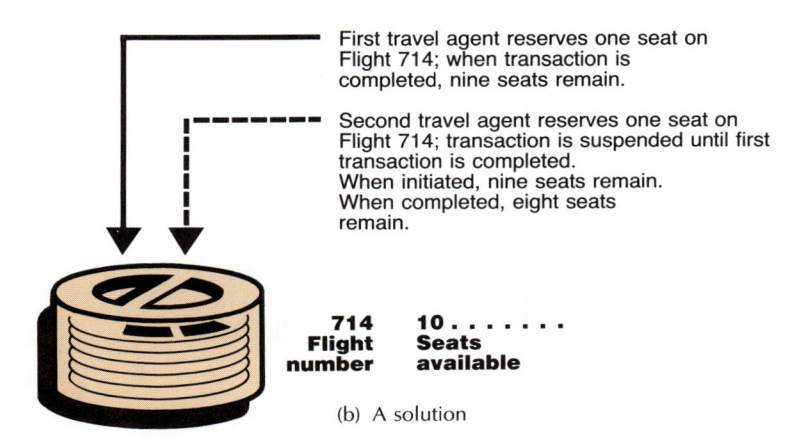

First travel agent reserves one seat on Flight 714; when transaction is completed, nine seats remain.

Second travel agent reserves one seat on Flight 714; transaction is suspended until first transaction is completed. When initiated, nine seats remain. When completed, eight seats remain.

714 Flight number — 10 . . . . Seats available

(b) A solution

Uses of Operations Information Systems

Operations information systems handle the data that keeps track of the organization's resources, such as goods and services purchased, goods and services sold, suppliers, customers, and employees. They provide the information needed to carry out clerical operations such as billing a customer and recording payment of bills. In addition, they provide summary information to help supervisors evaluate employees' performance and the performance of the department in general.

Within an organization, different levels of personnel require different types of information to function. For example, operations personnel in the accounts receivable department need to know how much each client owes, how long the bill has been outstanding, and whom to contact for payment. The supervisor of this department requires summary information concerning the total amount owed, the average amount owed, and the like. Many operations information systems furnish supervisors with information related to employee performance, such as number and total amount of bills sent out on a given day.

In addition, different departments need different kinds of information. Let's take another look at the example of an airline. An airline uses inventory, maintenance, and accounting information generated by operations information systems. Although it is a service organization and hence does not have a manufacturing department that produces an inventory of products, it has an inventory in the form of seats on its flights. The main operations data for its inventory department is the list of reservations for all available flights. The airline's maintenance department needs detailed records of every flight to determine when to carry out scheduled maintenance. In addition, it needs performance data for each airplane, both on the ground and in flight, to determine when to carry out additional maintenance. Finally, the accounting department uses reservation data as well as cost data to prepare bills for passengers. For each flight it

The pilot and co-pilot of a Boeing 767 interact continuously with several operations information systems. These systems improve flight safety and make the work of pilots easier and more pleasant. (Courtesy of Boeing Corp.)

Computer information systems are used to plan, organize, and control maintenance operations. They also indicate when unscheduled maintenance is appropriate. (© Roger Miller, The Image Bank.)

keeps track of revenue generated (by tickets sold) and expenses incurred (such as fuel, depreciation, food, and crew members' salaries).

Operational Control

Operations information systems can provide various types of information to enable the first level of management—supervisors who interact with operations personnel on a daily basis—to perform their tasks efficiently and effectively. The tasks include *planning* employees' work schedules and, in some cases, departmental budgets; *organizing* staff by dividing up the work; *leading* employees, sometimes taking a direct role in training them; and *controlling* the department by measuring employee performance and taking corrective action when necessary.

The information provided to supervisors by operations information systems consists of several kinds of reports, including *periodic reports* like the one shown in Figure 13-4. This report lists flights scheduled for the following week and crew requirements for each flight; another report lists personnel assignments for the following week. By comparing the two reports, the supervisor can schedule the crew. Another type of report, the *summary report* (shown in Figure 13-5), supplies the accounting department with the gross and net revenue for a given week or a given route. This type of report can also be used to summarize overtime expenses by department for a given week. An *exception report*, illustrated in Figure 13-6, helps supervisors

FIGURE 13-4

A Periodic Report

```
            R&D Airlines
    Flight and Crew Requirements          Week of July 8-14, 1990

    Date       Flight No.   Final Dest. Pilots    Flight Attend. Other Crew

    9 July        813       Newark        2            6              1
    0 July        818       Memphis       1            3              0
    0 July        912       Miami         2            8              2
    2 July        117       Boston        1            4              0
```

This report illustrates the flight and crew requirements for an airline during a given week. It is issued weekly for the following week. These reports can be used by operations personnel and supervisory management to prepare personnel schedules.

FIGURE 13-5

A Summary Report

```
            R&D Airlines
         Gross and Net Revenue           Week of July 8-14, 1990

         Day          Number            Gross           Net
                     of Flights        Revenue        Revenue

         9 July          1             $107,500       $13,800
        10 July          2             $235,127       $32,503
        12 July          1              $47,505       -$2,304
```

This report summarizes gross and net revenue for an airline during a given week. It can be used by supervisory and middle management to review financial performance.

PEOPLE AND SYSTEMS 490 PART 4

FIGURE 13-6

An Exception Report

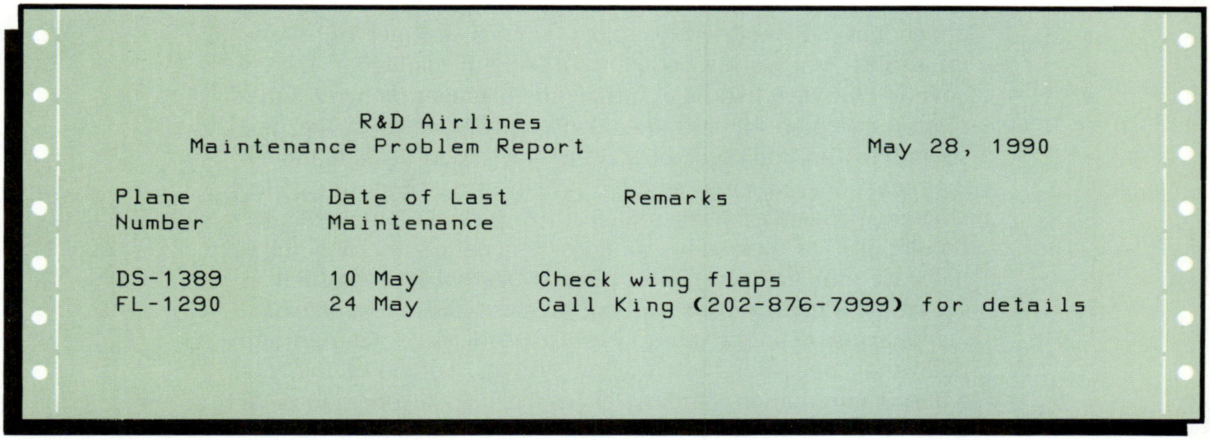

```
            R&D Airlines
       Maintenance Problem Report              May 28, 1990

  Plane        Date of Last        Remarks
  Number       Maintenance

  DS-1389      10 May              Check wing flaps
  FL-1290      24 May              Call King (202-876-7999) for details
```

This report lists only items that do not fall within the normal range, such as planes that require further servicing. The report can be used by supervisory and middle management to find problem areas rapidly.

pinpoint problem areas such as planes that may require further servicing or reservation agents who have made less than a specified amount in sales.

The scope of information furnished by an operations information system closely mirrors the activities of operations personnel and their supervisors. The information from the various reports provided by the system can be summarized but is rarely integrated, and these systems rarely process data from external sources such as the Federal Aeronautics Administration. The next level of the information system pyramid, management information systems, satisfies many of these requirements.

Management Information Systems

Management information system (MIS)
A computer information system that provides managers with integrated information on a scheduled basis.

Management information systems (MIS) are computer information systems that provide managers (usually middle managers) with integrated information on a scheduled basis. Although there is no clear line separating the activities of middle management from those of supervisory management, or management information systems from operations information systems, there are differences between the two levels of management and between the types of systems that supply them with information.

Like supervisory managers, middle managers plan, control, organize, and lead. But their activities involve longer time spans and provide more scope for individual initiative and independent judgment. For example, whereas a supervisor draws up a short-term work schedule for a flight or maintenance crew covering the next two weeks, a middle manager prepares a medium-range plan for the allocation of personnel over the next six months. In addition, supervisors may report items that need maintenance, whereas middle managers propose policy changes such as a lower frequency of preventive maintenance on aircraft. For their tasks, supervisors generally use only internal data, but managers must access external sources such as government regulations regarding frequency of maintenance.

Management information systems are harder to design and build than operations information systems. For one thing, operations information systems reflect the clerical operations for which they are designed, and such tasks as calculating the pay of a flight attendant or airline pilot are fairly straightforward. But management information systems deal with processes that are complicated, not fully understood, and often beyond the control of the organization. For example, to determine the financial feasibility of adding Wednesday and Friday morning flights to Chicago to an airline schedule, a manager may be able to say what general information is required but will not know all the specifics, such as how many competitors will be attempting to add such a flight or the price of fuel two months from today.

Management information systems begin where operations information systems end: They integrate, consolidate, and summarize information produced by operations information systems in the form of periodic reports and exception reports, along with appropriate external information. The content and form of the information provided by an MIS are designed to meet the needs of the user. To help meet those needs, management information systems often apply advanced techniques such as data-base management systems and fourth-generation programming languages.

Although management information systems may be used by any level of management, they are most often used by middle managers. In general, middle managers require broader, more summarized information than supervisory managers do. For example, a manager who has been asked to determine the profitability of an airline route over a period of several months does

FIGURE 13-7

A Predictive Report

```
              R&D Airlines                    July 30, 1990
     Gross and Net Revenue Forecast Report

  Week         Gross          Net
  Ending       Revenue        Revenue        Remarks

   6 July      $405,188       $57,200
  13 July      $390,132       $44,000
  20 July      $404,785       $54,908
  27 July      $513,204       $72,118
  ----------------------------------------------------------
  Ave. Aug.    $478,000       $61,000
  Ave. Sept.   $421,000       $57,000
  Ave. Oct.    $467,500       $64,700        Assumes daily flights to
                                             New Orleans starting first
                                             week in October.
```

Predictive reports present actual data and attempt to forecast the future. They are used by middle and upper management as a guide to planning.

not need daily reports on the specific number of seats sold on every flight but must have summary reports presenting the information by day, week, route, and so on.

Middle managers also use reports to analyze commercial situations, such as whether to expand the number of flights offered or to launch a new promotional campaign. *Predictive reports* forecast the future on the basis of past events and trends. The one shown in Figure 13-7 analyzes gross and net revenue from exisiting flights and adds a projected new flight in the near future. *Ratio analysis reports* show the relationship between two important variables. For example, Figure 13-8 shows the loading ratio for July, that is, the ratio of the number of seats available to the number sold. Other ratios that airline managers find useful are the amount of fuel consumed divided by the number of passenger miles flown, and the number of specially priced tickets sold divided by the total number of tickets sold. Some ratio analysis reports present a series of ratios.

FIGURE 13-8

A Ratio Analysis Report

```
            R&D Airlines
    Ratio Analysis Report    Week of July 8-14, 1990

    Date        Flight      Final          Seats       Seats       Loading
                Number      Destination    Available   Sold        Ratio

    9 July      813         Newark         38          36          0.947
    10 July     818         Memphis        72          72          1.000
    10 July     912         Miami          84          46          0.548
    12 July     117         Boston         31          34          0.912
```

This report indicates the ratio of seats available to seats sold (loading ratio) for several flights. Such reports help managers find problem areas rapidly.

Uses of Management Information Systems

Managers, especially middle managers, use management information systems to obtain the information they need to carry out the tasks of planning, controlling, organizing, and leading. MIS systems allow managers to set goals and objectives and determine whether they are being met.

We return to the airline example to show how an MIS can help middle management. Information from an MIS can be used by managers in the airline's inventory, maintenance, personnel, and accounting departments.

Inventory. Middle managers can examine summary and exception reports to identify flights that are candidates for elimination or may require an increased level of service. To make these sometimes difficult decisions, they interface with other departments such as accounting and may get help from decision support systems, which are described later in the chapter.

Maintenance. Management information systems serve the maintenance department by keeping a summary of maintenance activities and their costs for each plane, each type of plane, and each period of time. With the aid of an MIS, the maintenance department can examine different maintenance policies and decide, for example, when to retire a given plane. Such information should be passed on to the purchasing department to help it decide what types of planes to buy when the airline expands.

Personnel. With the aid of a management information system, personnel managers assist the airline's employees by logging employee flight times and administering contracts and letters of understanding that define the labor relations between the airline and its employees. The system may supply detailed labor cost reports to the accounting department.

Accounting. The accounting department uses a management information system to obtain detailed cost figures, which enable it to analyze the net revenue (or loss) generated by a particular flight or group of flights. These financial considerations are the major factor in deciding whether or not to extend or reduce service. It is interesting to note, for example, that one airline saved $100,000 a year by eliminating an olive from its salad.

External Data and the MIS

Unlike operations information systems, which use only data from within a company, management information systems may collect and analyze data from external as well as internal sources. No business, whatever its size, can afford to remain isolated from its constantly changing environment. The better a management information system can process external data, the greater the service it will render to its organization. Few management information systems can process data from all the external sources presented here, but most systems are able to use some of it.

Trends in the Economy. A company's profits are often directly related to general trends in the economy. To help determine the behavior of the economy, statistics such as the gross national product and the unemployment rate are available on magnetic tape and diskettes from a variety of sources, including the U.S. Department of Commerce and private suppliers like *Fortune* magazine. An airline would monitor economic conditions to determine its long-range sales of tickets for business and pleasure travel, both of which are affected by overall economic conditions.

Consumer Behavior. Businesses sell goods and services to fairly well-defined market segments. To determine appropriate market segments for their specific goods or services, they use the results of questionnaires and surveys, often prepared by marketing research specialists. A survey prepared for an airline might ask actual and prospective customers questions such as "How often have you flown in the last six months?" "How often do you plan to fly in the next six months?" and "How satisfied are you with the service provided by R&D Airlines?" The data gathered by such surveys is processed and summarized by the MIS.

Actions of Competitors. Businesses need to keep abreast of their competition. Information about competitors' activities can be obtained from such sources as newspapers, trade journals, and reports filed with regulatory agencies. In the airline industry, it is necessary to know about routes other airlines are adding (or taking away), new pricing policies, and additional or improved customer services.

Actions by Governments. Although the U.S. economy is known as a free-enterprise economy, or one in which the marketplace plays an essential role, all businesses and public organizations are affected by government actions. For many businesses the most visible government activity is taxation. Changes in tax rates affect a business directly by increasing or decreasing its after-tax profits. They may also affect it indirectly by increasing or decreasing the amount of money available to its potential customers. It is important to realize that for many businesses the government is a major and sometimes the only customer. Furthermore, the government regulates many industries, defining what they may and may not do.

Even though the airlines industry has been partially deregulated, government policy continues to affect it. For example, the nature and frequency of aircraft maintenance are determined largely by government rules and regulations.

Actions of Suppliers. Businesses that transform raw materials into finished products are directly dependent on their suppliers—they cannot stay in business long without access to raw materials at reasonable prices. If a steel mill is faced with a shortage of pig iron or a restaurant is faced with a shortage of bacon, it must find new sources of supply or modify its product line. In the case of an airline, the prices charged for seats depend to a large extent on the prices charged by suppliers, including aircraft manufacturers and oil companies. A good example is the surcharge that was added to air fares as a result of the spectacular increase in oil prices beginning in 1973.

Financing. A large corporation like an airline may need to deal with dozens of sources of short-, medium-, and long-term financing. The computer can be a valuable tool for analyzing and comparing the different financing options available and determining their tax implications and true cost to the company.

Actions of Environmental Protection Groups. Many industries are required to file a statement describing the potential impact of their actions on the environment before beginning a new operation. For example, an airline may have to prepare an environmental impact statement before buying a plane with a new type of jet engine. Computer models can indicate the environmental impact of such a purchase for varying periods and under a variety of conditions.

Actions of Stockholders. No publicly owned corporation can operate completely independently of its stockholders. Computer information systems can be designed to maintain a file of stockholders' names, addresses, and phone numbers to enable the company to contact stockholders in the case of a takeover bid by another corporation, or to obtain data about stockholders' attitudes toward its dividend policies.

Actions of Labor Unions. A substantial portion of operating expenses for many corporations, including airlines, consists of employee salaries and fringe benefits, which are often specified in contracts negotiated with labor unions. Management information systems can help minimize total labor cost and provide data for use in labor negotiations.

The MIS Department

The importance of management information systems is demonstrated by the fact that many computer departments are now called *MIS departments* and are responsible for developing and maintaining management information systems as well as operations information systems. An MIS department is organized to meet the needs and management style of the business it serves. Since the first computer applications were developed for such purposes as accounts receivable and payroll management, many computer departments were initially under the control of the chief financial officer. (See Figure 13-9.) This meant that

FIGURE 13-9

Traditional Approach to Placement of Computer Services Department

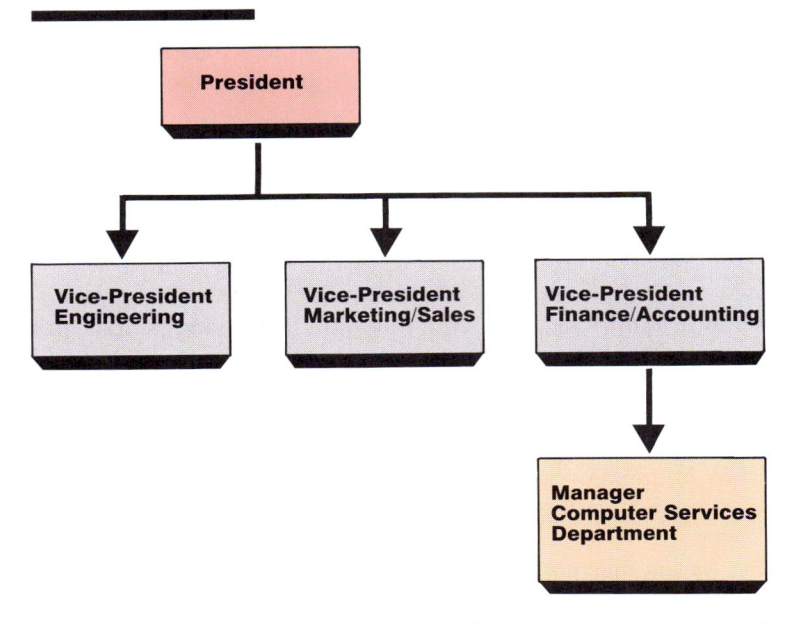

accounting and finance needs were better met than those of other departments. Some organizations have since adopted the *service center* approach, in which the MIS department is organized to meet needs of all departments. (See Figure 13-10.) Although this approach makes MIS services available on a more equitable basis, it views the MIS department as a provider of services rather than as a major part of the organization. Because the MIS must spend so much time solving the immediate information needs of the other departments (this is often referred to as "putting out fires"), it usually is unable to develop long-range plans.

Today, as a result of the increased importance of computer systems in all phases of a company's activities, the MIS department is often a separate group reporting directly to upper management. (See Figure 13-11.) This approach has the advantage of relating the MIS department to the company as a whole instead of to a single department such as accounting or finance. In many companies the director of the MIS department is a member of upper management and reports to the president or vice-president. Under these conditions the MIS department is expected to develop long-range information policies and plans for the entire company.

FIGURE 13-10

Service Approach to Placement of Computer Services Department

- President
  - Vice-President Engineering
  - Vice-President Marketing/Sales
  - Vice-President Finance/Accounting
- Manager Computer Services Department

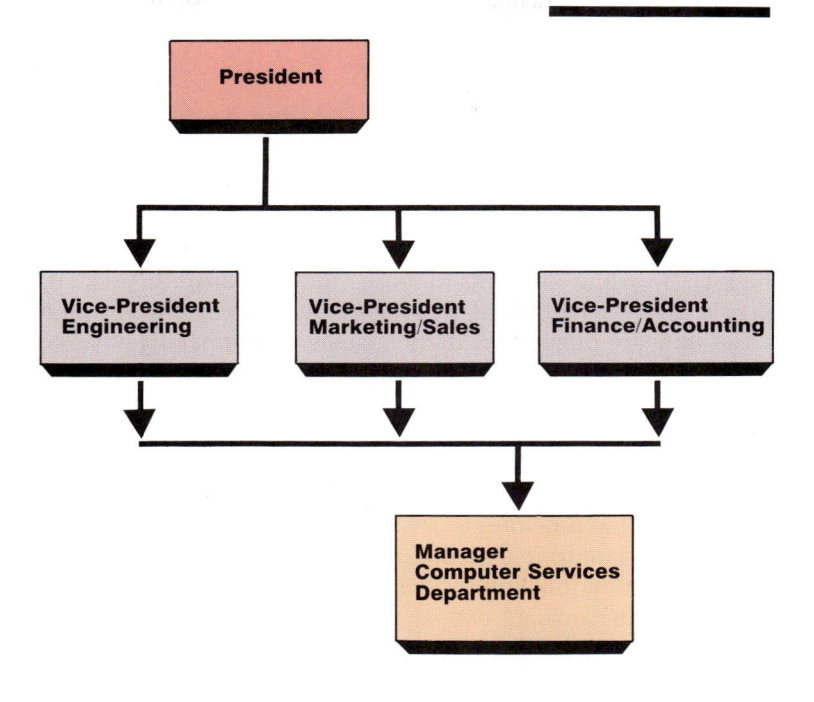

FIGURE 13-11

Contemporary Approach to Placement of Computer Services Department

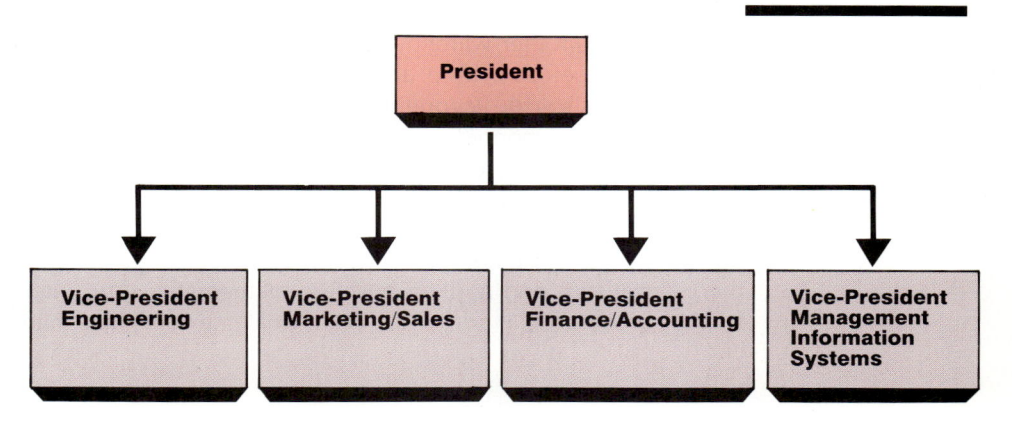

- President
  - Vice-President Engineering
  - Vice-President Marketing/Sales
  - Vice-President Finance/Accounting
  - Vice-President Management Information Systems

Decision Support Systems

Decision support systems (DSS) are computerized systems that provide middle and upper management with information to help them make decisions, especially strategic decisions. They permit managers to develop models and ascertain what might happen if various elements in those models change. In general, they answer "what if?" and "what causes?" questions. In some cases they are outgrowths of management information systems; in others, they have been developed independently. A key difference between these two types of information systems is that an MIS provides reports on a scheduled basis whereas a DSS provides information on an ad hoc or as-needed basis. With a DSS, a manager may obtain an answer to a question that has never been asked before.

It is important to realize that operations information systems, management information systems, and decision support systems are not totally separate entities but, rather, form a continuum. (See Figure 13-12.) The output generated by an operations information system may be further processed by a management information system, whose output, in turn, may be further processed by a decision support system. In its own way, each of these systems helps selected personnel get the job done.

Just as the decisions made by upper management cut across departmental divisions, the information supplied by decision support systems cuts across departmental divisions. For example, a manager may be wondering whether the company should build another warehouse. Making this decision requires a wide range of data from areas such as sales and marketing (how much is sold?), accounting (how much profit is made on what is sold?), personnel (how much are warehouse employees paid?), and buildings (how much will it cost to build or lease the proposed warehouse?).

Decision support systems depend on several technologies and disciplines, including behavioral sciences, organizational theory, statistics and applied business mathematics, and information processing. And, to an even greater extent than man-

Decision support system (DSS)
A computer information system that provides middle and upper management with information to be used in making decisions.

FIGURE 13-12

A Continuum of Computer Information Systems

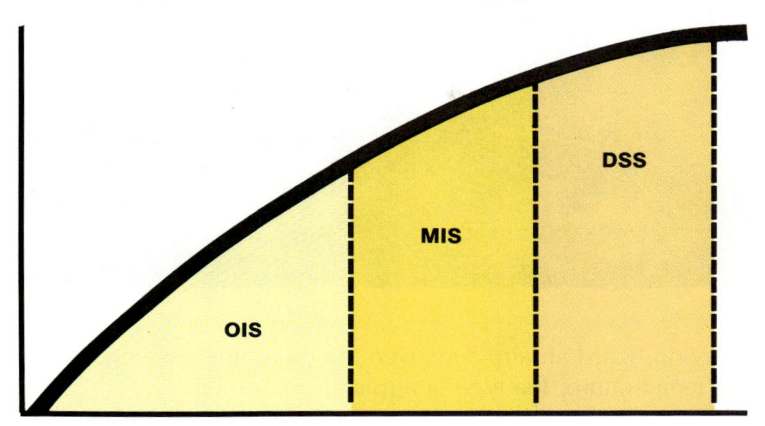

Each succeeding level relies on the previous level for data and information in much the same way that each succeeding level of personnel in an enterprise relies on previous levels.

agement information systems, they rely on external sources of data. Furthermore, these systems are continuously changing and never reach a state of completion.

Decision support systems are particularly useful in two steps of the decision-making process—processing the data and evaluating the alternatives. The other steps—defining the problem and the decision criteria, identifying the alternatives, gathering the data, making the decision, implementing the decision, and finally evaluating the decision—are best performed by the executives themselves.

Types of Decisions

There are three basic types of decisions: structured, semi-structured, and unstructured. The type of computer information system used and its role in the decision-making process depend on the type of decision to be made.

Structured Decisions. Structured decisions are made by applying one or a few well-defined rules to a situation. An example is a travel agent deciding to call a credit bureau when the amount of a credit card purchase exceeds a predetermined limit. Another example is the calculation of how much fuel to

This air traffic controller is using a computer information system to make semistructured decisions that are communicated to pilots. In cases like this there is no room for error. (© Mike Yamashita, Woodfin Camp.)

carry on board an airplane given the route, the passenger load, the temperature, the type of airplane, and so on.

Semistructured Decisions. Semistructured decisions are informed decisions based on partial information. For example, an airport manager makes a semistructured decision when deciding whether or not to close the airport during a severe snowstorm. In this situation it is impossible to have complete information. On the other hand, the airport manager can calculate the costs and benefits of closing the airport or keeping it open, thus making a relatively informed decision.

Unstructured Decisions. An unstructured decision is one to which rules do not apply. Generally, the number of variables is too large and their interaction too ill-defined for the problem to be analyzed by computer. For example, the decision to deregulate the U.S. airlines industry was basically an unstructured one. In spite of claims made by interested parties during the debate over deregulation, no one knew for certain what the effect would be.

Characteristics of Decision Support Systems

Decision support systems are geared toward helping managers make decisions by supplying specific information rather than the general reports furnished by management information systems. Although there is some overlap between the two types of systems, decision support systems are more closely associated with semistructured decisions, mathematical tools, future orientation, and user-friendliness.

Semistructured Decisions. Unstructured decisions are too complicated and require too great a quantity and variety of data to be aided substantially by computer systems. Because of their relative simplicity, structured decisions can use information supplied by management information systems or operations information systems. Semistructured decisions occupy the middle ground between unstructured decisions and structured decisions. They often require large quantitites of external data and sophisticated mathematical analysis. These decisions therefore are often made with the aid of decision support systems.

Mathematical Tools. Decision support systems enable executives who are not trained in mathematics to use mathematical tools to help them make decisions. For example, a DSS can calculate return on investment, enabling users to compare the financial aspects of two or more investment projects. An airline faced with the choice of buying or leasing an additional airplane could use a decision support system to compare the financial implications of the two alternatives. Additional mathematical tools include probability analysis, which is used, for example, in evaluating the probable success of a proposed strategy such as opening a new route.

Future Oriented. Decision support systems provide information about future performance rather than a record of the past such as is generated by most management information systems. A DSS uses a model to describe reality. The better the model and the more complete the sources of data, the more accurate its predictions are likely to be.

User-Friendly. Decision support systems are intended for busy executives who cannot waste time leafing through documentation and reports and want to obtain the overall picture quickly. They therefore offer not only rapid response but a variety of user-friendly aspects, including graphics, nonkeyboard input devices, and menus. Electronic spreadsheets, a rudimentary form of decision support system, became successful largely because of their user-friendliness. Armed with an electronic spreadsheet, a manager can explore the implications of a budgetary change. Such calculations are not feasible for managers who must depend on more traditional systems such as OIS and MIS.

FIGURE 13-13

Information Requirements

This diagram relates the information requirements of workers and various levels of management to the responsibilities that are typical of each. Source: Reprinted from Journal of Systems Management, *November 1986, p. 8.*

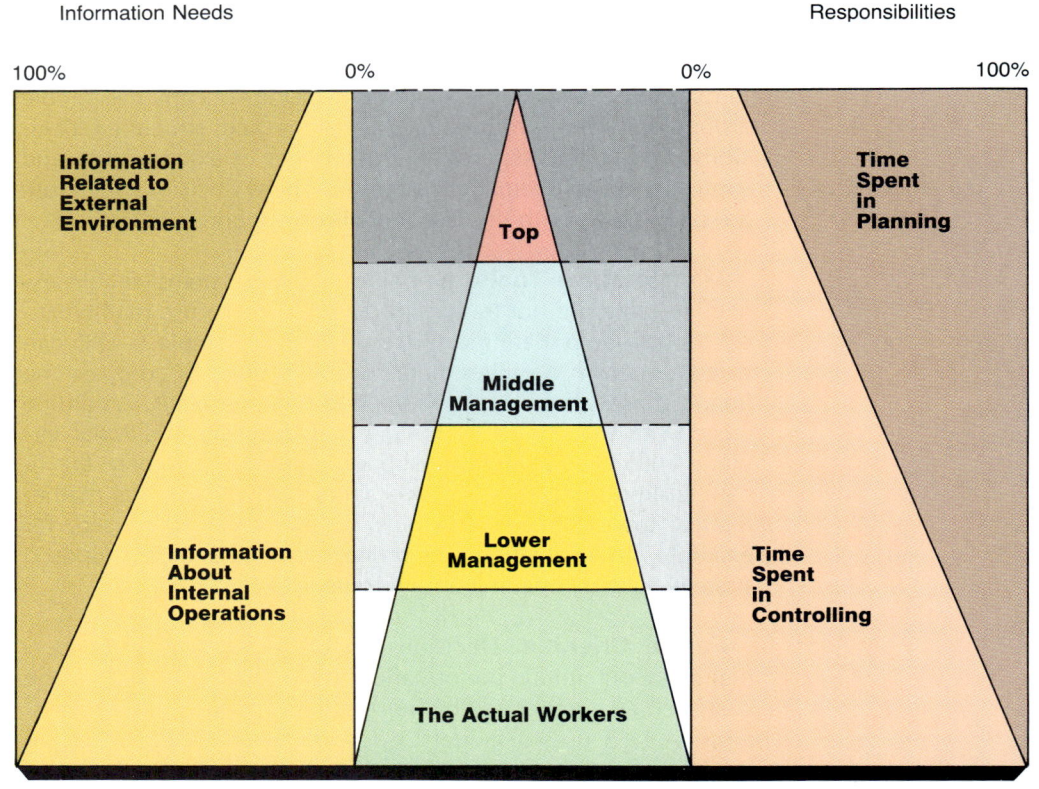

Information Needs — Responsibilities

- Information Related to External Environment
- Information About Internal Operations
- Top
- Middle Management
- Lower Management
- The Actual Workers
- Time Spent in Planning
- Time Spent in Controlling

Uses of Decision Support Systems

Decision support systems meet the specific information needs of middle and upper management. (See Figure 13-13.) Properly used, they can help managers in many ways, but as Box 13-1 points out, such systems can sometimes be misused.

Many organizations have one management information system that meets a wide variety of needs, but they may have a series of decision support systems, each of which meets a specific set of needs. For example, decision support systems pro-

BOX 13-1

MANAGING CHANGE

Uses and Misuses of Information Systems

The management process is often said to consist of four functions: planning, organization, leadership, and control. Computerized decision support systems have many uses in connection with each of these functions—but they also have some potential misuses. Much of what is said here about the DSS used by top management also applies to the use of MIS by middle management.

Planning. Management information systems and decision support systems have become key planning tools in most large organizations and in many small ones. Their greatest utility lies in their ability to make "what if?" projections based on alternative assumptions. What if mortgage interest rates fall? What will happen to the demand for home insulation? What if the value of the dollar rises in foreign currency markets? What will happen to raw-materials costs?

But even the best DSS cannot tell managers what people will do in the future. A DSS might tell a textile firm that if women decide to wear longer skirts, then more yards of cloth must be woven to make them. But it cannot forecast style changes.

Organizing. In a large firm, a DSS may help top managers see the relationships among various departments and help them work together. The availability of such a system may also affect the degree of centralization that is feasible for organization.

Leadership. One aspect of leadership is staffing—getting the right people for the right jobs. Here a DSS can be very useful. For example, a large multiplant firm may keep computerized records of any job openings within the organization and the skills of employees already on the payroll. This may permit the firm to fill vacancies through promotion from within. However, a DSS cannot supply the human contact that is essential for motivating employees and getting them to do their best.

Control. Controlling means checking to see that an organization is progressing toward its goals and taking corrective action if it is not. It is here that a well-designed DSS can make perhaps its greatest contribution. A DSS can vastly increase the timeliness and accuracy of reports, allowing management to spot and correct negative trends, or seize unexpected opportunities, much faster than in the past.

But the unprecedented power of a DSS to pull up detailed information from the depths of an organization has dangers, too. The greatest potential problem is that excessive oversight and control will be perceived by subordinates as meddling and even as spying. Brand managers may feel that they are being denied the opportunity to be creative if their activities are monitored too closely. Customer service personnel may feel pressured to be rude and impatient with customers if they know that the length of each phone call is being recorded and displayed on a terminal in the boss's office.

In short, no matter how good the DSS, managers must always remember that management is the art of *getting things done through people*.

vide sales and marketing departments with information for planning and organizing promotional campaigns. Such a system will indicate the potential payoff for a new campaign, such as a plan to advertise an airline on television instead of in newspapers. Purchasing departments also use information provided by decision support systems. An airline's purchasing group can use a DSS to compare airplanes produced by different manufacturers with respect to cost and frequency of maintenance, fuel consumption, mileage logged before retirement, and so on, taking into account the routes flown by different planes and unusual weather conditions.

Since decision support systems cut across departmental lines and provide information in an integrated form, they are particularly useful for *task forces*, groups of people from different departments who are assigned to work together on a specific project. For example, a task force of people from the accounting, sales and marketing, and flight scheduling departments can be set up to analyze potential new routes for an airline.

In practice, when a task force is set up it may be necessary to modify and expand existing decision support systems. If these systems were designed, built, and implemented according to the system development life cycle described in Chapter 12 and the programs were designed, built, and implemented according to the program development process described in Chapter 7, it should be possible to adapt them to the needs of the task force reasonably quickly. The use of data-base management systems or fourth-generation programming languages can further reduce the time needed to adapt an existing system. Figure 13-14 shows the components of a typical decision support system.

Executive Information Systems

The term *executive information system* is sometimes used to refer to decision support systems designed to meet the needs of top management. Executive information systems primarily monitor strategic information such as the company's financial picture and market share. Their chief advantage is their user-friendly presentation of information that can be used by executives in making strategic decisions.

FIGURE 13-14

Components of a Typical Decision Support System

Source: Reprinted from *Journal of Systems Management*, December 1986, p. 28.

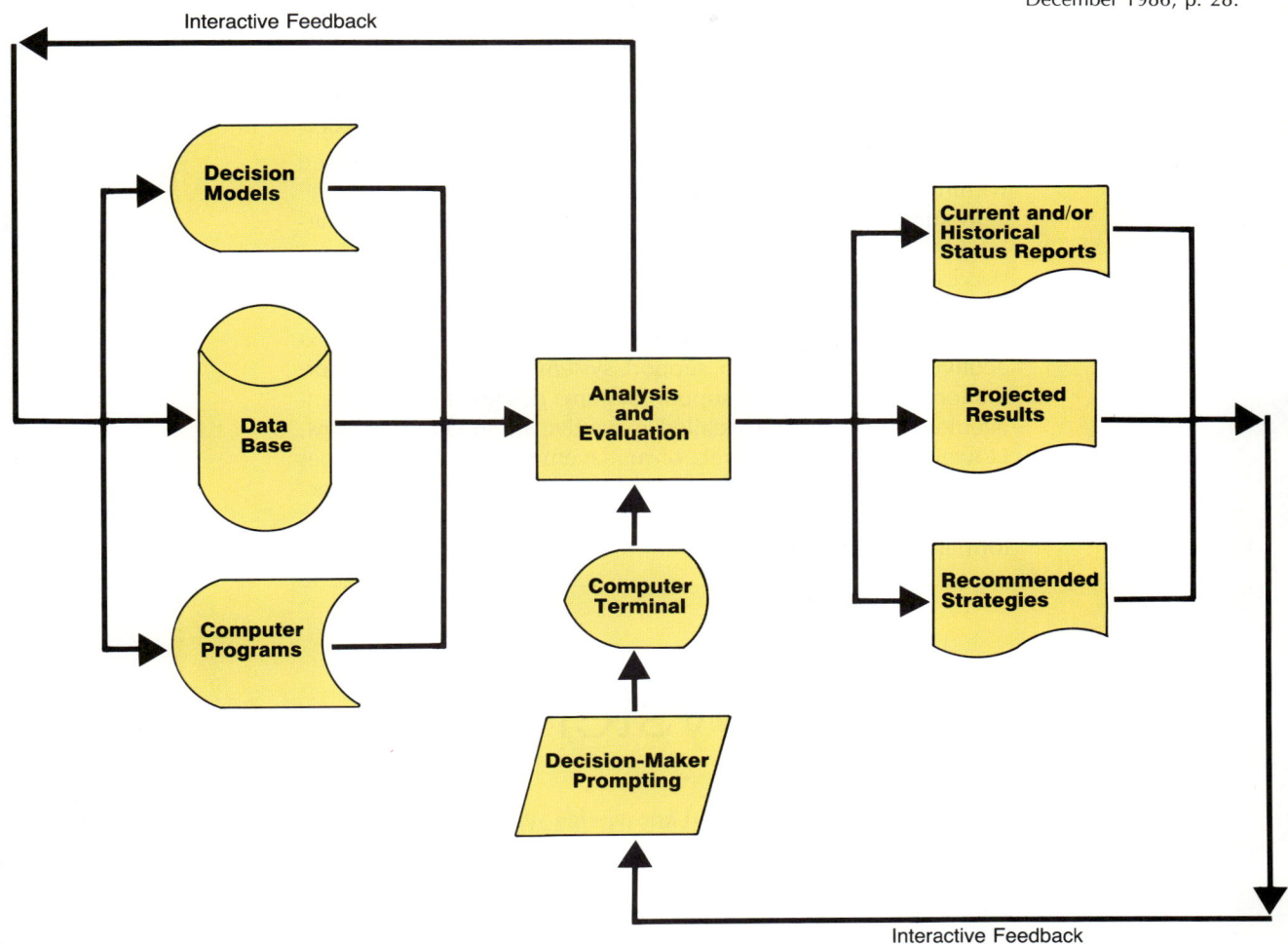

CHAPTER 13 507 MANAGEMENT SUPPORT AND EXPERT SYSTEMS

An executive information system is tailored to the organization it serves. Shell Oil Company, for example, created an EIS that processes data furnished by an external data base devoted to the oil industry. It consists of several mainframe and microcomputer software packages, including a fourth-generation query language, and a graphics package, which run on a mainframe computer. It also includes Lotus 1-2-3 and dBASE III, which run on microcomputers, and a commercially available communication program that enables users to access the system from terminals or personal computers. The system is used by a vice-president, three general managers, and six to eight senior managers to monitor current business conditions and keep abreast of price trends and histories. All the available screens and supporting data contained in the system can be accessed within twenty seconds.

In sum, several types of information systems can serve various information needs within an organization. Clerks and supervisors use reports furnished by operations information systems. Middle managers often access management information systems to obtain information. Other middle managers and executives look to decision support systems to meet their information needs. Decision support systems designed for top management are sometimes called executive information systems. However, like all the levels of management, all of these types of information systems are interrelated and depend on correct data and appropriate information from other systems in the information systems hierarchy.

Expert Systems

Expert systems, also called *knowledge systems*, are computer systems that imitate the reasoning abilities of humans, thereby supplementing or replacing the work of human experts. Expert systems are an application of *artificial intelligence (AI)*, the use of a computer to emulate human thinking.

Conventional expert systems have three parts. The first, the *knowledge base*, represents the knowledge and experience of human experts. The knowledge base is expressed by *IF . . . THEN* rules such as IF 747 THEN USE PREMIUM FUEL. The amount of knowledge contained in the system varies, depending on the nature and complexity of the human expertise that the system emulates. It may range from a dozen to over 1000

Expert system
A computer system that simulates the reasoning of human experts.

This aircraft designer is aided by an expert system. In effect, the computer is able to apply dozens of years of human experience in aircraft design. (Courtesy of Hewlett-Packard.)

rules, with sophisticated systems allowing a measure of certainty (e.g., 90 percent) to be associated with each rule and, consequently, with each conclusion the system draws.

The second part of an expert system, the *inference engine*, or *expert system shell*, is the proprietary program that processes the knowledge base by applying the rules to solve a problem. An example of an inference engine is *Mycin*, which is used in applications such as diagnosing respiratory diseases, teaching medical students, and locating failures in telecommunication networks. (See Figure 13-15.)

The third part of an expert system is the *interface*, the means by which it interacts with people who use it. The interface often takes the form of a series of questions and answers. For example, when diagnosing a medical problem, an expert system may ask the user to enter symptoms and, if necessary, to clarify them. The system then provides a diagnosis.

Sophisticated expert systems show users their reasoning on demand. For example, when an expert system used in a bank refused to grant a loan to the bank's president, the system was able to demonstrate that the president should not be granted the loan because he leased a condominium and did not own any real estate. After some rules were changed, the loan was granted.

FIGURE 13-15

Some Rules from the MYCIN Expert Diagnostic System

IF: (1) The site of the culture is blood, and
(2) The identity of the organism is not known with certainty, and
(3) The stain of the organism is gramneg, and
(4) The morphology of the organism is rod, and
(5) The patient has been seriously burned,
THEN: There is weakly suggestive evidence (0.4) that the identity of the organism is pseudomonas.

IF: (1) The infection which requires therapy is meningitis, and
(2) The patient has evidence of a serious skin or soft tissue infection, and
(3) The organisms were not seen on the strain of the culture, and
(4) The type of infection is bacterial,
THEN: There is evidence that the organism (other than those seen on cultures or smears) which might be causing the infection is staphylococcus-coagpos (.75) or streptococcus (.5).

Source: Reprinted from Journal of Systems Management, July 1985, p. 10.

Since the knowledge base and the inference engine are separate entities, it is easy to add rules to reflect changing conditions. Unlike traditional programs, whose instructions must be written in the correct order, the rules in a knowledge base may be in any order. This flexibility makes it possible for people with no programming experience to modify the knowledge base after a short period of training.

Expert systems are available on computers of all sizes. However, those that run on personal computers are limited to small and medium-sized applications, since most personal-computer systems have difficulty accommodating more than 100 rules. Many expert systems run on specially designed workstations, but because these workstations are relatively expensive and cannot be used for other applications, their usefulness tends to be limited.

Expert systems are used in various fields and for many applications, including evaluating sites for petroleum and mineral resources, helping salespeople select computer systems to meet customers' needs, providing estate planning and portfolio management, and helping scientists plan and simulate gene-splicing experiments. IBM uses an expert system to assemble and test disk drives for its mainframe computers. The system was written by two technicians with no previous programming experience. It is credited with a 94 percent success rate in diagnosing errors on the first try.

Expert System

Simulates the reasoning of human experts

Decision Support System

Provides middle and upper management with information to be used in making decisions

Management Information System

Provides managers with integrated information on a scheduled basis

Operations Information System

Collects, processes, and stores data for routine record-keeping purposes

Computer Information Systems

Benefits of Expert Systems

Although it is possible to build a microcomputer-based expert system with a moderate investment of time and money, most expert systems require a major commitment. Before deciding whether to install an expert system, an organization should consider the potential benefits and drawbacks. The following are some of the benefits:

1. *Continuity of knowledge.* An expert system enables a company to continue to draw upon the expertise of employees who have left the company.

2. *Decreased overhead.* Although few companies lay off personnel and replace them with expert systems, they may hire fewer people and decide not to replace those who retire or leave.

3. *Easy transport.* It is considerably quicker and less expensive to ship diskettes or magnetic tapes containing an expert system than to move experts and their families. Expert systems enable organizations to diagnose problems that occur thousands of miles away.

4. *Employee training.* Expert systems can train new and existing employees, particularly if the system explains its reasoning and conclusions on demand. Such training can be tailored to a company's needs.

5. *Knowledge of others.* Expert systems can represent and apply the knowledge and experience of large numbers of experts. For example, physicians use expert systems for medical diagnoses: They compare their knowledge to that of the system, which is actually that of other physicians and experts.

6. *Competitive edge.* Expert systems can provide services that exceed the abilities of human experts. For example, the expert system XCON, which is used by Digital Equipment Corporation to configure minicomputer systems, can supply proposed solutions faster than human analysts.

Drawbacks of Expert Systems

Like other types of computer solutions, expert systems have drawbacks that may counteract their advantages. Therefore, it is necessary to make a detailed comparison of the benefits and the drawbacks of an expert system before deciding whether or not to install one. The drawbacks of expert systems include the following:

1. *Hardware.* Expert systems make great demands on hardware. Some simple expert systems can be run on PCs, but

BOX 13-2

FRONTIERS IN TECHNOLOGY
Personal Workstations

The personal workstation is a relatively new arrival in the computing world—the first commercial units, from Apollo Computer Systems (Chelmsford, Massachusetts), Sun Microsystems (Mountain View, California), and Xerox Information Systems (Pasadena, California), appeared in 1981. By 1986, 57,000 such workstations had been sold. By 1990, says analyst Kathleen Hurley of Dataquest (San Jose, California), close to 350,000 workstations will be sold annually.

Personal workstations usually come with sophisticated graphics displays, a keyboard, and a mouse, and frequently are attached to high-speed networks. The network gives rapid access to other users (and to files and data on their workstations), to massive data storage, and often, to mainframe computers or even supercomputers. Consequently, workstation users have at their fingertips computing power exceeding that of a personal computer several times over.

The first users of personal workstations were engineers and designers. For example, mechanical engineers can use their workstations to design, analyze, and simulate products and even generate the instructions for driving the machine tools that will make the product's parts. Now the range of applications is broadening into finance and general management.

Inference Corporation (Los Angeles) has developed a workstation-based expert system for American Express that can conduct sophisticated credit checks that previously were possible only with the expertise of a senior corporate officer. Such financial and business applications are a new area of activity for workstations. "I believe that workstations are just beginning to make an impact on corporate America," says Don Sinsabaugh of Swergold, Chefitz and Sinsabaugh, a New York–based investment company. With the increases in computing power that workstations will shortly bring, AI applications like intelligent stock trading systems and rule-based merger and acquisitions systems will become available to a much wider marketplace.

"An individual can get greater responsiveness from a machine under his control than if he has to share computing resources through a multiterminal system," says Vicki J. Brown, a program manager at International Data Corporation (Framingham, Massachusetts). The possibilities for management applications are exciting in view of the fact that the performance of workstations is beginning to encroach on the territory now occupied by minicomputers, while their price—$15,000 or less as of 1987—is dropping close to that of a top-of-the-line PC.

Source: Reprinted with permission from *High Technology*, March 1987. Copyright © 1987 by Infotechnology Publishing Corp., 214 Lewis Wharf, Boston, MA 02110.

they are quite limited. On the other hand, when expert systems are run on mainframe machines, they may monopolize the CPU for long periods. In some cases these problems can be overcome by the use of personal workstations like those described in Box 13-2.

2. *Software.* Since expert systems usually are written in special programming languages, developing and maintaining the system may require a separate programming staff. This results in higher costs, and it may be difficult to recruit and train the programmers.

3. *Data.* In general, expert systems will not process data contained on a corporate data base. Data must be recoded into a special data base, a time-consuming operation. If the data is extensive, storage and maintenance can also be expensive.

4. *Human reactions.* Although the success of the best expert systems can match or surpass that of the best human experts in many areas, many individuals shy away from relying on the computer. In the field of medicine, for example, an expert system can apply the combined knowledge and experience of several world-class practitioners; nevertheless, most patients prefer to deal with a human physician.

Although expert systems have yet to prove themselves for most commercial applications, they are playing an increasing role in many areas. As the costs of this technology and the associated hardware and software decrease while the salaries and fringe benefits of human experts increase, we may expect the use of expert systems to expand. In general, such systems are most valuable in helping human experts, rather than replacing them.

Information Centers

As computer technology has become increasingly sophisticated, the *applications backlog*, or the time users have to wait for their computer information requests to be met, has either remained constant or increased. Each new type of information system and each advance in computer technology, whether it involves faster and more powerful hardware or easier to use software, promises to reduce this backlog but fails to do so. The

information center, a department set up to train end-users to access their own data and generate their own reports, is another means by which computer experts hope to reduce the applications backlog. With the rise of the personal computer, a major focus for many information centers is helping users choose personal-computer hardware and software.

Information centers have been available at universities for at least two decades, but the first commercial center was not developed until 1973. At first the concept progressed slowly in the business world, but its popularity increased with the emergence of microcomputers in the late 1970s and early 1980s. At this writing, there are more than 6000 information centers in the United States. (See Figure 13-16.)

The variety of information centers is great; in fact, no two information centers are likely to be exactly the same because the needs they are designed to meet are not the same from one organization to another. Many information centers have their own hardware resources, ranging from one or a few personal computers to a complete mainframe computer system. They may contain a wide variety of software, usually chosen for ease of use. They are generally available to all users who need the computer for their work, and as a result some information centers serve hundreds or even thousands of users ranging from neophytes to power users.

The San Diego Gas and Electric Company information center, for example, has a staff of twelve that supports about 2500 users who operate 230 IBM personal computers and 1200 terminals linked to two large IBM mainframes. They are able to use this equipment for applications ranging from engineering and accounting studies to electronic spreadsheets. Because the information center helps users identify their needs and develop detailed requirements for new systems, the MIS staff can spend its time refining the data base or developing major applications that users cannot develop themselves.

Perhaps the major value of information centers is teaching users to access the computer on their own, thereby reducing the we-must-have-it-this-afternoon report requests that take up so much of computer specialists' time. Information centers enable many users to get started with personal computers, which also frees computer specialists for other tasks. However, although a major goal of information centers is to reduce the applications backlog, they often fail to meet this goal. When users develop a better feel for the computer and what it can do, they ask for more complex applications, thereby increasing the waiting time for results. Furthermore, as users gain confidence, their expectations become higher. Sometimes users' expectations are so high that they become unrealistic.

Information center
A department whose funtion is to train end-users to access their own data and generate their own reports.

FIGURE 13-16

Common Applications of Information Centers

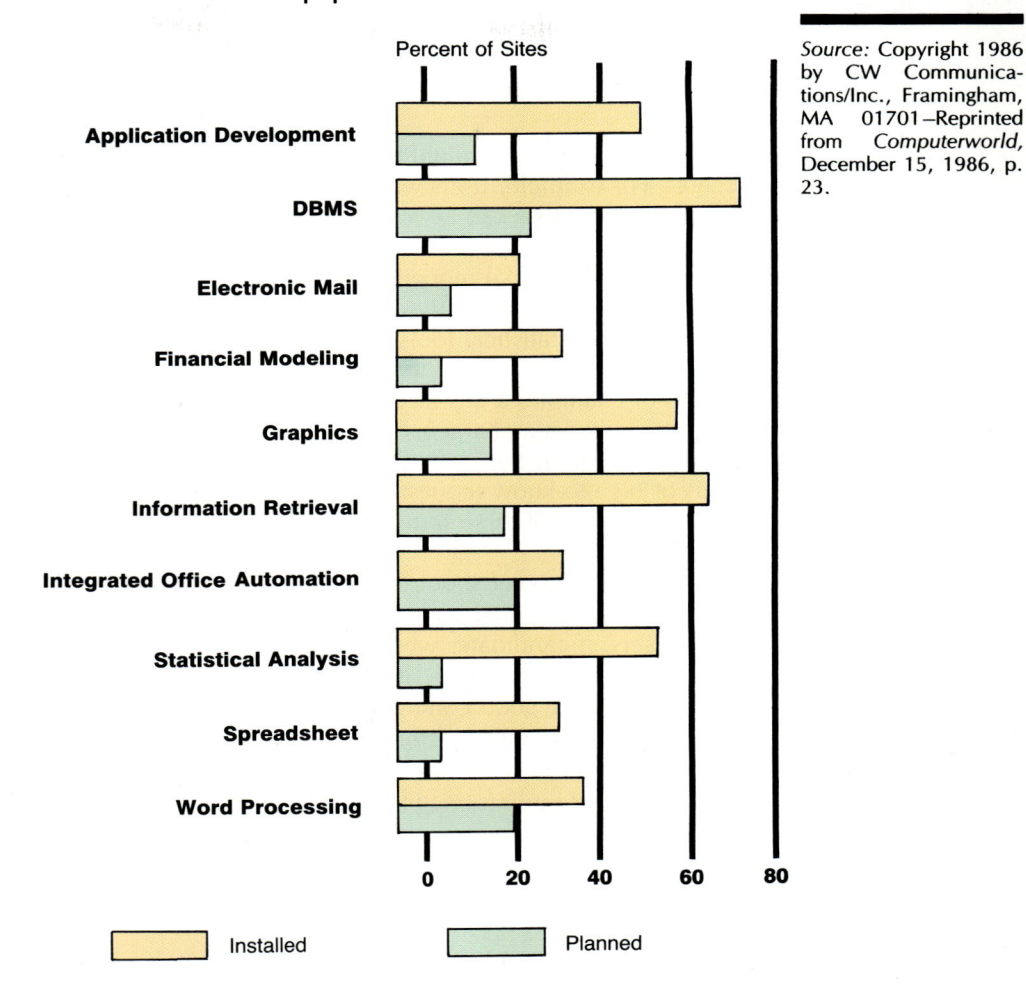

Source: Copyright 1986 by CW Communications/Inc., Framingham, MA 01701—Reprinted from *Computerworld,* December 15, 1986, p. 23.

Percent of Sites

- Application Development
- DBMS
- Electronic Mail
- Financial Modeling
- Graphics
- Information Retrieval
- Integrated Office Automation
- Statistical Analysis
- Spreadsheet
- Word Processing

☐ Installed ☐ Planned

Guidelines for Information Centers

Traditionally, information centers have been established for two purposes:

1. To give users training in fourth-generation programming languages so that they can produce their own queries and reports without needing help from systems analysts and programmers; in other words, to help users engage in what is often called *end-user computing.*

CHAPTER 13 515 MANAGEMENT SUPPORT AND EXPERT SYSTEMS

2. To serve as a clearinghouse for the purchase, use, and maintenance of personal-computer hardware and software.

It takes only about two or three years for these objectives to be largely achieved as users become familiar with a few essential software packages and as the number of personal computers in the organization reaches a saturation point. For an information center to continue to succeed once it has met its initial objectives, the organization must apply certain guidelines:

1. Improved productivity should be a long-term objective of the center. For example, users who have learned to work with electronic spreadsheets can be trained to audit their worksheet models and apply more sophisticated personal-productivity software such as financial modeling programs, which enable them to perform financial analyses with the aid of advanced mathematical and statistical tools.

2. The organization must treat the information center as a business. For example, a key factor in the success of an information center is a *chargeback policy* in which users pay for services rendered. Such a policy tends to eliminate frivolous or nice-to-know requests and makes it easier to justify the existence of the information center to upper management.

3. The information center should be staffed with personnel who are technically skilled and able to work well with a wide variety of users. If candidates who combine these qualifications are not available, it is advisable to favor applicants who have good communication skills. If necessary, technical problems can be referred to the MIS department.

4. The organization needs to agree on general-purpose, easy-to-use software for the information center. A major problem of the personal-computer revolution is the difficulty of exchanging data and programs that have been developed on different computers using different software packages. Standardizing the software will make it easier for users to exchange data and programs; in addition, it can lead to reduced purchase costs (e.g., volume discounts).

5. The information center must develop procedures for accessing production data. Often end-users are not allowed to access data such as invoice or payroll files.

6. Information centers need to help users develop a programmer's outlook. Although many users apply personal-productivity packages and other software successfully, they are not trained in problem analysis. For example, they may try to use an electronic spreadsheet to solve a problem because it is the software that they know best, not because it is the best means of solving that problem. Users must also be encouraged to develop good testing habits, to back up their files and to document their work, both for use by others and for their own later use.

7. The people in the information center need to develop good relationships with those in the MIS department. This goal may be difficult to achieve, since MIS personnel often feel that the information center is invading their territory and may resent losing some of their best personnel to the center. In practice, however, a properly run information center can serve the MIS department by absorbing time-consuming user requests.

Now that we have explored the nature of computer information systems and information centers in detail, we are ready to examine the impact of computer systems on office work and production processes. These subjects are discussed in the next two chapters.

SUMMARY

1. Within an organization, data is generated and information processed by several interdependent systems. **Operations information systems (OIS)** process files or data bases and produce documents that help keep track of basic resources. **On-line transaction-processing systems (OLTPS)** are systems in which several users can make inquiries and updates of a shared data base.

2. Operations information systems provide various types of information needed to carry out clerical operations and enable supervisors to plan, organize, lead, and control efficiently and effectively. They furnish periodic reports, summary reports, and exception reports.

3. Management information systems (MIS) begin where operations information systems end. They integrate, consolidate, and summarize information produced by operations information systems. They are often used by middle managers, whose activities tend to involve longer time spans and more scope for individual judgment than those of supervisors. Management information systems may use predictive reports and ratio analysis reports. An MIS is usually set up to integrate data from various departments and may also process data from external sources.

4. The organization of the MIS department depends on the needs and management style of the company it serves. Many computer departments were first placed under the control of the chief financial officer. Some companies have adopted the service center approach, in which the MIS department also responds to the needs of departments other than accounting and finance. Today, as a result of the increased importance of computer systems in all phases of a company's activities, the MIS department is often a separate group reporting directly to upper management.

5. Decision support systems (DSS) are computerized systems that provide middle and upper managers with information to help them make strategic decisions. In general, decision support systems are used to make semistructured decisions, to apply mathematical tools, and to provide information about future performance. The term *executive information system* is sometimes used to refer to decision support systems designed to meet the needs of top management.

6. Expert systems simulate the reasoning of human experts. They typically consist of three parts: a knowledge base, which represents the knowledge and experience of human experts; an inference engine, which is a proprietary program that processes the knowledge base; and an interface with the people who use the product. Many expert systems permit the user to interrogate the computer.

7. An **information center** is a department whose purpose is to train end-users to access their own data and generate their own reports. Information centers rarely reduce the applications backlog, but they do free computer specialists for other activities. Recently information centers have begun to serve as clearinghouses for the purchase, use, and maintenance of personal-computer hardware and software.

KEY TERMS

operations information system (OIS)

on-line transaction-processing system (OLTPS)

management information system (MIS)

decision support system (DSS)

expert system

information center

REVIEW QUESTIONS

1. What is the information systems pyramid? How does it relate to the different levels of management in a typical organization?

2. Compare and contrast two types of operations information systems. What type of personnel do such systems supply with information?

3. Describe management information systems. List some possible sources of external information used by these systems.

4. Describe decision support and executive information systems. How do they differ from systems that are lower on the information systems pyramid?

5. What are expert systems? List and describe each of their component parts. Identify some of the potential benefits and drawbacks of expert systems.

6. Explain the information center concept. What are the initial objectives of most information centers? Why is it necessary to go beyond these goals to ensure the survival and growth of the center?

APPLICATIONS

1. Find an article that describes how supervisors use computer systems. What types of systems do they use? What kind of information do they receive?

2. Find an article that describes how middle managers use computer systems. Answer the same questions as in application 1.

3. Find an article that describes how top managers use computer systems. Answer the same questions as in application 1.

4. Discuss the following statement: Expert systems will eliminate the need for human experts.

CASE FOR DISCUSSION

Consolidated Tube is a leading manufacturer of plumbing supplies. It has a sales organization that spans the entire United States. Its sales representatives call on wholesalers (who in turn sell Consolidated's products to individual plumbing contractors) and on a number of large retail hardware chains.

Consolidated's representative in Oklahoma is Wilson Flynn. Flynn attended Oklahoma University in Norman, where he majored in business. He now makes Norman his home base, but he spends many nights a month away from his family because his sales territory covers the entire state.

A typical night on the road finds him in a motel in Muscogee or Tulsa. After a dinner that makes him look forward to home cooking, he returns to his room, snaps open the case of his portable computer, and continues a long day that began with a working breakfast. Using software supplied by the company, he prepares the day's report. The report includes a list of clients visited, sales closed on each product line, and a forecast of future sales potential for each client. When the report is finished, he calls a special number at corporate headquarters in Rockville, Illinois. A computer at the other end answers with a tone. Flynn connects the modem of his computer to the telephone and transmits his report.

The next day Jill Soderbach, Midwest regional sales manager for Consolidated, arrives for work in her office in Rockville. Soderbach's job is to give the firm's traveling representatives the support they need to do the job. Her management duties also include a control function: She must make sure that all potential clients are visited regularly and that all sales representatives are performing up to the company's standards.

Her first task of the day is to review the reports that the sales representatives have called in during the night. The computer that answered the telephone when Flynn called has already prepared a summary for the region as a whole. Soderbach looks at this first. Then she goes through the sales territories one by one. When she calls up the Oklahoma file, she is able to review not only Flynn's report but a variety of other data as well. She sees that Flynn's sales this year are running well ahead of last year's mark. In fact, his territory has become one of the busiest in the entire Midwest region. Perhaps the territory should be subdivided, she thinks; it is getting to be too large for one person to handle. As she goes through the reports other ideas occur. Certain product lines are not being given a high enough priority. A competitor's vigorous campaign in Iowa is cutting into Consolidated's sales—something should be done about that. She makes some notes concerning these matters.

The notes are for a luncheon meeting she has scheduled with T. H. White, vice-president for strategic planning. White reports directly to the president of the company and is responsible for such basic decisions as what lines of business to enter and how to deal with competition from other firms. Competition from imports has been a particular problem recently. White wants to know if Soderbach has any insights that will help the company formulate a plan for dealing with this competitive threat.

mic view of the firm's manufacturing facilities and looks over the notes that Soderbach brought to lunch. A pattern begins to emerge from the data. White sees a possible approach to the problem that faces him—an approach that, when implemented, will have effects that ripple through the entire company.

CASE QUESTIONS

1. Flynn, Soderbach, and White have different functions within the company and different tasks to perform. How are their varying functions and tasks reflected in the different types of computer systems they will use? Answer in terms of concepts introduced in this chapter.

2. Consolidated's computer system plays an important role in tying together decision making at many different levels in the company. How will data generated at each level of the information pyramid affect information systems and decisions at other levels of the pyramid?

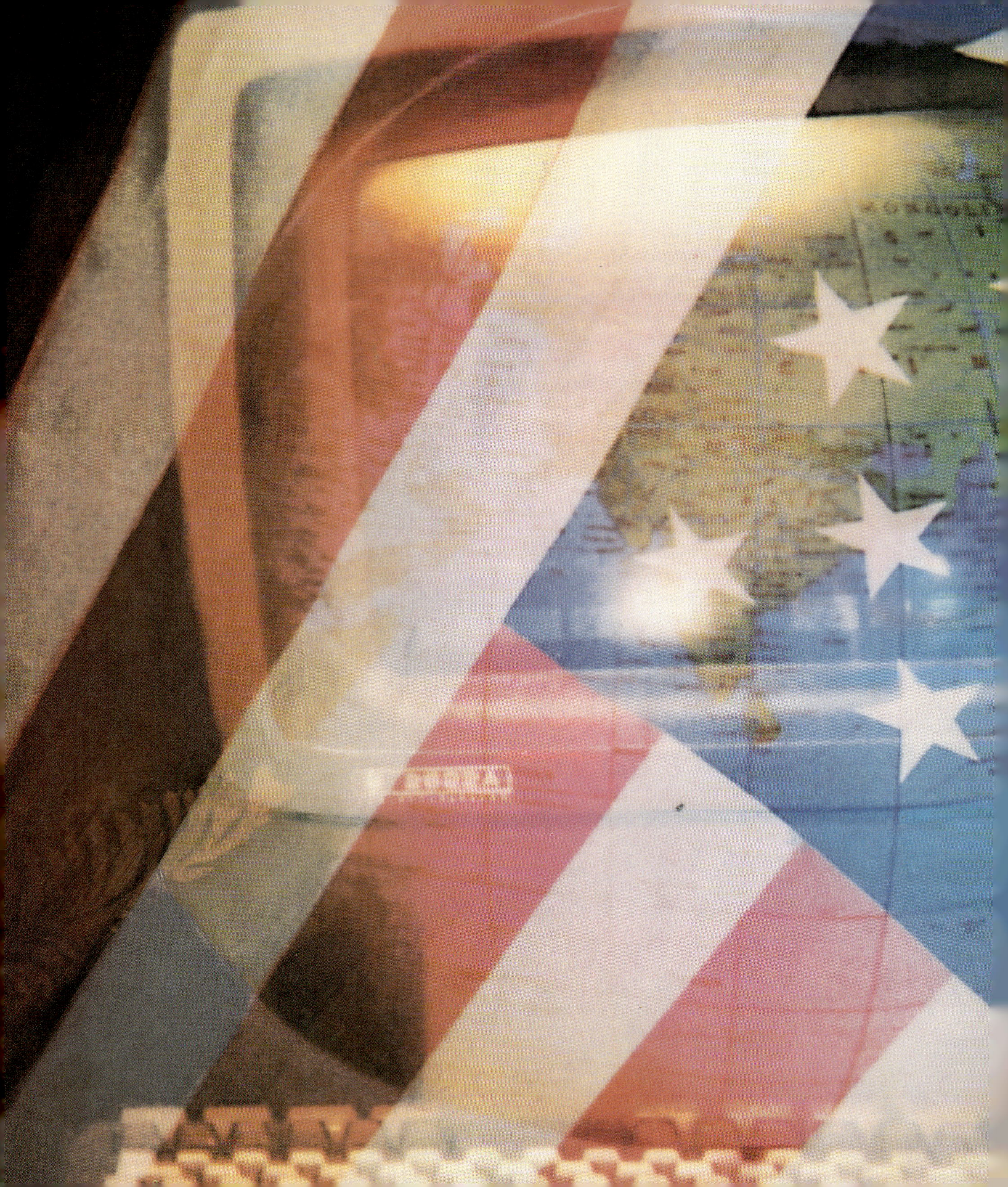

The Automated Office

CHAPTER

14

As Karen Dowling drives along the parkway, the stone needle of the Washington Monument is etched in black against a sky streaked with pink and orange. Beside it, the rim of the sun is peeping over the horizon. It takes an early start to beat the rush hour traffic into Washington, D.C.

Dowling parks a few blocks from the Capitol, and by 7:45 A.M. she is showing her pass to the guard at the entrance of the building that houses the offices of the Voice of America. She walks down a corridor past a window through which visitors can see a team of engineers working at a long control console. A lighted map of the world shows the locations of transmitters and the countries to which the Voice of America broadcasts daily in forty-two languages.

At her desk, the first thing Dowling does is to activate a terminal connected to the agency's Source News and Programming (SNAP) system. A flashing message on the screen tells her that two messages are waiting. She calls up the first message. It is from her boss, Terry Holman, requesting that copies be made of testimony that the agency will present to a Senate subcommittee that afternoon. The second message is from a friend, Alyosha Primorov, who is a broadcaster in the USSR division: "Ты свободно сегодня вечером?"

A key feature of the SNAP system, which was developed for the Voice of America by Xerox, is its ability to handle word processing in all of the languages in which broadcasts are made—Russian, French, Arabic, whatever. Primorov, a native speaker of Russian, uses the system to type the scripts for his daily news broadcasts. He knows that Dowling was a Russian language major in college, so he often sends her messages in Russian.

"Да, судовольствием." Dowling replies. She then gets to work on the testimony. Holman went over it the evening before, after Dowling had gone home, and he made some changes. Dowling makes the necessary corrections in page formats and sends the document to a laser printer in the next room. In a few minutes a very professional-looking document is ready for copying.

Other copies of the testimony must go to people at other agencies. Dowling calls up a master address file, selects the university and other-agencies categories and prints them on a sheet of labels using a dot-matrix printer. By this time it is nine o'clock. In preparing the final copy of the testimony and the mailing, she has already done what would have been a full day's work in a traditional office.

Ours is an information society, one in which more than half of the active population is engaged in the processing of information. Like Karen Dowling, most of these people work in offices and are making increasing use of computer information systems. Chapter 12 explained how such systems are developed, and Chapter 13 presented an overview of the different types of systems used in organizations. This chapter focuses on computer information systems used in office environments. It examines the ways in which office automation can increase the productivity of workers in thousands of offices in business and government, as it has for workers at the Voice of America. Since one of the essential components of any system is the human factor, the chapter also discusses the impact of office automation on different levels of personnel.

When you have read this chapter you should be able to:

1. Show how office automation affects managers and professionals.
2. List and explain the tools of office automation.
3. Describe the features of integrated workstations.
4. Discuss the importance of integrated office automation systems in business and other organizations.
5. Describe the impact of office automation on secretaries and managers.
6. Describe desktop publishing, including its applications and limitations.
7. Understand and use the key terms listed at the end of the chapter.

In the late 1980s office expenses account for more than 25 percent of the cost of doing business for most companies, and this percentage is expected to almost double by the beginning of the 1990s. Although the rate of increase in office productivity accelerated rapidly during the early and mid-1980s compared to the 1970s, much improvement remains to be made. For businesses to remain competitive in today's environment they must make further increases in the productivity and cost-effectiveness of their office operations.

Increasing cost is not the only problem in modern business and administrative offices. For decades managers have been complaining about the low quality and high turnover rate of clerical personnel. They also complain of poor postal service and hours spent commuting rather than doing productive work. The automated office resolves many of these problems of traditional offices.

Contrast the traditional office, in which the only equipment was typewriters and a telephone, with the modern office. Notice that stacks of paper have been replaced by magnetic media. [(top) Culver Pictures; (bottom) © Sepp Seitz, Photo Researchers.]

CHAPTER 14 525 THE AUTOMATED OFFICE

The first attempts at **office automation (OA)**, the process of applying computers, communications, and related technologies to increase productivity in offices, were directed at secretaries and clerical workers. But recently office automation has increasingly been applied to managers, professionals, and technical workers. Office automation may be applied in a wide variety of offices, ranging from a corner of an apartment, where the occupant pays bills and files correspondence, to the executive suite of a multinational corporation.

Office automation (OA)
The process of applying computers, communications, and related technologies to increase productivity in an office.

Benefits of Office Automation

Office automation provides two types of benefits in comparison with a traditional office. First, it reduces the time required to complete a given activity, thereby increasing the number of activities that can be carried out. This benefit is particularly significant for repetitive activities. For example, word processing, one component of office automation, substantially decreases the time and effort required to produce a general mailing in which the contents of the letters are essentially the same.

Second, office automation enables workloads to be tailored to individuals' levels of competence. As a result, high-level and

Dozens of operators use word-processing programs in this New York bank. More modern equipment does not necessarily mean better working conditions. (© Tom Hollyman, Photo Researchers.)

PEOPLE AND SYSTEMS   526   PART 4

TABLE 14-1

Managers' Tasks in Traditional and Automated Offices

Task	Traditional Office	Automated Office
Management	30%	35%
Specialized professional work	16	20
Routine professional work	13	15
Administrative and support work	16	15
Clerical work	7	5
Nonproductive activity	18	10

Source: Based on Peter G. Sassone and A. Perry Schwartz, "Cost-Justifying Office Automation," *Datamation,* February 15, 1986, pp. 83–88.

skilled personnel can sharply reduce the time they spend on tasks that do not require people with their expertise. For example, in a traditional office, managers may proofread letters, search for filed material, and make phone calls. An automated office reduces the amount of time and effort spent on such activities.

In a study published in the February 15, 1986, issue of *Datamation* magazine, Peter G. Sassone and A. Perry Schwartz reported that typical managers spend more than 40 percent of their time on activities that could be classified as underemployment, that is, activities that might be automated or delegated to subordinates. The authors propose that through office automation, managers' time could be reallocated so that they spend only 30 percent on such activities. Table 14-1 shows the tasks managers perform and how they would be allocated in a traditional and an automated office. Tables 14-2 and 14-3 illustrate Sassone and Schwartz's findings for several categories of office personnel.

Sassone and Schwartz also estimate that the increased managerial productivity that results from automating an office has an annual value of just under $14,000 when salary, fringe benefits, and direct overhead are taken into account, whereas the increased productivity of secretaries would have a value of under $150. Although not all researchers and organizations report the same findings, it is increasingly clear that the major thrust of office automation in the future will be toward increasing the productivity of managers and professional and technical personnel because of the greater financial benefits that accrue from such increases.

TABLE 14-2

Baseline Composite Work Profile Matrix (N = 587, Four Departments)

	Higher-Value Work			Lower- and No-Value Work		
Employee Class	Mgt. & Supv.	Spec. Prof.	Rout. Prof.	Admin. & Support	Cler'l	Nonprod.
Managers	30%	16%	13%	16%	7%	18%
Senior Professionals	2	35	26	13	12	12
Junior Professionals	1	10	50	13	14	12
Administrators and Technicians	0	0	1	58	27	14
Secretaries	0	0	0	10	76	14

Source: Peter G. Sassone and A. Perry Schwartz, "Cost-Justifying Office Automation," *Datamation,* February 15, 1986, p. 84.

TABLE 14-3

Anticipated Post OA Composite Work Profile Matrix

	Higher-Value Work			Lower- and No-Value Work		
Employee Class	Mgt. & Supv.	Spec. Prof.	Rout. Prof.	Admin. & Support	Cler'l	Nonprod.
Managers	35%	20%	15%	15%	5%	10%
Senior Professionals	2	42	29	11	8	8
Junior Professionals	1	15	55	11	10	8
Administrators and Technicians	0	0	1	65	25	10
Secretaries	0	0	0	12	78	10

Source: Peter G. Sassone and A. Perry Schwartz, "Cost-Justifying Office Automation," *Datamation,* February 15, 1986, p. 84.

Tools of Office Automation

An automated office is a system, and like any system it relies on the proper functioning and coordination of its individual

Word Processing

Electronic Mail

Electronic Filing

Image Processing

Teleconferencing

Telecommuting

Automating the Office

components. Among the most important components of the automated office are tools that handle word processing, electronic mail, electronic filing, image processing, teleconferencing, and telecommuting.

Word Processing

Word processing is the cornerstone of the automated office. Originally it was performed on specialized machines called dedicated word processors (see Chapter 9), which are still an important part of many automated offices. However, many people now work with microcomputers, which can also be used for other office functions such as electronic spreadsheets and data-base management.

Opinions are mixed concerning the profitability of word processing for managers and professionals. On the one hand, they can save time typing and correcting documents; on the other hand, the notion of managers and professionals typing their own material goes against the concept of division of labor, and in most cases nonclerical personnel are unable to enter the material fast enough. Many organizations therefore have developed arrangements in which a secretary enters the original document and the manager makes corrections using the word processor.

Electronic Mail

Electronic mail
The sending, storing, and delivering of messages by electronic means.

Electronic mail (or *E-mail*) is the sending, storing, and delivering of messages electronically, replacing telephone calls and mail service. Many office employees start their day by switching on a workstation and asking for a display of their electronic mail such as messages or memos, which they can file or discard by pressing a few keys. To reply, they can use a word processor. There are basically two categories of electronic mail services: in-house E-mail, which is run on a firm's computer system, and commercial E-mail, which is supplied by organizations such as General Electric Information Services and MCI Communication. As its name implies, in-house E-mail is limited to use within an organization. A commercial E-mail service enables subscribers to contact other organizations as well as commercial news services.

In the mid-1980s electronic mail was still a small but rapidly growing communication method; there were 225,000 commercial subscribers generating an estimated $150 million in revenue, in comparison to the 500,000 Telex machines generating

CHAPTER 14   **529**   THE AUTOMATED OFFICE

$700 million for Western Union and almost 500,000 facsimile transmission machines generating an estimated $650 million for the telephone companies. It is estimated, however, that electronic mail revenue will climb to $5 billion by 1992, with a corresponding increase in number of users.

Advantages. Electronic mail is expected to grow rapidly because it offers several advantages compared to traditional methods of communication. Among the advantages of E-mail are the following:

1. *The recipient need not be present.* In many cases the benefits of being able to receive messages while one is absent may be great enough to warrant the use of electronic mail. According to AT&T, 75 percent of all business calls are not completed because of busy signals or unavailability of the intended party. Electronic mail makes it possible to transmit messages whenever the sender wishes.

2. *Potentially lower cost.* Electronic mail systems that operate on a company's existing computer network tend to be relatively inexpensive. For example, some in-house systems send messages for as little as 5 to 7 cents each.

3. *Written communication.* Unlike telephone conversations, electronic mail produces hard copy. Both the sender and the recipient can request a permanent copy, which can be retrieved at any time. Many systems record the time when the recipient first accesses the message, making it impossible for him or her to claim, "I'm sorry, I never got your memo dated March 17."

4. *Many recipients.* A major advantage of electronic mail is the ease with which a single message can be sent to several recipients. In general, the greater the number of people who receive the message, the greater the savings in preparing and sending the message by electronic mail compared to traditional communication methods.

5. *Speed.* Electronic mail travels at the speed of light. This is particularly important for long-distance communication, for which mail or courier services are likely to be too slow and the telephone is inconvenient because of differences in time zones.

6. *Succinctness.* Senders can edit electronic communication until it conveys the exact message desired, thereby saving the recipient time and energy when reading the message.

Disadvantages. In spite of electronic mail's many advantages over traditional methods of communication, it has certain disadvantages that limit its use. The disadvantages of E-mail include the following:

1. *Not easy to use.* Potential users may find electronic mail systems intimidating, especially if they don't know how to type. Some older systems require users to dial the phone number and possibly the recipient's access code, key the message at the terminal, and manually set a modem to transmit the message.
2. *Sender and recipient must be connected.* Unlike telephone lines, which are linked and can be used by subscribers all over the world, not all workstations are linked electronically. Many organizations that have in-house E-mail facilities do not subscribe to commercial electronic mail services. In addition, not all electronic mail services are compatible.
3. *Furnishes text only.* Most electronic mail systems do not provide graphics, which can be supplied by facsimile services.
4. *Cost.* If electronic mail requires new hardware, it may be too expensive for an organization to install.
5. *Lack of response and dialog.* Unlike the telephone, electronic mail doesn't permit instantaneous responses. In addition, messages transmitted by electronic mail are not accompanied by a tone of voice, which often says as much as the message itself.

Electronic Filing

Businesses in the United States generate an estimated 70 billion paper documents a year. Although most documents, such as memos and letters, are used for relatively short periods, for legal reasons it is usually necessary to retain documents for a number of years. In many cases inactive documents are stored on microfilm or on microfiche. Retrieving the desired information from a manual system employing microfilm or microfiche is often a painstaking, time-consuming operation and may require specialized personnel and equipment. Although these technologies are gradually being integrated with computer technology, the majority of records stored on microfilm or microfiche are not computerized, that is, are not part of an electronic filing system.

Electronic filing is the storage, retrieval, duplication, and transmission of records from one workstation to another by electronic means. In the past, electronic filing was restricted by the relatively high cost and limited storage capacity of magnetic disks. (Recall that whereas magnetic tape offers less expensive and almost unlimited storage capacity, it does not provide direct access and therefore is impractical for many applications.) In the last few years the cost of magnetic-disk storage has declined sharply and its capacity has increased. Depending on the sophistication of the system, a user might be able to retrieve a document in a few seconds instead of spending hours looking for it in a filing cabinet.

Offices are particularly interested in the storage facilities offered with personal computers. The storage capacity of personal-computer systems is sufficient for many applications, and managers can store confidential data on floppy disks, which can be locked in a desk drawer. In addition, special software enables users to access and transmit files rapidly.

Among the most important advantages of electronic filing systems are the following:

1. *Faster access to information.* In many cases access to desired information is almost instantaneous.

2. *Reduction in required storage space.* With the rapid decline in the cost of magnetic material, it is much less expensive to store documents on fixed disks than in filing cabinets.

3. *Integration with other office automation technologies.* Once the document has been retrieved, it may be edited on a word processor and transmitted via electronic mail to a list of recipients. The updated document may be refiled on the system.

4. *Less misfiling.* A well-designed system permits users to find a document in a variety of ways. A related advantage is the reduced dependence on a single individual's filing techniques.

On the other hand, some important disadvantages limit the use of electronic filing. They include the following:

1. *Unfamiliarity.* Many office employees are reluctant to use this technology because it requires mastering unfamiliar equipment and new methods of communicating.

2. *Lack of security.* If the system has not been created with proper safeguards, intruders may gain access to sensitive information.

3. *Proliferation of files.* As many owners of personal computers can testify, computerization may actually increase the amount of data stored. To reduce storage costs it is necessary to adopt a document retention policy, such as storing rarely used documents on magnetic tape.

To a certain extent, these disadvantages can be reduced by training programs. As is so often the case when new equipment is installed and new work methods applied, proper training of personnel will more than pay for itself.

Image Processing

Originally, computers were used to process numbers, in much the same way that calculators are now used. Then the

This image-processing system handles securities for Chemical Bank in New York City, increasing operator speed and reducing processing time. (© Guy Gillette, Photo Researchers.)

power of the computer was extended to process words, creating what amounted to a high-powered typewriter, or word processor. But a substantial amount of business information is conveyed in images such as graphs and drawings, rather than in words. Therefore, *image processing*, the ability of a computer system to process an image composed of a picture, business form, or text that can be stored, retrieved, transmitted, edited, and printed, was developed and became one of the tools of the automated office.

Applications of image processing abound. For example, production facilities may use "computer vision" systems to check or sort parts. Image processing is of particular interest to "paper-intensive" industries such as insurance companies, banks and other financial institutions, government agencies, and engineering firms.

Image-processing systems are composed of special hardware devices and associated software. (See Box 14-1.) These devices convert a picture or image and any associated text into electronic signals that are stored within the unit. Some of the larger systems can store millions of pages on-line. Depending on the system's specific characteristics, the stored images may be retrieved within a few seconds and transmitted to personal computers or specialized workstations for further processing. An image-processing system can accomplish the following tasks:

1. *Scan a paper document to capture the image on disk.* An image, whether a picture or text, is made up of tiny dots. The more detailed the image, the more dots there are per inch and the more sophisticated the scanner required to capture the image.

2. *Compress and store images on disk.* Image-processing systems enable offices to store a large number of images in a small space. For example, the contents of a four-drawer file cabinet could be placed on one side of a 12-inch disk.

BOX 14-1

FRONTIERS IN TECHNOLOGY
Hardware for Image Processing

Electronic mail and word processing alone are not enough to create the "paperless office"—an ideal that has often been promised but has not yet arrived. A major barrier to the paperless office is the need, in many organizations, to keep millions of pages of records that are not generated on the organization's word-processing system, including drawings, incoming letters, tax returns, signature-bearing financial documents, and so on. This need has created a demand for image-processing hardware; that demand is being filled by a variety of devices, including scanners, image controllers, storage devices, and output devices.

Scanners. Scanners are the primary input devices of an image-processing system. Image scanners are quite different from optical character readers (see Box 4-1, p. 113) because scanned documents are not converted into alphanumeric characters. Instead, each line of the document is converted to thousands of picture elements, or *pixels*, which can be stored electronically as 1s or 0s. (See figure.) For most purposes, a scanning density of 200 pixels per inch is sufficient, although for some documents, such as engineering drawings, higher resolutions are required.

Image scanners have an advantage over OCRs in that they can handle a variety of type styles, pictures, signatures, and sometimes even colors. But they have a disadvantage in that documents stored in nonalphanumeric form cannot be edited using a word processor or searched for key words. Hence some advanced systems include both image scanners and OCR devices, the former to pick up letterheads, signatures, and so on, and the latter to permit future processing and searching of text.

Image controllers. An image controller, which may be anything from an embedded microprocessor to a minicomputer, provides enhancement, compression, and decompression of scanned images. It is an essential part of every image-processing system on the market.

Storage devices. The storage requirements of image-processing systems are enormous. Whereas a typed page stored alphanumerically requires about 2.5 KB of storage, the same page scanned at 200 pixels per inch requires about 50 KB. The most popular means of storing such vast quantities of information is the optical disk. (See Box 5-2, p. 154.) These write-once, read-many-times devices provide greater data security than documents filed on paper. When a user needs to inspect a document, a paper or on-screen copy is generated while the original remains securely on file. This feature also permits more than one user to look at the same document at the same time.

For enormous files that exceed the capacity of a 12-inch optical disk (about 40,000 pages), disks are kept in "jukeboxes." These are electromechanical devices that pull the required disk out of a slot and insert it in a reader as required.

An alternative to optical disks is automated microfiche or microfilm. Images are written on the film by a laser beam. When they need to be retrieved, they are digitally scanned.

Output devices. A limitation of image-processing systems is their reliance on high-resolution workstations. Data that is stored as pixels rather than in alphanumeric form often cannot be displayed successfully on the low-resolution monitors of typical PCs or video display terminals. Overcoming the need to keep two workstations on a desktop is considered a high priority by vendors of image-processing systems.

Meanwhile, the alternative to displaying the stored image on a high-resolution workstation is to make a paper copy. This can be done with a modified laser printer. Other laser devices can be used to transfer data that no longer needs to be accessed actively from optical disks to microfiche or microfilm.

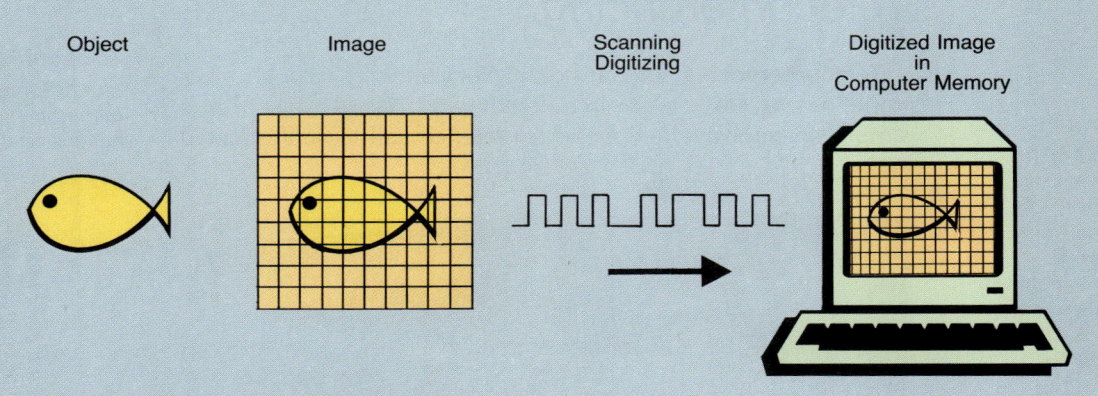

Object   Image   Scanning Digitizing   Digitized Image in Computer Memory

An electronic digitizing camera functions as the computer's "eyes," translating images into computer-readable digital code.

Source: Copyright 1986 by CW Communications/Inc., Framingham, MA 01701—Reprinted from Connie Moore, "System Components: Scanners, Lasers Build an Image," *Computerworld*, June 23, 1986, p. 73. Diagram excerpted from Administrative Management, July 1986, p. 24. © 1986 by Dalton Communications Inc., New York.

3. *Retrieve and display images on a screen.* Image-processing systems enable people to show rotated or reversed images, to zoom in on an image from any angle, and to display both the front and back of an image simultaneously. Some systems permit the display of several images at once.

4. *Edit the image and create or modify accompanying text.* Editing options include changing the size or colors of the image. This is useful, for example, in modifying a photograph to convey a certain mood. Associated word-processing features enable text to be modified as well.

5. *Route images to different workstations or printers.* Some image-processing systems include software that enables users to send images back and forth among workstations within a network. This facility is useful when several employees are required to handle the image at different points in its processing—for example, a graphic artist who edits the photograph and an advertising copy writer who edits the accompanying text.

6. *Print copies of images and accompanying text.* Printing is typically done with laser printers, which, because of their high resolution, are best able to approach the quality of the original image.

Teleconferencing

Teleconferencing, or the holding of meetings through electronic means, takes place in different ways. These range from a simple, inexpensive telephone conference call to sophisticated

Teleconferencing
The holding of meetings by electronic means.

This laser-printed image can be stored, modified, or transmitted to branch offices within seconds. (© A. Upitis, The Image Bank.)

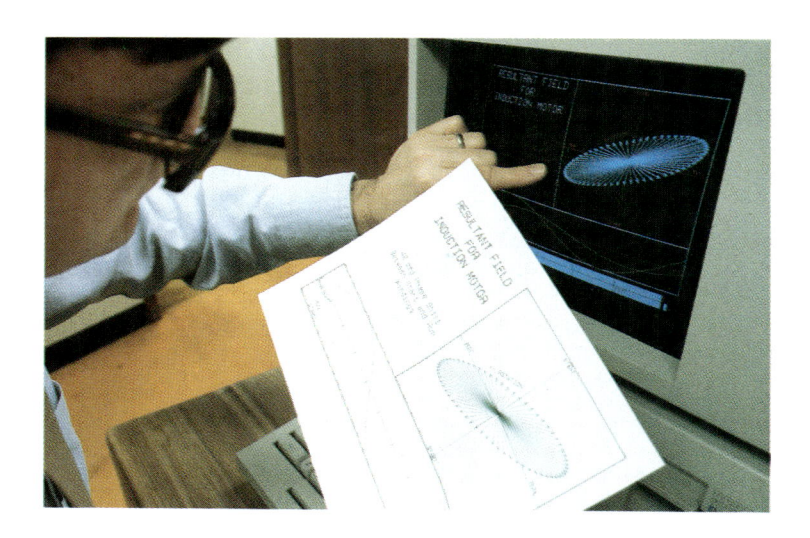

PEOPLE AND SYSTEMS 536 PART 4

and expensive *video conferencing*, in which participants can see and hear each other as if they were in the same room. Precision video conferencing requires specially designed rooms, high-quality cameras and multiple viewing screens for the video transmission, and sensitive microphones for audio transmission.

Specialized personnel are required to operate this sophisticated equipment. As is the case with most systems, user satisfaction depends above all on the human element. Successful video conferences therefore usually include highly trained moderators to coordinate the participants and put them at ease if necessary.

For video conferencing to be successful, the participants must learn new ways of communicating. A basic feature is that the speakers see each other. It usually takes a while for people to adapt to this type of conferencing, that is, to acquire the habit of introducing themselves before speaking and to avoid distracting facial expressions and movements.

An interesting development in automated offices is the combined use of teleconferencing and other office automation technologies. For example, participants can join an ongoing teleconference and obtain a record of the prior proceedings via electronic mail. The entire conference proceedings or selected portions of them can be filed electronically and sent by E-mail to people who are unable to attend. The combination of teleconferencing and electronic mail is sometimes called *computer conferencing*.

Teleconferencing and video conferencing are promising methods for reducing business travel for several reasons. Among them are the following:

The participants in this teleconference are using a system developed at Bell Labs to "meet" electronically without leaving their home offices. (© Sepp Seitz, Woodfin Camp.)

1. *Reduced cost.* When teleconferencing is suitable, it represents a much less expensive way of getting together than traditional business travel. While video conferencing is relatively expensive, it may be more cost-effective than sending participants to out-of-town meetings.
2. *Increased productivity.* A substantial portion of business travel is spent in nonproductive ways such as waiting in airports. Furthermore, many executives face a period of reduced efficiency after long business trips.
3. *Faster response time.* While it may take days to convene participants for a business meeting, it is possible to set up a teleconference in a very short time. Organizing a video conference usually requires more time than organizing a teleconference.
4. *Reduced energy requirements.* Forty percent of air travel is for business trips. A large proportion of these trips could be avoided through the use of conferencing techniques.
5. *Special applications.* Various conferencing techniques have been used to provide special applications such as teaching bedridden students; enabling doctors in different locations to consult in diagnosing illnesses and proposing treatment; and servicing a wide variety of equipment, including computers and airplanes, from remote locations. Many of these applications would be unfeasible without the use of conferencing.

It should be noted that computer conferencing has not lived up to its initial promise. This is largely because of some inherent disadvantages, including the following:

1. *Difficulty of use.* Successful use of video conferencing requires training. Most business executives do not make successful television personalities.
2. *Lack of suitability.* Many applications, such as negotiation or conflict resolution, are best carried out in the physical presence of all the parties involved.
3. *Expense.* High-quality video conferences are expensive to run and may not be financially justified.

Telecommuting

Just as the use of conferencing techniques can save time and energy expended on business trips, employees can use computer and communication facilities to reduce commuting to a local office. **Telecommuting** is the use of a remote workstation equipped with a modem and telephone lines to work at home or in a satellite office instead of in a central office. Given the millions of people who are familiar with personal computers and software such as electronic spreadsheets and graphics pro-

Telecommuting
Using a remote workstation, communications lines, and related facilities to work at home or in a satellite office instead of in a central office.

grams, together with the increasing costs of transportation and centralized offices, it is not surprising that telecommuting has grown rapidly in the last decade.

Telecommuting often means operating a workstation located at home instead of one located in the central office. For example, technical personnel such as architects can prepare and revise drawings, estimates, and reports at home and go to the office once or twice a week for meetings. Perhaps the biggest advantage of telecommuting is the reduction in the time and expense of commuting. In many urban areas commuting means fighting traffic for two or three hours. The time spent commuting is wasted.

In addition, telecommuting enables people who cannot come to the office to perform work at home, and it offers people the opportunity to determine their own working hours. It also reduces the consumption of energy and the wear and tear on highways.

Perhaps the main disadvantage of telecommuting is that it requires new methods of supervision. Many managers feel that if they cannot see their employees, they cannot be sure that the employees are performing efficiently. On the other hand, many employees find it difficult to work at home, that is, to separate office work time from home activity time and to avoid the distractions present in their homes. Also, they may miss the office setting, which provides human interaction that is both personally satisfying and an informal means of obtaining information and making decisions. In addition, trade unions, among other organizations, have raised questions about working conditions, claiming that people who work at home will not be able to obtain the same wages and benefits as those who work in offices and factories because of the difficulty of negotiating and policing contracts.

Integrated Workstations

In a recent issue of *Computerworld Focus*, Donald D. Bentley described an ideal workstation for an automated office.[1] In

---

[1] From Donald D. Bentley, "Universal Workstations: Fact or Fantasy," *Computerworld Focus*, February 6, 1985.

general, an *integrated workstation* in an automated office will meet the needs of several categories of people, including executives, managers, and professional, secretarial, and clerical staff. It will replace existing office tools such as the telephone, calculator, word processor, and dictaphone, and will enable users to switch from one function to another with relative ease and to perform more than one activity at a time.

Characteristics of Integrated Workstations

For a workstation to be truly integrated, it must have the following characteristics:

1. It must be easy to use.
2. It should be designed and set up for users' individual needs and comfort. User-friendliness is particularly important because many office workers will be using this equipment eight hours a day or more.
3. The user interface should be consistent for all applications; for example, a given function key should have the same meaning for all applications.
4. The system should be available in both portable and network versions.
5. Users should have a choice of input devices, such as a mouse or a keyboard, instead of being limited to a single device.
6. If a printer is not directly connected to the workstation, one must be available within easy walking distance. Printed output should be available within seconds.
7. The workstation should provide a visible signal when the user has received electronic mail, ordinary mail, or telephone calls.
8. The system should provide automatic backup of the user's files. This will enable each user to operate the system without the fear of hitting a few incorrect keys and destroying valuable files.
9. The system should permit users to work on several applications at once, such as modifying a business letter via a word-processing program and, in the process, accessing an electronic spreadsheet to obtain figures to be inserted in the letter.
10. The integrated workstation should run a wide variety of applications, including word processing, data management, electronic mail, electronic filing, project management, and an *electronic calendar* that enables employees to review their schedules and organize meetings without having to contact the other parties by telephone.

Office Automation Systems

Although automated offices with fully integrated workstations do not yet exist, there are workstations that incorporate many of the tools of the automated office. Moreover, the integrated workstation is becoming more of a reality. For example, Digital Equipment Corporation (DEC), a major vendor of minicomputers, provides an integrated office automation system known as the All-In-1. It includes electronic mail, calendar management, and basic word processing, and also works with DEC's Business Operations Support System, which provides spreadsheet, report generation, and graphics capabilities. United Telephone Company in Florida uses All-In-1 on a network of more than 300 users at twelve locations. Its system consists of 120 Decmate word processors, over 70 graphics terminals, and about two dozen DEC PCs. These machines communicate with each other and various models of IBM PCs via a network; users can also access the system via telephone lines.

Integrated office automation systems are often built by combining products from several different vendors. Consider the following example, which describes the activities of an employee at Westinghouse Electric Corporation:

> Using a Sun Microsystems, Inc. workstation and Applix, Inc.'s Alis integrated office automation program, [administrative assistant Marilyn] Gruen can create text, graphics, spreadsheets and freehand drawings in a compound document. Through icons and multiwindowing, she can rearrange the presentation, change the graphics or recalculate the spreadsheet without leaving the original screen. Using a style selection guide, she can choose a predetermined text format with multiple fonts and can change formats as she creates the document.
>
> Once she finishes, Gruen can mail the document to a distribution list of other Alis users or can store it in a multilevel filing system. Data base access and the option of using a mouse or keyboard also lie at her disposal.[2]

The author of the article just quoted estimates that in 1996 many managers, secretaries, and professionals will have access

---

[2]Copyright 1986 by CW Communications/Inc., Framingham, MA 01701—Reprinted from Michael Sullivan-Trainor, "Integrated OA Systems," *Computerworld*, June 30, 1986, p. 33.

to integrated office automation systems. In the meantime, most companies and organizations do not have systems like the one at Westinghouse Electric. A typical organization might have an IBM mainframe computer, several VAX or other incompatible minicomputers, and hundreds of incompatible terminals and microcomputers. This hardware generally is supported by a variety of software packages, each of which has its own user interface and produces files that are difficult to transfer from one piece of equipment to another automatically.

The major challenge of office automation, then, is to put together hardware and software to produce a viable, integrated system. For many users an acceptable level of system integration would consist of the following:

1. *Integrated applications* that enable even relatively inexperienced users to move from one application to another, for example, from word processing to data-base management and back. A key aspect of such integration is the use of the same commands to perform similar operations in each application.

2. *Systems connectivity*, which enables users to transfer files either manually or electronically from one computer or terminal to another, converting their format if necessary. For example, a computer in a meat-packing plant could generate a disk with payroll data to be sent to a government computer for income tax processing.

3. *Communication with the IBM PC and compatibles*. This means that a user working on a PC could access mainframe data and programs on demand. Another user working on a terminal attached to the mainframe could access data and programs associated with a PC.

These three criteria should be considered together. In other words, system integration means that a relatively inexperienced user can think of the computer as a single tool and not have to consider such details as which program is active, how the files are stored, or whether the workstation is a microcomputer or a computer terminal.

The Impact of Office Automation

Installing a system that will increase productivity enough to justify its cost will inevitably lead to widespread and often unforeseen change within the organization. It will affect all levels of office personnel in one way or another. Office automation systems can have a substantial impact on employees' morale, productivity, career paths, and interactions with peers, superiors, and subordinates. Some observers claim that office automation can also have a negative impact on employee health.

Changes in Secretarial and Clerical Work

Secretarial and clerical work will be affected significantly by office automation. Physical aspects of the job, which are related to comfort and health, will change. In addition, some traditional duties will no longer be necessary, and secretaries and clerks will have to learn to perform new tasks. For example, in a traditional office secretaries and clerks are always in motion: answering the telephone, walking to the copy machine, bending to put something in a filing cabinet, and so on. Such activities have a hidden benefit: They tend to keep muscles and eyes relaxed. In contrast, in an automated office secretaries and clerks will be able to perform these and other activities without getting up from their chairs and in many cases without taking their eyes off their monitors. There is some evidence that the constant use of video display terminals (VDTs) and other office automation equipment can create health hazards. For example, although the National Institute for Occupational Safety and Health (NIOSH) has concluded that the radiation emitted by workstations presents no threat to human health, it has found

This secretary is an obvious candidate for electronic mail. (© Jon Halaska, Photo Researchers.)

that employees who use VDTs have more health complaints, such as eyestrain and backaches, than those who do not. NIOSH recommends that employees who use VDTs take regular rest periods and have their eyes examined both before starting to use VDTs and regularly afterwards. Some labor unions have been active in implementing guidelines for the use of VDTs.

The installation of office automation systems also produces changes in the traditional work performed by clerks and secretaries. They may do less typing because managers and other professionals may decide to enter and correct documents themselves. Furthermore, with the aid of an electronic calendar, participants may schedule meetings themselves, relieving secretaries of the need to perform this time-consuming activity. At the same time, automated offices create new activities related to data processing, such as making backups of computer files and creating parallel filing systems for hard copy and magnetic material.

The arrival of the automated office may bring new challenges to secretaries. For example, they are commonly the first employees to become familiar with the new system, and as a result they may become trainers, showing their bosses and others how to use word processing, receive or transmit electronic mail, and save files, and even how to use the keyboard. Depending on the personalities of the secretary and the boss, this change in operations may lead to a more balanced working relationship. It is not unusual for secretaries in automated offices to assume new administrative functions to replace those that have been eliminated or reduced by automation.

Effects on Managers, Professionals, and Technical Personnel

Office automation inevitably affects the way managers, professionals, and technical personnel work. Not only are working relationships with secretaries and clerical personnel likely to change, but those with peers, superiors, and technical associates may also change. In addition, modifications in work habits can lead to greater productivity and increased autonomy.

Greater Productivity. We noted at the beginning of the chapter that a major reason for implementing office automation is to increase the productivity of managerial, professional, and technical personnel (see Tables 14-1, 14-2, and 14-3). The automated office can reduce the amount of time spent in unproductive activities such as proofreading a document more than once, trying to reach people by telephone, and excessive business travel.

At the same time that the use of automated office tools increases productivity, it leads to a corresponding increase in expectations. For example, a manager looking for a file in a filing cabinet does not expect to find it in a few seconds. However, the same manager is likely to become impatient with file retrieval software if it doesn't deliver the desired file within a few seconds. The higher level of productivity has become the new norm.

Increased Autonomy. Managers in an automated office may find that they need not rely on subordinates as much as they did in a traditional office. For example, managers can use electronic spreadsheets to perform financial analyses, which traditionally have been delegated to technical specialists, and salespeople can use graphics programs to prepare presentations without having to deal with a graphics designer. These changes increase the speed and may decrease the cost of obtaining desired information.

Potential Problems. In spite of the many potential benefits of office automation, many managers, professionals, and technical personnel are opposed to it. Managers in traditional offices do not use typewriters and may resist the idea of using a keyboard to access and update documents, spreadsheets, or data bases. In addition, they may be unwilling to learn the procedures and standards of an automated office, such as the requirement that files be named consistently. And it is not surprising that many managers resent the organizational changes that often accompany office automation.

Computers have not yet been developed that can duplicate the thought processes of a manager making a decision. (© Don Klumpp, The Image Bank.)

The automated office has other potential problems as well. Some procedures may actually become less efficient and more subject to error. For example, managers may wait until the last minute to prepare reports, expecting secretaries to compensate for the delay by using automated equipment. Also, the ease with which documents and revisions can be produced causes some people to revise documents over and over again, thereby wasting both time and money.

New Support Functions

Technological advances typically create new employment opportunities and expand existing ones at the same time that they reduce some traditional employment opportunities. For example, the automobile eliminated the need for buggy whip makers but created millions of jobs in the manufacture, repair, and sale of automobiles. Similarly, automated offices will reduce the number of jobs in some fields and create new jobs in others.

Administrative Support Tasks. Successful implementation of office automation requires a capable, respected administrator called an *office automation administrator*. This person's role is similar to that of the data-base administrator discussed in Chapter 10. The duties of an office automation administrator include the following:
1. Determining and implementing standards and procedures for the automated office.
2. Developing guidelines for using shared resources such as laser printers and files.
3. Creating and coordinating a training program for all levels of users.
4. Maintaining a liaison with the management information systems and telecommunication departments.
5. Managing clerical and technical support functions.

Clerical Support Tasks. Clerical support tasks for office automation systems include keeping track of the equipment, noting, for example, what equipment has been borrowed by employees for use at home or on the road. Support personnel may also gather statistics on the use of facilities such as electronic mail. A related task is maintaining an inventory of supplies and consolidating orders from various departments in order to obtain quantity discounts.

Technical Support Tasks. Technical support tasks include debugging software, handling hardware problems, maintaining hardware and software, evaluating system usage, and preparing plans for future acquisition of hardware and software. Technical support personnel may make recommendations regarding when additional workstations should be acquired, as well as identifying the equipment that would best meet present and future needs.

Consolidating Tasks. Many organizations are consolidating the support personnel responsible for office automation with those responsible for telecommunication and management information systems. The result is a *corporate information systems department (CIS)* that handles all of the organization's information needs. Often the head of this new department, the *chief information officer (CIO)*, reports directly to the organization's chief executive officer.

Desktop Publishing

The information explosion has generated an estimated 2.5 trillion pages of paper and shows no sign of abating. According to InterConsult of Cambridge, Massachusetts, publishing ranks second only to personnel on the list of companies' major expenses, consuming from 6 to 10 percent of gross revenues. Legend has it that the documentation for a Boeing 747 weighs more than the plane itself. Clearly any strategy for controlling office costs and operations must view publishing as a major item. Three technological breakthroughs—inexpensive workstations, easy-to-use software, and inexpensive laser printers—have made it possible to automate the corporate publishing process. The resulting procedure is referred to as **desktop publishing**.

Desktop publishing
A system that enables an organization or individual to produce professional-looking documents using relatively inexpensive hardware and software.

Desktop publishing allows an individual or organization to produce professional-looking documents using relatively inexpensive hardware and software. These documents can be reproduced on high-quality copying machines or sent to a commercial typesetting firm. A key aspect of desktop publishing is its What-You-See-Is-What-You-Get (WYSIWYG) feature: The text and graphs displayed on the monitor represent exactly what the printed output will look like.

Desktop publishing systems have become very popular, in part because they often result in enough savings to pay for themselves within a short time. Many systems pay for themselves through savings on typesetting costs, which for many applications can easily exceed $50 per page. The more a document is subject to revision, the greater the potential saving in time and money.

Desktop publishing systems can satisfy a variety of printing needs. They can be used to prepare in-house newsletters, brochures, sales literature, and even books. Regardless of the final output, people use desktop publishing systems to do tasks that have traditionally been done by editors, designers, typesetters, proofreaders, indexers, and printers.

The following are some typical applications of desktop publishing systems:

1. *Newsletters*. Simple but handsome newsletters can be produced with a carefully selected combination of typefaces and sizes. More sophisticated newsletters can contain text, graphics, and even photographs.

2. *Instructional materials*. Training materials ranging from handouts to technical manuals and audiovisual aids such as transparencies can be produced using a desktop publishing system. An advantage to producing these materials in-house is that they can be kept up to date relatively inexpensively.

3. *Internal communication*. Documents for a company's personnel, such as rules and regulations, memos, and bulletins, can be prepared with a desktop publishing system and revised without having to be fitted into a printer's schedule.

4. *Marketing materials*. Desktop publishing is often used to prepare brochures and other promotional material. It makes individualized marketing campaigns for small target groups economically feasible.

Limitations

Desktop publishing, even in its infancy, is changing the way many businesses prepare printed materials. As more advanced hardware and software become available, even more uses and benefits will be discovered for this technique. But desktop publishing is not suitable for all of a firm's printing needs. The following are some limitations on desktop publishing:

1. *Long documents*. A rule of thumb states that desktop publishing works best for documents of up to 50 pages. Longer documents should be handled by traditional methods. (Note, however, that this can be expected to change as desktop systems become more sophisticated.)

2. *Complex documents*. Documents that contain graphics, computer-generated drawings, and mathematical formulas may

exceed the capabilities of the laser printers used with desktop publishing systems. In addition, the available software may not allow an untrained user to produce a professional-looking document without a major expenditure of time and effort.
3. *Color output.* The most widely used laser printers do not provide color output.
4. *Heavy usage.* Laser printers generally should not be required to print more than 10,000 copies per month, and many models need a major overhaul after 100,000–150,000 copies.

Types of Systems

Because of the wide range of hardware and software that can be used to put together a desktop publishing system, a system can be designed to meet the user's specific needs. Individual publishing needs can be met by an inexpensive system consisting of a home computer, a near-letter-quality printer, and word-processing and low-capacity desktop publishing software, often called *personal publishing software*. These systems can produce documents such as multilingual greeting cards, posters, and informal newsletters. An inexpensive graphics printer makes it possible to produce many other kinds of output.

Somewhat more sophisticated output can be produced using a *basic desktop publishing system*, which consists of a microcomputer equipped with a hard disk, a graphics monitor, and a laser printer. An example of software designed for this type of system is Microsoft Word, which includes both a word processor and a very elementary page composition program. This al-

This computer system is used to set type at a large printing company in Pennsauken, New Jersey. Such systems require more sophisticated hardware than microcomputer-based desktop publishing systems. (© Joseph Nettis, Photo Researchers.)

lows the user to design pages that combine several different typefaces and graphics.

Midrange desktop publishing systems are driven by more powerful computers like the IBM AT with an enhanced graphics adapter. They use special page composition software packages, such as PageMaker or Ventura Publisher. In addition, a digitized scanner can be used to include photographs in the documents. Still more sophisticated systems, known as *high-level publishing systems*, require an IBM AT and a specialized typesetting program such as MagnaType. These systems are operated by professionals and can handle the typesetting requirements of newspapers and magazine publishers. Finally, *very-high-level publishing systems*, also known as *corporate electronic publishing systems*, are in effect full-scale printing operations that can be used to produce books. These systems can include a powerful dedicated workstation, a monitor large enough to display an 8½ by 11 inch page, a powerful laser printer, an image scanner, and a video camera. In some cases a corporate electronic publishing system can be more than just a cost-saver. As Box 14-2 illustrates, such a system can be crucial to the firm's entire way of doing business.

In this chapter we have explored the major applications of information systems and computer technology in office environments. We examined some of the tools of office automation and their benefits, both actual and potential. Chapter 15 describes another major application of computer information systems: the automation of production processes.

Appendix: Computer Graphics

Shortly after businesspeople began using computers, they found that an existing problem was aggravated: Instead of reducing the amount of paper used in offices, the use of computers tends to result in an increase in the number of reports and documents produced. Although many of these reports can be very useful, managers and technical personnel do not have time to wade through reams of paper looking for a few significant pieces of information. Moreover, computer-generated reports often are not well adapted for presenting information to top

BOX 14-2

USING COMPUTERS

Corporate Electronic Publishing Saves the Ace Catalog

Ace Hardware Corporation of Oak Brook, Illinois, is one of today's most committed users of electronic publishing. In 1981, there was real doubt whether Ace would be able to continue producing its 45,000-item, 4000-page catalog for its thirteen regional warehouses. "Producing this book was becoming almost cost prohibitive. Despite the word-processing systems, it was very laborious," remembers Chris DeBoo, the company's office systems manager. "Until the new system, there were days when I wondered if we were a publishing company or a hardware company."

The catalogs that Ace sends out to its 48,000 dealers must be tailored to specific regions because some products are suitable only for certain areas—snowblowers in New England, for example. Thirteen word-processing operators and thirteen graphic artists manually prepared each region's catalogs. Also working feverishly to pull the books together were seven paste-up people, five illustrators, and two clerks who assisted the WP operators. The $1 billion hardware company updates the important catalog checklists, rotating the various departments, such as housewares or hand tools, throughout the year.

"Each time we added a warehouse," says DeBoo, "we had to add five people. At the time, we were adding a warehouse a year, so the preparation was very cumbersome, the books were enormous," recalls DeBoo, who supervised much of the conversion work.

Ace started looking for automated alternatives and found the Xerox XPS 700 publishing system, a mainframe-based setup built around the Xerox 9700 high-speed laser printer. Now all the catalog checklist information is stored on the corporate IBM 3081 mainframe that runs Xerox's XIS software. Pages are composed on the XPS 700 system, with output to the 9700.

During the demanding two and one-half year conversion period, Ace's DP shop wrote 50 to 60 custom programs. It was also necessary to keep producing the catalog by the old manual methods, so temporary staffing was high. The new system has cut down on those personnel costs. "One operator in half a day of keyboarding does what dozens of operators and clerks used to do full time," explains DeBoo. "We've saved $600,000 and every year that grows by leaps and bounds."

The publishing system has helped Ace do more than produce its mammoth catalogs. It has created several new marketing tools the company has used to good advantage, such as a catalog without prices that local dealers can give to their commercial and industrial accounts.

Source: Connie Winkler, "Desktop Publishing," *Datamation*, December 1, 1986, pp. 92–96. Copyright © Cahners Publishing Company.

management or to clients, and they tend to be dull and colorless. Today computer graphics are widely used to overcome these drawbacks.

Graphic output has numerous business applications, including internal analysis and decision making, sales presentations, and publications. With the aid of easy-to-use software, users can create and modify graphics after a few hours of training.

The range of computer-generated graphics is enormous. Simple graphics such as line, bar, and pie charts can be used in making business decisions. More sophisticated pictures may be used for presentations, whether visual or published. And special systems may be used to create animated effects.

Categories of Graphics

Graphic applications are frequently divided into two basic categories: analytical graphics and presentation graphics. The main difference between these categories is the type of person who will use them. This in turn determines the types of hardware and software required.

Analytical Graphics. *Analytical graphics* are simple, low-resolution[3] graphics such as line graphs, bar charts, and pie charts. Their purpose is to present information in an easy-to-use form as an aid in the decision-making process, not to impress top management or clients. Analytical graphics may be produced on microcomputers with some graphics hardware and popular software such as Lotus 1-2-3 or SuperCalc3. Such programs enable users to present electronic spreadsheets in graphic form, adding labels and titles if desired. Analytical graphics could readily convert any of the reports illustrated in Chapter 13 into graphs.

Presentation Graphics. *Presentation graphics* are high-quality graphics whose objective is to convince managers or clients to approve a particular decision or buy a particular product or service. They may include figures ranging from line charts to three-dimensional drawings. Presentation graphics are suitable for publication in reports or sales brochures. A middle manager for a snack food company might include presentation graphics in a report suggesting that the company introduce a new product line. Other managers might use presentation graphics to prepare advertisements for the new product line.

---

[3]*Resolution* refers to the quality of a graphic image. It is measured in *pixels*, or number of dots and lines. The more pixels, the sharper the image.

Requirements for Graphics

Hardware. A special circuit board is required to generate graphic images, and a special monitor may be needed to display them. An example of the former is IBM's enhanced graphics adapter (EGA), which, when combined with an appropriate color monitor, produces relatively high-quality graphics. The EGA board, when equipped with at least 128K of memory, permits 16 colors with a resolution of 640 × 350 pixels. The popularity of this board has led to the production of dozens of replacement boards or clones.

A more recent development is the introduction of the multiscan monitor, which reads the input signal and displays it automatically. The user need not indicate any technical details about the signal and can easily switch from one graphics mode to another. The picture quality of multiscan monitors is much sharper than that of EGA monitors.

Most graphics systems include a facility for producing hardcopy output. Relatively inexpensive dot-matrix printers generally are used for analytical graphics, whereas more sophisticated, higher-priced plotters (see Chapter 4) or specialized devices such as slide makers are used for presentation graphics.

Software. Analytical graphics software is an integral part of products such as Lotus 1-2-3 and SuperCalc3. Special programs are used for presentation graphics. In general, software for presentation graphics is more expensive and harder to use than software for analytical graphics. However, the graphics marketplace is so dynamic that excellent software for presentation graphics is appearing almost daily.

Each graphics program has its own special features. As always, in choosing a product it is essential to determine the user's specific needs. Good presentation graphics software can perform the following functions:
- Producing three-dimensional drawings.
- Processing files produced by popular electronic spreadsheets.
- Creating a library of drawings for future access.
- Rotating a figure to any desired angle.
- Zooming in on a desired portion of the figure.
- Moving, resizing, formatting, and positioning text.
- Controlling a wide variety of output devices such as plotters and slide makers.
- Automatically making design decisions such as size of text or color combinations.

With each improvement in graphics hardware and software, the number of office workers who are relying on computer graphics to help them get the job done continues to grow.

SUMMARY

1. If businesses are to remain competitive, they must increase the productivity and cost-effectiveness of their office operations. **Office automation (OA)** is the process of applying computer, communication, and related technologies in order to increase productivity in offices.

2. The first attempts at office automation were directed at secretaries and clerical workers. Recently office automation has also been applied to managers, professionals, and technical workers, enabling them to spend more time on management and professional work and less time on nonproductive activities.

3. The components of an automated office include word processing, electronic mail, electronic filing, image processing, teleconferencing, and telecommuting. **Electronic mail** is the sending, storing, and delivering of messages by electronic means. **Teleconferencing** is the holding of meetings by electronic means ranging from telephone conference calls to video conferencing in which participants see and hear each other. **Telecommuting** is the use of a remote workstation equipped with a modem and telephone lines to enable employees to work at home or in a satellite office instead of in a central office.

4. An integrated workstation can be used by executives, managers, professionals, and secretarial and clerical staff. It replaces the telephone, calculator, word processor, dictaphone, and other desktop equipment and enables each user to switch from one function to another with relative ease.

5. The major challenge of office automation is to combine hardware and software so as to produce a viable, integrated system. For many users, an acceptable level of integration includes integration of applications, connectivity among systems, and support for personal computers such as the IBM PC and compatibles.

6. A system that will increase productivity enough to justify its cost will inevitably change the nature of work within the organization. Secretaries are most directly affected by office automation, but the work habits of managers and technical personnel are also likely to change.

7. Office automation creates the need for a variety of support functions. Successful implementation of OA requires an office automation administrator. Clerical support functions include keeping track of equipment, maintaining inventory and supplies, and gathering statistics on usage of facilities. Technical support functions include debugging and maintaining software and hardware, evaluating present system usage, and planning future hardware and software acquisition. Some organizations have formed corporate information systems departments to handle all of the organization's information needs.

8. Desktop publishing systems produce professional-looking documents using relatively inexpensive hardware and software. Typical desktop publishing applications include newsletters, instructional materials, internal communication, and marketing materials.

KEY TERMS

office automation

electronic mail

teleconferencing

telecommuting

desktop publishing

REVIEW QUESTIONS

1. What is office automation? Why is it necessary for businesses to increase office productivity?

2. What was the initial focus of office automation? What is it today? What is the reason for this change?

3. List and describe the components of an automated office. Relate them to traditional office equipment and activities.

4. Compare electronic mail with traditional communication methods. List the advantages and disadvantages of electronic mail.

5. What is an integrated workstation? Describe how an integrated workstation could be used by different categories of personnel in an office.

6. Explain the concept of integrated office automation. Why is this concept important?

7. Compare and contrast the effects of office automation on secretaries and on managers.

8. Describe the new functions created by office automation systems. What is the effect of office automation on the MIS department?

9. What is desktop publishing? Why is it important? Identify three applications of desktop publishing.

APPLICATIONS

1. Assume that you are the director of office services for an export-import firm. Write a letter to the secretarial staff announcing the installation of an office automation system. How can you dispel the staff's fears concerning the new system?

2. Write a similar letter to the managers and professional staff.

3. Find examples of documents prepared using desktop publishing systems. Compare them with documents prepared using traditional printing methods.

4. Discuss the following statement: Telecommuting will eliminate the need for people to work in offices.

CASE FOR DISCUSSION

The ability of secretaries to use computers is bringing them expanded duties and higher-level responsibilities—but not necessarily higher pay, according to more than 1250 secretaries surveyed by *The Secretary* magazine, a publication of Professional Secretaries International (PSI).

Traditionally, workers are told that higher-level skills mean higher salary. Yet more than half of the respondents (58 percent) said that their ability to use computers—dedicated word processors, PCs, and the like—had not brought them better wages. Instead, their salary increases were achieved through promotions or by changing employers.

The survey results would not be surprising if it were true that computers have made secretarial jobs "easier" and have reduced the skills needed to perform them. But responses to the survey provide a much different picture. Ninety percent of the respondents indicated that computers have not reduced the level or number of skills needed in their jobs. In fact, 72 percent said that their roles have expanded because of computer-based equipment. Thirty-five percent said they now do work formerly done by their managers or other departments in their companies, and nearly 80 percent said that working with computers requires more analytical and problem-solving abilities.

Also, respondents wrote that since computers make individual tasks easier and quicker, they are required to do more of them. The result is that while many managers may think their secretaries' workloads have been decreasing, they actually have been increasing. Secretaries now do more work with spreadsheets, do more budget-related work, have more administrative and supervisory duties, prepare more reports, originate more letters, do more research, and work more often on special projects, the study claims.

A large majority of respondents were pleased with the changes that computers had brought to their jobs: 80 percent said they were enjoying their duties more now that they were using computers; 87 percent said their jobs were more challenging; and 73 percent believed that computer skills would increase their career mobility.

Source: Adapted, by permission of the publisher, from "Secretaries and Their Computers," *Management Review*, January 1987, p. 7, © 1987 American Management Assoc., New York. All rights reserved.

CASE QUESTION

Using the information given in this article (supplemented by your own experience if you have worked in an office environment), write a dialog between a representative of a secretarial workers' union and a manager. The representative of the union takes the position that increasing the skills and responsibilities associated with a job should bring higher pay. The manager takes the position that making a job more pleasant is not normally a reason to increase pay. Because secretaries are pleased with the changes that computers bring to their jobs, says the manager, there is no need to pay them more.

hot cold
WATER

Automating Production

CHAPTER

15

General Electric's vast home dishwasher plant in Louisville, Kentucky, has chalked up some impressive achievements since its conversion from the standard manual assembly line to automated production:
- Point-of-use parts manufacturing has slashed inventory by some 60 percent. Redesigning the company's line of dishwashers, meanwhile, has cut the number of required parts from about 5600 to only 850.
- The average number of dishwasher customer service calls has been trimmed by 53 percent since 1982.
- Whereas the plant needed five to six days to produce a dishwasher two years ago, it now requires only about eighteen hours.
- Overall employee productivity has increased by more than 25 percent.
- Production capacity at the plant has grown by 20 percent.

The entire manufacturing process—parts production, unit assembly, warehousing—is now controlled and tracked by thirty-four Series Six programmable controllers, developed by GE's industrial electronics division and used for the first time at Louisville. Assembly is monitored from an overhead control booth equipped with three computer terminals run by a DEC PDP 11/44. Among other features, the custom software provides a color graphics display of every machine on the floor.

During the assembly, the parts for each of the thirteen dishwasher models made at Louisville are moved through a series of stations (21 for the tub assembly, 13 for the door) by a 3-mile-long nonsynchronous overhead conveyor network.

The assembly process incorporates several optical devices. For example, the status of each unit is tracked through assembly via laser-scanned bar codes on the conveyor hangers. At the final inspection stage, any unit that has experienced special problems during assembly is automatically diverted into a separate repair area.

Predictably, the project wasn't without its problems, especially during its early months. "If we were starting over again, we'd probably spend more time simulating the plant process," says Raymond L. Rissler, general manager of the program.[1]

---

[1]Reprinted with permission from Garrett DeYoung, "GE: Dishing Out Efficiency," *High Technology* magazine, May 1985, pp. 32–33. Copyright © 1985 by Infotechnology Publishing Corp., 214 Lewis Wharf, Boston, MA 02110.

Chapters 13 and 14 described the impact of computers on businesses, and specifically on office workers and managers. This chapter discusses the impact of computers on manufacturing. It examines how computers and robots are involved in the manufacturing process, from initial design to distribution of the finished product. It also explores the information systems that accompany manufacturing systems.

When you have read this chapter you should be able to:
1. Describe computer-aided design systems.
2. Discuss the impact of computer-aided manufacturing on production.
3. Compare and contrast materials requirements planning and manufacturing resource planning.
4. Explain what robots are and how they are used in industry.
5. Describe flexible manufacturing systems and their impact on manufacturing.
6. Explain just-in-time and discuss its effects on inventory management and the entire production process.
7. Discuss computer-integrated manufacturing.
8. Discuss the manufacturing automation protocol and its impact on factory communication.
9. Understand and use the key terms listed at the end of this chapter.

This picture illustrates several manufacturing operations in a textile plant of the 1830s. Many of these operations are computerized in modern factories. (Culver Pictures.)

Computer-Aided Design

One of the reasons that computers and robots can be applied successfully to all phases of the manufacturing process is the wide variety of tools available. These tools range from computer-aided design systems, which can be used on microcomputers to do drafting, to computer-integrated manufacturing systems, which are used on mainframes and are suitable for large-scale industrial production.

Computer-aided design (CAD) is the use of a workstation with graphics capability and special graphics software to design, draft, and document products ranging from contact lenses to Olympic bobsleds and airplanes. Some CAD systems are used on mini- and microcomputers, others on mainframes. Many corporations use microcomputer CAD systems in conjunction with mainframe CAD systems.

Computer-aided design (CAD)
The use of a workstation with graphics capability and special graphics software to design, draft, and document products.

Elements of a CAD System

Computer-aided design systems consist of a computer, one or more input devices, one or more graphics output devices, and

CHAPTER 15   561   AUTOMATING PRODUCTION

A sophisticated CAD system is used by the Boeing Corporation to develop aircraft. (Courtesy of Boeing Corp.)

specialized software. The most widely used input devices are the keyboard, the mouse, and the light pen; output is produced by dot-matrix printers, laser printers, and plotters. The computer that drives the system may be a microcomputer used by a drafter or designer, or a dedicated mainframe-based system serving dozens of users at once. The complexity and cost of the software depends on the nature of the hardware.

Features of CAD Systems

CAD software that runs on microcomputers offers the following features:

Text Capabilities. Users can insert text in any size and at any angle they wish. They can also choose from different fonts (that is, type styles) and character sets, such as those for mechanical engineering, mathematics, or architecture. The text can be entered directly onto the drawing or read in from a file created on a word processor.

Editing Functions. Selected parts of a drawing can be moved, copied, or erased. For example, an architect can use this feature to determine the best location for a room or staircase. In addition, two or more drawings can be combined, and all or part of a drawing can be saved.

Zooming. On a monitor, the user can look at any level of detail, depending on specific needs. For example, a user can start with a map of the United States and zoom in on a single state, then a county, a city, and finally a particular street. The final view of the street appears thousands of times larger than it did on the map of the United States.

Scale Drawings. The user can choose a specific scale of measurement, such as ¼ inch = 1 foot, and size of output, such as standard 8½ by 11 inch paper or plotter output ranging up to 36 by 48 inches or more. The height-to-width ratio of the drawing can be changed, for example, when an engineer is trying to determine the strongest structural design for a bridge. In addition, the drawing can be presented in a slanted version or mirror image.

Standard Output. To allow drawings from different CAD systems to be interchangeable, a standard for CAD has been devised, called Initial Graphics Exchange Standard (IGES). CAD software used with microcomputers enables users to translate their output into IGES format.

Users of CAD systems generally create a library of objects that they use frequently, such as transistors for an electronic circuit or windows for a house, and call up a drawing from the library whenever it is needed. This method saves time and energy. A drawback, however, is that inexperienced users may have difficulty coordinating library drawings with items drawn from scratch. Some programs automatically convert the units of library items into the units used within the drawing. This means that a user working with metric dimensions can insert a figure drawn in inches without having to convert units.

This CAD system is used by the Chrysler Corporation to design automobiles. The automobile industry is a major user of automated systems in all phases of development and production. (Courtesy of Chrysler Corp.)

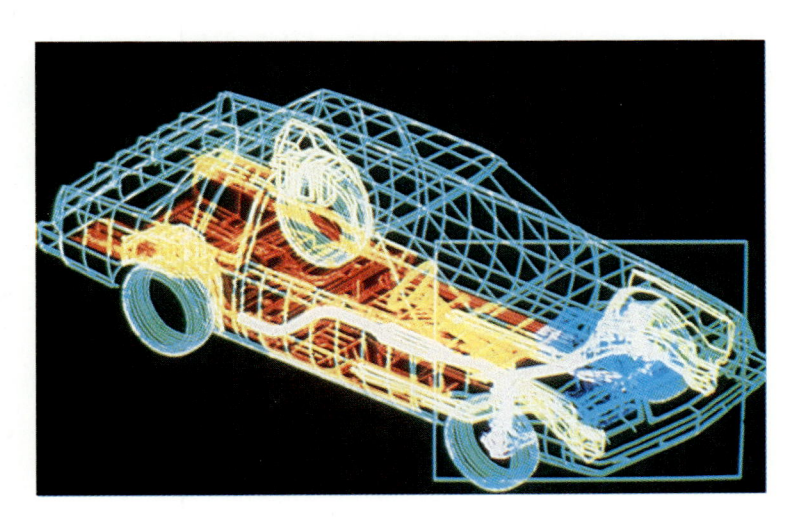

Advantages and Disadvantages of CAD

An advantage of a CAD system is that the drawings are dynamic: The designer can zoom in on any part, view it from any angle, and enlarge details. Another advantage is that the user can vary the design and observe the effects of changing variables such as temperature and mechanical stress. With the aid of CAD systems, designers can create and test many variations of a product and reject unsuitable designs without having to build costly prototypes. Also, with many systems the documentation can be prepared at the same time as the design, permitting easy updating of both.

Major drawbacks of microcomputer-based CAD systems include their slow speed compared to most mainframe-based systems and their basic stand-alone quality: They generally do not provide networking or multiuser capabilities. In the mid-1980s they offered only medium-range screen resolution, and most systems were unable to present three-dimensional views and solid models of objects such as drive shafts. Also, some systems cannot draw parallel lines, ellipses, or regular polygons and do not provide for drawing or plotting wide lines or curves.

An Application

Grinnell College in Grinnell, Iowa, has a policy of encouraging computer use on campus, especially in disciplines that are not traditionally associated with computers, such as the social sciences and humanities. In the mid-1980s Grinnell's theater department purchased a microcomputer-aided drafting and design system known as AutoCAD, distributed by Autodesk, Inc., of Sausalito, California. AutoCAD has been marketed widely for use by architects, engineers, and systems and graphics designers. But since the stage design process is similar to architectural and engineering design, the software can easily be applied to theatrical stage design.

At the beginning of the stage design process, the designer meets with a representative of the theater department to gather enough information to prepare a preliminary drawing of the stage set using AutoCAD. The drawing is then presented to the theater's technical director and changes are discussed and made. A main advantage of using the AutoCAD system rather than paper-and-pencil drawings is that the effects of changes can be seen immediately. By simply moving the cursor, walls can be moved, furniture changed, and actors and actresses placed in various locations. When the design has been approved, it is saved on a disk, from which it can be retrieved at any time to be reused or modified.

Although Grinnell's theater department uses a CAD program to design stage sets, the actual construction of the sets is not computerized but is done by the stage crew with hammers and saws. However, theater sets, as well as other products, can be built by computerized systems. This approach to production is known as computer-aided manufacturing.

Computer-Aided Manufacturing

Computer-aided manufacturing (CAM) is the use of a computer system to plan, manage, and control manufacturing operations. It may be used in operations of varying complexity, ranging from machine shops employing one or two people to huge state-of-the-art factories employing thousands of workers. Depending on the scope of the application, CAM may employ computers of any size. Graphics monitors frequently are included so that the user can see what the product will look like before the computer actually produces it. Commonly used input devices include the light pen, the mouse, and specialized sensors such as temperature or pressure indicators.

Computer-aided manufacturing (CAM)
The use of a computer system to plan, manage, and control manufacturing operations.

CAD/CAM systems proceed from product design to manufacturing in an integrated fashion. (Photo Researchers.)

Like the hardware, the software can vary greatly. For example, many applications use a computer that runs a single program; an example is process control in an oil refinery. Other applications may require dozens or even hundreds of interlocking programs. Prospective users may choose off-the-shelf software or may develop their own software or hire a specialist to develop it for them.

The term *CAD/CAM system* is used to describe systems in which a product is first designed using CAD techniques and then manufactured using CAM techniques. This approach eliminates much of the duplication of effort that usually occurs when the design and manufacturing phases are separate, even if both are computerized. An integrated CAD/CAM data base includes data generated during product design, such as size and shape of components and materials specifications, and manufacturing data such as the machine tools to be used and the scheduling of machines and human operators.

Advantages and Disadvantages of CAM

The advantages of using CAM or CAD/CAM systems include improved productivity, ability to prepare designs or finished products more quickly, ability to modify existing designs or finished products more easily; and improved communication among designers, engineers, and management. The major disadvantage of this approach is that choosing and installing these systems is a lengthy, error-prone process.

An Application

Webster Tool & Die of Webster, New York, is a custom machine shop that produces parts ranging from a tiny battery contact for a Kodak camera to a 3-foot-long panel for optical machinery. To increase its market share in a highly competitive industry, in the mid-1980s Webster purchased an expensive laser cutter that can cut through sheet steel at 500 inches per minute with an accuracy of 1/500 of an inch. But although it took only a few minutes to cut the metal with the new equipment, it took up to two days to calculate exactly where the laser should cut it. To solve this problem, Webster purchased an IBM PC with CAM software from Comprep of Orange, California, to perform the calculations and give the resulting instruction to the laser cutter. The CAM system reduced the total time it took to go from a blueprint to a finished product from several days to a few hours.

To use the CAM software, an operator enters data in the form of points, lines, and circles into the computer. The software processes the data and draws a picture of the part; the operator then edits the drawing. Next the system produces a data file, which is transmitted to the laser's numerical control to direct the cutting operations.

Materials Requirements and Manufacturing Resource Planning

Designing and producing products is only part of the manufacturing process. The process also includes gathering the raw materials and the parts to be assembled. One of the computer information systems that can be used to guide this aspect of manufacturing is known as materials requirements planning.

Elements of an MRP System

Materials requirements planning (MRP)
A method of scheduling purchases and deliveries of raw materials and parts.

Materials requirements planning (MRP) is a method of scheduling purchases and deliveries of raw materials and parts in the most efficient manner.

Inputs to an MRP system include the master production schedule, the structure for each product, and the inventory file. The major output is the report listing all parts to be ordered. Additional outputs include performance reports such as actual costs compared to projected costs, exception reports such as overdue orders, and inventory forecasts. MRP applications can be used on a variety of computer systems, depending on the complexity of the manufacturing operation, the volume of input data, and the quantity and nature of the output reports desired.

Potential benefits of MRP include a substantial reduction in inventory, a sharp reduction in late orders, greater productivity of people and machines, and quicker response to changes in the marketplace. However, traditional MRP systems are not integrated with other computer information systems such as capacity planning, shop floor control, and financial systems. These shortcomings may be overcome by manufacturing resource planning systems.

Manufacturing Resource Planning

Whereas MRP systems are used to determine when to purchase materials to meet a production schedule, **manufacturing resource planning (MRP II)** systems indicate whether or not it makes financial sense for the firm to try to meet a particular schedule. MRP II is a planning and operating system that includes all manufacturing functions—materials, capacity, finance, engineering, sales, distribution, and marketing. When the required resources are available, the MRP II system issues the shop-floor and inventory instructions necessary to begin production. As production proceeds, MRP II collects and analyzes data, evaluating performance and making changes where necessary.

For example, at any point during the production process the value of raw materials or work-in-progress may be calculated and adjustments made in the production plan if necessary. MRP II systems provide "what if?" simulations to help managers make production decisions. Because of their great scope, MRP II systems are usually quite expensive, requiring large mainframe computers and sophisticated software.

MRP II systems treat manufacturing information as a corporate resource, simulate alternative courses of action, and, if properly designed, respond rapidly to changes in the marketplace. These systems have some disadvantages, however: They are expensive, take a long time to implement, and require extensive user training.

Manufacturing resource planning (MRP II)
A planning and operating system that includes all manufacturing functions—materials, capacity, finance, engineering, sales, distribution, and marketing.

An Application

Pratt & Whitney Aircraft Company in East Hartford, Connecticut, uses an MRP II system in which numerical control machines on shop floors are on-line to IBM mainframes in the management information systems department in the company's head office. Data from the shop floor (e.g., the production status of engine components) is used to generate work schedules, forecast production of various parts, schedule machine time to produce those parts, and identify manufacturing bottlenecks. Every two weeks the company produces a new schedule listing the engines to be shipped and any spare parts required, and the manufacturing resource planning system creates a new work schedule for the shop floor.

Robots

Robot
A computer-controlled device used for manipulating objects.

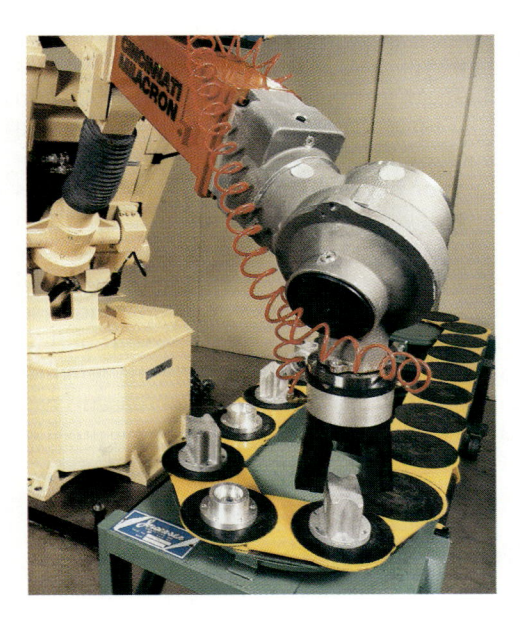

One of the most misunderstood applications of computer technology is the robot. Movies and science fiction portray robots as humanoids destined either to attack or to save humanity. In reality, few of the approximately 20,000 industrial robots in the United States resemble people. **Robots** are simply computer-controlled devices used to manipulate objects. They often take the form of a mechanical arm.

This robotic arm selects items from a moving conveyor belt. (Courtesy of Cincinnati Milacron.)

The automobile industry is the most important user of robots, accounting for over half the robotics industry. Robots are also used in the electronics, furniture, contact lens, and plastics industries and, increasingly, in small machine shops. They are particularly useful for tedious or dangerous tasks such as spot-welding, which is carried out at extremely high temperatures in the presence of noxious fumes.

CHAPTER 15　569　AUTOMATING PRODUCTION

Using robots for spot welding frees human workers from a very unpleasant activity. (The Image Bank.)

Programming Robots

Traditionally, programming or reprogramming a robot meant having someone put the robot through its paces, causing its arm to make the required motions. This usually required that the production line be shut down, and therefore occurred infrequently, such as once a year in preparation for the new models of automobiles. By using microcomputers, however, users can create, edit, test, and store programs for robots off-line, thereby reducing the time the robot is not in use. In addition, powerful engineering workstations provide the graphics capabilities to create three-dimensional images of a robot and its surrounding work area and simulate the robot's operations. When a program is ready it can be transmitted to the robot. This increased flexibility enables robots to accomplish several tasks on the production line rather than being single-purpose devices.

Robot Vision Systems

Although robots can, in principle, be reprogrammed to do several tasks, in practice most robots are used to carry out one highly specialized task day after day. Such specialization is very efficient for tasks that do not change. For example, robot welders are three times as productive as human welders and are used to relieve humans of a dirty and dangerous job. But for many tasks robots that can adapt to their environment by means of vision systems will be needed. (See Box 15-1.) Trucks, for example, have many optional accessories and therefore are

BOX 15-1

FRONTIERS IN TECHNOLOGY

Why Do Robots Need to See?

Ironically, manufacturers have made relatively little use of the feature that distinguishes robots from conventional fixed automation: the ability to reprogram their movements. Instead, they are often bolted to the floor and fitted with a one-purpose hand. There, they follow the same pattern of motion day after day.

One reason is the current method of programming. Programming is typically done "on-line." A human worker literally holds the robot's hand and guides it through a task. The robot then remembers, and repeats the task. Reprogramming requires shutting down the assembly line.

An alternative is to reprogram off-line using a computer simulation of the robot's movements. This approach is limited, however, by the fact that each robot has a characteristic "arm signature" that causes it to respond slightly differently than its fellows to the same command. Where tolerances of a few thousandths of an inch are required, off-line programming does not work well.

A solution is to equip the robot with a vision system or tactile feedback that allows it to correct a near miss. For example, a robot may have to stick a bolt in a hole. If it can see the hole, near misses can be avoided.

But the impact of vision and other sensors will go beyond improving a robot's accuracy. At least as significant will be their role in correcting for the inevitable variations in the manufacturing process. Parts don't always reach the robot in the same position or orientation; they may not even be the right parts. "Most of the things you could do with a sensorless robot have already been done," says Victor Scheinman, vice-president for advanced systems at Automatix (Billerica, Massachusets), which makes sensor-based systems. Eric Mittelstadt, president of GMF Robotics (Troy, Michigan), echoes that thought. "By 1990," he asserts, "a robot that doesn't have vision will not be called a robot."

Although a robot that relies on sensor input will generally work more slowly than a nonsensing robot, the speed issue can cut both ways. A sighted robot that can swivel its wrist to pick up a part, regardless of orientation, eliminates the need to fix the part in a predetermined position. Moreover, by detecting its own errors, a sensor-equipped robot can correct them on the spot, lessening the need for time-consuming inspection and repair further downstream.

Source: Reprinted with permission from Herb Brody, "The Robot: Just Another Machine?" *High Technology* magazine, October 1986, p. 32. Copyright © 1987 by Infotechnology Publishing Corp., 214 Lewis Wharf, Boston, MA 02110.

A robot places a part in the correct position in the Saab-Scania factory in Sodertalje, Sweden. Western Europe has made a major commitment to robotics. (© Tom McHugh, Photo Researchers.)

highly customized; it is unlikely that two trucks on an assembly line will be exactly the same. A robot programmed to do one specific task would be unable to apply it to all trucks. One way of increasing robot flexibility is to install vision systems that will allow robots to inspect each truck and determine what it needs. Along these lines, Ford Motor Company is planning to use a robot to rivet parts onto truck chassis. The robot will use a vision system to inspect each truck, determine its type by the pattern of holes in the chassis, and then rivet the parts accordingly.

Robot vision may enable robots to be more cost effective. They enable the robot to pick up a part regardless of its position on the conveyor belt. It is usually less expensive to equip a robot with a vision system than to design a conveyor belt that presents each part in a predetermined orientation. And it is easier and less expensive to reprogram a robot than to reprogram a conveyor belt.

Touch-Sensitive Robots

Another human sense that has been simulated in robots is the sense of touch. Many assembly operations consist of inserting a piece into a hole. A *touch-sensitive robot* can mimic this operation by circling around the target point, trying from time to time to insert the piece. Grinding operations can also make use of touch-sensitive robots. In a grinding operation, a robot can measure the resistance of bumps felt by the grinding wheel and continue to grind as long as it senses a predetermined degree of resistance. Robots equipped with vision or tactile capabilities can often be programmed to detect their own errors and correct them on the spot, thereby reducing the need for expensive, time-consuming inspection and repair later in the production process.

However, in applications of robots as in other applications of high technology, it is necessary to avoid the trap of throwing technology at a problem. When considering the application of robots to meet an industrial need, it is necessary to use the systems approach, determining the nature of the problem and the desired objectives before focusing on a technological solution.

An Application

The 12-pound laptop IBM PC Convertible is the first computer to be built entirely by robots. The computer is assembled, tested, packed, and shipped in a specially designed facility in Austin, Texas, without ever being touched by human hands. IBM specifically designed the Convertible with fewer than 70 components, using special chips and advanced mounting technology to permit easy assembly by robots. Even the boxes containing the parts were redesigned so that a robot could open them quickly.

The Austin facility has two assembly lines for the Convertible, each with thirteen robots producing a computer every two minutes. The robots, which were custom-built by IBM, can handle a multitude of tasks, and the production line can be used to build any electronic product whose measurements do not ex-

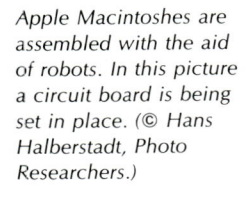

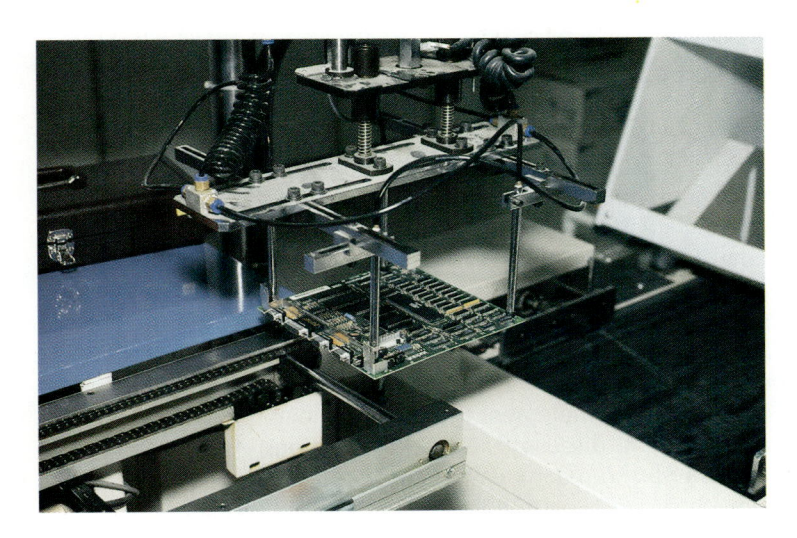

Apple Macintoshes are assembled with the aid of robots. In this picture a circuit board is being set in place. (© Hans Halberstadt, Photo Researchers.)

ceed 2 feet by 2 feet by 14 inches. This flexibility enables the manufacturer to respond rapidly to shifts in the demand for its products.

Flexible Manufacturing Systems

A **flexible manufacturing system (FMS)** is an automated system that machines a variety of items as determined by product demand. Two examples are IBM's Charlotte, North Carolina, printer facilities and its Lexington, Kentucky, keyboard facilities. Similar manufacturing techniques using FMSs are being implemented by chemical and pharmaceutical companies.

An FMS eliminates the need for manual setup of machine tools by using a central computer to direct each machine tool in the system. In effect, the central computer sets up each station to receive a particular part and then routes the processed part to the next station. Unlike traditional assembly lines, which require large lot sizes to be cost-effective, flexible manufacturing systems can efficiently produce lot sizes as small as a single item. This enables manufacturers to produce custom products at or below the unit cost of mass-produced items.

Flexible manufacturing system (FMS)
An automated system that machines a variety of items as determined by product demand.

Implementing FMS

A successful way of implementing flexible manufacturing systems is to start with an analysis of the work flow on the factory floor and make simple but often neglected changes such as moving sequential work areas closer together. At the same time, the product design needs to be examined and simplified and the number of parts and operations reduced wherever possible. Next, small-scale automation, such as using a robot to load and unload parts and a computer to control related machine tools, can be implemented. (At this point it may be worthwhile to implement the just-in-time approach to inventory management, discussed in the next section.) As engineers, programmers, and machine operators gain experience with the system, they can expand it to solve additional problems.

Advantages and Disadvantages of FMS

Flexible manufacturing systems enable companies to change their products rapidly in response to changes in demand for their products. Sophisticated systems can run an entire manufacturing plant with only a few employees. They offer the additional advantage of providing cost savings before the entire system has been installed. Flexible manufacturing systems may be particularly cost-effective for companies that manufacture products with multiple options, such as consumer packaged goods and automobiles. An FMS simplifies the task of tracking a specific item as it passes through different operations within the plant, and it reduces the error rate in manufacturing.

Among the problems associated with flexible manufacturing systems are the cost and time required to put an entire system into service. Such systems often cost between $15 million and $20 million and require eighteen to twenty-four months for development and installation. Moreover, some manufacturers have found that an FMS does not provide the promised degree of flexibility. (See Box 15-2.) For example, an FMS may be unable to meet the precision requirements for laser sights on tank guns. In such cases operations have to be done manually.

An Application

Beginning in 1984, Vought Aero Products Division of LTV Aerospace and Defense in Dallas implemented a flexible man-

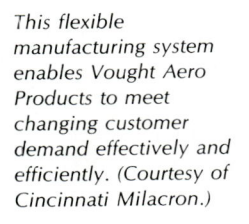

This flexible manufacturing system enables Vought Aero Products to meet changing customer demand effectively and efficiently. (Courtesy of Cincinnati Milacron.)

BOX 15-2

MANAGING CHANGE

Flexible Manufacturing, a Step at a Time

Squeezed by inflation and import competition, in the 1970s and early 1980s a number of U.S. firms embraced flexible manufacturing systems (FMS) as a sort of cure-all. But many of the most ambitious projects were disappointments. They were more expensive and less flexible than promised, and took much longer than planned to implement. Many attempts ended as monuments to unrealistic expectations. Now manufacturers are looking at what was learned from early failures and are taking a more cautious, step-by-step approach.

For one thing, firms have learned the importance of designing products to fit the capabilities of FMS. For example, in 1979 Deere & Company installed a $20 million FMS in Waterloo, Iowa, to make eight types of transmission and clutch housings for its tractors. But the control sequence for totally random part sequences proved too complex for the system's software to handle. Vice-president James Lardner blames this problem on Deere's failure to design simpler parts that have more common features.

"The FMS was a retrofit to a design problem that shouldn't have existed in the first place," says Lardner. "We can cut capital investment for automation by 50 to 60 percent just by getting the design and manufacturing people together from the beginning."

Today, many FMS projects begin with "cells" of automation that can be fully connected later. For example, Deere now identifies families of parts that have similar characteristics—although they may have very dissimilar uses. When parts are close enough in size, shape, and configuration to be machined at a single station, Deere dedicates a cell to that family. One such cell, making fifteen different medium-sized gearcase and housing covers, retains a human operator, making it an "imitation of a flexible machining system without the high level of electronic sophistication," says Lardner. "We can make a much lower level of investment and get 70 to 80 percent of the cost advantage."

Richard T. Lindgren, president of Cross & Trecker, a leading machine tool maker, concedes that there are always teething problems in an FMS. To reduce these problems, rather than going for all-out flexibility, Cross now pushes "appropriate flexibility."

"Flexibility is a good word," says Deere's Lardner, "but you need to be precise about how much flexibility you're looking for. Infinite flexibility means infinite cost."

Source: Reprinted with permission from Jeffrey Zygmont, "Flexible Manufacturing Systems: Curing the Cure-All," *High Technology* magazine, October 1986, pp. 22–27. Copyright © 1986 by Infotechnology Publishing Corp., 214 Lewis Wharf, Boston, MA 02110.

ufacturing system to make parts for the U.S. Air Force B-1B bomber. It was estimated that it would take two hundred thousand hours of conventional machining to produce the required 500–600 components. The FMS is expected to cut that time to approximately seventy thousand hours and to generate savings of about $15 million after recovering the $10 million cost of installation. Shortly after the initial implementation Vought expanded its system to make commercial aircraft components, more than doubling the number of parts produced.

Just-in-Time

Just-in-time (JIT)
An approach to production scheduling and inventory control that enables companies to keep inventory to a minimum.

The high inventory levels that are typical of conventional systems can cover up low quality and inefficient operating techniques. For example, if there are twenty surplus bolts available, a few defective ones or late deliveries of additional stock will not slow production. **Just-in-time (JIT)** is an approach to production scheduling and inventory control that enables companies to keep inventory to a minimum. Basically, it makes it possible for companies to arrange for the delivery of parts to the assembly line just before they are to be used, thus controlling quality and eliminating waste. Successful implementing of the just-in-time approach requires a computer information system that provides continuous feedback from the factory floor to the business office.

Hewlett-Packard uses the just-in-time approach to product scheduling and inventory control in manufacturing computers and computerized laboratory instruments. (Courtesy of Hewlett-Packard.)

CHAPTER 15 577 AUTOMATING PRODUCTION

JIT entails placing all the machines necessary to make the finished product close together to avoid expensive, time-consuming transportation of work-in-progress. An improved manufacturer-supplier relationship is also required in order to increase the reliability of raw materials and components supplied. Another important aspect of JIT is employee training that focuses on quality production.

The just-in-time approach to inventory control was first used in 1957 by Mitsubishi Heavy Industries for the production of diesel engines. In the 1980s, one of the main subscribers to the JIT approach is the Toyota Motor Company. In fact, Toyota is widely viewed as having the most efficient and market-responsive production system in the world, partly because of its use of JIT. For example, the JIT method has enabled Toyota to reduce the setup time for a 1000-ton press from four hours to three minutes.

For the just-in-time approach to be effective, the company has to establish close relationships with its suppliers. If suppliers fail to deliver goods on schedule, the entire production line may have to be shut down. The key factors in choosing a supplier are the quality of its products and its ability to deliver them on demand. Computer systems can be used to keep detailed records on supplier performance.

An example of a successful manufacturer-supplier relationship is the one between Nissan in Smyrna, Tennessee, and its suppliers. Nissan uses the JIT approach to inventory control in its chassis plant. When the plant was being built, Nissan requested bids from truck seat manufacturers; the successful bidder was expected to build a plant nearby to supply seats on an as-needed basis. The selected supplier, Hoover Universal's North American Seat Division of Saline, Michigan, built a plant in Murfreesboro, Tennessee, only 18 miles from the Nissan plant. Orders for seats are sent from Nissan's computer to a printer in Hoover's shipping department. At the same time, the order information is transmitted to a robot, which goes to the rack and picks out the requested seats. Trucks make the trip from the Hoover plant to the Nissan plant every hour during the work day.

Advantages and Disadvantages of JIT

Just-in-time inventory systems are installed for the express purpose of cutting inventory, if not eliminating it entirely. For example, by applying JIT, General Motors has cut its annual inventory-related costs from $8 billion to $2 billion. A related advantage is more available warehouse and factory floor space for other uses. Also, the inventory that is created with JIT usually takes the form of raw materials or finished products (as opposed to work-in-progress with other systems), both of which are relatively easy to count and evaluate; this reduces accounting costs. Furthermore, by reducing the time lost in replacing defective material and transporting work-in-progress, JIT speeds up the production process.

Possible disadvantages of JIT include the need for extensive employee training and a significant change in attitudes toward quality. It may also be necessary to renegotiate labor contracts because of the change in job activities, and relocating machines to eliminate long-distance transportation of work-in-progress can be costly.

An Application

In 1984 Centronics Data Computer Corporation, a New Hampshire printer manufacturer, implemented a just-in-time inventory system. The system took about a month to implement and cost less than $100,000. Within a year the firm was able to report the following results:

1. A decrease in the time it takes to fill an order from an average of ninety days to thirty days.
2. A decrease in the time necessary to produce and test a printer from almost eight days to two days.
3. An eightfold increase in the annual inventory turnover.
4. A fourfold increase in daily printer production.

Since the system has been implemented, suppliers that formerly made deliveries once or twice a month now deliver twice a week. Centronics has not eliminated inventory entirely, but has reduced it to a maximum of one week's supply for most items.

Computer-Integrated Manufacturing

Computer-integrated manufacturing (CIM)
The implementation of a fully integrated data base that describes and controls the entire manufacturing process.

Computer-integrated manufacturing (CIM) is the implementation of a fully integrated data base that describes and controls the entire manufacturing process. In the context of computer-integrated manufacturing, the term *manufacturing* has come to

FIGURE 15-1

Components of Computer-Integrated Manufacturing

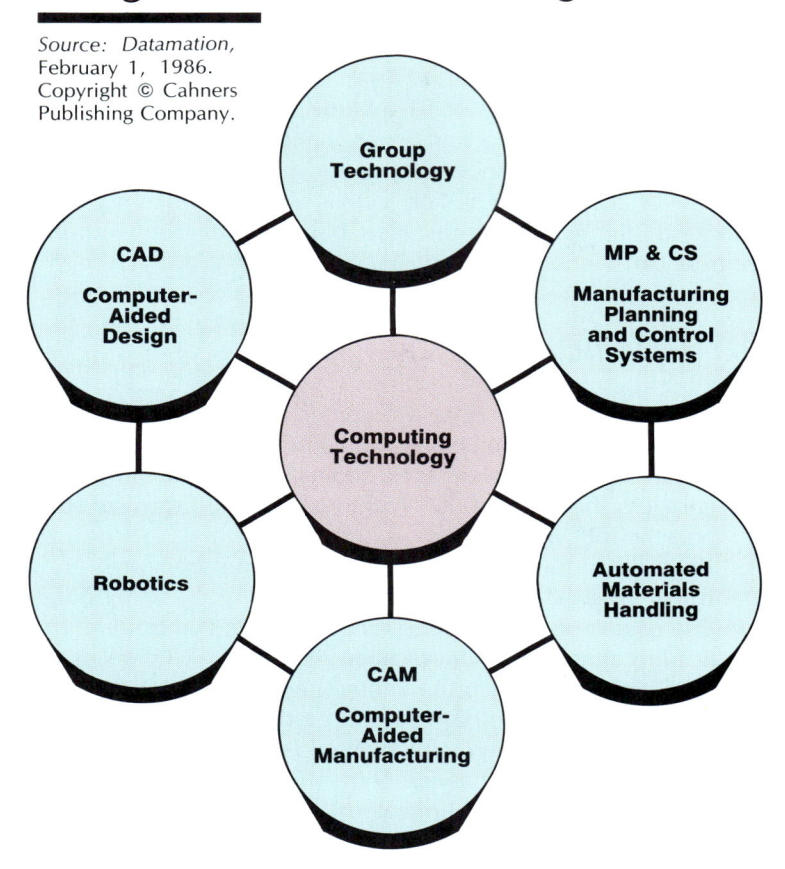

Source: Datamation, February 1, 1986. Copyright © Cahners Publishing Company.

- Group Technology
- CAD — Computer-Aided Design
- MP & CS — Manufacturing Planning and Control Systems
- Computing Technology
- Robotics
- Automated Materials Handling
- CAM — Computer-Aided Manufacturing

mean activities ranging from design to distribution. (See Figure 15-1.) CIM systems include financial information related to each of these activities, both individually and in combination.

Because of their complexity, computer-integrated manufacturing systems are rarely sold as off-the-shelf packages but may be an extension of already existing factory automation systems like those described earlier in the chapter. Depending on the exact nature of the factory to be automated, these systems may be based on powerful minicomputers or mainframes. While some software may be purchased off the shelf, installation of CIM almost always requires extensive custom software development.

In a CIM system, each stage of the manufacturing process acts as the starting point for the next stage. For example, a designer initiates the process by drawing an automobile body. Next an engineer calculates specifications for the parts shown in the drawing; these specs are then used to generate electronic blueprints, three-dimensional drawings, structural analyses, and, finally, the numerical-control instructions that will cut the metal to be used in building the car.

To be successful, CIM systems must take into account the company's competitive situation and objectives, and the selection of hardware, software, and operating procedures must be based on these factors. For example, a company whose product line consists of a few basic, unchanging items will require a vastly different CIM system than one that manufactures a wide variety of products on order.

Developing a CIM system is a major undertaking, often involving millions of dollars, several calendar years, dozens of managerial and technical specialists, and perhaps most important, major changes in the way the company does business. These changes will affect many other departments besides engineering and manufacturing. The process of developing and implementing a computer-integrated manufacturing system is similar in many respects to the system development life cycle presented in Chapter 12. The development process for CIM systems starts with a clear definition of system objectives and, like the system development life cycle, is an ongoing process.

Extensive training of personnel is necessary if a CIM system is to be successful. Industry experts suggest spending about $1000 a year to train each employee who will be affected by the technical and cultural changes brought about by the installation of a CIM system. Such training generally represents about 5 to 10 percent of the cost of capital equipment. It can take various forms, including seminars, computer simulations, and on-the-job training after the system has been installed.

Advantages and Disadvantages of CIM

Among the advantages of computer-integrated manufacturing are the following:
1. Easy access to business, engineering, and factory data.
2. A substantial reduction in data redundancy.
3. Simpler updating of data.
4. A reduction in the time required for new-product design and engineering changes.
5. Close coordination of automated production and materials-

handling equipment with the manufacturing planning and control system.

The primary disadvantage of CIM is its extremely high cost without a guaranteed return. When organizations are considering a capital investment in a new system or product, standard cost-benefit analyses require that the investment justify itself within two to five years. Few CIM systems are able to meet this requirement. Another disadvantage is the extensive change that the organization must undergo. For many manufacturers, however, refusal to implement CIM systems may weaken their competitive position and even lead to bankruptcy.

An Application

Chrysler Corporation uses five primary computer centers in the greater Detroit area, each of which is equipped with mainframe computers. At its Technical Computer and Instrumentation (TCI) Center, about 2500 designers and engineers can access a single integrated computer system. They use the system to invent cars, equip them at will, test them in simulated crashes at any speed desired, and modify the design. Because the system eliminates the need to build a clay model of the automobile, Chrysler's managers can examine prototypes much faster than was possible before the introduction of the computer into the design process. In addition, the cutting of fabric for car upholstery and the cutting of wood for wooden panels on prototype models are carried out in full-scale computer-integrated manufacturing.

Chrysler's CIM system has increased the productivity of its designers and engineers by 25–30 percent over a three-year period. Some activities show an even greater productivity gain; for example, in selected engineering tests, a one-day computer simulation replaces the four-month process of building and testing a physical model.

Manufacturing Automation Protocol

Perhaps the largest and most troublesome problem facing users and suppliers of factory automation systems is communi-

This typical factory floor contains several types of robots, computers, and computerized equipment. A communication standard like MAP would simplify the effort required to get these machines to work together. (Courtesy of Cincinnati Milacron.)

Manufacturing automation protocol (MAP)
A proposed standard for communication among computers, robots, and other devices used in industrial settings.

cation: If robots, machine tools, and computer information systems are unable to communicate with each other efficiently and effectively, factory automation is doomed to failure. One approach to solving this problem, a standard for factory communication known as **manufacturing automation protocol (MAP)**, is currently under development.

Much of the impetus for MAP has come from the world's largest manufacturer, General Motors Corporation. In 1980, General Motors set up a task force to investigate local area networks (see Chapter 6) to interconnect computers, robots, and other electronic gear that work together in a factory or an office. In 1984, it began implementing MAP in its plants, which then contained about 40,000 programmable devices. By 1990, most of GM's 200,000 computers and control devices will be attached to a MAP network.

General Motors is not the only company using a MAP standard: Other suppliers of factory automation equipment have announced products that will conform to part of the MAP standard. In addition, some semiconductor manufacturers are producing circuit boards to link existing equipment to MAP-based networks. About 400 companies are committed to making MAP-compatible hardware such as robots and other automated factory equipment, as well as the software to operate it. MAP is particularly advantageous for industries with a high degree of product change. Industries that produce products that are modified less often, such as office equipment, may find that less all-encompassing communication standards are more profitable.

An Application

General Motors has fifteen plants scheduled to implement MAP. A plant in Saginaw, Michigan, produces front-wheel-drive axles. In its completed network, 55 manufacturing cells (a *cell* is a group of machines that work closely together) will be connected via a MAP network to perform light assembly and metal working. All materials will be moved from station to station by automatically guided vehicles. Robots, material handling devices, numerical control machines, and other equipment will be attached to the local area network, and engineers will be able to implement model changes in ten minutes or less by downloading programs from CAD/CAM workstations.

In this concluding chapter of Part 4 we have explored some of the applications of computer and robot technologies to production processes. Those applications range from computer-assisted design to computer-integrated manufacturing systems. In the final part of the book we will take a look at some applications—and abuses—of computers outside of office and factory settings.

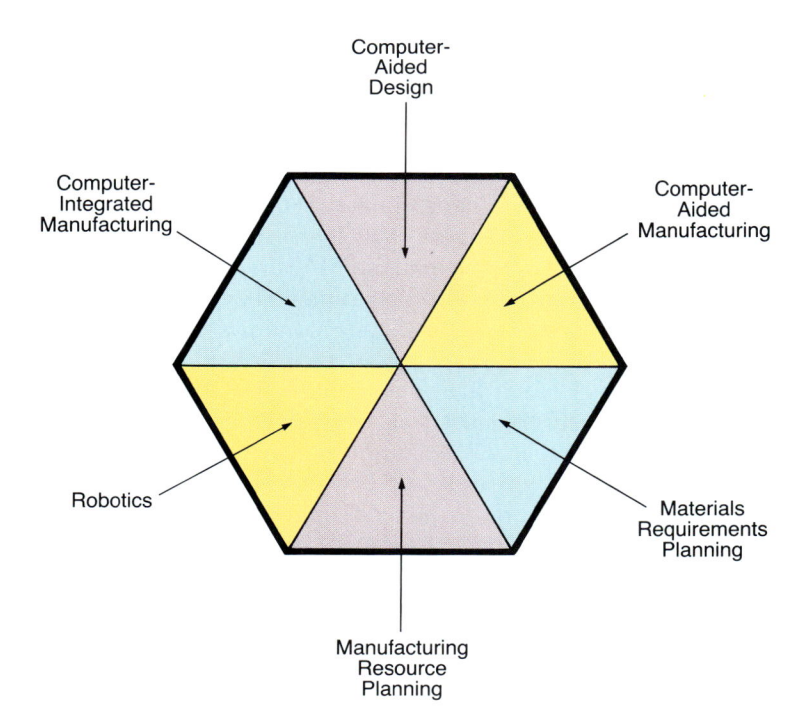

Automating Production

SUMMARY

1. **Computer-aided design (CAD)** is the use of a workstation with graphics capability and special graphics software to design, draft, and document products. It allows the user to make precise, detailed drawings. CAD systems consist of a computer, one or more input devices, one or more graphics output devices, and specialized software. Features offered by CAD software designed for microcomputers include text capabilities, editing functions, zooming, scaling drawings, and production of standard graphics output.

2. **Computer-aided manufacturing (CAM)** is the use of a computer system to plan, manage, and control manufacturing operations. Computer-aided manufacturing capabilities are often associated with computer-aided design capabilities in what are known as CAD/CAM systems.

3. **Materials requirements planning (MRP)** is a method of scheduling purchases and deliveries of raw materials and parts. Inputs to the MRP system include the master production schedule, the structure of each product, and the inventory file. The primary output is a report listing all parts to be ordered. Potential benefits include substantial reduction in inventory, sharp reduction in late orders, greater productivity, and quicker response to changes in product demand.

4. **Manufacturing resource planning (MRP II)** is a planning and operating system that includes all manufacturing functions—materials, capacity, finance, engineering, sales, distribution, and marketing. MRP II systems provide "what if?" simulations to help managers make production decisions.

5. **Robots** are computer-controlled devices used for manipulating objects. Although they can be programmed for various tasks, individual robots are usually devoted to carrying out a single, highly specialized task. Robot vision may make robots more cost effective.

6. A **flexible manufacturing system (FMS)** is an automated system that machines a variety of items as determined by product demand. It eliminates manual setup of machine tools and instead uses a central computer to direct each machine tool in the system. An FMS makes possible rapid product changes in response to changes in demand for the product.

7. **Just-in-time (JIT)** is an approach to production scheduling and inventory control that enables companies to keep inventory to a minimum. JIT speeds the production process, increasing cash flow and enabling the company to meet marketing challenges. It requires that the company establish close relationships with suppliers, which play a key role in the new system. It is also necessary to review the plant's inventory and operating procedures and to initiate a training program to change the attitudes as well as the functions of employees.

8. **Computer-integrated manufacturing (CIM)** is the implementation of a fully integrated data base that describes and controls the entire manufacturing process. Among the advantages of CIM are easy access to

SUMMARY CONTINUED

business, engineering, and factory data; a substantial reduction in data redundancy; simpler updating of data; a reduction in the time required for new-product design and engineering changes; and coordination of automated production and materials-handling equipment with the manufacturing planning and control system.

9. Communication within the factory is probably the largest and most troublesome problem facing users and suppliers of factory automation systems. In 1980 General Motors set up a task force to investigate the use of local area networks to interconnect computers, robots, and other electronic gear that must work together in a factory or an office. In 1984 it started implementing **manufacturing automation protocol (MAP)**, a communication standard for factory applications. MAP is particularly advantageous for industries with a high degree of product change, such as automobiles and packaged consumer goods.

KEY TERMS

computer-aided design (CAD)

computer-aided manufacturing (CAM)

materials requirements planning (MRP)

manufacturing resource planning (MRP II)

robot

flexible manufacturing system (FMS)

just-in-time (JIT)

computer-integrated manufacturing (CIM)

manufacturing automation protocol (MAP)

REVIEW QUESTIONS

1. Describe computer-aided design and how it can be used in designing a product.

2. What is computer-aided manufacturing? How can it be associated with computer-aided design?

3. Compare and contrast materials requirements planning and manufacturing resource planning and describe their role in the manufacturing process.

4. What is a robot? What is the role of robots in manufacturing?

5. Describe flexible manufacturing systems and their impact on manufacturing.

6. Explain the concept known as just-in-time and its effect on inventory and the entire production process. Describe the relationship between computer systems and JIT.

7. Discuss computer-integrated manufacturing and its benefits.

8. What is meant by manufacturing automation protocol? Why is it important?

APPLICATIONS

1. Report on a computer-aided design package for microcomputers. What features are required to run the program? Describe advantages, disadvantages, and typical applications.

2. Compare the descriptions of robots that appear in science fiction and movies to the description presented in this chapter. What do you think accounts for the differences between them?

3. Find a recent article on MAP. How successful are its applications? Has it gained acceptance among manufacturers and users?

4. Discuss the following statement: In the long run the use of computers and robots will increase employment opportunities in manufacturing.

CASE FOR DISCUSSION

Banks Corporation is a medium-sized manufacturer located in an industrial park on the edge of a medium-sized midwestern town. Its principal product is small electric motors. The motors are sold to manufacturers of appliances, hand tools, transportation equipment, and similar products. Motors for different purposes have some parts in common, but each also has certain custom features specified by the buyer. Depending on the flow of orders, Banks's production line must frequently switch from making one model to making another.

Banks, like many U.S. manufacturers, lost market share to import competition during the early 1980s. During that period the U.S. dollar was soaring in the foreign exchange markets, making U.S. exports expensive and imports from abroad cheap. After 1985, a falling dollar gave the company some breathing room. Don Wold, vice-president for manufacturing at Banks, is determined to make use of this breathing room to cut production costs. The next time international market conditions take an unfavorable turn, Wold wants to make sure the firm is positioned to meet the import competition head on in terms of production costs.

Because of the characteristics of Banks's product—many customized models with some basic parts in common—Wold thinks the firm should look at flexible manufacturing systems. He has a general idea of the capabilities and limitations of such systems, but he is not an expert. Thus, his first move is to hire Floyd Perkins, a consultant who specializes in flexible manufacturing systems.

After several visits to the plant and many conversations with Wold and his subordinates, Perkins completes a preliminary proposal. Wold invites him to make a presentation to a group of senior executives. They ask many technical questions about how the proposed system will work. They have heard about failures at other firms where overly ambitious projects were undertaken. Perkins emphasizes that his proposal takes a conservative, step-by-step approach. One by one, he deals with all technical objections in a manner that he thinks is persuasive.

He leaves the meeting satisfied that his proposal will be accepted.

The next day Wold calls Perkins and asks him to drop by. When Perkins arrives, Wold tells him that the proposal was voted down in a stormy management meeting that ran until late in the evening. Wold was the only one of Banks's senior executives who supported the proposal. Perkins asks what reasons were given.

"Nobody gave their true reasons for turning down the proposal," says Wold, "but if I could read their minds, here's what I think was going on."

"Stanke, the company president, has been running this outfit for forty years, ever since he took it over from his father. He has two years to go until retirement. I think he wants to leave a decision on this to his successor—but the successor hasn't been named yet.

"Stanke also feels a lot of pressure from middle managers who are afraid the FMS will undermine their authority. They know how to deal with a guy out there running a lathe. You look over his shoulder and you can tell if he's doing his job right or not. With the FMS, there will be fewer people running lathes and more people doing programming, designing, and troubleshooting. The middle managers don't know how to monitor people like that. They're afraid of losing control.

"Dorothy Connors is our financial vice-president. She's a real bean counter. The only thing she thinks about is the next quarter's earnings statement and what it will do to our stock price. I'm convinced that your FMS proposal will pay for itself in two years, but that's way too long for her way of thinking.

"Jason Richards is in charge of labor relations. He's afraid of the union. He hasn't talked to them about this thing, but he's full of objections. They'll never agree to change their work rules, he says, and without a change in work rules, there won't be any savings. He thinks the union will see FMS as a threat to job security. I think that if we can upgrade the quality of our product, our sales will rise enough to provide plenty of jobs for everyone."

CASE QUESTIONS

1. How does this case illustrate the idea that management is a matter of getting things done through people?

2. If you were Wold, what would you do to give the FMS system a fighting chance?

P

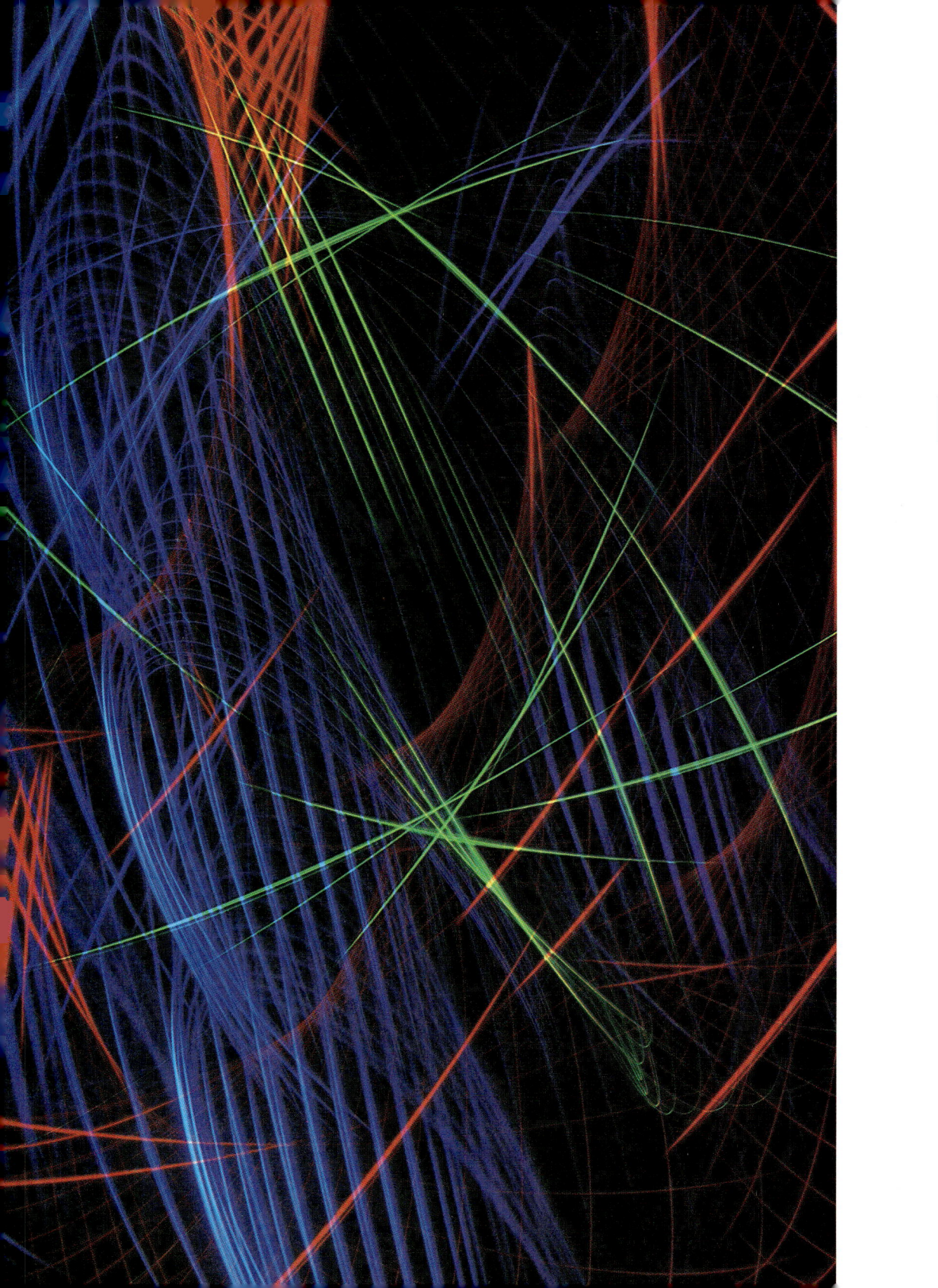

PART 5

Our Automated Lives

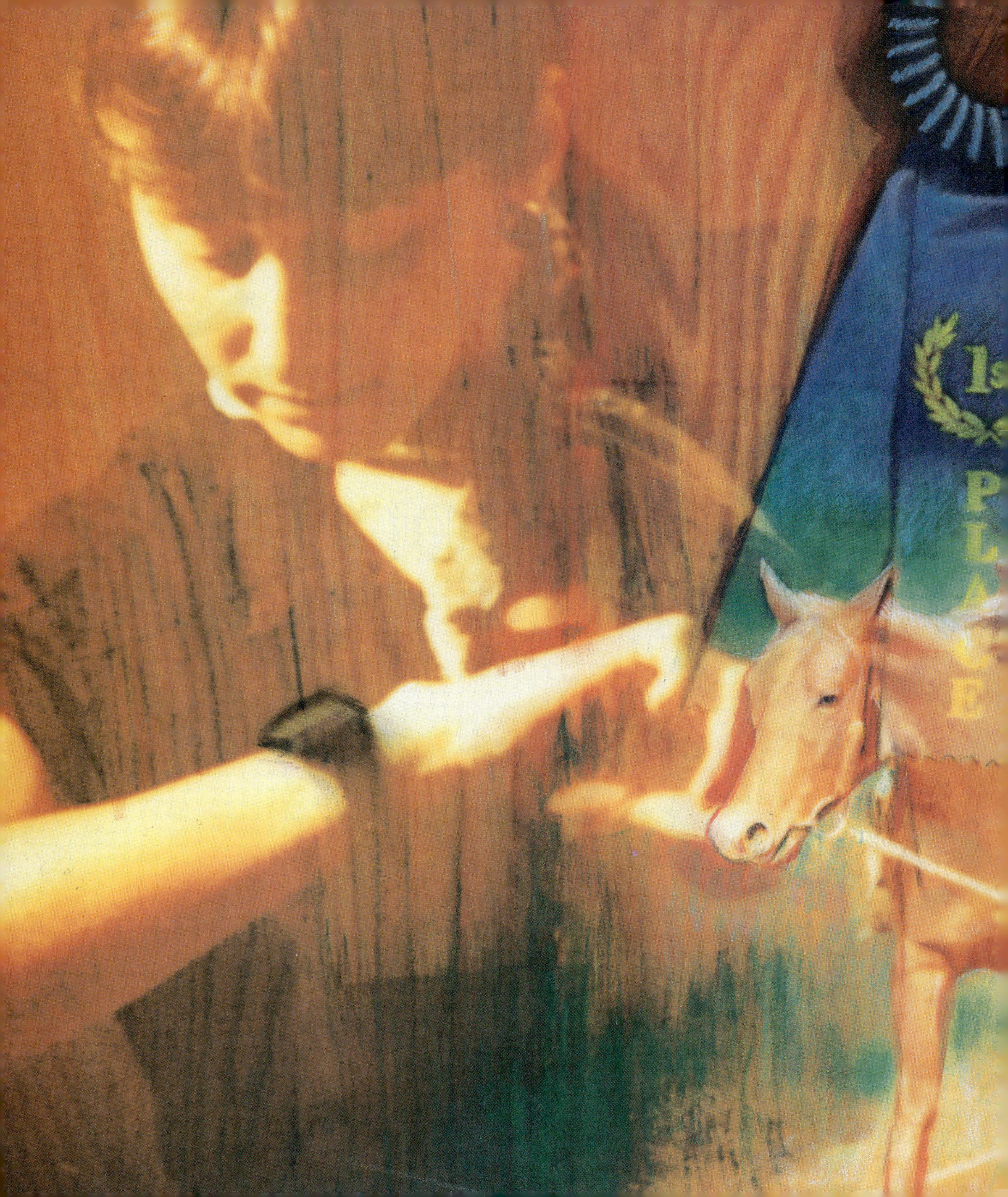
PLACE

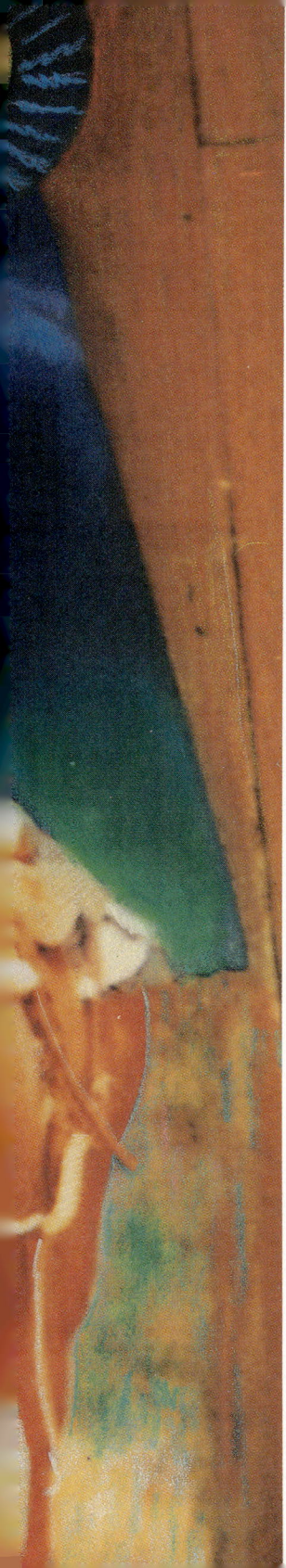

Uses of Computers: Some Applications

CHAPTER

16

The trail is steep and stony. To the right is hardwood forest dappled with autumn colors. To the left is a steep drop that provides a spectacular view of another ridge to the west. But Foxtrot's mind is not on the view. It's on the tail of the horse ahead, which is about to disappear around a bend 50 yards up the trail. Foxtrot surges forward. He doesn't like the horse in front of him to get out of sight.

Sandy Mason, Foxtrot's rider, glances at an instrument on her wrist. Its liquid-crystal digital display reads 165. Foxtrot's heart rate is 165 beats per minute now. That's high. As a veterinarian specializing in equine sports medicine, Mason has conducted extensive computer studies of horse physiology. Horses that go all-out in short races use an anaerobic energy pathway that "burns" chemical fuel stored in the muscle tissue. But this is a 50-mile endurance race. Mason wants to keep Foxtrot in a more efficient aerobic energy mode that uses oxygen from the air.

How does she know what's going on deep in Foxtrot's powerful body? By looking at the read-out unit on her wrist. The horse wears a sensor unit attached to his saddle pad. The sensor sends a radio signal that is picked up by the wrist unit. A tiny chip analyzes the data from the sensor and filters out extraneous noise. Right now it's telling Mason that Foxtrot is overdoing it.

Without coming to a halt, Mason slips out of the saddle and drops back to take a light hold on Foxtrot's tail. She jogs behind as he continues his trot up the ridge. Mason weighs only 110 pounds, but that is 15 percent of Foxtrot's weight, enough to make a difference. Foxtrot's heart rate drops to 145.

Five miles down the trail Mason's caution pays off. There they come to a "gate" where a race official checks the horses for signs of undue stress. Horses can't get through the gate until their heart rate drops to 64. The horse that disappeared around the bend has reached the gate ahead of them, but he's breathing hard. His rider is sponging him with water from a stream and anxiously checking his pulse.

Mason takes Foxtrot to the stream and sponges him, too. In four minutes her computer shows that his heart rate has fallen to 64. The official verifies this and they are on their way. Looking back, Mason sees the other rider still resting his horse.

Throughout this book we have emphasized the use of computers in business. But while it is true that computers are used extensively in business, it is equally true that computers affect life outside the office and factory in numerous ways. The photo essay that appears between Parts 3 and 4 of this book indicates the variety of ways in which computers affect everyday life. In this chapter we explore applications of computers in many fields: in medicine, where they help doctors and administrators diagnose diseases and manage hospitals, and in sports, where they help riders like Sandy Mason, yachtsmen like America's Cup winner Dennis Connor, and the managers of Vermont's Ski Limited Resort. We will also see computers in action in education, music, and finance. In fact, computers are almost everywhere these days.

When you have read this chapter you should be able to:

1. Describe some typical computer applications in the fields of health care, sports, music, and finance.

2. Show how the use of computers has led to changes in these fields.

3. Describe other computer applications that affect your life.

4. Understand and use the key terms listed at the end of the chapter.

Computers and Health Care

Computers play a variety of roles in the field of health care. They are used to maintain medical and financial records in hospitals, doctors' offices, insurance companies, government bureaus, and research institutions. They are used in training health-care practitioners—not only doctors, surgeons, and nurses but also administrative and clerical personnel. And they have come into widespread use in many areas of medical care. For example, they have made it possible for some patients to be treated at home, rather than in hospitals, thereby reducing the cost of health care and physicians' workloads. Computerized decision support systems help hospital administrators determine the best mix of treatments to provide in the light of patient needs and financial and personnel constraints. On-line medical data bases can be consulted by health-care practitioners, and similar data bases are available to hospital administrators who need to be aware of rules and regulations affecting health care. In the following pages we'll take a closer look at some of these applications.

Home Health Care

Computers have been an essential element in the rapid expansion of the home health-care industry, which has been transformed from a service furnished by charitable organizations to a business operated for profit. Like other businesses, providers of home health care can choose from a wide range of hardware and software options. The most popular hardware for this application is microcomputer-based systems, often linked together in a network. Commercial software is also available for home health-care applications.

Extensive computerization is a relatively recent phenomenon in the home health-care industry. The earliest applications were in such areas as accounts receivable and work scheduling. As in other businesses, such applications do not generate revenue but may reduce costs. Recently, however, home health-care agencies have been implementing computer information systems that are specifically designed to generate revenue. A good example is the use of computers to obtain electrocardiograms (EKGs). Typically a caregiver visits a patient at home and records EKG data with a hand-held data acquisition device. After returning to the office the caregiver connects the device to the agency's computer, which processes the data and generates a report. The report is then submitted to the patient's physician.

A typical home health-care agency, St. Mary's Home Health Care of Knoxville, Tennessee, uses a computer information system to obtain the following reports and services:

1. *Management*: a productivity report per division, a visit summary per patient, a comprehensive employee activity report, and others.

2. *Clinical*: master scheduling, clinical histories and update reports by patient, treatment plans, discharge summaries with details, and several reports required by the federal government.

3. *Financial*: payroll; quarterly cost reports; accounts payable and receivable; revenue/expense reports by month, by quarter, and year-to-date; insurance logs; balance sheets; and others.

St. Mary's system enables it to produce the forms required for Medicare billing forty-eight hours sooner than previously. The system has also virtually eliminated billing errors and produces accurate, up-to-date clinical information daily. The agency anticipates that it will expand its services and is considering entering the medical-equipment business with the support of its information system.

Decision Support Systems for Hospitals

You will recall from Chapter 13 that decision support systems are characterized by semistructured decisions, use mathematical tools, rely extensively on external data, and are user-friendly and future oriented. Hospital administrators are increasingly using computerized decision support systems to help them decide what services to provide and to document those decisions for hospital boards of directors, physicians, governmental agencies, and the general public.

It is common for information systems designed for health-care administrators and practitioners to serve as both planning and control tools. Such systems are part of many hospital decision support systems. They must be flexible enough to meet needs that vary from one user to another and change over time. Some administrators, for instance, need information such as cost per patient or cost per disease, whereas others want forecasts of average length of patient stay and statistics on hospital bed uti-

Hospitals use computer information systems to keep track of such things as availability of beds and levels of medical supplies. (© William Hubbell, Woodfin Camp.)

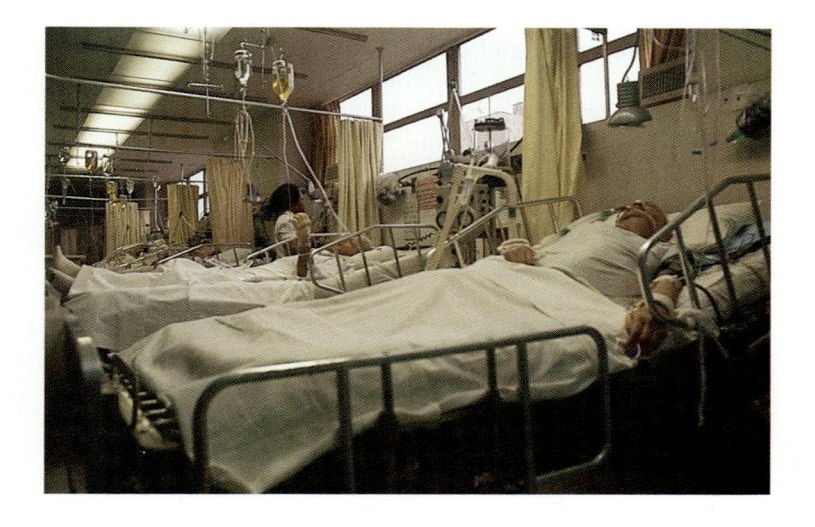

lization. Doctors and medical researchers may need information on the death and recovery rates for different diseases and how these are affected by different treatments.

An example of a hospital decision support system is the one installed by the MacNeal Hospital in suburban Chicago in 1983. The system analyzes the hospital's services by product line and diagnosis group, taking into consideration data obtained from financial and medical records. This decision support system runs on an IBM mainframe linked to hundreds of workstations. A major use of the system is the transfer of data on patient visits from the mainframe data base to the workstations. Analysts employ this data to study the usage rate of various hospital services and verify the performance of physicians and nursing stations. The system also helps departmental managers determine the profitability of each service offered.

The hospital relies on other microcomputer-based information systems to provide statistical estimates of length of patient stays based on tests conducted prior to admission. The patient's medical profile is monitored constantly, making possible immediate action if his or her condition changes suddenly. Among the financial applications is a system that estimates the utilization of a wide variety of medical services, calculating projected revenue and expenses.

Data Bases for Health-Care Professionals

Health-care professionals such as doctors, nurses, and medical researchers use on-line data bases to obtain information on diseases, diagnoses, and drugs, without having to spend long hours in medical libraries or wait for reports to arrive through the mail. The data bases supply up-to-date information provided by specialists at locations throughout the world. Hospital administrators use data bases to familiarize themselves with government regulations and to obtain econometric and public health data for use in making decisions about the nature and extent of the services they provide.

AMA/NET is an example of a health-care data base. It contains extensive information on drugs used in medical practice. The user can search the data base according to several different criteria, including desired action of the drug (e.g., as an antidote to bee stings), adverse reaction (e.g., possible danger when the drug is taken in the presence of penicillin), brand name, and generic name. This data base also includes information on 3500 diseases.

Another health-care data base, Medlars (Medical Literature Analysis and Retrieval System), is actually a collection of sixteen data bases with over 6 million references to publications in the health sciences. A researcher can use Medlars to obtain information on a particular virus or biological system. One of Medlars's components, Medline, contains references to more than 3000 technical journals.

Often the decision to build or expand a health-care institution depends on characteristics of the surrounding population, including its distribution by age, race, family status, and family income. This data, as well as statistical software to process it and produce meaningful information, is available from sources such as CompuServe's Executive Information Service. Hospital administrators can obtain data from this service in either numeric or graphic form on such subjects as the rate of population growth and employment figures within a particular region.

The Centers for Disease Control

An important application of computers in health care can be seen in the Centers for Disease Control (CDC) located in Atlanta, Georgia. The Centers' branches track communicable and other diseases, design programs to combat them, and monitor the effectiveness of those programs. Their main product is information, and therefore computer systems play an important role in their operations. CDC employs a wide assortment of computer hardware, including an IBM mainframe computer for batch processing and electronic mail, a network of Wang computers for secretarial and administrative word processing, and a variety of microcomputers. CDC's software is even more varied

At the Centers for Disease Control computers help in the fight against disease, both in laboratories and in administrative offices. (Courtesy of Centers for Disease Control.)

than its hardware. For example, the mainframe computer runs over 100 administrative applications, including purchasing and vaccine inventories.

A major activity of the CDC is conducting research on AIDS (acquired immune deficiency syndrome). It has provided personal computers for all of its AIDS researchers to assist them in collecting data, testing multiple hypotheses, and communicating with other researchers.

Confidentiality of data is important in the health-care industry. Therefore, only a small percentage of the data processed at the Centers for Disease Control can be identified by individual. In the case of diseases like AIDS, the names of affected individuals are coded and kept on a file separate from the disease data.

Computers and Sports

It comes as no surprise to athletes and sports enthusiasts that computers are playing an important role in sports. We saw in Chapter 1 how a journalist used a portable computer to file a story about a football game before the fans had left the stadium parking lot. Other computer applications in sports include keeping track of scores, ticketing matches, providing instant replays, analyzing statistics to help coaches develop game tactics, and assisting in the training of players. Other kinds of sports also are affected by computers; many people use home computers to develop training programs and track their progress in sports like weight lifting, high jumping, and long-distance running. In addition, handicapped and injured athletes can use computerized training systems that allow them to exercise specific muscles without endangering themselves. In this section we will consider applications in football, boating, and skiing.

Computers and Football

In most sports, the degree of computerization depends on the level at which the sport is practiced. Even "pick-up" football games played on neighborhood fields are indirectly affected by the computer revolution: The football itself and the players' equipment probably were designed and marketed according to a strategy developed with the aid of a decision support system. And many communities use a microcomputer to schedule the use of their playing fields.

At the high school and college levels, many teams depend on computers to help them analyze and choose tactics, taking into account statistical information from previous games. Football leagues draw up their game schedules with the aid of computer-based scheduling programs.

Microprocessors make it possible to custom-design athletic equipment to meet individuals' needs. (Focus on Sports.)

Professional football is a big business, and like many big businesses it relies heavily on computers for a variety of applications. Computers have helped transform professional football from an art to a science. Only professional teams can afford to hire specialists to develop customized applications for ticketing, marketing, and sportscasting. Computers also provide information for use in negotiations with players and television networks, and in developing individualized training programs for the players.

An important application of computers in football is in scouting. Because of the relatively short careers of most professional football players, teams must constantly be on the lookout for new players. Two organizations, the National Scouting Combine Inc. and Blesto Scouting Inc., provide information on potential players to National Football League teams. In a typical year they report on the future prospects of over 10,000 college football stars, of whom only about 3 percent will be drafted. It would be cumbersome and time-consuming to consider all these prospective players without the help of computer information systems.

Figure 16-1 shows a form used by Blesto to collect data on college football players. Shaded areas refer to the most important qualities required for a given position. In the case of quarterbacks, for example, arm strength, quick release, accuracy, and certain other qualities are essential. Taking into account the weighting factors that each team assigns to these qualities, the computer calculates a grade for each player. This computer-generated grade may be accompanied by an additional grade representing the scout's assessment of the player.

The scouting process consists of several stages, each of which uses computers in some way. The initial evaluation begins in February. Prospective players are evaluated in several rounds, and only the most promising candidates are retained. Representatives of the scouting organization meet with coaches from the different teams and obtain information to complete the computer reports. After these meetings and, in some cases, after viewing the games themselves or game films, the final step of player selection begins. In January of the following year the two scouting organizations and all twenty-eight NFL teams take part in a *combined workout*, in which the top 300 prospective players display their skills and undergo extensive medical examinations. The data gathered in these ways helps the teams make their selections in May. (See Figure 16-2.) Computerized scouting systems have by no means eliminated the need for human judgment; instead, they provide an example of how computers can be used as a tool to improve human performance.

FIGURE 16-1

Player Evaluation Form

Source: Reprinted from *Journal of Systems Management,* May 1986, p. 28.

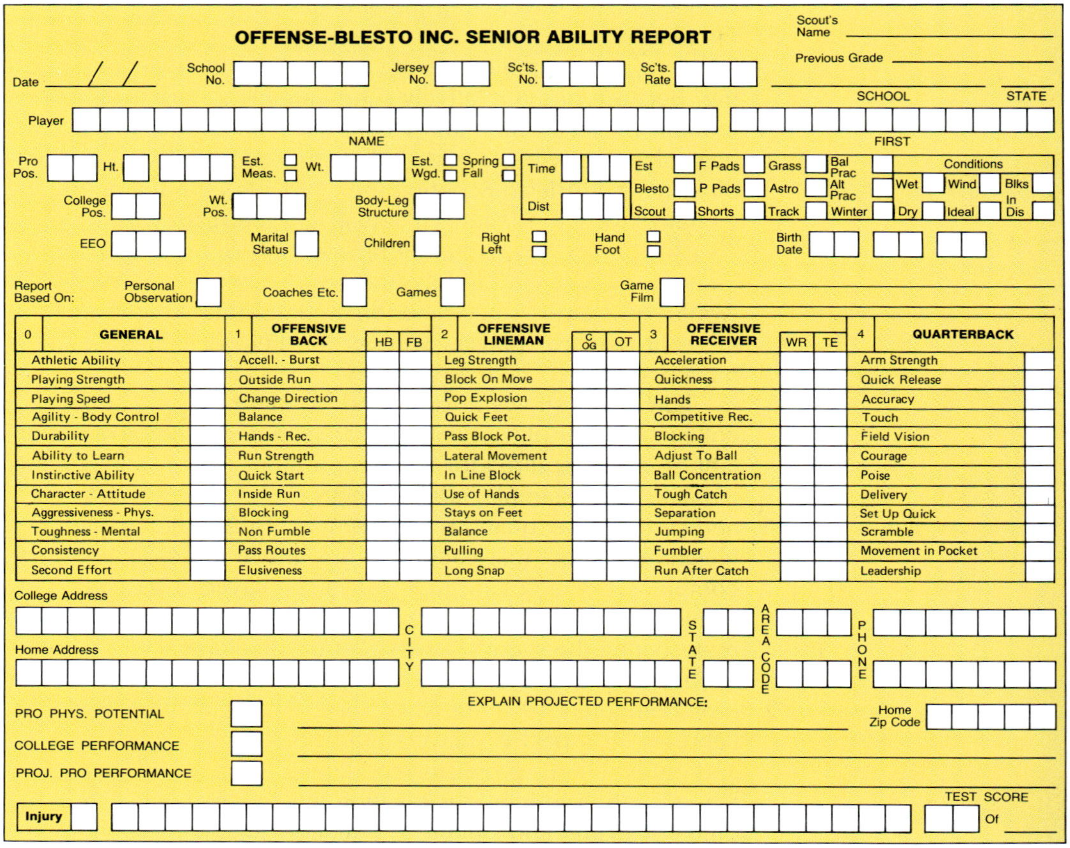

OFFENSE-BLESTO INC. SENIOR ABILITY REPORT

Scout's Name ______ Previous Grade ______

Date __/__/__ School No. Jersey No. Sc'ts. No. Sc'ts. Rate

SCHOOL STATE

Player NAME FIRST

Pro Pos. Ht. Est. Meas. Wt. Est. Wgd. Spring Fall Time Dist Est Blesto Scout F Pads P Pads Shorts Grass Astro Track Bal Prac Alt Prac Winter Conditions Wet Dry Wind Ideal Blks In Dis

College Pos. Wt. Pos. Body-Leg Structure

EEO Marital Status Children Right Left Hand Foot Birth Date

Report Based On: Personal Observation Coaches Etc. Games Game Film

0 GENERAL		1 OFFENSIVE BACK	HB	FB	2 OFFENSIVE LINEMAN	C OG	OT	3 OFFENSIVE RECEIVER	WR	TE	4 QUARTERBACK	
Athletic Ability		Accell. - Burst			Leg Strength			Acceleration			Arm Strength	
Playing Strength		Outside Run			Block On Move			Quickness			Quick Release	
Playing Speed		Change Direction			Pop Explosion			Hands			Accuracy	
Agility - Body Control		Balance			Quick Feet			Competitive Rec.			Touch	
Durability		Hands - Rec.			Pass Block Pot.			Blocking			Field Vision	
Ability to Learn		Run Strength			Lateral Movement			Adjust To Ball			Courage	
Instinctive Ability		Quick Start			In Line Block			Ball Concentration			Poise	
Character - Attitude		Inside Run			Use of Hands			Tough Catch			Delivery	
Aggressiveness - Phys.		Blocking			Stays on Feet			Separation			Set Up Quick	
Toughness - Mental		Non Fumble			Balance			Jumping			Scramble	
Consistency		Pass Routes			Pulling			Fumbler			Movement in Pocket	
Second Effort		Elusiveness			Long Snap			Run After Catch			Leadership	

College Address CITY STATE AREA CODE PHONE

Home Address

PRO PHYS. POTENTIAL EXPLAIN PROJECTED PERFORMANCE: Home Zip Code

COLLEGE PERFORMANCE

PROJ. PRO PERFORMANCE

Injury TEST SCORE Of

Computers and Boating

Computers have been used aboard ships for a long time. As we noted in Chapter 1, in 1822 Charles Babbage designed a specialized calculating machine called the difference engine to generate mathematical tables for navigation. Modern computer applications for boats and ships of all sizes include controlling the engines and other equipment, keeping track of fuel and cargo, and monitoring nearby ships to reduce the chances of collision.

FIGURE 16-2

Pro Football's MIS Model

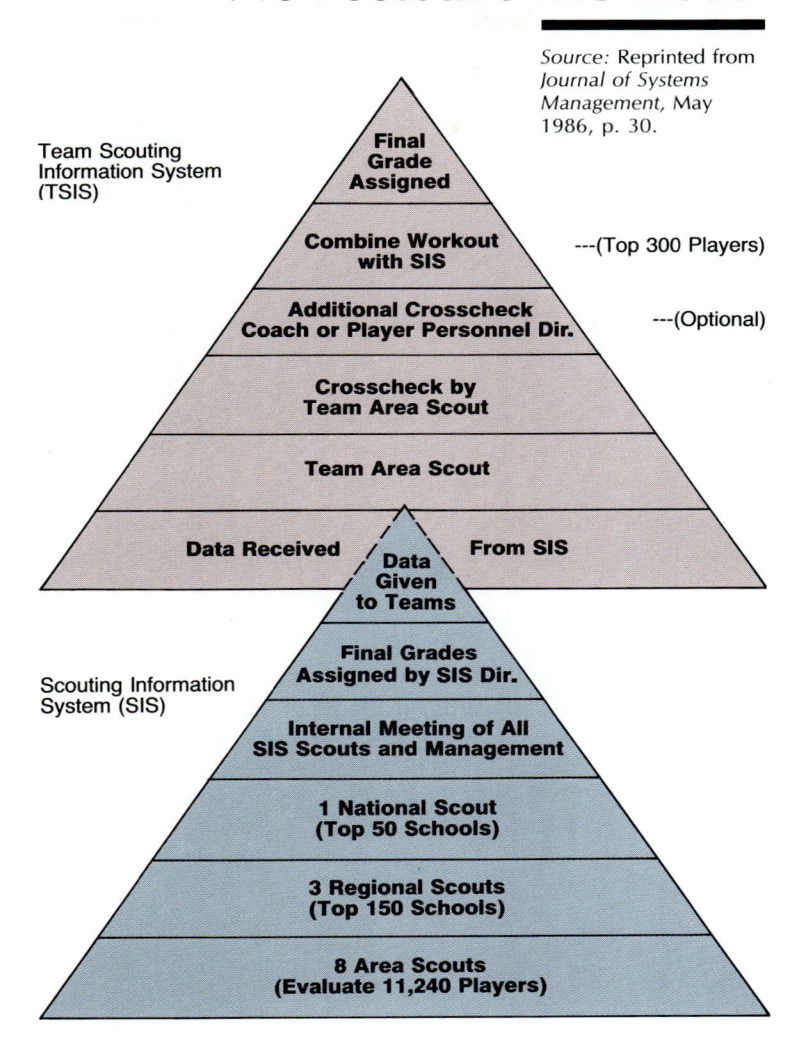

Source: Reprinted from *Journal of Systems Management,* May 1986, p. 30.

Team Scouting Information System (TSIS)

- Final Grade Assigned
- Combine Workout with SIS ---(Top 300 Players)
- Additional Crosscheck Coach or Player Personnel Dir. ---(Optional)
- Crosscheck by Team Area Scout
- Team Area Scout
- Data Received / Data Given to Teams / From SIS

Scouting Information System (SIS)

- Final Grades Assigned by SIS Dir.
- Internal Meeting of All SIS Scouts and Management
- 1 National Scout (Top 50 Schools)
- 3 Regional Scouts (Top 150 Schools)
- 8 Area Scouts (Evaluate 11,240 Players)

An example of the use of computers in boating can be found in the world's best-known yacht race, the America's Cup. This annual race was won in 1983 by *Australia II*, possibly because of its radical "winged keel," which was inspired by an aircraft

This on-board computer was used by the crew of the yacht Stars and Stripes to analyze wind and weather conditions and make tactical decisions. Stars and Stripes won the America's cup in 1987. (© Daniel Forster, Duomo.)

wing design created at NASA. In 1987 the race was won by the American yacht *Stars and Stripes* with the aid of a computer program that determines the hydrodynamic flow of sailboat hulls. This program enables scientists to view a three-dimensional model of a boat from any angle and to test its design under different sailing conditions.

Before computers became available, testing a boat design meant building an expensive prototype and spending weeks gathering and analyzing data. Today computer-aided design can help create a hull that offers minimum resistance to waves, thereby enabling the yacht to make maximum use of the prevailing winds. In addition, computerized testing can provide information on a design's performance under a wide range of conditions. Many companies have donated computer time, software, and expertise to participants in the America's Cup.

After a yacht has been designed, its actual performance is monitored by on-board microcomputers that collect data on such factors as wind speed and wave types and transmit this data to minicomputers, also on board. The minicomputers process the data and furnish the crew with up-to-the-minute information comparing the yacht's performance to that of competitors, including suggestions regarding the choice and positioning of sails. Today, as a result, most professional yacht crews would no sooner set sail without computers than they would with a leaky hull.

Computers and Skiing

Every type of business has its own special requirements, and the ski resort industry is no exception. But unlike most businesses, ski resorts have only a limited number of weeks, perhaps twenty to thirty, each year in which to generate their annual income. Although many of its expenses must be paid during the entire year, a ski resort cannot earn much income in the summer. Furthermore, its revenues during the ski season are highly dependent on weather conditions.

In the last few years many ski resorts have installed computer systems to help them run their business and increase customer satisfaction. The systems are used in accounting, marketing, and personnel applications. More progressive ski resorts are developing computerized snow-making systems to increase the length of the ski season.

Ski Limited, located in Killington, Vermont, uses computer information systems for a wide variety of applications. Ski Limited's computers enable the company to take the greatest possible advantage of natural and artificial snow conditions. For example, they provide information that helps the resort's managers decide when to open their various facilities such as ski lifts and trails.

Unlike many of its competitors, Ski Limited uses computers to operate its snow-making system. To maximize the efficiency of the snow-making process, the company has installed equipment that measures the depth of the snow at intervals of a few meters, and sensors that record wind velocity and humidity every few seconds. These specialized instruments are linked to minicomputers. Other computer systems keep track of the ski lifts, speeding them up or slowing them down according to frequency of use. Ski lift usage data is summarized by computer to help the resort's managers decide when to expand existing lifts or install additional ones.

A key factor in the success of a resort is customer satisfaction. Besides providing skiers with well-groomed slopes and reducing the wait for ski lifts, Ski Limited has installed computer systems that display the images of different trails so that skiers can choose among them on the basis of ability. Other systems speed up the reservation and checkout process and provide repeat customers with favored locations whenever possible. Computer systems keep track of "points" so that repeat customers can obtain free passes to ski lifts. In sum, Ski Limited has improved its competitive position by furnishing an increased level of service to its customers, largely as a result of its skillful use of computer information systems.

Computers and Education

Computers are being used in teaching millions of students at all levels, from nursery school to graduate school, as well as in nontraditional learning situations. As Box 16-1 shows, they may be applied in situations that straddle the fields of education and medicine. They are also being used by schools and colleges in nonteaching applications such as accounting and financial systems for school administrators. The applications that we will examine in this section include computer-assisted instruction and computer-managed instruction. We will also discuss some of the problems associated with the use of computers in schools.

Computer-Assisted Instruction

A major application of computers in schools and colleges is **computer-assisted instruction (CAI)**, or the use of a computer to help students learn, with or without a human teacher. CAI encompasses a wide variety of techniques, including drill and practice, computerized tutorials, and simulation. Drill and practice typically is used to free teachers from the time-consuming task of verifying addition and multiplication tables. Computerized tutorials allow students to advance at their own pace. In a learning situation supported by a network of microcomputers or terminals, teachers can review students' progress and focus their efforts on those who can best profit from extra help. Hundreds of CAI systems are available for computers ranging from small home computers to mainframes.

The most widely used CAI system is Programmed Logic for Automatic Teaching Operations (PLATO), which was developed at the University of Illinois, Champaign-Urbana, in conjunction with Control Data Corporation. Although some PLATO lessons may be accessed from microcomputers, PLATO lessons usually are run on special terminals designed for touch input so that they can be used by people who do not type. Students can choose among hundreds of PLATO lessons ranging from accounting to zoology.

Computer-assisted instruction (CAI)
The use of computers to help students learn.

BOX 16-1

FRONTIERS IN TECHNOLOGY
Computers Help Teach the Deaf to Speak

For 18-year-old Leann Gilroy of Birmingham, Alabama, such words as "church" and "sheep" were once an impassable barrier to normal speech. Gilroy was born almost totally deaf. With the help of a hearing aid she had learned to utter low-frequency sounds like a "g" or a "k." But high-frequency sounds were beyond even her aided hearing, and she had no concept of the high-frequency whistling of "s," "sh," "c," or "ch." Moreover, it was physically impossible for parents, friends, or teachers to show her exactly how one shapes and places the tongue to produce such sibilant sounds.

In 1980, however, Gilroy volunteered for an experiment at the University of Alabama. The experiment's success can be gauged by the fact that Gilroy now can clearly and distinctly utter a phrase like "I see my sheep," attend a regular high school (with the help of a sign language interpreter), and be easily understood by classmates. "She has to go slow and needs a lot of practice, but now she knows how to control the thrust of her tongue," says her mother.

Gilroy is one of the first beneficiaries of a research effort that uses computerized devices to teach the hearing-impaired how to speak. In her case Samuel Fletcher and his colleagues at the university's biocommunications department used an electronic palate to show Gilroy how to curl the tip of her tongue against the roof of her mouth, leaving a small passageway for sibilant sounds to whistle through.

The electronic palate is a thin plastic plate that fits to the roof of the mouth and is wired to a computer. The palate is studded with 96 tiny electronic sensors, each of which is activated when touched by the tongue. The computer, scanning the sensors 100 times a second, can display on a television monitor a pattern of bright dots showing exactly where the tongue is touching the palate when the person is uttering any sound.

The computer can also display a pattern showing how people normally place the tongue to produce, say, an "s" sound. A deaf person can try to match the pattern by placing the tongue against the electronic palate. With careful coaching and trial and error, children can learn how to make sounds that require placing the tongue against the roof of the mouth.

Other computerized devices are used for vowels and for consonant sounds that do not bring the tongue into contact with the roof of the mouth. And other people besides the hearing-impaired may benefit from the new technologies. Fletcher tells of a lisping child with normal hearing who had spent three years in speech therapy trying to pronounce an "s" sound. A single half-hour session with one of Fletcher's computerized devices showed him the proper tongue configuration. "All the instruction he'd been receiving suddenly made sense to him," Fletcher says. The boy then learned to overcome his lisp.

Source: Jerry E. Bishop, "Computerized Devices Teach Deaf People Art of Speaking," *Wall Street Journal*, December 19, 1986, p. 25. Reprinted by permission of *The Wall Street Journal*. Copyright © Dow Jones & Company, Inc. 1986. All rights reserved.

A key technique of CAI is **simulation**, in which a computer model is used to represent a real-life situation. Simulations can be used at all levels of education, from games in elementary school to business and scientific problem solving in graduate school. Simulations enable students to conduct experiments that might otherwise be too expensive or dangerous. For example, medical students can simulate the reactions of patients to several drugs taken separately or together. Such experiments could not be performed using live patients. Similarly, a marketing student can ask "what if?" questions about how consumers in various potential markets might respond to a particular product.

Computer-assisted instruction offers several advantages. Many systems are available at night and on weekends as well as during regular school hours. They make possible individualized instruction—systems can be programmed to meet the needs of particular students. And they provide almost instantaneous feedback: Students receive immediate verification or correction of their answers to review or test questions.

CAI also has some disadvantages. These include the high cost of many systems, which may require mainframes, specialized workstations, and communication facilities. In addition, the quality of CAI software is uneven. Many CAI programs are of rather poor quality; for example, they will reject the answer "Henry the 8th" or "Henry The 8th" when the answer "Henry the Eighth" is expected.

Simulation
A technique used in computer-assisted instruction in which a system is represented by a model.

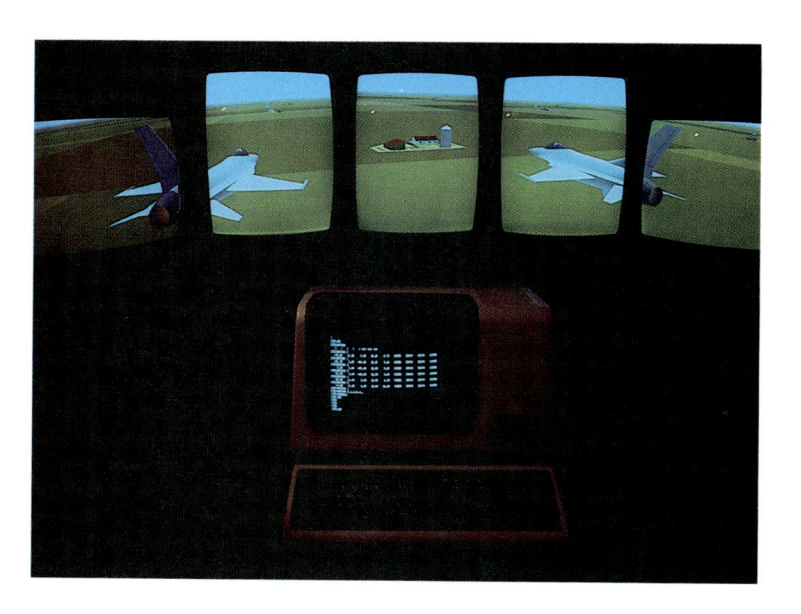

A major component of airline pilot training is the use of sophisticated computer programs to simulate flight situations. (© Chuck O'Rear, Woodfin Camp.)

Computer-Managed Instruction

Computer-managed instruction (CMI)
The use of computers by educational institutions to store and process administrative data.

Computer-managed instruction (CMI) is the use of computers by educational institutions to store and process administrative data. CMI systems range from modified electronic spreadsheets that calculate grades for a small class to mainframe-based systems that manage school districts or universities with thousands of students. The major application of CMI is for record keeping, freeing teachers from this responsibility. With the aid of CMI, teachers can identify test questions that are answered incorrectly by an unusually large percentage of students, indicating that the questions should probably be reworded. Some computer-managed instruction systems are used by administrators to perform tasks related to registration, class scheduling, and staffing. CMI and CAI may be combined, for example, in systems that direct students to additional sources of information when they experience undue difficulty in understanding instructional material.

Challenges to the Use of Computers in Education

Clearly, computers have great potential for providing instruction in ways that are unfeasible or impractical for human teachers. The coming years will bring new challenges to the use of the computer as a partner in the educational process. One of those challenges is in the area of hardware. Many of the computers that are currently used in classrooms are small by today's standards. Their small CPUs and memory capacity make it difficult for them to run high-quality educational software, and they cannot be used to introduce students to commonly used business software. An additional problem is the difficulty of linking together a series of workstations within a single classroom. With a local area network, a teacher could send the same exercise to each student's workstation without having to prepare a series of diskettes.

The development of high-quality instructional software is another challenge that must be overcome in the near future. An educational software development team might include an expert on pedagogy, a specialist in a particular subject, an expert on computer graphics, a programmer, a technical writer, and a project manager to coordinate the team's efforts. It is not surprising, therefore, that software development costs sometimes exceed $500,000, even when multimedia equipment such as cassettes and slides are not included. Because of the tight budget constraints imposed on most schools, it is necessary to keep costs down even when the goal is to create high-quality software.

A further challenge related to the use of computers in education is to increase the computer literacy of teachers. Only a small fraction of the nation's 2 million teachers have been exposed to computer education in a systematic way. Even the best software will not work in the hands of a teacher who is unable or unwilling to use a computer. As computer literacy increases and classrooms are equipped with improved hardware and software, more teachers will begin to think of the computer as a valuable educational tool, one that can free them from routine activities and allow them to focus on teaching.

Students also will find computers playing a greater role in their education. Perhaps the most important effect of computers on students will be a decrease in the distinction between studying and doing. The growing availability of courses taught by computer and the flexibility of computers in meeting individual students' needs and aptitudes mean that computers will become essential to students as well as to teachers and educational administrators.

Computers and Music

Computers have been applied to many aspects of musical composition and performance. Designers of musical instruments can use computer-aided design systems to help recreate ancient instruments or produce new ones. An especially useful application of computers in music is the teaching of music theory. Students can see notes on a monitor at the same time that they hear them produced by a computer-driven loudspeaker. Other computer-based systems have greatly increased the quality of recorded sound. Finally, musicologists use computers to assist them in determining the authorship of disputed musical works.

The first musical composition created on a computer dates back to the late 1950s. In the mid-1960s the Moog synthesizer, an electronic device for imitating musical sounds or creating new ones, gained considerable popularity. But this synthesizer and others available at the time required frequent adjustments,

Musical Instrument Digital Interface (MIDI)
A standard that describes the way the hardware of electronic musical instruments is interconnected and the software for data interchange.

Computer synthesizers allow musicians to imitate a variety of instruments or invent new ones. (© Chuck O'Rear Woodfin Camp.)

and their bulk made them difficult to operate; moreover, their cost put them out of the reach of the average musician. With the development of digital synthesizers, the flexibility and reliability of the equipment increased but the cost remained high until the advent of microcomputers.

In 1983 several manufacturers of electronic musical instruments adopted a standard known as **Musical Instrument Digital Interface**, or **MIDI.** This standard applies to both hardware and software. MIDI-based musical systems range from systems that teach introductory music on home computers to specialized systems used by professional musicians. A common way to use a MIDI-based musical system is for a musician or music student to type notes at the keyboard. The notes are processed by the system and output as music by a synthesizer. Depending on the sophistication of the hardware and software used, some MIDI systems are able to capture a particular musician's keyboard touch and produce very high-quality music.

Many MIDI-based musical systems include programs that allow the user to manipulate notes in much the same way that a word processor manipulates words. For example, the user can move a portion of a musical composition from one point to another. Similar operations enable rapid copying or deletion of melodies. Additional features permit more sophisticated musical manipulation. For example, the musician can replace a series of notes or modify the pitch of every fourth note. Because the system lets them hear and sometimes see the effects of such experiments almost immediately, musicians have more freedom and flexibility than was possible in the past.

An important application of MIDI is a computerized music teacher, Musicom, that is used in music schools to supplement human teachers. Musicom has several components: an IBM PC or compatible equipped with color graphics, special MIDI hardware (including a velocity-sensitive keyboard), and a microphone for singing lessons. The music lessons, which are available on diskettes, cover a series of subjects, including keyboard basics, beginning and intermediate music theory, and singing. Additional lessons in such subjects as jazz and rock music are being developed.

The first lesson, Rapid Piano, helps students learn the letter name of each note and the corresponding sound. Then it introduces the student to musical notation and ends by presenting note lengths and rhythm. More advanced lessons listen to the student's voice or playing and provide a critique; for example, the computer indicates whether a tone is sharp or flat.

Another application of MIDI is the Kurzweil 250 digital synthesizer, a moderately expensive device that is capable of producing professional-quality sound. For example, it can imitate

The user of this microcomputer is running MUSICALC, a computer software package that uses graphics as an aid to musical composition. (© Jerry Mason, Photo Researchers.)

a concert grand piano, taking into account its acoustical properties under a wide variety of conditions. The Kurzweil 250 synthesizer contains millions of digital samples of music in its ROM and is therefore able to duplicate the musical effects of dozens of instruments.

Sound engineers and musicians use the Kurzweil synthesizer to make digital recordings and mix sound tracks. It can combine several versions of the same sounds to create the illusion of several instruments playing at the same time, a feature called *chorusing*, and can switch almost instantaneously from one musical instrument to another. It can also transpose music from one key to another. A feature that is particularly useful for writers of television commercials is time compression/expansion, with which, for example, a musical piece that is thirteen seconds long can be lengthened to fill exactly fifteen seconds.

Computers and Finances

For decades computers have been used in monetary applications ranging from payroll and accounting systems to helping the U.S. Mint produce money and the Federal Reserve Bank control the amount of money in circulation. Numerous software packages are available to help individuals manage their personal and family finances, calculate their taxes, and forecast their future net worth. Specialized packages keep investors informed of the latest financial news and assist them in tracking securities and developing investment strategies.

Personal Finances

Computers have long been used for personal financial activities ranging from balancing checkbooks to managing an entire family's financial affairs. Personal-finance software packages vary widely in complexity, speed of operation, accounting knowledge required, and features offered. Many people initially use personal-finance programs to balance their checkbooks. Although this takes longer to do on a computer than manually, computerization of this activity offers some important benefits. Besides cutting down on arithmetic errors, personal-finance programs can generate useful reports such as income/expense statements. Unlike a list of checks, such reports provide users with a clear picture of how they are handling their money. The electronic spreadsheets included with many personal-finance software packages allow users to ask "what if?" questions and see the financial effects of buying or selling a second car, getting a part-time job, and the like.

The features offered by personal-finance software vary considerably and can include one or more of the following:

- **Checkbook balancing.** While most personal-finance programs allow the user to balance a checkbook, they differ in flexibility and power. One program may allow a maximum of 500 checks a year while another can handle ten different checking accounts. Some checkbook-balancing programs are suitable for use in a small business as well as for managing personal finances.
- **Recurring payments.** Some products allow for recurring payments such as mortgage or rent. Checks for such items are prepared and records are updated automatically.
- **Calculator.** The program is able to function as an electronic calculator.
- **Special functions.** The program can be used to calculate special financial functions such as loan amortizations.
- **Tax returns.** Many programs produce standard tax schedules. Some more sophisticated programs can calculate the tax implications of financial transactions such as the purchase or sale of a home. These programs are typically sold with annual updates to reflect changing tax rules and regulations.

- **Forecasting.** Many personal-finance packages generate financial forecasts based on various assumptions regarding inflation, interest rate, and the like. A typical calculation is the amount of money that will be needed at retirement to maintain a person's present standard of living.
- **Family finances.** Some programs calculate, update, and report on the financial situation of family members both individually and as a whole. Such programs can monitor financial data such as Social Security benefits and the tax implications of setting up a college trust fund.
- **Net worth.** An important feature of many personal-finance packages is the ability to compute the net worth of an individual or family. Such information may be useful in obtaining bank loans.

Investment Software

It is estimated that at least one out of five Americans invests in the stock market, and millions of investors have access to microcomputers at home or in the office. In the past several years software vendors have attempted to tap this market by producing a variety of investment software packages. These programs serve clients ranging from casual investors with a few stocks that they hold onto for years to professionals with portfolios containing hundreds of stocks that are bought or sold almost every day. A popular feature of investment software is access to one or more investment news services. A strike by miners in Colorado or the failure of a bank in California can

This investor is using a computer to analyze and purchase stocks. The program produces a variety of reports to help manage the portfolio. (© Michael Salas, The Image Bank.)

have a major impact on investments. Such news may not be reported in newspapers but is a regular feature of investment news services.

A popular type of investment software consists of portfolio management programs. These programs require the user to enter a considerable amount of data, including the details of each stock transaction and dividends or stock splits. Once the data has been entered, it can be processed in several ways, depending on how sophisticated the program is. Some programs can dial a commercial data base and extract the market price for each individual stock. Within a short time it generates a report giving the total value of the investor's holdings, the amount of capital gains realized on any given sale, and estimated tax liability. It is typical for such programs to indicate when a particular stock holding is nearing long-term status—information that is important for tax purposes. Many programs automatically remind the user to consider selling or buying a stock on certain dates. Some programs used by brokerage houses provide for electronic buying and selling of stocks for users with accounts at that particular house. These and similar programs can also be used to manage other investment vehicles, such as corporate bonds.

Another type of financial management program consists of investment advice programs, which provide suggestions regarding which stocks should be bought or sold. One such program provides a daily list of the ten most overvalued and undervalued stocks, the five most highly and least highly recommended industries for investment, and an analysis of potential winners and losers in each of these industries. Also available are investment analysis programs, which do not actually recommend sales or purchases of stocks but help investors analyze stocks using traditional investment analysis techniques such as fundamental analysis and technical analysis. *Fundamental analysis* is an approach to stock market trading that makes use of trends in the overall economy and specific industries as well as individual stocks. *Technical analysis* is an approach to stock market trading that involves studying the behavior of other investors as reflected in past stock prices. Several investment programs collect the data necessary for technical analysis and process it according to a specific set of formulas.

Although investment analysis programs that run on microcomputers are available for home use, professional financial planners often confront problems that are too complex for these small-scale packages. By using more advanced software running on specialized hardware, they can tap the full power of artificial intelligence, as discussed in Box 16-2.

BOX 16-2

USING COMPUTERS

Artificial Intelligence Aids Financial Planners

After years of development, applications that make use of artificial intelligence (AI) are finally reaching the desks of ordinary computer users. One such application is in the area of financial planning.

Developing a financial plan for an individual is a complicated and time-consuming task. The planner must balance each client's unique financial situation and long-term goals with numerous interrelated factors such as taxes, prior investments, insurance coverage, and real estate holdings. "It's such a complex field that we tend to operate a lot on intuition and rules of thumb," says Harold Evensky, a certified financial planner and president of Evensky & Brown of Miami, Florida. "Otherwise, it would take forever to create a plan."

To help manage this process, in early 1986 Evensky & Brown became one of the first buyers of PlanPower, an expert system sold by Applied Expert Systems (APEX) of Cambridge, Massachusetts. Designed to assist in the creation of financial plans, the system is sold with the Xerox 1186 LISP machine for about $45,000. Using PlanPower, the firm's staff can produce a plan in about a quarter of the time previously required, Evensky says; a moderately complex plan that once took about fifty hours of computer time to produce can now be generated in ten or fifteen hours.

PlanPower's knowledge base contains information on such things as interest rates, expected inflation rates, and tax laws, as well as standard investment strategies to realize specific objectives. Nevertheless, Evensky prefers to use PlanPower only as a tool, backed up by the expertise of his firm's qualified planners. "It's just an assistant," he says, "but a phenomenal assistant."

Of all the system's capabilities, Evensky rates its ability to do "what if?" projections as among the most important. If a client asks for advice about, say, whether to buy or lease a car, the system can quickly model and compare the five-year impact of each option.

Another key benefit of the system, according to Evensky, is that all data resides in the same data base. The conventional planning software that the company used previously didn't allow for the integration of different data bases—for instance, those that contained mortgage algorithms and those that contained stock investment information. If a change was made in one area, it was difficult to track its effect in others. With PlanPower, all the information is combined, and the stand-alone system can even make connections that are sometimes overlooked by human planners.

Source: Reprinted with permission from Dwight B. Davis, "Artificial Intelligence Goes to Work," *High Technology* magazine, April 1987, pp. 16–27. Copyright © 1987 by Infotechnology Publishing Corp., 214 Lewis Wharf, Boston, MA 02110.

Electronic Funds Transfer

Electronic funds transfer (EFT)
The transfer of funds from one individual, business, or bank to another by electronic means.

Another use of computers in financial management is **electronic funds transfer (EFT)**, or the transfer of funds from one individual, business, or bank to another by electronic means. Electronic funds transfer systems can take several forms. Automatic teller machines (see Chapter 4) employ EFT to allow customers to deposit or withdraw cash from an account or receive an instant loan on their credit card. Banks use electronic funds transfer systems to transmit billions of dollars every day. Investors use EFT facilities when they buy stocks by computer and the system automatically debits their account. Still another example of EFT is the system used by the federal government to transfer Social Security funds directly to recipients' bank accounts, thereby reducing the possibility of loss or theft.

Proponents of electronic funds transfer systems originally looked forward to a "checkless" society. However, because of some unanticipated drawbacks of EFT systems they now refer to a "less check" society.

EFT systems reduce customer waiting time. Automatic teller machines allow customers to avoid long lines at the bank. They also increase access to funds. Many automatic teller machines can be accessed around the clock. One consequence of easier access is that many customers withdraw less cash per transaction. In addition, the use of EFT reduces *float*, the time it takes for a check to clear. It also reduces paperwork. Once the system is in place, paper records are virtually eliminated.

Electronic funds transfer systems have some very real disadvantages, however. For one thing, they have an impact on privacy. EFT systems enable banks and the government to access an individual's financial transactions. They also have the potential for criminal misuse. In view of the vast amounts of money processed by EFT systems, criminals can be expected to focus their attention on these systems. There are also technical problems associated with some EFT equipment. Still other disadvantages include the increased cost of transactions and the discomfort that many people feel when interacting with a machine instead of a human being.

This chapter has described several applications of computers in several fields, including health care, sports, education, music, and finance. In each case it is clear that computers have a major impact on people's daily lives. In the case of the final application, electronic funds transfer systems, the use of computers has a potentially major impact on individuals' private lives and offers new opportunities for criminal behavior. The relationship between computers and these two subjects, privacy and crime, is the subject of the next chapter.

SUMMARY

1. Computers play a major role in health care. To a large extent they have made possible the rapid expansion of the home health-care industry. Hospitals, health-care administrators and practitioners benefit from computer-based decision support systems. Health-care professionals also use on-line data bases to obtain information on diseases, diagnoses, and drugs as well as government rules and regulations related to health care.

2. Computers also play an important role in many sports. Professional football teams rely on computers for a variety of applications, including scouting for new players. Computer-aided design systems are used to design yachts, and computer systems help racers monitor their yacht's performance and make tactical decisions. Some ski resorts use computers to assist in the snow-making process and keep track of ski lifts.

3. Computers are used in teaching students at all grade levels, from nursery school to graduate school, as well as students in nontraditional learning situations such as in the home and on the job. **Computer-assisted instruction (CAI)** is the use of computers to help students learn. A key technique of CAI is **simulation**, in which a computer model is used to represent a real-life situation. **Computer-managed instruction (CMI)** is the use of computers by educational institutions to store and process administrative data.

4. Computers have been applied to many aspects of musical composition and performance. In 1983 several manufacturers of electronic musical instruments adopted a standard known as **Musical Instrument Digital Interface (MIDI).** This standard has been applied to a variety of products and systems, including the teaching of music and the production of synthesizers that can produce professional-quality sound.

5. Computers are used for monetary applications ranging from payroll and accounting systems to specialized systems used by the U.S. Mint and the Federal Reserve System. Individuals use computers to manage their personal finances. Software packages are also available for use in managing investments; they include portfolio management programs, investment advice programs, and investment analysis programs. **Electronic funds transfer (EFT)** is the transfer of funds from one individual, business, or bank to another by electronic means. It offers many advantages, but it can have negative effects on privacy and has the potential for criminal misuse.

KEY TERMS

computer-assisted instruction (CAI)

simulation

computer-managed instruction (CMI)

Musical Instrument Digital Interface (MIDI)

electronic funds transfer (EFT)

REVIEW QUESTIONS

1. Describe how computers are used in health care. What impact has computerization had on health care?

2. Describe three ways in which the computer has been applied to various sports. What impact has computerization had on sports?

3. How are computers used in education? What is the difference between computer-assisted instruction and computer-managed instruction?

4. How have computers been applied to music? What is the significance of the MIDI standard?

5. Describe three types of systems for managing bank accounts and other financial resources. What are some advantages and disadvantages of electronic funds transfer systems?

APPLICATIONS

1. Describe the advantages of computerization for doctors and for nurses. Can you think of any disadvantages?

2. Report on a computer application that is designed to improve athletic performance. Do you believe such applications should be banned because they give an unfair advantage to those who can afford computers?

3. Listen to a musical recording produced with the aid of a synthesizer. How does it compare to music produced with traditional instruments?

4. Can computers replace human teachers? Why or why not?

CASE FOR DISCUSSION

For years the newspapers have been full of stories about the prospect of banking at home. The idea is to let customers take care of a lot of banking chores using a computer and a modem. In exchange for a monthly fee of $5 to $12, customers can access account information and pay bills through interaction with the bank's computer.

From the standpoint of the banks, the arguments for electronic home banking are persuasive. The cost of printing, processing, and returning the 41 billion checks that Americans write every year averages nearly $1 per check. The $41 billion tab is equal to almost 20 percent of the annual revenues of the 5800 banks that belong to the Federal Reserve System.

To customers, however, the arguments seem less convincing. First, customers are reluctant to give up "float," that is, the period between the time a check is written and the time it is cleared, during which the funds remain in the customer's account. In paying by computer, the funds are debited immediately to the customer's account even if they are not immediately credited to the payee's account. Second, the computer and modem are still a major investment. There are not as many home computers as bankers once thought there would be, and only an estimated 10 percent of those have modems. And third, it's a matter of opinion—not fact—whether paying bills using a personal computer is more convenient than writing paper checks. Home banking still doesn't get rid of paper checks. It merely shifts the checkwriting burden from the bank customer to the bank. There is no universal technology for keying in transactions and transmitting data from payer to bank to payee. After a customer has authorized a payment and his or her account has been debited, the bank then writes out its own check and mails it to the payee.

The banks are now exploring new delivery devices and alternative marketing strategies. Since electronic ventures such as these are profitable only with a high transaction volume, banks and other companies are joining forces to offer a host of electronic services.

Some banks hope to solve the hardware problem with low-cost stand-alone terminals. One, made by Sharp for AT&T, can be sold by banks for as little as $100. New York's Citibank is testing a pocket terminal that weighs only a few ounces and can be plugged into any telephone jack.

But the fact remains that from the customer's viewpoint, home banking must save time or money to justify the monthly service fee and equipment costs. Customers who write many checks each month, are willing to group many transactions at a time, or have very high balances may find home banking worthwhile. The others will have difficulty justifying home banking.

Source: Efrem Sigel, "Is Home Banking for Real?" *Datamation*, September 15, 1986, pp. 128–134. Copyright © Cahners Publishing Company.

CASE QUESTIONS

1. Why has home banking failed to bring about a "checkless society"?

2. Do you think it is realistic for banks to charge customers for the use of electronic banking facilities when the point of the service is to save the banks money?

3. How is home banking of the type described here related to electronic funds transfer?

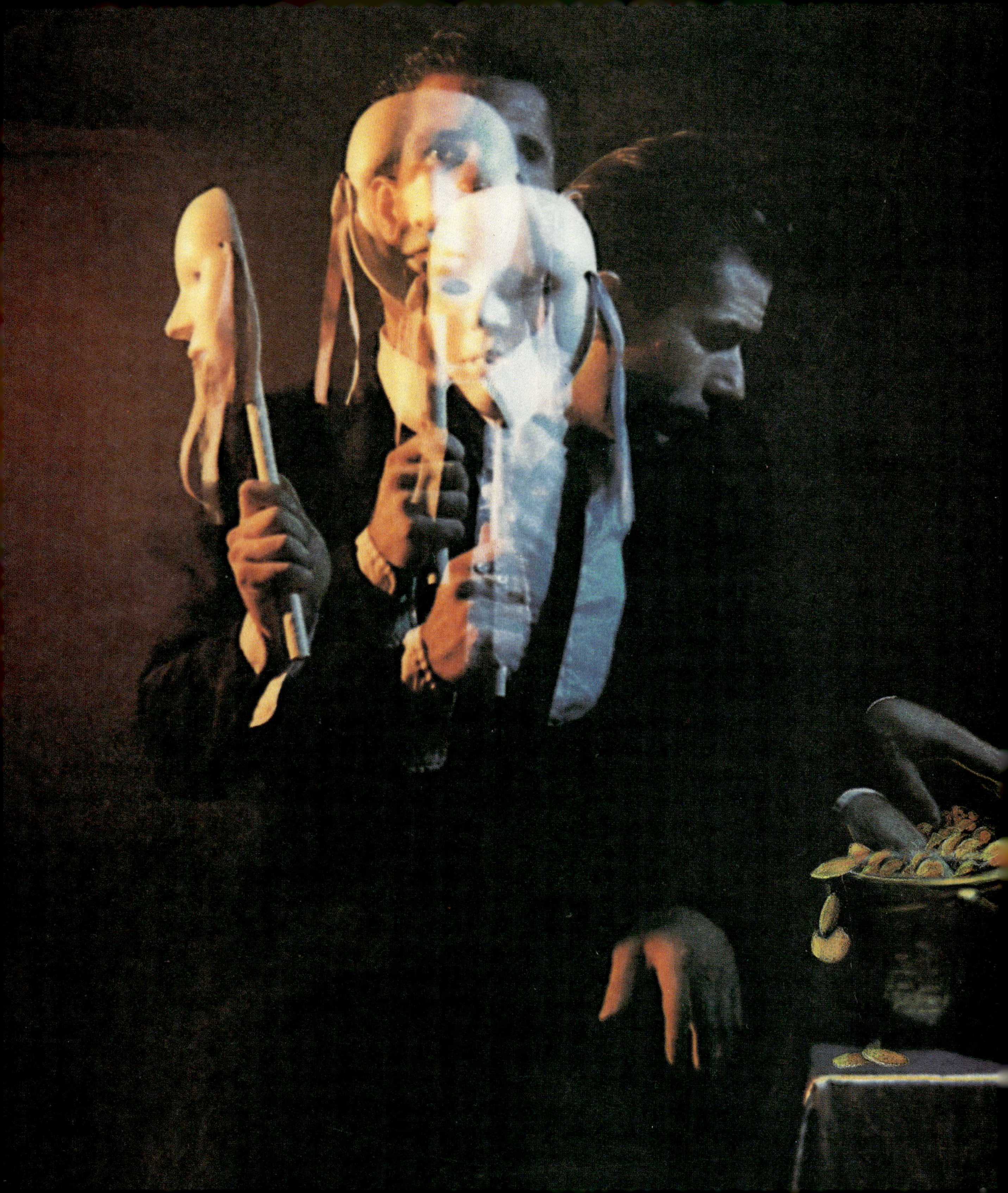

Privacy, Computer Crime, and Security

CHAPTER

17

WOLFSBURG, WEST GERMANY—Volkswagen AG last week said it discovered that a corporate foreign-exchange loss of as much as $259 million had been fraudulently covered up through the alteration of computer programs and erasure of data tapes.

The case appears to be the biggest reported example of computer fraud in history.

The fraud was apparently perpetrated by a currency trader or traders, either within Volkswagen or with an outside financial firm, which handled Volkswagen corporate funds in 1984.

Volkswagen will include a provision for the estimated amount of the loss in its 1986 financial results.

In a radio interview in West Germany, Volkswagen board member Karl Gustaf Ratjen said that the fraud involved computer programs and storage tapes, according to published reports.

"I would speculate that someone made some bad moves in currency trading and, to cover it up and impress the boss, fabricated the computer records so the reports continued to look good," according to Jack Bologna, who is a noted computer crime consultant and professor of management at Siena Heights College in Adrian, Michigan.

The person or persons involved would probably have had to rewrite processing software as well as alter output, Bologna said. "In a company of Volkswagen's size, they would have needed sophisticated skills in applications programming and maybe systems programming as well," he said.

Volkswagen said it filed fraud, breach of trust, and forgery charges against individuals outside the company but did not rule out the involvement of its own employees.[1]

---

[1] Copyright 1987 CW Communications/Inc., Framingham, MA 01701—Reprinted from Clinton Wilder, "Altered Systems, Data, Blindside Volkswagen in Record-Breaking $259 Million Computer Fraud," *Computerworld*, March 16, 1987, p. 4.

In this book we have seen many examples in which computerized systems have changed the way businesses carry out their activities, record and analyze the results, and plan for the future. However, computer applications go far beyond meeting business needs. As Chapter 16 demonstrated, computers have had a profound effect on many aspects of everyday life. We have described several beneficial computer applications in such diverse fields as health care, sports, education, music, and money. This chapter presents the other side of the picture.

Although computer applications can yield enormous benefits to both commercial and individual users, they can also have negative effects. The $259 million fraud perpetrated against Volkswagen provides a dramatic example. In addition to the problem of computer crime, this chapter also focuses on the computer as a means for invading privacy, both personal and corporate. The chapter ends with a discussion of computer security, that is, the methods and techniques used to decrease the possibility of harmful or criminal uses of computers.

When you have read this chapter you should be able to:

1. Describe the impact of computers on individual and corporate privacy.
2. Explain the concept of a standard universal identifier and its relevance to individual privacy.
3. Discuss ways in which privacy can be protected.
4. Present the nature and types of computer crime.
5. Discuss ways in which computer crime can be reduced.
6. Describe measures that a business may take to increase computer security.
7. Understand and use the key terms listed at the end of the chapter.

Privacy

Although the impact of computers on business is far-reaching, their impact on individuals may be more important. Computers have enormous potential for misuse, particularly in terms of invasion of privacy. For example, a government or organization that wanted to keep track of people's movements around the country could use data stored on computerized airline reservation files. In this instance most people would agree that the government had overstepped its bounds and invaded individual privacy. Similarly, while we expect the government to access payroll data for income tax purposes, such data should not become public knowledge. For example, privacy would be invaded if salary information were made available to an employee's co-workers or sold to a marketing company. These examples are not the unjustified fears of pessimists; they are very real possibilities, as will become clear in this section of the chapter.

Vast quantities of data can pass through this satellite dish almost instantaneously. The question is, who is processing the data and for what purpose? (© Chuck O'Rear, Woodfin Camp.)

The Meaning of Privacy

The word *privacy* is not used in the United States Constitution. However, in 1928 Supreme Court Justice Louis D. Brandeis wrote that "the right to be let alone is the most comprehensive of rights and the right most valued by civilized men." Since then the Court has held on numerous occasions that the right of privacy is implied by several phrases in the Bill of Rights.

The right of privacy is not absolute. Most people are willing to release some information about themselves or their families in exchange for the benefits offered by organized society. For example, students readily fill out forms with their names, addresses, and other personal details in order to register for college courses. If they apply for financial aid, they furnish other "private" data. But while most students will accept the fact that their professors know their name and perhaps their chosen field of study, they would not want their professors to know their family's income or even their home address. In short, the right of individual privacy means that people can *choose* who will have access to certain information about themselves and can determine exactly what that information will be.

Like individuals, businesses often find it necessary to release information about themselves in order to obtain certain benefits. For example, a business must provide some details about a new invention before it can obtain a patent on it. Likewise, a request for incorporation must be accompanied by specific financial information. Judging from the number of patent applications and requests for incorporation that are processed each year, it is evident that many businesses, like individuals, are willing to give up some of their privacy in order to obtain the benefits provided by the society in which they operate.

Before the advent of the computer, individual and corporate privacy was relatively easy to protect, for the following reasons:
1. It generally was not feasible to collect large quantities of data about individuals or businesses.
2. Whatever data was collected was usually kept in decentralized files. Moreover, often this data was not kept up to date and hence became useless in a few years.
3. It was not always easy to gain access to existing data.
4. It was difficult to keep track of people and businesses in a mobile society.
5. Most outsiders were unable to interpret available data so as to obtain useful information from it.

The widespread use of computer systems has greatly increased the potential for abuse of both personal and corporate privacy. Computers make it possible to gather data bases that include fairly complete pictures of millions of individuals. In addition, it is easy to use a computer to search an entire data base relatively quickly. Any "interesting" data found in this way can be compared with data contained on other data bases. Moreover, the computer can update records on a data base in just a few seconds. And unless special protective measures are taken, access to such data bases may be very easy to obtain, even for casual users of the system. For example, an unauthorized employee may be able to access a corporation's payroll records.

Privacy in Business Situations

Despite the risk of invasion of privacy by means of computers, protection of privacy is not given very high priority in most organizations. The head of the management information systems department is generally too busy supervising personnel, maintaining information systems, and coordinating the purchase and installation of new equipment to devote much time to issues of privacy. The same is true of office automation system administrators. Moreover, in most organizations the MIS department does not control the use of microcomputers in other departments.

A variety of factors contribute to the risk of invasion of privacy in business situations. They include unprotected physical environments, access to highly processed information, a wide range of users, uncontrolled data communication, and links to corporate data bases.

Unprotected Physical Environments. Many office automation and microcomputer systems are characterized by a low level of physical protection. For example, it is typical for both

This magnetic-tape library at the computer center of the Cigna Insurance Company contains millions of records. (© Leif Skoogfors, Woodfin Camp.)

hardware and storage media to be readily accessible. In many cases of unauthorized access, members of the organization are not even aware that the files have been copied. It is easy for an intruder to copy sensitive files and process them on another computer at home.

Access to Highly Processed Information. Microcomputers and office automation systems often contain large amounts of highly processed data. For example, they may contain the results of a major marketing survey, which could be more valuable to a competitor than the original data. A 20-MB hard disk has enough capacity to store a 10-page record for each of 1000 clients. Devices like the Bernoulli box (see Chapter 5) make it possible to access enormous amounts of data in a few seconds.

A Wide Range of Users. The first computers could be accessed only by specialists. Time-sharing systems made computers available to more users, but those users were usually limited to one or a few applications, and the system was often protected by specialists who were aware of security issues. Microcomputers and office automation have brought the power of the computer to a much wider range of users. Many of those users do not realize the potential value of the data to which they have access and have not been trained in ways of preventing unauthorized access.

Uncontrolled Data Communication. Abuses of privacy become even more likely when data is being transmitted from one user or system to another. In many cases communication lines are the least protected parts of a system, and it is not difficult or expensive for outsiders to tap into standard computer networks. Data communication systems are also open to abuse by insiders. For example, supervisors could use such a system to access employees' electronic mail.

Links to Corporate Data Bases. The power of the computer is magnified when it is linked to a corporate data base. In a poorly protected system, a user in a branch office can access data that "belongs" to the head office, such as confidential personnel data, thereby violating both individual and corporate privacy.

Standard Universal Identifiers

The use of a **standard universal identifer (SUI)** to specify data records for a particular individual makes possible rapid linking

Standard universal identifier (SUI)
An identifier that is used to specify all data records for a particular individual, making possible the linking of records stored on different files.

of different files containing information about that individual. Organizations such as credit bureaus find standard universal identifiers useful in carrying out their operations, but the use of SUIs poses a clear threat to personal privacy. A standard universal identifier makes it easy to use data for reasons other than the purpose for which it was gathered. For example, the Selective Service System has asked motor vehicle departments to furnish the names, addresses, and Social Security numbers of all young men who are eligible for draft registration.

With the aid of an SUI it is relatively simple to link records from dozens of sources, such as medical, credit, and education files, in order to obtain a detailed picture of an individual's life style. An error in any one of those files could have serious implications. If, for example, a high school student had been arrested for driving without a license, information concerning that incident could have a negative effect on his or her chances of getting a job many years later.

The Social Security number is widely used as a means of identification. However, there are some major problems associated with this practice. Because an individual may have more than one Social Security number and several people may share a particular number, a person could be refused employment because of the criminal record of another person with the same Social Security number. Nevertheless, numerous organizations use Social Security numbers for purposes of identification. For example, employers are required by law to report earnings to the Internal Revenue Service and state unemployment compensation boards according to the employee's Social Security number. Credit bureaus, insurance companies, hospitals and doctors, schools and colleges, banks, and motor vehicle depart-

Your Social Security number is on dozens of files, some of which could be used in ways that you do not approve of. (The Image Bank.)

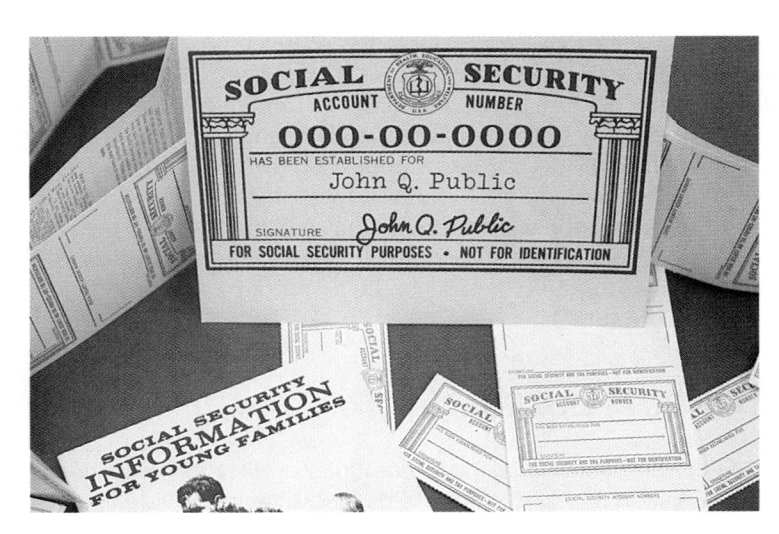

The automated teller machine is a great convenience to people who want to do their banking in a hurry. It also makes it possible to obtain information about the financial affairs of private citizens. (Courtesy of Citibank.)

ments also make extensive use of this means of identification. In sum, the Social Security number has become a *de facto* SUI.

Electronic Funds Transfer Systems

Chapter 16 mentioned the use of computerized systems to transfer funds from one individual or institution to another. These systems, known as electronic funds transfer (EFT) systems, offer major benefits to the banking industry. However, they also can be used to invade privacy. For example, by keeping track of an individual's income and expenses, the government could gain a clear picture of that person's activities. Although financial privacy is protected to some extent by the use of paper checks, EFT systems can analyze and store many kinds of financial data. EFT systems combined with the use of standard universal identifiers pose a powerful threat to individual liberties. A dictatorial government that had control over the nation's electronic funds transfer systems could outlaw cash transactions and arbitrarily confiscate the assets of particular individuals and institutions.

Privacy Legislation

As the number and scope of computer applications expanded during the 1960s and early 1970s, prominent individuals and representatives of government and industry met to discuss ways of protecting personal privacy against invasion through computerized systems. A key development was the formation of an Advisory Committee on Automated Personal Data Systems to study the impact of computer data banks on individual privacy. In 1973 the committee produced a report entitled "Records, Computers, and the Rights of Citizens," which recommended a federal "Code of Fair Information Practice" based on five principles:

1. There must be no personal data record-keeping systems whose very existence is secret.
2. There must be a way for an individual to find out what information about him or her is in a record and how it is used.
3. There must be a way for an individual to prevent personal information that was obtained for one purpose from being used or made available for other purposes without his or her consent.
4. There must be a way for an individual to correct or amend a record of identifiable information about him or her.
5. Any organization creating, maintaining, using, or disseminating records of identifiable personal data must make sure that data is reliable and must take precautions to prevent its misuse.[2]

Largely on the basis of this report, Congress passed the Privacy Act of 1974. In the second half of the 1970s additional laws, such as the Tax Reform Act of 1976 and the Right to Financial Privacy Act of 1978, expanded the provisions of the 1974 Act. During this period several European countries enacted their own privacy laws, some of which went much further than the American laws.

Many people feel that laws enacted in the 1970s are no longer adequate. When those laws were passed, the bulk of computer applications consisted of batch processing on mainframe computers in government agencies and large corporations. At that time the majority of business users did not run their own programs or maintain their own data bases. Today many of them do. Under these conditions, it will take more than a series of federal laws to protect individuals against abuses of this readily available information.

Most businesses agree that is is essential to protect both individual and corporate privacy against invasion via computer systems. Generally, they favor self-regulation over governmental legislation. At present, however, few industries or companies have established guidelines for protecting privacy. An exception is IBM, which in 1981 established the following principles for handling personal data:

---

[2]*Records, Computers, and the Rights of Citizens*, Report of the Secretary's Advisory Committee on Automated Personal Data Systems. Washington, DC: U.S. Department of Health, Education and Welfare, 1973.

1. Purpose of file clearly defined and in support of valid company business.
2. Collection only of required personal data and by fair, lawful means and reliable services.
3. Use limited to defined purposes.
4. Information relevant, correct, complete, and up-to-date.
5. Right of access to data subject compatible with valid business interests of company.
6. Security measures adequate and relevant to classification of data.
7. Person responsible for file identified.[3]

Computer Crime

$500,000
Average Computer Crime

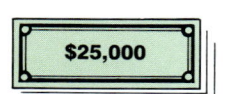

$25,000
Average Bank Fraud

$3,000
Average Bank Robbery

The use of computers to invade personal or corporate privacy is often related to the use of computers for criminal purposes. The immense data bases that have been created by government and private agencies are easy targets for criminal abuse. In addition, the microcomputer revolution has given criminals a powerful new tool. In contrast to the data in mainframe computer systems, the data in most microcomputer systems is not well protected. Moreover, data that was originally in a mainframe system is often transferred to microcomputers in edited or summarized form. Paradoxically, therefore, as data becomes more valuable it becomes less secure. Once data has been transferred to a microcomputer, a criminal can gain access to it relatively easily.

Computer crime is a big business. The average reported computer crime involves an estimated $500,000, in contrast to the average incident of bank fraud, which involves less than $25,000, and the average bank robbery, which nets a little over $3000. However, not all computer criminals are big-time operators. In fact, as Box 17-1 shows, many computer criminals are ordinary people, including unemployed individuals and unskilled workers. The second largest category of computer criminals consists of students!

The reluctance of victims to report computer crimes makes it difficult to obtain convictions and thus contributes to the frequency of such crimes. However, as businesses and society in general have begun to realize the magnitude and impact of

---

[3]*ComputerData*, December 1985, p. 13.

computer crime, there has been greater willingness to prosecute criminals and increasing pressure for legislation to prevent such crime.

Computer crimes are often difficult to trace; expert criminals not only can create evidence that the crime never happened, as was done in the Volkswagen case, but also can create evidence that shifts the blame for the crime to another party, almost as if the criminal had stolen someone's fingerprints and left them at the site of the crime. In fact, the computer is the perfect accomplice: It does whatever it is programmed to do without requiring anything in return but maintenance and electricity.

Types of Computer Crime

Many observers divide computer crime into six categories: financial crime, information crime, theft of computer services, vandalism, theft of computer hardware, and theft of computer software. Here we will take a brief look at each of these categories.

Financial Crime. Financial crime involves the use of computers to divert funds or goods from their intended destinations and to hide the diversions from auditors. An early example of computer crime was the Equity Funding scheme, which was uncovered in 1972. In that case employees of an insurance company created 50,000 fictitious life insurance policies and sold them to other insurance companies in a practice known as reinsurance. The value of the policies has been estimated at $200 million. This held the record for reported computer crime for fifteen years, until the $259 million fraud against Volkswagen mentioned at the beginning of this chapter was reported. In the Equity case, the perpetrators of the fraud were able to escape detection because the bogus policies were coded in such a way that the company's auditors could not distinguish them from genuine ones. The computer was also used to generate an appropriate number of deaths and policy cancellations.

Information Crime. Information crime involves the theft of valuable information with the aid of a computer. In many instances it entails invasion of personal or corporate privacy. For example, a disgruntled employee may offer to sell the company's master mailing list or the results of a multimillion-dollar marketing survey to a competitor. This kind of crime can be difficult to detect because it does not destroy the information but merely makes a copy of it.

BOX 17-1

USING COMPUTERS FOR CRIME
Who Does It? Who Gets Hit?

Computer crime is becoming more common because computer technology is becoming more accessible. Unfortunately, as computers become more user-friendly, they also become more "abuser-friendly." This is evident in the results of a survey made by the National Center for Computer Crime Data, a nonprofit research institute located in Los Angeles.

The accompanying charts show, perhaps as expected, that programmers lead the list of computer criminals. But others with more modest levels of computer sophistication are close behind—including students, input clerks, bank tellers, and unskilled workers. (See the chart at the right.) The survey showed that commercial users and banks are the most common victims. (See the chart on the opposite page.)

Many computer criminals benefit from on-the-job training. Far and away the greatest number of computer criminals are employees of the firms they defraud. These criminals have the system-specific information they need to carry out their crimes, as well as access to the system.

Unfortunately, employees also often have

Who commits computer crimes?
Number of cases brought to trial nationwide before February 1986.

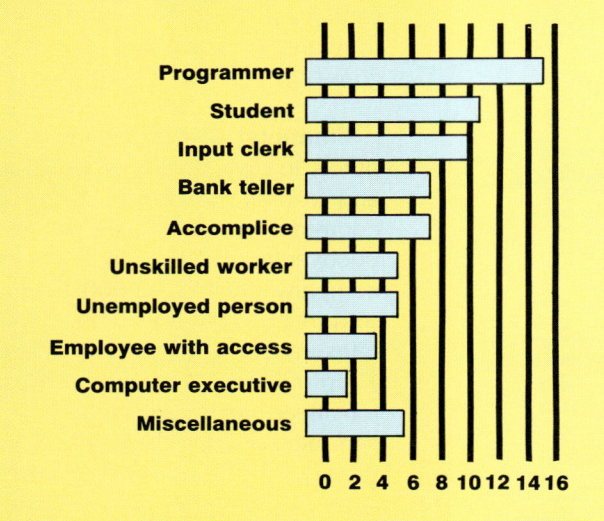

Programmer	
Student	
Input clerk	
Bank teller	
Accomplice	
Unskilled worker	
Unemployed person	
Employee with access	
Computer executive	
Miscellaneous	

0 2 4 6 8 10 12 14 16

real or imagined grudges against the firms they work for. These provide them with the psychological motive they need to carry out their misdeeds.

Who are the victims?
Number of cases brought to trial nationwide before February 1986.

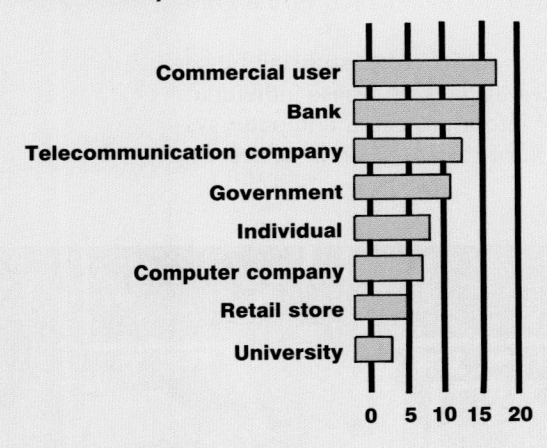

Commercial user	~17
Bank	~15
Telecommunication company	~13
Government	~10
Individual	~8
Computer company	~7
Retail store	~4
University	~2

(scale: 0 5 10 15 20)

Also, it is often harder to prosecute employees than nonemployees, especially when the crime is one of theft of information or computer services, rather than theft of money. Laws in several states require prosecutors to prove that the crime entailed unauthorized access. For example, a California law provides that "any person who intentionally and without authorization accesses any computer system . . . with knowledge that the access was not authorized shall be guilty of a public offense. This subdivision shall not apply to any person who accesses his or her employer's computer system, computer network, computer program, or data when acting within the scope of his or her employment."

The difficulty of prosecuting crimes involving authorized access by employees is thought to be one factor contributing to the underreporting of computer crime.

Source: J. J. Buck BloomBecker, "New Federal Law Bolsters Computer Security Efforts," *Computerworld*, October 27, 1986, pp. 53–62.

Theft of Computer Services. Theft of computer services involves unauthorized use of a computer, such as processing and storing data or printing information for personal use. For example, dishonest but enterprising individuals sometimes develop their own computer service companies, using their employers' computer systems to provide services to their clients. Because of the widespread use of microcomputers and the large number of activities that are carried out simultaneously on minicomputers and mainframes, this type of crime can be difficult to detect.

Vandalism. Vandalism, or inflicting intentional damage on a computer system, is most likely to occur when an insider with technical skills damages programs or data. Fired employees, for example, have been known to plant "logic bombs" in a company's software: After a specific interval, the affected programs destroy themselves or erase important data stored in the computer system.

Many computer installations are subject to trespassing by sophisticated computer users known as *hackers*. These individuals consider it a challenge to break into a protected computer system; they may have no intention of diverting funds or destroy-

The dangers of unauthorized access are illustrated in the movie War Games, in which a high school student taps into an army simulation program called Global Thermonuclear War and comes very close to causing one. (Phototeque.)

ing data. The advent of microcomputers has greatly increased the number of hackers and the ease with which they are able to operate.

Theft of Computer Hardware. Easy access to microcomputer systems and their components has increased the frequency of hardware theft. Whereas few people have any use for a printer driven by a mainframe computer, dishonest microcomputer owners do not hesitate to buy illegally acquired printers. And while it is difficult to sell a printer for a mainframe without arousing suspicion, printers for microcomputers can readily be sold through the classified ads in daily newspapers.

A related crime is the illegal sale of certain types of computer hardware to countries like the Soviet Union or to terrorist organizations. Because of the strategic value of advanced computer systems, such sales can yield enormous profits.

Theft of Computer Software. Theft of computer software, also known as *software piracy*, is probably the most widespread form of computer crime. It is estimated that up to ten pirated copies of popular software packages exist for each legally obtained copy. This type of crime deprives software manufacturers of the revenue they need to develop and market new software. In the last few years software manufacturers have sued companies accused of software piracy for large amounts of money, and in some cases they have won large sums, either awarded by the courts or received in out-of-court settlements. Software manufacturers have also tried to reduce piracy by means of *copy protection*, or techniques that make it difficult to copy the software. However, copy protection tends to impede legitimate use of the software and is not very effective as a means of preventing the making of copies.

When the software in question is more specialized and expensive than the personal-productivity software available at the local computer store, there can be even greater conflict between the vendor's desire to prevent theft and the user's interest in using and maintaining the program. Box 17-2 discusses one possible solution to this growing problem.

Another strategy that is used by software manufacturers to discourage illegal copying of software is *site licensing*. This term refers to a type of contract under which a company that needs a large number of copies of a particular piece of software may make those copies for a relatively low fee per copy. Site licences for several hundred copies of popular software are not unusual. Some software manufacturers also offer discounts for large-volume purchases.

BOX 17-2

MANAGING CHANGE

Programs in Escrow

Consider the following scenario: You are a maker of scientific instruments. You buy a control program from a startup software company and incorporate it into a new, top-of-the-line oscilloscope. A few months later, users complain that under certain conditions that occur frequently but did not come up in your testing procedures, a defect in the control software causes the instrument to give an inaccurate reading.

The software vendor is obligated by its contract to fix any such bugs. However, when you contact the firm, you find that it has gone out of business. Can your own programmers fix the problem? No, they tell you. As is often the case, the software company provided you only with a machine-readable object code for the software. The human-readable source code and documentation that are needed to debug the program were retained by the seller. There is nothing to be done. You must pull your product off the market until a new control program can be written from scratch.

Farfetched? Not really. When Art Benjamin and Associates went out of business in 1982, it left some 80 users of its products without support or maintenance. But software piracy is not unusual either. Somehow the conflicting interests of software vendors and users need to be reconciled.

One way to manage the problem is by means of a software escrow agreement. In the most common type of escrow agreement, a third party accepts critical information and holds it. The information placed in escrow includes the source code for the program; all necessary documentation regarding the software, the type of hardware used, and so on; and all updates to the program.

If the software firm goes out of business, the user is given access to the escrowed materials and can use them as the basis for maintaining and modifying the program in the future. But business failure is not the only contingency that may trigger the escrow agreement. Other problems short of bankruptcy may make the vendor unwilling or unable to maintain the software properly. The vendor may lose key personnel. It may face financial difficulties that cause it to cut back on its service operations. Or it may simply abandon the product. A properly drawn escrow agreement must be flexible enough to handle all of these situations.

Of course, the vendor and user may disagree as to whether the vendor has defaulted on maintenance obligations. For that reason, an escrow agreement should include an arbitration clause. Under such a clause, each side must present its arguments to the arbitrator within a certain time. The arbitrator too must observe a time limit in rendering a decision. This procedure avoids lengthy court proceedings.

The cost of the escrow agreement is negotiable. It may be borne by the vendor, by the user, or partly by each. Sometimes vendors set up multiuser escrows to ensure continuity of maintenance of products that are widely sold. An escrow is not the answer to every security problem, but it can help.

Source: Reginald Weller and Shelley Wall, "Source Code under Lock and Key," *Computerworld*, June 2, 1986, pp. 70–72.

Legislation to Reduce Computer Crime

One reason computer crime has become so widespread is that for years people have been able to commit such crimes without much fear of punishment. Many companies choose not to prosecute because of the lack of strong laws in this area. For example, the New York Superior Court dismissed a theft-of-services charge against an employee who had used his employer's computer system to study the genealogy of thoroughbred horses as part of a betting system. The court ruled that because the employee was entitled to use the system, no theft had occurred.

As computer crime has become more widespread, it has attracted more attention. Companies are under increasing pressure to press charges against computer criminals, and the federal government and almost all the states have passed laws prohibiting specific computer-related activities. Both the nature of those activities and the severity of the punishments associated with them vary widely. For example, in Ohio and Georgia unauthorized computer access is considered a felony, whereas in Maryland it is considered a misdemeanor and in some states, such as Utah and Virginia, unauthorized computer access is not even mentioned in the criminal code. Many computer crime laws deal specifically with the problem of nonmalicious but unauthorized access by hackers. The New Jersey law, for example, defines as a "disorderly person" one who "purposely and without authorization accesses a computer . . . and this action does not result in altering, damage, or destruction of any property or services."

In 1984, after several years of discussion, the first federal law dealing with computer crime was passed. It defined as criminal any unauthorized access to classified national security information as well as data contained in certain financial records, but it did not apply to computers operating in interstate commerce. The Computer Fraud and Abuse Act of 1986 goes much further. It defines a variety of computer-related activities as criminal and includes punishments in the form of fines or jail sentences ranging from five to twenty years, depending on the nature of the offense and whether or not it is a first offense.

The 1986 Act applies only to computers used by the federal government and federally insured financial institutions and to interstate computer crimes. This law makes it a felony to access such a computer in order to alter or destroy data such as medical records or to use the computer to steal amounts over $1000. It also makes it a misdemeanor to trespass in a "federal interest computer" or to traffic in stolen passwords.

Security

The incidence of computer crime can be reduced only through a combination of legislation, heightened public awareness of the seriousness of computer crime, and the adoption of appropriate security measures. **Computer security** refers to the protection of computer systems from unauthorized access and from the effects of accidents such as power shortages or surges, fires, or earthquakes. Although it is impossible to make a computer system entirely secure, the more detailed and better enforced an organization's security program is, the lower the risk of computer crime and invasions of privacy. Properly designed security measures also help protect computer systems against human error.

Before setting up a computer security program, it is necessary to evaluate potential security risks and the cost of reducing those risks to an acceptable level. When the organization's security goals have been outlined, the necessary funds must be allocated. However, successful implementation of a security

Computer security
The protection of a computer system against unauthorized access and against damage caused by electrical problems or natural disasters.

Many organizations sell hardware, software, and expertise to increase computer security. As these ads illustrate, the computer industry is engaging in a major campaign to stop software piracy. (© Chris Pullo.)

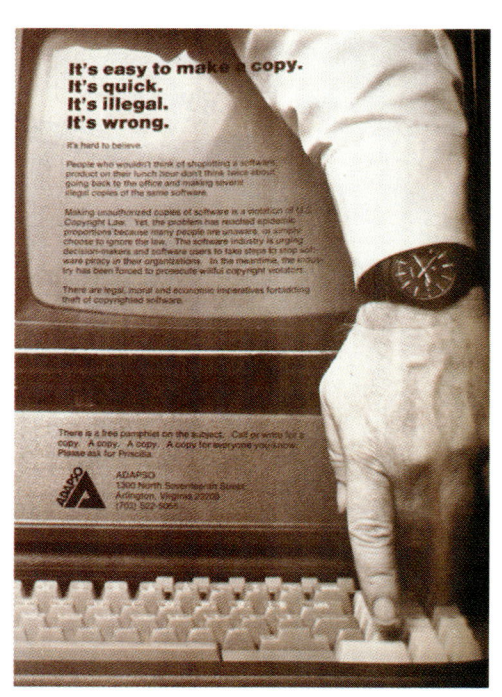

OUR AUTOMATED LIVES 640 PART 5

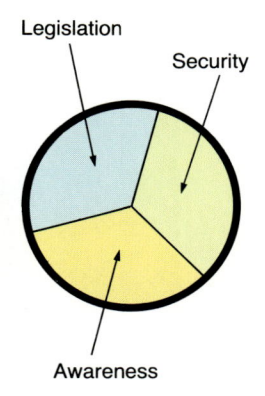

Computer Crime: The Solution

program requires more than money. The support of management is essential. If the organization's managers are not interested in creating a secure environment and enforcing security procedures, the computer system will not be secure, no matter how much money is spent on technical solutions.

In this section we consider three types of security measures: administrative, physical, and technological. We also discuss the need for employee awareness to ensure that security measures are implemented in practice as well as in theory.

Administrative Measures

Administrative security measures consist of policies and procedures set up for the specific purpose of increasing computer security. They typically include the following:

1. Careful screening of job applicants before hiring.
2. Separation of duties. For example, programmers may be prevented from operating the computer in order to reduce the possibility of illegal program modifications.
3. Guidelines indicating which department is responsible for guarding the security of each file or data base. Each department should also be furnished with a list of individuals who are authorized to access particular files or data bases.
4. Specific procedures for backing up data. Many organizations insist that data backups be performed by people who do not work with the data on a regular basis. This reduces opportunities for making unauthorized copies.
5. Policies for eliminating files in accordance with government regulations, including shredding documents that are no longer needed.
6. Assignment of responsibility for different aspects of the security program. This may include the appointment of a *security administrator* to oversee the program.

Physical Measures

Physical security measures consist of a variety of techniques that protect the computer system itself. These include preventing unauthorized access to the system and protecting the system against such hazards as fires or floods. Because the computer depends on electric power, special measures must be taken to protect the power supply.

Limiting Access to the Computer. In the past, unauthorized use of a computer system required that the intruder have access to the equipment itself. Batch systems can be protected against intruders by having a security officer at a single entry point admit only individuals who can furnish proper identification. The use of communication facilities has reduced the effectiveness of such security measures, however; it is no longer necessary to be physically present to abuse a computer system. As a result, technological devices (to be discussed shortly) are required to protect computer systems from abuse by people who may be located thousands of miles away.

Protection Against Natural Disasters. It is impossible to make a computer system completely immune to natural disasters such as floods, fires, and earthquakes. However, the damage caused by such events can be reduced through the choice of a protected site and specific types of building materials. Organizations that depend on having a computer system in operation at all times may invest in an alternative processing site equipped with a complete set of backup files. The availability of such a site enabled a large Canadian food distributor to run the payroll for its 28,000 employees within two days after a fire had largely destroyed the company's headquarters.

Protecting the Power Supply. Computer systems also need to be protected against the effects of electrical problems such as power interruptions and power surges. Various devices have been developed for this purpose. *Surge suppressors*, for example, reduce random fluctuations in the power supply that may damage data or computer equipment. *Uninterruptible power supplies* are equipped with batteries that provide backup in the event of a power failure.

Technological Measures

Technological security measures are applications of software and hardware that reduce the probability of computer abuse. These measures include the use of passwords, call-back systems, cards and keys, validation of personal attributes, and data encryption techniques.

Passwords. A password system requires a prospective user to furnish a series of characters, typically eight or less, that are known only to the user and perhaps a security officer. Passwords may also be used to restrict access to sensitive data in files or data bases. But while the use of passwords undoubtedly reduces unauthorized access to computer systems, the level of protection they provide is often unsatisfactory. For example,

With this restricted-entry card system individual cardholders are assigned access privileges (doors and times) on a door-by-door basis. A central CPU stores all authorizations and records all access activity by each cardholder. (Courtesy of Schlage Electronics.)

many users are unwilling to use hard-to-remember passwords like VDS67BA but insist on using passwords such as MARY-BETH or DLANODcM (McDonald spelled backwards). The user is unlikely to forget such a password, but compared to a random series of letters and numbers, it offers relatively little protection. Even a password like VDS67BA is vulnerable to a serious criminal armed with a program that systematically generates such passwords and a modem that automatically redials a telephone number after the line has been disconnected.

Call-Back Systems. *Call-back systems* receive requests for computer access, note the user's password, and terminate the call. After verifying the password, the system calls the user back and grants access to the computer. If the password cannot be verified, the call-back does not occur. Call-back systems reduce the ability of unauthorized users to gain access to a computer simply by composing a series of passwords. However, they also deny access to some legitimate users, such as traveling salespeople whose hotel telephone numbers are not on the authorized list.

Cards and Keys. Many security systems require that the user present some form of identification, such as a special card, before being granted access to the computer. The simplest example is a magnetic identification card similar to a credit card. Cards and card readers are relatively inexpensive, but the cards

CHAPTER 17   643   PRIVACY, COMPUTER CRIME, AND SECURITY

can easily be forged by experts. More expensive laser cards are harder to copy and offer the added benefit of a memory that can be used to store information about the user, such as security level and number of attempts to access a given file. Some cards, known as "smart cards," contain a microprocessor, RAM, and ROM. Basically, they are individual computers that contain data that can be updated each time the user accesses the computer system.

Many applications—for example, automatic teller machines in banks—require that the user enter a password as well as provide an identification card. To reduce the possibility of fraud, the card should not include the password in any form that is legible either to people or to computers.

Some microcomputer systems and terminals require that the user insert a key similar to a car key. High-security systems may require the use of two separate keys, thereby reducing the possibility of abuse by a single individual.

Cards and keys have certain disadvantages. They can be lost or stolen. Some of them may be easily forged. Moreover, a security system based on cards or keys must include a series of readers or locks at various entry points. To increase their effectiveness, they are usually accompanied by another verification device such as a numeric keypad on the door.

Personal Attributes. Several identification systems rely on unique personal attributes such as fingerprints and voice. Unlike passwords and keys, these attributes cannot be forgotten, stolen, or copied. Equipment that verifies fingerprints is fairly expensive and is limited to systems with very high security requirements. Voice recognition systems (see Chapter 4) are less expensive, but they will reject an authorized person who has a cold or sore throat. As their quality improves, voice recognition systems should become more useful as identification devices. Other identification systems rely on personal attributes such as hand shape, retinal scanning, or the patterns of muscle pressure involved in handwriting.

Data Encryption. The coding of data to prevent reading by unauthorized individuals is called **data encryption**. It became popular during World War II, when methods were developed to encode and decode military data. Data encryption relies on two basic techniques: replacing a character with one or more other characters, and transposing the order of characters. These techniques may be combined. The data is encoded according to an algorithm or formula and then transmitted or stored for future use.

Data encryption
The coding of data to prevent reading by unauthorized individuals.

Encrypted data is decoded by applying the algorithm that was used to code it. Individuals without access to the algorithm can sometimes decode the data by analyzing it for patterns or using "brute force," that is, trying a series of substitutions until one works. The difficulty of "cracking" the code depends on the type of algorithm chosen and the skill and resources of the code breaker.

The *Data Encryption Standard (DES)* was adopted by the National Bureau of Standards in 1977. It is used by the federal government for nonmilitary applications, and by some businesses for sensitive data. At present there is some doubt as to whether this standard is sufficiently unbreakable for military applications. DES is implemented in several microcomputer programs, such as Superkey, that enable users to encrypt their files.

Individual Awareness

As we have emphasized throughout this book, the success of a new system requires the active cooperation of all the personnel involved. A well-functioning security system relies to a large extent on individual awareness. A password system will not work if users write their passwords on their desks or "lend" their passwords to others. The most sophisticated door has no value if users hold it open for passersby. Likewise, data encryption is useless if users of the system give the encryption algorithm to outsiders.

An important aspect of the fight against computer crime is the attitude of users and the general public. If people treat hackers as heroes, they should not be surprised when they are asked to pay the increased cost of making computer systems secure. Management can also help in the fight against computer crime by prosecuting individuals who commit such crimes.

Data Security for Microcomputer Users

A negative aspect of the personal-computer revolution is the increased potential for computer crime and invasion of personal and corporate privacy. Organizations that use microcomputers need to develop and enforce special security guidelines. An example is the following set of guidelines, which were suggested by Joel S. Zimmerman in a recent article published in *Datamation* magazine:

1. Establish clear organizational policy on what types of data are to be considered sensitive. As a matter of policy, make sure every sensitive data set [file] has a designated custodian to bear responsibility for its safekeeping.
2. Establish a policy that no sensitive information may be stored in a file, either temporarily or permanently, on a fixed hard disk. All sensitive information is to be recorded either on specially colored floppies or on specially designated and distinctly marked removable hard disks.
3. Make sure that a locked area or cabinet is available for all media containing sensitive information. Access should be possible only for the data custodian. Arrange this either by individually controlled locks and keys or by using a centrally secured data library.
4. Place PCs in private offices for work with sensitive data.
5. Encourage the use of encryption for sensitive data.[4]

Data Integrity

An issue that is related to data security is *data integrity*, or the assurance that data is, in fact, correct. It is pointless to go to great lengths to protect data if it contains errors. In the article just mentioned, Zimmerman addressed the matter of data integrity by suggesting the following guidelines:

1. All customized microcomputer programs should be validated and certified for accuracy.
2. All corporate data bases, whether stored on micros, minis, or mainframes, should have user-accessible date and time fields to indicate the last time the data base was modified.
3. All output from PCs should be marked clearly with date and time of production. If the report draws upon any external data base, the report should note that data base's date and time stamp.
4. All analytical data reports done on PCs should have independent validations of data input and embedded formulas. Analytical models are to be checked for conceptual accuracy as well as clerical accuracy. The checkers should initial the reports and note the date and time.
5. As a matter of policy, no corporate decisions shall be made on the basis of any PC-based data unless they meet all the conditions set above.[5]

---

[4]"PC Security: So What's New?" *Datamation*, November 1, 1985, p. 92.

[5]Ibid., p. 92.

SUMMARY

1. The right of privacy is not absolute. Most people are willing to release some information about themselves or their families in exchange for the benefits provided by organized society. Like individuals, businesses often find it necessary to release financial and other information about themselves in order to obtain certain benefits. Privacy means that people have the right to choose who has access to information about themselves, and can determine exactly what that information will be.

2. The widespread use of computer systems has increased the potential for invasion of personal and corporate privacy. Computer systems make it possible to gather data bases containing information about millions of individuals. They also make it easier to gain access to corporate data bases.

3. Most organizations do not give high priority to privacy protection. Among the factors that reduce privacy in microcomputer and office automation systems are unprotected physical environments, access to highly processed information, a wide range of users, uncontrolled data communication, and links to corporate data bases.

4. The use of a **standard universal identifier (SUI)** to specify data records for a particular individual makes possible rapid linking of records stored on different files. In practice, the Social Security number has become a *de facto* standard universal identifier. Electronic funds transfer systems also have implications for privacy. By keeping track of an individual's income and expenses, the state could obtain a clear picture of his or her activities and associates.

5. Congress passed the first Privacy Act in 1974. Additional laws such as the Tax Reform Act of 1976 and the Right to Financial Privacy Act of 1978 expanded the provisions of the 1974 Act and applied them to other agencies. Many people feel that the laws enacted in the 1970s are no longer adequate for protecting privacy, and most businesses prefer self-regulation over governmental legislation.

6. The use of computers to invade personal or corporate privacy is often related to the use of computers for criminal purposes. Computer crimes often involve large sums of money or goods and are quite difficult to trace. The main categories of computer crime are financial crime, information crime, theft of computer services, vandalism, theft of computer hardware, and theft of computer software. Both the federal government and the states have passed laws defining forbidden computer-related activities, but those laws vary widely.

7. Computer security refers to the protection of computer systems against unauthorized access and accidental damage. Administrative security measures are policies and procedures whose goal is to increase computer security. They include careful screening of job applicants, separation of duties,

SUMMARY
CONTINUED

guidelines indicating responsibility for the security of each file, frequent file backups, procedures for purging files, and appointment of a security administrator to oversee the entire security operation.

8. Physical security measures are techniques that protect the computer system itself. They include limiting access to the computer and protecting it against natural disasters and electrical problems. Technological security measures are techniques that reduce the probability of computer abuse. They include limiting access to the system to individuals who are able to identify themselves via passwords, cards and keys, or physical attributes, and **data encryption**, or coding data to prevent reading by unauthorized individuals.

KEY TERMS

standard universal identifier (SUI)

computer security

data encryption

REVIEW QUESTIONS

1. Define privacy. What kinds of information are you willing to provide to government agencies or businesses? What kinds of information would you refuse to provide?

2. Describe how the advent of computers has increased the potential for invasion of individual and corporate privacy. How is the threat to privacy increased by the widespread use of microcomputers?

3. What is a standard universal identifier? Indicate how the use of SUIs can endanger personal privacy.

4. Report briefly on the history of privacy legislation.

5. Define computer crime and list the main categories of computer-related crime. Give an example for each category.

6. What are the goals of computer security? Describe administrative, physical, and technological measures for protecting computer security.

7. What is data encryption? Where is it used?

8. Discuss ways of increasing data security and data integrity for microcomputer systems.

APPLICATIONS

1. Locate several data bases that include information about you. Try to find out the exact content of those records. What procedures are available for modifying erroneous data?

2. Give an example of a computer crime. Indicate how you would have prevented that crime if you had been the organization's security director.

3. Determine what laws exist in your state to deal with computer crime. Do you think those laws are adequate? Why or why not?

4. Discuss the following statement: In view of the high cost of software, exchanging copies of software with friends is justified.

CASE FOR DISCUSSION

The security industry has come a long way from night watchmen and guard dogs. Now businesses and government are turning to "electronic access control" devices like computerized card readers and fingerprint scanners, largely because traditional security systems are often costly and less reliable. "The development of access systems based on computers has probably been the single most important driving force in the industry," says Joseph Freeman, a Newtown, Connecticut, security consultant.

Electronic access cards have emerged as the most popular high-tech security method. A computer-linked device "reads" an identification card that is typically placed into a slot or waved in front of a sensor. The computer then releases the door lock and records the time.

The card systems are also attractive because electronic access devices are less expensive than security guards. Nynex Corporation has saved $1 million a year by installing card access devices in fifty New York buildings, says Albert Larsen, a maintenance manager. The buildings are also safer, especially for employees working night shifts, Larsen contends.

Meanwhile, more exotic "biometric" systems are emerging that read fingerprints or even the retina of the eye. A wide range of businesses use the machines. La Reserve, a pricy hotel in White Plains, New York, installed a fingerprint scanner in its wine cellar because thieves walked away with more than $3000 worth of wine each year. And in Omaha, Nebraska, a day-care center uses a fingerprint reader to identify people authorized to pick up children.

Interstate Airlines, which installed three fingerprint scanners in its Little Rock, Arkansas, headquarters, found that some employees were skittish about using the machines. "They said, 'Oh my gosh, they're putting my fingerprint on file. What are they going to use that for?'" recalls William Willoughby, director of information systems.

The workers' paranoia soon wore off, however, partly because the scanner is easier to use than the company's previous security device, a card access system. "You'd have a briefcase in one hand and you're trying to whip your wallet out" to get at the card, Willoughby says.

The future for electronic access systems looks promising because the devices are versatile. St. Mary's Hospital of Richmond, Virginia, expects to use a card access system just like a time clock; the machines might also guard its narcotics supply. But making sure employees are doing their job might become a more common, albeit controversial, application.

Employees' movements can be traced by placing sensors at the entrance of each room in a building. "The tracking device would document the fact that [the employee] has gone to the cafeteria," says Freeman, the security consultant. Employers "don't really want to do this, but the pressures of running a large organization are so immense that the question sooner or later has to be confronted."

Says Jerry Berman, legislative counsel for the American Civil Liberties Union in Washington, "It's not technology based on trusting your employees, it's based on 'We trust no one.'"

Source: Hank Gilman, "Sense of Security," *Wall Street Journal*, November 10, 1986, p. 40D. Reprinted by permission of *The Wall Street Journal*, copyright © Dow Jones & Company, Inc. 1986. All rights reserved.

CASE QUESTION

A restaurant with a fingerprint scanner on its wine cellar finds that wine is still being stolen. With the aid of the police department, it checks the fingerprints of employees who have authorized access to the cellar against FBI records. The check reveals that Tim Sanders, who has been employed as a wine waiter at the restaurant for five years, was convicted of shoplifting fifteen years earlier and received a suspended sentence. Sanders is fired on the ground that he lied on his employment application. Is firing Sanders a legitimate security precaution? Or do you think that his privacy was unreasonably invaded?

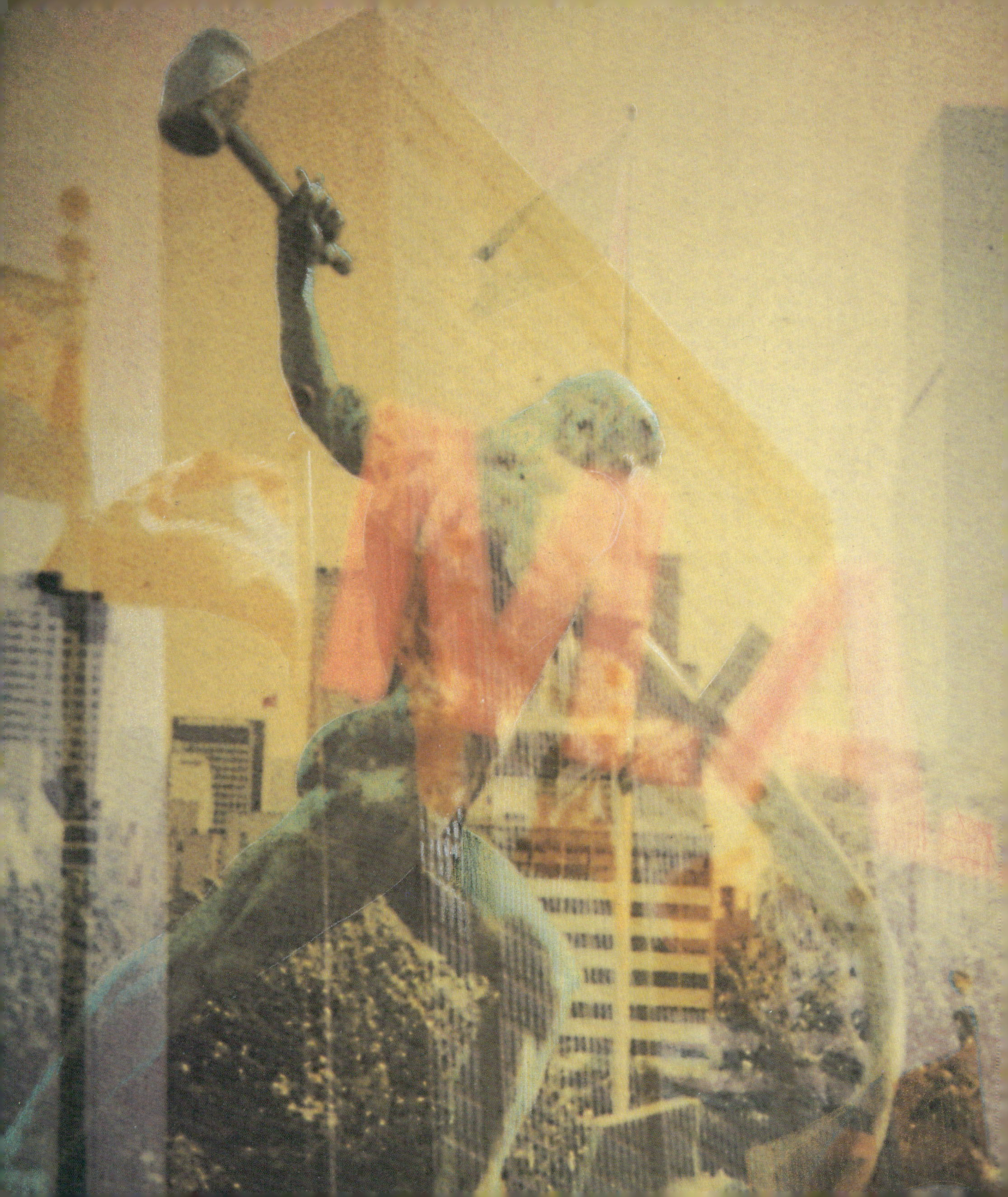

The Future of Computing: Trends and Prospects

CHAPTER

18

The scene is a computer science class in the year 2000. Professor Marianne Askari is showing the class a recorded movie. The plot involves an attempted takeover of the world government by the main computer of the United Nations. Housed in a forty-story skyscraper in Manhattan, this machine, whose name is Max, has the unimaginable memory capacity of 10 million bytes and runs at the incredible speed of 10 million instructions per second. Max has analyzed human history and concluded that humans are too irrational to be trusted to govern themselves.

Max has laid down an ultimatum: Either its directives will be accepted as law, or it will begin turning off the food synthesis factories in one country after another.

As the film's climax approaches, the hero is trying to reach the control room and turn off Max's power supply. Max has blocked all the corridors and entrances to the building by closing automatic doors. Our hero has gained access to the building through an emergency manual service hatch. He climbs story after story through acres of circuit boards studded with transistors, resistors, capacitors, and diodes. Finally he reaches the control room. It is a vast space filled with blinking lights, oscilloscope screens, and thousands upon thousands of magnetic-tape drives. Our hero makes for an emergency power cutoff switch.

"I sense irrational human brainwaves!" announces Max in a sinister voice. "I analyze them as the brainwaves of Carson Telluride. Telluride, halt!"

"I take orders from no machine!" says Telluride as he lunges for the switch.

"No!" says Max's mechanical voice. "No, I don't want to die! I don't . . ."

Clunk! goes the switch. The world is saved.

The classroom lights go on. Professor Askari stands at the front of the room and places her hand on a briefcase-sized portable computer. "What are some differences between my Compaq Model 21 here and Max, the computer in the movie?"

"Yours is smaller," says one student.

"Smaller," says another, "but a lot more powerful. Your Compaq operates at 1 billion instructions per second and has 2.5 billion bytes of memory."

"I think you're forgetting the most important thing," says a student in the back of the room. "The biggest difference between Max and your Compaq portable is that the Compaq doesn't *want* to take over the world. It doesn't *care* what people do. It can't care, or think, or feel, or fear death. It can only compute!"

Predicting the future is dangerous. Twenty years ago writers made many mistakes in their predictions about the evolution of computers. In some ways they wildly underestimated the pace of progress in this field. The failure to predict that computers would shrink in size as they grew in power was one of the most common mistakes that they made. In other ways they vastly overestimated the pace of progress. Twenty or thirty years ago, computers that you could talk to seemed just around the corner. In practice, speech synthesis and recognition have posed thorny problems that are still years away from resolution, although progress is being made.

But in one way past predictions about the future of computing were right on the mark: Computers, as predicted, have come to play an ever-larger role in almost every area of life, from business to government to education to leisure activities. This chapter concurs with that safe prediction. It discusses trends in hardware and software and in the role of computers in life and work.

When you have read this chapter, you should be able to:

1. Discuss emerging technologies that may affect computer hardware in the future.

2. Discuss the differences between the software techniques known as artificial intelligence, on the one hand, and human intelligence, on the other.

3. Make informed speculations about the future roles of computers in life and work.

4. Discuss the risks that computers pose for society.

5. Understand and use the key term listed at the end of the chapter.

Trends in Hardware

If past trends in computer hardware are taken as a guide, the future is clear: Computers will become more powerful, cheaper, and smaller. These trends are illustrated in Box 18-1. Today's most powerful desktop computers are the equivalent of yesterday's minicomputers and the mainframes of just a few years before that.

Past trends toward increased power and reduced weight and cost have involved several revolutionary changes in technology. First vacuum tubes were replaced by transistors and magnetic core memories, then these in turn were replaced by silicon-based integrated circuits. Recent progress has come largely in the form of packing more and more elements onto silicon-based chips. The 80286 and 80386 chips that power the latest generation of personal computers are part of that trend. Let's begin by taking a look at these new, more powerful personal computers, or "personal systems," as some prefer to call them.

When IBM introduced the Personal System/2, users of existing IBM microcomputers often were unwilling to convert to the new equipment, which requires different-sized disks. (Courtesy of International Business Machines.)

CHAPTER 18　655　THE FUTURE OF COMPUTING

BOX 18-1

FRONTIERS IN TECHNOLOGY
The Downward Migration of Computer Technology

In predicting future developments in computer technology, David Nelson, chief technical officer at Apollo Computer, classifies computers into seven tiers, each separated from the other by a factor of 10 in cost (see chart). The aggregate improvement in performance across the tiers is about 35 percent a year, so a tenfold improvement (across one tier) occurs every seven years. Thus, the virtual-memory capability of a $1 million IBM 370 mainframe computer, which first emerged in 1970, became available on the DEC VAX in 1977 (for approximately $100,000) and in the Apollo DN300 workstation in 1984 (for approximately $10,000). By extrapolation, claims Nelson, that same capability ought to be available in 1991 for close to $1000.

At the higher end of the workstation market, he says, there will be increasing performance for constant cost. Thus, a $50,000–$100,000 workstation, which approaches the performance of a mainframe today, should have the capabilities of a minisupercomputer by 1991.

Nelson also believes that a tenfold performance increase is matched by a weight decrease of the same order. "Computers seem to cost about $200 per pound, independent of their size," says Nelson, "a figure that has been valid for the last thirty years when adjusted for inflation." As computers become more of a "commodity," perhaps one day it will be possible to buy them by the pound.

Source: Reprinted with permission from Jeffrey Bairstow, "Personal Workstations Redefine Desktop Computing," *High Technology* magazine, March 1987, p. 20. Copyright © 1987 by Mark Alsop.

CHAPTER 18 THE FUTURE OF COMPUTING

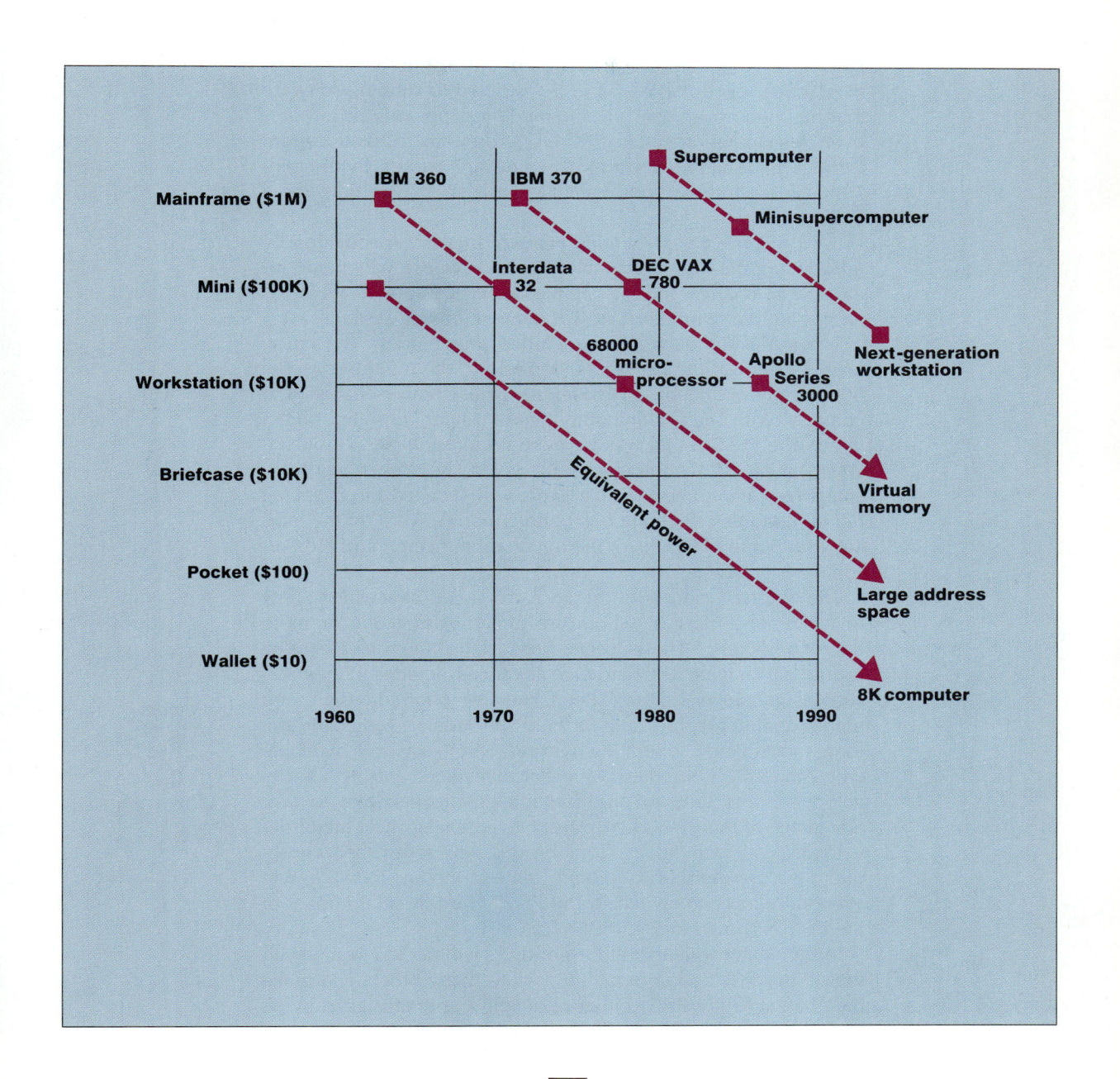

The IBM PS/2

The IBM family of personal computers, introduced in 1981, played a key role in the development of personal computing. Although this series did not represent a technological breakthrough, it was largely responsible for the widespread use of microcomputers in business. But by the mid-1980s hundreds of manufacturers, some located in garages or basements, were producing compatibles at a fraction of the cost of IBM products. In practice, even the PC AT was restricted to running software that had been developed for the much less powerful PC. Moreover, the operating system, PC-DOS, drew its inspiration from CP/M, which had been developed a decade earlier. By the mid-1980s most industry observers agreed that it was time for a change.

In April of 1987 IBM ended years of industry speculation by introducing the PS/2 (Personal System/2), whose very name indicated a change in basic philosophy. Customers were no longer buying computers; now they were buying systems.

The initial announcement included four models: the entry-level Model 30, the single-user Model 50, the multiuser Model 60, and the 80386-based Model 80, whose power enables it to compete with many minicomputers. A major, unstated objective of the PS/2 design was to make it more difficult for outsiders to copy IBM equipment. But given the stakes involved, sooner or later some manufacturers will succeed in producing full compatibles. Partially compatible models were on the market within a few months of the initial announcement of the Personal System/2.

The different models of the PS/2 are aimed at a wide variety of customers, most of whom are already using one or more microcomputers. These users are asking themselves, Why should we change? The hardware advances included in the PS/2, such as greater processing speed, more ergonomic design, and higher-quality graphics, are far from spectacular. Moreover, the long-awaited new operating system, OS/2, was not available when the PS/2 computers were first delivered, and it took developers some time to produce applications software to take advantage of the PS/2's hardware. Nevertheless, most major developers will focus their efforts on this new series, and consequently customers who require state-of-the-art software will eventually have to switch to the PS/2. The potential impact of the PS/2 is shown in Figure 18-1.

In the next few years millions of users will decide to stay with their older PCs and compatibles, while many others will make the change to the PS/2, either reluctantly or enthusiastically. A key question that they will be asking is what is involved in

FIGURE 18-1

Potential Impact of the PS/2

What percentage of your PC unit purchases during the next 12 months will be the new IBM Personal System/2?

Other Systems 61%

PS/2 39%

Based on answers from 78% of respondents.

Information provided by a Computerworld survey of 101 MIS managers. Based on answers from 78% of respondents. (Source: Copyright 1987 by CW Communications/Inc., Framingham, MA 01701—Reprinted from Computerworld.)

changing from the PC to the PS/2. The answer to this question is not a simple one.

Perhaps the biggest difficulty in changing models is that the PS/2 uses 3½-inch diskettes instead of the 5¼-inch diskettes found on the IBM PC. Many software manufacturers are already supplying software on diskettes of either size. Several methods are available for converting existing program and data diskettes, none of them ideal, especially for users with hundreds of 5¼-inch diskettes. For example, IBM offers an external 5¼-inch disk drive for the PS/2, but many software manufacturers will not guarantee that their software will work on these drives.

Some observers believe that the conversion process offers an ideal opportunity to eliminate unauthorized software, while others are afraid that PS/2 users will give away software on 5¼-inch diskettes to people who are still using the older series of microcomputers. In short, as we have seen so often, the real challenge offered by the new hardware and software has to do with managing change.

CHAPTER 18   THE FUTURE OF COMPUTING

Gallium Arsenide[1]

The IBM PS/2 is not the limit in silicon technology. Further increases in speed and power can be expected. Nevertheless, research efforts are beginning to look beyond the silicon era to other technologies that are on the horizon. For even though silicon is the material on which the computer age has been built, it has its shortcomings.

One shortcoming is that no practical way has yet been developed for getting silicon to emit light, so it is useless for making lasers and light-emitting diodes needed for fiber optics, optical disk readers, and other state-of-the-art devices. Silicon also has speed limitations. It performs poorly, if at all, at microwave frequencies. These limitations put a ceiling on the number of bits per second that a circuit can handle.

The leading candidate to overcome silicon's limitations in at least some applications is gallium arsenide (GaAs). GaAs shines where silicon slumps. Electrons are about five times as mobile in GaAs as in silicon, allowing proportionately higher operating speeds. Moreover, GaAs devices can emit light, withstand higher temperatures, and survive higher doses of radiation.

Unfortunately, GaAs has its own drawbacks: It is difficult to produce and to work with. Whereas silicon crystals can be grown several inches in diameter, GaAs can be produced only in much smaller sizes. Also, GaAs is soft and fragile. It tends to break during slicing, scratch during polishing, and chip during handling. These difficulties have caused GaAs to remain expensive and have limited its applications mainly to military systems in which high speed and radiation resistance are essential.

Researchers have not given up hope for GaAs, however. Current efforts focus on ways to combine its desirable properties with the handling characteristics of silicon. One promising approach is to deposit a thin layer of GaAs on a silicon chip, thus giving the composite chip the desirable properties of both materials. This technique, if successful, may bring GaAs out of the realm of the exotic. Already makers of supercomputers are testing GaAs devices such as ultrafast memories and "gate arrays" for use in their next generation of machines.

Superconducting Computers

One way to speed up computers and make them more powerful is to pack the components closer together on a chip and

---
[1]This section is based on John G. Posa, "Uniting Silicon and Gallium Arsenide," *High Technology*, March 1987, pp. 38–41.

to pack chips closer together within the computer. This process has been the basis for much of the improvement of silicon-based semiconducting devices in recent decades. However, the ability to pack components closely together is limited in some cases by the heat given off by electrical resistance within the devices.

Theoretically, one way to overcome this problem would be to make the conductors that connect the components, or even the components themselves, from a superconducting material. Superconductors are materials that have no electrical resistance and therefore give off no heat when an electric current is passed through them. However, until recently the known superconductors would operate only when cooled to about the temperature of liquid helium, near absolute zero. This made superconducting computers impractical.

Beginning in 1987, however, major advances in superconductor technology were reported. It was discovered that certain exotic ceramic materials exhibits superconductivity at temperatures much higher than that of liquid helium. The prospect of superconductors that would operate at the temperature of relatively inexpensive liquid nitrogen, or even higher, renewed interest in superconducting computers. At this writing, the potential for this technology is largely a matter of speculation. However, the new superconductors have become the focus of an enormous research effort. The payoffs in terms of enhanced computational power could be substantial.

Optical Computing

All computers depend on electrical signals to process information. In principle, however, one can imagine a computer in which electrical signals are replaced by light. Writing in a recent issue of *High Technology*,[2] Jeff Hecht summarizes the possible advantages of such an approach as follows:

Speed. The fastest electronic transistors take several picoseconds (trillionths of a second) to switch between on and off states. Light beams, however, have been switched far more rapidly; the shortest optical pulse so far is a 0.008-picosecond flash generated at AT&T Bell Laboratories. Moreover, light travels faster than electricity, and there is no optical equivalent of some of the electrical effects that slow down signals in conductors. And while electronic devices speed up as they shrink, the

---

[2]This section is based on Jeff Hecht, "Optical Computers," *High Technology*, February 1987, pp. 44–49.

wires that connect them do not. It takes at least fifty nanoseconds (billionths of a second) for an electronic signal to move between two circuit boards on a computer; light, which travels at thirty centimeters per nanosecond, could make the same trip much faster.

Parallelism. Ten thousand independent light beams can pass through an ordinary lens. Thus, an optical device can accept numerous inputs at the same time. In most electronic computers, by contrast, the data for all computations pass "single file" through the main processor.

Interconnection. Light rays, unlike electric currents, do not affect each other. Optics could therefore allow denser arrays of interconnections to, and within, a chip than are possible with electronic conductors.

An all-optical computer is years away, if indeed such a thing will ever be built. However, researchers are hard at work on ways to graft optical components onto conventional computers. The computers could pass along especially demanding problems, such as matrix processing or image recognition, to these optical components. Also, it may be possible to use optical methods to make connections between or within conventional electronic components.

The Future of Desktop Computing

A generation ago the very idea of personal computing eluded the imagination of futurists and science fiction writers, who thought of future computers mainly in terms of ever larger and more powerful mainframe machines. In the last years of the twentieth century and beyond, new technologies will probably continue to be applied to mainframes first, but the lag in putting such things as gallium arsenide chips into desktop computers will not be long.[3]

Aside from the certainty that personal computers will continue to improve in both speed and memory capacity, future desktop systems will be distinguished from those of today by the range and power of their input and output peripherals. Here are some things to expect:

- Read/write optical disks will replace magnetic storage media.

---

[3]For a survey of what is coming in desktop computing, see "Special Report: The Future of Computing," *PC World*, May 1987, pp. 260–286.

The ubiquitous floppy disk may survive as a convenience device, but tape drives will probably be relegated to museums.
- Flat displays will become standard, with increased resolution and better color.
- Laser printers will increase in power and decrease in price. The technology to build high-resolution, color laser printers already exists. Holographic laser printers that make three-dimensional hard copy are a definite possibility.

The increasing power of top-of-the-line microcomputers does not mean that everyone will have such machines, any more than BMW's state-of-the-art technology means that everyone drives a BMW. There will be plenty of jobs, such as simple word processing and record keeping, that can be done on a machine with little more inherent power than today's microcomputer. Even these basic machines will change, however. They will be less expensive. They will have a smaller "footprint," taking up less room on a desktop. And they will have better ergonomics: better screen resolution, more convenient keyboards, and so on.

Trends in Software

We have repeatedly pointed out that computer hardware is useless without software. When hardware advances faster than software, as was the case with the introduction of 80386-based microcomputers, the full potential of the new machine cannot be realized at first. Software will not be written before machines are available to run it, so in a sense we can expect that software will continue to play a catch-up game as hardware develops. What will this software of the future look like when it does become available?

Personal-Productivity Software

Software is valuable because it makes people more productive. Today's office worker is already more productive than yesterday's because of word processing, spreadsheets, and database programs. Writing in *PC World*, Charles Seiter and Daniel Ben-Horin give this vision of personal productivity in the office of the future:

This keyboard allows the user to enter data and commands in English, Chinese, or Japanese. (Courtesy of Hewlett-Packard.)

If nothing else, the software of the future will meet you more than halfway. When you walk into an office in 1998, the PC will sense your presence, switch itself on, and promptly deliver your overnight E-mail, sorted in order of importance. For a lot of people, the workday could start all too smoothly.

Suppose that the most urgent message concerns a lost shipment from Osaka. You load an English-to-Japanese word processor, speak into a microphone, and "write" a letter simultaneously in both languages. End the session, and the program automatically telecommunicates the message to the client in Japan, CC's your boss, and files a copy away in the company's cross-indexed optical disk archives. If the shipment were from an English or American supplier, you might set up a voice/video teleconference via PC and direct the program to transcribe the conversation and display a summary of past meetings and transactions to all those electronically present.[4]

With a note of caution, Seiter and Ben-Horin add that "human imagination has a way of outstripping constraints. What makes the future exciting are those things we can't yet imagine." They quote an industry observer as saying that "the really dazzling new application is probably something none of us have thought of yet. And the author of that program is probably a ten-year-old kid in Nebraska who will drop out of college in disgust at our stodgy corporate software—and revolutionize the business!"

---

[4]Charles Seiter and Daniel Ben-Horin, "Software," *PC World*, May 1987, pp. 272–273. Reprinted with permission.

Artificial Intelligence

Artificial intelligence
The use of a computer to emulate human capabilities such as thinking.

In the past decade much progress has been made toward developing computer systems that can handle tasks that go far beyond numerical calculations and word processing. These directions in software development, which come under the heading of **artificial intelligence (AI)**, will continue to be vigorously pursued in the future. Some developments in AI have been mentioned in earlier chapters, including expert systems, natural programming languages, robotics, and game-playing programs. Of these, expert systems are most widely used today (Box 18-2 illustrates a typical expert system application of AI.)

Research on AI began shortly after the appearance of the first commercial computers. At the same time that industry observers were underestimating the computer's commercial potential, many researchers were overestimating its ability to carry out sophisticated activities such as translating poetry or deciding where to drill for oil. As recently as 1965, Herbert Simon, a pioneer in the field of AI, asserted that "machines will be capable, within 20 years, of doing any work that a [person] can do."[5] While we can safely say that by the end of the century machines will not yet be capable of doing many types of work that people perform, progress in the type of work (or play) that machines can do has been steady, and the commercial importance of AI is increasing.

One of the first areas of research in AI was teaching computers to play games such as chess and checkers. Although the economic implications of a chess-playing computer are minor, game-playing served as a good starting point for research in AI because games are governed by a small set of rules. It soon became evident that it is impossible to devise a computer that is fast enough to play chess by examining every possible move; there are simply too many possibilities. The computer has to be supplied with "rules of thumb" like those a beginner uses in learning to play chess. In 1968 the Scottish chess champion David Levy bet that no computer could ever beat him. It was ten years before a computer program was finally victorious (although Levy won a rematch). No computer program has yet defeated a world chess champion. Some experts believe that it is merely a matter of time before a computer accomplishes this feat, but others claim that it will never happen, at least not during their lifetimes. On the other hand, in the early 1980s a computer program defeated the world backgammon champion by a score of 7 to 1.

---

[5]Quoted in Tom Alexander, "Artificial Intelligence," *Popular Computing*, May 1985, p. 69.

BOX 18-2

USING COMPUTERS
AI Integration

The TOLAS-Telestream system, developed by Carnegie Group for GSI-Transcomm (Pittsburgh), shows how AI components can be integrated with an existing data processing application. The AI module contains six expert systems that perform functions previously handled by human specialists, plus a communications expert to manage the exchange of information. When a customer calls in an order, it enters the system as a "problem statement." Each expert system, under the arbitration of a system scheduler/planner, tries to solve the problem with its own special knowledge. Most have goals, which are based on rules from a rule base, knowledge from the knowledge base, and facts stored in the conventional data base. For example, realizing the goal of not selling to credit-risk customers requires that the caller's rating be determined on the basis of conventional data such as annual sales. Once the AI module has arrived at a solution that meets both the customer's needs and the vendor's goals, the solution is sent to the terminal screen to be relayed to the customer.

Source: Reprinted with permission from Dwight B. Davis, "Artificial Intelligence Enters the Mainstream," *High Technology* magazine, July 1986, p. 20. Copyright © 1986 by Graphic Ideas, Inc.

AI module

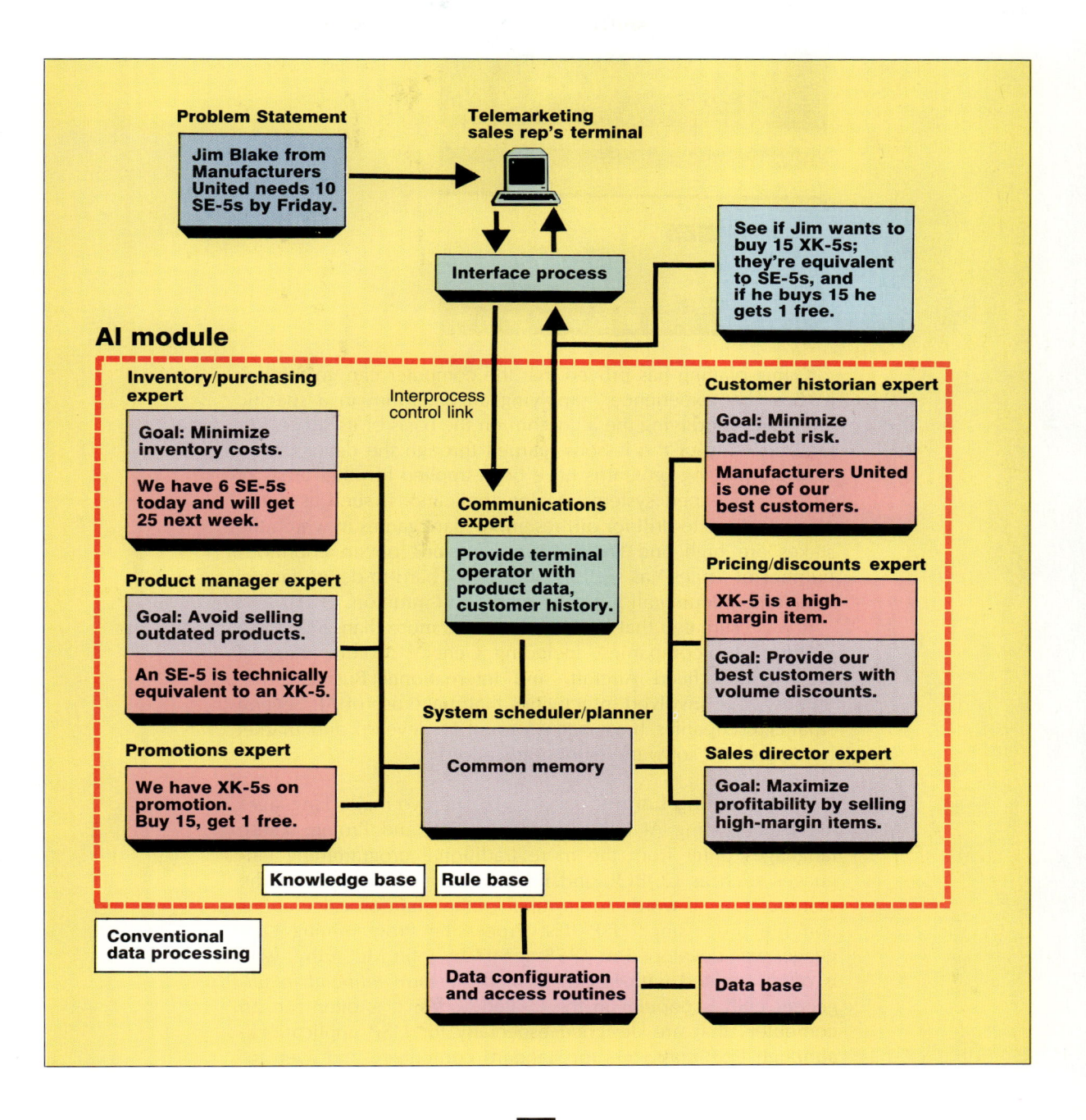

Problem Statement
Jim Blake from Manufacturers United needs 10 SE-5s by Friday.

Telemarketing sales rep's terminal

Interface process

See if Jim wants to buy 15 XK-5s; they're equivalent to SE-5s, and if he buys 15 he gets 1 free.

Inventory/purchasing expert
Goal: Minimize inventory costs.

We have 6 SE-5s today and will get 25 next week.

Product manager expert
Goal: Avoid selling outdated products.

An SE-5 is technically equivalent to an XK-5.

Promotions expert
We have XK-5s on promotion. Buy 15, get 1 free.

Interprocess control link

Communications expert
Provide terminal operator with product data, customer history.

System scheduler/planner
Common memory

Customer historian expert
Goal: Minimize bad-debt risk.

Manufacturers United is one of our best customers.

Pricing/discounts expert
XK-5 is a high-margin item.

Goal: Provide our best customers with volume discounts.

Sales director expert
Goal: Maximize profitability by selling high-margin items.

Knowledge base Rule base

Conventional data processing

Data configuration and access routines — Data base

Chess-playing computer programs range in performance capability from the level of a beginning player to that of a participant in international tournaments. (© David W. Hamilot, The Image Bank.)

Game-playing has proved that the computer can go through a "learning experience," applying an algorithm in a specific game and modifying the algorithm on the basis of its success or failure. Many of the lessons learned through the development of game-playing programs have been applied to other areas of AI such as expert systems. Major applications, such as determining where to drill for oil, resemble giant games in which the stakes are high and the outcome depends on an enormous number of "rules" as well as on a set of hard-to-define factors that some people call luck and others call intuition.

It was estimated that by the mid-1980s more than 200 of the Fortune 500 companies, including General Motors, General Electric, Lockheed Aircraft, and International Business Machines, were involved in activities that make use of AI. Several smaller companies have been formed to develop and market hardware and software for AI applications.

Programming Languages for AI. The two major languages for programming AI applications are LISP and Prolog. These languages differ from the more traditional programming languages such as COBOL and BASIC in that they focus on the manipulation of words and symbols rather than on calculations and file processing. LISP (List Processing Programming Language) was developed in 1958 at MIT by John McCarthy, who is often credited with having coined the term *artificial intelligence*. LISP is popular in the United States. It is often run on computers that are designed especially for LISP applications, although LISP compilers for standard computers, and even for

Students in this training course are learning LISP, a major programming language for artificial-intelligence applications. (Courtesy of Texas Instruments.)

some powerful microcomputers, are beginning to compete successfully with the specialty machines. Prolog (Programming in Logic) was developed in the 1960s by Alain Colmerauer and Philippe Rousel at the University of Montreal and later at the University of Marseilles. Prolog is favored in Europe, Canada, and Japan. Several versions of Prolog are available for all sizes of computers, and one popular version, Turbo Prolog, runs on microcomputers. Advances in programming languages associated with artificial intelligence will lead to more applications as it becomes more cost-effective to use AI to solve business problems.

Interest in AI is widespread, especially in Western Europe, the Soviet Union, and Japan, which in 1982 launched the multibillion-dollar Fifth-Generation Computing Project with the goal of producing a truly new generation of computers. These computers are expected to handle spoken input and to have improved reasoning ability. The fifth-generation project is an effort on the part of the Japanese to overcome their reputation of being good at hardware development but weak in software development. If it is successful, the project will enhance Japan's position as a major player in the world computer market.

But Can Computers Think?

The term *artificial intelligence* connotes a machine that can *think* in the sense that a human can think. But can computers think? And if so, how would we know?

The classic view, supported by many of the pioneers of AI, is that thinking is information processing; information processing is computation; computation is the manipulation of symbols;

and in this sense what goes on in the brain and what goes on in a computer are pretty much the same thing.[6] This point of view, which Tufts University philosopher Daniel C. Dennett has dubbed "high-church computationalism," suggests that we can learn whether a computer can think by conducting the "Turing test."

Devised in 1950 by the British mathematician Alan Turing, the Turing test works as follows: You are seated in a room at a standard workstation. Wires lead from the workstation either to a computer or to another person seated at a similar workstation in the next room. You don't know which; your job is to find out by asking a series of questions. The answers to your questions appear on the screen of your workstation. If you are communicating with a computer, but no amount of questioning allows you to be sure, then the computer has passed the Turing test: It can think.

But there are those who consider the Turing test a fraud. According to Hubert Dreyfus, John Searle, and others whom Dennett calls "Zen holists," thinking "is not computation at all: thinking is something holistic and emergent—and organic and fuzzy and warm and cuddly and mysterious." Even if a machine could pass the Turing test, it wouldn't be thinking in the sense intended by holists, because the symbols it manipulated wouldn't *mean* anything to it. It would be in the same situation as a person who became skilled at sorting cards marked with Chinese characters by looking at the shape and number of lines in each character, but without understanding a word of the Chinese language.

What is more, say the Zen holists, computers lack the property of *intentionality*. They don't do things for a purpose or because they want to, but just because they are programmed in a certain way. The output of the machine reflects the intentions of the programmer, not the intentions of the machine itself.

This debate is one that is not likely to be resolved, because at its roots it is a debate over values and beliefs as much as over scientific issues. Perhaps, as M. Mitchell Waldrop, an expert in the field has suggested, the proper answer to the question of whether computers really think is "Who cares?" After all, says Waldrop, the important thing is whether or not a machine does its job. We don't go around asking whether taxis can walk, so why should we ask whether computers can think?

---

[6]This section is based on M. Mitchell Waldrop, "If I Compute, Therefore Am I?" *Washington Post*, February 22, 1987, p. C3.

Risks in the Computerized Future

Herbert Simon was off the mark in thinking that computers would be able to do everything people can do by the 1980s. But it is increasingly true that there are few things that people do that cannot be *aided* by computers. This has made life easier, more pleasant, and more productive for people throughout the world. Even people who may live all their lives without seeing a computer are likely to benefit from genetically engineered seed for their crops or perhaps an advance in preventive medicine that was developed with the aid of computers. Nevertheless, as we have indicated at various points in this book, there are risks in the computerized future. These are worth recalling here.

Computers Are Only as Good as Their Programmers

In Chapter 1 we emphasized that computers can do only what they are told to do. This means that computers are only as good as their software, and software is only as good as the programmers who write it. "Computer errors," which are really errors made by people, become more of a threat as we become more dependent on computers. Medical tests can be misread by a misprogrammed computer; a misprogrammed computer can fail to warn of an impending airplane collision. A favorite theme of fantasy writers is to have a misprogrammed computer start a world war. Let us hope this remains only a fantasy. At the same time, as the speed and range of modern weapons systems grow we do become more and more dependent on computers to control them.

Can anything be done about the software problem? Researchers are certainly hard at work on it. Programs that help programmers eliminate the drudgery of writing thousands of lines of routine code may reduce some kinds of errors. Critical applications like medical technology will someday incorporate artificial intelligence features that help computers recognize the

CHAPTER 18 671 THE FUTURE OF COMPUTING

absurdity of, for instance, a recommendation to increase an X-ray machine's intensity 100 times. If the scope of computer applications stood still, our ability to purge these applications of software "bugs" could surely be expected to improve.

Applications will not stand still, however. Applications designers will always be pushing the limits of what can be accomplished. There will always be some applications that strain the ability of software designers, and therefore there will always be new opportunities for errors. The risk of programming errors in large and complex systems will not go away.

Threats to Privacy and Freedom

Few people worry seriously today about the danger of a computer taking over the world as they did in 1950s' science fiction stories. We are protected from this danger by our inability to build a computer that is capable of wanting to take over the world or even one that is capable of caring whether it is turned on or off. However, it is unfortunate but true that there will continue to be *people* who want to invade our privacy and violate our freedom. And these people, just like the rest of us, will often find ways in which their work can be aided by computers.

Chapter 17 discussed problems of privacy and crime at some length. There we saw how important it is that computers be programmed with safeguards that protect privacy and security. However, we are always faced with the fact that computers don't *care* whether they divulge sensitive information to individuals with authorized access or to others who are up to no good. As long as the troublemakers know the codes with which the computer has been programmed, the machine will hum and blink and spill out the contents of its storage registers without a touch of remorse.

The saying that the price of freedom is eternal vigilance was not coined with computers in mind. But it fits.

Is Anything Safe from Computers?

Warnings about programming errors that might cause a computerized construction crane to drop a load of bricks on our heads, or about data bases that might allow a secret police force to trace our every footstep, make it sound as if nothing is safe from computers. On the contrary, although we cannot afford to be careless with these powerful machines any more than we could afford to be careless with a chainsaw, there is reason to believe that some things will remain safe from computers; indeed, there is reason to believe that computers will make life in the future better rather than worse. Why is this so?

Writer and futurist Isaac Asimov provides the following analogy: Billions of dollars and many hours of research have been spent on developing cars and other machines that roll on wheels; by comparison, hardly any effort has been devoted to developing machines that walk. Surely walking machines could be devised, given the effort. Why is the effort not made? Because, says Asimov, most people can already walk easily and effortlessly by themselves, but they can't roll by themselves. It is the same with computers. Most efforts in the future, as in the past, will be devoted to designing computers that can do things that humans find difficult, tedious, or impossible, like performing complex numerical calculations or handling dangerous materials. Efforts to design computers that can do things that people can already do fairly easily—such as give one another comfort and friendship, write poetry or music, or play games—will remain on the sidelines of research.

Take chess-playing programs, for example. Why were these developed? In part they were developed because the principles learned by doing so could be applied elsewhere. In part, also, they were developed because doing so was itself a challenge, a sort of game. But they were not developed so that people could be freed from the need to play chess or deprived of the opportunity to play chess.

Chess is safe from computers because people find playing chess enjoyable even if most of them don't do it as well as a computer can. What is more, the principles of artificial intelligence that were learned by writing chess programs can free people from routine, tedious tasks like approving credit applications or allocating warehouse space, thereby leaving them more time to play chess.

The same is true of most other activities that humans are good at or that they find enjoyable. In these areas we may find ways for computers to aid us, but they will not displace us. A computerized dating service may put us in touch with someone who likes cats, lasagna, and baseball. That is all to the good. But few if any of us will ever actually want to go on a date with a computer—even one that could pass the Turing test!

In the future computers will continue to bring change to our life and work. For the most part, that is also good. Change is one of the things that people find enjoyable, provided that it is managed change, not chaotic, disruptive, threatening change. This, then, will remain the biggest job reserved for humans in the age of computers: managing change.

SUMMARY

1. Advances in hardware have made computers smaller, cheaper, and more powerful at a steady rate, and these trends are likely to continue. (The recently introduced IBM PS/2 is an example of this process.) The possibilities of silicon semiconductors have not yet been exhausted. Beyond them such exotic technologies as gallium arsenide chips, superconductors, and optical computers await practical development. Optical storage devices are already a reality and will continue to improve. Input and output devices also will advance. Voice recognition and synthesis will be improved, and holographic printers are on the horizon.

2. As more powerful desktop computers become available, personal-productivity software will increase productivity even more than it does now. Greater user-friendliness, including natural-language interfaces, will become more common. Software will become increasingly integrated. Further advances will be made in the area of artificial intelligence, although many observers maintain that computers will never "think" in the sense that people do.

3. As computers become more widely applied, there will be risks to be faced. "Computer errors," which are almost invariably errors made by human programmers, will continue to be a problem because software complexity will continue to push the limit of programers' ability to "debug" programs. Vigilance will be necessary to minimize threats to privacy and security. Computers will make life better in the future, provided that the changes they bring are properly managed.

KEY TERM

artificial intelligence

REVIEW QUESTIONS

1. Compare the advantages and disadvantages of silicon and gallium arsenide computer chips.

2. How might recent advances in superconductor technology be applied to computers?

3. What would be the advantages of an all-optical computer?

4. What is meant by *artificial intelligence*? What programming languages are used for AI, and how do they differ from such languages as BASIC and COBOL?

5. What risks must be guarded against as the use of computers becomes increasingly widespread?

APPLICATIONS

1. Review such publications as *Computerworld, Datamation, High Technology,* and *PC World* for information on trends in hardware and software. Are any products being advertised that incorporate gallium arsenide technology? superconductors? artificial intelligence?

2. Pick one of the magazines listed in application 1. Find an issue of the magazine from five years ago. What advances are apparent from a comparison of the articles and ads then and now?

3. Read Robert Heinlein's novel *The Moon Is a Harsh Mistress* or Arthur C. Clark's *2001*. In what ways are the computers featured in these works of fiction represented realistically or unrealistically?

CASE FOR DISCUSSION

The pattern room in Winer Industries Inc.'s Paterson, N.J., building is cramped and frenetic. Workers breeze through pushing mannequins and carrying garments. Racks of clothing are in perpetual motion. No one sits—except a cluster of women behind sewing machines. Hunched over her workbench is Brenda Hester Small, the head pattern maker for the women's clothing division.

The Oscar de la Rentas, Calvin Kleins and Carolina Herreras may reap the fame and fortune of the fashion world, but it is the anonymous pattern maker such as Mrs. Small who translates designers' concepts into reality and fiscal reason. Working from a designer's rough sketch, the cutter must turn the drawing into a three-dimensional garment, which then goes to full production.

The job straddles the gap between art and manufacturing. While sticking to the designer's intent, the pattern maker must be mindful of production costs, which climb sharply as the design becomes more complex. Mrs. Small recently told a designer, for example, that a double-needle stitch on a shirt would be too expensive, and she recommended instead a less expensive way of stitching.

The post also is impervious to computerization. Machines can't be programmed to sense the hang and balance of a dress, or to ensure that a blouse won't be too revealing. "You have to interpret what the designer wants," says Mrs. Small, 27. "That's why this would be hard to computerize. It isn't always cut and dried."

Charles F. Sortino, who heads his own New York pattern-making company and who trained Mrs. Small, says the job requires a knack for "making the patterns fit while still keeping the style. If you don't have both, it won't sell."

Subject to fashion's ever-changing whims, the job also is subject to constant deadline pressure. Mrs. Small tells a visitor that she is still recovering from a week of designing more than 100 patterns for buyers at Sears, Roebuck and J.C. Penney, the company's two biggest customers. " 'As soon as possible' means nothing to me because everything is A.S.A.P.," she says.

Despite its strains, Mrs. Small loves her job, which she says pays in the mid $40,000 range. She recognized her affinity for such work as a child cutting out paper dolls. Growing up in New York City in the borough of Queens, she attended the High School of Fashion Industries and the Fashion Institute of Technology and worked at several apparel firms before joining Winer Industries in 1983.

She says her ultimate satisfaction is in seeing one of her garments on a store rack. "There's the result of all my hard work, and people are buying it."

Take the designer's sketch for a polyester pleated blouse she is working on. She outlines half of the back of the blouse on a piece of soft paper, draping it over a lifesize mannequin to check for proper proportions. She repeats the process for the front, which is slightly shorter than the back to account for a dropped shoulder, and for the left sleeve. Mrs. Small drapes the paper cutout on the mannequin and marks where the pleats appear best—usually over the apex of the bust.

Although she confesses that her own eclectic tastes don't include polyester blouses (she is wearing a Western-cut, tie-died silk dress adorned with brass studs), "it still must look fabulous."

Mrs. Small transfers the paper pattern to a piece of muslin, which will allow the first chance to view the design in three dimensions. She drapes the muslin over the mannequin, checking for the placement of the pleats and the proper hang. Once everything checks out, she transfers the paper pattern to hard cardboard, which is sent to the pattern cutters who make a sample garment in the actual material. With the buyer's approval, the garment will go into full production.

Source: Seth H. Lubove, Pivotal People: In the Computer Age, Certain Workers Are Still Vital to Success," *Wall Street Journal*, August 3, 1987, p. 1. Reprinted by permission of *The Wall Street Journal*, © Dow Jones & Company, Inc., 1987. All rights reserved.

CASE QUESTIONS

1. What characteristics of the pattern cutter's job make it resistant to computerization?

2. Can you think of any ways in which the process of turning a design into a pattern might be aided by computers?

3. What other jobs can you think of that resist computerization?

Programming in BASIC

APPENDIX

This appendix presents several series of related BASIC programs. In each series an elementary version of the problem is solved using relatively elementary BASIC syntax. Then the limitations of the solution are indicated and more advanced syntax is applied to produce a more complete solution to the problem.

Mastery of a programming language entails the ability to modify existing programs to meet changing needs. It also implies the ability to find and correct programming errors without introducing any additional errors. Each series of programs is accompanied by an illustration of program modifications and some common programming errors.

Rudimentary BASIC

Our first series of programs illustrates the rudiments of BASIC. We will learn how to perform simple arithmetic operations. We will also learn some basic techniques for inputting data and outputting information.

Jill Dupuis wants to know how much money she will make this summer if she takes a job paying $175 a week for 8 weeks. While she could calculate this amount by hand or with an electronic calculator, she chose to write a small BASIC program as follows:

First Program

```
100 REM SIMPLE ARITHMETIC PROGRAM
200 LET T = 175 * 8
300 PRINT T
999 END
```

BASIC programs are composed of a series of numbered *instructions*, also called BASIC *statements*. The numbers, called *line numbers*, serve to identify the instructions. In the most common version of BASIC that runs on the IBM PC, line numbers must be positive whole numbers in the range 0 to 65529. Most programs use 3- or 4-digit line numbers. Typically programmers number their instructions by 10s. This choice of line numbers enables them to insert new instructions between two existing instructions without renumbering. Whenever possible, a given instruction is identified by the same line number for each program in a series. Before examining this program line by line, we introduce two key elements of BASIC: constants and variables.

Constants. *Constants* are items whose values do not change during the life of the program; in the example just given, 175 and 8 are constants. These constants are also called *numeric constants* because they have numeric values and may be used in arithmetic. Other examples of numeric constants include 3.14159, 1.80, and −40. In addition to numeric constants, BASIC can process strings. A *string* is a combination of numbers, letters, and other characters such as the comma or the dollar sign. Strings may be used for identification purposes; they are not normally used for arithmetic.

Variables. *Variables* are items whose value may change during the life of the program. This sample program contains a single numeric variable, here given the label T. During program execution a storage location in main memory is set aside for the variable T. Whenever the program refers to the variable T, the computer processes the current contents of that specific memory location. The programmer does not know the precise location of the variable T in memory. The computer does not "know" that the program is using the variable T to refer to the total income.

We next proceed to dissect the program line by line.

```
100 REM SIMPLE ARITHMETIC PROGRAM
```

REM is an abbreviation for remark. This instruction is included in the program for documentation purposes. Removal of the entire line does not affect program results. However, REM statements are important because they can be used to describe in plain English what the program is supposed to do. Both beginning and experienced programmers are advised to use REM statements liberally to clarify details that may not be obvious from looking at the undocumented program.

```
200 LET T = 175 * 8
```

The LET statement is used for arithmetic operations. This statement directs the computer to multiply 175 by 8 and place the result in the memory location T. In technical terms, the variable T is *assigned* the value 175 times 8. Note the use of the symbol * for multiplication. The computer generates the result 1400 (and not 1,400). This result is stored in the computer in the variable T but is not output until a PRINT statement is executed.

```
300 PRINT T
```

The PRINT statement directs the computer to generate output, in this case the result of the summer earnings calculation. Programmers can invoke different options of the PRINT statement to control the form of the output. In this simplest case the result 1400 is displayed on the monitor without any explanation.

```
999 END
```

FIGURE A-1

An Elementary BASIC Program

This program contains two BASIC commands, LIST and RUN. The program produces an unidentified result.

```
LIST
100 REM   SIMPLE ARITHMETIC PROGRAM
200 LET T = 175 * 8
300 PRINT T
999 END
Ok
RUN
 1400
Ok
```

This statement is used to indicate the end of the program. In most versions of BASIC the END statement must have the largest line number in the program. Many programmers choose line numbers such as 999 or 9999 to identify the END statement.

Once the program has been entered, it is easy to display and test. First enter the BASIC command LIST. LIST displays the program statements in numerical order, independently of the order in which they were entered into the computer. The results of this command are shown at the top of Figure A-1. In this version of BASIC the Ok signifies that the computer is waiting for a BASIC command or an instruction to be entered. Next enter the BASIC command RUN, producing the results shown at the bottom of Figure A-1.

Enter, LIST, and RUN the program. If no errors occurred during program entry, when the program is run it displays the number 1400 on the monitor. If the program produces a result other than 1400, reexamine the list of program statements and determine the probable cause of error. Then correct the program by retyping the entire BASIC statement that is in error. It may take a while to determine the cause of error, but once it is determined, the program can be retested rapidly. When making several modifications it is a good idea to LIST the modified program.

Second Program

The first sample program is abstractly correct but leaves much to be desired. For example, the output produced is unintelligible (except perhaps to the programmer). Even if the programmer can understand the output generated, he or she will probably forget the significance of 1400 a few days after writing the program. The next program introduces the use of character or string constants to make the output clearer. Before modifying the program output, we modify the documentation by adding several REM statements that identify the names of the variables. We also render the program more flexible by changing the way that it obtains the data to be processed. The results of running this program are shown in Figure A-2.

```
100 REM    ARITHMETIC PROGRAM
110 REM    VARIABLE NAME
120 REM    T   TOTAL INCOME
130 REM    S   SALARY PER WEEK
140 REM    W   WEEKS WORKED
190 READ S,W
200 LET T = S * W
300 PRINT "The total income =";T
800 DATA 175,8
999 END
```

We consider only the lines in the program that illustrate points that have not been previously covered.

```
120 REM    T   TOTAL INCOME
```

The rules for composing variable names differ from one version of BASIC to another. However, no version of BASIC permits the "natural" name TOTAL INCOME. Such a name is illegal because the computer interprets the blank space as a separation between two items. The REM statement allows the programmer to associate a "natural" name such as TOTAL INCOME with a legal variable name such as T. Many teachers and installations refuse to consider a BASIC program complete unless it includes REM statements that describe every variable used within the program.

```
200 READ S,W      and     800 DATA 175,8
```

This program uses the pair of statements known as the READ statement and the DATA statement to assign the value 175 to the variable S and the value 8 to the variable W. The effect of these two statements is equivalent to the two statements LET S = 175 and LET W = 8.

```
300 PRINT "The total income =";T
```

This PRINT statement provides more understandable output than the PRINT statement of the first program. It consists of three parts:
1. The string constant or *literal*, "The total income =", is printed exactly as it appears, except for the quotes. This phrase describes the numeric value printed.
2. The current value of the variable T, namely, 1400, is printed. Proper coordination of literals and variables printed is an essential element of legible output.
3. The semicolon causes the next item to be printed immediately after the last item. In this case the space that follows the equal sign stems from the fact that a positive number is always preceded by a space when printed.

Modifying the Program. Students can test their understanding of a program by making changes in it. For example, to calculate James O'Leary's summer earnings at $160 a week for 9 weeks, replace line 800 with the following BASIC statement:

FIGURE A-2

A Program with Named Variables

This BASIC program calculates a student's summer earnings.

```
LIST
100 REM    ARITHMETIC PROGRAM
110 REM    VARIABLE NAME
120 REM    T   TOTAL INCOME
130 REM    S   SALARY PER WEEK
140 REM    W   WEEKS WORKED
190 READ S,W
200 LET T = S * W
300 PRINT "The total income =";T
800 DATA 175,8
999 END
Ok
RUN
The total income = 1400
Ok
```

800 DATA 160,9. The rest of the program remains unchanged. We could produce more complete output by adding the following instructions:

    280 PRINT "Weekly Salary";S

and

    290 PRINT "Number of Weeks Worked";W

Common Errors. Although BASIC is considered one of the easiest programming languages to learn, making and correcting errors is an inevitable part of the programming process. We present some common errors here. It is advisable to keep track of all errors made to avoid making the same error twice.

Typing errors occur frequently. If words such as READ, REM, or LET are misspelled, the program will not run to completion. For example, in the preceding program if we typed 210 LTE T = S * W the system would produce a message such as

    Error in line 210

This is an example of a syntax error. (We misspelled LET.) A more difficult error to locate is using a DATA statement that does not contain enough items to satisfy the accompanying READ statement. For example, if we incorrectly coded the DATA statement

    800 DATA 175

the program would read the value of S in line 190 correctly. However, when it tried to read W there would be no data item to read. A typical error message in this case is

```
Out of data in line 190
```

The READ statement has failed.

Another error is inverting the order of the lines 190 and 200, calculating the value of T before obtaining the values of S and W. This is an example of a logic error; the program cannot calculate the summer earnings without knowing both the weekly rate and the number of weeks worked. Finding logic errors in large programs can be a lengthy, painstaking task.

Third Program

The power of the computer comes from its ability to process data under different conditions, for example, to award a bonus to some employees and not others. We consider the case in which an employee who has worked more than 10 weeks is paid a bonus of $50. An employee who has worked 10 weeks or less does not get any bonus, in other words gets a bonus of $0. The following program introduces a new BASIC instruction, the IF . . . THEN instruction, to produce the correct pay for all employees, including both those who earn a bonus and those who do not. The results of running this program are shown in Figure A-3.

```
100 REM    ARITHMETIC PROGRAM
110 REM    VARIABLE NAMES
120 REM    T   TOTAL INCOME
130 REM    S   SALARY PER WEEK
140 REM    W   WEEKS WORKED
150 REM    B   BONUS   $50 if worked more than 10 weeks
160 REM                $0  if worked 10 weeks or less
190 READ S,W
210 LET B = 0
220 IF W > 10 THEN B = 50
250 LET T = S * W + B
280 PRINT "Weekly Salary";S
290 PRINT "Number of Weeks";W
300 PRINT "The total income =";T
800 DATA 175,8
999 END
```

```
150 REM    B   BONUS $50 if worked more than 10 weeks
160 REM                $0  if worked 10 weeks or less
```

Whenever a new variable is introduced in the program, it should be documented with the aid of one or more REM statements. Note that these REM statements not only indicate the variable name but also describe the values taken in different cases.

```
210 LET B = 0
```

FIGURE A-3

IF . . . THEN Statements

This BASIC program employs an IF statement to calculate a student's summer earnings, printing both intermediate and final results (a). Then the weekly salary and number of weeks worked are changed and the program is rerun, producing a different result (b).

```
LIST
100 REM   ARITHMETIC PROGRAM
110 REM   VARIABLE NAMES
120 REM   T   TOTAL INCOME
130 REM   S   SALARY PER WEEK
140 REM   W   WEEKS WORKED
150 REM   B   BONUS   $50 if worked more than 10 weeks
160 REM               $0  if worked 10 weeks or less
190 READ S,W
210 LET B = 0
220 IF W > 10 THEN B = 50
250 LET T = S * W + B
280 PRINT "Weekly Salary";S
290 PRINT "Number of Weeks Worked";W
300 PRINT "The total income =";T
800 DATA 175,8
999 END
Ok
RUN
Weekly Salary 175
Number of Weeks Worked 8
The total income = 1400
Ok
```

There are several equivalent ways of programming the bonus calculation for this problem. We initially accord a bonus of $0 to every employee (line 210). This policy does not lead to overpayment of any employees but simplifies the IF . . . THEN statement used in the next line.

```
220 IF W > 10 THEN B = 50
```

The *IF . . . THEN statement* asks a Yes or No question and selects an activity to perform depending on whether the answer was Yes or No. It is an example of the selection structure discussed in Chapter 7. In this case the question asked is, "Is the number of weeks worked greater than (>) 10?" If the answer is Yes, bonus B is set to $50. If the answer is No, no change is made; in other words, the bonus B remains at $0.

```
250 LET T = S * W + B
```

This statement is carried out for all employees. It calculates the total income T including the bonus for everyone; however, the bonus is $0 for those who have not worked more than 10 weeks. The program proceeds to print T. The program has fully isolated the bonus question and never raises the matter of weeks worked again. The coming together of the Yes and No cases is an important aspect of structured programming.

Testing Programs. It is rare for a large program to work properly when it is first written. Chapter 7 discussed how important it is for programmers to test all programs with sample data called *test data*. The more complicated the program, the greater the volume and complexity of test data required in order for the programmer to be reasonably certain that the program performs as desired. A rule of thumb states that each IF . . . THEN statement should be tested for both the Yes and No branches. In other words, the above program should be tested for at least one employee who has worked more than 10 weeks and at least one employee who has worked 10 weeks or less. Note the use of statements 280 and 290 to identify the different cases.

Programs to Modify

1. Modify the bonus program to calculate a bonus of $25 a week for each week worked over 10 weeks.
2. Modify the bonus program to deduct income tax at the rate of 15 percent on the first $1000 of income and 20 percent on any income over $1000. Use appropriate PRINT statements to indicate the amount of income tax deducted, the gross salary, and the net salary. Be sure to use adequate test data.

Programs to Write

1. Write a BASIC program that reads a student's numeric grades and calculates the average grade. Indicate whether or not the student has failed one or more courses (grade < 50). Assume that each student takes exactly four courses.
2. Write a BASIC program that reads a student's four numeric grades and assigns the letter grade. The program assigns the student a letter grade according to the following scale:

90 – 100	A
80 – 89.9	B
65 – 79.9	C
50 – 64.9	D
below 50	F

Include test data for the five different grades.

Branching to Another Instruction

We stated earlier that the IF . . . THEN statement asks a Yes or No question and carries out one of two activities depending on whether the answer is Yes or No. But what if we want to carry out two or more activities in the case of a Yes or a No answer? For example, what if we want to award each employee who worked more than 10 weeks a bonus of $50 and print the message that the employee has earned a bonus? There are several ways to handle this common situation, depending on the version of BASIC used. Some methods are considered better than others.

Since the invention of BASIC in 1964, it has been discovered that the originally supplied version of the IF . . . THEN statement can cause programming problems. Consequently, its use is no longer recommended. We present this "solution" because many versions of BASIC do not provide a better one.

```
220 IF W > 10 THEN 240
230 GOTO 250
240 LET B = 50
245 PRINT "Bonus of $50"
250 LET T = S * W + B
```

This five-line program segment is somewhat complicated. In fact, its very complication is the reason why it is not recommended. Line 220 asks a Yes or No question, namely, whether the number of weeks worked is greater than 10. If it is greater than 10, the program next executes line 240. In this case the program calculates the bonus of $50 and then prints "Bonus of $50" before calculating the total salary in line 250. If the number of weeks worked is 10 or less, there is no bonus. In this case the program ignores the latter part of line 220 and continues to the next instruction at line 230, which directs the computer to skip over the two subsequent instructions. Line 230 commands the program to proceed to line 250, the calculation of the total salary. Because lines 240 and 245 were skipped, there is no bonus and the message "Bonus of $50" is not printed.

Many people find it difficult to code and even understand the preceding BASIC program segment. For example, it is easy to forget to enter line 230, which may not seem to be an essential part of the program. If line 230 is forgotten, the program calculates the salary correctly for employees who worked 10 weeks or more, and incorrectly for the others. The difficulty of applying the IF and GOTO statements correctly is compounded when the program contains a series of interrelated IFs. The following version of the IF statement, the IF . . . THEN . . . ELSE statement, is somewhat easier to work with. It is available on the version of BASIC supplied with the IBM PC and compatibles but not on the version of BASIC supplied with the Apple II series of computers.

The IF . . . THEN . . . ELSE Statement. The IF . . . THEN . . . ELSE statement is illustrated in the following program segment.

```
220 IF W > 10 THEN 240 ELSE 250
240 LET B = 50
245 PRINT "Bonus of $50"
250 LET T = S * W + B
```

Line 220 now indicates two line numbers. The first, line number 240, identifies the instruction to be executed in the case of a Yes answer to the Yes or No question. The second, line number 250, identifies the instruction to be executed in the case of a No answer to the Yes or No question. This program segment is easier to write than the previous one because an instruction redirecting the computer (line 230) has been eliminated.

Many programming students and programmers find the use of line numbers confusing. It is more straightforward to tell the computer *what* to do next, rather than telling it *which line number* to execute next, as we did in the previous example.

Some recent versions of BASIC, such as Microsoft's QuickBASIC 3.0 and Borland's TurboBasic, allow the programmer to work with or without line numbers and to set up the following type of IF statement:

IF Yes or No question
THEN actions to take in case of a Yes answer
ELSE actions to take in case of a No answer
END of the IF statement

Intermediate BASIC

This section contains three programs that calculate the true rate of interest on an installment loan. Students who are thinking of borrowing money for an installment purchase can apply these programs to calculate the true rate of interest.

The true annual interest rate (R) depends on several variables: the number of payments per year (P), the total finance charges (C), the amount financed (F), and the total number of payments (N). To simplify matters, we assume that there is no down payment. The formula follows:

$$R = \frac{PC \times 100}{F \times (N+1)}$$

First Program

Dom Pelligrini, a business student at XYZ State University, wants to buy his first car. The model he likes costs $3000. Since Pelligrini spent his existing assets on tuition and books, he'll have to negotiate a loan. The salesperson suggests purchasing the car with no money down and payments of $100 a month for 36 months. Pelligrini does a quick mental calculation and figures that he will pay $600 in finance charges on a $3600 loan, or about 16.6 percent. But since the loan is for three years, he estimates that he will pay about 5.5 percent a year. He thinks this is a good interest rate, but before buying the car he writes a BASIC program to find out the true interest rate charged for the car loan. The results of running this program are shown in Figure A-4.

```
010 REM Initial Program to Calculate
020 REM    The Annual Interest Rate
030 REM List of Variables
040 REM   P   Payments per Year
050 REM   C   Total Finance Charges
060 REM   F   Amount Financed
```

```
070 REM   N   Number of Payments
080 REM   R   Annual Interest Rate
230 PRINT "Enter Number of Payments per Year"
240 INPUT P
250 PRINT "Enter Total Finance Charges"
255 PRINT "Do Not Enter a $ or a ,"
260 INPUT C
270 PRINT "Enter Amount Financed Do Not Enter a $ or a ,"
280 INPUT F
290 PRINT "Enter Number of Payments Over Life of Loan"
300 INPUT N
310 LET R = 2*P*C*100/(F*(N+1))
320 PRINT "Annual Interest Rate (%) ";R .
999 END
```

This program allows the user to enter data at the workstation and obtain different results; depending on variables such as the number of payments, the user reruns the program, changing the data entered. It is important to realize that the user need not be the one who wrote the program. In fact, the user may not know BASIC at all. The programmer must write the program in such a way that the user can apply it easily. The PRINT statements provide the output seen by the user. They are the means by which the programmer communicates with the user, who has no access to the REM statements.

```
230 PRINT "Enter Number of Payments per Year"
240 INPUT P
```

During program execution line 230 will cause the computer to output the following message:

```
Enter Number of Payments per Year
```

This statement, known as a *prompt*, explains in plain English (or other human language) the type of data that the user should enter in response to line 240.

Line 240 contains an INPUT statement, which accepts data from a user at the keyboard. When the program executes an instruction such as 240 INPUT P, it stops and displays a question mark. The computer is waiting for the user at the keyboard to enter a value designating the number of payments per year. This value will be assigned to the variable P, which is available for later reference in the program.

The INPUT statement replaces a LET statement or the pair of statements READ . . . DATA. The INPUT statement has the advantage of permitting flexible data entry. It has the disadvantage of stopping the program, which cannot proceed until the user has entered data. Easily understood, unambiguous prompts are necessary for user satisfaction.

In response to the prompt issued by line 230, Pelligrini enters the value 12. The program then resumes execution with line 250.

```
250 PRINT "Enter Total Finance Charges"
255 PRINT "Do Not Enter a $ or a ,"
260 INPUT C
```

FIGURE A-4

INPUT Statements

```
800 DATA 150,11
RUN
Weekly Salary 150
Number of Weeks Worked 11
The total income = 1700
Ok
            (a)


LIST
10 REM Initial Program to Calculate
20 REM    The Annual Interest Rate
30 REM List of Variables
40 REM   P   Payments per Year
50 REM   C   Total Finance Charges
60 REM   F   Amount Financed
70 REM   N   Number of Payments
80 REM   R   Annual Interest Rate
230 PRINT "Enter Number of Payments per Year"
240 INPUT P
250 PRINT "Enter Total Finance Charges"
255 PRINT "Do Not Enter a $ or a ,"
260 INPUT C
270 PRINT "Enter Amount Financed Do Not Enter a $ or a ,"
280 INPUT F
290 PRINT "Enter Number of Payments Over Life of Loan"
300 INPUT N
310 LET R = 2*P*C*100/(F*/(N+1))
320 PRINT "Annual Interest Rate (%) ";R
999 END
Ok
RUN
Enter Number of Payments per Year
? 12
Enter Total Finance Charges
Do Not Enter a $ or a ,
? 600
Enter Amount Financed Do Not Enter a $ or a ,
? 3000
Enter Number of Payments Over Life of Loan
? 36
Annual Interest Rate (%)   12.97297
Ok
            (b)
```

This BASIC program employs INPUT statements to calculate the true rate of interest, in response to data entered by the user at the keyboard.

In response to the prompts, Pelligrini enters the value 600, the difference between the total amount repaid, 3600, and the amount financed, 3000. The programmer specifically stated in lines 250 and 255 that the user must not enter a dollar sign or a comma. In the absence of this indication, the user is likely to enter a dollar sign or a comma, which the program is unable to process.

```
270 PRINT "Enter Amount Financed Do Not Enter a $ or a ,"
280 INPUT F
```

In response to the prompt, Pelligrini enters 3000. To avoid possible confusion, the prompt repeats the message not to enter a dollar sign or a comma.

```
290 PRINT "Enter Number of Payments Over Life of Loan"
300 INPUT N
```

In response to the prompt, Pelligrini enters 36.

```
310 LET R = 2*P*C*100/(F*(N+1))
320 PRINT "Annual Interest Rate (%) ";R
```

Hierarchy of Operations. BASIC uses a set of rules known as the *hierarchy of operations* to determine the order in which to carry out arithmetic operations. These rules are as follows:

1. First perform operations within parentheses. If there are several sets of parentheses, begin with the innermost set and proceed to the outermost set.
2. Next carry out exponentiation. [*Note*: In this version of BASIC, 3 to the power of 2 (commonly called 3 squared) is written 3^2.]
3. Next perform multiplication and division. If there are several multiplication and division operations, work from left to right.
4. Finally, perform addition and subtraction. If there are several addition and subtraction operations, work from left to right.

The LET instruction expresses the formula for the true annual rate of interest. It is evaluated according to the hierarchy of operations. The PRINT statement provides the output. By examining the program output we see that instead of 5.5 percent, Pelligrini would be paying almost 13 percent annual interest.

Common Errors. One common error that is likely to occur when a program undergoes frequent revision is failure to coordinate a prompt with the data to be entered. For example:

```
270 PRINT "Enter Amount Financed Do Not Enter a $ or a ,"
280 INPUT N
```

where N is the number of payments per year. Another common error with formulas like the one in line 310 is omitting parentheses. Try rerunning the program with the following incorrect instruction:

```
310 LET R = 2*P*C*100/F*N +1
```

Second Program

You will recall from the discussion of structured programming in Chapter 7 that there are three fundamental building blocks of structured programming: sequence, selection, and repetition. All previous programs illustrated the sequential structure, in which the instructions follow each other in sequential order. Some of these programs illustrated the selection structure, in which an IF statement directs the computer to carry out one or another activity depending on the answer to a Yes or No question. The next BASIC program illustrates the repetitive structure known as the FOR . . . NEXT loop. We illustrate use of the FOR . . . NEXT loop with a short program before applying it to the interest rate calculation.

The FOR . . . NEXT Loop. In the *FOR . . . NEXT loop* all instructions enclosed within the FOR and the NEXT are repeated. The FOR statement indicates the number of repetitions.

```
300 FOR I = 1 TO 4
310 PRINT "Counter is now";I
320 NEXT I
350 PRINT "The End"
999 END
```

This program prints

```
Counter is now 1
Counter is now 2
Counter is now 3
Counter is now 4
The End
```

Let's see how this program works. First the program executes line 300. It sets the variable I to 1 and then checks to see if I exceeds the limit of 4. Because this variable is used to count the number of repetitions, it is called a *counter*. Since the counter does not exceed the limit, the program proceeds to instruction 310, printing the first line of output. Then the program executes line 320 NEXT I, increasing the value of I to 2 and returning to the FOR in line 300. Once again the program checks the counter to see if it exceeds the limit of 4. The program then repeats the previous steps of printing output in line 310, increasing the counter in line 320, and returning to line 300 to see if the counter exceeds the limit. This repetitive processing is known as *looping*. The program keeps looping until finally the NEXT statement sets the value of I to 5. Then the program returns to check the value of I against the limit of 4. Because I is greater than 4, the program proceeds to the line after the NEXT, in this case the PRINT statement at line 350. It prints the closing message and the program terminates.

With a slight modification, the FOR . . . NEXT loop can count by increments other than 1. This procedure is handled by the *STEP* clause. If the first line in the preceding example is changed to

```
300 FOR I = 1 TO 4 STEP 2
```

the counter I would be increased by 2 at each repetition and the program would print

```
Counter is now 1
Counter is now 3
The End
```

To count backwards, a negative STEP is used. While it is legal to write an instruction such as

```
300 FOR I = 1 TO 4 STEP 1
```

in practice this is rarely done because a STEP of 1 is assumed when the STEP is not used.

Character Variables. *Character variables*, also known as *string variables*, are variables that may take on alphanumeric values such as "Robert" or "1245 First Avenue." Character variables are denoted by a letter followed by a $, for example, N$. Some systems permit a wider range of character variables, such as N4$. Character variables are assigned values as in the following statement:

```
100 LET N$ = "Robert"
```

The following program uses a FOR . . . NEXT loop and character variables to perform four different calculations for Dom Pelligrini and his friend Nancy Watson. The results of running this program are shown in Figure A-5.

```
010 REM Initial Program to Calculate
020 REM    The Annual Interest Rate
030 REM List of Variables
040 REM  P  Payments per Year
050 REM  C  Total Finance Charges
060 REM  F  Amount Financed
070 REM  N  Number of Payments
080 REM  R  Annual Interest Rate
090 REM  I  Counter FOR...NEXT loop
100 REM  H  How Many Calculations
110 REM  N$ Name of Individual Requesting the Calculation
130 PRINT "Enter the Number of Calculations Desired"
160 INPUT H
200 FOR I = 1 TO H
210     PRINT "Enter Name of Person Requesting Calculation"
220     INPUT N$
230     PRINT "Enter Number of Payments per Year"
240     INPUT P
250     PRINT "Enter Total Finance Charges"
255     PRINT "Do Not Enter a $ or a ,"
260     INPUT C
270     PRINT "Enter Amount Financed Do Not Enter a $ or a ,"
280     INPUT F
290     PRINT "Enter Number of Payments Over Life of Loan"
300     INPUT N
```

```
310     LET R = 2*P*C*100/(F*(N+1))
320     PRINT "Annual Interest Rate (%) ";R
330     PRINT "Calculation Done For ";N$
400 NEXT I
999 END

210     PRINT "Enter Name of Person Requesting Calculation"
220     INPUT N$
```

It is not necessary to place quotes around a string such as "Robert" entered via the INPUT statement. However, quotes are necessary in the case of a string such as "Jones, Robert" to inform the computer that a single name is being entered. This restriction is necessary because in BASIC the comma is normally used to separate items. In the absence of quotes, the program assumes that there are two data items, Jones and Robert.

```
200 FOR I = 1 TO H; 400 NEXT I
```

This program performs H interest rate calculations. Each calculation involves the instructions in lines 200 to 400. It is highly recommended that all instructions within a FOR . . . NEXT loop be indented. This makes the program clearer and can be quite helpful in finding errors.

Common Errors. A common syntax error is writing a FOR without a corresponding NEXT or vice versa. A more difficult error to detect is the incorrect placement of instructions with respect to the FOR . . . NEXT loop. (Remember that lines inside the FOR . . . NEXT loop are executed H number of times, whereas lines outside the FOR . . . NEXT loop are executed only once.) For example, if we placed lines 210 and 220 before the FOR statement, the resulting program would prompt for the name of the person requesting the calculation only once. Placing the prompt (line 210) prior to the FOR statement and placing the INPUT statement (line 220) after the FOR statement also results in a single prompt for the name of the person requesting the calculation. However, at each execution of the FOR . . . NEXT loop the program stops and waits for unspecified input. The user will definitely be confused by such a program.

Third Program

In this program we examine an alternative way of handling repetition, the WHILE . . . WEND loop. We also look at the two processes of counting and taking a total. These processes do not involve any new instructions but rather a new way of combining familiar instructions. First we look at a new way of looping.

The WHILE . . . WEND Loop. The very useful FOR . . . NEXT loop has an important drawback: It requires that either the programmer or the user state how many repetitions are required. In many cases no one knows in advance the number of repetitions required; perhaps the calculations should continue as long as data remains to be calculated. Many users react to the prompt "Enter the number of

FIGURE A-5

FOR . . . NEXT Statements

This BASIC program employs a FOR . . . NEXT loop to calculate the true rate of interest, in response to a series of data entered by users at the keyboard.

```
LIST
10  REM  Initial Program to Calculate
20  REM     The Annual Interest Rate
30  REM  List of Variables
40  REM    P   Payments per Year
50  REM    C   Total Finance Charges
60  REM    F   Amount Financed
70  REM    N   Number of Payments
80  REM    R   Annual Interest Rate
90  REM    I   Counter FOR...NEXT loop
100 REM    H   How Many Calculations
110 REM    N$ Name of Individual Requesting the Calculation
130 PRINT "Enter the Number of Calculations Desired"
160 INPUT H
200 FOR I = 1 TO H
210     PRINT "Enter Name of Person Requesting Calculation"
220     INPUT N$
230     PRINT "Enter Number of Payments per Year"
240     INPUT P
250     PRINT "Enter Total Finance Charges"
255     PRINT "Do Not Enter a $ or a ,"
260     INPUT C
270     PRINT "Enter Amount Financed Do Not Enter a $ or a ,"
280     INPUT F
290     PRINT "Enter Number of Payments Over Life of Loan"
300     INPUT N
310     LET R = 2*P*C*100/(F*(N+1))
320     PRINT "Annual Interest Rate (%) ";R
330     PRINT "Calculation Done For ";N$
440 NEXT I
999 END
Ok
RUN
Enter the Number of Calculations Desired
? 4
Enter Name of Person Requesting Calculation
? Dom
Enter Number of Payments per Year
? 12
Enter Total Finance Charges
Do Not Enter a $ or a ,
? 600
Enter Amount Financed Do Not Enter a $ or a,
? 3600
Enter Number of Payments Over Life of Loan
? 36
Annual Interest Rate (%)   10.81081
Calculation Done for Dom
```

```
Enter Name of Person Requesting Calculation
? Dom
Enter Number of Payments per Year
? 12
Enter Total Finance Charges
Do Not Enter a $ or a ,
? 1000
Enter Amount Financed Do Not Enter a $ or a ,
? 3000
Enter Number of Payments Over Life of Loan
? 48
Annual Interest Rate (%)   16.32653
Calculation Done for Dom

Enter Name of Person Requesting Calculation
? Nancy
Enter Number of Payments per Year
? 6
Enter Total Finance Charges
Do Not Enter a $ or a ,
? 600
Enter Amount Financed Do Not Enter a $ or a ,
? 3000
Enter Number of Payments Over Life of Loan
? 18
Annual Interest Rate (%)   12.63158
Calculation Done For Nancy

Enter Name of Person Requesting Calculation
? Nancy
Enter Number of Payments per Year
? 6
Enter Total Finance Charges
Do Not Enter a $ or a ,
? 1000
Enter Amount Financed Do Not Enter a $ or a ,
? 3000
Enter Number of Payments Over Life of Loan
? 24
Annual Interest Rate (%)   16
Calculation Done For Nancy
Ok
```

calculations desired" by asking, "Why should I be bothered counting the number of data items to process? I thought that's why we got the computer, so it can relieve me of the tiresome and error-prone job of counting."

The WHILE . . . WEND loop repeats a series of instructions as long as a given variable, called the *control variable*, is not equal to 0. When the control variable is equal to 0, the program stops looping and then executes the instruction following the WEND. The control variable must initially have a value other than 0 for the WHILE . . . WEND loop to function properly. During program execution the control variable must attain the value 0. If not, the program contains an *infinite loop*; it repeats calculations until the computer is shut off.

The next program illustrates the use of the WHILE . . . WEND loop to calculate the interest rate for an unspecified number of cases. The results of running this program are shown in Figure A-6. Before examining this program in detail we consider two important processes: counting and summing.

Counting and Summing. The two somewhat similar processes of counting and summing a series of values are found in almost every application. Remember that the average of a series of values is their sum divided by their count. The count and the sum are obtained in a three-step process:

1. Before entering the WHILE . . . WEND loop, *initialize* the count T and the sum S to 0. In this program these variables are initialized in lines 160 and 170.
2. Within the WHILE . . . WEND loop, *increase* the count by 1 and the sum by F, the amount financed. In this program these variables are increased in lines 340 and 350. Note that the variable S is increased by F only after the most recent value of F has been input (see line 280).
3. After exiting the WHILE . . . WEND loop, *print* the count and the sum. In this program these variables are printed in lines 420 and 430.

Note that neither counting nor summing requires any new BASIC instructions. However, each requires three sets of instructions, which must be placed in the right order for correct results. A detailed explanation of the WHILE . . . WEND loop in this program follows:

```
180 LET MORE = 1; 200 WHILE MORE
```

The variable MORE carries one of two values during the program, namely, 1 or 0. The value 1 signifies "Yes, there are more sets of data to enter and process." The value 0 signifies "No, there are no more sets of data to enter and process." These values are documented in line 105. Line 180 initializes MORE to 1 as a prelude to processing. LINE 200 repeats processing of instructions in the WHILE . . . WEND loop, namely, lines 210 to 390. Repetition occurs as long as MORE = 1.

```
390     IF (R$="Y") OR (R$="y") THEN MORE=1 ELSE MORE = 0
```

This statement can be interpreted as follows: If the string variable R$ is equal to either Y or y, then the variable MORE is set to 1; otherwise it is set to 0. Note the use of quotes and parentheses, which are both mandatory in this case.

```
440 LET A = S / T
```

The average of a series of items is equal to the sum of the items divided by the number of items. It is calculated only after all items have been counted and totaled, in other words, after exiting the loop.

```
010 REM Third Program to Calculate
020 REM    The Annual Interest Rate
030 REM List of Variables
040 REM  P  Payments per Year
050 REM  C  Total Finance Charges
060 REM  F  Amount Financed
070 REM  N  Number of Payments
080 REM  R  Annual Interest Rate
090 REM  R$ More calculations if Yes Y or y
100 REM  MORE control variable for WHILE...WEND loop
105 REM   MORE = 1 continue   MORE = 0 stop repetition
110 REM  N$ Name of Individual Requesting the Calculation
130 REM  T Total Number of Calculations
140 REM  S Sum of Amount Financed
150 REM  A Average Amount Financed
160 LET T = 0
170 LET S = 0
180 LET MORE = 1
200 WHILE MORE
210    PRINT "Enter Name of Person Requesting Calculation"
220    INPUT N$
230    PRINT "Enter Payments per Year"
240    INPUT P
250    PRINT "Enter Total Finance Charges"
255    PRINT "Do Not Enter a $ or a ,"
260    INPUT C
270    PRINT "Enter Amount Financed Do Not Enter a $ or a ,"
280    INPUT F
290    PRINT "Enter Number of Payments"
300    INPUT N
310    LET R = 2*P*C*100/(F*(N+1))
320    PRINT "Annual Interest Rate (%) ";R
330    PRINT "Calculation Done For ";N$
340    LET T = T + 1
350    LET S = S + F
360    PRINT "Do You Want Another Calculation?"
370    PRINT "Enter Y for Yes or N for No"
380    INPUT R$
390    IF (R$="Y") OR (R$="y") THEN MORE=1 ELSE MORE=0
400 WEND
410 PRINT
420 PRINT "Total Number of Calculations = ";T
430 PRINT "Total Amount Financed = $";S
440 LET A = S / T
450 PRINT "Average Amount Financed $";A
999 END
```

FIGURE A-6

WHILE . . . WEND Statements

This BASIC program employs a WHILE . . . WEND loop to calculate the true rate of interest, in response to a series of data entered by users at the keyboard.

```
LIST
10 REM Third Program to Calculate
20 REM    The Annual Interest Rate
30 REM List of Variables
40 REM   P  Payments per Year
50 REM   C  Total Finance Charges
60 REM   F  Amount Financed
70 REM   N  Number of Payments
80 REM   R  Annual Interest Rate
90 REM   R$ more calculations  if Yes  Y or y
100 REM   MORE control variable for WHILE...WEND loop
105 REM     MORE = 1 continue   MORE = 0 stop repetition
110 REM   N$ Name of Individual Requesting the Calculation
130 REM   T Total Number of Calculations
140 REM   S Sum of Amount Financed
150 REM   A Average Amount Financed
160 LET T = 0
170 LET S = 0
180 LET MORE = 1
200 WHILE MORE
210     PRINT "Enter Name of Person Requesting Calculation"
220     INPUT N$
230     PRINT "Enter Payments per Year"
240     INPUT P
250     PRINT "Enter Total Finance Charges"
255     PRINT "Do Not Enter a $ or a ,"
260     INPUT C
270     PRINT "Enter Amount Financed Do Not Enter a $ or a ,"
280     INPUT F
290     PRINT "Enter Number of Payments"
300     INPUT N
310     LET R = 2*P*C*100/(F*(N+1))
320     PRINT "Annual Interest Rate (%) ";R
330     PRINT "Calculation Done For ";N$
340     LET T = T + 1
350     LET S = S + F
360     PRINT "Do You Want Another Calculation?"
370     PRINT " Enter Y for Yes or N for No"
380     INPUT R$
390     IF (R$="Y") OR (R$="y") THEN MORE = 1 ELSE MORE = 0
400 WEND
410 PRINT
420 PRINT "Total Number of Calculations = ";T
430 PRINT "Total Amount Financed = $";S
440 LET A = S / T
450 PRINT "Average Amount Financed $";A
999 END
Ok
```

```
RUN
Enter Name of Person Requesting Calculation
? Dom
Enter Payments per Year
? 12
Enter Total Finance Charges
Do Not Enter a $ or a ,
? 600
Enter Amount Financed Do Not Enter a $ or a ,
? 3000
Enter Number of Payments
? 36
Annual Interest Rate (%)   12.97297
Calculation Done For Dom
Do You Want Another Calculation?
Enter Y for Yes or N for No
? y
Enter Name of Person Requesting Calculation
? Nancy
Enter Payments per Year
? 6
Enter Total Finance Charges
Do Not Enter a $ or a ,
? 600
Enter Amount Financed Do Not Enter a $ or a ,
? 3000
Enter Number of Payments
? 18
Annual Interest Rate (%)   12.63158
Calculation Done For Nancy
Do You Want Another Calculation?
Enter Y for Yes or N for No
? n
Total Number of Calculations = 2
Total Amount Financed = $ 6000
Average Amount Financed $ 3000
Ok
```

Common Errors. As mentioned previously, a common error is the infinite loop, which occurs if the statement that may eventually set MORE to 0 (line 390) is deleted. Interestingly enough, if line 390 were not deleted but placed after the WEND statement at line 400, the result would be the same. In this case the program never gets a chance to set MORE to 0 because it never leaves the loop. As discussed earlier, the placement of statements that initialize, increase, and print the count and the sum are critical. Improperly placing one of these statements can generate incorrect results.

A more sophisticated error is the following:

```
390 IF R$="Y" THEN MORE=1 ELSE MORE=0
```

This instruction will treat a y input as equivalent to N for No, in response to the prompts "Do you want another calculation?" and "Enter Y for Yes or N for No." Here is an example of a program that is not user-friendly. The user enters what seems to be an appropriate response, and the program stops instead of continuing. Proper program testing will uncover this error.

Programs to Modify

1. Modify the program containing the FOR . . . NEXT loop so that it calculates the average amount financed and the average finance charges. Is it necessary to count the number of interest rate calculations?

2. Modify the program containing the WHILE . . . WEND loop so that it processes at most five interest rate calculations.

Programs to Write

1. Write a BASIC program that uses a FOR . . . NEXT loop to process a series of student grades. For each student, the program reads his or her numeric grades and calculates the average grade. Indicate whether or not the student has failed one or more courses (grade < 50). Assume that each student takes exactly four courses. Calculate the total number of courses taken and the average grade for the entire group of students. Supply appropriate test data.

2. Write a BASIC program that uses a WHILE . . . WEND loop to process a series of student grades. For each student, the program reads his or her four numeric grades and assigns the letter grade. The program assigns the student a letter grade according to the following scale:

90 – 100	A	50 – 64.9	D
80 – 89.9	B	below 50	F
65 – 79.9	C		

Include test data for the five different grades. Calculate the total number of courses taken and the average grade for the entire group of students.

3. *Optional.* Process student grades as in the previous two programs but use a

FOR . . . NEXT loop to handle the separate students and a WHILE . . . WEND loop to handle each individual student's grades. Do not assume that each student takes exactly four courses. Supply appropriate test data.

Arrays

Arrays are collections of numbers or strings. Common examples of arrays include income tax rates, insurance rates, sales figures per vendor or region, and student grades. The simplest type of array is a one-dimensional array, also called a *list*. An example of a one-dimensional array is a list of sales figures for each vendor in a sales office. Once a single identification, the vendor, has been supplied, the appropriate sales figure can be obtained. Two-dimensional arrays, also called *tables*, are commonly used to represent situations for which more detail is required. An example of a two-dimensional array is a table of monthly sales figures for each vendor in a sales office. A user who wants to access data from a two-dimensional array must supply two separate pieces of information: in this case the vendor and the month. A sales office could organize data in a three-dimensional array, for example, a table containing monthly sales figures for each product line for each vendor in the sales office. In theory, there is no limit to the number of dimensions that an array or table can have. In practice, most commercial applications involve arrays of three dimensions or less.

Arrays are very useful because they are an organized way to store data in memory and access it on demand. Data in arrays can be readily summarized for managers who do not need to know the details but want to see the big picture. For example, data in the two-dimensional array containing monthly sales figures for each vendor in a sales office can be summarized to produce one-dimensional arrays that contain total sales figures by month or by vendor. We will consider a series of programs illustrating arrays that might be used by a travel agency to inform its clients of the temperature at a winter destination.

The Sun Travel Agency handles flights to Kilookoo Island in the Caribbean. This site is particularly popular during the winter months because of its warm climate. Many clients want to know the temperature before deciding where to spend their winter vacation. In order to inform its clients, Sun asked the island's weather bureau to send the daily temperature reading. Because Kilookoo Island is a former British colony, the weather bureau takes the daily readings in Centigrade degrees. Most of Sun's customers prefer Fahrenheit readings. The sister-in-law of the agency's owner is a programming student and has offered to write BASIC programs for the travel agency. The following program converts Centigrade temperatures to Fahrenheit temperatures for the month of February. It does not use arrays but serves as an introduction to the other programs in the section. The results of running this program are shown in Figure A-7. (Note: Data such as 91.39999 is generated by the particular version of BASIC used. Other versions of BASIC will produce the expected value of 91.4.)

```
100 REM KILOOKOO ISLAND PROGRAM
110 REM    CONVERTS CENT. TO FAHR.
130 REM    LIST OF VARIABLES
140 REM    C  Centigrade Temperature
150 REM    F  Fahrenheit Temperature
160 REM    D  Day of the Month
170 REM    T  Total Fahrenheit Temperature
180 REM    A  Average Fahrenheit Temperature
200 LPRINT "Temperatures during February"
210 LPRINT "Day", "Degrees F", "Degrees C"
290 LET T = 0
300 FOR D = 1 TO 28
310    READ C
320    LET F = 1.8 * C + 32
330    LET T = T + F
340    LPRINT D, F, C
350 NEXT D
360 LET A = T / 28
440 LPRINT "Average Temperature = ";A
800 DATA 30,31,29,28,34,32,31
810 DATA 33,29,29,34,34,31,29
820 DATA 34,32,32,29,27,29,31
830 DATA 33,33,30,31,31,29,30
999 END
```

This program provides a report on the daily temperatures and the average temperature. Once data is printed, it may not be accessed again by the program. For example, we can compare a particular daily temperature with the average temperature only manually, not by computer.

```
200 LPRINT "Temperatures during February"
```

The BASIC statement LPRINT works in exactly the same way as the BASIC statement PRINT except that LPRINT directs output to the line printer whereas PRINT directs output to the screen. Other versions of BASIC may use different methods to direct output to the line printer.

```
340 LPRINT D, F, C
```

Note the use of the comma in this instruction. A comma places the value that follows it at the beginning of a *print zone*. The exact width of the print zone depends on the version of BASIC used. In this case the print zone is 14 characters wide.

Second Program

This program performs the same calculations as the preceding program, but it uses arrays. The program illustrates how arrays are *declared* or set up as well as the initialization and referencing of individual array items. The results of running this program are shown in Figure A-8.

FIGURE A-7

Temperature Conversion Program

This BASIC program calculates Fahrenheit temperatures for a resort area. Note: Data such as 91.3999 is generated by this particular version of BASIC. Other versions will produce the expected value of 91.4.

```
LIST
100 REM    KILOOKOO ISLAND PROGRAM
110 REM      CONVERTS CENT. TO FAHR.
130 REM    LIST OF VARIABLES
140 REM    C  Centigrade Temperature
150 REM    F  Fahrenheit Temperature
160 REM    D  Day of the Month
170 REM    T  Total Fahrenheit Temperature
180 REM    A  Average Fahrenheit Temperature
200 LPRINT "Temperatures during February"
210 LPRINT "Day", "Degrees F", "Degrees C"
290 LET T = 0
300 FOR D = 1 TO 28
310    READ C
320    LET F = 1.8 * C + 32
330    LET T = T + F
340    LPRINT D, F, C
350 NEXT D
360 LET A = T / 28
440 LPRINT "Average Temperature = ";A
800 DATA 30,31,29,28,34,32,31
810 DATA 33,29,29,34,34,31,29
820 DATA 34,32,32,29,27,29,31
830 DATA 33,33,30,31,31,29,30
999 END
Ok
RUN
Temperatures during February
Day           Degrees F     Degrees C
 1              86             30
 2              87.8           31
 3              84.2           29
 4              82.4           28
 5              93.2           34
 6              89.6           32
 7              87.8           31
 8              91.39999       33
 9              84.2           29
10              84.2           29
11              93.2           34
12              93.2           34
13              87.8           31
14              84.2           29
15              93.2           34
16              89.6           32
17              89.6           32
18              84.2           29
19              80.6           27
20              84.2           29
21              87.8           31
22              91.39999       33
23              91.39999       33
24              86             30
25              87.8           31
26              87.8           31
27              84.2           29
28              86             30
Average Temperature =  87.60713
```

```
100 REM    KILOOKOO ISLAND PROGRAM
110 REM      CONVERTS CENT. TO FAHR.
120 REM      Uses arrays
130 REM    LIST OF VARIABLES
140 REM     C Centigrade Temperature
150 REM     F Fahrenheit Temperature
160 REM     D Day of the Month
170 REM     T Total Fahrenheit Temperature
180 REM     A Average Fahrenheit Temperature
190 DIM C(28), F(28)
200 LPRINT "Temperatures during February"
210 LPRINT "Day", "Degrees F", "Degrees C"
290 LET T = 0
300 FOR D = 1 TO 28
310    READ C(D)
320    LET F(D) = 1.8 * C(D) + 32
330    LET T = T + F(D)
340    LPRINT D, F(D), C(D)
350 NEXT D
360 LET A = T / 28
440 LPRINT "Average Temperature = ";A
800 DATA 30,31,29,28,34,32,31
810 DATA 33,29,29,34,34,31,29
820 DATA 34,32,32,29,27,29,31
830 DATA 33,33,30,31,31,29,30
999 END
```

```
190 DIM C(28), F(28)
```

The program contains two arrays: one for the 28 daily Centigrade temperatures and one for the 28 daily Fahrenheit temperatures. This DIM statement reserves space in main memory for each array. It allows the programmer to reference storage locations in a systematic manner.

The exact nature and use of DIM statements vary from one version of BASIC to another. For example, some versions of BASIC reserve an additional storage location for each array that may be used for bookkeeping purposes. Moreover, the use of the DIM statement may be optional for arrays of ten elements or less. Experienced programmers tend to use the DIM statement to indicate the presence of an array even though it is not required.

Declaring an array with the DIM statement does *not* place any values in the array itself. To place data within the array or access it from the array, we refer to individual locations in memory known as array elements. In BASIC this reference is made as follows: C(3) is the third element in the array C. In our example, C(3) is the Centigrade temperature on February 3. The Fahrenheit temperature on February 12 is written F(12).

The value within parentheses indicating the array element referenced is called the *subscript*. The subscript may be either an integer constant, as in the preceding examples, or a variable assigned integer values, as in our program. The subscript's value must be greater than 0 (or equal to 0 in some versions of BASIC) and may not exceed the number of items in the array as declared in the DIM statement.

FIGURE A-8

A Program Using Arrays

This BASIC program employs an array to calculate Fahrenheit temperatures for a resort area.

```
LIST
110 REM    KILOOKOO ISLAND PROGRAM
110 REM       CONVERTS CENT. TO FAHR.
120 REM       Uses arrays
130 REM    LIST OF VARIABLES
140 REM     C   Centigrade Temperature
150 REM     F   Fahrenheit Temperature
160 REM     D   Day of the Month
170 REM     T   Total Fahrenheit Temperature
180 REM     A   Average Fahrenheit Temperature
190 DIM C(28), F(28)
200 LPRINT "Temperatures during February"
210 LPRINT "Day", Degrees F", "Degrees C"
290 LET T = 0
300 FOR D = 1 TO 28
310    READ C(D)
320    LET F(D) = 1.8 * C(D) + 32
330    LET T = T + F(D)
340    LPRINT D, F(D), C(D)
350 NEXT D
360 LET A = T / 28
440 LPRINT "AVERAGE Temperature = ";A
800 DATA 30,31,29,28,34,32,31
810 DATA 33,29,29,34,34,31,29
820 DATA 34,32,32,29,27,29,31
830 DATA 33,33,30,31,31,29,30
999 END
Ok
RUN
Temperatures during February
Day            Degrees F     Degrees C
 1               86             30
 2               87.8           31
 3               84.2           29
 4               82.4           28
 5               93.2           34
 6               89.6           32
 7               87.8           31
 8               91.39999       33
 9               84.2           29
10               84.2           29
11               93.2           34
12               93.2           34
13               87.8           31
14               84.2           29
15               93.2           34
16               89.6           32
17               89.6           32
18               84.2           29
19               80.6           27
20               84.2           29
21               87.8           31
22               91.39999       33
23               91.39999       33
24               86             30
25               87.8           31
26               87.8           31
27               84.2           29
28               86             30
Average Temperature =   87.60713
```

APPENDIX 705 PROGRAMMING IN BASIC

Examples of illegal subscripts for our program are −3, 0, 1.5, and 34. These correspond to meaningless values, namely, the temperatures on February −3, February 0, February 1.5, and February 34.

```
310    READ C(D)
```

This statement directs the computer to read element D of the array C. The value of D is determined by the FOR . . . NEXT loop in lines 300 to 350. The first time the loop is executed, the variable D is set to 1 and line 310 reads the first element in the array of Centigrade temperatures. In other words, the Centigrade temperature for February 1 is set to 30 degrees. This data item is processed in the next line.

```
320    LET F(D) = 1.8 * C(D) +32
```

The first time through the FOR . . . NEXT loop, the Fahrenheit temperature for February 1 is calculated from the Centigrade temperature for February 1. (The Fahrenheit temperature for February 1 equals 1.8 * 30 + 32 = 54 + 32 = 86 degrees.) These Fahrenheit and Centigrade temperatures are printed in line 340. In succeeding passages through the loop, the program does several things: It reads (line 310) the Centigrade temperatures day by day; it calculates (line 320) the corresponding Fahrenheit temperatures; it keeps a running total (line 330) of the Fahrenheit temperatures for subsequent averaging; and it prints (line 340) both the Fahrenheit and Centigrade temperatures with the day for the entire month of February. The following program presents an application that would be impractical without the use of arrays.

Third Program

Items stored within an array are available for processing over and over again during the life of the program. An example of this is determining which days are hotter than average. The average cannot be calculated until the data for the entire month of February is processed. Although BASIC, unlike most other programming languages, provides a mechanism for rereading the data, it is common practice to access array elements from memory two or more times as required. Results of running the next program are shown in Figure A-9.

```
100 REM   KILOOKOO ISLAND PROGRAM
110 REM     CONVERTS CENT. TO FAHR.
120 REM     Uses arrays; indicates hotter than average days
130 REM   LIST OF VARIABLES
140 REM   C  Centigrade Temperature
150 REM   F  Fahrenheit Temperature
160 REM   D  Day of the Month
170 REM   T  Total Fahrenheit Temperature
180 REM   A  Average Fahrenheit Temperature
190 DIM C(28), F(28)
200 LPRINT "Temperatures during February"
210 LPRINT "Day", "Degrees F", "Degrees C"
290 LET T = 0
```

```
300 FOR D = 1 TO 28
310     READ C(D)
320     LET F(D) = 1.8 * C(D) + 32
330     LET T = T + F(D)
350 NEXT D
360 LET A = T / 28
400 FOR D = 1 TO 28
410     LPRINT D, F(D), C(D),
420     IF F(D)>>A THEN LPRINT "Hotter than aver." ELSE LPRINT
430 NEXT D
440 LPRINT "Average Temperature = ";A
800 DATA 30,31,29,28,34,32,31
810 DATA 33,29,29,34,34,31,29
820 DATA 34,32,32,29,27,29,31
830 DATA 33,33,30,31,31,29,30
999 END

410     LPRINT D, F(D), C(D),
```

Notice the comma at the end of this instruction. It is used to position output generated by the next LPRINT command (in line 420) at the same line. In the absence of this comma output generated by the LPRINT command of line 420 would go on the next line, producing results that are much harder to read.

Common Errors. A common error in processing arrays is to code an array variable as a simple variable, for example, writing line 320 as follows:

```
320 LET F = 1.8 * C + 32
```

Most versions of BASIC would assign a value of 32 to the variable F because the variable C has not been assigned a value and is treated as 0. Another error that is common when processing arrays is generating illegal subscripts.

Programs to Modify

1. The programs just presented have been written to process temperature data for the 28 days of February. Modify the second program so that it processes data for the 31 days of March.
2. Modify the third program so that it calculates the average temperature for days that are hotter than average. Call this value the hot-days average. Indicate the days that are hotter than the hot-days average.

Programs to Write

1. The formula for accumulation of capital invested at simple interest is:

Capital = Initial Investment * (1 + Interest Rate * Years Invested)

FIGURE A-9

Using Arrays for an Average

This BASIC program employs an array to calculate Fahrenheit temperatures and the days that are hotter than average for a resort area.

```
LIST
100 REM   KILOOKOO ISLAND PROGRAM
110 REM     CONVERTS CENT. TO FAHR.
120 REM     Uses arrays; indicates hotter than average days
130 REM   LIST OF VARIABLES
140 REM   C  Centigrade Temperature
150 REM   F  Fahrenheit Temperature
160 REM   D  Day of the Month
170 REM   T  Total Fahrenheit Temperature
180 REM   A  Average Fahrenheit Temperature
190 DIM C(28), F(28)
200 LPRINT "Temperatures during February"
210 LPRINT "Day", "Degrees F", "Degrees C"
290 LET T = 0
300 FOR D = 1 TO 28
310    READ C(D)
320    LET F(D) = 1.8 * C(D) + 32
330    LET T = T + F(D)
350 NEXT D
360 LET A = T / 28
400 FOR D = 1 TO 28
410    LPRINT D, F(D), C(D),
420    IF F(D)>A THEN LPRINT "Hotter than aver." ELSE LPRINT
430 NEXT D
440 LPRINT "Average Temperature = ";A
800 DATA 30,31,29,28,34,32,31
810 DATA 33,29,29,34,34,31,29
820 DATA 34,32,32,29,27,29,31
830 DATA 33,33,30,31,31,29,30
999 END
Ok
RUN
Temperatures during February
Day           Degrees F        Degrees C
 1               86              30
 2               87.8            31             Hotter than aver.
 3               84.2            29
 4               82.4            28
 5               93.2            34             Hotter than aver.
 6               89.6            32             Hotter than aver.
 7               87.8            31             Hotter than aver.
 8               91.39999        33             Hotter than aver.
 9               84.2            29
10               84.2            29
11               93.2            34             Hotter than aver.
12               93.2            34             Hotter than aver.
13               87.8            31             Hotter than aver.
14               84.2            29
15               93.2            34             Hotter than aver.
16               89.6            32             Hotter than aver.
17               89.6            32             Hotter than aver.
18               84.2            29
19               80.6            27
20               84.2            29
21               87.8            31             Hotter than aver.
22               91.39999        33             Hotter than aver.
23               91.39999        33             Hotter than aver.
24               86              30
25               87.8            31             Hotter than aver.
26               87.8            31             Hotter than aver.
27               84.2            29
28               86              30
Average Temperature =  87.60713
```

Write a BASIC program that creates a 10-member array whose element Y contains the capital generated by an initial investment of $1000 at an interest rate of 10%, where Y is the number of years invested and varies from 1 to 10. Print the contents of this array with appropriate identification.

2. The formula for accumulation of capital invested at compound interest is:

Capital = Initial Investment * (1 + Interest Rate ** Years Invested)

Write a BASIC program that creates two 10-member arrays as in Program 1; the first array contains the capital accumulated at simple interest and the second contains the capital accumulated at compound interest. Print the contents of these arrays with appropriate identification.

Additional Topics

We conclude this chapter with an examination of several topics that are elements of intermediate BASIC. They include nested FOR . . . NEXT loops and the related two-dimensional arrays, subroutines, and random numbers.

Nested FOR . . . NEXT Loops

Recall that FOR . . . NEXT loops are used to repeat one or a series of instructions a fixed number of times. When the contents of a FOR . . . NEXT loop include another FOR . . . NEXT loop, the resultant structure is called a *nested FOR . . . NEXT loop*. Nested FOR . . . NEXT loops are often used with multidimensional arrays. Few business applications involve FOR . . . NEXT loops nested more than three deep. The following program segment illustrates how the computer processes a nested FOR . . . NEXT loop.

```
100 FOR I = 1 TO 2
110     FOR J = 1 TO 3
120         PRINT "I = ";I," J = ";J
130     NEXT J
140 NEXT I
150 END
```

The program prints the following:

```
I = 1        J = 1
I = 1        J = 2
I = 1        J = 3
I = 2        J = 1
I = 2        J = 2
I = 2        J = 3
```

Note that the innermost loop (J loop) is processed first. Indentation is particularly important in programs that contain one or more nested FOR . . . NEXT loops. Inverting the two NEXT statements in lines 130 and 140 produces a syntax error. We will apply this structure after examining a related topic, two-dimensional arrays.

Two-Dimensional Arrays

Recall that an example of a two-dimensional array is a table of monthly sales figures for each vendor in a sales office. Assume that the array contains monthly sales data for six vendors during the previous three months. This array can be declared by the statement

```
100 DIM S(6,3)
```

The 6 indicates that there are 6 rows (vendors); the 3 indicates that there are 3 columns (months). The array element that represents the sales figure for the first vendor during the second month is

```
S(1,2)
```

In the same way, S(5,1) refers to the sales figures for the fifth vendor during the first month. We can modify the second Centigrade-to-Fahrenheit temperature conversion program to make use of two-dimensional arrays and nested FOR . . . NEXT loops. The FOR . . . NEXT loop that spans lines 305–345 processes the three readings for a given day; the variable H assumes a value from 1 to 3. The FOR . . . NEXT loop that spans lines 300–350 instructs the computer to process the inner loop for each of the 10 days; the variable D assumes a value from 1 to 10. Results of processing this program are shown in Figure A-10.

```
100 REM KILOOKOO ISLAND PROGRAM
110 REM    CONVERTS CENT. TO FAHR.
120 REM    Uses two-dimensional arrays
130 REM LIST OF VARIABLES
140 REM   C  Centigrade Temperature
150 REM   F  Fahrenheit Temperature
160 REM   D  Day of the Month
165 REM   H  Hour of the Day
170 REM   T  Total Fahrenheit Temperature
180 REM   A  Average Fahrenheit Temperature
190 DIM C(10,3), F(10,3)
200 LPRINT "Temperatures during February"
210 LPRINT "Day", "Degrees F", "Degrees C"
290 LET T = 0
300 FOR D = 1 TO 10
305     FOR H = 1 TO 3
310         READ C(D,H)
320         LET F(D,H) = 1.8 * C(D,H) + 32
```

```
330          LET T = T + F(D,H)
340          LPRINT D, F(D,H), C(D,H)
345       NEXT H
350    NEXT D
360    LET A = T / 30
440    LPRINT "Average Temperature = ";A
800 DATA 30,33,33
810 DATA 31,33,32
820 DATA 29,29,29
830 DATA 28,27,27
840 DATA 34,33,33
850 DATA 32,33,33
860 DATA 31,34,32
870 DATA 33,32,32
880 DATA 29,31,32
890 DATA 29,29,29
999 END
```

This program processes hourly temperature readings at Kilookoo Island. Hourly readings for the 28 days of February comprise 672 pieces of data, an unwieldy amount. To limit the amount of data, we will consider only three daily readings for the first 10 days of February. For ease of reference, each DATA line in the program contains the three readings for a given day. The nested FOR . . . NEXT loops process the data day by day.

The following program segment could be used in calculating the average daily temperature for the 28 days of February (assuming one reading per hour).

```
130 REM LIST OF VARIABLES
150 REM   C  Centigrade Temperature
160 REM   D  Day of the Month
165 REM   H  Hour of the Day
185 REM   S  Sum Daily Centigrade Temperature
195 DIM C(28,24), S(28)
370 FOR D = 1 TO 28
380    LET S(D) = 0
390 NEXT D
400 FOR D = I TO 28
410    FOR H = 1 TO 24
420       READ C(D,H)
430       LET S(D) = S(D) + C(D,H)
440    NEXT H
450    LPRINT "Average Daily Temperature for Feb. ";D;S(D)/28
460 NEXT D
```

We see that a FOR . . . NEXT loop can be used to process a two-dimensional array (such as C), producing a one-dimensional array (such as S) in summary. Interested readers may write a similar program segment to calculate the average hourly temperature.

FIGURE A-10

A Two-Dimensional Array

This BASIC program employs a two-dimensional array to calculate the average temperature for a resort area.

```
LIST
100 REM   KILOOKOO ISLAND PROGRAM
110 REM      CONVERTS CENT. TO FAHR.
120 REM      Uses two-dimensional arrays
130 REM   LIST OF VARIABLES
140 REM    C  Centigrade Temperature
150 REM    F  Fahrenheit Temperature
160 REM    D  Day of the Month
165 REM    H  Hour of the Day
170 REM    T  Total Fahrenheit Temperature
180 REM    A  Average Fahrenheit Temperature
190 DIM C(10,3), F(10,3)
200 LPRINT "Temperatures during February"
210 LPRINT "Day", "Degrees F", "Degrees C"
290 LET T = 0
300 FOR D = 1 TO 10
305    FOR H = 1 TO 3
310       READ C(D,H)
320       LET F(D,H) = 1.8 * C(D,H) + 32
330       LET T = T + F(D,H)
340       LPRINT D, F(D,H), C(D,H)
345    NEXT H
350 NEXT D
360 LET A = T / 30
440 LPRINT "Average Temperature = ";A
800 DATA 30,33,33
810 DATA 31,33,32
820 DATA 29,29,29
830 DATA 28,27,27
840 DATA 34,33,33
850 DATA 32,33,33
860 DATA 31,34,32
870 DATA 33,32,32
880 DATA 29,31,32
890 DATA 29,29,29
999 END
Ok

RUN
Temperatures during February
Day           Degrees F      Degrees C
 1              86             30
 1              91.39999       33
 1              91.39999       33
 2              87.8           31
 2              91.39999       33
 2              89.6           32
 3              84.2           29
 3              84.2           29
 3              84.2           29
 4              82.4           28
 4              80.6           27
 4              80.6           27
 5              93.2           34
 5              91.39999       33
 5              91.39999       33
 6              89.6           32
 6              91.39999       33
 6              91.39999       33
 7              87.8           31
 7              93.2           34
 7              89.6           32
 8              91.39999       33
 8              89.6           32
 8              89.6           32
 9              84.2           29
 9              87.8           31
 9              89.6           32
10              84.2           29
10              84.2           29
10              84.2           29
Average Temperature = 87.92
```

Subroutines

Subroutines are small programs within a BASIC program. They are often employed when a group of instructions is used repeatedly within a program. They work as follows: Upon encountering the instruction GOSUB, the program transfers control to the beginning of the subroutine. The subroutine executes until it encounters the RETURN instruction, at which point the computer returns to the first instruction after the GOSUB. Unlike the GOTO statement, which operates in a single direction, the GOSUB directs the computer to transfer control to a subroutine and come back when the program is finished. Many people think of the GOSUB as an opening parenthesis and the RETURN as a closing parenthesis. These two statements must always come in pairs.

Recall the program segment presented in the first group of programs (page 686) to calculate a student's summer earnings:

```
220  IF W > 10 THEN 240
230  GOTO 250
240  LET B = 50
245  PRINT "Bonus of $50"
250  LET T = S * W + B
```

We replace this program segment with a subroutine (lines 300 to 320):

```
220  IF W > 10 THEN GOSUB 300
250  LET T = S * W + B
290  STOP
300  LET B = 50
310  PRINT "Bonus of $50"
320  RETURN
```

If the number of weeks worked is greater than 10, the program proceeds to the subroutine starting at line 300. Then lines 300 to 320 are executed in order. At this point the program returns to the instruction after 220, namely, line 250. The instruction STOP in line 290 stops program execution. It is necessary to prevent the program from continuing to line 320, at which point it would encounter the RETURN a second time compared to a single GOSUB.

Other Features

This program presents some very useful features of BASIC: random numbers, new versions of the PRINT statement, and functions. The program calculates potential winnings or losses from a dice game and presents these values with a dollar sign, as we expect financial data to be presented.

Random Numbers. *Random numbers* are numbers that occur in accordance with the laws of probability, such as rolls of dice. Strictly speaking, random numbers generated by computer are not truly random, but they are useful for many purposes. For example, the following program uses random numbers to simulate the rolls of dice in order to play a game. We can reroll the dice to play the game again. Similar but more complicated simulations may be used to help determine marketing strategy or whether or not to drill for oil at a given location.

The exact processing of random numbers may vary slightly from one version of BASIC to another. In this version the function RND(1) produces a value ranging from 0 to slightly less than 1. The actual value may be different every time the function is executed but is fairly random; in other words, it is less than .05 as often as it is greater than .95 and has the same chance of being less than .5 that it has of being greater than this value. To simulate a single die, it is necessary to transform numbers such as .05 into numbers such as 1, 2, 3, 4, 5, or 6. This transformation is carried out in lines 310 and 320 using BASIC's INT function.

This program simulates a game of dice in which the player rolls two dice and wins $1.20 if he or she rolls a 2, 3, 4, 5, or 6. If the player rolls a 7, 8, 9, 10, 11, or 12, he or she must pay $1.00. The game goes on for ten rolls. The program that simulates this dice game follows. The results of running this program are shown in Figure A-11.

```
100 REM PROGRAM THAT SIMULATES DICE
110 REM   USES RANDOM NUMBERS
120 REM VARIABLE LIST
130 REM    N TABLE OF RESULTS
140 REM      EXAMPLE N(10) NUMBER OF 10s
150 REM    C COUNTER FOR TABLE
160 REM    R ROLL NUMBER
170 REM    D1, D2 VALUE FOR EACH DIE
180 REM    T TOTAL FOR THE ROLL
190 REM    W WINNINGS
200 RANDOMIZE
210 DIM N(12)
220 LET W = 0
230 FOR C = 1 TO 12
240    LET N(C) = 0
250 NEXT C
300 FOR R = 1 TO 100
310    LET D1 = INT(6*RND(1)+1)
320    LET D2 = INT(6*RND(1)+1)
330    LET T = D1 + D2
340    LET N(T) = N(T) + 1
350    IF T > 6 THEN W = W - 1 ELSE W = W + 1.2
360 NEXT R
400 PRINT "TOTAL ROLL", "TIMES ROLLED"
410 FOR C = 1 TO 12
420    PRINT C, N(C)
430 NEXT C
490 PRINT TAB(5);"Winnings (losses with - sign) ";
500 PRINT USING "$$##.##";W
999 END

200 RANDOMIZE
```

This statement allows us to repeat a series of random numbers if desired, for example, if we want to see the effect on the payoff of changing the rules. In this version of BASIC the user enters a whole number varying from -32768 to 32767. The computer uses this number, called a *seed*, to generate the rolls of the dice. The use of the same seed always generates the same series of random numbers and, consequently, the same rolls of the dice. The use of a different seed will probably generate a different series of random numbers and different rolls of the dice.

```
310     LET D1 = INT(6*RND(1)+1)
320     LET D2 = INT(6*RND(1)+1)
```

These statements are used to convert the random numbers varying from 0 to slightly less than 1 into whole numbers ranging with equal probability from 1 to 6, in other words, the roll of a die. Because there are two dice, this conversion is done twice.

```
330     LET T = D1 + D2
340     LET N(T) = N(T) + 1
```

The two dice are summed and the appropriate array element is increased by 1. For example, if a 3 and a 4 were rolled, the sum is 7 and the seventh element of the array is increased by 1. (Note that the program keeps a record of the total rolls but not the way they were obtained; rolling a 1 and a 6 is exactly the same as rolling a 3 and a 4.)

```
350     IF T > 6 THEN W = W - 1 ELSE W = W + 1.2
```

This statement calculates the financial impact of the roll according to the rules of the game. We can modify this instruction and produce a new game, to be tested by generating the same series of random numbers.

```
490 PRINT TAB(5);"Winnings (losses with - sign) ";
500 PRINT USING "$$##.##" ;W
```

TAB Function. The TAB function enables the programmer to obtain additional control over the placement of output. In the above program, the output generated by line 490 starts in column 5. The TAB function is used with both the PRINT and LPRINT statements but may not appear in the same instruction as PRINT USING, discussed below.

PRINT USING. The PRINT USING statement is a very important option of BASIC for presenting the results of many calculations of financial and other quantities. It enables the programmer to produce results positioned at will on the report. The exact form of this option varies from one version of BASIC to another; the BASIC supplied with the Apple II series of computers does not provide for PRINT USING. This particular instruction is used to provide a dollar sign with the numeric results. Note that the dollar sign appears next to the leftmost digit of the result. LPRINT USING works in exactly the same way as PRINT USING except that it sends output to the printer.

FIGURE A-11

A Dice Game Simulation

This BASIC program employs random numbers and PRINT USING to simulate a dice game.

```
LIST
110 REM PROGRAM THAT SIMULATES DICE
110 REM   USES RANDOM NUMBERS
120 REM VARIABLE LIST
130 REM   N TABLE OF RESULTS
140 REM   EXAMPLE N(10)  NUMBER OF 10s
150 REM   C COUNTER FOR TABLE
160 REM   R ROLL NUMBER
170 REM   D1, D2 VALUE FOR EACH DIE
180 REM   T TOTAL FOR THE ROLL
190 REM   W WINNINGS
200 RANDOMIZE
210 DIM N(12)
220 LET W = 0
230 FOR C = 1 TO 12
240     LET N(C) = 0
250 NEXT C
300 FOR R = 1 TO 100
310     LET D1 = INT(6*RND(1)+1)
320     LET D2 = INT(6*RND(1)+1)
330     LET T = D1 = D2
340     LET N(T) = N(T) + 1
350     IF T > 6 THEN W = W - 1 ELSE W = W + 1.2
360 NEXT R
400 PRINT "TOTAL ROLL", "TIMES ROLLED"
410 FOR C = 1 TO 12
420     PRINT C, N(C)
430 NEXT C
490 PRINT TAB(5);"Winnings (losses with - sign) ";
500 PRINT USING "$$##.##"; W
999 END
Ok
RUN
Random number seed (-32768 to 32767)? 32767
TOTAL ROLL      TIMES ROLLED
 1               0
 2               2
 3               4
 4              11
 5               7
 6              15
 7              18
 8              15
 9               7
10              10
11               8
12               3
     Winnings (losses with - sign) -$14.20
Ok
```

```
RUN
Random number seed (-32768 to 32767)? 32766
TOTAL ROLL      TIMES ROLLED
   1               0
   2               3
   3               7
   4              15
   5              12
   6              13
   7              13
   8              15
   9               9
  10               7
  11               3
  12               3
        Winnings (losses with - sign)   $10.00
Ok
RUN
Random number seed (-32768 to 32767)? 0
TOTAL ROLL      TIMES ROLLED
   1               0
   2               6
   3               5
   4               8
   5              10
   6              13
   7              18
   8              14
   9              12
  10               4
  11               5
  12               5
        Winnings (losses with - sign)   -$7.60
Ok
```

Functions. The above program used the BASIC functions RND and INT to perform useful calculations. Other functions that are often used include SRT(N), to find the square root of the number N; SIN(X), to find the trigonometric sine of the angle X; and LEN(X$), to find the length of the string variable X$. Depending on the application, BASIC programmers may make use of functions to determine the position of the cursor or the light pen or to read a character from the keyboard. The use of functions simplifies programming considerably; it enables programmers to take advantage of prewritten, tested, efficient code rather than writing and testing their own. The following example illustrates the use of string functions.

String Functions. String functions are functions that return a string value. An example of a string function is LEFT$(X$,n), which returns the leftmost n characters of the string X$. It is illustrated in the following program segment:

```
100 REM LIST OF VARIABLES
110 REM    X$   Original String
120 REM    L$   Left Segment of String
200 LET X$ = "GORGEOUS GEORGE"
210 LET L$ = LEFT$(X$,1)
220 PRINT "Leftmost character in ";X$;" is ";L$
230 LET L$ = LEFT$(X$,2)
240 PRINT "Leftmost two characters in ";X$;" are ";L$
999 END
```

The result of running this program is:

```
Leftmost character in GORGEOUS GEORGE is G
Leftmost two characters in GORGEOUS GEORGE are GO
```

Other commonly used string functions are MID$(X$,n,m), which returns m characters from X$ starting at position n; RIGHT$(X$,n), which returns the rightmost n characters of X$; and SPACE$(n), which returns a string of n spaces. Two of these functions and the LEN function, which returns the length of a string, are illustrated in the following program segment. The results of running this program are shown in Figure A-12.

```
100 REM       STRING MANIPULATION PROGRAM
110 REM    X$   Original String
120 REM    L$   Left Segment of String
130 REM    R$   Right Segment of String
140 REM    M$   Middle Segment of String
150 REM    L    Length of String
160 REM    M    Position of Middle of String
200 LET X$ = "GORGEOUS GEORGE"
210 LET L$ = LEFT$(X$,1)
220 PRINT "Leftmost character in ";X$;" is ";L$
230 LET L$ = LEFT$(X$,2)
240 PRINT "Leftmost two characters in ";X$;" are ";L$
250 LET R$ = RIGHT$(X$,3)
260 PRINT "Rightmost three characters in ";X$;" are ";R$
270 LET L = LEN(X$)
280 PRINT "Length of string ";X$;" is ";L
290 LET M = INT((L+1)/2)
300 LET M$ = MID$(X$,M,1)
310 PRINT "Middle character in string ";X$;" is ";M$
999 END
```

```
290 LET M = INT((L+1)/2)
```

Line 290 is necessary to assign the middle value to the variable L. In this case the length of the string is 15, so the position of the middle character is calculated as INT(16/2), or 8. If the string were 20 characters long, the position of the middle character would be calculated as INT(21/2), or 10.

FIGURE A-12

A String Manipulation Program

```
LIST
100 REM     STRING MANIPULATION PROGRAM
110 REM     X$  Original String
120 REM     L$  Left Segment of String
130 REM     R$  Right Segment of String
140 REM     M$  Middle Segment of String
150 REM     L   Length of String
160 REM     M   Position of Middle String
200 LET X$ = "GORGEOUS GEORGE"
210 LET L$ = LEFT$(X$,1)
220 PRINT "Leftmost character in ";X$;" is ";L$
230 LET L$ = LEFT$(X$,2)
240 PRINT "Leftmost two characters in ";X$;" are ";L$
250 LET R$ = RIGHT$(X$,3)
260 PRINT "Rightmost three characters in ";X$;" are ";R$
270 LET L = LEN (X$)
280 PRINT "Length of string ";X$;" is ";L
290 LET M = INT((L+1)/2)
300 LET M$ = MID$(X$,M,1)
310 PRINT "Middle character in string ";X$;" is ";M$
999 END
Ok
RUN
Leftmost character in GORGEOUS GEORGE is G
Leftmost two characters in GORGEOUS GEORGE are GO
Rightmost three characters in GORGEOUS GEORGE are RGE
Length of string GORGEOUS GEORGE is 15
Middle character in string GORGEOUS GEORGE is S
```

ON GOTO Statement. The case structure is expressed in BASIC by the ON GOTO statement illustrated below. In this example, employees will be given a bonus according to a performance code. Employees with a performance code of 1 get a bonus of $100; employees with a performance code of 2 get $50; and so forth.

```
100 REM    LIST OF VARIABLES
110 REM      C   PERFORMANCE CODE
120 READ     C
130 ON C GOTO 200,300,400,500
200 PRINT "Bonus of $100"
210 GOTO 999
300 PRINT "Bonus of $50"
310 GOTO 999
400 PRINT "Bonus of $20"
410 GOTO 999
500 PRINT "Bonus of $10"
800 DATA
999 END
```

Glossary

Access
The process of finding data stored in a computer system.

Address
The location of data in a computer storage medium.

Algorithm
A set of well-defined rules for solving a problem in a finite number of steps.

Alphanumeric
A term used to refer to data composed of letters and numbers and a few special characters.

Analog computer
A computer that processes continuous data, such as pressure or temperature, by measuring it.

Arithmetic operation
An activity such as addition, subtraction, multiplication, or division that is performed by the arithmetic-logic unit of the CPU.

Artificial intelligence
The use of a computer to emulate human capabilities such as thinking.

Assembler
A program that translates assembly-language programs into machine language.

Assembly languages
Programming languages that allow the programmer to use letters and symbols to replace the 0s and 1s of machine language.

Audio response unit
An output device that produces sound.

Backup copy
A copy of data on a file or series of files that is made to ensure continuity in case of data loss.

BASIC (*B*eginner's *A*ll-purpose *S*ymbolic *I*nstruction *C*ode)
A programming language that was invented in 1964 for the purpose of enabling students to use the computer.

Basic structures
The programming structures necessary for coding a structured program, including the sequential structure, the selection structure, the looping structure, and often the case structure.

Batch processing
A technique by which data and programs are collected in groups, known as batches, and processed periodically.

Baud
The speed at which data is transmitted in a data communication system.

Binary system
A number system that contains only two digits, 0 and 1.

Bit
A binary digit that can take on either of two values, arbitrarily called 0 and 1.

Byte
A group of bits in storage that represents a number, a character, or a program instruction.

C
A hybrid language that combines many features of high-level languages with the power of assembly languages.

Central processing unit (CPU)
The core of the computer, composed of the arithmetic-

logic unit, the control unit and primary storage.

Chip
A single electronic circuit that serves as the building block of modern computers.

COBOL (COmmon Business Oriented Language)
The most widely used programming language for commercial and administrative applications on mainframe computers.

Coding
The process of translating an algorithm into a computer language such as COBOL, FORTRAN, or BASIC. The word code is often used to refer to the finished program.

Command
A precise statement or set of keystrokes that instructs a software package to perform a particular operation.

Compatible
A term used to describe a group of computers that can run all or most of the same software and process data on the same storage media.

Compiler
A program that translates an entire high-level language program into machine language before attempting to perform any operations.

Computer
An electronic machine that processes raw data to produce information for people or for other machines.

Computer-aided design (CAD)
The use of a workstation with graphics capability and special graphics software to design, draft, and document products.

Computer-aided manufacturing (CAM)
The use of a computer system to plan, manage, and control manufacturing operations.

Computer-assisted instruction (CAI)
The use of computers to help students learn.

Computer-integrated manufacturing (CIM)
The implementation of a fully integrated data base that describes and controls the entire manufacturing process.

Computer-managed instruction (CMI)
The use of computers by educational institutions to store and process administrative data.

Computer network
A data communication system that links computer systems and their workstations.

Computer output microfilm (COM)
An output device that produces microfilm or microfiche.

Computer security
The protection of a computer system against unauthorized access and against damage caused by electrical problems or natural disasters.

Console
A workstation for an operator of a mainframe or supercomputer.

Cursor
A special symbol that highlights an area on a screen.

Daisy-wheel printer
A printer that forms letter-quality characters when a removable print head strikes the ribbon and paper.

Data
The facts and figures that make up the raw material supplied to a computer for processing.

Data base
A collection of data that has been organized to permit ready access by both technical personnel and end-users.

Data-base administrator (DBA)
The person or group that is responsible for

721 GLOSSARY

designing, installing, and controlling a data base.

Data-base management program
A program that is designed to store, retrieve, and manipulate data from one or more files.

Data-base management system (DBMS)
The software that controls the creation, maintenance, and use of a data base.

Data communication
The transmission of data, information, and programs from one location to another.

Data dictionary
An organized collection of information about all the data elements within a data base.

Data encryption
The coding of data to prevent reading by unauthorized individuals.

Data entry
The process of inputting data into a computer.

Data processing
The manipulation of data to produce information.

Debugging
The process of finding bugs, or errors, that prevent a program from doing what it is supposed to do.

Decimal system
The commonly used number system based on the digits 0 through 9.

Decision support system (DSS)
A computer information system that provides middle and upper management with information to be used in making decisions.

Desktop publishing
A system that enables an organization or individual to produce professional-looking documents using relatively inexpensive hardware and software.

Digital computer
A computer that processes discrete items of data via a counting procedure. The majority of computers used in business are digital computers.

Direct-access file
See random-access file.

Distributed data processing (DDP)
A data communication system in which more than one computer is used to process applications. programs.

Documentation
A detailed written description of a program or a system.

Dot-matrix printer
A printer that forms characters when pins in a rectangular grid strike the ribbon and paper.

Electronic funds transfer (EFT)
The transfer of funds from one individual, business, or bank to another by electronic means.

Electronic mail
The sending, storing, and delivering of messages by electronic means.

Electronic spreadsheet
A program that converts a computer monitor into part of a worksheet, to be used in calculations such as budgeting and financial analysis.

Ergonomics
The study of the relationship of people to their work environment, particularly to computing.

Expert system
A computer system that simulates the reasoning of human experts.

Feasibility study
A study that determines whether or not a particular problem can be solved with the resources allocated by management.

GLOSSARY 722

Field
A contiguous group of characters that has a meaning.

File
A collection of related records.

File-processing system
A computerized system consisting of files that are designed and organized to meet specific needs, such as accounting, sales, and marketing applications.

Flexible manufacturing system (FMS)
An automated system that machines a variety of items as determined by product demand.

Flowchart
A diagram using standard symbols that expresses the relationships among processing activities within a program.

FORTRAN (FORmula TRANslator)
A high-level programming language that was developed primarily to enable scientists and engineers to express problems in mathematical formulas.

Graphics
Data or information that is composed of pictures and diagrams.

Hard copy
Permanent output such as that generated by a printer.

Hierarchical model
A data model in which each data record can have one or more subordinate data records.

High-level programming languages
Programming languages that resemble English or mathematical notation and permit more natural communication between the programmer and the computer than assembly languages do.

Icon
A visual symbol that indicates a computer operation.

Indexed-sequential file
A type of file whose records can be accessed rapidly via a series of indexes.

Information
Processed data that is available for use by an individual.

Information center
A department whose function is to train end-users to access their own data and generate their own reports.

Information utility
A collection of specialized information that is available on a fee basis to subscribers via personal computers or computer terminals.

Input
The data that is entered into a computer.

Interactive processing
A technique by which data and programs are processed on demand.

Interpreter
A program that translates a high-level language program one instruction at a time, executing it if possible.

Just-in-time (JIT)
An approach to production scheduling and inventory control that enables companies to keep inventory to a minimum.

Keyboard
The most commonly used input device, similar to a typewriter keyboard.

Key field
A field that identifies each record in a file.

Laser printer
A printer that is driven by a laser unit.

Local area network (LAN)
A data communication network that covers a geographically limited area, often connecting microcomputers, peripheral devices, and other office machines.

Logic operation
An activity such as a comparison or test that is performed by the arithmetic-logic unit of the CPU.

Machine language
A programming language that is composed entirely of 0s and 1s. The computer itself can respond only to machine language.

Magnetic ink character recognition (MICR)
A data entry technique in which a specialized machine reads a standard set of 14 characters— 0–9 and four banking symbols.

Mainframe computer
A large computer with immense primary storage capacity that can serve hundreds of users at once.

Management information system (MIS)
A computer information system that provides managers with integrated information on a scheduled basis.

Manufacturing automation protocol (MAP)
A proposed standard for communication among computers, robots, and other devices used in industrial settings.

Manufacturing resource planning (MRP II)
A planning and operating system that includes all manufacturing functions—materials, capacity, finance, engineering, sales, distribution, and marketing.

Materials requirements planning (MRP)
A method of scheduling purchases and deliveries of raw materials and parts.

Memory
A part of the central processing unit in which data and programs may be stored for a short period.

Message
Data that is sent from a transmitter to a receiver, including the user's transaction and control information for the data communication system.

Microcomputer
A microprocessor that is fitted with an input device, an output device, and primary storage.

Microprocessor
A computer on a chip; it can serve as the heart of a microcomputer or be used to computerize equipment such as microwave ovens.

Microsecond
One-millionth of a second.

Millisecond
One one-thousandth of a second.

Minicomputer
A computer whose processing power and storage capacity is between that of microcomputers and mainframe computers.

Modem
A device that converts an analog signal into a digital signal or vice versa. The word modem is an abbreviation of modulation-demodulation.

Mouse
A small object that is rolled or stroked to move a cursor and select items from a menu.

Musical Instrument Digital Interface (MIDI)
A standard that describes the way the hardware of electronic musical instruments is interconnected and the software for data interchange.

Nanosecond
One one-billionth of a second.

Network model
A data model in which data records can have one or more subordinate data records and can themselves be subordinate to one or more data records.

New master file
The file that contains basic data for a computer application after an update has been carried out.

Office automation (OA)
The process of applying computers, communications, and related technologies to increase productivity in an office.

Old master file
The file that contains basic data for a computer application before an update is carried out.

One-line transaction-processing system (OLTPS)
A computer information system in which several users can make inquiries and updates of a shared data base at the same time.

Open architecture
An approach in which a computer's specifications are made public in order to encourage independent hardware and software developers

to create material that can be used on that computer, thereby increasing its market.

Operating system
Systems software that supervises the input, output, storage, and processing functions of a computer system.

Operations information system (OIS)
A computer system that enables an organization to process files or data bases and produce documents that keep track of employees, customers, goods and services, cash, buildings and equipment, and the like.

Optical character recognition (OCR)
A technique in which a specialized device is used to scan handwritten or typed characters and convert them into electronic signals that a computer can process.

Output
The information that is generated by a computer.

Pascal
The first programming language to be designed after the development of structured programming, whose concepts it incorporates.

Password
A code that permits a user to access a computer system.

Personal computer
A microcomputer that can be used by individuals in homes, schools, and offices.

PL/I (Programming Language I)
A high-level programming language developed by IBM in the mid-1960s. It includes features of COBOL, FORTRAN, and assembly languages.

Plotter
An output device that produces hard-copy graphics.

Point-of-sale (POS) terminal
A computerized cash register.

Portable computer
A microcomputer that a user can transport to various locations, usually without requiring access to an electrical outlet.

Printer
A computer output device that produces permanent or hard copy.

Program maintenance
The process of revising a program to meet new requirements and eliminate bugs.

Programming languages
Specialized languages that enable people to

prepare computer programs.

Pseudocode
An informal language that is used to express algorithms in a natural fashion. The word pseudocode *is often used to refer to the document itself as well as to the language in which it is expressed.*

Random-access file
A file in which any record can be processed without processing all preceding records or accessing an index. Also called direct-access file.

Record
A collection of related fields.

Relational model
A data model composed of tables that represent the relationships among the data items.

Robot
A computer-controlled device used for manipulating objects.

Sequential file
A file whose records must be accessed in order, starting with the first record on the file.

Simulation
A technique used in computer-assisted instruction in which a system is represented by a model.

Software
The programs, procedures, and documentation used to run the hardware of a computer system.

Sorting
The process of arranging data in a useful sequence.

Source data automation
The use of specialized data entry equipment to collect data at the source and transmit it to a computer.

Source document
A form that contains data for entry into a computer system.

Standard universal identifier (SUI)
An identifier that is used to specify all data records for a particular individual, making possible the linking of records stored on different files.

String
A collection of characters.

Structure chart
A graphic representation of a program's modules and their interrelationships.

Structured programming
A technique for designing and writing programs that divides programs into logical, readily identifiable modules.

Supercomputer
The fastest type of computer, often used for scientific and engineering applications.

System
An organized set of machines, people, and procedures designed to meet one or more specific objectives.

System acquisition
The stage of the system development life cycle in which the approved hardware and software are acquired or custom programs are developed.

System design
The stage of the system development life cycle in which the hardware and software components of the new system are specified in detail.

System development life cycle
A set of activities whose goal is to produce an information system.

System implementation
The stage of the system development life cycle in which the system is actually put into service.

System investigation
The stage of the system development life cycle that consists of defining the problem to be solved and determining whether a feasible solution exists.

System maintenance
The stage of the system development life cycle that consists of correcting errors and modifying the information system to meet users' needs.

Systems analysis
The stage of the system development life cycle in which the systems analyst, in conjunction with users, determines how the existing information system functions in order to design and develop a new system.

Telecommunication
See data communication.

Telecommuting
Using a remote workstation, communication lines, and related facilities to work at home or in a satellite office instead of in a central office.

Teleconferencing
The holding of meetings by electronic means.

Teleprocessing
A data communication system in which only one computer processes applications programs.

Testing
The process of determining whether a program contains errors that prevent it from doing what it was intended to do.

Time-sharing
A processing method in which large numbers of users share a teleprocessing system or network, with each user charged only for the resources that are actually used.

Top-down design
A technique in which a large problem is subdivided into modules and each module, which represents a specific aspect of the problem, is broken down into smaller modules.

Track
The circular area on a magnetic disk or diskette on which data may be recorded.

Transaction file
A file that contains changes to be made in a master file.

Universal product code (UPC)
A standard bar code that appears on many products. This code is used with point-of-sale terminal systems.

Updating
The process through which data on a master file is modified to reflect changed conditions such as customer payments or purchases.

User
A person who requests information from a computer.

Very-high-level programming languages
Programming languages that allow people to specify what they want a computer to do rather than how the computer should do it.

Video display terminal (VDT)
A device in which output is displayed on a screen. Also known as a cathode-ray tube (CRT).

Voice recognition system
An input device that accepts and decodes human speech.

Word processing
The use of a computer program to enter text, modify its content and appearance, and print it.

Index

Abacus, 7
Access (access data), 135
  electronic access control, 650–651
  of indexed-sequential files, 159
  of a magnetic disk, 150
Accounting (as a business subsystem), 423
  computer information systems for, 426, 427, 428–432
Accumulator, 163
Acoustic coupler, 186
Ada (programming language), 264–265
Addresses, 135
Advantages of computers, 14, 15–16
Advisory Committee on Automated Personal Data Systems, 631
Agriculture, fully automated farming, 436–437
Aiken, Howard, 10
ALGOL (ALGOrithmic Language), 265, 266
Algorithm, 217–218, 235
Alphabetic characters, 52
Alphanumeric output, 118
Altair 8800 (microcomputer), 74
AMA/NET (health-care data base), 598
Analog computers, 71
Analog signals, 184, 185
Analytical engine, 8–9
Analytical graphics, 552
APL (A Programming Language), 265–266, 267
Apple Computer, Inc., 36, 74, 75, 76, 277
Application generators, 267–272
Applications backlog, 513
Applications software, 46–49
Arithmetic-logic unit (ALU), 39, 133, 134
Arithmetic operations, 134
Artificial intelligence (AI), 508, 665–670
  for financial planners, 616
  programming languages for, 668–669
Arrays, 701–707, 710–712
ASCII code, 138, 163
Assemblers, 253–254
Assembly languages, 253–254
Asynchronous transmission, 184
Atari, 74

Audio response units, 119, 124–125
AutoCAD, 564
Automated office, see Desktop publishing; Integrated workstations; Office automation
Automated teller machines, 110
Auxiliary storage, 33, 42–45, 137, 138, 139–153
  for large computers, 146–153
  for microcomputers, 139–145
  protecting storage media, 143, 145
  special storage techniques, 145

Babbage, Charles, 8–9, 602
Backup and recovery, 197
Backup copy, 143
Banking at home, 620–621
Bardeen, John, 74
BASIC (Beginner's All-purpose Symbolic Instruction Code), 23, 74, 219, 259–261, 668
BASIC commands, 678
BASIC functions, 717–719
BASIC statements, 678
  DATA, 682
  DIM, 704
  GOSUB, 713
  GOTO, 686
  FOR . . . NEXT loop, 691, 694–695, 709–710
  IF . . . THEN, 683–684
  IF . . . THEN . . . ELSE, 686–687
  INPUT, 688, 689
  LET, 679
  LPRINT, 702
  ON GOTO, 719
  PRINT, 679
  PRINT, USING, 715
  READ, 682
  REM, 679
  RETURN, 713
  STEP clause, 691
  WHILE . . . WEND loop, 693, 696, 698–699
Basic structures, 235–237
Batches, 53
Batch processing, 53–54, 483
Baud, 178
Bernoulli box, 143–145, 628

Binary system, 134, 164
Bits, 51, 297
BIX (BYTE Information Exchange), 176
Blocking, 146–147
Boating, computers and, 602–604
Branching, 685
Break key, 107
Bricklin, Dan, 75, 320, 321
Buffers, 123
Burning, 137
Business subsystems, 419–427
  computer information services in, 424–427
Bus networks, 190
Bytes, 51–52, 138, 297
  gigabytes, 86
  kilobytes, 72
  megabytes, 73

C (programming language), 263–264
CAD/CAM system, see Computer-aided design and computer-aided manufacturing
Calculating machines, 7–8
Call-back systems, 643
Cards (security measure), 643–644
Cassette tapes, 43
Cathode-ray tube (CRT), 38, 118–120
CD-ROM (Compact Disk/Read-Only Memory), 154
CD-WORM (Compact Disk/"write once, read many times"), 154
Centers for Disease Control (CDC), 598–599
Central processing unit (CPU), 33, 39–42, 133–138
  arithmetic-logic unit, 39, 133, 134
  codes, 137–138
  control unit, 133
  primary storage, 133, 134–137
Channel, 173, 174
Character printers, 38, 120–121
Characters (bytes), 52, 138
Chargeback policy, 516
Chief information officer (CIO), 547
Clock speed, 133
Clones, 69, 77
Coaxial cables, 180
COBOL (COmmon Business Oriented

INDEX 728

Language), 23, 219, 257–259, 260, 668
COBOL generators, 236
Code generators, 272
Codes, 137–138, 163
Coding, 219–220
Collision, 157
Command, 313
Command flow, 162–163
Command consistency, 336
Commercial E-mail, 529
Common programming errors, 682, 690, 693, 700, 707
Communication channels, 178–182
Communication satellites, 182
Communication terminology, 182–185
Communications controllers, 186
Compaq Computer Corporation, 75, 81
Compatibles, 77–78
Compiler, 255–257
Computer, definition of, 5
Computer-aided design (CAD), 402–405, 561–565
Computer-aided design and computer-aided manufacturing (CAD/CAM), 201, 566
Computer-aided manufacturing (CAM), 565–567
Computer-assisted instruction (CAI), 606–608
Computer chips, 69, 77, 655–656
Computer conferencing, 175, 537
Computer crime, 632–639, 672
  criminals and victims, 634–635
  legislation to reduce, 639
  types, 633–638
Computer down time, 486
Computer errors, 18, 220–222, 671–672
Computer file, *see* File
Computer Fraud and Abuse Act of 1986, 639
Computer generations, 11–12
Computer graphics, 14, 118, 550–553
Computer information systems, 24, 416–419, 427–433
  accounting, 426, 427, 428–432
  in business, 424–427
  inventory control and management, 427, 432–433
  sales analysis, 427–429, 433
Computer-integrated manufacturing (CIM), 579–582
Computer-managed instruction (CMI), 609
Computer management titles, 425
Computer networks, 189–203
  distributed data processing, 198–200
  local area network, 200–202

multiuser systems, 202–203
network configurations, 189–193
network suppliers, 194
teleprocessing, 195–198
Computer output microfilm (COM), 119, 124
Computer security, 197–198, 640–646
  administrative measures, 641
  data integrity, 646
  data security for microcomputer users, 645–646
  electronic access control, 650–651
  individual awareness, 645
  physical measures, 641–642
  technological measures, 642–645
Computer services (as a business subsystem), 424
Computer services department, 497–499
Computer services information systems, 427
Computer services, theft of, 636
Computer specialists, 23–24
Computer systems, selecting, 93
Concentrators, 187
Concurrency, 336
Concurrent update, 486, 487
Conference on Data System Languages (CODASYL), 361
Console, 86
Constants, 679
Content, 309
Contention, 183
Control unit, 39, 133
Convex C-1 (superminicomputer), 89
Corporate electronic publishing systems, 550
Corporation information systems (CIS), 547
Counting, 696
CP/M (Control Program for Microcomputers), 277, 285
Cursors, 119
Cylinder, 150–151

Daisy-wheel printers, 40, 122
Data, 6
Data bank, 173
Data base, 53, 297, 298
Data-base administrator (DBA), 354
Data-base management programs, 48, 293–295
  mechanics, 297–309
Data-base management system (DBMS), 352–378
  advantages, 372–373
  data dictionary, 356–357
  data models, 358–363

disadvantages, 373–374
DBMS personnel, 354–356
installing, 377–378
programming languages for, 354–355
selecting, 374–377
special hardware for, 375
structured query language, 363–371
technical challenges, 374
Data communication, 33, 45–46, 173–175
  applications, 175–177
  basic concepts, 178–189
Data communication software, 188–189
Data compatibility, 336
Data definition language (DDL), 355
Data dictionary, 356–357
Data encryption, 198, 644–645
Data Encryption Standard (DES), 645
Data entry, 34–36, 101–102
Data entry box, 300
Data entry operators, 24
Data entry professionals, 35
Data flow, 161
Data flow diagrams, 456, 460
Data-gathering techniques, 452–454
Data hierarchy, 51–53
Data management function, 278, 279
Data management programs, 14
Data manipulation language (DML), 355
Data processing, 19–22
  functions of, 21–22
dBASE II, 226
dBASE III, 48, 264, 295–307
Deaf children, computers aiding the deaf to speak, 607
Debugging, 216, 220–221
Decimal system, 134, 164
Decision support systems (DSS), 416, 419, 500–508
  characteristics, 502–503
  components, 506, 507
  executive information system, 506–508
  types of decisions, 501–502
  uses and misuses of, 504–506
Dedicated lines, 180
Dedicated word processors, 307–308
Demodulation, 185
Desk-checking, 241–242
Desktop publishing, 547–550
  limitations, 548–549
  types of systems, 549–550
Destination, 173, 174
Dial-up lines, 180
Difference engine, 8
Digital computers, 71
Digital Equipment Corporation (DEC), 12, 82, 345, 511, 514

Digital lines, 180
Digital signals, 184, 185
Direct-access files, 156–158
Direct-connect modems, 185
Direct product-profitability analysis, 115
Disk caching, 145
Disk drives, 42, 149
Diskettes, 42
Distributed data processing (DDP), 198–200
Division/remainder method, 157
Documentation, 217
Dot-matrix printers, 40, 74, 121–122
Double-density (DD), 140
Downloading, 200
Drum plotters, 123, 124
Dumb terminals, 108

EBCDIC code, 138, 163
Eckert, J. Presper, 10
Econograph, 249–250
Economic data banks, 176
Economics, computer-aided instruction program for, 276
Education, 388–389, 606–610
  challenges to computer use, 609–610
  computer-assisted instruction, 606–608
  computer-managed instruction, 609
  use of home computers for, 13
Egoless programming, 242–243
80286 chip, 77, 655
80386 chip, 77, 655
Electrocardiograms (EKGs), 596
Electronic access control, 650–651
Electronic conferencing, 176
Electronic Delay Storage Automatic Computer (EDSAC), 11
Electronic filing, 531–532
Electronic funds transfer (EFT) systems, 176, 617, 630
Electronic mail, 529–531
Electronic Numerical Integrator and Computer (ENIAC), 10–11
Electronic shopping, 176
Electronic spreadsheets, 14, 47–48, 320–335
  mechanics, 322–335
  use of, 322
Embedded computers, 71
End-user computing, 516
Enhanced graphics adapter (EGA), 553
Entertainment, use of home computers for, 13
Erasable programmable read-only memory (EPROM), 136, 137
Ergonomics, 55–60
  system development life cycle and, 461

Escape (Esc) key, 107
Exception report, 489, 491
Execution cycle (E-cycle), 162
Executive information system, 506–508
Expansion boards, 76
Expert systems, 508–513
  benefits, 511
  drawbacks, 511–513
External data and the MIS, 495–497
External disks, 142
Extracting records, 304–307

Factory data-collection devices, 110
Fault-tolerance, 486
Feasibility study, 448
Fiber optics cables, 180–181
  for local area networks, 201
Field, 52, 297
Field engineers, 24
Fifth-Generation Computing Project, 12, 669
File, 6, 53, 297
File design, 462
File-management programs, 48, 294, 295
File organization, 153–160, 347–351
  indexed-sequential files, 158–160, 347, 349
  random-access files, 156–158, 347, 349, 351
  sequential files, 155–156, 347–349
File-processing systems, 53–55, 347–352
  drawbacks of traditional file processing, 351–352
  types of file organization, 347–351
File updating, 54
Finance (as a business subsystem), 423
Finances, 612–617
  artificial intelligence for financial planning, 616
  electronic funds transfer, 176, 617, 630
  home banking, 620–621
  investment software, 614–615
  personal finances, 13, 613–614
Financial crime, 633
Financial information, 175
Fingerprint scanners, 650–651
Firmware, 137
First-generation computers, 11–12
Fixed disks, see Hard disks
Flatbed plotters, 123–124
Flat-panel displays, 120
Flexible manufacturing systems (FMS), 574–577
Float, 617
Floppy disks (floppies), 42, 139, 140–141
Flowcharts, 233, 234, 235

system flowcharts, 454, 455–456, 458
Food Marketing Institute, 115
Football, computers and, 600–601, 602, 603
Format of text in word-processing, 309
FORTRAN (FORmula TRANslator), 219, 257, 258
Fourth-generation programming languages, 268
Framework, 48
Frankston, Robert, 75, 320, 321
Front-end processors, 187–188
Full-duplex channels, 183
Function keys, 107
Fundamental analysis (investment analysis technique), 615

Gallium arsenide (GaAs), 660
GFLOPS (billions of floating-point operations per second), 88
Gigabytes, 86
GO TO instructions, 237–241
Government, computers and, 384–387
Grammar/style checkers, 318, 320
Graphics, see Computer graphics
Grid charts, 456, 457

Hackers, 636–637
Half-duplex channels, 183
Hand-held computers, 79
Hard copy, 38, 118
Hard disks, 43, 76, 139, 141–143
Hardware, 33–46
  auxiliary storage devices, 33, 42–45, 137, 138, 139–153
  central processing unit, 33, 39–42, 133–138
  data communication systems, 33, 45–46, 173–175
  ergonomics and, 55–56
  for graphics, 553
  for image processing, 534–535
  input devices, 33, 34–38, 103–117
  output devices, 33, 38–39, 118–125
  theft of, 637
  trends in, 655–663
Hashing, 157–158
Health care, 399–401, 595–599
  data bases for, 597–599
Help screens, 313, 314–315
Hewlett-Packard Touch Screen computer, 36, 116
Hexadecimal system, 164
Hierarchical model, 358–360
Hierarchical networks, 190–192
Hierarchy of operations, 690
High-level programming languages, 252, 254–267

INDEX 730

High-level publishing systems, 550
History of computing, 6–14
  early calculating devices, 7–8
  first computing devices, 8–11
  first three generations of computers, 11–12
  personal computers, 13–14
Hollerith, Herman, 10
Hollerith code, 109
Hollerith tabulator, 9–10, 37
Home banking, 620–621
Home computers, see Personal computers (PCs)
Home health care, 595–596
Home management, 13
Hospitals, decision support systems for, 596–597
Human resources (as a business subsystem), 424
Human resources information systems, 427

IBM (International Business Machines), 10, 266, 485, 514
  privacy principles for handling personal data established by, 631–632
  system architecture study of, 446–447
  use of expert systems by, 510
IBM AT, 77, 550
IBM PC Convertible, 80
IBM PCs, 69, 72–76
IBM Personal System/2 microcomputers, 77, 658–659
IBM Series/360, 12, 87
IBM Series/370, 656
IBM XT, 76–77
IBM 1401, 12
IBM 4341, 85
Icons, 49, 119, 120
Image processing, 532–536
  hardware for, 534–535
Image scanners, 534
Impact printers, 121
Indexed-sequential files, 158–160, 347, 349
Inference engine (expert system shell), 509
Infinite loop, 700
Information, 6
Information centers, 513–517
  common applications, 514, 515
  guidelines, 515–517
Information crimes, 633
Information services, use of home computers for, 13
Information systems pyramid, 483, 484
Information utilities, 175–176

In-house E-mail, 529
Input, 19, 33, 34–38, 101–102
Input design, 461–462
Input devices, 33, 34–38, 103–117
  computers that read, 113
  keyboards, 36, 104–107
  other data entry devices, 108–110
  other input devices and techniques, 114–117
  scanners, 111–114
  terminals, 19, 107–108
Inputting, 21
Insert (Ins) key, 107
Instruction cycle (I-cycle), 162
Instruction flow, 161–162
Instructions, BASIC, 678
Integrated software, 48
Integrated workstations, 539–540
Integrating environments, 337
Intel Corp., 74
Intel 8088 microprocessor, 72
Intelligent terminals, 108
Interactive access, 86
Interactive processing, 55
Interblock gaps, 146
Internal clock, 133
Internal disks, 142
Internal workings of a computer, 160–164
Interpreter, 255–256
Inventory control and management, computer information systems for, 427, 432–433
Inverted files, 350–351
Investment software, 614–615
Iverson, Ken, 265

Jacquard, Joseph Marie, 8
Jacquard loom, 8
Job management function, 278
"Jukeboxes," 535
Just-in-time (JIT), 577–579

Kemeny, John, 74, 259
Keyboard enhancer, 107
Keyboard redefinition option, 107
Keyboards, 36–37, 104–107
Keyboard software, 107
Key field, 52, 155
Keypunch, 37
Keypunch machines, 108–109
Keys (security measure), 643–644
Key-to-disk systems, 110
Key-to-floppy disk systems, 110
Key-to-tape systems, 109
Knowledge base, 508–509
Knowledge systems, see Expert systems
Kurtz, Thomas, 74, 259

Kurzweil 250 digital synthesizer, 611–612

Laptop computers, 75, 80–81
Laser printers, 40, 122–123
Leibnitz, Gottfried von, 8
Light pens, 116
Limitations of computers, 14, 16–19
Line numbers in programs, 678
Line printers, 39, 120–121
Linked lists, 349–350
LISP (List Processing Programming Language), 616, 668–669
Literal, 682
Local area network (LAN), 200–202
  fiber optics for, 201
  multiuser systems versus, 202–203
Logic errors, 220–221, 683
Logic operations, 134
Looping, 691
Looping structures, 237, 240
Lotus 1-2-3, 23, 47, 322, 324, 553
  electronic spreadsheet program for, 322–335
  screen, 60
Lovelace, Lady Ada, 9, 264
Low-level programming languages, 252–254

McCarthy, John, 668
Machine languages, 252–253
Macintosh computers, 36, 72, 277
Magnetic bubble memory, 153
Magnetic core memory, 12
Magnetic-disk drive, 44
Magnetic disks, 44–45, 139, 149–152
  accessing data on, 150
  cylinders on, 151
Magnetic identification cards, 643
Magnetic ink character recognition (MICR), 111
Magnetic-tape backup systems, 145
Magnetic-tape drive, 43
Magnetic tapes, 43–44, 139, 146–149
Mail merge programs, 320
Mainframe computers, 5, 84–87, 89
  applications software for, 48–49
  systems software for, 50
  user interaction on, 282–283
Mainframe CPUs, 42
Management information systems (MIS), 416, 418–419, 491–499
  external data and, 495–497
  MIS departments, 497–499
  misuses of, 505
  operations information systems compared to, 492
  uses of, 494–495, 505

Managers, systems development and, 443
Manufacturing automation protocol (MAP), 582–584
Manufacturing resource planning (MRP II), 568–569
Marketing (as a business subsystem), 423
Marketing information systems, 426
Mark I computer, 10, 11
Mass storage devices, 152
Master file, 53–54, 147
Materials requirements planning (MRP), 567–568
Mauchly, John, 10
Medlars (Medical Literature Analysis and Retrieval System), 598
Megahertz (MHz), 133
Memory, 134–135
Message, 173
Menu, 49, 116
Microcomputers, 5, 13, 72, 79, 89
  applications software for, 46–48
  data security for, 645–646
  minicomputers versus, 82–84
  storage devices for, 139–145
  systems software for, 49–50
Microprocessors, 71–72, 89
Microsecond, 15
Microsoft Word, 47, 549
Microwave transmission, 181–182
Middle management, reshaping the functions of, 420–421
Midrange desktop publishing systems, 550
Migration, software, 364
Millisecond, 15
Minicomputers, 5, 82–84, 89
  user interaction on, 282–283
MIPS (millions of instructions per second), 85
MIS departments, 497–499
Modems, 45–46, 76, 185–186
Modulation, 185
Monitors, 38
Mouse, 36, 116
MS-DOS, 49, 277, 285
Multifunction packages, 337
MultiMate (word-processing program), 47, 309–311
Multiplexers, 186–187
Multiprocessing, 284
Multiprogramming, 283–284
Multiuser systems, 202–203
Music, 610–612
Musical Instrument Digital Interface (MIDI), 611
MX-80 dot-matrix printer, 74

Mycin (expert diagnostic system), 509, 510

Nanosecond, 15
National Center for Computer Crime Data, 634
National Institute for Occupational Safety and Health (NIOSH), 543
National Superspeed Computer Project, 89
Natural language interface, 272–273
Natural languages, 272–273
Network model, 358, 361–362
Neumann, John von, 11
New master file, 54, 147
Nomad 2 (fourth-generation data-base management system), 270–271
Nonimpact printers, 121
Nonkeyboard devices, 37
Nonprocedural programming languages, 268
Normalization, 363
Numbering systems, 164
Numeric characters, 52
Numeric keypad, 106

Observations, 453–454
Office automation (OA), 390–395, 526
  benefits, 526–527
  electronic filing, 531–532
  electronic mail, 529–531
  image processing, 532–536
  impact of, 542–547, 556–557
  integrated workstations, 539–540
  telecommuting, 538–539
  teleconferencing, 536–538
  tools of, 528–539
  word processing, 529
Office automation administrator, 546
Office automation systems, 541–542
Off-line systems, 53
Old master file, 54, 147
One-dimensional array, 701
On-line program development systems, 197
On-line query systems, 195
On-line systems, 55
On-line thesaurus, 318, 319
On-line transaction-processing systems (OLTPS), 195, 483–486
Open architecture, 76
Operating systems, 277–285
  commands, 279–283
  functions, 278–279
  special features, 283–284
  standardization, 285
  types, 277–278

Operations information systems (OIS), 416, 417, 483–491
  management information systems compared to, 492
  on-line transaction-processing systems, 195, 483–486
  operational control, 489–491
  uses of, 487–489
Operators, 24
Opportunity costs, 474–475
Optical character recognition (OCR), 112
Optical character recognition, devices, 37–38
Optical computing, 661–662
Optical disk storage media, 75, 152–153, 154
Optical mark recognition, 111–112
Organizational applications, 412–413
Organization chart, 452, 453
Osborne I portable computer, 79
Output, 19, 33, 38–39, 117
Output design, 461
Output devices, 33, 38–39, 118–125
  audio response units, 119, 124–125
  computer output microfilm systems, 119, 124
  plotters, 119, 123–124
  printers, 38–39, 40, 119, 120–123
  video display terminals, 38, 118–120

Page printers, 39, 120, 121
Pascal (programming language), 262–263
Pascal, Blaise, 7–8, 262
Pascaline, 8
Passwords, 197–198, 642–643
PC-DOS, see Personal Computer Disk Operating System (PC-DOS)
PC-File III (file-management program), 48
PC World, 663
PDP-1 (minicomputer), 12
People as element of computer systems, 53–60
Periodic reports, 489, 490
Peripherals, 81
Personal applications, 411–412
Personal Computer Disk Operating System (PC-DOS), 49, 277, 285, 337
Personal computers (PCs), 13–14
  business applications, 14
  buyer guidelines, 90–93
  future of, 662–663
  IBM PCs, 62, 72–76
  integration of, 337
  other IBM models, 76–77
  technological advances in, 74–75
  in use in United States (1987), 78
  user interaction on, 279–282

INDEX 732

Personal finances, 13, 613–614
Personal-productivity software, 47, 663–664
  integrating, 336–337
  See also Data-base management programs; Electronic spreadsheets; Word processing
Personal publishing software, 549
Personal System/2 (PS/2), 77, 658–659
Personal workstations, 512
Personnel for DBMS interaction, 354–356
Personnel placement programs, 382–383
PFS-File (file-management program), 48
PL/1 (Programming Language 1), 261–262
PLATO (Programmed Logic for Automatic Teaching Operations), 606
Platters, 149
Plotters, 119, 123–124
Pocket computers, 79
Pointing, 36, 116
Point-of-sale (POS) terminals, 37, 114
Polling, 183
Portable computers, 78–81
  problems with, 81
Power user, 23
Predictive reports, 493
Prescription farming, 436–437
Presentation graphics, 552
Primary storage, 39–42, 133, 134–137
Prime numbers, 157
Print buffers, 123
Printers, 38–39, 40, 80–81, 119, 120–123
Printer spacing chart, 228–229
Privacy, 625–632, 672
  in business situations, 627–628
  electronic funds transfer systems and, 630
  legislation, 630–632
  standard universal identifier, 628–631
Privacy Act of 1974, 631
Private networks, 194
Procedure manuals, 452
Processing, 160–163
Processing design, 462
Product families, 337
Production (as a business subsystem), 424
Production data, 483
Production information systems, 426
Programmable read-only memory (PROM), 136, 137
Program maintenance, 222–224

Programmers, 23–24, 214–215
  computer errors by, 671–672
  programs for, 236
  system development and, 443
Programming languages, 251–257
  for artificial intelligence, 668–669
  for DBMS, 354–355
  high-level, 252, 254–267
  low-level, 252–254
  selecting the most suitable, 274–277
  very high-level, 252, 268–274
Programming process, 215–224
  coding the program, 216, 219–220
  defining the problem, 215, 216–217
  designing the solution, 215, 217–219
  implementing and maintaining the program, 216, 222–224
  testing and debugging the program, 216, 220–222
Prolog (Programming in Logic), 668, 669
Prompts, 110, 688
Prototype development, 473
Pseudocode, 218, 231–232
PS/2, *see* Personal System/2 (PS/2)
Punched cards, 8, 9

Query languages, 268–269, 356
  structured, 363–371
Questionnaires, 453

Radio Shack's TRS-80 microcomputer, 74
RAM disks, 145
Random-access (direct-access) files, 156–158, 347, 349, 351
Random-access memory (RAM), 42, 136–137
Random numbers, 713–714, 716–717
Random processing, 44–45
Ratio analysis reports, 493, 494
Ratliff, C. Wayne, 226
R:base 5000 (data-base management program), 48
Reader response cards, 295, 296
Reading, teaching computers to read, 113
Read-only memory (ROM), 42, 136, 137
Ready-made software packages, 465–467
Receiver, 173, 174
Record, 52, 297
Record layout form, 229
Record structure, 298–299
Registers, 133
Relational model, 358, 362–363
  migration software for, 364

Relative record location, 157
Remote batch systems, 195
Remote data collection, 79
Research and development (as a business subsystem), 424
Research and development information systems, 426
Research data banks, 176
Resource management (of operating systems), 278–279
Right to Financial Privacy Act of 1978, 631
Rigid disks, *see* Hard disks
Ring networks, 190, 193
Robots, 569–574
  applications, 573–574
  programming robots, 570
  touch-sensitive robots, 572–573
  vision systems for, 570–572
RPG (Report Program Generator), 266
Run-time error, 220, 221

SABRE (Semi-Automatic Business Research Environment), 55
Sales analysis, computer information systems for, 427–428, 433
Sampling, 454
Satellites, 182
Scanners, 111–114, 534
Screen layout forms, 230
Second-generation computers, 12
Secretaries
  computer skills of, 556–557
  technological advances and, 128–129
Secretary, The, 556
Security, *see* Computer security
Seed, 715
Selection structure, 237, 239
Semicolon, use of in BASIC, 682
Semistructured decisions, 502
Sequential files, 155–156, 347–349
Sequential processing, 43
Sequential structure, 237, 238
Sequential update, 147, 149
Silicon-based computer chips, 655–656
Simplex channels, 183
Simulation, 608
Single-density (SD), 140
Site licensing, 637
Skiing, computers and, 605
"Smart cards," 644
Smart terminals, 108
Software, 46–50
  applications software, 46–49
  custom software, 467
  data communication, 188–189
  desktop publishing, 549

ergonomics and, 58–60
for graphics, 553
keyboard, 107
migration, 364
ready-made software packages, 465–467
systems software, 49–50
theft of, 637
trends in, 663–670
user-friendly, 58–60
Software Arts Inc., 75
Software bugs, 18
Software escrow agreement, 638
Solution design report, 218–219
Sorting, 21, 155
Source data automation, 102–103
Source documents, 101
Spaghetti programs, 241
Special characters, 52
Spelling checkers, 318–319
Sports, computers and, 396–398, 599–605
Spreadsheets, 320–321, 324
 See also Electronic spreadsheets
Standards manuals, 452
Standard universal identifier (SUI), 628–631
Star networks, 190, 192–193
Start-stop transmission, 184
Storage, see Auxiliary storage
Stored-program computer, 11
Strings, 317–318, 679
Structure charts, 231, 232
Structured decisions, 501–502
Structured programming, 225–227
Structured query language (SQL), 363–371
Structured walkthrough, 233
Subroutines, 713
Subscript, 704
Summary report, 489, 490
Summing, 696
SuperCalc3, 553
Supercomputers, 6, 88–90
Superconducting computers, 660–661
Superminicomputer systems, 84, 89
Symphony (integrated software), 48
Synchronous transmission, 184
Synonyms, 157–158
Syntax errors, 220, 682
System, 33, 414–419
System acquisition, 444, 465–468
System acquisition report, 468
System architecture study of IBM, 446–447
System design, 444, 459–464
System development life cycle, 444–473

acquisition, 444, 465–468
analysis, 444, 452–459
design, 444, 459–464
dos and don'ts of, 472
implementation, 444, 469–471
investigation, 444, 445–461
maintenance, 444, 471–473
opportunity costs and, 474–475
prototyping, 473
system architecture study, 446–447
throwaway systems and, 474–475
System flowcharts, 454, 455–456, 458
System personnel, 442–444
System testing design, 463
Systems analysis, 444, 452–459
Systems analysts, 24, 214–215, 236
 system development and, 442
Systems Network Architecture (SNA), 194
Systems software, 48–50

Table for structured query language, 365–370
Tape librarians, 146
Tate, Ashton, 295
Tax Reform Act of 1976, 631
Telecommunication, 173
 See also Data communication
Telecommuting, 538–539
Teleconferencing, 536–538
Telegraph lines, 178–179
Telephone lines, 179–180
Telephone systems, 45
Teleprocessing, 195–198
Terminal, 19, 107–108
Testing, 220–222
 programs, 685
ThinkJet (printer), 80–81
Third-generation computers, 12
Throwaway systems, 474–475
Time-sharing, 197
Top-down design, 227–228, 231
Touch-sensitive robots, 572–573
Tracks, 140, 141
Transaction, 53
Transaction file, 147
Transistors, 12, 74
Transmitter, 173, 174
Transportable computers, 81
Turbo Lightning (spelling checker), 319
Turing test, 670
Two-dimensional arrays, 710–712

U.S. Bureau of the Census, 9, 10
U.S. Department of Agriculture, 436
U.S. Department of Commerce, 495
U.S. Department of Defense, 264

UNIVAC I, 12
Universal product code (UPC), 37, 114
UNIX, 50, 285
Unstructured decisions, 502
Updating, 147–148
Upgrading computers, 73–76
User-friendly software, 58–60
Users (end-users), 19, 22–23
 system development and, 443

Vacuum, tubes, 11–12
Value-added networks, 194
Vandalism, 636–637
Variables, 679
 character, 692
 control, 696
 string, 692
Vendor networks, 194
Verifier, 109
Very-high-level programming languages, 252, 268–274
 cost justification for, 270–271
 disadvantages, 273–274
Video conferencing, 537
Video display terminal (VDT), 38, 118–120
 health hazards of, 543–544
Virtual storage, 284
VisiCalc, 59, 320–321
VisiCalc spreadsheet program, 75
Vision systems, robot, 570–572
Voice-grade lines, 180
Voice recognition system, 116–117

Weaving, automation of, 8
What if? questions, 332
Wilkes, Maurice, 11
Wirth, Niklaus, 262
Word processing, 307–320
 additional features, 318–320
 mechanics, 309–318
 programs, 14, 47
 role in office automation, 529
Word-processing programs, 14, 47
 See also names of programs
Word processors, 308
WordStar, 47
Word wrap, 313
Worksheet, 324
Workstations, 19, 656–657
 integrated, 539–540
 personal, 512
Wristwatch computers, 75
WYSIWYG ("what-you-see-is-what-you-get"), 318, 547

XCON (expert system), 511

Yachting, computers and, 602–604

INDEX 734